Learning Functional Programming in Go

Change the way you approach your applications using functional programming in Go

Lex Sheehan

BIRMINGHAM - MUMBAI

Learning Functional Programming in Go

Copyright © 2017 Packt Publishing

All rights reserved. No part of this book may be reproduced, stored in a retrieval system, or transmitted in any form or by any means, without the prior written permission of the publisher, except in the case of brief quotations embedded in critical articles or reviews.

Every effort has been made in the preparation of this book to ensure the accuracy of the information presented. However, the information contained in this book is sold without warranty, either express or implied. Neither the author, nor Packt Publishing, and its dealers and distributors will be held liable for any damages caused or alleged to be caused directly or indirectly by this book.

Packt Publishing has endeavored to provide trademark information about all of the companies and products mentioned in this book by the appropriate use of capitals. However, Packt Publishing cannot guarantee the accuracy of this information.

First published: November 2017

Production reference: 1221117

Published by Packt Publishing Ltd.
Livery Place
35 Livery Street
Birmingham
B3 2PB, UK.

ISBN 978-1-78728-139-4

www.packtpub.com

Credits

Author
Lex Sheehan

Reviewer
John Pradeep

Commissioning Editor
Merint Mathew

Acquisition Editor
Karan Sadawana

Content Development Editor
Rohit Kumar Singh

Technical Editor
Pavan Ramchandani

Copy Editor
Pranjali Chury

Project Coordinator
Vaidehi Sawant

Proofreader
Safis Editing

Indexer
Rekha Nair

Graphics
Jason Monteiro

Production Coordinator
Shraddha Falebhai

About the Author

Lex Sheehan has a B.S. in Computer Science from Auburn University, resides in Atlanta, GA, and works as a senior software engineer with over 20 years of experience. He has a deep understanding of functional programming; His first encounter was using high-order functions in Ruby, Scala, JavaScript, Haskell, Java, and Go.

Lex worked for IBM Software Group and IBM Global Business Services, designing and building various enterprise business systems. He is the author of eight US patents (IT security and data transformations) and he writes a blog titled *Application Development with Lex Sheehan*.

Lex is available to consult and meet with your CTO, or provide in-house training on the information in this book.

Acknowledgments

I would like to acknowledge the people who helped me during the writing of this book.

Thank you, Rohit, for editing my writing and providing your insight, guidance, and words of encouragement.

Thank you, John and Wayne, for reviewing this book for technical accuracy. Thank you to all other reviewers who helped improve the quality of this book's content.

Thank you, Mac, for being my wise counsel.

Thank you, Marty, for being my sounding board.

Thank you, Erik, for providing legal counsel regarding the Forgetful Functor.

Thank you all who lifted me up in your prayers during this endeavor.

Thank you, Salim, for your support. Your leadership style has earned my trust and loyalty.

Thank you, to the one who would say, *"Lex Brilliance"*.   That was and still is a great source of inspiration. Words matter.

We are all given talents. Some fear failure and suffer for it; others invest their talents.

This book is dedicated to those who invest in themselves and go on to help others.

"Do or do not. There is no try".

- Yoda

About the Reviewer

John Pradeep is a software engineer with over 10 years of experience in designing and developing various applications in an agile way.

After working on multiple languages (Lisp being his favorite), he has recently started using Go for its clear set of design goals and simplicity. Now, Go has become his language of choice for most projects that he works on.

He loves finding simple solutions to complex problems, and he is also a huge fan of methodologies that help build elegant systems such as functional programming, domain-driven design, CQRS, reactive architectures, and so on.

www.PacktPub.com

For support files and downloads related to your book, please visit www.PacktPub.com.

Did you know that Packt offers eBook versions of every book published, with PDF and ePub files available? You can upgrade to the eBook version at www.PacktPub.com and as a print book customer, you are entitled to a discount on the eBook copy. Get in touch with us at service@packtpub.com for more details.

At www.PacktPub.com, you can also read a collection of free technical articles, sign up for a range of free newsletters and receive exclusive discounts and offers on Packt books and eBooks.

https://www.packtpub.com/mapt

Get the most in-demand software skills with Mapt. Mapt gives you full access to all Packt books and video courses, as well as industry-leading tools to help you plan your personal development and advance your career.

Why subscribe?

- Fully searchable across every book published by Packt
- Copy and paste, print, and bookmark content
- On demand and accessible via a web browser

Customer Feedback

Thanks for purchasing this Packt book. At Packt, quality is at the heart of our editorial process. To help us improve, please leave us an honest review on this book's Amazon page at `https://www.amazon.com/dp/1787281396`.

If you'd like to join our team of regular reviewers, you can e-mail us at `customerreviews@packtpub.com`. We award our regular reviewers with free eBooks and videos in exchange for their valuable feedback. Help us be relentless in improving our products!

Table of Contents

Preface — 1

Chapter 1: Pure Functional Programming in Go — 11
- **Motivation for using FP** — 12
- **Getting the source code** — 13
  - The directory structure of the source files — 13
  - How to run our first Go application — 14
- **Imperative versus declarative programming** — 15
- **Pure functions** — 18
- **Fibonacci sequence - a simple recursion and two performance improvements** — 19
  - Memoization — 21
- **The difference between an anonymous function and a closure** — 24
  - FP using Go's concurrency constructs — 26
- **Testing FP using test-driven development** — 28
  - A note about paths — 30
  - How to run our tests — 31
- **A journey from imperative programming to pure FP and enlightenment** — 36
  - Benchmark test for the imperative SumLoop function — 37
  - Benchmark test for the SumRecursive function — 37
  - A time of reckoning — 38
    - A quick example of a function literal — 39
- **Summary** — 40

Chapter 2: Manipulating Collections — 41
- **Iterating through a collection** — 42
- **Piping Bash commands** — 44
- **Functors** — 45
  - Functions that modify functions — 46
    - A coding example of functions that modify functions — 46
    - A visual example of functions that modify functions — 47
      - Composition in Mindcraft — 48
  - Tacit programming — 48
    - Tacit programming with Unix pipes — 49
    - Programming CMOS with Unix pipes — 49
    - Tacit programming with FP — 50
      - Non-TCO recursive example — 50

Table of Contents

TCO recursive example	51
The importance of recursion	52
Various intermediate and terminal functions	53
Reduce example	54
Intermediate functions	54
Common intermediate functions	55
Map Example	55
Terminal functions	56
Common terminal functions	56
Join example	56
GroupBy example	57
Reduce example	57
Predicates	**57**
Reflection	60
Combinator pattern	61
Map and filter	**61**
Contains	**67**
Iterating over a collection of cars	68
The empty interface	68
The Contains() method	69
If Go had generics	**70**
Map function	71
Testing our empty interface-based Map function	71
Itertools	**72**
Go channels used by the New function	74
Testing itertool's Map function	74
Testing iterators for element equality	75
Functional packages	**76**
Another time of reflection	**76**
Go is awesome	76
Go is awesome, but	76
The cure	**77**
Gleam - distributed MapReduce for Golang	77
LuaJIT's FFI library	78
Unix pipe tools	78
Processing Gleam collections	79
Summary	**80**
Chapter 3: Using High-Order Functions	**81**
Characteristics of FP	**81**
Function composition	92
Monads allow us to chain continuations	93

[ii]

Generics	94
First-class functions	95
Closure	96
Dynamically scoped	97
Pure function	98
Immuable Data	98
Persistent data structures for Go	99
Use of expressions	101
Sample HOF application	**101**
The chapter4 application code	102
Build and runtime instructions	103
More application code	104
The Filter function	105
Reality check	106
FilterFunc	107
Filter function	107
RESTful resources	108
Chaining functions	109
More cars	110
Reality check	110
The Map function	111
Improved performance from the Map function	112
The Reduce function	113
More high-order functions	114
Generators	115
RESTful server	116
The GenerateCars function	116
Currying Goroutine	118
A closer look at currying	118
Extending our currying example	120
Using a WaitGroup variable to manage concurrency	121
Finishing up the GenerateCars function	121
Handling concurrency	122
The final HOF example	123
Summary	**124**
Chapter 4: SOLID Design in Go	**125**
Why many Gophers loath Java	**125**
More reasons for loathing Java	127
Digging deeper into error handling	128
A conversation - Java developer, idiomatic Go developer, FP developer	129
Software design methodology	**132**
Good design	133
Bad design	134
Good versus bad design over time	134

Table of Contents

SOLID design principles — 135
Single responsibility principle — 136
Function composition — 138
Open/closed principle — 138
Open / close principle in functional programming — 141
FantasyLand JavaScript specification — 142
Setoid algebra — 142
Ord algebra — 143
The expression problem — 143
Liskov substitution principle — 144
This OOP method stinks — 144
Our FP function smells like roses — 145
In FP, contracts don't lie — 146
Duck typing — 150
What can go wrong with inheritance? — 150
Interface segregation principle — 152
Dependency inversion principle — 152
The big reveal — 153
MapReduce — 154
MapReduce example — 155
What else can Monads do? — 157
Viva La Duck — 158
Pass by value or reference? — 161
Type embedding with Go interfaces — 163
Interface embedding to add minor features — 164
A Go error handling idiom — 164
It's time to run our program — 165
Summary — 168

Chapter 5: Adding Functionality with Decoration — 169
Interface composition — 170
Go's complimentary Reader and Writer interfaces — 170
Example usages of the Reader and Writer interfaces — 171
Design with Duck Typing — 171
More reasons to design using interfaces — 172
Using the Reader and Writer interfaces — 174
Decorator pattern — 176
Type hierarchy UML — 177
How Procedural design compares to functional Inversion of Control (IoC) — 178
Procedural design example — 179
Functional IoC example — 179
A decorator implementation — 180

The main.go file	180
The decorator/simple_log.go file	182
Example InitLog calls	183
Back to our main package	184
Understanding our statistics using the easy-metrics GUI	187
Quick look at the Dot Init update	188
Easy-metrics - 1 of 3	189
The decorator/decorator.go file	190
A framework to inject dependencies	191
Wrapping a client request with decorators (in main)	191
Authorization decorator	192
Logging decorator	192
LoadBalancing decorator	193
Strategy pattern	193
Inversion of control and dependency injection	195
Our first failure	196
Easy metrics - 2 of 3	196
Groking our trace log file	197
The rest of the graph	198
Easy metrics - 3 of 3	199
Examining the trace log	200
The decorator/requestor.go file	200
The job variable declared in main()	201
Back to the requestor.go file	201
Using channels to manage the life cycle	202
All requests done	204
Launching our makeRequest goroutine	204
Our DI framework in action	205
Summary	206
Chapter 6: Applying FP at the Architectural Level	**207**
Application architectures	208
What is software architecture?	209
Client-server architecture	209
Cloud architecture	210
Why does architecture matter?	211
The role of systems engineering	212
Real systems	212
IT system specialty groups	212
Systems engineering is lean	213
Requirements, scope and terms	213
Defining terms	213
Software requirements	214
System	214
System architecture	214

System elements	214
System Boundaries	214
Managing Complexity	214
The best tool for the job	215
Divide and conquer	215
Designing for state management	216
Add a microservice	216
FP influenced architectures	219
Domain Driven Design	219
Dependency rule	220
Cyclic dependency	221
Working code	221
Code with cyclic dependency error	222
The Golang difference	223
Solution for cyclic dependencies	224
Domain Driven Design	224
Interface-driven development	225
Hollywood principle	226
Observer pattern	226
Dependency injection	229
A cloud bucket application	230
Directory structure	230
main.go	231
func HandlePanic	232
Dependency injection	233
func main()	234
Layers in the architecture	234
Domain layer	235
Use cases layer	240
Compatible interfaces	242
Interfaces layer	244
Why global variables are bad	252
Format the response	253
Testing our interfaces	258
Infrastructure layer	262
Context object	264
Benefits of DDD	266
Adaptablity	266
Sustainability	267
Testability	267
Comprehensibility	267
A solid architectural foundation	267
FP and Micyoservices	267
Message passing	268

All parties must participate	269
Communication across boundaries	**269**
Polyglot Persistence	269
Lambda architecture	**270**
Speed	270
Batch	270
Servicing	271
Next generation big data architecture	271
CQRS	**271**
Benefits of CQRS	272
Infrastructure architecture	**273**
Share nothing architecture	**274**
Integrating services	**274**
Agreed upon protocol	274
Circuit breakers	274
Functional reactive architecture	**275**
Go is ideal for building microservices	**276**
Size matters	277
Benefits of gRPC	278
Who is using Go?	278
Summary	**279**
Chapter 7: Functional Parameters	**281**
Refactoring long parameter lists	**282**
What's wrong with a function signature with more than seven parameters?	282
Refactoring - the book	283
Edsger W. Dijkstra says OOP is a bad idea	284
What else did Edsger W. Dijkstra say?	285
The underlying OOP problem	287
OOP inconsistency	288
Functional programming and cloud computing	288
A closer look at f(x)	290
A closer look at refactoring	290
Passing every parameter a function requires to do its job is not a good idea	290
Methods can query other objects' methods internally for data required to make decisions	291
Methods should depend on their host class for needed data	291
Pass a whole object with required attributes to reduce the number of required parameters	291
Replace parameter with method technique to reduce the number of required parameters	292
Before applying Replace Parameter with Method technique	292
After applying Replace Parameter with Method technique	292
Use a parameter object when we have unrelated data elements to pass	292

Long parameter lists will change over time and are inherently difficult to understand	294
The solution	295
Three ways to pass multiple parameters	296
Simply passing multiple parameters	296
Passing a configuration object/struct that contains multiple attributes	296
Partial application	297
Functional parameters	298
Contexts	302
Context limitations	305
Report example	306
Writing good code is not unlike a good game of soccer	306
Functional parameters - Rowe	308
Report example	308
A more practical Context use case	308
src/server/server.go	310
The src/server/server_options.go file	316
Summary	319
Chapter 8: Increasing Performance Using Pipelining	**321**
Introducing the pipeline pattern	322
Grep sort example	322
Pipeline characteristics	323
Examples	324
Website order processing	324
Boss worker pattern	324
Load balancer	325
Data flow types	325
Building blocks	326
Generalized business application design	326
Example implementations	327
Imperative implementation	328
Decrypt, authenticate, charge flow diagram	328
Concurrent implementation	331
Buffered implementation	332
Leverage all CPU cores	334
Improved implementation	334
Imports	335
BuildPipeline	335
Immediately executable Goroutine	336
Receive order	336
Filterer interface	336
A Filterer object	337
Authenticate filter	337
Decrypt filter	338
Complete processing	338

The ChargeCard helper function	339
Charge filter	339
The encrypt and decrypt helper functions	340
Testing how the application handles invalid data	341
Invalid credit card cipher text	341
Invalid password	342
Changing the order of authenticate and decrypt filters	343
Attempting to charge before decrypting credit card number and authentication	343
Attempting to charge before authentication	344
Further reading	344
Summary	345
Chapter 9: Functors, Monoids, and Generics	**347**
Understanding functors	347
An imperative versus pure FP example	348
What did that Map function do for us?	348
What possible benefits can this afford us?	349
A magical structure	349
Color blocks functor	350
Fingers times 10 functor	350
Definition of a functor in Haskell	351
Kinds of types	352
Maybe	353
Polymorphism at a higher level	353
No Generics results in a lot of boilerplate code	354
Solve lack of generics with metaprogramming	355
Generics code generation tool	357
The clipperhouse/gen tool	357
If Go supported generics	362
Adding new methods	363
Defining a filter function	363
Nums revisited	364
The slice typewriter	367
Aggregate[T]	367
Generics implementation options	368
We used the gen tool	369
The shape of a functor	369
Functor implementation	370
ints functor	370
Functor definition	374
Identity operation	375
Composition operation	375
Composition example in Go	376

Haskell version of compose	377
(g.f)(x) = g(f(x)) composition in Go	381
The (g.f)(x) = g(f(x)) implementation	382
A note about composition naming conventions in Go	383
The directions of the arrows are significant	385
EmphasizeHumanize ordered incorrectly	385
Function composition is associative	387
Functional composition in the context of a legal obligation	**387**
Decisions determine state transitions	388
Category theory review	389
Categorical rules	389
Results oriented	389
The forgetful functor and the law	390
The rule of law	390
Lucy's forgetful functor	391
Larry's forgetful functor	391
Build a 12-hour clock functor	**392**
Clock functor helpers	393
The Unit function	393
The AmPmMapper function	394
The AmHoursFn helper	394
The String helper function	394
main.go	395
Terminal output log	397
Functor summary	397
The car functor	**397**
The functor package	397
main.go	400
Compare one line of FP to a bunch of imperative lines	401
Car functor terminal session	402
Monoids	**402**
Monoid rules	402
Closure rule	402
Closure rule examples	403
Closure axiom	403
Associativity rule	403
Identity rule	403
Identity rule examples	404
An identity of 0	404
Writing a reduction function	404
A semigroup is a missing neutral value	405
Converting binary operations into operations that work on lists	405
Using monoids with divide and conquer algorithms	406
Referential transparency	406

Handling no data	407
More examples of monoids	407
What are not monoids?	407
Monoid examples	**409**
Name monoid	410
Name monoid terminal session	411
Int slice monoid	411
Lineitem slice monoid	413
Int slice monoid terminal session	415
Summary	**416**
Chapter 10: Monads, Type Classes, and Generics	**417**
Mother Teresa Monad	**418**
The bind operation	421
The lift operation	422
Monadic functions	430
Basic monadic functions	432
Monadic list functions	432
Monadic workflow implementation	**434**
Lambda calculus	447
Y-Combinator	**453**
The Y in Y-Combinator	453
How the Y-Combinator works	454
The Lexical Workflow solution	455
Is our ProcessCar method idomatic Go code?	456
The non idiomatic parts	456
The idiomatic parts	456
An alternative workflow option	**457**
Business use case scenarios	**459**
Y-Combinator re-examined	**460**
What is tail recursion?	465
Big-Oh notation	466
InternationalizatioN (I18N) package	468
Type classes	**474**
Base class definitions	474
Int base class	475
String base class	475
Our main.go file	476
Sum parent type class	476
Sum base classes	476
Generics revisited	**479**
Impact of Golang	482

Table of Contents

Personal opinion	483
Summary	484
Where to go from here	485
Chapter 11: Category Theory That Applies	**487**
Our goal	488
Break it down	490
Algebra and the unknown	490
Real-world application of algebra	493
Linear equation and the law of demand	493
Quadratic equations all around us	494
Function composition with linear and quadratic functions	495
More examples of quadratic equations	497
The golden ratio	497
Basic laws of algebra	499
Correspondence in mathematics	500
Proof theory	501
Logical connectives	501
Logical inconsistency	502
Partial function	503
Truth table	503
Conditional propositions	503
Logical equivalence	504
Converse of a conditional proposition	505
Order matters	505
The Curry Howard isomorphism	505
Examples of propositions	506
Not propositions	506
Lambda calculus	506
Why so formal?	507
The importance of protocol	507
Historical Events in Functional Programming	507
George Boole (1815 - 1864)	508
Augustus De Morgan (1806 - 1871)	508
Friedrich Ludwig Gottlob Frege (1848 – 1925)	509
Modus Ponens	509
Charles Lutwidge Dodgson (1832 –1898)	510
Alfred Whitehead and Bertrand Russell (1903)	511
Moses Schonfinkel (1889–1942)	512
Haskell Curry - 1927	513
Gerhard Gentzen (1936)	514
Alonzo Church (1930, 1940)	514

Alan Turing (1950)	515
MacLane and Eilenberg (1945)	516
John McCarthy (1950)	516
Curry-Howard-Lambek Correspondence (1969)	517
Roger Godement (1958)	519
Moggi, Wadler, Jones (1991)	520
Gibbons, Oliveira (2006)	521
The history of FP in a nutshell	523
Where to go from here	524
Programming language categories	**525**
A declarative example	525
An imperative example	525
An OOP example	526
Venn diagram of four programming paradigms	526
Five generations of languages	527
The Forth language	528
The LINQ language	530
Type systems	530
The Lambda Calculus	**531**
Lambda Expressions	531
Anonymous function example and type inference	532
Lambda expression ingredients	532
Visualizing a lambda expression	534
A Lambda calculus is like chocolate milk	536
Lambda examples in other languages	536
JavaScript	536
JavaScript (ES6)	537
Ruby	537
The importance of Type systems to FP	**539**
Static versus dynamic typing	540
Type inference	540
Haskell	541
Type classes in Haskell	542
Domains, codomains, and morphisms	**544**
Set theory symbols	**546**
Category theory	**547**
Algebra of functions	548
Abstract functions	548
Official definition of a function	548
Intuitive definition of a function	549
Function composition with sets	549
Composition operation example using travel expenses	550

Table of Contents

A Category — 550
    Category axioms — 551
    Category laws — 551
    More rules — 552
    More examples — 552
        Invalid categories — 552

Morphisms — 554
    The behaviors of morphisms — 554
        Composition operation — 554
        Identity operation — 555
    Law of associativity — 556
        Only concerned with morphisms — 557
            Interface-driven development — 557
    More morphisms — 557
    A review of Category theory — 559
    Even more correspondence — 560
    Table of morphisms — 561
        Morphism examples — 561
        Modens ponens — 561
            Type theory version — 562
            Logic version — 562
        Correspondence between logic and type theory — 562
        Cartesian closed category — 562
        Unit type — 563

Homomorphism — 564
    Homomorphisms preserve correspondence — 565
    Homomorphic encryption — 566
        An example of homomorphic encryption — 566
            Lesson learned — 567
    Isomorphism — 567
        Injective morphism — 568
        Surjective morphism — 568
        Endomorphism — 568
        SemiGroup homomorphism — 568
        SemiGroup Homomorphism Algebra — 569
    Homomorphism table — 569
        Car crash analogy — 571

Composable concurrency — 571
    Finite state machines — 572

Graph Database Example — 574

Using mathematics and category theory to gain understanding — 575
    Laws of exponentials for building a lambda expression — 579
        Table legend — 580
        For the top right law... — 580

Sums and products	580
Isomorphic equations	581
Fun with Sums, Products, Exponents and Types	**582**
Big data, knowledge-driven development, and data visualization	**588**
Data visualization	588
Summary	**593**
Appendix: Miscellaneous Information and How-Tos	**595**
How to build and run Go projects	**595**
TL;DR	595
Development workflow	596
Dot init features and benefits	596
Aliases available	597
Functions available	598
Motivation for using goenv	599
Motivation for using the init script	599
Ways to manage Go dependencies	599
The go get tool	600
The Godep tool	600
Vendoring in Go	601
Glide - the modern package manager	601
Each dot init step in detail	602
The cd command to project root directory	602
Using homebrew to install Go	602
Examining the initial directory structure and files	603
The init script contents	603
Running the init script	607
Re-examining the initial directory structure and files	608
The goenv shows what's been updated	609
Running glide-update to get third-party dependency files	609
Adding standard library imports	611
The Go standard library	612
Adding third-party imports	613
Importing statement referencing go_utils	614
Development workflow summary	**617**
Troubleshooting dot init	617
How to propose changes to Go	**623**
The first step - search specs	623
Second step - Google search	624
The official Golang change proposal process	624
Search for existing issues	625
Reading existing proposals	626
Adding a comment to the existing TCO proposal	628

Creating a new proposal	629
Creating a design document	630
Sending an email to notify the golang-dev group	630
An example proposal	631
Monitoring a proposal until the resolution is reached	631
FP resources	632
Minggatu - Catalan number	632
An explanation and call to action	634
Index	637

Preface

Until recently, the message has been *Go and functional programming—don't do it*.

Functional programming (FP) is a perfect fit for multicore, parallel processing. Go is a concurrency baller (with Goroutines, channels, and so on) and already runs on every available CPU core. FP reduces complexity; simplicity is one of Go's biggest strengths.

So, what can FP bring to Go that will actually improve our software applications? Here's what it offers:

- **Composition**: FP shows us how to decompose our apps and rebuild them by reusing small building blocks.
- **Monads**: Using monads, we are able to safely order our workflows into pipelines of data transformations.
- **Error handling**: We can leverage monadic error handling and still maintain compatibility with idiomatic Go code.
- **Performance**: Referential transparency is where we can evaluate our function once and then subsequently refer to its pre-computed value.
- **Expressive code**: FP allows us to concisely express business intent in our code. We declare what our functions do, without the clutter of error checking after every function call, and without having to follow state changes (pure FP means immutable variables).
- **Simpler code**: No shared data means not having to deal with semaphores, locks, race conditions, or deadlocks.

Most people have difficulty grasping FP.

I did too. And when I got it, I wrote this book. Take this journey with me. We'll see hundreds of illustrations, read easy-to-understand explanations, and implement FP in Go code along the way.

I enjoyed coaching soccer. The litmus test I used to determine whether I succeeded as a coach was the answer to this simple question: *Did they all register for next season and request me to be their coach?* Just like planning practice, I planned each chapter, starting with simple concepts and adding to them. Read this book, then you too will be able to say, *I got it*.

Preface

If you want to improve your FP skills, this book is for you.

What this book covers

Chapter 1, *Pure Functional Programming in Go*, introduces the declarative style of programming and demonstrates recursion, memorization, and Go's concurrency constructs using the Fibonacci Sequence. We will learn how to benchmark/performance test your recursive code and we will get some bad news.

Chapter 2, *Manipulating Collections*, shows us how to use intermediate (Map, Filter, and Sort) and terminal (Reduce, GroupBy, and Join) functions to perform data transformations. We use a Mocha-like BDD Go framework to test predicate functions. Itertools helps us grasp the breadth of FP collection manipulating function and we look at a distributed MapReduce solution: Gleam = Go + LuaJIT + Unix Pipes.

Chapter 3, *Using High-Order Functions*, covers a list of 27 FP characteristics: Anonymous function, closures, currying, Either data type, first-class functions, functions, functional composition, Hindley-Milner type system, Idempotence, immutable state, immutable variables, Lambda expressions, List Monad, Maybe data type, Maybe Monad, Monadic error, handling, No side-effects, operator overloading, option type, parametric polymorphism, partial function application, recursion, referential transparency, sum or union types, Tail Call Optimization, typeclasses, and Unit type. It also covers an example of Generics, and illustrates its value to FP programmers. We implement the Map, Filter, and Reduce functions, as well as lazy evaluation using Goroutines and a Go channel.

Chapter 4, *SOLID Design in Go*, talks about why Gophers loath Java, principles of good software design, how to apply the Single Responsibility principle, function composition, the open/closed Principle, FP contracts, and duck typing. It also covers how to model behavior using interfaces, compose software using the Interface Segregation principle and embedded interfaces. We will learn about the law of Associativity with a purple Monoid chain and get the big reveal—Monads chain continuations.

Chapter 5, *Adding Functionality with Decoration*, illustrates interface composition using Go's complimentary Reader and Writer interfaces. Next, we will learn how procedural design compares to functional Inversion of Control. We will implement the following decorators: authorization, logging, and load balancing. Also, we will add easy-metrics to our app to see our decorator pattern in action.

Chapter 6, *Applying FP at the Architectural Level*, builds an application framework using a layered architecture, which solves cyclical dependency errors. We will learn how to apply the Hollywood principle and the difference between the observer pattern and dependency injection. We will use Inversion of Control (IoC) to control the flow of logic and build a layered application. Also, we will build an effective table-driven framework to test our application's API.

Chapter 7, *Functional Parameters*, enlightens us as to why a lot of we've learned from Java and object-oriented programming does not apply to Go, teaches us a better way to refactor long parameter lists using functional options, and helps us understand the difference between currying and partial application. We will learn how to apply partial application to create another function with a smaller arity. We will use a context to gracefully shut down our server and see how to cancel and roll back a long-running database transaction using a context.

Chapter 8, *Increase Performance Using Pipelining*, covers data flow types (Read, Split, Transform, Merge, and Write) and teaches us when and how to build a data transformation pipeline. We use buffering to increase throughput, goroutines and channels to process data faster, improve API readability using interfaces, and implement some useful filters. We also implement and compare imperative and functional pipeline designs for processing credit card charges.

Chapter 9, *Functors, Monoids, and Generics*, gives us an appreciation for the lack of support for Generics in Go. We will see how to use a code generation tool to solve the repetitive boilerplate code problem. We will dive deep into function composition, implement a few functors, and learn how to map between worlds. We will also learn how to write a Reduce function to implement an invoice processing monoid.

Chapter 10, *Monads, Type Classes, and Generics*, shows us how a Monad works and teaches us how to compose functions using the Bind operation. It shows us how Monads process errors and deal with Input/Output (I/O). This chapter works through a monadic workflow implementation in Go. We cover what The Lambda Calculus is and what it has to do with Monads, see how The Lambda Calculus implements Recursion, and learn how the Y-Combinator works in Go. Next, we use the Y-Combinator to control a workflow and learn how to handle all errors at the end of the pipe. We will learn how type classes work and implement a few in Go. Finally, we review the pros and cons of generics in Go.

Preface

Chapter 11, *Category Theory That Applies*, gives us a working understanding of category theory. We will learn to appreciate the deep connection between category theory, logic, and type theory. We will increase our understanding with a journey through the history of FP. This chapter uses a Venn diagram to help explain various categories of programming languages. We come to understanding of what binding, currying, and application mean in the context of a lambda expression. This chapter shows us that the Lambda Calculus is like chocolate milk. This chapter covers the type system implications of FP, shows us different categories of homomorphisms and when to use them, and uses mathematics and the flight of a soccer ball to increase our understanding of morphisms. We will cover function composition with linear and quadratic functions, and we will learn about interface-driven development. We'll explore the value in knowledge-driven systems, and we will learn how to apply our understanding of category theory to build better applications.

Appendix, *Miscellaneous Information and How-Tos*, shows us how the author suggests that we build and run the Go projects in this book. It shows us how to propose changes to Go, introduces the Lexical Workflow Solution: a Go-compatible way to handle errors in one place, provides a place to go to provide feedback and an FP resources page, discusses the Minggatu-Catalan Number, and offers a solution for world peace.

What you need for this book

If you want to run the Go projects discussed in each chapter, you need to install Go. If you're on a Mac, visit here. Next, you need to get your Go development environment running and start writing code.

Read the *TL;DR* subsection of the *How to build and run Go projects* section of the *Appendix*. Go to Chapter 1, *Pure Functional Programming in Go* in the book and start reading the *Getting the source code* section. Continue reading on how to set up and run your first project.

Other Go resources include:

- Tour of Go (https://tour.golang.org/welcome/1)
- Go by Example (https://gobyexample.com/)
- Learning Go book (https://www.miek.nl/go/)
- Go language specification (https://golang.org/ref/spec)

When I think of other things to add, I'll put that information here: https://lexsheehan.blogspot.com/2017/11/what-you-need-for-this-book.html.

Who this book is for

A lot of the information in this book requires only a high school education.

For the programming sections in this book, you should have at least one year programming experience. Proficiency with Go or Haskell is ideal, but experience with other languages such as C/C++, Python, Javascript, Java, Scala or Ruby is also sufficient. You should have some familiarity using the command line.

This book should appeal to two groups:

1. Non-programmers (read `Chapter 11`, *Category Theory That Applies*) If you are one of these:

- K-12 math teacher and want to see why what you are teaching matters
- Math teacher and want to see how what you are teaching relates to other branches of mathematics
- Student in law school and want to understand what you will be doing when you plead your client's case
- Soccer enthusiast and like math
- Person interested in learning category theory
- Lover of the Lambda Calculus and want to see it illustrated with diagrams, pictures, and Go code
- Manager of software projects and want to see a better correspondence between requirement gathering, implementation, and testing
- C-level executive and want to understand what motivates and excites your IT staff

2. Programmers: If you are one of these:

- Software enthusiast and want to learn Functional Programming
- Software tester and want to see a better correspondence between requirement gathering, implementation, and testing
- Software architect and want to understand how to use FP
- Go developer and like soccer
- Go developer and want to implement your business use case programming tasks with more expressive code
- Go developer and want to understand Generics
- Java developer and would like to understand why we say, *less is more*

- *Your_language_here* developer who knows FP and wants to transfer your skills to Go
- Go developer looking for a better way to build data transformation pipelines
- Go developer and would like to see a viable way to write less code, that is, fewer if *err != nil* blocks
- Experienced Go developer and want to learn FP or add some tools to your toolbox
- Person involved in software development and want to understand any of the terms below.

If you are a Go developer looking for working code, with line-by-line explanations for any of the following, this book is for you:

- Benchmark testing
- Concurrency (Goroutines/Channels)
- Currying
- Data transformation pipeline
- Decorator Pattern
- Dependency Injection
- Duck typing
- Embedding Interfaces
- Error handler
- Function composition
- Funcitonal parameters
- Functors
- Generics via code generation
- Hollywood Principle
- Interface-driven development
- I18N (language translation)
- IoC
- Lambda expressions in Go
- Layered application framework
- Log handler
- Monads
- Monoids
- Observer Pattern
- Partial application

- Pipeline to process credit card payments
- Recursion
- Reduce function to sum invoice totals
- Solve circular dependency errors
- Table-driven http API test framework
- Type Class
- Upload/download files to/from Google Cloud Buckets
- Y-Combinator

 If I decide to change the format or update this info, I'll put it here: http://lexsheehan.blogspot.com/2017/11/who-this-book-is-for.html.

Conventions

In this book, you will find a number of text styles that distinguish between different kinds of information. Here are some examples of these styles and an explanation of their meaning. Code words in text, database table names, folder names, filenames, file extensions, pathnames, dummy URLs, user input, and Twitter handles are shown as follows: "We update code, run the `glide-update` and `go-run` commands, and repeat until done." A block of code is set as follows:

```
func newSlice(s []string) *Collection {
   return &Collection{INVALID_INT_VAL, s}
}
```

When we wish to draw your attention to a particular part of a code block, the relevant lines or items are set in bold:

```
[default]
exten => s,1,Dial(Zap/1|30)
exten => s,2,Voicemail(u100)
exten => s,102,Voicemail(b100)
exten => i,1,Voicemail(s0)
```

Any command-line input or output is written as follows:

```
go get --help
```

Preface

New terms and **important words** are shown in bold. Words that you see on the screen, for example, in menus or dialog boxes, appear in the text like this: "In order to download new modules, we will go to **Files** | **Settings** | **Project Name** | **Project Interpreter**."

Warnings or important notes appear like this.

Tips and tricks appear like this.

Reader feedback

Feedback from our readers is always welcome. Let us know what you think about this book-what you liked or disliked. Reader feedback is important for us as it helps us develop titles that you will really get the most out of. To send us general feedback, simply e-mail feedback@packtpub.com, and mention the book's title in the subject of your message. If there is a topic that you have expertise in and you are interested in either writing or contributing to a book, see our author guide at www.packtpub.com/authors.

Customer support

Now that you are the proud owner of a Packt book, we have a number of things to help you to get the most from your purchase.

Downloading the example code

You can download the example code files for this book from your account at http://www.packtpub.com. If you purchased this book elsewhere, you can visit http://www.packtpub.com/support and register to have the files e-mailed directly to you. You can download the code files by following these steps:

1. Log in or register to our website using your e-mail address and password.
2. Hover the mouse pointer on the **SUPPORT** tab at the top.
3. Click on **Code Downloads & Errata**.
4. Enter the name of the book in the **Search** box.
5. Select the book for which you're looking to download the code files.

6. Choose from the drop-down menu where you purchased this book from.
7. Click on **Code Download**.

Once the file is downloaded, please make sure that you unzip or extract the folder using the latest version of:

- WinRAR / 7-Zip for Windows
- Zipeg / iZip / UnRarX for Mac
- 7-Zip / PeaZip for Linux

The code bundle for the book is also hosted on GitHub at https://github.com/PacktPublishing/Learning-Functional-Programming-in-Go. We also have other code bundles from our rich catalog of books and videos available at https://github.com/PacktPublishing/. Check them out!

Downloading the color images of this book

We also provide you with a PDF file that has color images of the screenshots/diagrams used in this book. The color images will help you better understand the changes in the output. You can download this file from https://www.packtpub.com/sites/default/files/downloads/LearningFunctionalProgramminginGo_ColorImages.pdf.

Errata

Although we have taken every care to ensure the accuracy of our content, mistakes do happen. If you find a mistake in one of our books-maybe a mistake in the text or the code-we would be grateful if you could report this to us. By doing so, you can save other readers from frustration and help us improve subsequent versions of this book. If you find any errata, please report them by visiting http://www.packtpub.com/submit-errata, selecting your book, clicking on the **Errata Submission Form** link, and entering the details of your errata. Once your errata are verified, your submission will be accepted and the errata will be uploaded to our website or added to any list of existing errata under the Errata section of that title.

To view the previously submitted errata, go to https://www.packtpub.com/books/content/support and enter the name of the book in the search field. The required information will appear under the **Errata** section.

Piracy

Piracy of copyrighted material on the Internet is an ongoing problem across all media. At Packt, we take the protection of our copyright and licenses very seriously. If you come across any illegal copies of our works in any form on the Internet, please provide us with the location address or website name immediately so that we can pursue a remedy. Please contact us at `copyright@packtpub.com` with a link to the suspected pirated material. We appreciate your help in protecting our authors and our ability to bring you valuable content.

Questions

If you have a problem with any aspect of this book, you can contact us at `questions@packtpub.com`, and we will do our best to address the problem.

Pure Functional Programming in Go

"Go is an attempt to combine the safety and performance of statically typed languages with the convenience and fun of dynamically typed interpretative languages."

- Rob Pike

Do you love Go? If so, why? Could it be better? Can you write your code better today?

Yes! Because Go is simple yet powerful; Go does not make me wait; its compiler is fast and cross-platform; Go makes concurrent programming easy; Go also provides useful tooling, and it has a great development community. Perhaps. Yes, that's what this book is about: using the **functional programming** (FP) style of coding.

In this chapter, I will share the benefits of pure FP as well as its performance implications in Go by working through Fibonacci sequence code samples. Starting with a simple imperative implementation, you will explore functional implementations and learn some test-driven development and benchmark techniques along the way.

The goal of this chapter is to:

- Become grounded in the theory of FP
- Learn how to implement functional solutions
- Determine what type of FP will best fit your business requirements

Motivation for using FP

The FP style of programming can help you write less code in a more concise and expressive way, with fewer errors. How is that possible? Well, FP treats computation as an evaluation of mathematical functions. FP leverages this computational model (and the work of some brilliant mathematicians and logicians) to enable optimizations and performance gains that are simply not possible using traditional imperative coding techniques.

Developing software is not easy. You must handle numerous **non-functional requirements** (**NFRs**) first, such as:

- Complexity
- Extensibility
- Maintainability
- Reliability
- Concurrency
- Scalability

Software is becoming more and more complex. What is the average number of third-party dependencies in your typical application? What did that look like 5 years ago? Our applications often must integrate with other services within our own company and with our partners as well as external customers. How can we manage this growing complexity?

Applications used to run on-site on servers that were given pet names, such as Apollo, Gemini, and so on. It seems like every client would have a different naming scheme. Nowadays, most applications are deploying into a cloud environment, for example, AWS or the Google Cloud Platform. Do you have a lot of software applications that run on a lot of servers? If so, you should treat your servers more like cattle; there's just so many of them. Also, since you've got auto scaling, what's important is not a single server but the herd. As long as you always have at least one server in your cluster running for the accounting department, that's all that really matters.

With numbers comes complexity. Can you compose your applications to fit together like Lego blocks, and do you find it easy to write useful tests that run really fast. Alternatively, do you ever feel like there's too much scaffolding/`for` loops in your code? Do you like handling the `err != nil` condition so frequently? Would you like to see a simpler, cleaner way to do the same thing? Do your applications have any global variables? Do you have code in place to always properly manage its state and prevent all the possible side effects? Have race conditions ever been a problem?

Are you aware of all the possible error conditions in your applications, and do you have code in place to handle them? Can you look at the function signature of any function in your code and immediately have an intuition as to what it does?

Are you interested in learning about a better way to achieve your NFRs and enjoy developing Go software even more than you do right now? Looking for the silver bullet? If so, please continue reading. (Note that the rest of this book will be written in first person plural since we will be learning together.)

Getting the source code

> The GitHub repository for this book's source code is https://github.com/l3x/fp-go.
>
> If you store your Go projects in the ~/myprojects directory, then run cd ~/myprojects; git clone https://github.com/l3x/fp-go.git.
>
> Next, run the cd command into the first project directory: cd ~/myprojects/fp-go/1-functional-fundamentals/ch01-pure-fp/01_oop.

The directory structure of the source files

Directories correspond to the book's units and chapters:

```
~/myprojects/fp-go $ tree -C -d -L 2
├── 1-functional-fundamentals
│   ├── ch01-pure-fp
│   ├── ch02-collections
│   └── ch03-hof
├── 2-design-patterns
│   ├── ch04-solid
│   ├── ch05-decoration
│   └── ch06-onion-arch
├── 3-functional-techniques
│   ├── ch07-func-param
│   ├── ch08-pipelining
│   └── ch09-refx-futr-lazy
├── 4-purely-functional
│   ├── ch10-category-thery-that-applies
│   ├── ch11-functor-monoid-tclass
│   └── ch12-monads
└── 5-appendix
```

Each chapter is divided into sequentially numbered directories that are in the order of their appearance in the book.

How to run our first Go application

First, let's make sure we have Go installed, our GOPATH is properly set, and that we can run a Go application.

> **TIP:** If you are using a macOS, then check out the instructions on how to use the brew command to install Go in the appendix; otherwise, to install Go, visit: http://golang.org/doc/install. To set your GOPATH, visit: https://github.com/golang/go/wiki/Setting-GOPATH.

Many people use a global GOPATH to store the source code for all their Go applications or, frequently, manually reset their GOPATH. I found this practice to be troublesome when working with multiple Go projects for multiple clients, each of which had differing Go versions and third-party dependencies.

The example Go applications that we'll use in this chapter do not have dependencies; that is, we don't have to import any third-party packages. So, all we have to do to run our first app--cars.go--is verify that Go is installed, set our GOPATH, and type go run cars.go:

```
~/myprojects/fp-go/1-functional-fundamentals/ch01-pure-fp/01_oop $ go version
go version go1.9 darwin/amd64
~/myprojects/fp-go/1-functional-fundamentals/ch01-pure-fp/01_oop $ export GOPATH=$(pwd)
~/myprojects/fp-go/1-functional-fundamentals/ch01-pure-fp/01_oop $ go run cars.go
Found &{Highlander} ~/myprojects/fp-go/1-functional-fundamentals/ch01-pure-fp/01_oop $
```

Using a global GOPATH is easy for projects that are super simple, like the examples in this chapter.

In Chapter 2, *Manipulating Collections*, our Go applications will start getting more complex, and we'll get introduced to a simple, more consistent way to manage our Go development environments.

Imperative versus declarative programming

Let's look at why the functional style of programming helps us be more productive than the imperative alternative.

"We are not makers of history. We are made by history."

- *Martin Luther King, Jr.*

Nearly all computer hardware is designed to execute machine code, which is native to the computer, written in the imperative style. The program state is defined by the contents of memory, and the statements are instructions in the machine language where each statement advances the state of computation forward, toward a final outcome. Imperative programs change their state over time, step by step. High-level imperative languages, such as C and Go, use variables and more complex statements, but they still follow the same paradigm. Since the basic ideas in imperative programming are both conceptually similar to low-level code that operates directly on computer hardware, most computer languages--such as Go, also known as *C of the 21st century*--are largely imperative.

Imperative programming is a programming paradigm that uses statements that change a program's state. It focuses on the step-by-step mechanics of how a program operates.

The term is often used in contrast to **declarative programming**. In declarative programming, we declare what we want the results to be. We describe what we want, not detailed instructions of how to get it.

Here's a typical, imperative way to find `Blazer` in a slice of cars:

```
var found bool
carToLookFor := "Blazer"
cars := []string{"Accord", "IS250", "Blazer" }
for _, car := range cars {
   if car == carToLookFor {
      found = true; // set flag
   }
}
fmt.Printf("Found? %v", found)
```

Here's a functional way of accomplishing the same task:

```
cars := []string{"Accord", "IS250", "Blazer" }
fmt.Printf("Found? %v", cars.contains("Blazer"))
```

That's nine lines of imperative code, compared to two lines in the **functional programming (FP)** style.

Functional constructs often express our intent more clearly than for loops in such cases and are especially useful when we want to filter, transform, or aggregate the elements in a dataset.

In the imperative example, we must code the *how*. We must:

- Declare a Boolean flag
- Declare and set a variable value
- Create a looping structure
- Compare each iterated value
- Set the flag

In the functional example, we declare *what* we want to do. We are able to focus on what we want to accomplish, rather than bloating our code with the mechanics of looping structures, setting variable values, and so on.

In FP, iteration is implemented by the library function `contains()`. Leveraging library functions means that we code less and allow library developers to focus on highly efficient implementations, which have been typically vetted and performance enhanced by seasoned professionals. We don't have to write, debug, or test such high-quality code for repetitive logic.

Now, let's look at how we could look for `Blazer` using the object-oriented programming paradigm:

```go
type Car struct {
    Model string
}
accord := &Car{"Accord"}; is250 := &Car{"IS250"}; blazer := &Car{"Blazer"}
cars := []*Car{is250, accord, blazer}
var found bool
carToLookFor := is250
for _, car := range cars {
    if car == carToLookFor {
        found = true;
    }
}
fmt.Printf("Found? %v", found)
```

First, we declare our object types:

```go
type Car struct {
   Model string
}
type Cars []Car
```

Next, we add our methods:

```go
func (cars *Cars) Add(car Car) {
   myCars = append(myCars, car)
}

func (cars *Cars) Find(model string) (*Car, error) {
   for _, car := range *cars {
      if car.Model == model {
         return &car, nil
      }
   }
   return nil, errors.New("car not found")
}
```

Here, we declare a global variable, namely `myCars`, where we will persist the state, that is, the list of cars that we will build:

```go
var myCars Cars
```

Add three cars to the list. The `Car` object encapsulates the data for each object, and the `cars` object encapsulates our list of cars:

```go
func main() {
   myCars.Add(Car{"IS250"})
   myCars.Add(Car{"Blazer"})
   myCars.Add(Car{"Highlander"})
```

Look for `Highlander` and print the results:

```go
    car, err := myCars.Find("Highlander")
   if err != nil {
      fmt.Printf("ERROR: %v", car)
   } else {
      fmt.Printf("Found %v", car)
   }
}
```

We are using `car` objects, but we are essentially doing the same operations as we were in the simple imperative code example. We do have objects that have state and to which we could add methods, but the underlying mechanisms are the same. We assign a state to object properties, modify the internal state by making method calls, and advance the state of execution until we arrive at the desired outcome. That's imperative programming.

Pure functions

"Insanity is doing the same thing over and over again and expecting different results."

- Albert Einstein

We can use this insanity principle to our advantage with pure functions.

Assigning values to variables during an imperative function's execution may result in the modification of a variable in the environment in which it has run. If we run the same imperative function again, using the same input, the result may differ.

Given the results of an imperative function and given the same input, different results may be returned each time it is run. Is that not insanity?

Pure functions:

- Treat functions as first-class citizens
- Always return the same result given the same input(s)
- Have no side effects in the environment in which they run
- Do not allow an external state to affect their results
- Do not allow variable values to change over time

Two characteristics of a pure function include referential transparency and idempotence:

- **Referential transparency**: This is where a function call can be replaced with its corresponding value without changing the program's behavior
- **Idempotence**: This is where a function call can be called repeatedly and produce the same result each time

Referentially transparent programs are more easily optimized. Let's see whether we can perform optimizations using a caching technique and Go's concurrency features.

Fibonacci sequence - a simple recursion and two performance improvements

The Fibonacci sequence is a sequence of numbers where each number is equal to the previous two numbers added together. Here's an example of this:

```
1   1   2   3   5   8   13   21   34
```

So, 1 plus 1 is 2, 2 plus 3 is 5, 5 plus 8 is 13, and so on.

Let's use the Fibonacci sequence to help illustrate a number of concepts.

A **recursive function** is a function that calls itself in order to break down complex input into simpler ones. With each recursive call, the input problem must be simplified in such a way that eventually the base case must be reached.

The Fibonacci sequence can be easily implemented as a recursive function:

```
func Fibonacci(x int) int {
    if x == 0 {
        return 0
    } else if x <= 2 {
        return 1
    } else {
        return Fibonacci(x-2) + Fibonacci(x-1)
    }
}
```

In the preceding recursive function (`Fibonacci`), if the input is the simple case of 0 then it returns **0.** Similarly, if the input is 1 or 2 then return 1.

An input of 0, 1 or 2 is called the **base case** or **stopping condition**; else, `fib` will call itself twice, adding the previous value in the sequence to the one preceding it:

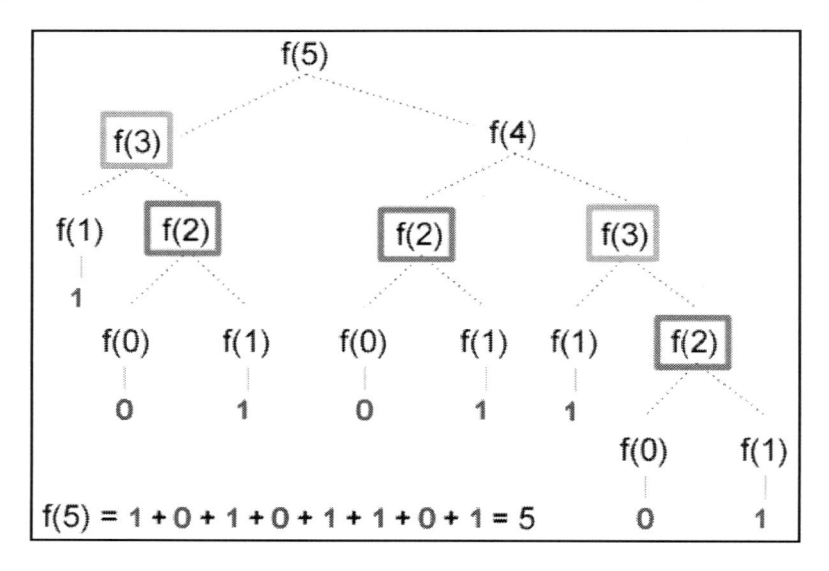

Fibonacci(5) calculation graph

In the preceding figure *Fibonacci(5) calculation graph*, we can visually see how the fifth element in the Fibonacci sequence is calculated. We see **f(3)** is calculated twice and **f(2)** is calculated thrice. Only the final leaf nodes of **1** are added together to calculate the sum total of **8**:

```
func main() {
    fib := Fibonacci
    fmt.Printf("%vn", fib(5))
}
```

Run that code and you'll get 8. Recursive functions perform identical calculations over and over again; **f(3)** is calculated twice and **f(2)** is calculated thrice. The deeper the graph, the more redundant calculations get executed. That is terribly inefficient. Try it yourself. Pass a value greater than 50 to `fib` and see how long you have to wait for the final result.

Go provides many ways to improve this performance. We'll look at two options: memoization and concurrency.

Memoization is an optimization technique used to increase performance by storing the results of expensive function calls and returning the cached result when the same input occurs again.

Memoization works well because of the following two properties of pure functions:

- They always return the same result given the same input(s)
- They have no side effects in the environment in which they run

Memoization

Let's utilize a memoization technique to speed up our Fibonacci calculation.

First, let's create a function type named `Memoized()` and define our Fibonacci variable to be of that type:

```
type Memoized func(int) int
var fibMem Memoized
```

Next, let's implement the `Memoize()` function. The key thing to realize here is that as soon as our application starts, even before our `main()` function is executed, our `fibMem` variable get *wired up*. If we were to step through our code we'd see that our `Memoize` function is called. The cache variable is assigned and our anonymous function is returned and assigned to our `fibMem` function literal variable.

```
func Memoize(mf Memoized) Memoized {
        cache := make(map[int]int)
        return func(key int) int {
                if val, found := cache[key]; found {
                        return val
                }
                temp := mf(key)
                cache[key] = temp
                return temp
        }
}
```

Memoize takes a `Memoized()` function type as its input and returns a `Memoized()` function.

In the first line of Memoize, we create a variable of the type `map` to act as our cache in order to hold computed Fibonacci computations.

Next, we create a closure that is of the type `Memoized()`, which is *return*ed by the `Memoize()` function. Note that a **closure** is an inner function that closes over or that has access to variables in its outer scope.

Inside the closure, if we find the computation for the passed integer, we return its value from the cache; else we call the recursive Fibonacci function (`mf`) with the integer parameter (`key`), whose return value will be stored in `cache[key]`. Next time, when the same key is requested its value will be returned directly from the cache.

An anonymous function is a function defined with no name. When an anonymous function includes logic that can access variables defined in its scope, for example, `cache`, and if that anonymous function can be passed as an argument or returned as the value of function calls, which is true in this case, then we can refer to this anonymous function as a lambda expression.

We'll implement the logic of the Fibonacci Sequence in a function named `fib`:

```
func fib(x int) int {
   if x == 0 {
      return 0
   } else if x <= 2 {
      return 1
   } else {
      return fib(x-2) + fib(x-1)
   }
}
```

The last thing we do in our `memoize.go` file is to create the following function:

```
func FibMemoized(n int) int {
   return fibMem(n)
}
```

Now, it's time to see if our wiring works properly. In our `main()` function when we execute our `println` statement, we get the correct output.

```
println(fibonacci.FibMemoized(5))
```

The following is the output:

```
5
```

We can verify that 5 is the correct answer by glancing back at our `Fibonacci(5)` *calculation graph* shown earlier in this chapter.

If we were to step through our code using a debugger, we'd see that
fibonacci.FibMemoized(5) calls the following

```
func FibMemoized(n int) int {
    return fibMem(n)
}
```

And the value of n variable is 5. Since fibMem is pre-wired, we start executing at the return statement (and we have access to the cache variable that has already been initialized). So, we begin executing at the return statement shown in the following code (from the Memoize function):

```
return func(key int) int {
    if val, found := cache[key]; found {
        return val
    }
    temp := mf(key)
    cache[key] = temp
    return temp
}
```

Since this is the first time through, there are no entries in the cache and we skip past the body of the if block and run temp := mf(key)

That calls the fib function:

```
func fib(x int) int {
    if x == 0 {
        return 0
    } else if x <= 2 {
        return 1
    } else {
        return fib(x-2) + fib(x-1)
    }
}
```

And since x is greater than 2 we run the last else statement that recursively calls fib twice. Recursive calls to fib continues until the base conditions are reached and the final result is calculated and returned.

The difference between an anonymous function and a closure

Let's look at a few simple code examples to understand the difference between an anonymous function and a closure.

Here's a typical named function:

```
func namedGreeting(name string) {
   fmt.Printf("Hey %s!n", name)
}
```

The following is an example of the anonymous function:

```
func anonymousGreeting() func(string) {
    return func(name string) {
          fmt.Printf("Hey %s!n", name)
    }
}
```

Now, let's call them both and call an anonymous inline function to say `Hey` to Cindy:

```
func main() {
   namedGreeting("Alice")

   greet := anonymousGreeting()
   greet("Bob")

   func(name string) {
      fmt.Printf("Hello %s!n", name)
   }("Cindy")
}
```

The output will be as follows:

```
Hello Alice!
Hello Bob!
Hello Cindy!
```

Now, let's look at a closure named `greeting` and see the difference between it and the `anonymousGreeting()` function.

Since the closure function is declared in the same scope as the `msg` variable, the closure has access to it. The `msg` variable is said to be in the same environment as the closure; later, we'll see that a closure's environment variables and data can be passed around and referenced at a later time during a program's execution:

```
func greeting(name string) {
    msg := name + fmt.Sprintf(" (at %v)", time.Now().String())

    closure := func() {
        fmt.Printf("Hey %s!n", msg)
    }
    closure()
}

func main() {
    greeting("alice")
}
```

The output will be as follows:

```
Hey alice (at 2017-01-29 12:29:30.164830641 -0500 EST)!
```

In the next example, instead of executing the closure in the `greeting()` function, we will return it and assign its return value to the `hey` variable in the `main` function:

```
func greeting(name string) func() {
    msg := name + fmt.Sprintf(" (at %v)", time.Now().String())
    closure := func() {
        fmt.Printf("Hey %s!n", msg)
    }
    return closure
}

func main() {
    fmt.Println(time.Now())
    hey := greeting("bob")
    time.Sleep(time.Second * 10)
    hey()
}
```

The output will be as follows:

```
2017-01-29 12:42:09.767187225 -0500 EST
Hey bob (at 2017-01-29 12:42:09.767323847 -0500 EST)!
```

Note that the timestamp is calculated when the `msg` variable is initialized, at the time the `greeting("bob")` value is assigned to the `hey` variable.

So, 10 seconds later, when `greeting` is called and the closure is executed, it will reference the message that was created 10 seconds ago.

This example shows how closures preserve state. Instead of manipulating the state in the outside environment, closures allow states to be created, passed around, and subsequently referenced.

With functional programming, you still have a state, but it's just passed through each function and is accessible even when the outer scopes, from where they originated, have already exited.

Later in this book, we'll see a more realistic example of how closures can be leveraged to maintain a context of application resources required by an API.

Another way to speed up our recursive Fibonacci function is to use Go's concurrency constructs.

FP using Go's concurrency constructs

Given the expression `result := function1() + function2()`, parallelization means that we can run each function on a different CPU core and the total time will be approximately the time it takes for the most expensive function to return its result. Consider the following explanation for parallelization and concurrency:

- **Parallelization**: Executing multiple functions at the same time (in different CPU cores)
- **Concurrency**: Breaking a program into pieces that can be executed independently

> I recommend that you check out the video *Concurrency is Not Parallelism*, by Rob Pike at `https://player.vimeo.com/video/49718712`. This is where he explains concurrency as a decomposition of a complex problem into smaller components, where individual components can be run simultaneously resulting in improved performance, assuming communication between them is managed.

Go enhances the concurrent execution of Goroutines with synchronization and messaging using channels and provides multiway concurrent control with the `Select` statement.

The following language constructs provide a model in Go for concurrent software construction that is easy to understand, use, and reason about:

- **Goroutine**: A lightweight thread managed by the Go runtime.
- **Go statements**: The `go` instruction that starts the execution of a function call as an independent concurrent thread of control, or Goroutine, in the same address space as the calling code.
- **Channel**: A typed conduit through which you can send and receive values with the channel operator, namely `<-`.

In the following code, `data` is sent to `channel` in the first line. In the second line, `data` is assigned the value received from `channel`:

```
channel <- data
data := <-channel
```

Since Go channels behave as FIFO queues, where the first items in are the first items out, and since the calculation for the next number in a Fibonacci sequence is a small component, it seems that our Fibonacci sequence function calculation is a great candidate for a concurrency implementation.

Let's give it a go. First, let's define a `Channel` function that uses a channel to perform Fibonacci calculations:

```
func Channel(ch chan int, counter int) {
    n1, n2 := 0, 1
    for i := 0; i < counter; i++ {
        ch <- n1
        n1, n2 = n2, n1 + n2
    }
    close(ch)
}
```

First, we declare the variables `n1` and `n2` to hold our initial sequence values of `0` and `1`.

Then, we create a loop for the total number of times given. In each loop, we send the next sequential number to the channel and calculate the next number in the sequence, until we reach our counter value, which is the last sequential number in our sequence.

The following `FibChanneled` function creates a channel, namely `ch`, using the `make()` function and defines it as a channel that contains integers:

```
func FibChanneled(n int) int {
    n += 2
    ch := make(chan int)
    go Channel(ch, n)
    i := 0; var result int
    for num := range ch {
        result = num
        i++
    }
    return result
}
```

We run our `Channel` (Fibonacci) function as a Goroutine and pass it the `ch` channel and the `8` number, which tells `Channel` to produce the first eight numbers from the Fibonacci sequence.

Next, we range over the channel and print any values that the channel produces for as long as the channel has not been closed.

Now, let's take a breather and examine what we've accomplished with our Fibonacci sequence examples.

Testing FP using test-driven development

Let's write some tests to verify each technique (simple recursive, memoized, and channeled) works properly. We'll use TDD to help us design and write better code.

TDD, a software development method where the developer starts with requirements and first writes a simple test that will fail. Then, it writes just enough code to make it pass. It continues this unit testing pattern repeatedly until there are no more reasonable tests that validate the code satisfies the requirements. The concept is to *get something working now and perfect it later*. After each test, refactoring is performed to implement a little more of the feature requirement.

The same or similar test(s) are performed again as well as introducing new test code to test the next piece of the feature. The process is iterated as many times as necessary until each unit is functioning according to the desired specifications:

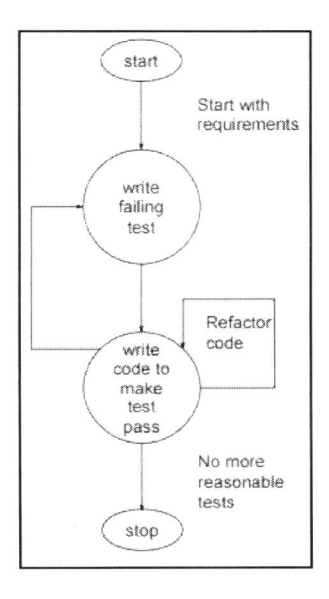

TDD workflow diagram

We can start using a table of input values and their corresponding result values to verify that the function under test is working properly:

```go
// File: chapter1/_01_fib/ex1_test.go
package fib

import "testing"

var fibTests = []struct {
    a int
    expected int
}{
    {1, 1},
    {2, 2},
    {3, 3},
    {4, 5},
    {20, 10946},
    {42, 433494437},
}

func TestSimple(t *testing.T) {
```

```
        for _, ft := range fibTests {
            if v := FibSimple(ft.a); v != ft.expected {
                t.Errorf("FibSimple(%d) returned %d, expected %d", ft.a, v,
    ft.expected)
            }
        }
    }
```

Recall that the Fibonacci sequence looks like this: 1 1 2 3 5 8 13 21 34. Here, the first element is 1 {1, 1}, the second element is 2 {2, 2}, and so on.

We use the range statement to iterate through the table, row by row, and check each calculated result (`v := FibSimple(ft.a)`) against the expected value (`ft.expected`) from that row.

Only if there is a mismatch do we report the error.

Later in the `ex1_test.go` file, we find the benchmark testing facility in action, which allows us to examine the performance of our Go code:

```
    func BenchmarkFibSimple(b *testing.B) {
        fn := FibSimple
        for i := 0; i < b.N; i++ {
            _ = fn(8)
        }
    }
```

Let's open a terminal window and write the `cd` command to the first set of Go code, our book's source code repository. For me, that directory is `~/clients/packt/dev/fp-go/1-functional-fundamentals/ch01-pure-fp/01_fib`.

A note about paths

In the first example, I used the `~/myprojects/fp-go` path. The path that I actually used to create the code in this book is `~/clients/packt/dev/fp-go`. So, please don't be confused by those paths. They are the same thing.

Also, later in the book, when we start using KISS-Glide, the screenshots may reference the `~/dev` directory. That comes from the init script, that is, `MY_DEV_DIR=~/dev`.

Here are a few links in that directory:

```
01_duck@ -> /Users/lex/clients/packt/dev/fp-go/2-design-patterns/ch04-
solid/01_duck
01_hof@ -> /Users/lex/clients/packt/dev/fp-go/1-functional-
fundamentals/ch03-hof/01_hof
04_onion@ -> /Users/lex/clients/packt/dev/fp-go/2-design-patterns/ch07-
onion-arch/04_onion
```

For more information about KISS-Glide, see the appendix.

How to run our tests

In the first benchmark test, we examine the performance of computing the eighth number in the Fibonacci sequence. Note that we pass the -bench=. argument, which means run all benchmark tests. The ./... argument means to run all the tests in this directory and all the child directories as well:

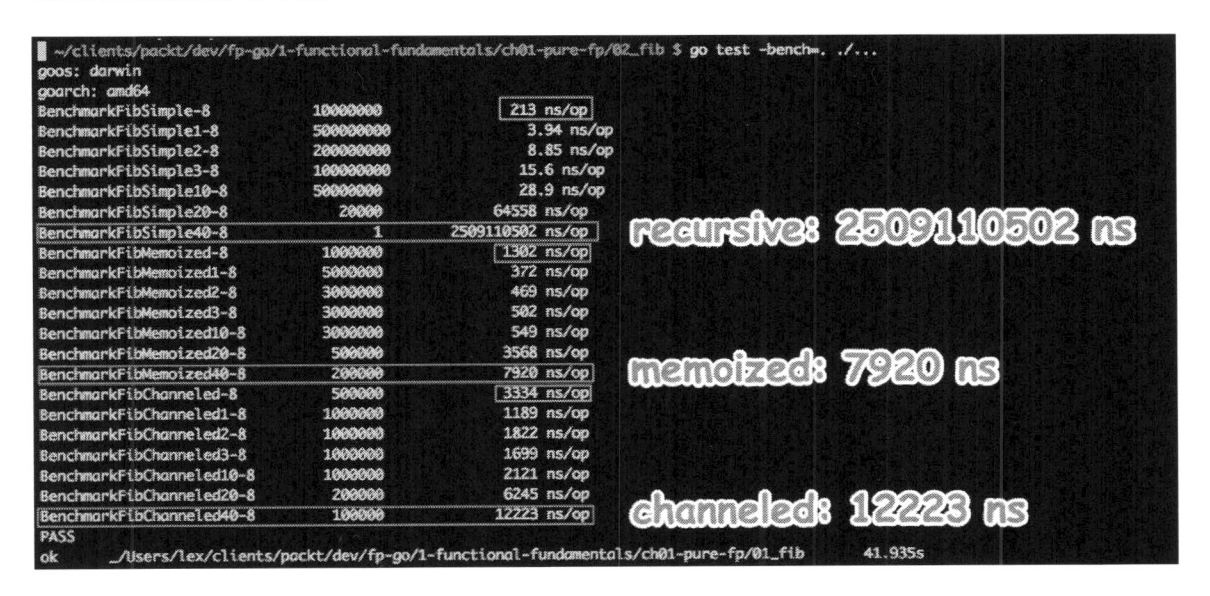

```
~/clients/packt/dev/fp-go/1-functional-fundamentals/ch01-pure-fp/02_fib $ go test -bench=. ./...
goos: darwin
goarch: amd64
BenchmarkFibSimple-8        10000000         213 ns/op
BenchmarkFibSimple1-8      500000000         3.94 ns/op
BenchmarkFibSimple2-8      200000000         8.85 ns/op
BenchmarkFibSimple3-8      100000000         15.6 ns/op
BenchmarkFibSimple10-8      50000000         28.9 ns/op
BenchmarkFibSimple20-8         20000         64558 ns/op
BenchmarkFibSimple40-8             1         2509110502 ns/op     recursive: 2509110502 ns
BenchmarkFibMemoized-8       1000000         1302 ns/op
BenchmarkFibMemoized1-8      5000000         372 ns/op
BenchmarkFibMemoized2-8      3000000         469 ns/op
BenchmarkFibMemoized3-8      3000000         502 ns/op
BenchmarkFibMemoized10-8     3000000         549 ns/op
BenchmarkFibMemoized20-8      500000         3568 ns/op
BenchmarkFibMemoized40-8      200000         7920 ns/op           memoized: 7920 ns
BenchmarkFibChanneled-8       500000         3334 ns/op
BenchmarkFibChanneled1-8     1000000         1189 ns/op
BenchmarkFibChanneled2-8     1000000         1822 ns/op
BenchmarkFibChanneled3-8     1000000         1699 ns/op
BenchmarkFibChanneled10-8    1000000         2121 ns/op
BenchmarkFibChanneled20-8     200000         6245 ns/op
BenchmarkFibChanneled40-8     100000         12223 ns/op          channeled: 12223 ns
PASS
ok    ./Users/lex/clients/packt/dev/fp-go/1-functional-fundamentals/ch01-pure-fp/01_fib    41.935s
```

When we request the eighth number in the sequence, the simple recursive implementation runs faster than the memoized and channeled (optimized) versions, `213 ns/op` compared to `1302 ns/op` and `2224 ns/op`, respectively.

Pure Functional Programming in Go

In fact, when the simple version is executed once, it only takes `3.94 ns/op`.

One very cool feature of Go's benchmark testing facility is that it is smart enough to figure out how many times to execute the function under test. The value of `b.N` will increase each time until the benchmark runner is satisfied with the stability of the benchmark. The faster the function runs under a test, the more times the benchmark facility will run it. The more times the benchmark facility runs a function, the more accurate the performance metric, for example, `3.94 ns/op`.

Take the `FibSimple` test for example. When it is passed with `1`, it means it only needs to execute once. Since it only takes `3.94 ns/op`, we see it is executed 10,000,000 times. However, when `FibSimple` is passed with `40`, we see that it takes 2,509,110,502 ns to complete one operation, and the benchmark facility is smart enough to only run it once. That way, we can be assured that running benchmark tests is as accurate as possible and they run within a reasonable time. How nice is that?

Since the `FibSimple` implementation is recursive and has not been optimized, we can test our assumption that the time it takes to calculate each successive number in the sequence will increase exponentially. We can do this using a common testing technique by calling the private function `benchmarkFibSimple`, which avoids directly invoking the test driver:

```go
func benchmarkFibSimple(i int, b *testing.B) {
    for n := 0; n < b.N; n++ {
        FibSimple(i)
    }
}

func BenchmarkFibSimple1(b *testing.B)  { benchmarkFibSimple(1, b) }
func BenchmarkFibSimple2(b *testing.B)  { benchmarkFibSimple(2, b) }
func BenchmarkFibSimple3(b *testing.B)  { benchmarkFibSimple(3, b) }
func BenchmarkFibSimple10(b *testing.B) { benchmarkFibSimple(4, b) }
func BenchmarkFibSimple20(b *testing.B) { benchmarkFibSimple(20, b) }
func BenchmarkFibSimple40(b *testing.B) { benchmarkFibSimple(42, b) }
```

We test the first four numbers in the sequence, `20` and then `42`. Since it takes about 3 seconds for my computer to calculate the 42nd number in the sequence, I decided not to go any higher. No need to wait longer than that when we can easily see the exponential growth pattern, without having to wait for more than a minute to get our results.

Our benchmark testing has proven that our simple, recursive implementation of the Fibonacci sequence behaves as expected. This behavior equates to poor performance.

Let's look at a few ways to increase performance.

We have observed that our `FibSimple` implementation always returns the same result, given the same input(s), and that there are no side effects in the environment in which it runs. For example, if we pass `FibSimple` an 8 value, we know that every time the result will be 13. We used this fact to leverage a caching technique called memoization to create the `FibMemoized` function.

Now, let's write some tests to see how effective `MemoizeFcn` is.

Since our `fibTests` structure has been defined in another test in our package, in `chapter1/_01_fib/ex1_test.go`, we don't need to define it again. This way, we only define the test table once, and we're able to reuse it in subsequent Fibonacci function implementations to get a reasonable apples-to-apples comparison of each solution.

Here's the basic unit test for the `FibMemoized` function:

```
func TestMemoized(t *testing.T) {
    for _, ft := range fibTests {
        if v := FibMemoized(ft.a); v != ft.expected {
            t.Errorf("FibMemoized(%d) returned %d, expected %d", ft.a, v,
ft.expected)
        }
    }
}
```

It won't return an error unless there is a bug in our code.

That's one of the great things about running unit tests. You don't hear about them unless something breaks.

> We should write unit tests in order to:
>
> - Ensure that what you implement meets your feature requirements
> - Leverage testing to help you think about how best to implement your solution
> - Produce quality tests that can be used in your constant integration process
> - Verify that your implementation meets interface requirements with other parts of your application
> - Make developing integration tests easier
> - Safeguard your work against other developers, who might implement a component that could break your code in production

Here are the benchmark tests:

```
func BenchmarkFibMemoized(b *testing.B) {
    fn := FibMemoized
    for i := 0; i < b.N; i++ {
        _ = fn(8)
    }
}
```

As before, in the `FibSimple` example, we examine the performance of computing the eighth number in the Fibonacci sequence:

```
func BenchmarkFibMemoized(b *testing.B) {
    fn := FibMemoized
    for i := 0; i < b.N; i++ {
        _ = fn(8)
    }
}

func benchmarkFibMemoized(i int, b *testing.B) {
    for n := 0; n < b.N; n++ {
        FibMemoized(i)
    }
}

func BenchmarkFibMemoized1(b *testing.B)   {
    benchmarkFibMemoized(1, b) }
func BenchmarkFibMemoized2(b *testing.B)   {
    benchmarkFibMemoized(2, b) }
func BenchmarkFibMemoized3(b *testing.B)   {
    benchmarkFibMemoized(3, b) }
func BenchmarkFibMemoized10(b *testing.B)  {
    benchmarkFibMemoized(4, b) }
func BenchmarkFibMemoized20(b *testing.B)  {
    benchmarkFibMemoized(20, b) }
func BenchmarkFibMemoized40(b *testing.B)  {
    benchmarkFibMemoized(42, b) }
```

As before, we carry out a test calling `FibMemoized`, using 1, 2, 3, 4, 20, and 42 as input.

Here's the complete listing for the `FibChanelled` function:

```
package fib

import "testing"

func TestChanneled(t *testing.T) {
    for _, ft := range fibTests {
        if v := FibChanneled(ft.a); v != ft.expected {
            t.Errorf("FibChanneled(%d) returned %d, expected %d",
ft.a, v, ft.expected)
        }
    }
}

func BenchmarkFibChanneled(b *testing.B) {
    fn := FibChanneled
    for i := 0; i < b.N; i++ {
        _ = fn(8)
    }
}

func benchmarkFibChanneled(i int, b *testing.B) {
    for n := 0; n < b.N; n++ {
        FibChanneled(i)
    }
}

func BenchmarkFibChanneled1(b *testing.B)  {
    benchmarkFibChanneled(1, b)  }
func BenchmarkFibChanneled2(b *testing.B)  {
    benchmarkFibChanneled(2, b)  }
func BenchmarkFibChanneled3(b *testing.B)  {
    benchmarkFibChanneled(3, b)  }
func BenchmarkFibChanneled10(b *testing.B)  {
    benchmarkFibChanneled(4, b)  }
func BenchmarkFibChanneled20(b *testing.B)  {
    benchmarkFibChanneled(20, b)  }
func BenchmarkFibChanneled40(b *testing.B)  {
    benchmarkFibChanneled(42, b)  }
```

We performed two optimizations on our original Fibonacci sequence logic using a caching technique and Go's concurrency features. We wrote both the optimization implementations. More optimizations are possible. In some cases, optimization techniques can be combined to produce even faster code.

What if all we had to do was write a simple recursive version and then when we compiled our Go code, the Go compiler would automatically generate object code with performance optimizations?

> **Lazy evaluation**: An evaluation strategy that delays the evaluation of an expression until its value is needed, which improves performance by avoiding needless calculations.

A journey from imperative programming to pure FP and enlightenment

Let's take a journey from imperative to a pure functional way of programming a `sum` function. First, let's look at the imperative `sum` function:

```go
func SumLoop(nums []int) int {
    sum := 0
    for _, num := range nums {
        sum += num
    }
    return sum
}
```

The integer variable `sum` changes or mutates over time; `sum` is not immutable. There are no for loops or mutating variables in pure FP.

So, how can we iterate through a series of elements using pure FP? We can do this using recursion.

> **Immutable variable**: A variable whose value is assigned during runtime and cannot be modified.

Note that Go does have constants, but they differ from immutable variables in that values are assigned to constants at compile time, rather than at runtime:

```go
func SumRecursive(nums []int) int {
    if len(nums) == 0 {
        return 0
    }
    return nums[0] + SumRecursive(nums[1:])
}
```

Notice that the last line of the preceding `SumRecursive` function calls itself: `SumRecursive(nums[1:])`. That's recursion.

Benchmark test for the imperative SumLoop function

We have heard that recursion in Go can be slow. So, let's write some benchmark tests to check it out. First, let's test the performance of the basic imperative function `SumLoop`:

```
func benchmarkSumLoop(s []int, b *testing.B) {
    for n := 0; n < b.N; n++ {
        SumLoop(s)
    }
}

func BenchmarkSumLoop40(b *testing.B) { benchmarkSumLoop([]int{1, 2, 3, 4,
5, 6, 7, 8, 9, 10, 11, 12, 13, 14, 15, 16, 17, 18, 19, 20, 21, 22, 23, 24,
25, 26, 27, 28, 29, 30, 31, 32, 33, 34, 35, 36, 37, 38, 39, 40}, b) }
```

Results: It took `46.1 ns/op`.

Benchmark test for the SumRecursive function

Now that we know how long the imperative function `SumLoop` takes, let's write a benchmark test to see how long our recursive version, namely `SumRecursive`, would take:

```
func benchmarkSumRecursive(s []int, b *testing.B) {
    for n := 0; n < b.N; n++ {
        SumRecursive(s)
    }
}

func BenchmarkSumRecursive40(b *testing.B) { benchmarkSumRecursive([]int{1,
2, 3, 4, 5, 6, 7, 8, 9, 10, 11, 12, 13, 14, 15, 16, 17, 18, 19, 20, 21, 22,
23, 24, 25, 26, 27, 28, 29, 30, 31, 32, 33, 34, 35, 36, 37, 38, 39, 40}, b)
}
```

Results: It took `178 ns/op`.

Tail call recursion is faster in languages such as Prolog, Scheme, Lua, and Elixir, and the ECMAScript 6.0-compliant JavaScript engines embrace the pure functional style of programming. So, let's give it a shot:

```
func SumTailCall(vs []int) int {
        if len(vs) == 0 {
                return 0
        }
        return vs[0] + SumTailCall(vs[1:])
}
```

Results of the benchmark test: It took `192 ns/op`.

> **TCO**: A tail call is where the last statement of a function is a function call. An optimized tail call has been effectively replaced with a `GoTo` statement, which eliminates the work required to set up the call stack before the function call and restore it afterward.

We could even use `GoTo` statements to further speed up the tail call recursion, but it would still be three times slower than the imperative version.

Why? This is because Go does not provide pure FP support. For example, Go does not perform TCOs, nor does it provide immutable variables.

A time of reckoning

Why would we want to use pure FP in Go? If writing expressive, easy-to-maintain, and insightful code is more important than performance, then perhaps.

What are our alternatives? Later, we'll look at some pure FP libraries that have done the heavy lifting for us and have made strides toward being more performant.

Is that all there is to functional programming in Go? No. Not by a long shot. What we can do with FP in Go is currently partially limited by the fact that the Go compiler currently does not support TCO; However, that may change soon. For details see the *How to Propose Changes To Go* section in the Appendix.

There is another aspect to functional programming that Go fully supports: function literals. And as it turns out, that is the single most important characteristic that a language must have to support FP.

Function literals: These are functions that are treated as first-class citizens of a language, for example, any variable type, such as int and string. In Go, functions can be declared as a type, assigned to variables and fields of a struct, passed as arguments to other functions, and returned as values from other functions. Function literals are closures, giving them access to the scope in which they are declared. When function literals are assigned to a variable at runtime, for example, `val := func(x int) int { return x + 2}(5)`, we can call that **anonymous function** a **function expression**. Function literals are used in lambda expressions along with currying. (For details about lambda expressions, see `Chapter 10`, *Functors, Monoids, and Generics*.)

A quick example of a function literal

See that `{ret = n + 2}` is our anonymous function/function literal/closure/lambda expression.

Our function literal:

- Is written like a function declaration, but without a function name following the `func` keyword
- Is an expression
- Has access to all the variables available in its lexical scope (n in our case)

```
package main

func curryAddTwo(n int) (ret int) {
    defer func(){ret = n + 2}()
    return n
}

func main()  {
    println(curryAddTwo(1))
}
```

The output is as follows:

```
3
```

Note that we used the `defer` statement to delay the execution of our function literal until after its surrounding function (`curryAddTwo`) is returned. Since our anonymous function has access to all the variables in its scope (n), it can modify n. The modified value is what gets printed.

Summary

When testing pure functions, we simply pass input arguments and verify the results. There is no environment or context to set up. There is no need for stubs or mocks. There are no side effects. Testing could not be easier.

Pure functions can be parallelized for performance gains in a horizontally scaled, multi-CPU environment. However, given that Go has not yet been optimized to support pure functional programming, a pure FP implementation in Go might not meet our performance requirements. We won't let that hinder us from leveraging Go's many effective non-pure functional programming techniques. We've already seen how we can gain performance by adding caching logic and leveraging Go's concurrency features. There are many functional patterns that we can use, and we'll soon see how. We'll also see how we can leverage them to meet stringent performance requirements.

In the next chapter, you'll learn about high-order functions as we explore different ways to manipulate collections using FP programming techniques.

2
Manipulating Collections

Handling lists of items is a common occurrence in life as well as in programming languages. When a list has associated functions that help us manipulate the items in the list, we often call that object a collection.

In this chapter, we will see how high-order functions can be used to greatly simplify the task of manipulating collections. We'll see how we can code using functional programming techniques and open source functional packages to create elegant solutions that are not only insightful, but also performant in today's distributed processing environments.

Our goal in this chapter is to:

- Iterate through a collection
- Learn about intermediate and terminal functors
- Use predicates to filter items in a collection
- Test using a Mocha-like BDD library
- Focus on Map functions
- Grasp the breadth of the collection-manipulating functions in Itertools
- Leverage routines and channels to iterate through a collection
- See how we can use Go to process big data collections

Iterating through a collection

In order to implement a collection, we must provide a way to access each element in the collection, which can be accomplished using the int index value shown in the following code. We will implement a **first in, first out** (**FIFO**) order queue. We will provide a way to store the elements using a slice data structure. Lastly, we will implement a Next() method to provide a way to traverse the elements in the collection.

In the following code, we define an interface for the Iterator object. It has one method, Next(), which will return the next element in the collection and a Boolean flag to indicate whether it's OK to continue iterating:

```
type CarIterator interface {
    Next() (value string, ok bool)
}
const INVALID_INT_VAL = -1
const INVALID_STRING_VAL = ""
```

Next, we define a collection object that has two properties: an int index used to access the current element and a slice of strings, that is, the actual data in the collection:

```
type Collection struct {
    index int
    List  []string
}
```

Now, we implement the collection's Next() method to meet the IntIterator interface's specification:

```
func (collection *Collection) Next() (value string, ok bool) {
    collection.index++
    if collection.index >= len(collection.List) {
        return INVALID_STRING_VAL, false
    }
    return collection.List[collection.index], true
}
```

The `newSlice` function is the constructor for the iterable collection `intCollection`:

```
func newSlice(s []string) *Collection {
        return &Collection{INVALID_INT_VAL, s}
}
```

Finally, we implement the `main()` function to test our `Collection`.

Let's open up a terminal window and use the `.init` toolset to run our simple Go application:

```
~ $ cd /Users/lex/clients/packt/dev/fp-go/1-functional-fundamentals/ch02-collections/01_iterator
~/clients/packt/dev/fp-go/1-functional-fundamentals/ch02-collections/01_iterator $ . init
+++ basename /Users/lex/clients/packt/dev/fp-go/1-functional-fundamentals/ch02-collections/01_iterator
++ PROJECT_DIR_LINK=/Users/lex/dev/01_iterator
++ ln -s /Users/lex/clients/packt/dev/fp-go/1-functional-fundamentals/ch02-collections/01_iterator /Users/lex/dev/01_iterator
Installed Go version: go version go1.9 darwin/amd64
Switching Go to version 1.9 ...
Exported GOBIN=/Users/lex/clients/packt/dev/fp-go/1-functional-fundamentals/ch02-collections/01_iterator/bin
You should only need to run this init script once.
Add Go source code files under the src directory.
After updating dependencies, i.e., adding a new import statement, run: glide-update
To build and run your app, run: go-run
~/dev/01_iterator $ go-run
CRV
IS250
Blazer
~/dev/01_iterator $
```

> The `.init` ("Dot Init") toolset ensures that we have Go installed and that our `GOPATH` and `GOBIN` directories are properly configured. First, we source the init script by typing `.init`. Since we have no import statements, there is no need to run glide-update. To run our application, we type `go-run`. For more details about Dot Init, see the `Appendix`, *Miscellaneous Information and How-Tos*.

The problem with this implementation is that we are mixing what we want to do with how we do it. We implement an explicit `for` loop to perform the mechanics of the iteration. We define and mutate the value of the index value in order to traverse the elements. We can immediately see that this is an imperative implementation.

In functional programming, we declare what to, rather than imperatively implementing each detail of each operation. We also avoid the sequential nature of `for` loops, which are difficult to fit into a concurrent programming model.

Go is not a functional programming language, but it has a lot of functional features and we can leverage those features to write concise, expressive, and hopefully, bug-free code.

A pure functional language does not maintain a state. Function calls are often chained, where input is passed from function to function. Each function call transforms its input in some way. These functions do not need to be concerned about the external state and do not produce side effects. Each function call can be very efficient at what it does. This style of programming lends itself to efficient testing.

Next, we'll see how function chaining is a lot like piping output through Bash commands.

Piping Bash commands

Executing a composition or chain of functions is very much like executing a series of Bash commands, where the output from one command is piped into the next command. For example, we might cat an input a file that contains a list of timestamps and IP addresses in an `awk` command. The `awk` command removes all but the seventh column. Next, we sort the list in descending order, and finally, we group that data by unique IP addresses.

Consider the following Bash command:

```
$ cat ips.log | awk '{print $7}' | sort | uniq -c
```

Let's give this command the following input:

```
Sun Feb 12 20:27:32 EST 2017 74.125.196.101
Sun Feb 12 20:27:33 EST 2017 98.139.183.24
Sun Feb 12 20:27:34 EST 2017 151.101.0.73
Sun Feb 12 20:27:35 EST 2017 98.139.183.24
Sun Feb 12 20:27:36 EST 2017 151.101.0.73
>Sun Feb 12 20:27:37 EST 2017 74.125.196.101
Sun Feb 12 20:27:38 EST 2017 98.139.183.24
Sun Feb 12 20:27:39 EST 2017 151.101.0.73
Sun Feb 12 20:27:40 EST 2017 98.139.183.24
Sun Feb 12 20:27:41 EST 2017 151.101.0.73
Sun Feb 12 20:27:42 EST 2017 151.101.0.73
Sun Feb 12 20:27:43 EST 2017 151.101.0.73
```

We will get the following output:

```
6 151.101.0.73
2 74.125.196.101
4 98.139.183.24
```

This is a very common pattern in functional programming. We often input a collection of data to a function, or chain of function calls, and get a result that has been transformed in some way.

Collections are used frequently. When we implement them in a concise manner, chaining function calls that explicitly declare what we want to accomplish, we greatly reduce code ceremony. The result is that our code is more expressive, concise, and easier to read.

Functors

Go has three predeclared/raw data types: `bool`, `string`, numeric (`float`, `int64`, and so on). Other data types in Go require type declarations, that is, they require we use the `type` keyword. Functions fall in the later category of data types along with array, struct, pointer, interface, slice, map, and channel types. In Go, functions are first-class data types, which means that can be passed around as parameters and returned as values. Functions that can take functions as arguments and return functions are called high-order functions.

We can write function factories--functions that return functions--and even function factory factories. We can also write functions that modify functions or create functions for specific purposes.

> **Functors**: A functor is a collection of X variables that can apply a function, f, over itself to create a collection of Y, that is, f (X) → Y. (To see what we're talking about here, take a quick look at the *Fingers times 10 functor* example in `Chapter 9`, *Functors, Monoids, and Generics*)

Manipulating Collections

Note that the Prolog software language defines a functor to simply be a function. The preceding definition comes from the *Category Theory* influence on functional programming. (For more details, see `Chapter 11`, *Category Theory That Applies*.)

Functions that modify functions

Before we explore intermediate and terminal functions lets' clarify the phrase *functions that modify functions* using a few examples.

A coding example of functions that modify functions

The following is a snippet of the code we might write to build a section of a page with two drop down lists, one for makes and the other for models of cars:

```
// http.Get :: String -> JSON
var renderPage = curry(func(makes, models) { /* render page */ })
// return two divs: one with makes and the other with models HTML/ULs
Task.Of(renderPage).Ap(http.Get("/makes")).Ap(http.Get("/models"))
```

Notice that each http.Get is a separate API call. Each API call is a partial application. In order for renderPage to wait for each call to complete we must curry our API calls.

Here's what the resulting HTML might look like:

- Honda
- Lexus
- Toyota

- Accord
- IS250
- Highlander

Chapter 2

A visual example of functions that modify functions

In the previous example we composed part of an HTML web page. In this example, let's immerse ourselves into a Railroading world and lay down some train tracks using function composition.

Immersive Railroading World

The following is our toolbox of reusable components. We modify our world by adding items from our toolbox. Thus, our immersive railroading *world* function is modified by adding and connecting a bunch of smaller *component* functions.

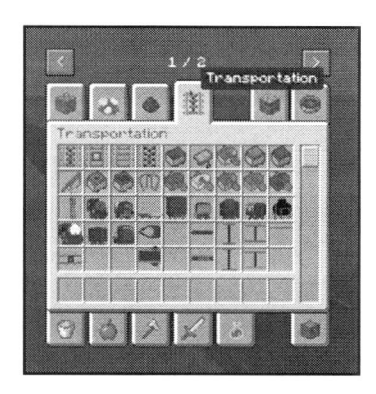

Manipulating Collections

Here's Christian laying down a railroad switch:

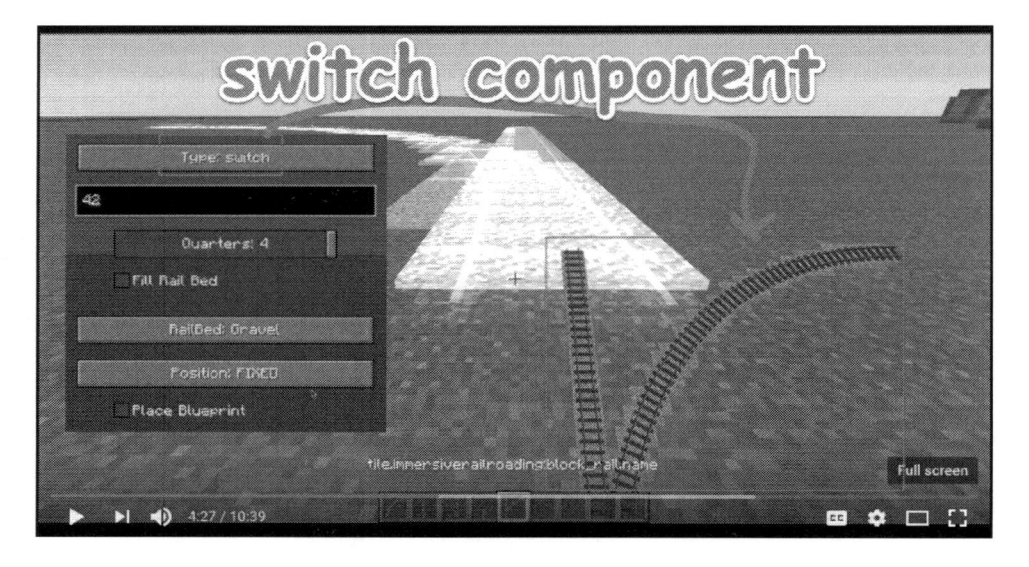

Composition in Mindcraft

We can find the source code for this Immersive Railroad application at `https://github.com/cam72cam/ImmersiveRailroading`.

Minecraft could have chosen to implement their world building UI exclusively with FP techniques by currying partial applications, but when we look closer we find more of an imperative implementation. Though generics are used:

```
// cam72cam.immersiverailroading.render.TileSteamHammerRender
public class TileSteamHammerRender extends
TileEntitySpecialRenderer<TileSteamHammer> {
    private List<String> hammer;
    private List<String> rest;
```

Tacit programming

Tacit programming is a style of programming where function definitions compose other functions and combinators manipulate the arguments. A combinator is a higher-order function that uses only function application and pre-defined combinators to define the result from its arguments. For more details, see the Moses Schonfinkel section in `Chapter 11`, *Category Theory That Applies*.

Tacit programming with Unix pipes

The following combinators are the functions in the pipeline, for example, head, awk, grep, and so on. Each combinator is a function that sends output to standard out and reads input from standard in. Note that arguments are not mentioned in the command.

```
$ cat access10k.log | head -n 1 | awk '{print $7}' | grep "\.json" | uniq -c | sort -nr
```

Programming CMOS with Unix pipes

Unix pipes can also be used to model the flow control of NAND gates of a CMOS device.

Assuming nil represents and electron then, /dev/zero (aka VSS) provides an infinite supply of electrons and /dev/null (aka VDD) will consume every electron sent to it.

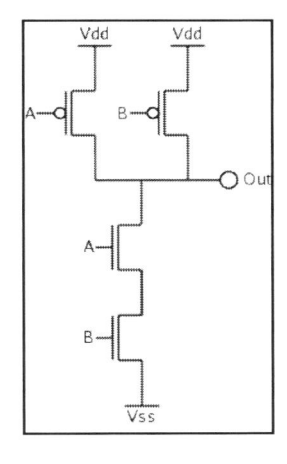

CMOS NAND gate

In our model, the UNIX pipe acts like a wire. When the pipe is connected to Vss, its buffer fills up with nil-bytes and the pipe acts like a negatively charged metal plate. When it is connected to Vdd, the pipe's buffer is drained, and the pipe acts like a positively charged metal plate. Unix pipes are used to model flow control in our NAND logic gate.

For more details, see http://www.linusakesson.net/programming/pipelogic/index.php.

Tacit programming with FP

We'll use Haskell to demonstrate a program that sums a list of integers. Both will be recursive, the second benefits from **Tail Call Optimization (TCO)**. We would use Go, but currently Go does not support TCO.

We loop over the list of numbers to accumulate the sum. In imperative programming, we would use a loop index to store the accumulated sum value. In functional programming, we implement loops using recursion where the accumulated sum is passed as a parameter to the next recursive call. What would be loop index variables/accumulator variables in an imperative language become *parameters* in the tail-recursive version.

Non-TCO recursive example

First, we'll look at the imperative example:

```
rSum :: [Integer] -> Integer
rSum (x:xs) = x + (rSum xs)
rSum [] = 0
```

Note that x:xs means we store the head of the list in x and the rest of the list is in xs.

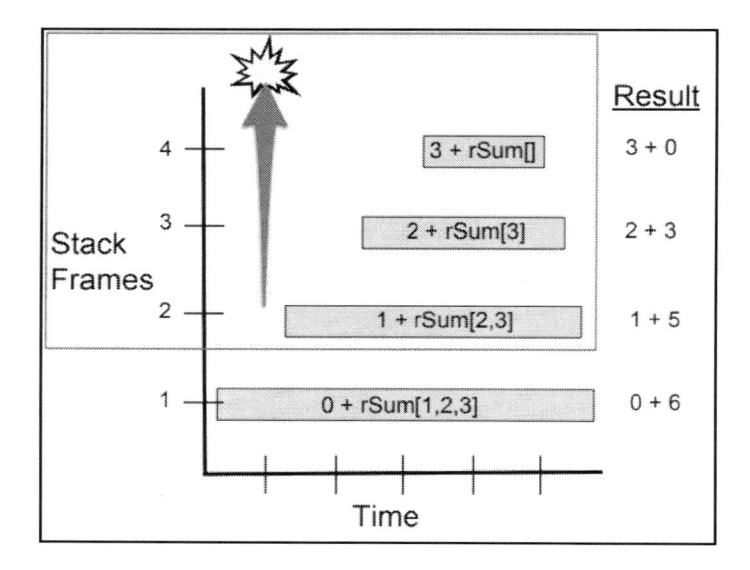

Each call to rSum needs to get the return value of the recursive call and add it to its x parameter before it can return. This means that each function must stay on the stack longer than the frame of any function that it calls. We had to create four stack frames to sum three numbers. Imagine the amount of RAM storage that this implementation will require when we process lists with a lot of values. Without TCO the our implementation will require **O(n)** of RAM storage space, based on the number of items in the list. (See Big-Oh notation in Chapter 10, *Monads, Type Classes, and Generics*)

TCO recursive example

In our tail recursive function, our stack frames do not need to be preserved.

```
tSum :: [Integer] -> Integer
tSum lst = tSum lst 0 where
    tSum (x:xs) i = tSum xs (i+x)
    tSum [] i = i
```

The following diagram illustrates that unlike the previous example (rSum), no action needs to be taken in the context of a frame after tSum makes its recursive call. rSum created a stack frame for each member of the list. tSum only needs to create one stack frame, which it reuses.

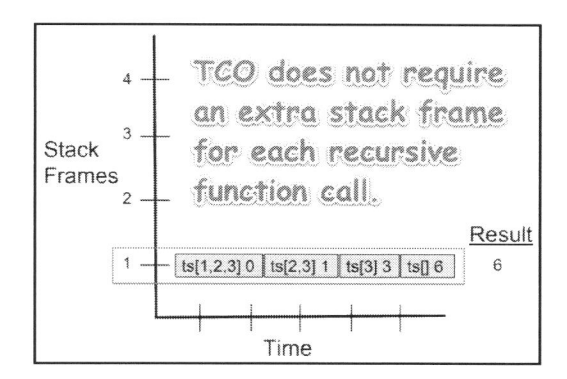

TCO avoids creating a new stack frame when the last call in a recursion is the function itself. Go currently does not support TCO. What is the implication? Without TCO, we should avoid using recursion to process lists with a lot of elements, that is, over a few thousand; Otherwise, our program will likely run out of RAM and crash. Why not replace recursive functions with functions that implement imperative loops? In other words, what is the importance of recursion in functional programming?

The importance of recursion

First, let's make sure we understand what recursion is. Let's think about how we pull apart Russian Dolls.

Recursion works like the process of finding the smallest doll. We repeat the same process, i.e., pulling apart the doll until we find a doll that is solid. Though our problems get smaller, the problem solving process is the same as the previous because the structure of the nesting dolls is the same. Each doll is a smaller than the previous one. Eventually, we get to a doll that's too small to have a doll inside it and we're done. That's the fundamental idea behind recursion.

We also need to understand how to to write a tail recursive function because that's the kind of recursion that's a candidate for TCO. When our recursive function that calls itself as its last action, then we can reuse the stack frame of that function. The tSum function in the previous section is an example of tail recursion.

Understanding recursion marks a transition for us from a programmer to a computer scientist. Recursion requires some mathematical sophistication to understand, but once we master it we'll find that it opens up a plethora of ways to solve important problems.

A soccer coach would not have his player practice kicking balls down hill to a target; that scenario will never occur in a game. Similarly, we will not spend a lot of time pursuing recursive implementations in Go.

> A tail recursive function is the functional form of a loop, and with TCO it executes just as efficiently as a loop. Without recursion, we must implement most loops using imperative programming techniques. Thus, having TCO in Go would actually be more beneficial to FP than Generics. We'll learn more about Generics in Chapters 9, *Functors, Monoids, and Generics* and Chapter 10, *Monads, Type Classes, and Generics*. See the *How to Propose Changes To Go* section in the Appendix or jump directly to the discussion regarding adding TCO to Go at https://github.com/golang/go/issues/22624.

Various intermediate and terminal functions

Look at the various intermediate and terminal functions in the following functor diagram. They are all functors. When a function, for example, Map, is provided with a set of values as input, it will apply a transformation on the elements and produce output that will be a different set of values.

In functional programming, given the same input, a given function will always return the same result set.

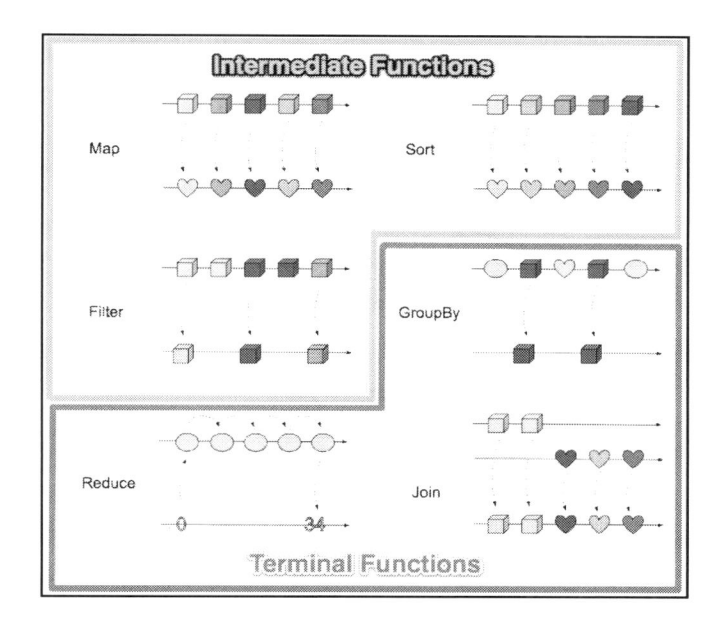

In the first row of preceding functors, Map and Sort, take a collection, transform it in some way, and return a collection of equal size.

In the second row of functors, `Filter` and `GroupBy`, take a collection and transform it into another collection of smaller size.

In the third row, `Reduce` takes a collection, performs computations over its elements, and returns a single result value.

Reduce example

Here's an implementation for reducing a collection, using the `alediaferia/go-collections` package, to find the maximum value:

```
numbers := []interface{}{
    1,
    5,
    3,
    2,
}

coll := collections.NewFromSlice(numbers)
min  := collections.Reduce(0, func(a, b interface{}) interface{} {
    if a > b { return a } else { return b }
})
```

The `Join` function takes two different collections and combines them into a single, larger collection.

There are two basic types of functors in functional programming: intermediate functions and terminal functions. They work together to transform the incoming collection into either another collection or a single value. Any number of intermediate functions can be chained together followed by the terminal function.

Intermediate functions

Intermediate functions are not evaluated until the terminal function has been processed.

> **Lazy evaluation** is an evaluation strategy that delays the processing of an intermediate function until its value is required. It can be combined with **memoization**, where the evaluation is first cached so that subsequent requests for that value return the cached value immediately without reevaluating the expression that originally created it.

A few of the more popular intermediate functions include `map`, `filter`, and `sort`.

We can create many other high-order functions to process the incoming stream, which is often a collection. We'll soon see functional programming libraries that provide a plethora of variations of these basic function types.

Common intermediate functions

Here's a table that describes some of the more common intermediate functions:

Function	Gleam	Preserves type	Preserves count	Preserves order	Description
map	Yes	No	Yes	Yes	This transforms each element in the list into another element in the resulting list of the same size.
filter	Yes	Yes	No	Yes	This calls a predicate function. If true, the current item is skipped and does not end up in the result list.
sort	Yes	Yes	Yes	Yes	This orders the result set by a criteria.

Map Example

Here's an example of mapping a collection using the `alediaferia/go-collections` package:

```
names := []interface{}{
    "Alice",
    "Bob",
    "Cindy",
}
collection := collections.NewFromSlice(planets)
collection = collection.Map(func(v interface{}) interface{} {
  return strings.Join([]string{ "Hey ", v.(string) })
})
println(collection)
```

The output is as follows:

```
Hey Alice
Hey Bob
Hey Cindy
```

Terminal functions

Terminal functions are eagerly executed. They execute immediately and once executed, they execute all the previous intermediate, lazy functions in the call chain. Terminal functions either return a single value or produce a side effect. The reduce example, we saw earlier, returns a single value: 1. The ForEach function does not return a value but can produce a side effect, such as printing out each item. The Collect, Join, and GroupBy functions group items in a collection.

Common terminal functions

Here's a table that describes some of the more popular terminal functions:

Function	Gleam	Groups items	Creates side effects	Gathers results	Description
Collect, Join, and GroupBy	Yes	Yes			Produce another collection
ForEach	Yes		Yes		Used for processing individual items
Reduce	Yes			Yes	Forces the required lazy expressions to fire and produce results

Join example

The following code shows an example of the Join() function:

```
// left collection:
0001, "alice", "bob"
0001, "cindy", "dan"
0002, "evelyn", "frank"
// right collection:
0001, "greg", "izzy"
0002, "jenny", "alice"

left.Join(right)
```

The output is as follows:

```
0001, "alice", "bob", "greg", "izzy"
0001, "cindy", "dan", "greg", "izzy"
0002, "evelyn", "frank", "jenny", "alice"
```

GroupBy example

The following code shows an example of the `GroupBy()` function:

```
// input collection:
 0001, "alice", 0002
 0001, "bob", 0002
 0003, "cindy", 0002

 GroupBy(1,3)
```

The output is as follows:

```
0001, 0002, ["alice", "bob"]
0003, 0002, ["cindy"]
```

Reduce example

Here's an implementation for reducing a collection, using the `alediaferia/go-collections` package, to find the maximum value:

```
numbers := []interface{}{
    1,
    5,
    3,
    2,
}
collection := collections.NewFromSlice(numbers)
min   := collection.Reduce(0, func(a, b interface{}) interface{} {
    if a > b { return a } else { return b }
})
```

Predicates

We can use predicates to perform operations on input data. Predicates can be used to implement many of the functions that we apply to collections to transform input data into the result collection or value.

> The `predicate` function is a function that takes one item as input and returns either true or false, based on whether the item satisfies some condition. They are often used conditionally to determine whether to apply certain operations in the execution chain.

Manipulating Collections

Let's create some predicate functions that we can use to manipulate a collection of cars.

The `All()` function returns `true` only if all the values in the collection satisfy the `predicate` condition:

```
package predicate

func All(vals []string, predicate func(string) bool) bool {
        for _, val := range vals {
                if !predicate(val) {
                        return false
                }
        }
        return true
}
```

The `Any()` function returns `true` as long as any one of the values in the collection satisfies the `predicate` condition:

```
func Any(vs []string, predicate func(string) bool) bool {
        for _, val := range vs {
                if predicate(val) {
                        return true
                }
        }
        return false
}
```

The `Filter()` function returns a new, smaller, or equal-sized collection containing all the strings in the collection that satisfy the `predicate` condition:

```
func Filter(vals []string, predicate func(string) bool) []string {
        filteredVals := make([]string, 0)
        for _, v := range vals {
                if predicate(v) {
                        filteredVals = append(filteredVals, v)
                }
        }
        return filteredVals
}
```

The `Count()` function is a helper function:

```
func Count(vals []string) int {
        return len(vals)
}
```

Now, let's use a Mocha-like BDD Go testing framework, named `goblin`, to test our predicates.

Declare the package and define the basic imports. We only need to define one function. Let's call it `TestPredicateSucceed`:

```
package predicate

import (
        "testing"
        "strings"
        . "github.com/franela/goblin"
)


func TestPredicateSucceed(t *testing.T) {
        fakeTest := testing.T{}
        g := Goblin(&fakeTest)
```

Let's wrap all our unit tests with a `Describe` block named `Predicate Tests`, where we define the `cars` variable to hold a list of our car models:

```
        g.Describe("Predicate Tests", func() {
            cars := []string{"CRV", "IS250", "Highlander"}
```

Here's our first test. It starts with a `Describe` block and contains one `It` block. Inside our `It` block, we assign our first-class function `bs`, the return value of calling the `Any()` function. Our predicate function is the function literal that calls the `strings.HasPrefix()` function. The last line of our unit test asserts that `bs` is `true`:

```
        g.Describe("Starts High", func() {
            g.It("Should be true", func() {
                bs := Any(cars, func(v string) bool {
                    return strings.HasPrefix(v, "High")
                })
                g.Assert(bs).Equal(true)
            })
        })
```

Our next unit test says `Highlander should be High` and asserts that it should be true. We pass the `strings.Contains()` function as our predicate to the `Filter()` function to return only those items in the list that contain the `High` substring:

```
        g.Describe("Highlander should be High", func() {
            high := Filter(cars, func(v string) bool {
                return strings.Contains(v, "High")
            })
```

Manipulating Collections

```
            highlander := []string{"Highlander"}
            g.It("Should be true", func() {
                    g.Assert(high).Equal(highlander)
            })
    })
})
```

This test counts the number of cars that contain the `High` substring and asserts that the count should be 1:

```
g.Describe("One is High", func() {
        high := Count(Filter(cars, func(v string) bool {
                return strings.Contains(v, "High")
        }))
        g.It("Should be true", func() {
                g.Assert(high).Equal(1)
        })
})
```

Our last test asserts that not all cars contain the `High` substring:

```
g.Describe("All are High", func() {
        high := All(cars, func(v string) bool {
                return strings.Contains(v, "High")
        })
        g.It("Should be false", func() {
                g.Assert(high).Equal(false)
        })
})
```

Let's take a moment to reflect on this implementation.

Reflection

Our implementation of predicates is performant but restrictive. Take the `Any()` function signature, for example:

```
func Any(vs []string, predicate func(string) bool) bool
```

The `Any` function only works for slices of `string`. What if we wanted to iterate over a tree or map structure? We'd have to write separate functions for each. This is a valid argument for requesting Go to support generics. If Go supported generics, our implementations would likely require much less code.

An alternative implementation could be to use empty interfaces. This would solve the problem of having to implement separate functions for each type of data we want to handle, given that an empty interface can take on a value of any type. To use a value of the `interface{}` type, you must use reflection or type assertion or a type switch to determine the type of value, and there will be a performance hit for any of those methods.

Another alternative implementation could be to use Goroutines and channels. Itertools uses empty interfaces, Goroutines, and channels.

The `github.com/ah15esoft/golang-underscore` is a package that uses a lot of reflection and empty interfaces to provide an underscore-like implementation of high-order functions.

Combinator pattern

Since Go supports passing functions around as values, we can create predicate combinators to build more complex predicates from simpler ones.

> **Combinator pattern**: Creating systems by combining more primitive functions into more complex functions.

We'll dive deeper into the composition and the combinator pattern later in the book. Now, let's look a little closer at the `map` and `filter` functions.

Map and filter

The next code example demonstrates the use of a few standard intermediate functions: `map` and `filter`.

> The code in this example can be copy/pasted into The Go playground, which is a service that takes your Go program, compiles, links, and runs your program with the latest version of Go inside a sandbox and then returns the output to the screen. You can find it at `https://play.golang.org/`.

Executable commands must always use `package main`. We can separate each import statement on a separate line for readability.

Manipulating Collections

External packages can be referenced using their remote GitHub repository path. We can preface long package names with a shorter alias. The `go_utils` package can now be referenced with the u letter. Note that if we aliased a package name with _, its exported functions can be referenced directly in our Go code without indicating which package it came from:

```
package main
import (
    "fmt"
    "log"
    "strings"
    "errors"
    u "github.com/go-goodies/go_utils"
)
```

> `iota`: A Go identifier used in `const` declarations that represents successive untyped integer constants. It is reset to 0 whenever the reserved word `const` appears:
>
> ```
> const (
>     SMALL = iota // 0
>     MEDIUM // 1
>     LARGE // 2
> )
> ```

We can apply expressions to iota to set increment values greater than 1. We do this as discussed in the next section.

Let's define a type of ints called `WordSize` and use an `iota` expression to create an enumeration from our constants. The first `iota` elements are assigned values that start at 0 and then increase by 1. Since we multiplied the `iota` element by 6, the sequence will look like 0, 6, 12, 18, and so on. We explicitly assign the value of 50 to the last element in the enumeration:

```
type WordSize int
const (
    ZERO WordSize = 6 * iota
    SMALL
    MEDIUM
    LARGE
    XLARGE
    XXLARGE  WordSize = 50
    SEPARATOR = ", "
)
```

The `ChainLink` type allows us to chain function/method calls. It also keeps data internal to `ChainLink`, avoiding the side effect of mutated data:

```
type ChainLink struct {
    Data []string
}
```

The `Value()` method will return the value of the referenced element or link in the chain:

```
func (v *ChainLink) Value() []string {
    return v.Data
}
```

Let's define `stringFunc` as a function type. This first-class method is used in the following code as a parameter to the `Map` function:

```
type stringFunc func(s string) (result string)
```

The `Map` function uses `stringFunc` to transform (up-case) each string in the slice:

```
func (v *ChainLink)Map(fn stringFunc) *ChainLink {
    var mapped []string
    orig := *v
    for _, s := range orig.Data {
        mapped = append(mapped, fn(s))
    }
    v.Data = mapped
    return v
}
```

This line is worth repeating:

```
mapped = append(mapped, fn(s))
```

We execute the `fn()` function parameter against each element in the slice.

The `Filter` function uses embedded logic to filter the slice of strings. We could have chosen to use a first-class function, but this implementation is faster:

```
func (v *ChainLink)Filter(max WordSize) *ChainLink {
    filtered := []string{}
    orig := *v
    for _, s := range orig.Data {
        if len(s) <= int(max) {           // embedded logic
            filtered = append(filtered, s)
        }
    }
    v.Data = filtered
```

Manipulating Collections

```
        return v
}
```

What's wrong, from a pure FP perspective, about our filter function in the preceding code?

- We are using an imperative loop
- We are saving the filtered results to the `Data` field our `ChainLink` structure

Why not use recursion? We discussed this earlier. The short version is that until Go gets TCO we need to avoid recursion if our list of elements we're processing could be over a few thousand elements.

Why are we storing the filtered data rather than returning it? Good question. This implementation of the filter function serves as a learning lesson. It shows us how we can chain functions in a non-pure FP way. We'll look at an improved filter implementation in the next chapter. Here's sneak peek:

```
func (cars Collection) Filter(fn FilterFunc) Collection {
    filteredCars := make(Collection, 0)
    for _, car := range cars {
        if fn(car) {
            filteredCars = append(filteredCars, car)
        }
    }
    return filteredCars
}
```

Let's display our constants using a here-doc with interpolation. Note that the first argument to the `fmt.Printf` statement is our here-doc, `constants`, and the remaining arguments are interpolated in `constants`.

```
func main() {
    constants := `
** Constants ***
ZERO: %v
SMALL: %d
MEDIUM: %d
LARGE: %d
XLARGE: %d
XXLARGE: %d
`
    fmt.Printf(constants, ZERO, SMALL, MEDIUM, LARGE, XLARGE, XXLARGE)
```

The output will be as follows:

```
** Constants ***
ZERO: 0
SMALL: 6
MEDIUM: 12
LARGE: 18
XLARGE: 24
XXLARGE: 50
```

Let's initialize `ChainLink` with our slice of words:

```
words := []string{
    "tiny",
    "marathon",
    "philanthropinist",
    "supercalifragilisticexpialidocious"}

data := ChainLink{words};
fmt.Printf("unfiltered: %#v\n", data.Value())
```

The output will be as follows:

```
unfiltered: []string{"tiny", "marathon", "philanthropinist",
"supercalifragilisticexpialidocious"}
```

Now, let's filter our list of words:

```
filtered := data.Filter(SMALL)
fmt.Printf("filtered: %#vn", filtered)
```

The output will be as follows:

```
filtered: &main.ChainLink{Data:[]string{"tiny"}}
```

Next, let's apply the `ToUpper` mapping to our small-sized words:

```
fmt.Printf("filtered and mapped (<= SMALL sized words): %#vn",
    filtered.Map(strings.ToUpper).Value())
```

The output will be as follows:

```
filtered and mapped (<= SMALL sized words): []string{"TINY"}
```

Manipulating Collections

Let's apply a `MEDIUM` filter and the `ToUpper` filter:

```
data = ChainLink{words}
fmt.Printf("filtered and mapped (<= MEDIUM and smaller sized words): %#vn",
    data.Filter(MEDIUM).Map(strings.ToUpper).Value())
```

The output will be as follows:

```
filtered and mapped (<= MEDIUM and smaller sized words): []string{"TINY", "MARATHON"}
```

Next, let's apply our `XLARGE` filter and map then `ToUpper`:

```
data = ChainLink{words}
fmt.Printf("filtered twice and mapped (<= LARGE and smaller sized words):
    %#vn",
    data.Filter(XLARGE).Map(strings.ToUpper).Filter(LARGE).Value())
```

The output will be as follows:

```
filtered twice and mapped (<= LARGE and smaller sized words):
[]string{"TINY", "MARATHON", "PHILANTHROPINIST"}
```

Now, let's apply our `XXLARGE` filter and map with `ToUpper`:

```
data = ChainLink{words}
val := data.Map(strings.ToUpper).Filter(XXLARGE).Value()
fmt.Printf("mapped and filtered (<= XXLARGE and smaller sized words): %#vn",
    val)
```

The output will be as follows:

```
mapped and filtered (<= XXLARGE and smaller sized words): []string{"TINY", "MARATHON", "PHILANTHROPINIST", "SUPERCALIFRAGILISTICEXPIALIDOCIOUS"}
```

The output will be as follows:

```
** Constants ***
ZERO: 0
SMALL: 6
MEDIUM: 12
LARGE: 18
XLARGE: 24
XXLARGE: 50
```

Here, we use the `Join()` function to join the items in the list to help with formatting our output:

```
fmt.Printf("norig_data : %vn", u.Join(orig_data, SEPARATOR))
fmt.Printf("data: %vnn", u.Join(data.Value(), SEPARATOR))
```

The output will be as follows:

```
orig_data  : tiny, marathon, philanthropinist, supercalifragilisticexpialidocious
    data: TINY, MARATHON, PHILANTHROPINIST, SUPERCALIFRAGILISTICEXPIALIDOCIOUS
```

Now, let's compare our original collection of words with the value that we passed through our chain of functions to see whether there were side effects:

This is what your terminal console should look like:

Contains

Let's consider another common collection operation: `contains`.

In Go, lists of things are often stored in a slice. Wouldn't it be nice if Go provided a `contains` method to tell us whether the item we are looking for is contained in the slice? Since there is no generic `contains` method for working with lists of items in Go, let's implement one to iterate over a collection of car objects.

Manipulating Collections

Iterating over a collection of cars

First, let's create a `Car` struct that we can use to define the `Cars` collection as a slice of `Car`. Later, we'll create a `Contains()` method to try out on our collection:

```
package main
type Car struct {
      Make string
      Model string
}
type Cars []*Car
```

Here's our `Contains()` implementation. `Contains()` is a method for `Cars`. It takes a `modelName` string, for example, `Highlander`, and returns `true` if it was found in the slice of `Cars`:

```
func (cars Cars) Contains(modelName string) bool {
      for _, a := range cars {
            if a.Model == modelName {
                  return true
            }
      }
      return false
}
```

This seems simple enough to implement, but what happens when we are given a list of boats or boxes to iterate over? That's right, we'll have to reimplement the `Contains()` method for each one. That's ugly!

This is yet another situation where it would be nice to have generics.

The empty interface

Another alternative would be to use the empty interface like so:

```
type Object interface{}
type Collection []Object
func (list Collection) Contains(e string) bool {
      for _, t := range list { if t == e { return true } }
      return false
}
```

However, reflection or typecasting would be required and that would again adversely affect the performance.

The Contains() method

Now, let's exercise our `Contains()` method:

```
func main() {
     crv := &Car{"Honda", "CRV"}
     is250 := &Car{"Lexus", "IS250"}
     highlander := &Car{"Toyota", "Highlander"}
     cars := Cars{crv, is250, highlander}
     if cars.Contains("Highlander") {
            println("Found Highlander")
     }
     if !cars.Contains("Hummer") {
            println("Did NOT find a Hummer")
     }
}
```

The output will be as follows:

```
Found Highlander
Did NOT find a Hummer
```

In order to understand how to make the leap from imperative programming to functional programming, let's look at pure functional programming languages and how to implement high-order functions such as `Map()` that manipulate collections.

With pure functional types, you had a function, `f`, that takes a cube and returns a heart, as shown in the following diagram:

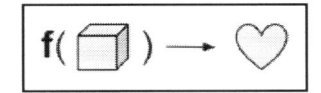

If you pass `f` a list of cubes, you could use `f` to return a list of hearts.

In order to implement this in Go, we can replace the cube with a string and the heart with a `bool` value:

```
func Map(f func(v string) bool, vs [] string) []bool {
     if len(vs) == 0 {
            return nil
     }
     return append(
            []bool{f(vs[0])},
            Map(f, vs[1:])...)
}
```

Manipulating Collections

First, we define a map of vowels that we later test for a key without retrieving the value, using an underscore in place of the first value:

```
func main() {
    vowels := map[string]bool{
        "a": true,
        "e": true,
        "i": true,
        "o": true,
        "u": true,
    }
    isVowel := func(v string) bool { _, ok := vowels[v]; return ok }
    letters := []string{"a", "b", "c", "d", "e"}
    fmt.Println(Map(isVowel, letters))
}
```

We define `isVowel` to be a literal function that takes a string and returns a `bool` result. We define letters to be a slice of strings (a, b,... e) and then call our `Map` function, passing our `isVowel` function and the list of strings to check.

This works well, but the problem is that we would have to rewrite our logic for every data type that we want to use. If we want to check whether a specific rune character exists in a list of runes, we would have to write a new `Map` function. We would have to be concerned about things such as this: does `len()` work with runes like it works with strings? If not, we would have to replace this logic. This would include a lot of effort and code, which would perform similar operations and would not be good style.

This is yet another example of why having generics in Go would be a delight.

If Go had generics

If Go had generics, we could have written a function signature like the following to replace strings with runes, and we would not have to rewrite the inner logic:

```
func Map(f func(v <string>) <bool>, vs [] <string>) []<bool>
```

However, Go does not have generics, so we can use empty interfaces and reflection to achieve the same result.

Map function

Let's create a `Map` function to transform the contents of a Collection.

First, let's define `Object` to be the empty interface type and create a `Collection` type to be a slice of objects:

```
package main
import "fmt"
type Object interface{}
type Collection []Object
func NewCollection(size int) Collection {
    return make(Collection, size)
}
```

The `NewCollection` function creates a new instance of the collection with the given size:

```
type Callback func(current, currentKey, src Object) Object
```

The `Callback` type is a first-class function type that returns the calculated result:

```
func Map(c Collection, cb Callback) Collection {
    if c == nil {
        return Collection{}
    } else if cb == nil {
        return c
    }
    result := NewCollection(len(c))
    for index, val := range c {
        result[index] = cb(val, index, c)
    }
    return result
}
```

The `Map` function returns a new collection where every element is the result of calling the `Callback` function.

Testing our empty interface-based Map function

We'll test our new empty interface-based `Map` function by defining a transformation function. This function will multiply every item in the collection by 10:

```
func main() {
    transformation10 := func(curVal, _, _ Object) Object {
        return curVal.(int) * 10 }
    result := Map(Collection{1, 2, 3, 4}, transformation10)
```

Manipulating Collections

```
        fmt.Printf("result: %vn", result)
```

We pass a collection of the numbers 1, 2, 3, and 4 as well as the transformation function.

The output will be as follows:

```
result: [10 20 30 40]
```

Now, let's pass our `Map` function a collection of strings:

```
        transformationUpper := func(curVal, _, _ Object) Object { return
    strings.ToUpper(curVal.(string)) }
        result = Map(Collection{"alice", "bob", "cindy"}, transformationUpper)
        fmt.Printf("result: %vn", result)
    }
```

This time we pass a collection of strings and transform each by calling `ToUpper`.

Here's the output:

`result: [ALICE BOB CINDY]`

Notice how in each case, we had to cast each `curVal`? With `transformation10`, we can cast each item in the collection to an `int` variable; with `transformationUpper`, we can cast each item to a `string` variable. We could choose to use reflection to avoid explicit casting, but that is even worse for performance than casting.

As with our earlier example, we could pass the collection to a chain of transformation functions to arrive at the result, which could be another collection or a single terminal value.

Instead of reinventing the wheel each time, we need another high-order function; let's use any one of the number of Go packages available that easily enable the functional style of programming in Go.

Itertools

Itertools is a Go package that provides many of the same high-order functions from the Python standard library.

Next, we see the different types of high-order functions provided by Itertools. High-order functions provide the vocabulary for the declarative coding style.

Infinite iterator creators:

- `Count(i)`: Infinite count from `i`
- `Cycle(iter)`: Infinite cycling of `iter` (requires memory)
- `Repeat(element [, n])`: Repeat the element `n` times (or infinitely)

Iterator destroyers:

- `Reduce(iter, reducer, memo)`: Reduce (or Foldl) across the iterator
- `List(iter)`: Create a list from the iterator

Iterator modifiers:

- `Chain(iters...)`: Chain together multiple iterators.
- `DropWhile(predicate, iter)`: Drop elements until predicate(el) = false.
- `TakeWhile(predicate, iter)`: Take elements until predicate(el) = false.
- `Filter(predicate, iter)`: Filter out elements when predicate(el) = false.
- `FilterFalse(predicate, iter)`: Filter out elements when predicate(el) = true.
- `Slice(iter, start[, stop[, step]])`: Drop elements until the start (zero-based index). Stop upon stop (exclusive) unless not given. Step is 1 unless given.

More iterator modifiers:

- `Map(mapper func(interface{}) interface{}, iter)`: Map each element to mapper(el).
- `MultiMap(multiMapper func(interface{}...)interface{}, iters...)`: Map all the iterators as variadic arguments to `multiMaper(elements...)`; stop at the shortest iterator.
- `MultiMapLongest(multiMapper func(interface{}...)interface{}, iters...)`: Same as `MultiMap`, except that here you need to stop at the longest iterator. Shorter iterators are filled with nil after they are exhausted.
- `Starmap(multiMapper func(interface{}...)interface{}, iter)`: If `iter` is an iterator of `[]interface{}`, then expand it to `multiMapper`.
- `Zip(iters...)`: Zip multiple iterators together.
- `ZipLongest(iters...)`: Zip multiple iterators together. Take the longest; shorter ones are appended with nil.
- `Tee(iter, n)`: Split an iterator into n equal versions.
- `Tee2(iter)`: Split an iterator into two equal versions.

Go channels used by the New function

In the `itertools.go` file, we see that the iterator uses Go channels to range over each element in the collection:

```go
type Iter chan interface{}
func New(els ... interface{}) Iter {
    c := make(Iter)
    go func () {
        for _, el := range els {
            c <- el
        }
        close(c)
    }()
    return c
}
```

The `New` function can be used as follows to take a list of values and turn it into a new iterable collection:

```
New(3,5,6)
```

Testing itertool's Map function

Let's test itertool's `Map` function by passing it a collection of words of various lengths and a literal function to operate on each word to return its length:

```go
package itertools
import (
    "testing"
    "reflect"
    . "github.com/yanatan16/itertools"
)
```

Let's not forget to run `go get -u github.com/yanatan16/itertools` to download the `itertools` package along with its dependencies.

Testing iterators for element equality

First, let's create the `testIterEq` function to test whether two collections are equivalent:

```
func testIterEq(t *testing.T, it1, it2 Iter) {
    t.Log("Start")
    for el1 := range it1 {
        if el2, ok := <- it2; !ok {
            t.Error("it2 shorter than it1!", el1)
            return
        } else if !reflect.DeepEqual(el1, el2) {
            t.Error("Elements are not equal", el1, el2)
        } else {
            t.Log(el1, el2)
        }
    }
    if el2, ok := <- it2; ok {
        t.Error("it1 shorter than it2!", el2)
    }
    t.Log("Stop")
}
```

In our test function `TestMap`, we define a `mapper` function literal that is passed to our `Map` function to perform the transformation. The `mapper` function returns the length of each string passed to it:

```
func TestMap(t *testing.T) {
    mapper := func (i interface{}) interface{} {
        return len(i.(string))
    }
    testIterEq(t, New(3,5,10), Map(mapper, New("CRV", "IS250", "Highlander")))
}
```

Let's go to the directory with this test file and run the following to verify that the `Map` function works as we expect. Here's what my console output looks like:

```
~/clients/packt/dev/go/src/bitbucket.org/lsheehan/fp-in-go-work/chapter2/itertools $ go test
PASS
ok  bitbucket.org/lsheehan/fp-in-go-work/chapter2/itertools 0.008s
```

Functional packages

There are many other Go packages that provide the high-order functions (HOF) that we've come to expect when writing declarative code for manipulating collections. They typically use empty interfaces and reflection, which have negative performance impacts. A well known HOF implementation is Rob Pike's `Reduce` package (see `https://github.com/robpike/filter`) where he states his preference for using for loops and clearly states, *don't use this.*

Another time of reflection

Are we frustrated yet? We learned how to code in a concise, declarative functional programming style only to learn that it would probably run too slow to be viable in production. We tried various techniques to speed it up, but nothing we've done thus far with pure functional programming can match the performance of old-school imperative programming.

Our goal is to find a way to program using the declarative functional programming style in Go with performance numbers that meet or exceed expectations.

Go is awesome

Go is our favorite language for many reasons including:

- Performance
- Fast and easy deployment
- Cross-platform support
- Protected source code
- Concurrent processing

Go is awesome, but

Since Go was not designed to be a pure functional language and lacks generics, we must take a performance hit to force Go into a functional style of programming, right? (Keep the faith! There's hope around the corner.)

We have covered the core principles of implementing and using collections. You learned that in functional programming, a single function can take input and return a result and transformations to the collection that occurs inside the function. You learned that we can compose functions by chaining them together.

If Go had generics that would simplify our implementation task, but more importantly, if Go were designed to perform **tail-call optimization** (TCO) and other performance-boosting optimizations, then it would be an easy decision to choose to program in the functional style in Go.

One of Go's best features is its performance, and if we are developing a solution that runs on a single server and performance is more important to us than having concise, intuitive, and declarative code, then most likely we would not program Go in the functional style.

The cure

However, if we are looking to implement a distributed computing solution using Go, then we're in luck.

Let's take a quick look at the features of a new Go package for performing distributed **MapReduce** for data processing at scale.

Gleam - distributed MapReduce for Golang

> *"First, generics are needed. Of course, we can use reflection. But it is noticeably slower, to the point that I do not want to show the performance numbers. Second, dynamic remote code execution is also needed if we want to dynamically adjust the execution plan. We could pre-build all the execution DAGs first and choose one of them during runtime. But it is very limiting. As everyone else here, I enjoyed the beauty of Go. How to make it work for big data?"*
>
> *- Chris Lu*

That's the right question.

Chris resolved the performance issues of reflection and the lack of Generics using a scripting language named LuaJIT. Rather than building the entire **directed acyclic graph (DAG)** and then choosing one branch during runtime, the scripting nature of LuaJIT allows dynamic remote code execution, allowing us to dynamically adjust the execution plan during runtime.

LuaJIT's FFI library

LuaJIT's FFI library makes it easy to call C functions and C data structures by parsing C declarations:

```
local ffi = require("ffi")
Load LuaJIT's FF library
ffi.cdef[[
int printf(const char *fmt, ...);
]]
Add a C declaration for the function.
ffi.C.printf("Hello %s!", "world")
```

Call the named C function. Simple!

Unix pipe tools

Gleam also leverages Unix pipe tools.

> **TIP**
> Gleam = Go + LuaJIT + Unix Pipes

Let's look at how we can use Gleam to process collections.

Processing Gleam collections

Let's see how Gleam processes collections. The input we'll use is a collection of lines that comprises words in the /etc/paths file:

```
$ cat /etc/paths
/usr/local/bin
/usr/bin
/bin
/usr/sbin
/sbin
```

Gleam reads the file content as lines and feeds each line into the flow. From this, it creates the stream through which the functions Map and Reduce are called to count the number of occurrences of each word:

```
package main
import (
    "os"
    "github.com/chrislusf/gleam/flow"
)
func main() {
    flow.New().TextFile("/etc/paths").Partition(2).FlatMap(`
        function(line)
            return line:gmatch("%w+")
        end
    `).Map(`
        function(word)
            return word, 1
        end
    `).ReduceBy(`
        function(x, y)
            return x + y
        end
    `).Fprintf(os.Stdout, "%s,%d\n").Run()
}
```

Here's the output of this:

```
bin,3
local,1
sbin,2
usr,3
```

> **TIP:** Disappointed? Were you hoping that there was a practical use of pure functional programming in pure Go? (Where practical means the performance of using recursion is not an issue and where you can write your business logic and control flow logic in a declarative style, free from empty interfaces, downcasting/unboxing and those noisy if err != nil blocks?) Keep working through the book and you'll find a solution in the last unit.

Summary

We manipulate collections constantly in our code. We often start with a list of items and need to transform our initial list into another list of different items. Sometimes, we want to map our list to another list of equal size. Sometimes, we want to group and sort our list. Other times, we need to arrive at a single result value.

In this chapter, we explored the different types (intermediate and terminal) of collection functors. We dived into a few key areas of collection manipulation, including iterators, the `map` function, the `contains` method, and chaining of functions.

We looked at a few Go packages that provide a cadre of high-order functions that we can use in our new functional style of programming.

We gained an appreciation for Unix pipes and discovered that a new distributed processing Go package, named Gleam, leverages pipe to deliver a lightweight Go-based functional solution.

In the next chapter, we'll dive deeper into pipelining and see how it can improve performance.

3
Using High-Order Functions

We frequently encounter questions such as, "Just curious, what are the benefits of applying pure functional programming concepts to imperative languages (other than making the code hard to read for others)?"

In this chapter, we will address this common misconception using high-order functions.

Our goal in this chapter is to:

- Understand the characteristics of **functional programming** (**FP**)
- Understand the purpose of generics
- Understand how FP improves performance
- Understand currying
- Implement `Map`, `Filter`, and `Reduce` functions
- Implement lazy evaluation using Goroutines and a Go channel

Characteristics of FP

Let's start by looking at the requirements for a pure FP language. A pure FP language must include support for things like:

- First-class functions
- **Tail-call optimization** (**TCO**)
- High-order functions
- Pure functions
- Immutable Data

Using High-Order Functions

In order to accomplish pure FP, a language must treat functions as it does any other variable type. How can an immutable language have variables that vary? The way we accomplish this in an FP way is by creating new variables, rather than modifying existing ones. We will see how to accomplish this later in the chapter, when we look at the Map function.

Go is a multidimensional language that supports imperative, object-oriented, and FP styles. We could write a purely imperative or functional program in Go. It is our choice of programming style that dictates this. This is one of the great things about Go and FP. It's not an all or nothing issue. We can migrate our code toward FP when and where it makes sense to do so.

Go requires **tail-call optimization** (**TCO**) to handle production performance requirements. Each time a recursive function calls itself, a new block is added to the stack frame; we soon feel the sluggish effects of this Go compiler omission. We will see how to mitigate this issue when we implement the Reduce function.

The last requirement is support for **high-order functions** (**HOF**). High-order functions take functions as arguments and/or return functions as their result. HOFs allow us to chain our functions together in a readable manner with less code.

HOFs are arguably the focal point of any FP language, and after a quick look at FP characteristics, we'll study how we can exploit them in Go:

Characteristic	Supported in Go?	Description

Anonymous Function	Yes	A function without a name. For example, this function call an anonymous function that prints a message.
		`func anonymousGreeting() func(string) {`
		`    return func(name string) {`
		`        fmt.Printf("Hey %s!n", name)`
		`    }`
		`}`

Closures	Yes	A closure is an inner function that closes over, that is, has access to, variables in its outer scope. In other words, a closure is a function's scope that is kept alive by a reference to that function.
Composition	Yes	Composition is what allows us to combine simple functions to build more complicated ones. Currying and pipelining are example implementations of the concept of composition.

| Continuations | Yes | Continuations are like a GOTO statements with arguments. A continuation is a function parameter (`next`) we pass to a function (`factorial`) that specifies where the function should return. The factorial function does not define a return value. It's a function that accepts an int and another function that passes along its current state.<br>```
func factorial(x int, next func(int)) {
   if x == 0 {
      next(1)
   } else {
      factorial(x-1, func(y int) {
         next(x * y)
      })
   }
}
```<br>Calls continue until a base condition is met (`x == 0`) and then all the partially executed next functions on the stack are popped off and evaluated.<br>We can call `factorial` like this:<br>```
factorial(4, func(result int) {
   fmt.Println("result", result)
})
```<br>It will print: **result: 24**<br>Programming with Monads is a form of **continuation passing style** (**CPS**) that gives us more control; Using the Lexical Workflow Solution, upon encountering an error we can direct execution to the error path (bypassing subsequent chained function calls) to our workflow's single idiomatic Go error handler.<br>CPS can also be programmed using Goroutines and channels. |
|---|---|---|
| **Currying** | Yes | Currying is where we get a function that accepts x parameters and return a composition of x functions each of which take 1 parameter. In FP, every function is a function of one argument. |
| **Declarative** | Yes | Declarative style, as opposed to an imperative style, means that we write expressions as opposed to step by step instructions. The imperative function is not used as data; Instead, it's used for its side effect, i.e., printing "Hello".
`Info.Println("Hello")` |

Either Data Type	Yes	Either is a type constructor that takes two arguments. It allows us to say a value is either one of two types. For example, `Either Car Truck`. We can use Either to create an error handling system if we make our result of type `Either Success Failure`. Slightly more complicated that the Maybe data type. `data Either a b = Left a	Right b`
First Class Functions	Yes!	First-class functions can be passed around as parameters and returned as values.
Functional Composition	Yes	Functional composition means that we decompose monolithic applications into our smallest units of computation. We can then re-combine our functions in new ways to create new functionality by chaining our function calls.

Hindley-Milner type system	No	HM infers types without requiring any type definitions. HM type systems support polymorphic types, where lists can contain items of different types. If Go used HM, then the type of b would be inferred as `float64` below (rather than throwing the runtime error, *constant 1.8 truncated to integer*)
		`a := 1`
		`b := a + 1.8`

Idempotence	Yes	Idempotence means that we can call our function repeatedly and it will produce the same result each time.
Immutable data	Yes	Immutable immutable data structures, once created, do not change. Data cannot be added, removed, or reordered. In order to make an *update* we need to create a copy with our changes. Immutability is a core tenant of FP because without it, the data flow in our applications become lossy and inconsistent. The true constant in FP (as in life) is change. Mutation hides change. For more reasons see the *Immutable Data* section below.

Immutable variables	Yes	Go has the const keyword, but that only works for ints and strings. In order to have a immutable object, we could to write it like this:
		`type Car struct {`
		`    const Make, Model string`
		`}`
		Or only allow access to fields via method calls that could be coded to prevent mutation.

| Lambda expressions | Yes | A Lambda expression is an anonymous function, often used as data, passed as a parameter, and returned as data and used to invoke another function. Note that a lambda expression executes in the context of their appearance, that is, they only have access to the variables in their lexical scope and they take only one parameter.<br>For an example of what is and what is not a lambda expression check: `2-design-patterns/ch04-solid/01_lambda/main.go`<br>**Tip 1**: If we can call a function without using its return value then it's impure.<br>**Tip 2**: If we need to pass more than one parameter, use a partially applied function.<br>**Tip 3**: When we see some code like that like the following, we're likely looking at a Lambda Expression:<br>```
return f(func(x int) int {
    return r(r)(x)
})
``` |
|---|---|---|
```

Using High-Order Functions

List Monad	Yes	List monads are used to model nondeterministic computations that can return an arbitrary number of results. A list monad can return zero or more results.
		The return function inserts a value into a list like this:
		`return a = [a]`
		The bind function pulls values from the list, applies a function to them and produces a new list like this:
		`[a] -> (a -> [b]) -> [b]`
		Given the following function definitions:
		`f :: String -> [String]`
		`f a = [a, prevChar a, nextChar a]`
		`g :: String -> [String]`
		`g a = [lower a, upper a]`
		The list monad allows us to compose **f** and **g** as follows:
		<pre> g | w
		       | W ---> |
		       | | W
		       |
		     f | g | x
		X --> | X ---> |
		       | | X
		       |
		       | g | y
		       | Y ---> |
		                | Y</pre>f looks like this:
		`f "X" --> ["W", "X", "Y"]`
		g looks like this:
		`map g (f "X") --> [["w", "W"], ["x", "X"], ["y", "Y"]]`
		When we compose f and g we get
		`["w", "W","x", "X","y", "Y"]`
		Using the composition operator "." we can write the List monad composition as follows:
		`f >=> g = concat . map g . f`

[86]

Maybe data type	Yes	Maybe represents a computation that might not return a result, i.e., an optional value. Maybe a is a value that either contains a value of type a (represented as Just a), or it is empty (represented as Nothing) The following definition of Maybe: `data Maybe a = Nothing	Just a` Says, `Maybe` a is either not there or it is there. If it's not there, its `Nothing`; If it is there is is Just a, where a is a value. Maybe is a polymorphic type that can be used to define a function that can produce a value of another type or nothing at all. `f :: a -> Maybe b`

Maybe Monad	Yes	The Maybe Monad is a type of error monad, where all errors are represented by `Nothing`. (The Either type provides more functionality.)
		Given the polymorphic nature of `Maybe` and associativity, we can say.
		`f :: a -> Maybe b`
		`g :: b -> Maybe c`
		`h :: a -> Maybe c`
		`h = f >=> g`
		h is the Monadic composition of **f** and **g**.
		The definition of the `Maybe` monad is a follows:
		`instance Monad Maybe where`
		`    return x = Just x`
		
		`    Nothing >>= f = Nothing`
		`    Just x >>= f = f x`

Monadic error handling	Yes	`Maybe` helps us handle errors. It represents something expected rather than an unexpected error. Either is like a `Maybe` that also lets us return an arbitrary value instead of `Nothing`. Instead of worrying about receiving a null from a function call, which could cause a null pointer exception, our type system will force to handle error conditions a type-safe way. Using Either as our return type, e can run a task, get a result, check for the value:
		`func runTask(success bool) maybe.Either {`
		And even if the task failed, we'll get a non-nil result.
		`func (e either) Succeeded() StringOption {`
		`    if e.err == nil {`
		`        return SomeString(e.val)`
		`    }`
		`    return EmptyString()`
		`}`
		For details, see `2-design-patterns/ch04-solid/02_maybe`

No side-effects	Yes	*No side effects* means that the only thing that occurs when we call a pure function is: • We pass in parameters • We get a result; `Nothing` else happens. **Tip 1:** If our function prints output it is impure. **Tip 2:** If any state/data changes anywhere else in our system as a result of calling our function then our function is impure. **Tip 3:** If our function has no return value then it is either impure or completely useless.
Operator overloading	No	Operator overloading, also known as *ad hoc polymorphism*, is a specific case of polymorphism, where different operators like +, = or == are treated as polymorphic functions and as such have different behaviors depending on the types of its arguments.

Option type	Yes	We can create an Option typeclass in Go:
		`fmt.Println("Has value:", option.SomeString("Hi"))`
		`fmt.Println("Is empty :", option.Empty())`
		The following is the output:
		`Has value: Hi`
		`Is empty : <EMPTY>`

Parametric polymorphism	No	Parametric Polymorphism means **Generics**. This is a style of datatype generic programming where we code our functions using non-specific data types. For example, we can implement generic algorithms that work on collections of non-specific types. Generics provides code reuse, type safety and easy-to-read code. See the following Generics section for a simple example.
Partial function application	Yes	Giving a function fewer arguments than it expects is called Partial function application. Here, our function accepts a function with multiple parameters and returns a function with fewer parameters.

Pure functions	Yes	Pure functions map inputs to outputs. When given the same input a pure function will always return the same output (also known as *determinism*) and will not have any observable side effects.
		The determinism of pure functions means that our FP programs' correctness can be proven formally, which is a great benefit for mission critical applications.
		Just like a mathematical function, the output of our function depends entirely on its input and nothing else.
		For example, the output of the function below will always return two more than the value (x) passed to it:
		`func addTwo(x int) int {`
		`    return x + 2`
		`}`

Pattern matching	No	Pattern matching enables the compiler to match a value against some patterns to select a branch of the code.
		`type ErrorMessage =`
		`| YourNameInvalid`
		`| YourPhoneInvalid`
		`| NoTicketsMustBeGreaterThan0`
		`| CreditCardNoInvalid`
		`| CreditCardExpDateInvalid`
		The value of our `ErrorMessage` in the preceding code will be one of five different error choices (`YourNameInvalid`, `YourPhoneInvalid`, and so on)
		In Go, we can accomplish this at runtime using a union type.

Pipelining	Yes	Pipelining allows us to pass the output of one function as input to another. Function calls can be chained in a sequence to implement a workflow. Pipelining encourages code reuse and parallel execution.
Recursion	Yes	Recursion is used by FP languages in place of loops where a function calls itself until an end condition is reached. In Go, every recursive call creates a call stack. TCO avoids creating a new stack by making last call in a recursion the function itself. Even though we can code recursively in Go without TCO, it's just not practical because of poor performance. Note that recursion in pure FP languages are abstracted from sight by HOFs.

Referential rransparency	Yes	Referential transparency is a property of pure functions where our function that always return the same output for the same inputs. Our function expression f(x) and the results of evaluating our function are interchangeable. For example, 1 + 1 is always equals 2. As we saw in Chapter 2, *Manipulating Collections*, this means that we can cache the results of the first function invocation and improve performance. **Tip:** If we can cache results from previous function calls then we have referential integrity.

Sum or Union types	Yes	We can implement a union type using an interface with Success() and Failure() methods that will return either Success or Failure. For details see 2-design-patterns/ch04-solid/02_maybe
		package maybe
		
		type SuccessOrFailure interface {
		   Success() bool
		    Failure() bool
		}

Tail Call Optimization	No	Tail Call Optimization makes recursive function calls performant. A tail call happens when a function calls another as its last action. TCO acts like a GOTO statement. For example: func f(x) {// some code;return g(x)} The program does not need to return to the calling function when the called function g(x) ends b/c there is no executable code after that last line. After the tail call, the program does not need any call stack information about g. Without TCO the program will create a needless call stack for g; A lot of recursive calls will cause a stack overflow. With TCO, the recursive program will be faster and consume far fewer resources.
Typeclasses	Yes	Type classes allow us to define functions that can be used on different types with a potentially different implementation for each type. Each class represents a set of types and is associated with a particular set of member functions. For example, the type class Eq represents the set of all equality types, which is precisely the set of types on which the (==) operator can be used.

| Unit type | Yes | A Unit type has exactly a one value. It is also known as the identity. The unit for multiplication is 1, for addition is 0, for string concatenation is the empty string.
How many values can a type defined as a tuple of of type int contain? Infinite. (-∞, ..., 0, 1, 2... ∞)
How many values can a type defined as the empty tuple contain? The value of a Unit type is that you can use it in places where we might otherwise return nil (or null). We return a Unit when we don't care what the value is. We don't return nil, we return a value; the Unit value. All functions return values; No more null pointer exceptions!
The Unit type is also useful in places that need an empty value. For example, in F# an Async action which may create side effects but does not return a value is an instance of type Async<unit> |
|---|---|---|

These are not all characteristics of a pure FP, just some of the more significant ones. Probably the most important one is support for first class functions.

> The preceding table introduces a lot of concepts that we'll cover in greater detail later in our book. Feel free to skip ahead if your curiosity is too great; Otherwise, just go with the flow and we'll eventually get to it.

In the *Supported in Go?* column in the preceding table:

- **Yes!**: Indicates that the FP characteristic exists in Go.
- **Yes**: Indicates that the characteristic or requirement can be achieved with some effort in Go.
- **No**: Indicates that this FP characteristic or requirement is missing and is difficult or not possible to achieve without a major upgrade to the Go compiler, or without using another technology in tandem with Go.

Using High-Order Functions

Function composition

Function composition is what happens when we combine functions. The output of one function is the the input of the next function. We can use objects and morphisms of category theory to help us get the order right. Take the following diagram for example...

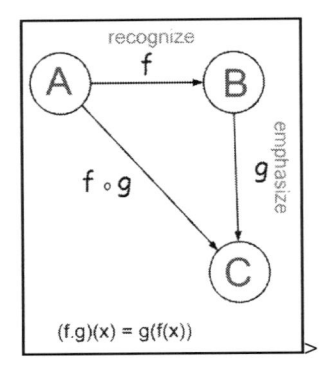

```
            recognize
               f
         A ─────────► B
          ╲           │
           ╲          │ emphasize
        f∘g ╲         │ g
             ╲        │
              ╲       ▼
               ╲───► C

      (f.g)(x) = g(f(x))
```

We see that we can combine our functions f and g to get from A to B to C. Note that the order matters. We must first go from A to B via f and then from B to C via g.

We express this with the following notation (f.g)(x). That reads, *f-compose-g with input x*. This expression equals g(f(x)), which reads *f of x of g*. So (f.g)(x) = g(f(x)).

This is what the compose function looks like in Go:

```
func Compose(f StrFunc, g StrFunc) StrFunc {
    return func(s string) string {
        return g(f(s))
    }
}
```

Where `StrFunc` is defined as:

```
type StrFunc func(string) string
```

In our `main.go`, we define our f and g functions, recognize and emphasize, respectively:

```
func main() {
    var recognize = func(name string) string {
        return fmt.Sprintf("Hey %s", name)
    }
    var emphasize = func(statement string) string {
        return fmt.Sprintf(strings.ToUpper(statement) + "!")
    }
```

[92]

We compose f and g as follows:

```
var greetFoG = Compose(recognize, emphasize)
fmt.Println(greetFoG("Gopher"))
```

The following is the output:

```
HEY GOPHER!
```

Note that order matters. What happens if we flip the order of f and g and then compose?

```
var greetGoF = Compose(emphasize, recognize)
fmt.Println(greetGoF("Gopher"))
```

The following is the output:

```
Hey GOPHER!
```

Monads allow us to chain continuations

Chaining continuations means that we can execute a series of functions, where the output of one function is the input of the next. Check out the following example of chaining high-order functions:

```
cars := LoadCars()
for _, car := range cars.Filter(ByHasNumber()).
    Filter(ByForeign()).
    Map(Upgrade()).
    Reduce(JsonReducer(cars), Collection{}) {
        log.Println(car)
}
```

You will see the following output:

```
{"car": {"make": "Honda", "model": " Accord ES2 LX"}}
{"car": {"make": "Lexus", "model": " IS250 LS"}}
{"car": {"make": "Lexus", "model": " SC 430 LS"}}
{"car": {"make": "Toyota", "model": " RAV4 EV"}}
```

How much more code would be required if we were to implement the for loops, error checking, and other scaffolding that is typically required when coding Go in the typical imperative style of programming?

Using High-Order Functions

Instead of telling Go how to filter, map, and reduce our collection, we declare what we want to accomplish. Later in this chapter, we do implement the `Filter`, `Map`, and `Reduce` functions, but what if the Go standard library already provides these for us?

How can we expect Go to provide HOF implementations for cars? That would not be reasonable, right? What's missing? The answer is *generics*.

> **TIP**
> The ChainLink implementation in this chapter is sort of a poor man's monad. We'll explore a real monad in the last chapter of this book and discover that there are more operations involved (Bind, Return, monadic error handling). Real monads also do not rely on global variables. What is similar is that they both allow us to execute operations in order, where the output of one function is the input to the next. That is a key concept to remember.

Generics

Parametric polymorphism means generics. A generic function or a data type can be written to handle any data value using the same logic, without having to cast the value to a specific data type. This greatly improves code reuse.

The following is a C# code example of a generic `IsEqual` implementation. The generic `IsEqual` function will accept any type (that implements `Equals`). We pass `IsEqual` integers and strings by simply indicating the type `T` during runtime, at the moment `IsEqual` is executed:

```
namespace Generics
{
   private static void Main() {
      if(Compute<int>.IsEqual(2, 2)) {
         Console.WriteLine("2 isEqualTo 2");
      }
      if(!Compute<String>.IsEqual("A", "B")) {
         Console.WriteLine("A is_NOT_EqualTo B");
      }
   }
    public class Compute<T> {
       public static bool IsEqual(T Val1, T Val2) {
          return Val1.Equals(Val2);
       }
    }
}
```

Currently, to do this in Go, we will have to use an empty interface and perform a type conversion. It's type conversion that will cause the performance hit that usually makes this sort of generics handling in Go impractical.

First-class functions

First-class functions allow us to make new functions by providing our base functions with function parameters. In the following code, our base function is `Filter`. By passing `ByMake("Toyota")` to `Filter`, we remove most of the car items from our collection, leaving only Toyota:

```
cars := Filter(ByMake("Toyota"))
```

We also have the ability to transform any function that works on single elements into a function that works on lists, by wrapping it with the `Map` function. Without our new functional style of programming, we might be tempted to implement a `for` loop and apply the `fmt.Sprintf` transformation on each individual car, as follows:

```
// cars: Honda Accord, Honda Accord ES2, Lexus IS250, Honda CR-V, Lexus SC 430,...
for _, car := range cars {
    thisCar := fmt.Sprintf("%s %s", car, map[string]string{
        "Honda": "LX",
        "Lexus": "LS",
        "Toyota": "EV",
        "Ford": "XL",
        "GM": "X",
    }[GetMake(car)])
    // upgrade a car by appending "LX" ... to the end of the model name
    mappedCars = append(mappedCars, thisCar)
}
// mappedCars: Honda Accord LX, Honda Accord ES2 LX, Lexus IS250 LS...
```

Instead, we can simply pass the `Upgrade` function to `Map` as we compose our data transformation:

```
Filter(ByMake("Toyota")).Map(Upgrade())
```

We no longer need to write `for` loops that manipulate arrays because we can call `Map` inline.

Using High-Order Functions

HOFs can greatly reduce the time that it takes to develop complex logic. We can quickly compose smaller, task-specific functions into solutions for complex business logic much faster, with less scaffolding code, which means we'll have fewer bugs to fix. Our functions are in essence reusable building blocks.

HOFs are independent, making them easy to reuse, refactor, and reorganize in our code base. This makes our programs more flexible and resilient to future code changes.

More readable code, faster implementation, fewer bugs. The benefits of FP are adding up!

Closure

A closure is a function that closes over variables in its outer scope. We really need an example to understand that statement! Here's a good one:

```
func addTwo() func() int {
        sum := 0
        return func() int {   // anonymous function
                sum += 2
                return sum
        }
}

func main() {
        twoMore := addTwo()
        fmt.Println(twoMore())
        fmt.Println(twoMore())
}
```

You will see the following output:

```
2
4
```

The preceding closure is formed by the `addTwo` function. Inside `addTwo`, both `sum` and the anonymous function are declared in the same lexical scope. Since `addTwo` closes over both `sum` and the anonymous function, and because `sum` was declared before the anonymous function, the anonymous function always has access to, and can modify, the `sum` variable. As soon as `addTwo` is assigned to `twoMore`, the `addTwo` functions's anonymous function gets access to the `sum` variable and holds on to it as long as the application continues to run.

Dynamically scoped

What if we accidentally initialized sum in an outer scope from where we defined our function? Notice that there is no sum variable initialization in the same scope as our anonymous function:

```
func addTwoDynamic() func() int {
    return func() int {
        sum += 2
        return sum
    }
}
```

When we run this in our main() function:

```
twoMoreDynamic := addTwoDynamic()
fmt.Println(twoMoreDynamic())
fmt.Println(twoMoreDynamic())
```

Our Go runtime looks in the environment in which the anonymous function was called, rather than where it was defined (as is the case in lexical scoping). If addTwoDynamic had been nested several stack frames deep, our Go runtime would look where addTwoDynamic was defined for sum. If it was not found there, it would continue up the stack until sum is found. So, we see that dynamic scoping adds complexity and might cause the value of sum to change in unpredictable ways, or at least in ways that are more difficult to debug.

The following is the output:

```
7
9
```

What happened? Since sum was not defined in the scope in which our anonymous function was defined, Go found it in the global scope. It's value was 5. addTwoDynamic added 2 to 5 and got 7. addTwoDynamic did it again and got 9. Probably not what we wanted.

Being able to pass around lexical context is powerful and guarantees that we won't have side effects that might occur with dynamic scoping. We'll look at a practical example where we create an application context, for example, database connection, logger, and so on, at application startup and pass that context around where needed throughout our application.

Pure function

A pure function is a function that when given the same input will always return the same output and will not have any observable side effects. How is that a benefit? Let's see. We can run any pure function in parallel since our functions do not need access to shared memory. Race condition due to side effects are not possible with pure functions. The performance gains of running our code concurrently on multiple cores is another awesome benefit of FP.

Immuable Data

Immutable data structures:

- Have one state and never change
- Are simpler to construct, debug, test, and reason about
- Are side-effect free
- Improve performance and are more scalable because they are easier to cache
- Are safer in that they prevent null pointer references
- Are thread safe
- Are always in a stable state

Since immutable data structures are never changed, that means that failures never occur during a data modification operation. When an immutable data structure is initialized it will either fail or succeed, returning a valid data structure that never changes.

In order to make changes to an immutable data structure, we must create a new tree. Suppose we want to update the value of g in the existing tree data structure (*previous root*). First, we would create the g' node and build the new tree by traversing the nodes connected to g and copying only those values necessary to rebuild the tree. References to other nodes can be created without creating new nodes (these are the nodes in white). With the new root in place, new leaf nodes are added to the new tree structure.

Once the new root has been created the previous/old root can be preserved or it can be marked for deletion.

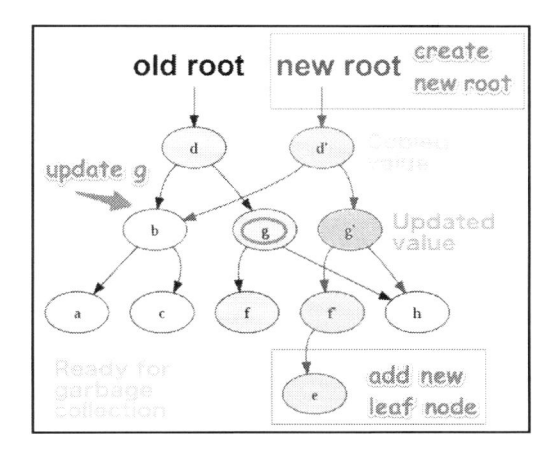

This may seem like a lot of work, but one of the greatest benefits is that we no longer need to worry about our data unexpectedly changing. For example, what if one Goroutine is looping through our data structure while another one is removing elements from it? We no longer need to concern ourselves with dealing with race conditions and verifying that our preconditions are still valid. When we use immutable data structures, our code becomes more robust and easier to reason about.

Can you think of any solutions today that make use of immutable data structures?

Ever wondered how git works?

Interested in full stack development? How does ReactJS update its models?

In the game of soccer, we may loose to a team because they have a player with specific skills. When we face the team again we may forget the past, but that does not change history; It is not possible to change the past. When the past is not preserved, we cannot learn from it and history will repeat itself. Mutability hides changes.

Persistent data structures for Go

Check out `https://godoc.org/github.com/mndrix/ps`

From it's documentation:

Fully persistent data structures. A persistent data structure is a data structure that always preserves the previous version of itself when it is modified. Such data structures are effectively immutable, as their operations do not update the structure in-place, but instead always yield a new structure.

Persistent data structures typically share structure among themselves. This allows operations to avoid copying the entire data structure.

ps has small but effective API for manipulating lists and maps of data:

```
type List interface {
   Cons(val interface{}) List
   ForEach(f func(interface{}))
   Head() interface{}
   IsNil() bool
   Reverse() List
   Size() int
   Tail() List
}
func NewList() List
type Map interface {
   Delete(key string) Map
   ForEach(f func(key string, val interface{}))
   IsNil() bool
   Keys() []string
   Lookup(key string) (interface{}, bool)
   Set(key string, value interface{}) Map
   Size() int
   String() string
   UnsafeMutableSet(key string, value interface{}) Map
}
func NewMap() Map
```

For more details see https://godoc.org/github.com/mndrix/ps

Use of expressions

Use of expressions (rather than statements) means that in FP, we pass a value to a function that typically transforms it in some way and then returns a new value. Since FP functions have no side effects, an FP function that does not return a value is useless and a sign of code smell. In Chapter 1, *Pure Functional Programming in Go*, we saw that imperative programming focuses on the step-by-step mechanics of how a program operates, whereas in declarative programming, we declare what we want the results to be.

Here's an example of imperative programming:

```
var found bool
car_to_look_for := "Blazer"
cars := []string{"Accord", "IS250", "Blazer" }

for _, car := range cars {
    if car == car_to_look_for {
        found = true;
    }
}
fmt.Printf("Found? %v", found)
```

Here's an example of declarative programming:

```
fmt.Printf("Found? %v", cars.contains("Blazer"))
```

We have less, declarative FP code that is easier to read.

Sample HOF application

Let's build a sample app that will demonstrate the benefits of applying functional programming concepts to Go.

Our app will read from the following `cars.csv` file:

```
"Honda Accord"
"Honda Accord ES2"
"Lexus IS250"
"Honda CR-V"
"Lexus SC 430"
"Ford F-150"
"Toyota Highlander"
"Toyota RAV4"
"GM Hummer H2"
"GM Hummer H3"
```

Using High-Order Functions

We will apply high-order functions and various functional programming constructs to the list of cars to filter, map, reduce, and transform it to our heart's content.

Our project is structured as follows:

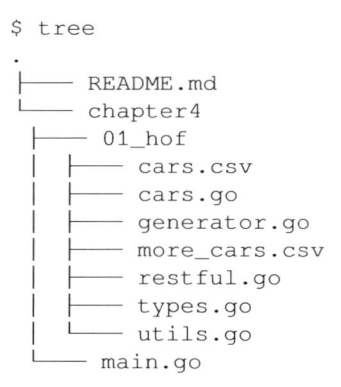

```
$ tree
.
├── README.md
└── chapter4
    ├── 01_hof
    │   ├── cars.csv
    │   ├── cars.go
    │   ├── generator.go
    │   ├── more_cars.csv
    │   ├── restful.go
    │   ├── types.go
    │   └── utils.go
    └── main.go
```

At the root of the `chapter4` directory is our `main.go` file. Since we plan to build a Go executable from `main.go` and run it, we use the package name of `main` and include a `main()` function.

The other files will be in a subdirectory named `01_hof`, where `hof` stands for high-order functions.

The chapter4 application code

Let's examine our `chapter4` implementation, starting with `main.go`:

```go
package main

import (
        . "github.com/l3x/learn-fp-in-go/chapter4/01_hof"
        "log"
        "os"
        "github.com/julienschmidt/httprouter"
        "net/http"
)
```

The dot (.) in the . "github.com/l3x/learn-fp-in-go/chapter4/01_hof" import keeps us from having to preface the functions in that directory with `hof`, which is the package name used by all the Go files in that directory:

```
func init() {
      log.SetFlags(0)
      log.SetOutput(os.Stdout)
}
```

We'll use the `log` package to log output to stdout. Passing a 0 value to `log.SetFlags` tells the logger to print without prepending timestamps. We also tell the logger to print to `stdout`, rather than the default `stderr` because we want all of the output to be consistently displayed for ease of reading. We'd likely not output any information to `stdout` for a production application because there isn't anything useful for the program to send on `stdout` other than command help and usage information.

> **TIP**: The `log` function can easily be configured to prepend timestamps and line numbers. The `log.SetFlags(log.Lshortfile | log.Ldate)` setting will print the output to `stdout`: `2017/04/07 utils.go:17: car: Honda Accord`.

Build and runtime instructions

After verifying that our Go environment is properly configured, we can change the directory to a project directory and start a RESTful web server with the following command:

```
$ RUN_HTTP_SERVER=TRUE ./chapter4
```

See the *My Go build and runtime process* section in the `Appendix`, *Miscellaneous Information and How-Tos*, for details regarding how I manage my Go environment.

We'll need to open another Terminal window to run our `chapter4` executable. Let's build and run our `chapter4` app to exercise our HOFs with the following command:

```
$ go build && ./chapter4
```

The top few lines of output should look like this:

```
ByMake - Honda
---------------------
car: Honda Accord
car: Honda Accord ES2
. . .
```

More application code

The first thing we do in the `main()` function is check the `RUN_HTTP_SERVER` environment variable. If it's set to `true`, then the program will set up two routes. The first route `/cars` returns the index page that displays all the cars that have been loaded from the `.csv` files. The second route `/cars/:id` retrieves an individual car object and returns its JSON representation:

```
func main() {
        if os.Getenv("RUN_HTTP_SERVER") == "TRUE" {
                router := httprouter.New()
                router.GET("/cars", CarsIndexHandler)
                router.GET("/cars/:id", CarHandler)
                log.Println("Listening on port 8000")
                log.Fatal(http.ListenAndServe(":8000", router))
```

The `IndexedCars` variable is defined in `types.go` as follows:

```
IndexedCar struct {
        Index int    `json:"index"`
        Car   string` json:"car"`
}
```

Before we look at the else logic, let's take a peek at the following `cars.go` file. We declare an exported package level variable `CarsDB` that is assigned a slice of `IndexedCars`:

```
package hof

import (
        "fmt"
        s "strings"
        "regexp"
        "log"
        "encoding/json"
)

var CarsDB = initCarsDB()

func initCarsDB() []IndexedCar {
        var indexedCars []IndexedCar
        for i, car := range LoadCars() {
                indexedCars = append(indexedCars, IndexedCar{i, car})
        }
        lenCars := len(indexedCars)
        for i, car := range LoadMoreCars() {
                indexedCars = append(indexedCars, IndexedCar{i + lenCars, car})
```

```
            }
            return indexedCars
    }

    func LoadCars() Collection {
            return CsvToStruct("cars.csv")
    }
```

Note that every Go source file in our `01_hof` directory uses the package name `hof`.

We preface the `strings` package with `s` so that we can easily reference string utility functions with `s` like this: `s.Contains(car, make)` rather than `strings.Contains(car, make)`.

Since `var CarsDB = initCarsDB()` is defined at the package level, it will be evaluated when we start our `chapter4` executable. The `initCarsDB()` function only needs to be referenced in this `cars.go` file, so we do not need to capitalize its first character.

The `LoadCars()` function, on the other hand, is referenced by the main package, so we need to capitalize its first character in order to make it accessible.

Now, let's turn our attention to the FP goodies in the else block.

The Filter function

The first HOF that we exploit is the `Filter` function:

```
    } else {
            cars := LoadCars()

            PrintCars("ByMake - Honda", cars.Filter(ByMake("Honda")))
```

You will see the following output:

```
ByMake - Honda
----------------------
car: Honda Accord
car: Honda Accord ES2
car: Honda CR-V
```

Using High-Order Functions

The `Filter` function is in the `cars.go` file. Observe the `fn` argument. It is passed into the `Filter` function and later called with a `car` parameter. If `fn(car)` --that is, `ByMake("Honda")`--returns `true`, then the car is added to the collection:

```
func (cars Collection) Filter(fn FilterFunc) Collection {
        filteredCars := make(Collection, 0)
        for _, car := range cars {
                if fn(car) {
                        filteredCars = append(filteredCars, car)
                }
        }
        return filteredCars
}
```

When we define the `Filter` function on the `cars collection` type, it's called a method. A Go method is a function with a special receiver argument. In our `Filter` function, the `cars` collection is the receiver. Notice that `cars` is in the first set of arguments, between the `func` keyword and the `Filter` name. Note that `cars` is a data structure that has a `Filter` behavior. The `Filter` method accepts `FilterFun` as its argument and returns a filtered collection.

Reality check

What? A `for` loop? A mutating `car` variable? What gives? We must face the facts. The Go compiler does not provide TCO, so a recursive implementation is simply not practical. Perhaps Go 2.0 will provide a pure functional library with all our favorite HOFs as well as generics. Until then, we will make do with using the functional programming style as much as possible with a bit of imperative programming where necessary. Another option that we'll explore later is an execution system named **Gleam**, which provides pure Go mappers and reducers that provide high performance and concurrency.

> Data transformations are so common that it's nice to have a shorthand for it. HOF's ability to simplify both writing and reading code that performs data transformations is one of FP's greatest benefits.

FilterFunc

In the `types.go` file, we see its definition:

```
FilterFunc func(string) bool
```

Looking back at the line in `main.go`, we see that we use the `ByMake` filter function:

```
PrintCars("ByMake - Honda", cars.Filter(ByMake("Honda")))
```

The `ByMake` function is defined in the `cars.go` file:

```
func ByMake(make string) FilterFunc {
    return func(car string) bool {
        return s.Contains(car, make)
    }
}
```

The `ByMake` function is a HOF because it returns a function. Recall that `Filter` is a HOF because it accepts a function. In this case, `ByMake` is that function, `fn`, as we will see in the next section.

Filter function

The `Filter` function is a HOF that takes another HOF, namely `ByMake`, and performs a data transformation.

```
func (cars Collection) Filter(fn FilterFunc) Collection {
    filteredCars := make(Collection, 0)
    for _, car := range cars {
        if fn(car) {
            filteredCars = append(filteredCars, car)
        }
    }
    return filteredCars
}
```

RESTful resources

Let's open `http://localhost:8000/cars` to see the full list of cars from both `cars.csv` and `more_cars.csv`:

```
{
  "IndexedCars": [
    {
      "index": 0,
      "car": "Honda Accord"
    },
    {
      "index": 1,
      "car": "Honda Accord ES2"
    },
    {
      "index": 2,
      "car": "Lexus IS250"
    },
    {
      "index": 3,
      "car": "Honda CRV"
    },
    {
      "index": 4,
      "car": "Lexus SC 430"
    },
    {
      "index": 5,
      "car": "Ford F-150"
    },
    {
      "index": 6,
      "car": "GM Hummer H2"
    },
    {
      "index": 7,
      "car": "GM Hummer H3"
    },
    {
      "index": 8,
      "car": "Chrysler 200"
    },
    {
      "index": 9,
      "car": "Chrysler Pacifica"
    },
    {
      "index": 10,
      "car": "Toyota 86"
    },
    {
      "index": 11,
      "car": "Toyota Highlander"
    },
    {
      "index": 12,
      "car": "Toyota RAV4"
    },
    {
      "index": 13,
      "car": "Dodge Charger"
    },
    {
      "index": 14,
      "car": "Dodge 330"
    },
    {
      "index": 15,
      "car": "GM Oldsmobile Cutlass Supreme"
    },
    {
      "index": 16,
      "car": "GM Oldsmobile Delta 88"
    },
    {
      "index": 17,
      "car": "GM Oldsmobile 442"
    }
  ]
}
```

Let's take a look at the next `Filter` function in action in `main.go`:

```
PrintCars("Numeric", cars.Filter(ByHasNumber()))
```

You will see the following output:

```
Numeric
---------------------
car: Honda Accord ES2
car: Lexus IS250
car: Lexus SC 430
car: Ford F-150
car: Toyota 86
car: Toyota RAV4
car: GM Hummer H2
car: GM Hummer H3
```

The `FilterFunc` method used in this case is `ByHasNumber()`. It operates like `ByMake` `FilterFunc` and uses Go's regexp `MatchString` function to return `true` if the car has a number in it:

```
func ByHasNumber() FilterFunc {
    return func(car string) bool {
        match, _ := regexp.MatchString(".+[0-9].*", car)
        return match
    }
}
```

Chaining functions

Now that we have the hang of it, let's chain a few filters together:

```
PrintCars("Foreign, Numeric, Toyota",
    cars.Filter(ByForeign()).
        Filter(ByHasNumber()).
        Filter(ByMake("Toyota")))
```

You will see the following output:

```
Foreign, Numeric, Toyota
---------------------
car: Toyota 86
car: Toyota RAV4
```

More cars

It's time to add more cars:

```
moreCars := LoadMoreCars()

PrintCars("More Cars, Domestic, Numeric, GM",
        cars.AddCars(moreCars).
            Filter(ByDomestic()).
            Filter(ByHasNumber()).
            Filter(ByMake("GM")))
```

The output of this is as follows:

```
More Cars, Domestic, Numeric, GM
-----------------------
car: GM Hummer H2
car: GM Hummer H3
car: GM Oldsmobile Delta 88
car: GM Oldsmobile 442
```

Wait, what? `AddCars`? How is that an HOF? `AddCars` neither takes a function nor returns a function. Even worse, it mutates the `cars` collection.

Reality check

It's not important that the cars collection remain *pure*; frankly, that's not feasible, given that the Go compiler currently does not provide TCO. What's important is that our code improves with the use of functional programming techniques. Granted, this one, `AddCars`, is the furthest function we have from pure, but it is useful and it does improve our programs' readability. We do need to be careful when we use non-pure functions, especially ones that mutate their state, but this usage is perfectly fine for our purposes.

We find `AddCars` in `cars.go`:

```
func (cars Collection) AddCars(carsToAdd Collection) Collection {
        return append(cars, carsToAdd...)
}
```

The Map function

Back to `main.go`. This time, you'll be introduced to the `Map` HOF. Whereas `Filter` acts to reduce the number of items in the resulting collection, `Map` will return the same number of items that it receives. The `Map` function transforms the collection into a new collection, where each item is changed in some way:

```
PrintCars("Numeric, Foreign, Map Upgraded",
    cars.Filter(ByHasNumber()).
        Filter(ByForeign()).
        Map(Upgrade()))
```

Here's the output of this:

```
Numeric, Foreign, Map Upgraded
----------------------
car: Honda Accord ES2 LX
car: Lexus IS250 LS
car: Lexus SC 430 LS
car: Toyota 86 EV
car: Toyota RAV4 EV
```

We pass a `MapFunc` function named `Upgrade` to `Map`:

```
func Upgrade() MapFunc {
    return func(car string) string {
        return fmt.Sprintf("%s %s", car, UpgradeLabel(car))
    }
}
```

`Upgrade` calls the `UpgradeLabel` function in order to append the appropriate upgrade label to the end of the cars' model name:

```
func UpgradeLabel(car string) string {
    return map[string]string{
        "Honda": "LX",
        "Lexus": "LS",
        "Toyota": "EV",
        "Ford": "XL",
        "GM": "X",
    }[GetMake(car)]
}
```

Improved performance from the Map function

One of the greatest benefits of FP is performance.

Programs today achieve better performance largely by performing more than one operation at a time using multiple CPU cores.

This means running code in parallel, and to do that, our code must be thread-safe. Programs that have a shared mutable state are not thread-safe. These programs will be bottlenecked in one core.

FP solves this bottleneck/thread safety issue by returning new instances of variables rather than changing the original instance.

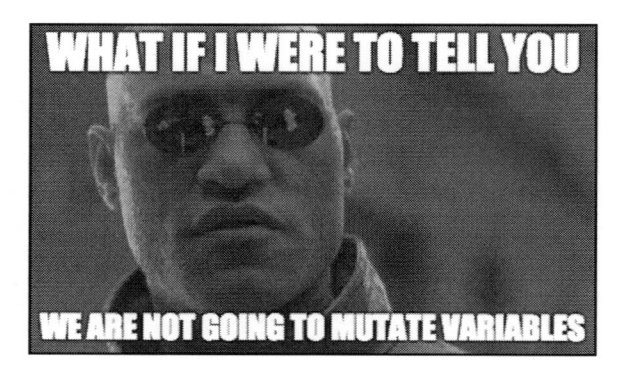

WHAT IF I WERE TO TELL YOU WE ARE NOT GOING TO MUTATE VARIABLES

Let's look at the Map function to see how we can pull this off using FP:

```
func (cars Collection) Map(fn MapFunc) Collection {
    mappedCars := make(Collection, 0, len(cars))
    for _, car := range cars {
        mappedCars = append(mappedCars, fn(car))
    }
    return mappedCars
}
```

Instead of appending to the cars collection, that Map receives a new variable mappedCars. The mappedCars collection is mutated, not the original cars collection.

What we are doing, tactically, when we call Map(Upgrade()) is pushing the moment that our data changes out to the last moment--in this example, after mappedCars has been populated.

We have been programming our way around FP concepts our entire career. Part of what we do in this chapter is to identify these FP patterns and see how and why we should exploit them.

The Reduce function

Next, let's look at the `Reduce` function. `Reduce` is the Swiss army knife of HOFs. With a `Reduce` function, we can do anything that can be done with `Filter` or `Map`.

A `Reduce` function, also known as a `fold`, `accumulate`, `aggregate`, `compress`, or `inject` takes a seed value and applies the logic of the reducer function to the seed, and potentially multiple calls to itself to arrive at a result. Often, the reduce function will combine the data elements to return a single aggregated value, hence the term `fold`. So, we fold all of the data into a single result.

Back in `main.go`, we apply the `ByMake` filter to filter out all the cars that are not a Honda product. Then, we call the `Reduce` function to transform the collection of Honda vehicles into a collection of JSON strings:

```
PrintCars("Filter Honda, Reduce JSON",
    cars.Filter(ByMake("Honda")).
        Reduce(JsonReducer(cars), Collection{}))
```

The output of this will be as follows:

```
Filter Honda, Reduce JSON
----------------------
car: {"car": {"make": "Honda", "model": " Accord"}}
car: {"car": {"make": "Honda", "model": " Accord ES2"}}
car: {"car": {"make": "Honda", "model": " CR-V"}}
```

The `Reduce` function is a method of the cars collection that accepts a `Reducer` function. Again, we see a `for` loop and recall, *No TCO, No recursion*. That's okay. So, the guts of our `Reduce` function is not *pure*. That's OK. It's still readable, performant, and safe; in the spirit of Go programming, it gets the job done:

```
func (cars Collection) Reduce(fn ReducerFunc, accumulator Collection)
Collection {
    var result = accumulator
    for _, car := range cars {
        result = append(fn(car, result))
    }
    return result
}
```

Using High-Order Functions

The second parameter `Collection{}` is the accumulator, which is the initial value assigned to the result. The `Reducer` function starts with the accumulator value, performs transformations on each item in the collection, and returns the result. This `Reduce` function provides the framework in which to perform a reduction, but it's the reducer function (`fn`) that does the heavy lifting. Note that we can pass any valid reducer function (`fn`) into the `Reduce` framework to get vastly different results.

Our `JsonReducer` function does the real work of transforming each item in the cars collection into a JSON string:

```
func JsonReducer(cars Collection) ReducerFunc {
    return func(car string, cars Collection) Collection {
        carJson := fmt.Sprintf("{"car": {"make": "%s", "model": "%s"}}", GetMake(car), GetModel(car))
        cars = append(cars, carJson)
        return cars
    }
}
```

Reduce is an HOF function that takes a function. `JsonReducer` is an HOF function that returns a function.

More high-order functions

Now, let's return to `main.go` to look at a few more HOFs in action.

We apply our `ByMake` filter and a new type of reducer. This reducer, `Reducer2`, will return a slice of `CarTypes` rather than JSON:

```
PrintCars2("Reduce - Lexus",
    cars.Filter(ByMake("Lexus")).
        Reduce2(CarTypeReducer(cars), []CarType{}))
```

Here's the output of this:

```
Reduce - Lexus
----------------------
car: {Lexus IS250}
car: {Lexus SC 430}
```

The following is another example that shows how easy chaining, also known as function composition, is:

```
PrintCars("ByModel - Accord up/downgraded",
       cars.Filter(ByModel("Accord")).
             Map(Upgrade()).
             Map(Downgrade()))
```

Here's the output of this:

```
ByModel - Accord up/downgraded
----------------------
car: Honda Accord
car: Honda Accord ES2
```

We saw how the `Upgrade` map function adds the appropriate label to the end of the car model. By applying `Downgrade` after `Upgrade`, we effectively undo `Upgrade`.

Generators

Time to check out generators. Generators are useful because they allow us to delay an expression evaluation. We only compute the expression(s) we need when we need them. Generators also conserve memory because with generators, we only create and use what we need, no more:

```
PrintCars("GenerateCars(1, 3)",
       cars.GenerateCars(1, 3))
```

We will find the implementation of `GenerateCars` in the `generate.go` file:

```
package hof

import (
        "sync"
        "log"
)

func carGenerator(iterator func(int) int, lower int, upper int) func() (int, bool) {
        return func() (int, bool) {
                lower = iterator(lower)
                return lower, lower > upper
        }
}

func iterator(i int) int {
```

Using High-Order Functions

```
        i += 1
    return i
}
```

We define our imports. The `sync` import is a clue that we have a need to synchronize our Goroutines. The `iterator` function will be passed to the `carGenerator` function and will track how many cars we've generated. We'll be creating cars as per need basis.

RESTful server

If we have our RESTful server running on port `8000`, we can open our web browser to `http://localhost:8000/cars/1` and see the following:

```
{
  "index": 1,
  "car": "Honda Accord ES2"
}
```

This is a representation of an `IndexedCar` struct. It has an index and a car make and model string.

Here's the actual `IndexedCar` struct in `types.go`:

```
IndexedCar struct {
    Index int    `json:"index"`
    Car   string `json:"car"`
}
```

The GenerateCars function

Here's the actual generator function:

```
func (cars Collection) GenerateCars(start, limit int) Collection {
    carChannel := make(chan *IndexedCar)
```

The `GenerateCars` is another method in the `cars` collection that makes it easy to compose data transformations with other HOFs. `GenerateCars` takes a start index and limit, which is the number of cars that we want to be returned. We create `carChannel` of pointers to `IndexedCars`:

```
var waitGroup sync.WaitGroup
```

We use `sync.WaitGroup` as a counting semaphore to wait for our collection of Goroutines to finish:

```
numCarsToGenerate := start + limit - 1
generatedCars := Collection{}
waitGroup.Add(numCarsToGenerate)
```

We calculate the number of cars we want to generate and pass that number to the `waitGroup.Add` function:

```
next := carGenerator(iterator, start -1, numCarsToGenerate)
```

Our `carGenerator` function returns a function that we assign to a variable named `next`:

```
carIndex, done := next()
```

The `next` variable returns two variables: `carIndex` and `done`. As long as there are more cars to generate, `done` will be `false`. So, we can use `done` to control a `for` loop that launches a Goroutine, one for each car to generate:

```
for !done {
    go func(carIndex int) {
        thisCar, err := GetThisCar(carIndex)
        if err != nil {
            panic(err)
        }
        carChannel <- thisCar
        generatedCars = append(generatedCars, thisCar.Car)
        waitGroup.Done()
    }(carIndex)

    carIndex, done = next()
}
```

The `next` variable returns two variables `GetThisCar(carIndex)` in the code block; immediately after this, the preceding code calls the RESTful car service that returns the requested car.

If an error is encountered, we use the built-in function `panic` to stop the execution of the current Goroutine. Since we used a deferred function, namely `csvfile.Close()`, in the call stack, it will be executed if a panic occurs. Note that we could have had more control over the termination sequence using the built-in recover function.

The `thisCar` variable is sent to `carChannel`, and the `Car` field is appended to the `generatedCars` collection.

[117]

Currying Goroutine

Notice anything special about the `generatedCars` collection? (Hint: Our Goroutine is an anonymous function).

That's right. We are currying the `generatedCars` collection. Our Goroutine covers over the `generatedCars` collection. That's what enables us to reference and append to it from the Goroutine, regardless of which core it happens to be running in.

We are standing on the shoulders of giants. We're using a Go channel and Goroutines to emulate an FP generator and other HOFs. Our code is readable, and it doesn't take much code to make it all work.

A closer look at currying

Before we move on, let's look at the following curried versus non-curried code example to improve our understanding of currying:

```go
package main

import "fmt"

// numberIs numberIs a simple function taking an integer and returning boolean
type numberIs func(int) bool

func lessThanTwo(i int) bool { return i < 2 }

// No curried parameters
func lessThan(x int, y int) (bool) {
   return x < y
}

func main() {
   fmt.Println("NonCurried - lessThan(1,2):", lessThan(1, 2))
   fmt.Println("Curried - LessThanTwo(1):", lessThanTwo(1))
}
```

You would immediately see that the curried example takes only one parameter, whereas the non-curried example requires two. The idea behind currying is to create new, more specific functions from smaller, more general, functions by partially applying them. We'll see more of this in `Chapter 8`, *Functional Parameters*.

Another take away is the use of a function type. The `numberIs` is a data type that is a function that takes an int and returns a bool. That's right. In FP, we are not scared of functions. We treat them as a regular old data type. In FP everything is data, and data never changes. It only gets passed around, created and returned.

> The value of angle x is equal to the length of the (A)djacent side divided by the length of the (H)ypotenuse (`http://www.mathopenref.com/cosine.html`):
>
> $\cos x = A / H$

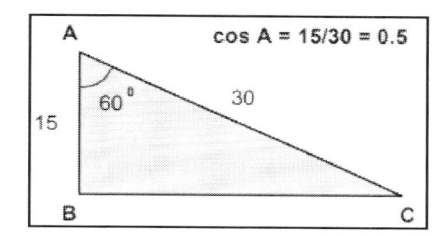

```
                A                    cos A = 15/30 = 0.5
                |\
                | \       30
             15 |  \
                |60°\
                |____\
                B     C
```

In imperative programming, we are led to believe that functions and data are different things. In FP, we see that functions have no side effects. A good FP example is the geometric cosine function. For a right-angle triangle, if we pass 15 for the (A)djacent side and 30 for the (H)ypotenuse, then we get 0.5 as the cosine of angle A. Since we can rely on that fact--pass 15 and 30 and get 0.5 every time--even with our imperative programming hats on, we know we can put those values in a lookup table. Imagine a spreadsheet where row numbers represent the A's and the columns represent the H's. The cell at row 15, column 30, would have the value 0.5.

See, functions are data! However, we don't always want to store every computed value for every possible parameter combination in every use case, just where it makes sense to do so.

Imagine the performance of a system where every function call is a table lookup. Now imagine our reuse potential, where the evaluation parts of the applications are generic. If your mind is still intact, wait until `Chapter 9`, *Category Theory That Applies*, where we will discuss the application of category theory and type classes.

Extending our currying example

But wait, there's more! Let's add the following, just above `func main()`:

```
func (f numberIs) apply(s ...int) (ret []bool) {
   for _, i := range s {
      ret = append(ret, f(i))
   }
   return ret
}
```

The `apply` function is a method bound to a function type, namely `numberIs`. Our apply function applies the `numberIs` function to each argument. Each calculated value is appended to the newly created array of bools that is then returned to the caller.

Next, we update `main()` as follows:

```
func main() {
   fmt.Println("NonCurried - lessThan(1,2):", lessThan(1,2))
   fmt.Println("Curried - LessThanTwo(1):", lessThanTwo(1))
   // use anonymous function
   isLessThanOne := numberIs(func(i int) bool { return i < 1 }).apply
   isLessThanTwo := numberIs(lessThanTwo).apply // use named function
   s := []int{0, 1, 2}
   fmt.Println("Curried, given:", s, "...")
   fmt.Println("isLessThanOne:", isLessThanOne(s...))
   fmt.Println("isLessThanTwo:", isLessThanTwo(s...))
}
```

Here's the output of this:

```
NonCurried - lessThan(1,2): true
Curried - LessThanTwo(1): true
Curried, given: [0 1 2]...
isLessThanOne: [true false false]
isLessThanTwo: [true true false]
```

In pure FP, every function is a function of one argument. We can use currying in Go to achieve this.

Now, back to cars.

Using a WaitGroup variable to manage concurrency

After appending `thisCar` to the `generatedCars` collection, we execute `waitGroup.Done()`. This decrements the count of the `WaitGroup` variable. This count corresponds to the iterator value we assign to the lower variable, and applies to the `lower > upper` expression that is assigned to the done return variable:

```
func carGenerator(iterator func(int) int, lower int, upper int) func() (int, bool) {
        return func() (int, bool) {
                lower = iterator(lower)
                return lower, lower > upper
        }
}
```

We use the iterator to know how many Goroutines to launch:

```
func iterator(i int) int {
        i += 1
        return i
}
```

Finishing up the GenerateCars function

At the end of our `GenerateCars` function, we execute another anonymous Goroutine. The purpose of this Goroutine is to wait for all the previously launched Goroutine generators to complete. We use `waitGroup.Wait` to know when the last generator was completed. Then, it's safe to close `carChannel`:

```
        go func() {
                waitGroup.Wait()
                println("close channel")
                close(carChannel)
        }()

        for thisCar := range carChannel {
                generatedCars = append(generatedCars, thisCar.Car)
        }
        return generatedCars
}
```

The `carChannel` will block until it receives a new car; this is a result of calling `GetThisCar(carIndex)`. Recall that `WaitGroup.Add(numCarsToGenerate)` told `WaitGroup` how many cars we'd process. The `waitGroup.Done()` function counts that number down to 0, at which time `waitGroup.Wait()` is executed and `carChannel` is closed.

We wait until all our Goroutines have fetched data from the RESTful HTTP server before returning the `generatedCars` collection. This is a common pattern in FP: we eliminate as much state change in our data transformation operation as possible. We wait until all of our data collection processing has completed and then we finally return the final result.

Our FP work is much like that of an electrician. Electricians turn off the power, hook up all the wires in the building, and when everything is in place, they flip the power switch and all the lights come on. Data is power. Don't let your data fly until the last possible moment.

In the `main.go` file, add the following code:

```
PrintCars("GenerateCars(1, 3)",
    cars.GenerateCars(1, 3))
```

The following is its output:

```
GenerateCars(1, 3)
---------------------
car: Honda CR-V
car: Honda Accord ES2
car: Lexus IS250
```

Handling concurrency

We are managing our `GetThisCar` Goroutines by counting how many we've launched, and we leverage a `WaitGroup` variable to decrement that count when they complete. While it is true that many of our `GetThisCar` Goroutines execute in parallel, what's important is the way we handle their concurrency. Using the next iterator and the `waitGroup` variable, we are able to simply and effectively deal with their life cycle: starting with each Goroutine, receiving their results and closing `carChannel` when our counter indicates all the Goroutines are completed. Ever tried managing multiple threads of operation using Java or C++? Notice how we don't have to deal with managing mutexes and hard-to-debug race conditions? The ease of concurrency implementation is one of Go's many strengths.

> **Concurrency**: A property of systems in which several processes are executing at the same time and potentially interacting with each other. Concurrency is about dealing with lots of things at once.
>
> **Parallelism**: This is a type of computation in which many calculations are carried out simultaneously, operating on the principle that large problems can often be divided into smaller ones, which are then solved in parallel. Parallelism is about doing lots of things at once.
>
> See Rob Pike's epic video, *Concurrency Is Not Parallelism*, at https://www.youtube.com/watch?v=cN_DpYBzKso.

The final HOF example

Our final HOF example is a doozy. We generate 14 cars, filter `ByDomestic`, map them with an `Upgrade` function, filter them by `ByHasNumber`, and reduce them to a collection of JSON strings:

```
PrintCars("GenerateCars(1, 14), Domestic, Numeric, JSON",
    cars.GenerateCars(1, 14).
        Filter(ByDomestic()).
        Map(Upgrade()).
        Filter(ByHasNumber()).
        Reduce(JsonReducer(cars), Collection{}))
```

The output of this is as follows:

```
GenerateCars(1, 14), Domestic, Numeric, JSON
---------------------
car: {"car": {"make": "Ford", "model": " F-150 XL"}}
car: {"car": {"make": "GM", "model": " Hummer H2 X"}}
car: {"car": {"make": "GM", "model": " Hummer H3 X"}}
```

That's six lines of code. How many lines of code do you think it would take to do this using an imperative coding style?

"This program is already so bloated a little more bloat won't hurt." No. Eventually, it will. And then it will be too late to fix."

- Rob Pike

"The problem is that adding more bloat is often much easier than integrating properly, which requires thought, time, and hard decisions."

- Roger Peppe

Summary

FP is a programming style that is declarative. It is more readable and usually requires much less code than our imperative or object-oriented implementation options.

In this chapter, we implemented the `Map`, `Filter`, and `Reduce` high-order functions. We studied closures and looked at how currying enables function composition.

Our `Reduce` implementation demonstrated how to use Goroutines and a Go channel to perform lazy evaluation. We managed its concurrency using a `WaitGroup` variable and some common sense.

In the next chapter, we'll consider the API software design. We'll look at how to build composable systems using interfaces and closures to enforce the single responsibility principle and the open/close principle.

4
SOLID Design in Go

Ever seen comments such as *If you like design patterns, use Java, not Go*?

In this chapter, we will address this common sentiment regarding software design patterns and how they fit with developing high-quality Go applications.

Our goal in this chapter is to understand the following topics:

- Why many Gophers loath Java
- Why Go does not support inheritance
- The principles of good software design
- How to apply the single responsibility principle in Go
- The open/closed principle
- Duck typing in Go
- How to model behavior in Go using interfaces
- How to compose software using the interface segregation principle
- Inner type promotion and how to embed interfaces

Why many Gophers loath Java

If you like design patterns, use Java, not Go.

Let's think about where this thinking comes from. Java (as well as C++) tends to focus on type hierarchies and type taxonomies.

Take the `ObjectRetrievalFailureException` class from the Spring Framework for example:

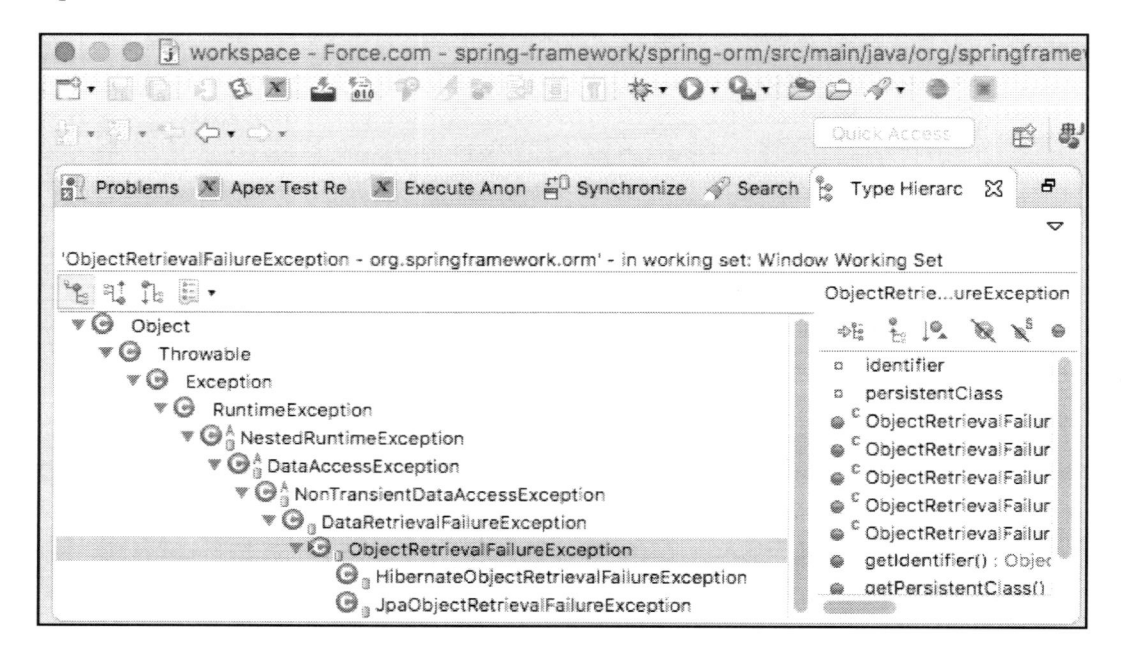

This looks far too complicated and over-abstracted, right?

Unlike Java, Go is designed to be a pragmatic language where we won't get lost in infinite levels of inheritance and type hierarchies.

When we implement a solution in a language that places so much emphasis on a type hierarchy, levels of abstractions, and class inheritance, our code refactorings tend to be much more time-consuming. It's best to get the design right before we begin coding. Leveraging design patterns can save a lot of time when implementing Java solutions.

Inheritance creates a high level of coupling in object-oriented programming. In the preceding example, a change in the `DataAccessException` class could cause unwanted side effects in every class above it in the hierarchy.

It's easy to see why anyone might think there is no place for design patterns in Go.

> *"If C++ and Java are about type hierarchies and the taxonomy of types, Go is about composition."*
>
> - Rob Pike

However, with careful use of abstraction, software design patterns can be entirely compatible with Go's composable simple design philosophy.

More reasons for loathing Java

Consider the following table:

	Java	Golang
Language specification (PDF)	788 pages (https://docs.oracle.com/javase/specs/jls/se8/jls8.pdf)	89 pages (https://golang.org/ref/spec)
Java JDK versus Go SDK (compressed)	279.59 MB (http://jdk.java.net/9/)	13 MB
Concurrency implementation complexity	Difficult	Easy

The following is a diagram that compares the Java and Go technology stacks from a high level:

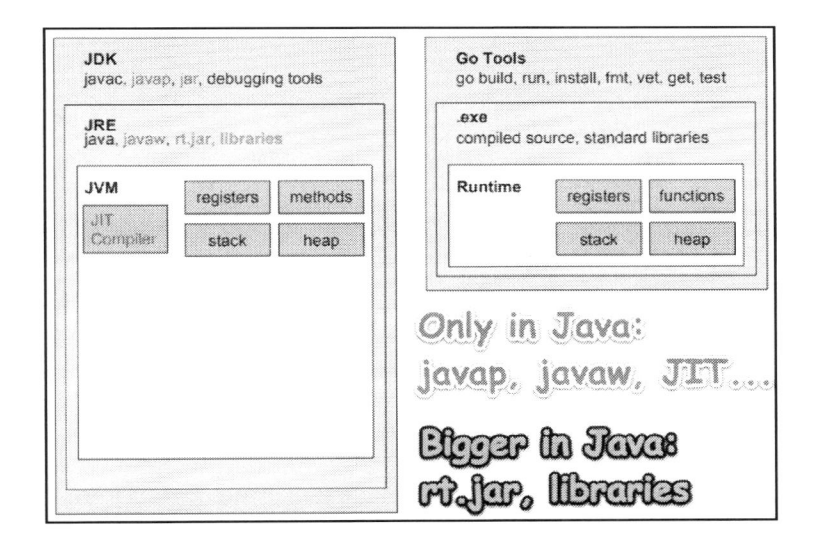

```
JDK
javac, javap, jar, debugging tools
    JRE
    java, javaw, rt.jar, libraries
        JVM     registers   methods
        JIT
        Compiler  stack      heap

Go Tools
go build, run, install, fmt, vet, get, test
    .exe
    compiled source, standard libraries
        Runtime   registers   functions
                  stack       heap
```

Only in Java: javap, javaw, JIT....

Bigger in Java: rt.jar, libraries

The Java/JVM alternative has a much bigger footprint; The JVM does more (some of which your application will use) and requires more RAM. Furthermore, since there is more raw source code to the Java/JVM solution than Go, that means that there is a larger attack surface for hackers to attack. Performance? It takes time for the JIT compiler to convert your application's source code to executable binary code than Go, which is natively compiled.

SOLID Design in Go

Go is smaller and simpler. Java was created for profit and has been aggressively marketed. Go is not marketed. There is a streamlined process for proposing changes to the Go language. See "How to Propose Changes To Go" in the Appendix. (I have found no such process for proposing changes to Java or the JVM, but I can only image that there would be much more time and effort involved).

Given the preceding comparisons of Go v. Java it seems to boil down to Simplicity v. Complexity. Gophers tend to prefer simplicity.

> "Less is exponentially more."
>
> - Rob Pike

Digging deeper into error handling

In Java, when an exception occurs in a method, the process of creating the exception object and handing it over to the runtime environment is called throwing an exception.

The normal flow of the program halts when this happens, and JRE tries to find a handler in the call stack that can process the raised exception.

The exception object contains a lot of debugging information, such as the line number where the exception occurred, type of exception, the method hierarchy, call stack, and so on.

Dozens of common exception handling antipatterns exist in Java largely due to the design and misunderstanding of proper use of Java's type hierarchy.

> "Don't just check errors, handle them gracefully."
>
> - Dave Cheney

Rather than asserting the error is a specific type or value and passing up the line, we can assert that the error implements a particular behavior:

```
type errorBehavior interface {
        Retryable() bool
}


func IsRetryable(err error) bool {
        eb, ok := err.(errorBehavior)
        return ok && eb.Retryable()
}
```

If the `IsRetryable` error occurs, then the caller would know they can retry the operation that generated the error. The caller does not need to import the library that implements the thrown error and attempt to understand the intricacies of its type hierarchy to handle the error properly.

> The `github.com/pkg/errors` package allows you to wrap errors with context so that later you can recover the cause like this:
> ```
> func IsRetryable(err error) bool {
>         eb, ok := errors.Cause(err).(errorBehavior)
>         return ok && eb.Retryable()
> }
> ```

Once the error value has been inspected, it should be handled once. Repackaging the error and throwing it up for another handler to deal with is not considered a best practice in Go.

A conversation - Java developer, idiomatic Go developer, FP developer

Java developer: I hate having to write `if err != nil` everywhere.

Go developer: Get used to it.

Java developer: Why not just throw an exception and let a handler up the call chain deal with it?

Go developer: All good programmers are lazy and that's extra typing.

Developer	Conversation
Java	I hate having to write `if err != nil` everywhere
Go	Get used to it.
Java	Why not just throw an exception and let a handler up the call chain deal with it? That's less typing and all good programmers are lazy, right?

Go	Errors should always be handled immediately.
	What if our `buggyCode` function returns an error yet we continue processing? Can you see how fragile and wrong that is?
	`val, err := buggyCode()`
	`// more code`
	`return val, err`

FP	What bothers me the most about throwing a Java exception is that when we throw an error up for another function to deal with we have just created a side effect. Our function is not pure. We have introduce indeterminism into our application. Since any caller in the call stack can handle an exception, how do we know which handler handles it? Since we wrote the code closest to the error, we should know better than any other developer what happened and how best to deal with it.
Java	Okay. I get it, but I am not only lazy but I all that extra `if err != nil` code looks like scaffolding that litters my code and makes me want to barf. Let me clarify my feelings with a couple of photos.

Our code:

with Exception Handling   with if **err != nil** scaffolding

Java	You can see the difference, right?
Go	Touche! But you need to realize I am mainly interested in programming backend systems where correctness trumps pretty. You can take your pretty J2EE enterprise business applications and wrap them with as many exception handlers as you like.
Java	Seriously? You say you like simplicity, but more code looks more complex to me. That's more code to maintain. That means that instead of having the option to handle all of my error handling in one place I have to insert little snippets of error handling code all throughout my application? Shit! I absolutely love Go's fast compiles times, Go's tiny footprint, the ease of programming concurrent applications, and so on. I am so frustrated. Is there no better error handling solution in Go?
FP	Glad you asked. Depending on what you want to accomplish, there is a better way. This way will not only allow you to handle all your errors in one place, but will also do so with the determinism of pure FP.
Go	B.S. I will stop reading this book now because there is no way this will work.
Java	Yeah! What's the catch?
FP	The solution requires thought, time, and hard decisions, but just like learning to ride a bike. Once you get up and running you'll keep doing it. It's fun and gets you where you want to go more efficiently and it's good for you.
Java	What's it called?
FP	The Lexical Workflow solution
Go	You caught me. I'm still reading. Just long enough to say, That's a ridiculous claim and the name is even more so.
FP	I know it sounds like magic and it sort of is. It's built on a things will even more ridiculous names: the Y-Combinator and Monads. But we have a way to go before we discuss the details. It will take thought and time and decision making skills.
Java	What's there to decide? If it works, I'll use it.
FP	The best use case for Lexical Workflow Solution is where you have data you want to transform. Do you have any workflows where you input data, transform it in some way and then produce an output? This covers a lot of business use case scenarios and some system level ones, too.
Java	Sounds good. What does it do and what does it not do?

FP	It handles your typical workflow use case where when you encounter an error, that error is handled and no further processing occurs in that workflow. If you want to keep processing even with errors, then we'd be better off using applicative functors. If Go supported TCO, then that would open up the door to many more FP possibilities. For now, we need to keep it real (and not worry about stack overflows or performance implications of using recursion). If/when Go does support TCO then us FP coders will be able to unleash a plethora of robust, expressive and performant FP solutions.

Software design methodology

Software design is where we:

- Gather requirements
- Create specifications from requirements
- Implement a solution based on the specifications
- Review results and iterate to improve the solution

Traditional waterfall development depends on a perfect understanding of the product requirements at the outset and minimal errors being executed in each phase. Source: `http://scrumreferencecard.com/scrum-reference-card/`

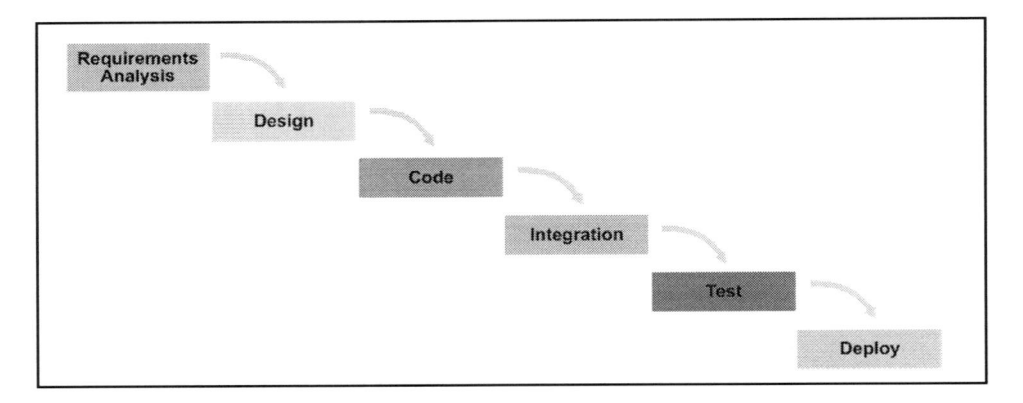

Scrum blends all the development activities into each iteration, adapting to discovered realities at fixed intervals:

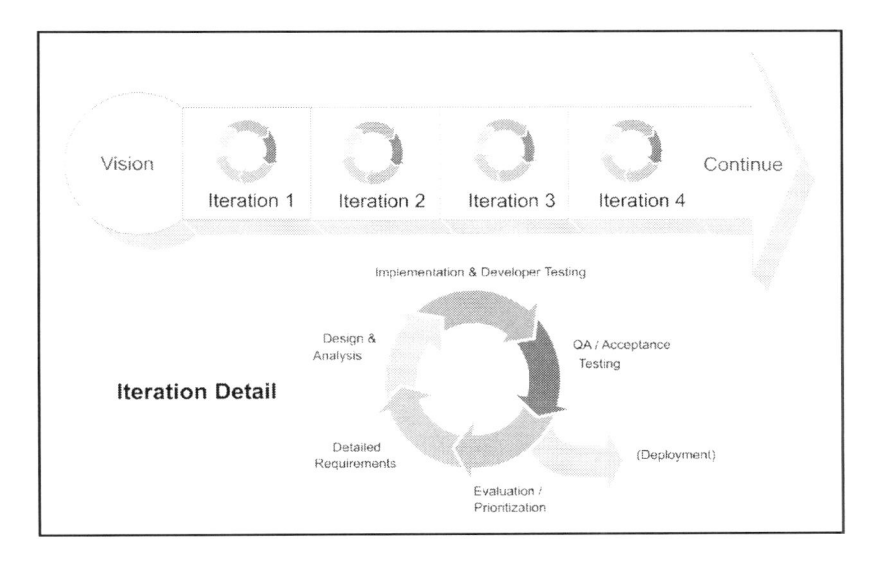

Source: http://scrumreferencecard.com/scrum-reference-card/

In the process of creating specifications, artifacts such as **Unified Markup Language** (**UML**) diagrams are often created to help us think about the problem and craft a viable solution.

Analysis is where we model real-world operations, breaking apart pieces into components. Design is where we craft a software solution based on the analysis work, our IT environment, and the frameworks/technology stacks at our disposal.

We abstract away all the concerns that are not pertinent. So, during analysis and design, we take away and break apart our problem into components that do simple things.

Implementation is when we put those simple things back together again.

Good design

Good design is about saving money in the long run.

If our project is small and the value of our time to market is high, then we can skip the design process. Otherwise, we should put effort into having a proper software design. This is a universal truth, regardless of the technology (Java, Go, and so on).

Bad design

If our application architecture diagram looks something like the following one, we have failed to properly design our application:

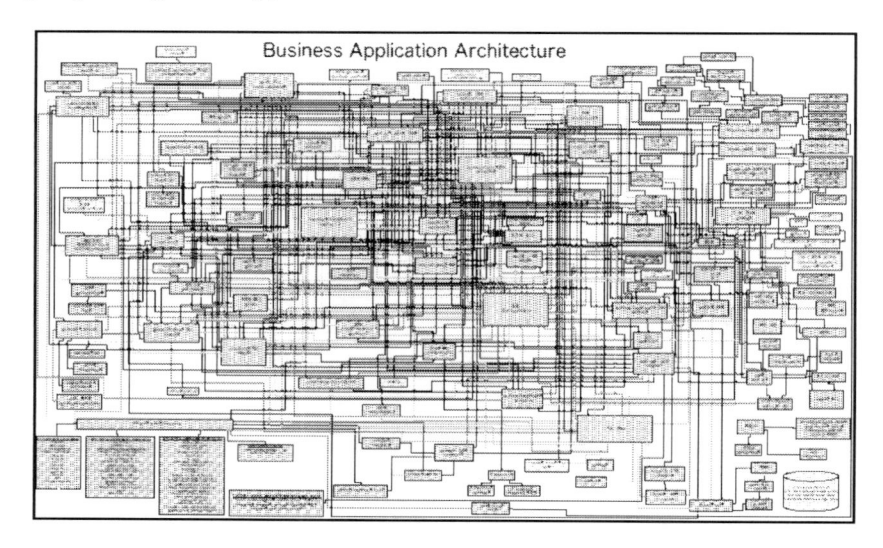

Simplicity is not easy, but it is worth striving for.

The more we add features to our already complex system, the more complex it becomes.

In a system like this, we cannot consider one thing at a time; we must think of everything together and all the possible weird interactions that may break our system.

Good versus bad design over time

The following diagram depicts the value of good design over time. As with most graphs, the x axis depicts the progression of time. The higher we go on the y axis, the more functionality and feature rich our application becomes. Below the **design payoff line**, applications with no design or poor design can quickly produce results.

However, there comes a point at which lack of design makes the application brittle, non-extensible, and difficult to understand:

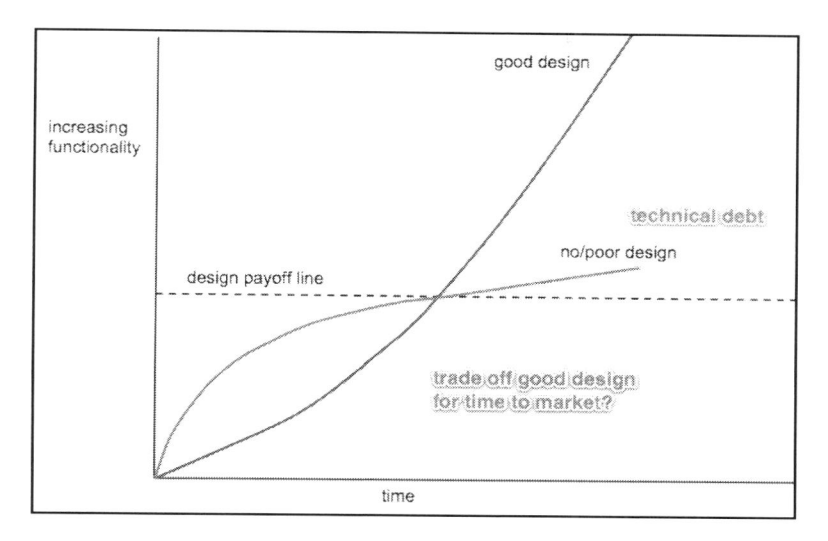

The application that has been properly designed can be extended easily and becomes much more maintainable in the long run.

"Over 90% of software cost happens during maintenance phase."

- Fred Brooks, Mythical Man Month

SOLID design principles

The SOLID design principles of **Object-Oriented Programming (OOP)** apply to designing Go software solutions.

SOLID Design in Go

Single responsibility principle

Single responsibility principle says, *Do One Thing and Do It Well*. We see the SRP at play in the Go standard libraries. Here're a few examples:

```
├── compress            ├── crypto           ├── encoding         ├── net
│   ├── bzip2           │   ├── aes          │   ├── ascii85      │   ├── http
│   ├── flate           │   ├── cipher       │   ├── asn1         │   │   ├── cgi
│   ├── gzip            │   ├── des          │   ├── base32       │   │   ├── cookiejar
│   ├── lzw             │   ├── dsa          │   ├── base64       │   │   ├── fcgi
│   ├── testdata        │   ├── ecdsa        │   ├── binary       │   │   ├── httptest
│   └── zlib            │   ├── elliptic     │   ├── csv          │   │   ├── httptrace
│                       │   ├── hmac         │   ├── gob          │   │   └── httputil
├── database            │   ├── md5          │   ├── hex          │   ├── mail
│   └── sql             │   ├── rand         │   ├── json         │   ├── rpc
│       └── driver      │   ├── rc4          │   ├── pem          │   │   └── jsonrpc
│                       │   └── rsa          │   └── xml          │   ├── smtp
│                                                                 │   └── url
```

If a pull request enhances the `aes/crypto` package, would you expect that code merge to affect the functionality of the `database/sql/driver` package (or any package)? No. Of course not. Each package is clearly name spaced and highly cohesive; they perform specific tasks and do not cross over into other concerns.

"A class should have one, and only one, reason to change."

– Robert C Martin

When Mr. Martin said that a class should have only one reason to change, it's obvious that he was talking about OOP design, but the same principle applies to our Go application. Should the tax calculation update affect the user interface or layout of any reports, other than showing a different amount? No. Why? Because one is cosmetic in nature and the other is not. Those are two separate responsibilities that should be handled by different, loosely coupled classes/modules.

Our classes/modules should be highly cohesive, performing as specific a role as possible. Code that has a single responsibility can handle the changing requirements better without adversely affecting other parts of our application. If we have a request to change our class/module and since it does only one thing then the reason for the change can only be related to its one responsibility.

Application of the SRP will drive our design towards smaller and smaller interfaces. Eventually, we will arrive at the ultimate interface. The interface with one method. For example, in `Chapter 5`, *Adding Functionality with Decoration*, we'll look at Go's complimentary Reader and Writer interfaces:

```
type Reader interface {
    Read(p []byte) (n int, err error)
}
type Writer interface {
    Write(p []byte) (n int, err error)
}
```

What the SRP means to FP is aligned with the Unix philosophy.

> *"Although that philosophy can't be written down in a single sentence, at its heart is the idea that the power of a system comes more from the relationships among programs than from the programs themselves. Many UNIX programs do quite trivial things in isolation, but, combined with other programs, become general and useful tools."*
>
> *- Rob Pike*

In lambda calculus, each function has exactly one parameter. It may look like our pure function accepts multiple parameters, but it's actually just currying the parameters. Our function takes the first argument in the list and returns a function which takes the rest of the arguments; It continues to process each argument until they are all consumed. Function composition works when every function accepts only one parameter.

```
three := add(1, 2)
func add1 := + 1
three == add1(2)
```

That was pseudo code for what happens when we curry. It converts a two parameter call into a one parameter call. Currying stores data (the number 1) and an operation (the addition operator) for use later. How is that like an object in OOP?

Function composition

Function composition is where we combine two smaller functions to create a new function that accomplishes the same goal as the two smaller ones. Both ways get us from an a to c. Below, f_1 accepts an a and returns a b. f_2 accepts a b and returns a c. We can compose/combine those two functions and get a single function that accepts an a and returns a c:

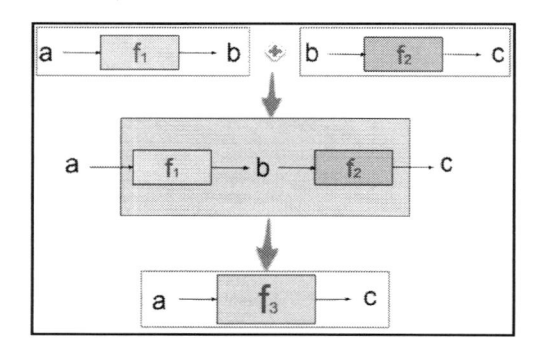

Function composition is the cornerstone to pure FP; It's what allows us to build larger abstractions out of smaller ones.

Open/closed principle

Software should be open for extension but closed for modification. Embedding fields in a struct allows us to extend one type with another. The object (CarWithSpare) that embedded the other (Car) has access to its fields and methods. The CarWithSpare object can call Car methods, but cannot modify the Car object's methods. Therefore, Go's types, while being *open for extension*, are *closed for modification*. Let's look at an example:

```
package car

import "fmt"

type Car struct {
    Make string
    Model string
}
func (c Car) Tires() int { return 4 }
func (c Car) PrintInfo() {
    fmt.Printf("%v has %d tires\n", c, c.Tires())
}
```

We defined our Car type and two methods, Tires and PrintInfo. Next, we'll define our CarWithSpare type and embed the Car type as an unnamed field:

```
type CarWithSpare struct {
    Car
}
func (o CarWithSpare) Tires() int { return 5 }
```

In our main.go file, we create a Honda Accord and call its PrintInfo method. As expected it returns 4 tires.

Next, we create a Toyota Highlander, but when we print its info, it prints 4 tires instead of 5. Why?

```
package main

import (
    . "car"
    "fmt"
)

func main() {
    accord := Car{"Honda", "Accord"}
    accord.PrintInfo()
    highlander := CarWithSpare{Car{"Toyota", "Highlander"}}
    highlander.PrintInfo()
    fmt.Printf("%v has %d tires", highlander.Car, highlander.Tires())
}
```

The following is the output:

```
{Honda Accord} has 4 tires
{Toyota Highlander} has 4 tires
{Toyota Highlander} has 5 tires
```

That's because PrintInfo is a method of Car, but since CarWithSpare is missing that method, when we call highlander.PrintInfo we're actually executing Car's method (not CarWithSpare).

In order to print the actual number of tires our highlander has, we must manually delegate the call by executing highlander.Tires directly from within our fmt.Printf statement.

SOLID Design in Go

Do we have other options? Yes. We can override the `PrintInfo` method. In other words, we can define a `PrintInfo` method for our `CarWithSpare` as follows:

```
func (c CarWithSpare) PrintInfo() {
    fmt.Printf("%v has %d tires\n", c, c.Tires())
}
```

The following is the output:

```
{Honda Accord} has 4 tires
{Toyota Highlander} has 5 tires
{Toyota Highlander} has 5 tires
```

What if we call `accord.PrintInfo()` again? We get the following output:

```
{Honda Accord} has 4 tires
```

So, Go allows us to:

- implicitly call an embedded object's method (if not defined)
- manually delegate to call our object's method
- override an embedded object's method

What about method overloading?

Not allowed. If we were to attempt to create another `PrintInfo` method with a different argument signature, Go would throw a compiler error:

```
func (c CarWithSpare) PrintInfo() {                               ⬅ 0 parameters
    fmt.Printf("%v has %d tires\n", c, c.Tires())
}
func (c CarWithSpare) PrintInfo(upCase bool) {                    ⬅ 1 parameter
    if upCase {
        fmt.Printf("%v HAS %d TIRES\n", c, c.Tires())
    } else {
        fmt.Printf("%v has %d tires\n", c, c.Tires())
    }
}
```

Using the decorator pattern in the next chapter, we'll see how we can extend functionality without modifying the existing code.

Open / close principle in functional programming

Similar to our preceding Go example where we added a new method (`PrintInfo`) to our base type (`Car`), pure functional programming languages also add new functions over existing data types without having to recompile existing code and while retaining static type safety.

> The *expression problem* also known as the *extensibility problem* addresses a software language's ability to add new methods and types to a program in a type safe manner. For details, see **Feature Oriented Software Development (FOSD)** Program Cubes where a base program (in a family of related programs called a **software product line**) (http://softwareproductlines.com/) is incrementally augmented with features to produce a complex program.

The following diagram shows how programs can be built by composing models from features and then transforming those models into executables:

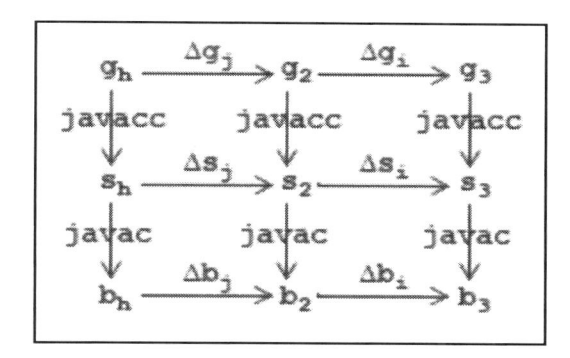

$$g_h \xrightarrow{\Delta g_j} g_2 \xrightarrow{\Delta g_i} g_3$$
$$\downarrow javacc \quad \downarrow javacc \quad \downarrow javacc$$
$$s_h \xrightarrow{\Delta s_j} s_2 \xrightarrow{\Delta s_i} s_3$$
$$\downarrow javac \quad \downarrow javac \quad \downarrow javac$$
$$b_h \xrightarrow{\Delta b_j} b_2 \xrightarrow{\Delta b_i} b_3$$

The FOSD methodology advocates that complex systems can be built by adding features incrementally where the domain models are functions and constants and the programs, which are represented as expressions, can be generated to perform specific tasks.

FantasyLand JavaScript specification

The `FantasyLand` project specifies interoperability of common algebraic structures:

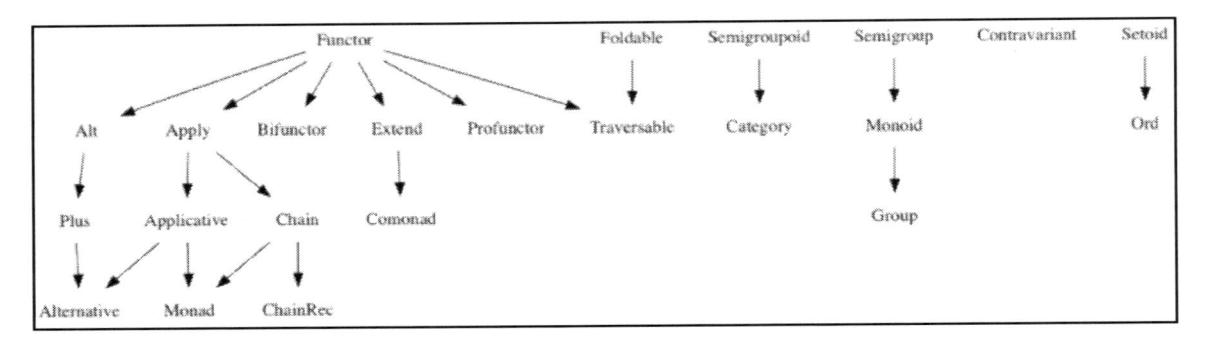

```
                        Functor                  Foldable    Semigroupoid   Semigroup    Contravariant   Setoid
                  ↙  ↙  ↓  ↓  ↘  ↘                 ↓             ↓             ↓              ↓           ↓
       Alt    Apply   Bifunctor  Extend   Profunctor  Traversable   Category     Monoid          Ord
        ↓    ↙  ↓  ↘                                                              ↓
       Plus Applicative Chain   Comonad                                          Group
        ↓    ↙  ↓  ↙
    Alternative Monad ChainRec
```

Each data type in the hierarchical diagram is called an algebraic data type because each consists of algebra, that is, a set of values, a set of operators that it is closed under, and the rules it must obey.

Let's take a simple example, the Setoid.

Setoid algebra

The following are the Setoid rules:

Name of rule	Description
Reflexivity	`a.equals(a) === true`
Symmetry	`a.equals(b) === b.equals(a)`
Transitivity	if `a.equals(b)` and `b.equals(c)`, then `a.equals(c)`
	If `b` is not the same `Ord`, behavior of `lte` is unspecified (returning false is recommended). `lte` must return a Boolean (`true` or `false`).

The values used in the rules are `a`, `b`, and `c`. A value which has an `Ord` must provide an `lte` method. The equals method is this algebra's operator and it takes one argument.

That's it. That's all there is to it!

Ord algebra

Here're the `Ord` rules:

Name of rule	Description
Totality	`a.lte(b)` or `b.lte(a)`
Anti-symmetry	If `a.lte(b)` and `b.lte(a)`, then `a.equals(b)`
Transitivity	If `a.lte(b)` and `b.lte(c)`, then `a.lte(c)`
	`b` must be a value of the same `Ord` as `a`. If `b` is not the same Setoid, then the behavior of equals is unspecified (returning false is recommended). The `equals` variable must return a Boolean (`true` or `false`).

The values used in the rules are `a`, `b` and `c`. A value which has a Setoid must provide an `lte` method. The `lte` method is this algebra's operator and it takes one argument.

From the preceding diagram, we see that an `Ord` is a Setoid, so the `Ord` has an `Equals` operator and the `Ord` must obey the same rules that a Setoid does, as well as its own rules.

Later in our book, we'll explore Haskell's type class hierarchy and look at the Functor, Monoid, and Monad algebras.

The expression problem

Different languages solve the expression problem in various ways:

- Open classes
- Multimethods
- Coproducts of functors
- Type classes
- Object algebras

The problem they solve is the same as what we looked at with our `CarWithSpare` example; It's all about how to add new functions over existing data types without having to recompile existing code and while retaining static type safety.

> Go has rudimentary support for the expression problem. Type classes, object algebras, and so on. are not part of Go's standard library, but there's nothing stopping us from building any of the aforementioned solutions. Here's a great start: https://github.com/SimonRichardson/wishful.

Liskov substitution principle

In OOP terms, the *Liskov Substitution Principle* says that objects of the same type or subtype should be substituted and can be replaced by the other, without affecting the caller. In other words, when we implement an interface, our class should implement all the methods defined in the interface and satisfy all interface requirements. And in even fewer words, *satisfy interface contracts*.

The compiler will enforce that our methods have the correct signatures. The LSP goes a bit further and demands that our implementation should also have the same invariant, postconditions, and other properties stated or implied by the documentation of the superclass or interface.

This OOP method stinks

This is what a method contract looks like in the OOP world:

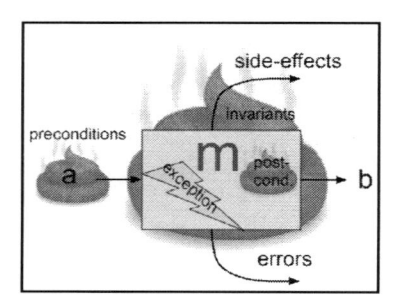

Our method m is passed an a, does some processing and returns b. An exception can occur, which may or may not be caught and handled and errors can be returned. Additionally, in order for the method to properly satisfy its contract, it's up to us to read the documentation (which of course will always be completely accurate and up-to-date.... not!) in hopes that we cover all the preconditions, invariant, and postconditions.

An **invariant** is something that must be always be true for the life of the method. For example, if our class has a duration member variable, that value must always be a positive float. Another example could be that our internal latitude and longitude values must always be in the northern hemisphere. We could go so far as to write invariance validator private methods to ensure our invariant are in compliance with their range of acceptable values.

A **precondition** is something that must be true at the time our method is called. For example, before we execute our `consummateMarriage` method we should ensure that our chosen `wouldBeSpouse` is not already married to another; Otherwise, we'd likely be in violation of our state's anti-polygamy laws. We would likely do our checking by executing another `verifyPersonIsSingle` method.

Let's not forget the **postconditions**. An example might be: After executing our `consummateMarriage` method we should ensure that the person with whom we consummate is actually the same person on our marriage certificate. Marrying the wrong person could cause all sorts of problems.

The last issue to deal with is *side effects*. A side effect is what happens when our method changes something other than the **b** (or the error) that it outputs. For example, if our postcondition check caused a credit card charge from a private investigation firm, that charge would be a side effect.

Our FP function smells like roses

This is what our function contract looks like in the FP world:

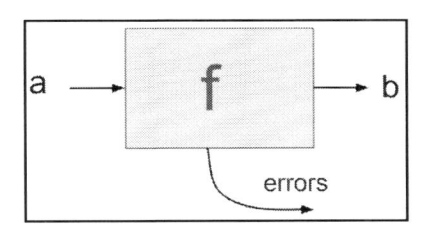

[diagram: a → f → b, with errors branching from f]

See the difference? We can almost smell the difference! Hey, wait a minute! (An OOP programmer might be thinking...)

This pure function is missing some stuff! This is an unfair comparison!

That's right. It's not fair, but it's real.

And what makes it real is our inputs type.

In FP, contracts don't lie

Let's look an example of some imperative code:

```
type Dividend struct {
   Val int
}
func (n Dividend) Divide(divisor int) int {
   return n.Val/divisor
}

func main() {
   d := Dividend{2}
   fmt.Printf("%d", d.Divide(0))
}
```

What is our contract in the preceding code?

The contract is our method's signature: `func (n Dividend) Divide(divisor int) int`

What three questions must our contract answer?

1. What does our contract expect?

    - Answer: It expects the following:
        - The `Dividend.Val` to be populated with an `int`
        - The divisor to be an `int`

2. What does our contract guarantee?

    - Answer: It promises to return an integer

3. What does the contract maintain?

    - Answer: Not applicable in this simple case

What happens when we run the preceding code?

```
panic: runtime error: integer divide by zero

goroutine 1 [running]:
main.Dividend.Divide(...)
    /Users/lex/clients/packt/dev/fp-go/2-design-patterns/ch04-solid/03_misc/misc.go:34
main.main()
    /Users/lex/clients/packt/dev/fp-go/2-design-patterns/ch04-solid/03_misc/misc.go:41 +0x11

Process finished with exit code 2
```

We get a runtime panic! Did our contract hold true, or did it lie to us?

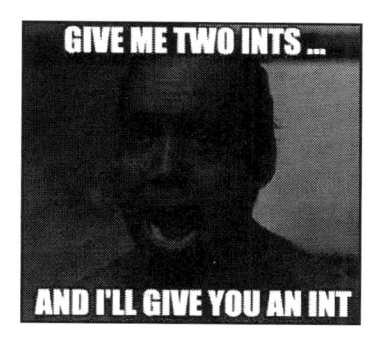

In pure FP, we don't rely on lowly types like int, char, or even string. We leverage the full power of an amazing type class system.

In a pure FP language like Haskell, we can define a `PostiveInt` type. So, instead of writing a method to validated that an input parameter is positive, we define a type named `PostiveInt` that guarantees that only positive integers will be input:

```
PositiveInt :: Int -> Maybe Positive
PositiveInt n = if (n < 0) then Nothing else Just (Positive n)
```

In FP terms, LSP says, *Contracts don't lie*;

In FP, we don't have to rely on our test suite to verify that our application properly enforces it requirements. In FP, assuming we have designed our software properly, if it compiles then it is correct. We let our type system enforce our requirements.

In an OOP courting relationship, the input (candidate spouse) is only verified to be Female. When we later discover that she is not the right type of woman, that is, she's already married, that would render the marriage contract invalid.

This is what happens when we don't properly type check our input:

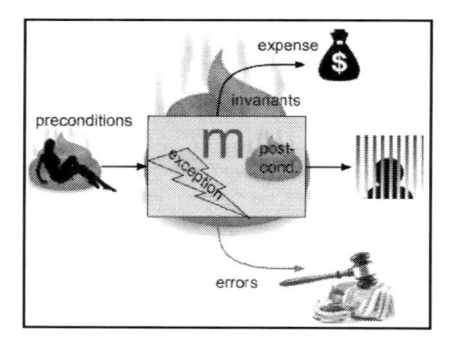

This is the picture when we use pure FP:

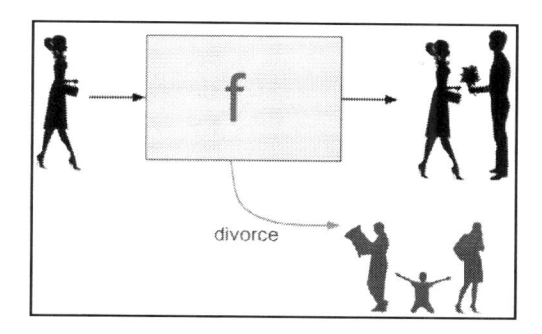

Looks simple, but where are the external interactions like in-laws that can lead to divorce? What about children? Aren't they what we might call side-effects of a marriage?

Monads provide a way for our couple to interact with the external world; To handle possibly harmful influences and generate beautiful side effects. It looks something like this:

The trick to Monads is that all external interactions are contained (in the box). We'll cover Monads in depth in our last chapter.

> This book is about learning *functional* programming in Go. Hence, we will embrace the full meaning of the term *functional*. Functional does not only mean *pure*. If we're using functions, we're doing functional programming. Go is a multi-paradigm language that does not force us to be completely pure or completely imperative. The vast majority of Go code these days is imperative... take the standard libraries as an example. There is a time and a place for implementing pure functional programming techniques. The more we learn about all aspects of Go's functional capabilities, and pure functional programming concepts, the better equipped we will be to prudently apply the proper style of coding to meet our application development requirements.

Let's see the LSP at work with a duck typing example.

Duck typing

Go does not have inheritance or subtypes, but we have interfaces. Functions that implement the methods of an interface satisfy the interface contract implicitly.

Go supports what's called **duck typing**. If it walks like a duck and quacks like a duck, then it's a duck. In other words, if we have a Go struct with methods that implement the Duck interface, that is, if it has the `Walk()` and `Quack()` methods, then for all intents and purposes, our struct is a duck.

In object-oriented languages, such as Java, we'd be tempted to design our ducks as follows.

What can go wrong with inheritance?

We are told that ducks can walk and quack. So we implement those behaviors in our parent class, namely `Duck`:

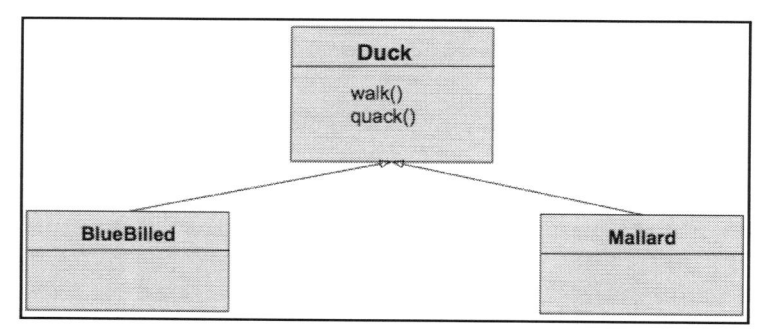

We start out with `Mallard` and `BlueBilled` ducks. We are able to reuse the `walk()` and `quack()` methods via inheritance.

Next, we hear that ducks can fly. So we implement the fly behavior in our Duck class and all the child classes inherit this new behavior:

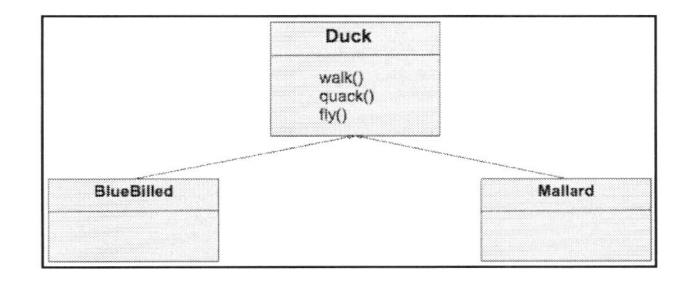

All is well until we add Pekins ducks to our flock.

The problem that we did not account for in our original design is that most domestically bred ducks cannot fly:

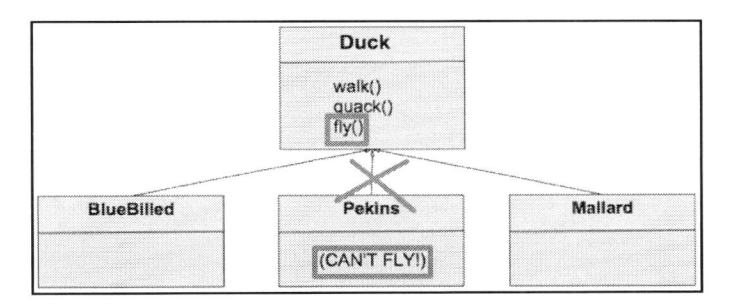

The good news for us is that this sort of a design flaw is not even a possibility in Go!

Interface segregation principle

It is better to have a lot of single purpose-specific interfaces than one general purpose interface. Our APIs should not accept references to structures that it does not need, and conversely, our client implementations should not depend on code that it does not use.

We'll see this soon in our Viva La Duck code example in the form of separate `EatBehavior` and `StrokeBehavior` interfaces.

When we strictly apply the integration segregation principle we end up with interfaces with a single method. Such objects represent data with behavior, but it can also be modeled as behavior with data, which is what closures are in FP.

This is another area where it would be nice if Go supported Generics. Why create boiler plate code to handle slices of `Int` types, `Customers`, or `AvailableWomen` when a single enumeration of `T` would work (with less code)?

Dependency inversion principle

The **dependency inversion principle** (**DIP**) states that we should depend upon abstractions, not concretions. DIP is about removing hardwired dependencies from our code.

For example, the following code violates DIP:

```
import "theirpkg"

func MyFunction(t *theirpkg.AType)

func MyOtherFunction(i theirpkg.AnInterface)
```

The `MyOtherFunction` function is not quite as bad as the `MyFunction` function, but both implementations couple our implementation with a type and an interface of another package.

In general, good software design relies on high cohesion, where we write functions that do one thing and do it well and are loosely coupled.

In pure functional programming, dependency injection is accomplished by passing partially applied functions around. Some call it the *hollywood principle*, as in, *Don't call us, we'll call you*. In JavaScript, this is frequently accomplished using callbacks.

Note that there is a subtle difference between callbacks and continuations. Callback functions may be called multiple times in the flow of an application and each time they return a result and processing continues. When a function calls another function as the last thing it does then the second function is called a continuation of the first.

The big reveal

A monad chains continuations.

Recall the monad from the hierarchy diagram of *Fantasy Land* algebras earlier in this chapter?

We'll talk a lot more about Monads in the last unit of our book, but for now let's take a sneak peak at the big picture.

Earlier we saw composition of functions:

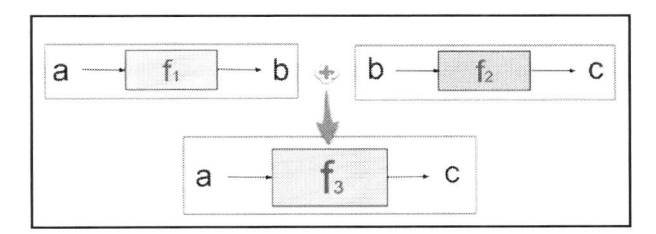

That's actually a problem because that's not a Monoid. A Monoid looks like this:

And that's the big reveal. Monads are purple!

Ha. Gotcha!

Besides the color, what can you see that's different between the monadic function and the ones above it?

What about the **a** going in and the **a** coming out? That means that if a Monoid accepts a parameter of type **A** (by convention, a lower case **a** variable is a value of type A), then it will spit out another **a** value.

Guess what that's called? When our function returns the same type that it's fed? We call that an *endomorphism* where *en* means *same* and *morphism* means *function*; So, it changes from an **a** to an **a**. Simple.

What about the *chain* word used in the *a monad chains continuations* statement?

How about a nice monoidal purple chain of functions?

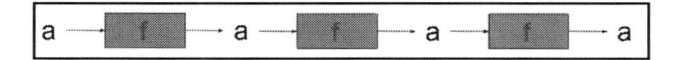

What else do we know about this purple monoid chain?

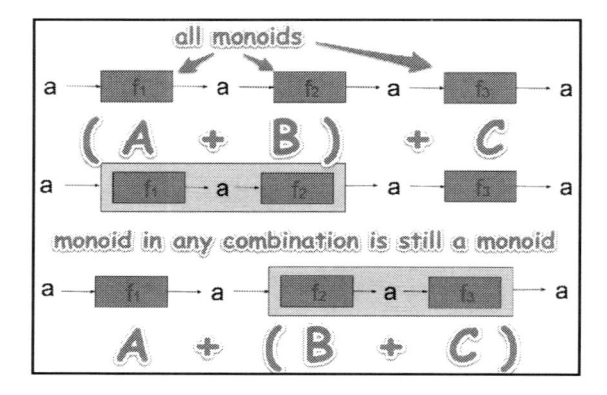

If all functions are monids then we can combine them in any order (associativity rule).

Great, but what can we do with a Monoid chain? Can we run the processes in parallel?

Run in parallel? Well, that depends on what we're dealing with. Many things can run in parallel.

In theory, yes but in practice we'll need to deal with the same considerations other Map/Reduce solutions such as Hadoop must deal with.

MapReduce

MapReduce is a technique that splits big datasets into many smaller ones. Each small dataset is separately, but simultaneously processed on different servers. The results are then gathered and aggregated to produce a final result.

How does it work?

Suppose we have a lot of web servers and we want to determine the top requested pages across all of them. We can analyze web server access logs to find all the requested URLs, count them, and sort the results.

The following are the good use cases for MapReduce:

- Gathering statistics from servers, for example, top 10 users, top 10 requested URL
- Compute the frequencies of all keywords found in your data

The following are the use cases not good for MapReduce:

- Jobs that require shared state
- Finding individual records
- Small data

MapReduce example

Suppose we have an Apache web server access log files with entries that look like this one:

```
198.0.200.105 - - [14/Jan/2014:09:36:51 -0800] "GET
/example.com/music/js/main.js HTTP/1.1" 200 614
"http://www.example.com/music/" "Mozilla/5.0 (Macintosh; Intel Mac OS X
10_9_1) AppleWebKit/537.36 (KHTML, like Gecko) Chrome/31.0.1650.63
Safari/537.36"
```

What if we are interested in knowing the top 5 most accessed JSON files?

We could perform a MapReduce directly from the terminal using standard Unix string processing commands:

```
$ cat access10k.log | while read line; do echo "$line" | awk '{print $7}' |
grep "\.json";done | sort | uniq -c | sort -nr
 234 /example.com/music/data/artist.json
 232 /example.com/music/data/songs.json
 227 /example.com/music/data/influencers.json
  28 /example.com/music-no-links/data/songs.json
  28 /example.com/music-no-links/data/influencers.json
  28 /example.com/music-no-links/data/artist.json
   8 /example.com/music/data/influencers2.json
```

SOLID Design in Go

That works great for a few thousand lines. If we type `time` in front of that last command we get something like the following:

```
real 1m3.932s
user 0m38.125s
sys 0m42.863s
```

But what if each server has millions of lines of code and we have a lot of servers?

Time for MapReduce!

On each server we can perform our mapping; Starting log file entries as input and resulting in a set of key value pairs:

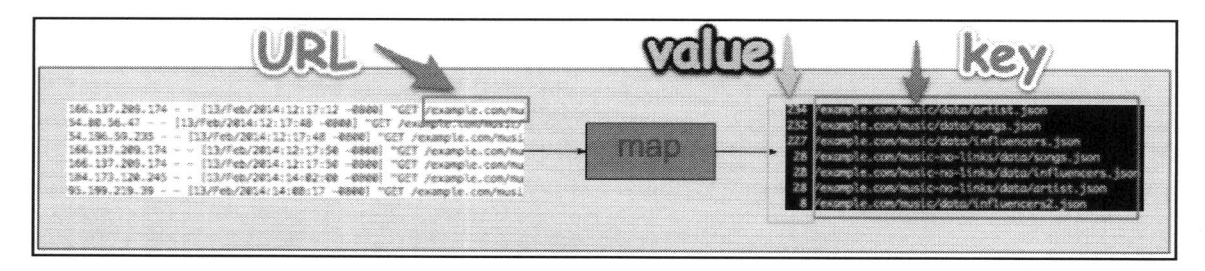

Next, we take each intermediate result from each server and feed them into our `reduce` function which then spits out the results:

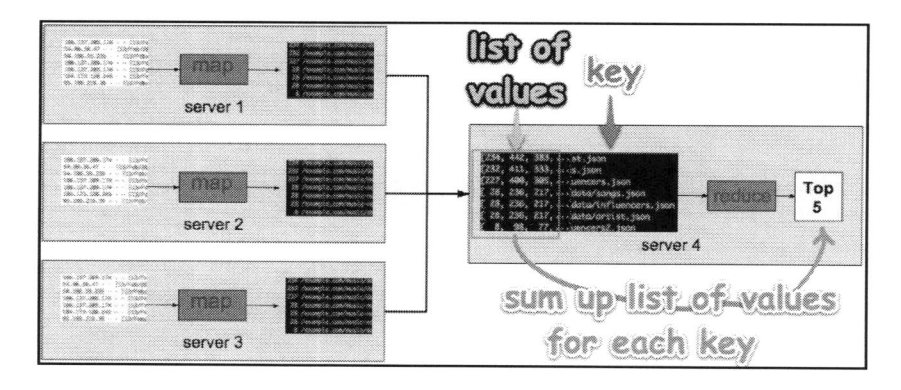

Our top 5 most requested JSON files might look like this:

```
85733 /example.com/music/data/artist.json
71938 /example.com/music/data/songs.json
57837 /example.com/music/data/influencers.json
17500 /example.com/music-no-links/data/songs.json
17500 /example.com/music-no-links/data/influencers.json
```

What can we glean from this example? It looks like good candidates for MapReduce include use cases where:

- We have so much data that running it all sequentially on one server would take too long
- Our output, from the `map` phase, consists of a list of key, value pairs
- We can run each `map` or `reduce` function in isolation, knowing that the output of our function relies only on its input

But what else is going on here that might not be readily apparent?

What else makes this process of Map/Reduce work?

What FP patterns are lurking in the shadows? (Hint: We've already seen it and it has to do with data types.)

What else can Monads do?

Monads can be used to clearly convey our business logic and manage our applications processing flows and more.

SOLID Design in Go

You know what I'm talking about. Consider the following piece of code:

```
if err != nil {
    return nil, fmt.Errorf("%s:%d: %v", sourceFile, sourceLine, err)
}
```

Those `if err != nil` blocks litter our code and obscure our code's original intent. If this is our happy path code:

```
happy path code
```

This is what it looks like after we add error checking:

```
add error checking
```

Guess what our FP code would look like after including error handling?

```
FP code including error handling
```

> **TIP**
> How can this be? No inline error checking? We'll cover this topic in `Chapter 9`, *Functors, Monoids, and Generics*.

Viva La Duck

Our next code example will illustrate several of the SOLID design principles applied to our Go implementation.

In our Viva La Duck application, our duck must visit a number of ponds looking for bugs to eat. To keep things simple, we'll assume that each stroke will require the duck to eat one bug. Each time the duck paddles its feet (one stroke), the duck's supply of strokes is decreased by one.

We're not concerned with how the duck moves from pond to pond, but rather the number of strokes the duck must make to traverse the length of the pond. If a pond has bugs to eat, they will be found on the other side of the pond. If the duck runs out of energy, it dies.

Our program is a self-contained runnable Go source file. Its package name is `main` and it has a `main()` function. We'll use the `DASHES` constant later when we print the statistics indicating what the duck encountered at each pond.

The `Pond` struct contains the state of each pond, that is, the number of bugs it supplies for the duck to eat and how many strokes are required to cross the pond:

```
package main

import (
        "fmt"
        "errors"
        "log"
)
const DASHES = "----------------------"

type Pond struct {
        BugSupply       int
        StrokesRequired int
}
```

One of the first things we should do is define our system's behaviors in the form of simple interfaces. We should think about how we can embed our interfaces into a larger set of interfaces as we compose our system's behavior patterns. It makes sense to categorize a thing by its abilities because a thing is defined by its actions.

Since this is a book about functional programming, now would be a good time to mention that a major benefit of using interfaces is that they allow us to group our application's functions in order to model real-life behaviors:

```
type StrokeBehavior interface {
        PaddleFoot(strokeSupply *int)
}

type EatBehavior interface {
        EatBug(strokeSupply *int)
}
```

Each interface (`StrokeBehavior` and `EatBehavior`) represents a fine-grained, well-defined behavior. Breaking apart our system into small parts will make our application more flexible and more easily composable:

```
type SurvivalBehaviors interface {
        StrokeBehavior
        EatBehavior
}
```

By declaring small, single purpose interfaces, we are now free to embed them in new, more feature-rich interfaces.

SOLID Design in Go

> Grouping interfaces is a common pattern we can find in the Go standard library. For example, in the `httputil` package, we find the following:
>
> ```
> type writeFlusher interface {
>     io.Writer
>     http.Flusher
> }
> ```

Next, we define our duck. Our duck is stateless and has no fields:

```
type Duck struct{}
```

We define two methods for our duck. The receiver, `Duck`, must be defined in the same package as our method, `Stroke`. Since we are only using a main package, that's not a problem.

Modeling our system after the real world, we define a `Foot` struct and a `PaddleFoot` method for that foot. Each time our duck paddles its foot, we'll decrement our duck's `strokeSupply` type:

```
type Foot struct{}
func (Foot) PaddleFoot(strokeSupply *int) {
    fmt.Println("- Foot, paddle!")
    *strokeSupply--
}
```

Similarly, we define a `Bill` type and its `EatBug` method that increments our duck's `strokeSupply` type:

```
type Bill struct{}
func (Bill) EatBug(strokeSupply *int) {
    *strokeSupply++
    fmt.Println("- Bill, eat a bug!")
}
```

For every stroke, our duck will paddle its foot.

Our `Stroke` method will return an error if the duck runs out of energy and gets stuck in the middle of a pond:

```
func (Duck) Stroke(s StrokeBehavior, strokeSupply *int, p Pond) (err error)
{
        for i := 0; i < p.StrokesRequired; i++ {
                if *strokeSupply < p.StrokesRequired - i {
                        err = errors.New("Our duck died!")
                }
                s.PaddleFoot(strokeSupply)
        }
        return err
}
```

Now, we define our duck's eating behavior. When our duck reaches the end of the pond, it gets to eat all the pond's bugs:

```
func (Duck) Eat(e EatBehavior, strokeSupply *int, p Pond) {
        for i := 0; i < p.BugSupply; i++ {
                e.EatBug(strokeSupply)
        }
}
```

The `SwimAndEat` method's signature is slightly different than that of `Eat` and `Stroke` methods. Notice the differences?

All three methods have a `Duck` as their receiver, but the `SwimAndEat` method defines the variable d. That's because we need to reference the `Stroke` and `Eat` methods within the `SwimAndEat` method.

Also, they all take an interface as their first parameter, but `SwimAndEat` takes a composed set of interfaces, namely `StrokeAndEatBehaviors`, which it uses polymorphically for both `Stroke` and `Eat`:

```
func (d Duck) SwimAndEat(se SurvivalBehaviors, strokeSupply *int, ponds
[]Pond) {
        for i := range ponds {
                pond := &ponds[i]
                err := d.Stroke(se, strokeSupply, *pond)
                if err != nil {
                        log.Fatal(err)   // the duck died!
                }
                d.Eat(se, strokeSupply, *pond)
        }
}
```

Pass by value or reference?

Here's the rule of thumb--if you want to share a state, then pass by reference, that is, use a pointer type; otherwise, pass by value. Since we need to update our duck's `strokeSupply` type in this `Stroke` method, we pass it as an `int` pointer (`*int`). So, pass a pointer parameter only when absolutely necessary. We should begin to code defensively, assuming that someone may try to run our code concurrently. When we pass our parameters by value, it's safe for concurrent use. When we pass by reference, we may need to add `sync.mutex` or some channels to coordinate concurrency.

Our duck builds its energy back by eating more bugs that it gets from the pond:

```go
func (Duck) Eat(e EatBehavior, strokeSupply *int, p Pond) {
    for i := 0; i < p.BugSupply; i++ {
        e.EatBug(strokeSupply)
    }
}
```

Since we are designing our software application to model the real world, things such as duck feet and duck bills are natural candidates for struct names to represent real-life objects. Feet are used to paddle and duck bills are used to eat bugs. Each paddle, that is, stroke, reduces our duck's supply of possible strokes. Each bug is worth one stroke.

We tell our duck's foot to paddle. As long as the duck has energy, that is, it's `strokeSupply` type is greater than zero, the duck will obey. However, if `strokeSupply` is zero, then our duck will be stranded in the middle of the pond before it gets to its next supply of bugs to eat:

```go
type Foot struct{}
func (Foot) PaddleFoot(strokeSupply *int) {
    fmt.Println("- Foot, paddle!")
    *strokeSupply--
}
```

Notice that we are passing a pointer to our supply of strokes. This means that our application is maintaining a state. We know that pure functional programming does not permit variable mutations. That's okay because this chapter is about good software design using Go. Pure functional programming in Go is covered in `Chapter 1`, *Pure Functional Programming in Go*:

```go
type Bill struct{}
func (Bill) EatBug(strokeSupply *int) {
    *strokeSupply++
    fmt.Println("- Bill, eat a bug!")
}
```

For every pond that our duck encounters, it must swim and eat bugs to survive.

Since our duck's `SwimAndEat` method requires both `StrokeBehavior` and `EatBehavior`, we pass the `SurvivalEatBehaviors` interface set as its first parameter:

```
func (d Duck) SwimAndEat(se SurvivalBehaviors, strokeSupply *int, ponds []Pond) {
        for i := range ponds {
                pond := &ponds[i]
                err := d.Stroke(se, strokeSupply, pond)
                if err != nil {
                        log.Fatal(err)   // the duck died!
                }
                d.Eat(se, strokeSupply, pond)
        }
}
```

Recall that the duck's `Stroke` method takes `StrokeBehavior`, not `StrokeEatBehavior`! How is this possible? This is part of the magic of type embedding.

Type embedding with Go interfaces

Go allows us to declare a type inside another type. In our `SurvivalBehaviors` interface, we have declared two fields of type interface. Through inner type promotion, the Go compiler performs interface conversions and the inner interface becomes part of the outer interface:

```
type SurvivalBehaviors interface {
        StrokeBehavior
        EatBehavior
}
```

The `d.Stroke` function takes a `SurvivalBehaviors` type as though it received `StrokeBehavior`, and the `d.Eat` function takes a `SurvivalBehaviors` type as if it received `EatBehavior`.

This means that the outer type, `SurvivalBehaviors`, now implements the interface of both `StrokeBehavior` and `EatBehavior`.

Interface embedding to add minor features

Here's another example of using interface embedding:

```
type BytesReadConn struct {
   net.Conn
   BytesRead uint64
}

func (brc *BytesReadConn) Read(p []byte) (int, error) {
   n, err := brc.Conn.Read(p)
   brc.BytesRead += uint64(n)
   return n, err
}
```

By embedding `net.Conn` in our `BytesReadConn` we are able to override its `Read` method not only perform the `Conn.Read` operation, but also to count the number of bytes read.

There's an ELO song that's ringing in my head now.

A Go error handling idiom

There's yet another common Go pattern at play in our code:

```
err := d.Stroke(se, strokeSupply, pond)
if err != nil {
       log.Fatal(err)    // the duck died!
}
```

Errors should be handled once and as soon as possible.

Some consider this as an antipattern that litters code with `if err != nil` blocks. We'll overlook that sentiment, for now, in favor of its simplicity and pragmatism.

Next, we'll define a `Capabilities` struct that embeds both behavior interfaces and all the important strokes fields. The `Capabilities` type defines what the duck can do. It has a number of strokes that it can use to cross each pond and two behaviors--one that increases its stroke count and the other that reduces the count but helps it to get close to its next source of food:

```
type Capabilities struct {
        StrokeBehavior
        EatBehavior
        strokes int
}
```

In Go, any method or field of an embedded/inner interface is accessible to the outer interface. Note that we're not saying parent or child, as that might imply inheritances. What we have is called inner type promotion, not inheritance. As long as an inner field or method name begins with a capital letter, it will be accessible to the outer object.

It's time to run our program

Now, it's time to provide the duck with its starting resources and a list of ponds to swim in and see whether our duck survives to live another day.

Let's assume our duck has five bugs in its belly, which is worth five strokes (we made our ponds and bugs very small to simplify our model):

```
func main() {
        var duck Duck
        capabilities := Capabilities{
                StrokeBehavior: Foot{},
                EatBehavior:    Bill{},
                strokes:        5,
        }
```

Our duck's first set of ponds will consist of two ponds. Each supplies only one bug. The first pond requires three strokes to reach the other side. The second pond requires two strokes:

```
ponds := []Pond{
        {BugSupply: 1, StrokesRequired: 3},
        {BugSupply: 1, StrokesRequired: 2},
}
duck.SwimAndEat(&capabilities, &capabilities.strokes, ponds)
displayDuckStats(&capabilities, ponds)
```

SOLID Design in Go

The call to the duck's `SwimAndEat` method uses the address of its capabilities because we want to share the duck's `Capabilities` object as our duck moves from one set of ponds to another.

At the end of each day, after the duck has crossed each pond and eaten the bugs it finds, we display the duck's statistics:

```
func displayDuckStats(c *Capabilities, ponds []Pond) {
    fmt.Printf("%s\n", DASHES)
    fmt.Printf("Ponds Processed:")
    for _, pond := range ponds {
        fmt.Printf("\n\t%+v", pond)
    }
    fmt.Printf("\nStrokes remaining: %+v\n", c.strokes)
    fmt.Printf("%s\n\n", DASHES)
}
```

Here's the output of this:

```
- Foot, paddle!
- Foot, paddle!
- Foot, paddle!
- Bill, eat a bug!
- Foot, paddle!
- Foot, paddle!
- Bill, eat a bug!
--------------------
Ponds Processed:
{BugSupply:1 StrokesRequired:3}
{BugSupply:1 StrokesRequired:2}
Strokes remaining: 2
--------------------
```

At the end of the first day, the duck crossed two ponds and has two strokes in reserve to start a new day.

The next day, our duck has only one pond to swim. Our duck has two bugs in its belly. There're two bugs in this pond. Let's see whether our duck makes it to the other side:

```
ponds = []Pond{
    {BugSupply: 2, StrokesRequired: 3},
}
duck.SwimAndEat(&capabilities, &capabilities.strokes, ponds)
displayDuckStats(&capabilities, ponds)
```

Here's the output of this:

```
- Foot, paddle!
- Foot, paddle!
- Foot, paddle!


2017/05/12 19:11:51 Our duck died!
exit status 1
```

Unfortunately, our duck did not have enough strokes to cross the pond. Bummer!

The moral of our story is as follows:

- Model applications in meaningful (like real world) ways
- Start by creating a set of behaviors as single responsibility interface types
- Compose simple interface types into larger, coherent sets of behaviors
- Ensure each function accepts only the types of behaviors it requires
- Don't be a duck

Summary

In this chapter, we saw how to use bad design using inheritance in Java and contrasted that solution to using composition in Go.

The **Gang of Four**'s (**GoF**) epic book, *Design Patterns: Elements of Reusable Object-Oriented Software*, discussed design patterns that addressed design flaws in the object oriented languages like Java. For example, in the *Putting Reuse Mechanisms to Work* section, the GoF book states, *Favor object composition over class inheritance*.

This design principle is not even applicable to Go. Go does not support inheritance. No extra thought or work is required for Go developers. Go promotes composition out-of-the-box.

> *"These compositional techniques are what give Go its flavor, which is profoundly different from the flavor of C++ or Java programs."*

> *- Rob Pike*

Composition is a software design pattern we should use to build better APIs.

We start by breaking our system into small parts: single responsibility interfaces. We can then put the pieces back together again. When we architect our APIs using composition, our applications have a better chance to grow and adapt to the requirements that may change over time. Our applications become easier to reason about and maintain.

In the next chapter, we'll persist in our pursuit of good design and will focus on the decorator pattern. We'll study Go's `Reader` and `Writer` interfaces and see why *less is more*. We'll implement channels in order to control the life cycle of a concurrent program and much more.

5
Adding Functionality with Decoration

In this chapter, we'll continue to address this remark: *If you like design patterns, use Java, not Go*. We'll do so with the help of the decorator and strategy patterns.

Our goal in this chapter is to understand:

- Go's Reader and Writer interfaces
- Why designing using the interface composition is better than type hierarchy design
- How to design with and implement the Decorator Pattern
- Inversion of Control (IoC) by implementing an IoC framework
- How to set up a request timeout using a proxy
- How to apply the Strategy Pattern when load balancing requests
- How to understand easy-metrics graphs
- How to implement a simple yet effective logger using standard library interfaces
- How to enrich HTTP requests with logging using dependency injection
- How to use channels to control the flow of events in a concurrent program
- A better way to extend our application's functionality

Adding Functionality with Decoration

Interface composition

Much like a writer composes a book from a set of chapters or a chapter from a set of sections, as Go programmers, we can compose our software applications using functional composition.

We can take the functional composition approach to design a software solution that enables us to design complex APIs from a set of smaller ones.

For example, in the Viva La Duck example from the previous chapter, we composed the `SurvivalBehaviors` interface from two smaller ones:

```
type SurvivalBehaviors interface {
     StrokeBehavior
     EatBehavior
}
```

Nothing is difficult. Complex things are simply built upon smaller, simpler things! When we approach all our software design problems from this perspective, we are able to more easily model the real world--our applications become much easier to read and reason about.

Go's complimentary Reader and Writer interfaces

To help us appreciate how Go encourages composition, let's look at Go's complimentary `Reader` and `Writer` interfaces:

```
type Reader interface {
     Read(p []byte) (n int, err error)
}
```

```
type Writer interface {
        Write(p []byte) (n int, err error)
}
```

What can we observe from these interface declarations? Simplicity.

They both have a single method that takes a single parameter and returns a single result (along with the requisite error value).

What does that buy us? For starters, we can compose broad interfaces by simply adding simpler interfaces.

Example usages of the Reader and Writer interfaces

The `Hash` interface from Go's standard library is composed of the `io.Writer` interface and four others. Therefore, `Hash` can be used anywhere the `io.Writer` interface is required:

```
type Hash interface {
        io.Writer
        Sum(b []byte) []byte
        Reset()
        Size() int
        BlockSize() int
}
```

Design with Duck Typing

As mentioned in the previous chapter, this is known as Duck Typing. It's a powerful design pattern. A thing is defined not by its type hierarchy but by its behaviors.

Here's an example of a `File` interface from the github.com/couchbase/moss package:

```
// The File interface is implemented by os.File. App specific
// implementations may add concurrency, caching, stats, fuzzing, etc.
type File interface {
        io.ReaderAt
        io.WriterAt
        io.Closer
        Stat() (os.FileInfo, error)
        Sync() error
        Truncate(size int64) error
}
```

Adding Functionality with Decoration

Here's another example of it from Go's `mime/multipart` project:

```
// File is an interface to access the file part of a multipart message.
// Its contents may be either stored in memory or on disk.
type File interface {
    io.Reader
    io.ReaderAt
    io.Seeker
    io.Closer
}
```

When composing with interfaces, keep things as simple as possible. Similarly, function signatures should be designed to only accept the smallest possible interface required to get the job done.

Note the application of the single responsibility principle and open/close principle in action: our software should be open for extension but closed for modifications.

More reasons to design using interfaces

As if that's not enough reason to design using interfaces.

We also get access to a plethora of functionality. For example, when working with readers and writers, we get the following for free:

Free functionality	Description

io.Copy	`// Copy copies from src to dst until either EOF is reached`
	`// on src or an error occurs. It returns the number of bytes`
	`// copied and the first error encountered while copying, if`
	`any.`
	`func Copy(dst Writer, src Reader) (written int64, err error)`
	`{`
	`        return copyBuffer(dst, src, nil)`
	`}`

io.LimitReader	`// A LimitedReader reads from R but limits the amount of`
	`// data returned to just N bytes. Each call to Read`
	`// updates N to reflect the new amount remaining.`
	`// Read returns EOF when N <= 0 or when the underlying R`
	`returns EOF.`
	`type LimitedReader struct {`
	`    R Reader // underlying reader`
	`    N int64  // max bytes remaining`
	`}`

`io.MultiReader`	```// MultiReader returns a Reader that's the logical concatenation of
// the provided input readers. They're read sequentially. Once all
// inputs have returned EOF, Read will return EOF. If any of the readers
// return a non-nil, non-EOF error, Read will return that error.
func MultiReader(readers ...Reader) Reader {
r := make([]Reader, len(readers))
copy(r, readers)
return &multiReader{r}
}```
`io.RuneReader`	```// ReadRune reads a single UTF-8 encoded Unicode character
// and returns the rune and its size in bytes. If no character is
// available, err will be set.
type RuneReader interface {
ReadRune() (r rune, size int, err error) }```
`io.ReadSeeker`	```// WriteSeeker is the interface that groups the basic Write and Seek methods.
type WriteSeeker interface {
Writer
Seeker
}```
`io.MultiWriter`	```// MultiWriter creates a writer that duplicates its writes to all the
// provided writers, similar to the Unix tee(1) command.
func MultiWriter(writers ...Writer) Writer {
w := make([]Writer, len(writers))
copy(w, writers)
return &multiWriter{w}
}```
`bufio.ScanBytes`	`ScanBytes` is a split function for a Scanner that returns each byte as a token.
`bufio.ScanLines`	`ScanLines` is a split function for a Scanner that returns each line of text, stripped of any trailing end-of-line marker. The returned line may be empty. The end-of-line marker is one optional carriage return, followed by one mandatory newline. In regular expression notation, it is \r?\n. The last non-empty line of input will be returned even if it has no newline.

Adding Functionality with Decoration

`bufio.ScanRunes`	`ScanRunes` is a split function for a Scanner that returns each UTF-8-encoded rune as a token. The sequence of runes returned is equivalent to that of a range loop over the input as a string, which means that erroneous UTF-8 encodings translate to `U+FFFD` = `"\xef\xbf\xbd"`. Because of the `Scan` interface, this makes it impossible for the client to distinguish correctly encoded replacement runes from encoding errors.
`ioutil.ReadDir`	`ReadDir` reads the directory named by `dirname` and returns a list of directory entries sorted by filename.
`ioutil.ReadFile`	The`addKeyFromFileToConfigMap` adds a key with the given name to a `ConfigMap`, populating the value with the content of the given file path; alternatively, it returns an error.

That's a lot of out-of-the-box functionality that we didn't have to test and code. Reusing Go standard library interfaces and functions is nearly always a win!

Using the Reader and Writer interfaces

Let's exercise what we've learned about the `io.Reader` and `io.Writer` interfaces:

```
package main

import (
        "io"
        "strings"
        "os"
)

type titlizeReader struct {
        src io.Reader
}

func NewTitlizeReader(source io.Reader) *titlizeReader {
        return &titlizeReader{source}
}
```

Recall that the `Reader` interface looks like this:

```
type Reader interface {
        Read(p []byte) (n int, err error)
}
```

When we implement the Read method, our titlizeReader struct now satisfies the Reader interface:

```
func (t *titlizeReader) Read(p []byte) (int, error) {
        count, err := t.src.Read(p)
        if err != nil {
                return count, err
        }
        for i := 0; i < len(p); i++ {
                if i == 0 {
                        if (p[i] >= 't' && p[i] <= 'z') {
                                p[i] = p[i] - 32
                        }
                } else {
                        if (p[i] >= 'A' && p[i] <= 'Z') {
                                p[i] = p[i] + 32
                        }
                }
        }
        return count, io.EOF
}
```

Our titlizeReader type will capitalize the first word in the sentence and change all the subsequent letters to lowercase. As we iterate through each byte, we check its ASCII value. The ASCII value of A is 97. The decimal value of a is 65. So, 97 minus 65 equals 32.

Here we use the string's NewReader method to create an io.Reader interface from the string, which is "this IS a tEsT":

```
func main() {
        var r io.Reader
        r = strings.NewReader("this IS a tEsT")
        r = io.LimitReader(r, 12)
        r = NewTitlizeReader(r)
```

We individually assigned the reader value on each line. We could have performed this in one line:

```
r := NewTitlizeReader(io.LimitReader(strings.NewReader("this IS a tEsT",
12))
```

We use three Readers: one from the strings package, another free one used to truncate our string to 12 characters, and the one we wrote ourselves.

Adding Functionality with Decoration

Given that we have separated our logic into individual function calls, Go's concurrency constructs enable us to process them independently to improve performance:

```
        var w io.Writer
    w = os.Stdout
        io.Copy(w, r)
}
```

We use the `os.Stdout` writer to output our results to standard output (our terminal console).

Since we are using the Reader and Writer interfaces, we get to use the `io.Copy` interface for free.

With `Readers` and `Writers` interfaces, we are able to process streams piece by piece. Granted, our example only used a 14-character string, but we could have handled more data than could fit in RAM at the same time.

> **Gang of Four (GOF)** refers to four authors who wrote the *Design Patterns: Elements of Reusable Object-Oriented Software* (https://en.wikipedia.org/wiki/Design_Patterns) book. Though the examples in the book are in SmallTalk and C++, the book is frequently referenced by many resourceful developers as they build object-oriented software. Languages such as Java, which supports inheritance, can greatly benefit from all the patterns in the GOF book. Not all patterns are equally important for Go. Though, as we saw in the previous chapter, we can definitely benefit from the structural Decorator pattern and the behavioral Strategy pattern.

Decorator pattern

Though it is easier to write quality Go code--than quality Java code--without an understanding of the GOF design patterns, it doesn't mean that we, as Go developers, cannot benefit from GOF's insight.

We'll soon see how we can put the Decorator pattern to good use in Go.

Type hierarchy UML

This is the type hierarchy UML that we might have created while designing the Decorator pattern back in the day that we used object-oriented languages:

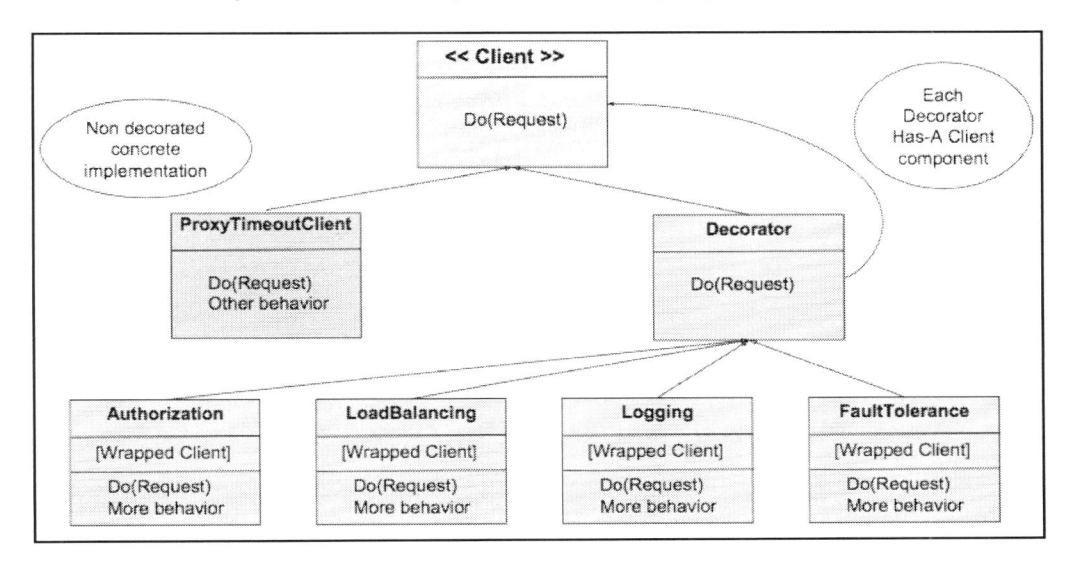

This is the design work needed to represent the same Decorator pattern using Go:

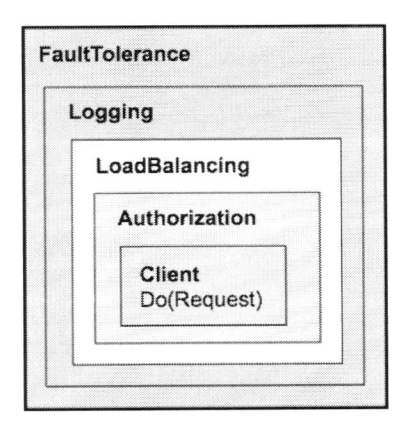

"Less is exponentially more"

- Rob Pike

How Procedural design compares to functional Inversion of Control (IoC)

The client request is wrapped by the `Authorization`, `LoadBalancing`, `Logging`, and `FaultTolerance` decorators. When a client request is executed, the functionality in those decorators will be injected into the flow by our Decorator framework, as shown in the following diagram:

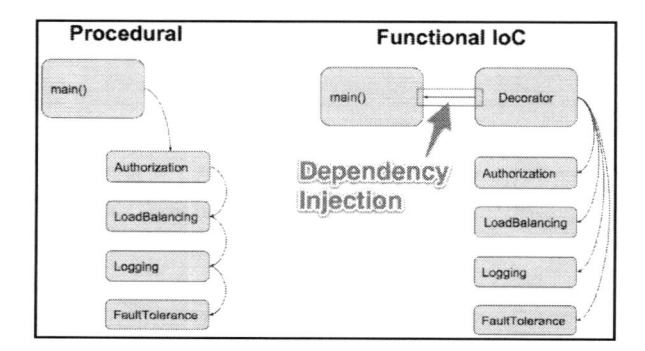

In procedural programming, the `main()` function would be in control of the flow of logic. The code would be monolithic and tightly coupled. For example, to implement `Authorization`, the programmer would insert the following line somewhere before the request is performed:

```
request.Header.Add("Authorization", token)
```

The logic of `FaultTolerance` and `LoadBalancing` would likely look like spaghetti code.

By programming the Decorator functions, we adhere to the client interface as follows:

```
type Client interface {
    Do(*http.Request) (*http.Response, error)
}
```

Each decorator will be a separate function-specific component.

Procedural design example

Procedural programming is like interacting with a Bash script in the terminal:

```
Pick a Product Type:
(1) Appliance
(2) Book
(3) Clothing
3

Pick a Clothing Type:
(1) Men
(2) Women
(3) Children
2
```

In procedural design, user interaction is predefined and sequential in nature.

Functional IoC example

Contrast the text-based Bash script example to a web application where the user is in control:

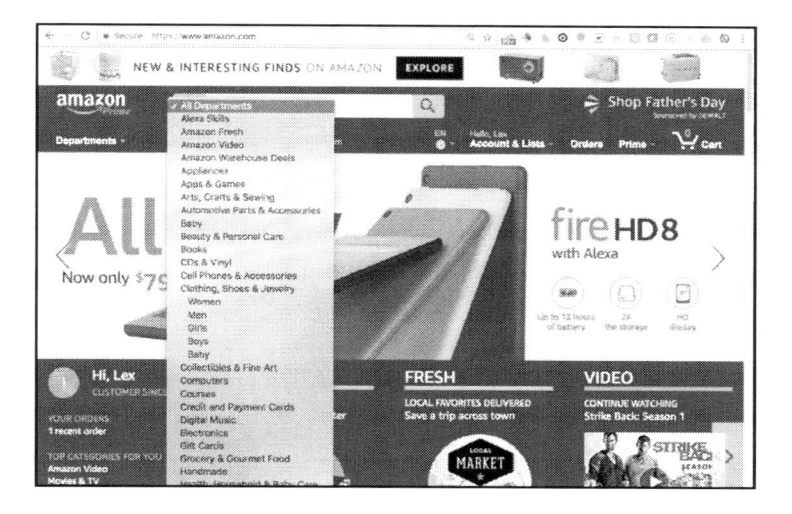

Adding Functionality with Decoration

In a GUI application, control is inverted. Instead of the program forcing the next user interaction, the user is mostly in control of what happens next. The IoC container is a web application framework that runs an event loop and handles the callback when the user clicks on controls, such as an item in the drop-down list or a submit button.

For some J2EE applications, IoC can also come in the form of XML configuration files that are injected into a Spring framework.

In a product shopping example, dependencies would be things such as **Select Product** or **Enter Shipping Address**. In our decorator implementation, dependencies include `Authorization`, `LoadBalancing`, etc., each of which decorate the request. Our IoC container is the decorator framework where functions like `Authorization` and `LoadBalancing` implement the Client interface.

A decorator implementation

Our decorator pattern example will be runnable, so we'll put it in the `main` package and define a `main()` function.

We use the easy-metrics package for recording and displaying our metrics. It comes out of the box with a nice GUI for displaying statistics.

We also import the decorator package and preface that import with a dot (.) in order to access the identifiers in the decorator package, in the local file block without a qualifier.

The main.go file

Let's have a look at the contents of `main.go`:

```
package main

import (
    "crypto/tls"
    "flag"
    "fmt"
    "io/ioutil"
    "log"
    "net/http"
    "net/url"
    "os"
```

```
    "os/signal"
    "time"
    "easy_metrics"
    . "decorator"
)

const (
    host = "127.0.0.1"
    protocol = "http://"
)
var (
    serverUrl string
    proxyUrl string
)
```

> This is what the imports looked like before using the init script and its aliases (and glide):
>
> ```
> import (
> ...
>     "time"
>     "github.com/l3x/fp-in-go/chapter5/02_decorator/easy_metrics"
>     . "github.com/l3x/fp-in-go/chapter5/02_decorator"
> )
> ```

I never liked long repository paths in my imports. I suppose it's time to give this technique a name. Let's call it **Keep It Simple Stupid-Glide** (**KISS-Glide**).

We define a host as a constant because we will always run this example code on our local workstation. We'll keep things simple and use the HTTP protocol (no SSL).

Our example uses a proxy server and also uses Go's standard library HTTP server implementation to listen to handle requests:

```
~/dev/02_decorator $ go-run --help
Usage of 02_decorator:
  -proxyPort int
        Server Port (default 8080)
  -serverPort int
        Server Port (default 3000)
```

Any function named `init()` will be executed before the `main()` function. We define default port numbers for our two servers and permit the user to specify different ports at runtime using the `flag` package, which implements command-line flag parsing:

```
func init() {
        serverPort := 3000
        proxyPort := 8080
        flag.IntVar(&serverPort, "serverPort", serverPort, "Server Port")
        flag.IntVar(&proxyPort, "proxyPort", proxyPort, "Server Port")
        flag.Parse()
        serverUrl = fmt.Sprintf("%s:%d", host, serverPort)
        proxyUrl = fmt.Sprintf("%s:%d", host, proxyPort)
}
```

`Simple Logger`

We'll implement a simple logger that will:

- Provide log file tracing
- Provide `Debug`, `Info`, and `Error` log levels
- Permit us to specify which log level(s) we want
- Enable us to more easily swap out our underlying logging framework

The decorator/simple_log.go file

Our logger leverages Go's `Logger` package, as follows:

```
package decorator

import (
        "io"
        "log"
        "os"
)

var (
        Debug       *log.Logger
        Info        *log.Logger
        Error       *log.Logger
        InfoHandler io.Writer
)
```

A simple logger exports one function, namely `InitLog`, which the calling package uses to enable the logging features:

```
func InitLog(
        traceFileName string,
        debugHandler io.Writer,
        infoHandler io.Writer,
        errorHandler io.Writer,
) {
```

Example InitLog calls

Here we pass the name of our trace file, called `trace-log.txt`, which will receive all of the logging output. We don't want `Debug` information, but we do want Info and Error output:

```
InitLog("trace-log.txt", ioutil.Discard, os.Stdout, os.Stderr)
```

This time we pass nil for the name of our trace log file, which tells our logger not to create a trace log file. We do want `Debug`, `Info`, and `Error` data displayed to standard out in our terminal console.

```
InitLog(nil, os.Stdout, os.Stdout, os.Stderr)
```

When we specify `traceFileName`, we'll need to create an `io.MultiWriter` interface to send the output to two places at the same time:

```
if len(traceFileName) > 0 {
        _ = os.Remove(traceFileName)
        file, err := os.OpenFile(traceFileName,
        os.O_CREATE|os.O_APPEND|os.O_WRONLY, 0666)
        if err != nil {
                log.Fatalf("Failed to create log file: %s", traceFileName)
        }
        debugHandler = io.MultiWriter(file, debugHandler)
        infoHandler = io.MultiWriter(file, infoHandler)
        errorHandler = io.MultiWriter(file, errorHandler)
}

InfoHandler = infoHandler

Debug = log.New(debugHandler, "DEBUG : ",
        log.Ldate|log.Ltime|log.Lshortfile)

Info = log.New(infoHandler, "INFO  : ",
        log.Ltime)
```

Adding Functionality with Decoration

```
Error = log.New(errorHandler, "ERROR : ",
        log.Ldate|log.Ltime|log.Lshortfile)
}
```

We'll preface each log line with `DEBUG`, `INFO`, or `ERROR` to indicate its log level.

Back to our main package

The first line of our `main` block calls our `InitLog` function:

```
func main() {
        InitLog("trace-log.txt",
                ioutil.Discard, os.Stdout, os.Stderr)
```

We use the `INFO` level to indicate which our server is listening.

We launch our server using a Goroutine, and since this is the `main()` function, we use the `log.Fatal` method, which is equivalent to `println` with a panic. This is because if we fail to start our server at this point, there are no buffers to flush, no outstanding defer statements, and no temporary files to process. We also wait for a second in order to give our server time to start:

```
Info.Printf("Metrics server listening on %s", serverUrl)
go func() {
        log.Fatal(easy_metrics.Serve(serverUrl))
}()
time.Sleep(1 * time.Second)
```

Next, we declare our request using `req`, which we'll later execute `NumRequests` times:

```
req, err := http.NewRequest(http.MethodGet, protocol + serverUrl, nil)
if err != nil {
        log.Fatalln(err)
}
```

In our example, we use a proxy server to pass all our requests through. This gives us the flexibility to handle proxy-level processing on a per-call basis. Our simple example does no such processing, but we do specify a proxy timeout of 1 second:

```
Info.Printf("Proxy listening on %s", proxyUrl)
proxyURL, _ := url.Parse(proxyUrl)
tr := &http.Transport{
        Proxy: http.ProxyURL(proxyURL),
        TLSClientConfig: &tls.Config{
                InsecureSkipVerify: true,
        },
```

}

Our client uses the decorator pattern to wrap our `proxyTimeoutClient` client with the `Authorization`, `LoadBalancing`, `Logging`, and `FaultTolerance` functionality:

```
tr.TLSNextProto = make(map[string]func(string, *tls.Conn)
http.RoundTripper)
proxyTimeoutClient := &http.Client{Transport: tr, Timeout: 1 * time.Second}
```

We do not modify our client implementation, rather extend its functionality (remember the open/close principle?):

```
client := Decorate(proxyTimeoutClient,
    Authorization("mysecretpassword"),
    LoadBalancing(RoundRobin(0, "web01:3000", "web02:3000", "web03:3000")),
    Logging(log.New(InfoHandler, "client: ", log.Ltime)),
    FaultTolerance(2, time.Second),
)
```

This is a declarative form of programming. There is no code ceremony. We chain our function calls, passing only the minimally required information to configure its behavior.

To get the load balancing working locally, you can add the following line to your `/etc/hosts` file:

```
127.0.0.1 localhost web01 web02 web03
```

Next, we define our job. We pass our client, request, the number of requests to process, and the time to wait before processing each request:

```
job := &Job{
    Client:       client,
    Request:      req,
    NumRequests:  10,
    IntervalSecs: 10,
}
```

In order to better comprehend the statistics, later in the easy-metrics web app, we'll set the `IntervalSecs` value to 10. There will 10 seconds between each of our 10 request-processing attempts.

Adding Functionality with Decoration

We set our start time and kick off our job processing with `job.Run()`. The `Run` function uses the `sync` package to wait until all the running jobs have completed before returning the control, at which time we print out how long the request-processing bit took:

```
start := time.Now()
job.Run()
Info.Printf("\n>> It took %s", time.Since(start))
```

Once our processing is complete, we call `DisplayResults` from the `easy_metrics` package, which displays a message like the following:

```
INFO    : 12:48:30 Go to http://127.0.0.1:3000/easy-metrics?show=Stats
```

```
Info.Printf("metrics")
err = easy_metrics.DisplayResults(serverUrl)
if err != nil {
        log.Fatalln(err)
}
```

Our server needs to keep running so that we can visit the easy-metrics URL to view our statistics with the user-friendly easy-metrics web app.

We create a channel to capture the *Ctrl + C* key sequence, which will signal our program to stop:

```
    Info.Printf("CTRL+C to exit")
    c := make(chan os.Signal, 1)
    signal.Notify(c, os.Interrupt)
    <-c
}
```

Chapter 5

Understanding our statistics using the easy-metrics GUI

The next few screenshots will display our terminal console and our web browser at `http://127.0.0.1:3000/easy-metrics?show=Stats` immediately after executing Go's `main.go` command:

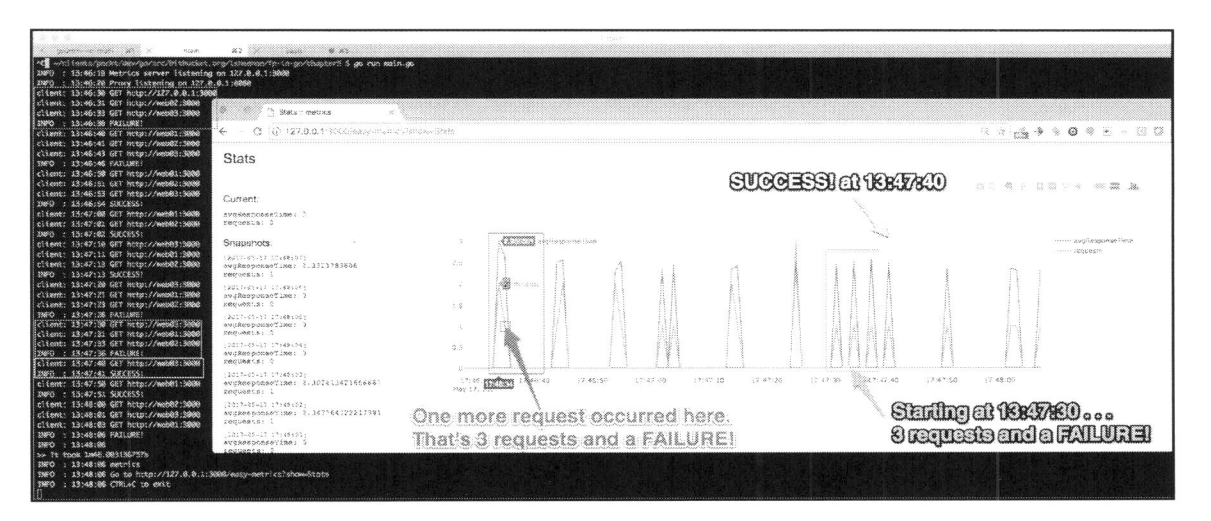

In the following sections, we'll split this image into three parts.

[187]

Adding Functionality with Decoration

Quick look at the Dot Init update

This is what our terminal looks like using the KISS-Glide toolset:

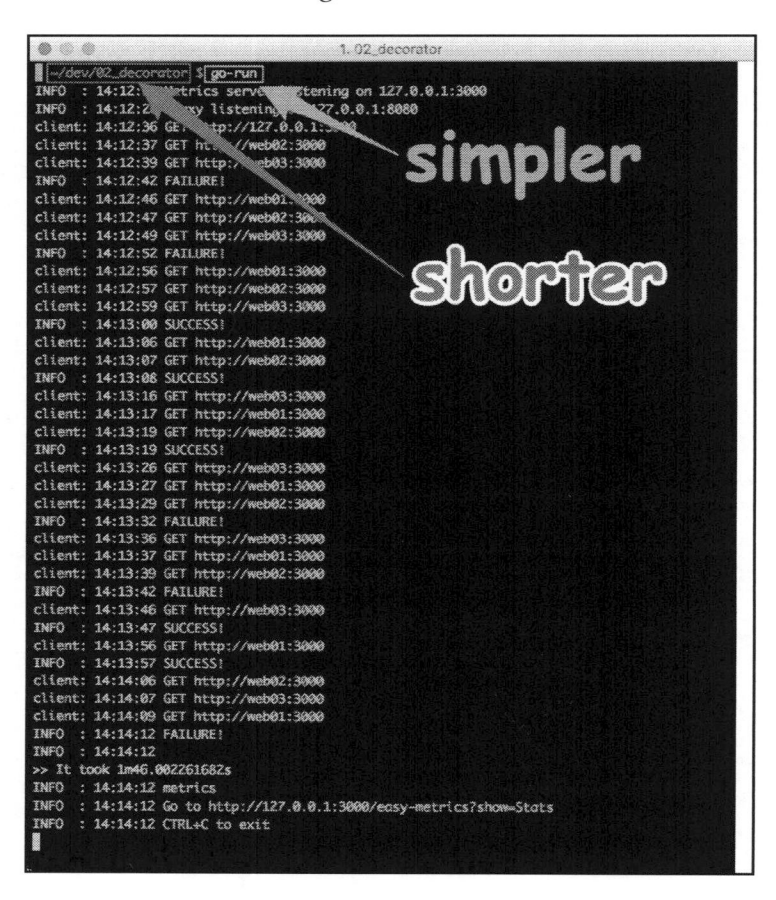

KISS-Glide makes it simpler and requires less typing to achieve the same result. That's a win-win situation.

> When I originally wrote this chapter, I used the standard `go get`, `go build`, and `go run main.go` commands. As the projects became more complicated (requiring more third-party dependencies), I found it helpful to create the KISS-Glide tool. Later, I returned to all the projects and simplified them using the KISS-Glide tool. Feel free to use any dependency management tool and build and run your Go applications as you prefer.

That's one of the great things about Go. As long as tool makers adhere to standard Go conventions, such as using the `GOPATH`, *and not break other Go tools, such as* `go test`, `go doc`, *and* `go vet`, *it's all good. I prefer simple, yet powerful (KISS-Glide).*

Easy-metrics - 1 of 3

This first screenshot is more about what we see in our terminal console than the easy-metrics GUI:

Adding Functionality with Decoration

The first two lines of output come from our `main.go` file. The next three lines come from this decorator: `Logging(log.New(InfoHandler, "client: ", log.Ltime))`,.

Each line is prefaced with either `INFO` or client. The `client` lines indicate an individual request attempt. The `INFO` lines indicate whether the initial request, which could have been tried twice, succeeded or failed.

The decorator/decorator.go file

Let's look at our `decorator.go` implementation. It's in the `02_decorator` directory, and the package name is `decorator`:

```
package decorator

import (
        "log"
        "net/http"
        "sync/atomic"
        "time"
)


type Client interface {
        Do(*http.Request) (*http.Response, error)
}

// ClientFunc is a function type that implements the client interface.
type ClientFunc func(*http.Request) (*http.Response, error)

func (f ClientFunc) Do(r *http.Request) (*http.Response, error) {
        return f(r)
}
```

The `ClientFunc` function is a function type that implements the `Client` interface.

We also define two additional methods that act as the getter and setter for the `ratelimitDuration` value:

```
var ratelimitDuration time.Duration

func (f ClientFunc) SetRatelimit(duration time.Duration) (error) {
        ratelimitDuration = duration
        return nil
}
```

```
func (f ClientFunc) GetRatelimit() (time.Duration, error) {
    return ratelimitDuration, nil
}
```

Next, we define the `Decorator` function type to wrap our `Client` with additional behavior:

```
type Decorator func(Client) Client
```

A framework to inject dependencies

Next, we'll look closer at the implementation of our IoC container framework.

We'll see that by wrapping decorators, which implement the `Client` interface, around our core client call and using the decorator pattern, our framework is able to extend our application functionality in a modular and easy-to-understand manner.

The `Decorator` notation indicates that this is a variadic parameter that can take any number of values. Remember our call in `main` where we passed in our decorators?

Wrapping a client request with decorators (in main)

```
client := Decorate(proxyTimeoutClient,
    Authorization("mysecretpassword"),
    LoadBalancing(RoundRobin(0, "web01:3000", "web02:3000", "web03:3000")),
    Logging(log.New(InfoHandler, "client: ", log.Ltime)),
    FaultTolerance(2, time.Second),
)
```

Our `Decorate` function extends our client's functionality by iterating over each decorator in order.

Note that there are several ways to implement this wrapping functionality. We could have used recursion, line-by-line wrapping, or inline wrapping like we did earlier in this chapter:

```
r := NewTitlizeReader(io.LimitReader(strings.NewReader("this IS a tEsT", 12))
```

Using a variadic parameter in conjunction with a range construct, when we are unsure of the number of decorators we need to wrap, is probably the best choice:

```
func Decorate(c Client, ds ...Decorator) Client {
    decorated := c
    for _, decorate := range ds {
```

Adding Functionality with Decoration

```
                decorated = decorate(decorated)
        }
        return decorated
}
```

Authorization decorator

Our first decorator is `Authorization`. We call the `Header` helper function that adds the `Authorization` header with the given token to each request at runtime:

```
func Authorization(token string) Decorator {
        return Header("Authorization", token)
}

func Header(name, value string) Decorator {
        return func(c Client) Client {
                return ClientFunc(func(r *http.Request)(*http.Response,
error) {
                        r.Header.Add(name, value)
                        return c.Do(r)
                })
        }
}
```

Logging decorator

The `Logging` decorator takes a pointer to the log from the `Logger` package, from Go's standard library. Note that we are able to pass our custom `InfoHandler` since we chose to implement it using the `io.Writer` interface:

```
Logging(log.New(InfoHandler, "client: ", log.Ltime)),
func Logging(l *log.Logger) Decorator {
        return func(c Client) Client {
                return ClientFunc(func(r *http.Request) (*http.Response,
error ) {
                        l.Printf("%s %s", r.Method, r.URL)
                        return c.Do(r)
                })
        }
}
```

We execute the `Printf` command just before running the client's `Do` method.

LoadBalancing decorator

We leverage the strategy pattern to implement our load balancing decorator.

The `LoadBalancing` decorator applies the strategy pattern to apply the logic that determines which backend server will receive the next incoming client request.

Strategy pattern

The strategy pattern uses composition rather than inheritance to choose which behavior is executed. The behavior in our example implements a load balancing algorithm. Production implementations of the strategy pattern often have an administrative application that is used to choose which strategy it selected during runtime:

Rather than using the context of the request or configuration instructions from an administrative application to selecting our load balancing strategy, we hardcode our example to use the `RoundRobin` behavior.

Here's the call:

```
LoadBalancing(RoundRobin(0, "web01:3000", "web02:3000", "web03:3000")),
```

The first parameter, `RoundRobin`, is the selected strategy. We pass the `RoundRobin` function We pass the iterating `RoundRobin` function in order over the backend server's host addresses. They are passed over the variadic parameter, namely backends.

Adding Functionality with Decoration

Instead of using a request to gather context to determine the strategy to employ, we define a `Director` function type that takes the request. We select the `RoundRobin` strategy and modify the request's embedded URL member to specify the server to connect to:

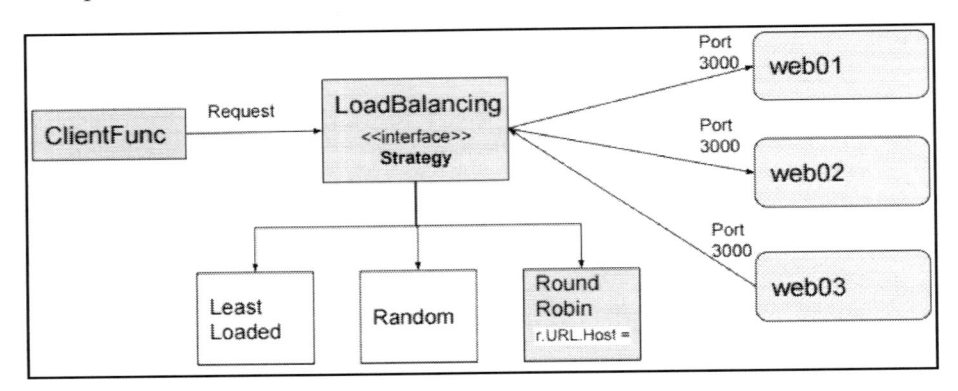

The following is the `RoundRobin` function where we make the `r.URL.Host` assignment:

```
func RoundRobin(robin int64, backends ...string) Director {
       return func(r *http.Request) {
              if len(backends) > 0 {
                     r.URL.Host = backends[atomic.AddInt64(&robin, 1) % int64(len(backends))]
              }
       }
}
```

Alternatively, if we had defined other load balancing strategies, such as **Least Loaded** or **Random**, we'd only need to implement that function and pass it to our `LoadBalancing` function as its director.

The `LoadBalancing` function returns a decorator that spreads client requests across multiple backend servers, based on the given director, that is, `RoundRobin` in our example:

```
func LoadBalancing(dir Director) Decorator {
       return func(c Client) Client {
              return ClientFunc(func(r *http.Request) (*http.Response, error) {
                     dir(r)
                     return c.Do(r)
              })
       }
}
```

The `Director` modifies each HTTP request to follow the chosen load balancing strategy:

```
type Director func(*http.Request)
```

Finally, we have our `FaultTolerance` decorator that extends a client with fault tolerance, based on the given attempts and backoff time duration:

```
func FaultTolerance(attempts int, backoff time.Duration) Decorator {
        return func(c Client) Client {
                return ClientFunc(func(r *http.Request) (*http.Response, error) {
                        var res *http.Response
                        var err error
                        for i := 0; i <= attempts; i++ {
                                if res, err = c.Do(r); err == nil {
                                        Info.Println("SUCCESS!")
                                        break
                                }
                                Debug.Println("backing off...")
                                time.Sleep(backoff * time.Duration(i))
                        }
                        if err != nil { Info.Println("FAILURE!") }
                        return res, err
                })
        }
}
```

We only want the `backing off` information output to our trace file, so we use our `Debug.Println` function.

Notice what each decorator has in common? They provide additional functionality and eventually call `c.Do(r)`. Some provide the additional functionality before calling `c.Do(r)`; some could do it before and after the call.

Inversion of control and dependency injection

This is a form **Dependency Injection (DI)**. DI is where a service; for example, `FaultTolerance`, is passed to a dependent object--for instance, the client--where it is used.

This can also be considered **Inversion of Control (IoC)** (DI is a subset of IoC). It's the director function that we pass into the `LoadBalancing` function that provides the flow of control. This determines which backend server to direct the request to.

IoC is a design principle where a framework determines the flow of control. Contrast that to procedural programming, where the custom code determines the application's flow of control in a predetermined manner.

Our first failure

Our first failure consisted of three requests:

```
client: 13:46:30 GET http://127.0.0.1:3000
client: 13:46:31 GET http://web02:3000
client: 13:46:33 GET http://web03:3000
INFO  : 13:46:36 FAILURE!
```

Easy metrics - 2 of 3

Our easy-metrics graph shows when the requests occurred and their average response time:

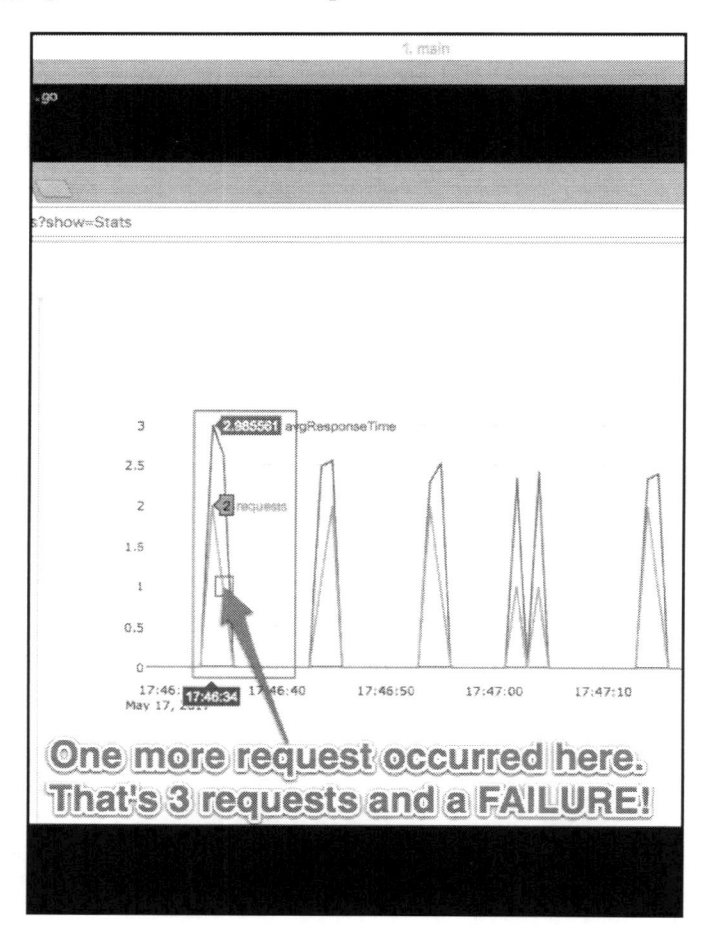

When you open the easy-metrics web application, move your mouse pointer over the lines for more context information. For example, when you move your mouse where the red arrow is pointing in the preceding screenshot, you'll see that another request occurred at that point.

Groking our trace log file

In order to get a deeper understanding of why our attempts failed, we can look in our trace file.

Groking is an old Scots term meaning to look at somebody while they're eating in the hope that they'll give you some of their food. In our case, we'll be looking intently at a trace log file in hope of getting some morsel of understanding:

```
INFO    : 13:46:19 Metrics server listening on 127.0.0.1:3000
INFO    : 13:46:20 Proxy listening on 127.0.0.1:8080
DEBUG   : 2017/05/17 13:46:30 requester.go:114: makeRequest:
client: 13:46:30 GET http://127.0.0.1:3000
DEBUG   : 2017/05/17 13:46:30 metrics.go:66: - randInt: 3081
DEBUG   : 2017/05/17 13:46:31 decorator.go:107: backing off...
client: 13:46:31 GET http://web02:3000
DEBUG   : 2017/05/17 13:46:31 metrics.go:66: - randInt: 2887
DEBUG   : 2017/05/17 13:46:32 decorator.go:107: backing off...
client: 13:46:33 GET http://web03:3000
DEBUG   : 2017/05/17 13:46:33 metrics.go:66: - randInt: 1847
DEBUG   : 2017/05/17 13:46:34 decorator.go:107: backing off...
INFO    : 13:46:36 FAILURE!
```

Here's the call to our call to the `FaultTolerance` function:

```
FaultTolerance(2, time.Second),
```

The key lines from our `FaultTolerance` decorator are as follows:

```
func FaultTolerance(attempts int, backoff time.Duration) Decorator
    . . .
        for i := 0; i <= attempts; i++ {
            if res, err = c.Do(r); err == nil {
                Info.Println("SUCCESS!")
                break
            }
            Debug.Println("backing off...")
            time.Sleep(backoff * time.Duration(i))
        }
        if err != nil { Info.Println("FAILURE!") }
        return res, err
```

Adding Functionality with Decoration

. . .

This indicates that if we don't succeed at first, we'll try again twice and wait for a second between each attempt.

The work is performed in the `metrics.go` file. Note that work can take anywhere from 0 to 5,000 milliseconds:

```
func work() {
        randInt := rand.Intn(5000)
        decorator.Debug.Printf("- randInt: %v", randInt)
        workTime := time.Duration(randInt) * time.Millisecond
        time.Sleep(workTime)
}
```

Lastly, recall that we set our per request timeout to 1 second when we defined `proxyTimeoutClient`:

```
proxyTimeoutClient := &http.Client{Transport: tr, Timeout: 1 * time.Second}
```

We tried thrice and none of our attempts took less than a second, so our first set of requests resulted in a failure.

The rest of the graph

The rest of the graph shows multiple requests. We'll focus on the following two:

```
client: 13:47:30 GET http://web03:3000
client: 13:47:31 GET http://web01:3000
client: 13:47:33 GET http://web02:3000
INFO   : 13:47:36 FAILURE!
client: 13:47:40 GET http://web03:3000
INFO   : 13:47:41 SUCCESS!
```

Notice that in the first set of requests, in green, we made three attempts. Note also, in red, the requests were load-balanced, in a round-robin manner, among `web03`, `web01`, and `web02`. `INFO` indicates a `FAILURE!`.

The first request of the next set of requests began 10 seconds later and was sent to the `web03` backend server. `INFO` indicates `SUCCESS!`

[198]

Easy metrics - 3 of 3

We can see the `FAILURE!` and `SUCCESS!` requests in the following easy-metrics graph:

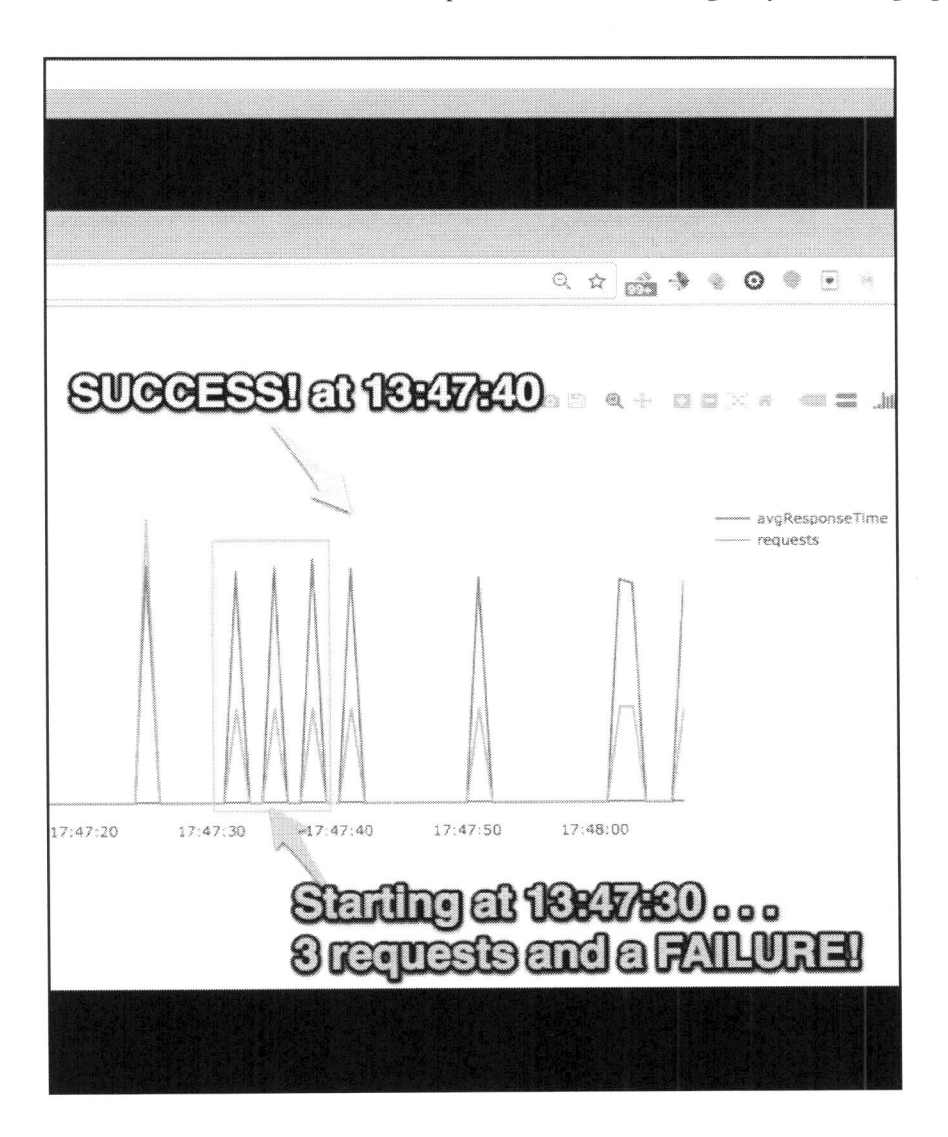

Adding Functionality with Decoration

Examining the trace log

Similar to the failed attempts we saw earlier, none of the three requests were performed in under a second. Thus, they failed.

However, the next request will take only 0.495 seconds and it will immediately succeed:

```
DEBUG   : 2017/05/17 13:47:30 requester.go:114: makeRequest:
client: 13:47:30 GET http://web03:3000
DEBUG   : 2017/05/17 13:47:30 metrics.go:66: - randInt: 1445
DEBUG   : 2017/05/17 13:47:31 decorator.go:107: backing off...
client: 13:47:31 GET http://web01:3000
DEBUG   : 2017/05/17 13:47:31 metrics.go:66: - randInt: 3237
DEBUG   : 2017/05/17 13:47:32 decorator.go:107: backing off...
client: 13:47:33 GET http://web02:3000
DEBUG   : 2017/05/17 13:47:33 metrics.go:66: - randInt: 4106
DEBUG   : 2017/05/17 13:47:34 decorator.go:107: backing off...
INFO    : 13:47:36 FAILURE!
DEBUG   : 2017/05/17 13:47:36 requester.go:65: > 7 requests done.
DEBUG   : 2017/05/17 13:47:40 requester.go:114: makeRequest:
client: 13:47:40 GET http://web03:3000
DEBUG   : 2017/05/17 13:47:40 metrics.go:66: - randInt: 495
INFO    : 13:47:41 SUCCESS!
DEBUG   : 2017/05/17 13:47:41 requester.go:65: > 8 requests done.
```

The last thing to observe in this trace output are the two lines that indicate how many requests have been performed: > 8 requests done.

Since this is DEBUG output, we don't need to guess which file and line this output came from.

The decorator/requestor.go file

The DEBUG output leads us to our last go source file, namely requestor.go:

```
package decorator

import (
        "io"
        "io/ioutil"
        "net/http"
        "os"
        "os/signal"
        "sync"
        "syscall"
        "time"
```

[200]

```
)

type response struct {
        duration       time.Duration
        err            error
}
```

The response struct is used to record the duration and any error from running our request. When we capitalize names of symbols, for example, the "J" in our struct named Job in the following code, we are telling Go to export it. When we import a package we will only be able to access exported symbols.

```
type Job struct {
        Client         Client
        NumRequests    int
        Request        *http.Request
        IntervalSecs   int
        responseChan   chan *response
}
```

The private field, responses, is a channel of response pointers with a buffer that has a size equal to NumRequests.

The job variable declared in main()

It begins with a capital J to export it. We use it in our main function to declare the total number of requests we want to run as well as how long to wait between making each request:

```
job := &Job{
        Client:        client,
        Request:       req,
        NumRequests:   10,
        IntervalSecs:  10,
}
```

Back to the requestor.go file

After the Job struct definition comes the displayProgress method:

```
func (b *Job) displayProgress(stopChan chan struct{}) {
        var prevResponseCount int
        for {
                select {
                case <-time.Tick(time.Millisecond * 500):
```

Adding Functionality with Decoration

```
                        responseCount := len(b.responseChan)
                        if prevResponseCount < responseCount {
                                prevResponseCount = responseCount
                                Debug.Printf("> %d requests done.",
responseCount)
                        }
                case <-stopChan:
                        return
                }
        }
}
```

Every 500 milliseconds, `displayProgress` checks to see whether a new response has been processed. It does this by checking the size of the job's response channel. If it finds a new response, it prints out a line like the following:

```
DEBUG : 2017/05/17 19:04:36 requestor.go:38: > 3 requests done.
```

It will continue to loop until a value is received on the `stopChan` channel.

Using channels to manage the life cycle

We use three channels to manage the life cycle of our requestor component:

- `responseChan chan *response`
- `stopChan chan struct{}`
- `interruptChan := make(chan os.Signal, 1)`

Every 5,000 milliseconds, we check `responseChan` to see whether we've received a new response. If so, we print a message indicating that the request is completed.

First, `stopChan` is used to stop the running of the `displayProgress` function.

Then, `interruptChan` is used to signal everything to shut down when the user presses *Ctrl + C*.

The `Run` method of `Job` makes all the requests, displays summary results, and blocks until all responses are received:

```
func (j *Job) Run() {
        j.responseChan = make(chan *response, j.NumRequests)
        stopChan := make(chan struct{})
        go j.displayProgress(stopChan)
```

We start by creating `responseChan` as a buffered channel with a size equal to the number of requests to process. Next, we create `stopChan` as a channel of empty structs. We use the empty struct because it takes up no space. We've seen in `displayProgress` that we are not concerned with the value in the channel. As long as anything, even the empty struct, is received on `stopChan`, that's enough to signal that it's time to stop processing. We launch `j.displayProgress(stopChan)` as a Goroutine.

We create `interruptChan` in a way it is unbuffered (with a size of 1). Since we want to catch `SIGTERM`, which is the default signal sent by the kill command (*Ctrl + C*), and since we wish this to work for both Unix and Windows systems, we use `syscall.SIGTERM` as the third parameter to `signal.Notify`:

```
interruptChan := make(chan os.Signal, 1)
signal.Notify(interruptChan, os.Interrupt, syscall.SIGTERM)
go func() {
        <-interruptChan
        stopChan <- struct{}{}
        close(j.responseChan)
        os.Exit(130)
}()
```

Our Goroutine blocks wait for a signal from `interruptChan`. If one is received, it will send an empty struct instance to `stopChan` and then close `j.responseChan` and finally run `os.Exit(130)`, indicating a fatal error caused by *Ctrl + C*.

For every `intervalSecs`, we add 1 to `WaitGroup` and launch the next request. Once we've iterated `j.NumRequests` times, we break out of our loop and run `wg.Wait()`. This blocks until all the requests have completed processing. Note that the last line of each request-processing Goroutine is the `wg.Done()` function, which is used to decrements the `WaitGroup` counter:

```
var wg sync.WaitGroup
intervalSecs := time.Duration(j.IntervalSecs)
requestsPerformed := 0
for range time.Tick(intervalSecs * time.Second)  {
        wg.Add(1)
        go func() {
                client := j.Client
                j.makeRequest(client)
                wg.Done()
        }()
        requestsPerformed++
        if requestsPerformed >= j.NumRequests {
                break
        }
```

Adding Functionality with Decoration

```
    }
    wg.Wait()
```

All requests done

When the `WaitGroup` counter reaches zero, `wg.Wait()` is unblocked and the processing continues to the next line, where we pass an instance of the empty struct to `stopChan`. As we've seen previously, `stopChan` signals to the `displayProgress` method of `Job` to stop processing:

```
        stopChan <- struct{}{}
        Debug.Printf("All requests done.")
        close(j.responseChan)
    }
```

Lastly, we use our `Debug` logger to print `All requests done.` and close `responseChan` of `Job`.

Launching our makeRequest goroutine

Our `Run` method launches a Goroutine `j.NumRequests` times. Each Goroutine runs this code:

```
    go func() {
            client := j.Client
            j.makeRequest(client)
            wg.Done()
    }()
```

The `makeRequest` function is called in a goroutine and passed to the client. We use our `Debug` logger to indicate that we are about to make a request and record the start time:

```
    func (j *Job) makeRequest(c Client) {
            Debug.Printf("makeRequest: ")
            start := time.Now()
            resp, err := c.Do(j.Request)
            if err == nil {
                    io.Copy(ioutil.Discard, resp.Body)
                    resp.Body.Close()
            }
            t := time.Now()
            finish := t.Sub(start)
            j.responseChan <- &response{
                    duration:    finish,
```

```
            err:       err,
    }
}
```

The key line is `resp, err := c.Do(j.Request)`.

Our DI framework in action

This is when we actually perform the request. This is when all the decorators are executed:

```
client := Decorate(proxyTimeoutClient,
    Authorization("mysecretpassword"),
    LoadBalancing(RoundRobin(0, "web01:3000", "web02:3000",
"web03:3000")),
    Logging(log.New(InfoHandler, "client: ", log.Ltime)),
    FaultTolerance(2, time.Second),
)
```

The decorators are executed in order. `Authorization` goes first, followed by `LoadBalancing`, `Logging`, and `FaultTolerance`.

We create our IoC framework by defining the client interface with a single `Do` method:

```
type Client interface {
    Do(*http.Request) (*http.Response, error)
}
```

Wrap each decorator around a return `c.Do(r)` statement that fires once the following line is executed in the `makeRequest` method of `Job`:

```
resp, err := c.Do(j.Request)
```

We created a simple framework for controlling the execution and enriching each HTTP request with our decorators wrapped around the client interface. This is IoC, and as we see, it's not too complicated.

Summary

In this chapter, we learned how no design or bad design using type hierarchies can lead to technical debt. We studied the decorator pattern and learned a great way to extend the functionality of our application using IoC.

We saw multiple examples of single method interfaces and learned to appreciate the fact that less is more and that good design is worthwhile.

Hopefully, by the end of this chapter, we can all agree that we can leverage design patterns to write better Go code.

In our next chapter, we'll use the adapter design pattern and other functional programming techniques to design and build better APIs.

6
Applying FP at the Architectural Level

Most Functional programming (FP) books only talk about the code level benefits but FP principles provide better returns when applied at the architecture level.

In this chapter, we will discuss some architectural styles that are based on the same ideas and philosophies of FP.

We'll also build a layered application that solves the problem of circular dependencies with the aid of Inversion of Control (IoC) to control the flow of logic. The application we build allows an admin to move files between two cloud storage service provider accounts.

Our goals in this chapter are as follows:

- Understand the basics of systems engineering and application architecture
- Discuss architecture styles that carry the same ideas of FP
- Prevent cyclic dependency errors
- Understand how to apply the Hollywood Principle
- Learn the difference between the observer pattern and dependency injection
- Use IoC to control the flow of logic
- Build a layered application architecture
- Create an effective table-driven framework to test our API
- Discuss where FP and Go fit into microservice architectures

Application architectures

Four years ago, I posted an article entitled *Application Architecture Considerations*.

Consider the following diagram:

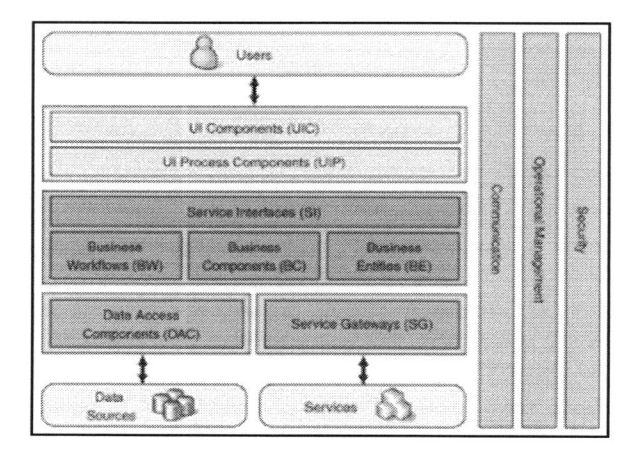

I had talked about things to consider when evaluating an application's architecture.

> For a list of things to consider when designing an application architecture, see http://lexsheehan.blogspot.com/2013/05/application-architecture-considerations.html.

Some of these things are listed as follows:

- **Functionality**: Does the application satisfy its business requirements?
- **Performance**: Does the application run fast enough? For example, if there are any views that take longer than 7 seconds to display, then you need to re-engineer something.
- **Scalability**: How well does your application scale? Can you easily add and remove components without affecting your application's performance or reliability? How loosely (or tightly) coupled is your application code?

It was all high level, mainly discussing nonfunctional requirements and cross-cutting concerns, for example, security, error handling, and logging.

> If you are only interested in pure functional programming techniques, you can safely skip this chapter. However, if you want to build an application framework in which you can place pure function programming components, this will be a good chapter for you.

What is software architecture?

Designing software architecture is the process of defining a structured solution to address our application's user, business, and system requirements. In each case, we must ask, "*What do you need?*" that is, the requirements, and "*Why do you need it?*" and document our understanding in a way that the business stakeholders understand. Finally, we must implement the "*How?*":

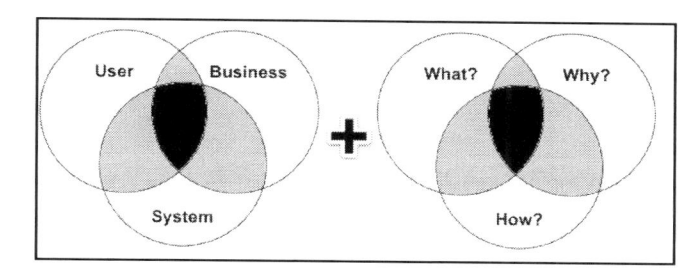

The art of software architecture lies in the ability to understand what is important, to make the key decisions in structuring application components and their interfaces, and to make the right decisions regarding things that are hard to change.

Whereas the *Application Architecture Considerations* article focused mainly on the "*What?*", this chapter focuses on the "*How?*" using Go.

Client-server architecture

The client-server model could be implemented as shown in the following diagram:

Applying FP at the Architectural Level

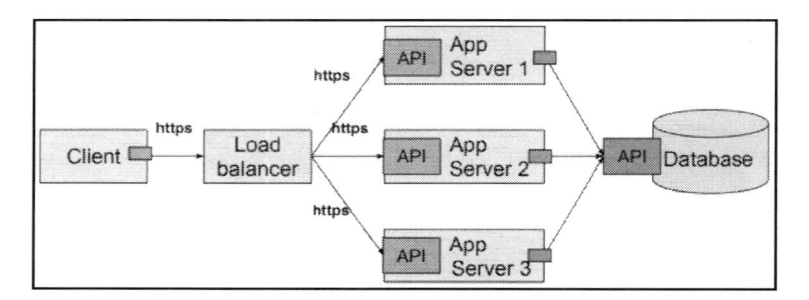

In our example, the client goes through a load balancer to talk to an application server's API. Each application server uses a database API client to interact with the database. The small, unlabeled boxes represent an API client. Some clients communicate directly to their server, for example, our database client. Others, like our application server client, go through intermediaries that provide services, for example, load balancing.

Cloud architecture

APIs expose the functions that are available and define the requirements that govern how applications or services can talk to each other.

As we move into cloud-based architectures, our systems begin to look more like this:

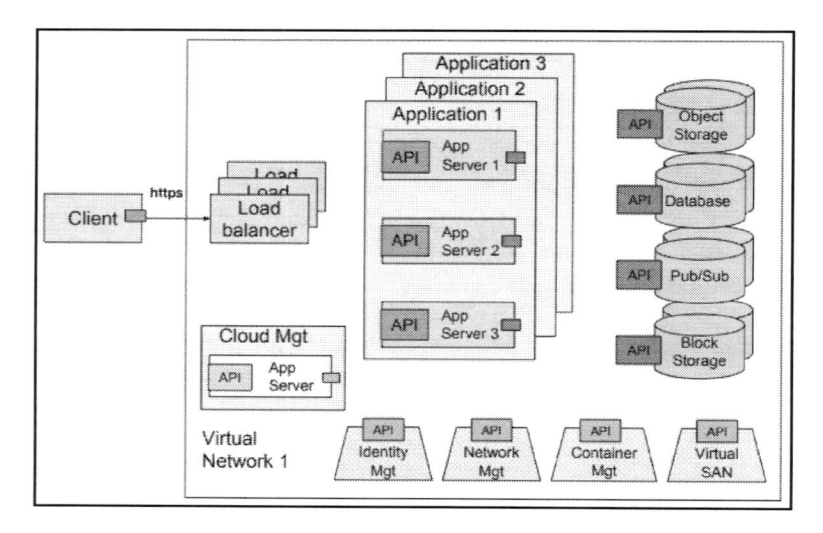

What do both the client/server and cloud architectures have most in common?

See all the APIs that expose the functionality of the underlying resources?

Go is well suited for server-side applications, that is, everything in the virtual network (the big gray box). That's pretty much the entire cloud infrastructure and everything running within it.

That's great for the big picture, but what about building applications? How much do APIs come into play when building an individual Go application?

It depends. Are we talking about a small utility application or an enterprise CRM application?

The interface to a small utility application can simply be defined by the command-line parameters that it accepts.

Large **customer relationship management** (**CRM**) applications will be composed of layers of functionality, not unlike the virtual network diagram we saw earlier. For example, the opportunity management system will need an API to the quote generation and electronic signatures components. The service and provisioning system will need API access to the billing and invoicing system.

If we intend to build large, complex applications, we must put effort into architecting our solutions.

Why does architecture matter?

Much like large buildings, complex software applications must be built on a solid foundation. In software, we sometimes call this our application framework.

If we do not consider the things mentioned in my article; things like functionality, security, extensibility, testability, and performance, then we will likely be unprepared for the consequences of our lack of forethought.

Our exposure to risk will increase as we find our application becomes more costly to test, deploy, and maintain over time.

Design takes some time and effort, but it does not take long before that effort pays off.

The role of systems engineering

Systems engineering is a discipline that focuses on the design and application of the whole system, which may be comprised of many parts.

Real systems

A real system includes things like:

- Products
- Processes
- People
- Information
- Techniques
- Resources
- Services

IT system specialty groups

Systems engineering focuses on identifying requirements early in the development life cycle. It considers the entire problem space. Taking all aspects and variables into account and relating the social to the technical aspects. Then it proceeds with design synthesis, integrating all the specialty groups such as:

• Cost	• Risk Assessment
• Development	• Schedule
• Disposal	• Support
• Manufacturing	• Test
• Operations	• Training
• Performance	• Verification
• Process Improvement	

Into a team effort in a structured development process that proceeds from concept, design synthesis, validation, deployment to production and operation.

Systems engineering is lean

Systems engineering is all about creating more value for our customer with fewer resources.

A lean IT department understands its customer's business and what customer value means and focuses its efforts to continuously increase it. The goal is to provide maximum value to the customer through a perfect value creation process that has zero waste.

For example, if your customer sells chicken to consumers, then every new project must start with this question: Will this project help our customer sell more chicken?

To accomplish this, lean thinking changes the focus of management from optimizing separate technologies, and vertical departments to optimizing the flow of products and services through entire value streams that flow horizontally across technologies and departments to customers.

Eliminating waste along entire value streams, instead of at isolated points, creates processes that requires less human effort, less capital, and less time to make products and services at far less costs and with much fewer defects, compared with traditional business systems. Lean companies are able to respond to changing customer desires with high variety, high quality, low cost, and with fast throughput times. Information management becomes simpler and more accurate.

Requirements, scope and terms

Everytime we develop software, we address both the business and technical needs of our customer with the goal of providing a quality product that meets our users' needs.

Some requirements are task-specific. For example, if we are required to write a script to move a specific log file from one server to another. Other times, we need may be required to write a command line input tool to parse the text a user types in their console input and count the characters, words, or lines they entered. This chapter is not about those types of applications. We'll consider system-level requirements only in this chapter.

Defining terms

Let's start by defining a few terms.

Software requirements
Conditions or capabilities needed by our customer to achieve an objective/solve problem(s).

System
An integrated set of subsystems and/or elements that accomplish a defined objective.

System architecture
The fundamental properties of a system in its environment embodied in its subsystems, elements, relationships along with the principles of its design and evolution.

System elements
Atomic elements that cannot to be broken down further

Decomposable: elements that can to be broken into smaller elements

System Boundaries
Defines the scope of a system, creating a distinction between the system and the environment in which a system exists.

Managing Complexity

As systems engineers, we must build and integrate elements and subsystems to achieve a desired objective. There can be a lot of moving parts: various APIs and communication protocols, various data schemas, various security interfaces to traverse. Our biggest challenge is, How do we manage all this complexity?

Chapter 6

The best tool for the job

The best tool we have to help manage complexity is composition. Functional programming to the rescue!

Our job is to decompose the elements of our system into atomic parts, fit them back together into subsystems and wire them together in a distributed, microservice based environment.

How do we know when have we sufficiently decomposed an element?

A: When we can treat the element as a black box, i.e., when we do not need visibility into the function to understand what it does.

Divide and conquer

FP gives us the tools and techniques we need to divide our monolithic applications into microservices.

In Chapter 4, *SOLID Design in Go*, we learned that our applications should be built from components that follow the Unix philosophy of doing one thing well. We follow the same precepts when building microservices. Furthermore, following the **Single Responsibility Principle (SRP)** we treat each microservice as a separate entity that, whose entire life cycle is kept separate within its predefined boundaries. This decoupling of our microservices is what allows us to create, move and restart our microservice, isolated from its surroundings.

> "This is the Unix philosophy: Write programs that do one thing and do it well. Write programs to work together." - Doug McIlroy

Designing for state management

Often, we find that application APIs are designed properly, giving the illusion that the application services are stateless. However, upon closer examination we find problems with their architecture.

Add a microservice

When they add one microservice it looks like this:

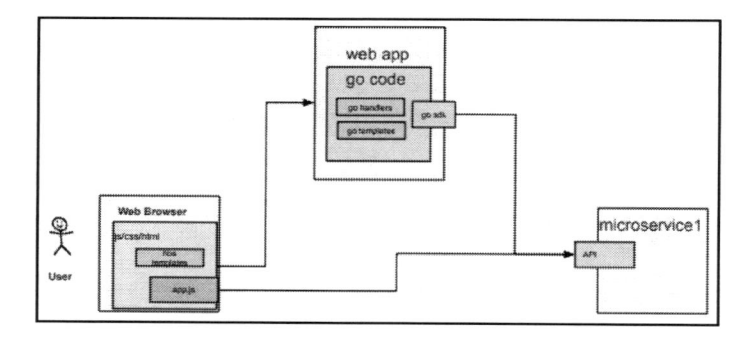

When they add two more it looks like this:

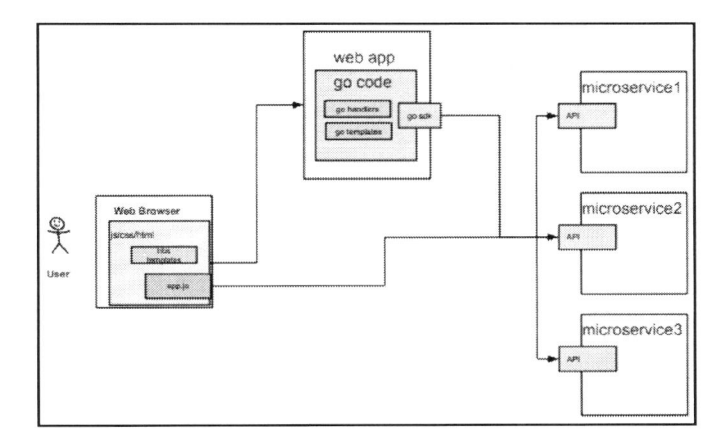

They are feeling good about their architecture until they launch their application and onboard users.

Problems begin to appear:

- Scalability
- Availability
- State management
- Data integrity issues

Rather than creating a stateless architecture, what really happened was that they pushed their application state down to a single database, which only complicated their issues.

Applying FP at the Architectural Level

All of their so supposedly stateless microservices are now coupled to the single, shared monolithic database.

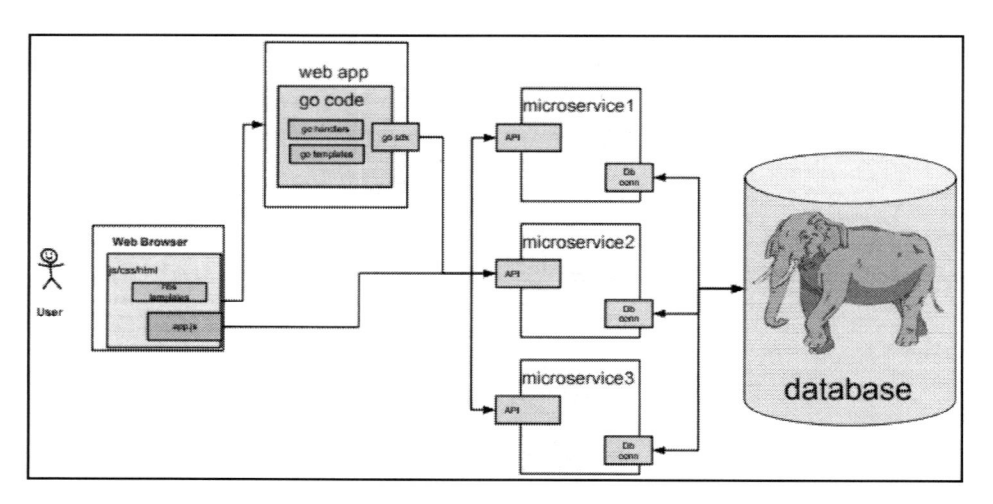

This is what they should have designed...

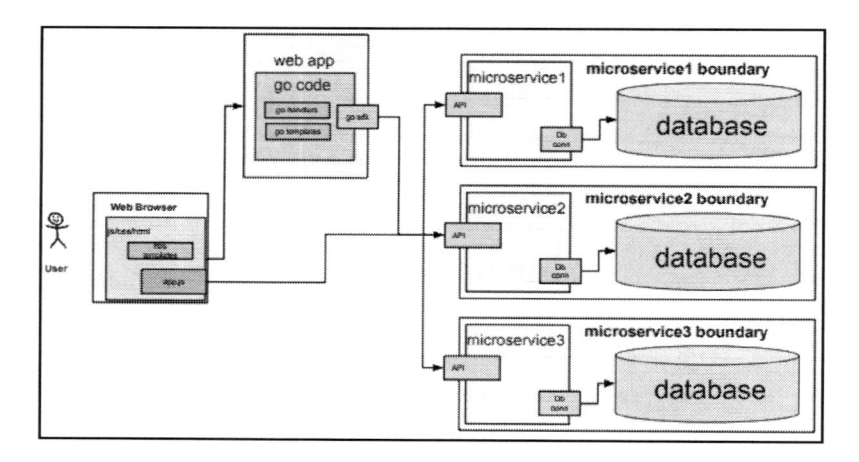

... where each microservice owns their own data. Lookup tables can be shared and managed with database replication, but the data in their domain remains isolated.

FP influenced architectures

Let's discuss a few popular architectures that borrow ideas from FP.

- Domain driven design (DDD)
- Event based architectures
- CQRS
- Functional reactive architecture

Let's start with DDD.

> Other names for DDD include Hexagonal Architecture, Clean Architecture, Ports and Adapters, Onion Architecture and Applicative-Style-Architecture. We'll call it DDD or layered architecture.

Domain Driven Design

In order to create good software, we must understand our customer's business. We cannot create a prospect management software application unless we have a good understanding of how a sales pipeline works; We must understand the domain of sales. This is what **Domain-Driven Design** (DDD) is about. Look for layered application architecture diagram later in this chapter. What's in the center?

A firm understanding of our business domain and our requirements is the key to successfully engineering a system solution.

In this model we consider two main layers. The inside, with applicative use case handlers, and business domain logic and the outside, with all our infrastructure code, with database connections, and messaging.

Combining this model with the dependency inversion principle which states that high level modules should not depend on low level modules. We see that our dependencies should always point inwards towards the domain layer.

Interactions between those two areas are achieved by ports and adapters. Clients requests or events arrive from the outside world at an API port and the technology specific adapter converts it into a function call or message that can be passed into the application layer.

Dependency rule

One issue that we soon face when building large Go applications is how to manage our dependencies. The larger your Go application gets, the more likely we are to encounter cyclic dependency errors unless our design accounts for the dependency rule.

What is the dependency rule and why does the Go compiler deem it so important?

The dependency rule says that source code in a lower-level layer can make use of code in higher-level layers yet higher-level layers may not make use of code in lower-level layers. Dependencies may only point in one direction.

What's the difference between a lower-level and a higher-level layer?

Consider the following diagram:

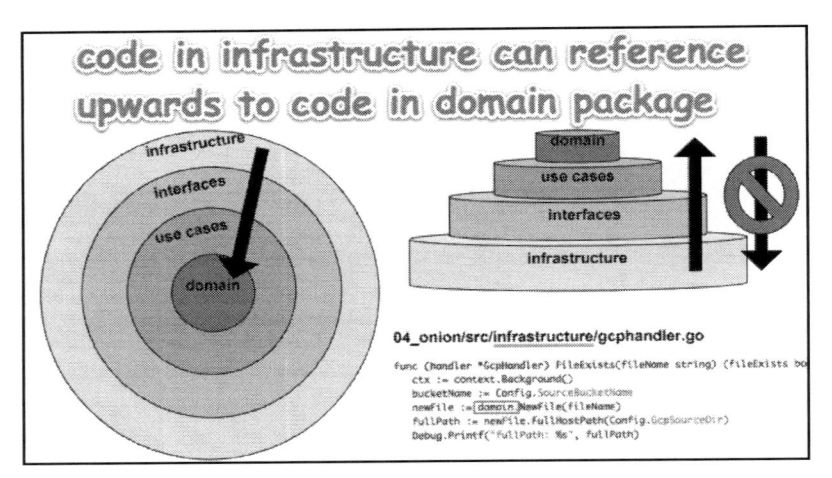

> We'll see the code above in action later in this chapter.

In functional terms, the dependency rule says that if function A (from package A) calls function B (from package B), then function B cannot call any function from package A.

However, the flow of application control could go in nearly any direction (between packages).

In practical terms, when writing a CRM application, we might find that our marketing campaign component may need to reference a function in our opportunity component. If our opportunity component needs to reference a function in our campaign component, then we could experience a circular dependency error.

Cyclic dependency

A cyclic dependency is a compilation error in Go. It indicates that our code has broken the dependency rule. It occurs when a package imports another package that in turn imports the original package. This can occur from package A to B to A or any combination that results in package A getting imported anywhere down the call chain.

Working code

Let's look at some example code to illustrate this concept. First, let's look at the working code. The `packageb` package has one, simple public function and no imports:

dependency-rule-good/src/packagea/featurea.go

```
package packageb

func Btask() {
   println("B")
}
```

The `packagea` package has one, simple public function and imports `packageb`:

```
// dependency-rule-good/src/packageb/featureb.go

package packagea

import b "packageb"

func Atask() {
   println("A")
   b.Btask()
}
```

Here's our main function where we run `Atask` from `packagea`:

```
// dependency-rule-good/main.go

package main

import a "packagea"

func main() {
   a.Atask()
}
```

Output:

```
A
B
```

Code with cyclic dependency error

This time, we will import `packagea` into `featureb.go`:

```
// circulardep/src/packageb/featureb.go

package packageb

import a "packagea"

func Btask() {
   println("B")
   a.Atask()
}
```

The `featurea.go` file remains unchanged:

```
package packagea

import b "packageb"

func Atask() {
   println("A")
   b.Btask()
}
```

The `main.go` file also remains unchanged:

```
package main

import a "packagea"

func main() {
    a.Atask()
}
```

The following is the output:

```
import cycle not allowed
package main
    imports packagea
    imports packageb
    imports packagea
```

We violated the dependency rule when we imported `packagea` into `featureb.go`.

The Golang difference

If you have spent most of your time up to now programming in other languages such as Ruby, you may be surprised when you get cyclic dependency errors.

Why are there no cyclic dependency errors in a language like Ruby?

First, Ruby is an interpreted language, so we will never get a compile error. Furthermore, Ruby determines the scope by namespaces. As long as Ruby has a unique reference to a block of code and that code has been loaded into memory, there should be no dependency reference errors.

Does that mean Ruby is better than Go in this respect?

It depends. Do we want to develop as quickly as possible without concerning ourselves with the dependency rule? Do we expect our application to grow complex over time? Do we want to put more time into design at the beginning of our project?

Go not only encourages us to write better code, like this instance, Go makes us write better code.

Solution for cyclic dependencies

How can we write Go code that adheres to the dependency rule and still reflect multi-directional flow of control that we frequently encounter in a business application logic?

We can accomplish this using a layered architecture, an interface-driven development and a form of the Hollywood Principle called dependency injection.

Let's take it one step at a time.

Domain Driven Design

We can use a layered domain driven architecture as a tool for structuring our large-scale functional programs in a modular and composable manner. This architecture helps us visualize the separate application concerns and enables us to write Go code whose source code dependencies only point inwards.

All references, that is, import statements must point inwards. An import **domain** statement can be found in all other packages. Import **use cases** can be found in the **interfaces** and **infrastructure** packages. Import **interfaces** can be found in the **infrastructure** package and no package (except the `import_test` package that we'll cover later) is permitted to import the **infrastructure** package:

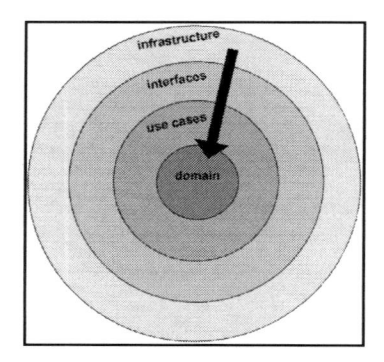

The preceding diagram is somewhat of a paradox. The more we move inwards, the higher level our software becomes. The **domain** entities are high-level concepts. Whereas, the more we move outwards, the more low-level our software is. The **infrastructure** is where we interact with the filesystem, cloud provider, or other data repositories, for example, databases or cloud storage.

When we adhere to the dependency rule, our source code dependencies only point inwards. Our system becomes highly cohesive, that is, components with closely related responsibilities are separated into the appropriate layer, thereby increasing cohesion. By programming to interfaces and leveraging dependency injection, we create a loose coupling that enables us to swap out pieces of the system without affecting other components.

Interface-driven development

Recall the following quote from Chapter 4, *SOLID Design in Go*?

> "It makes sense to categorize a thing by its abilities, because everything is defined by its actions."

Since this is a book about functional programming, now would be a good time to mention that a major benefit of using interfaces is that they allow us to group our application's functions in order to model real-life behaviors.

In the previous chapter, we modeled the behavior of a duck:

```
type StrokeBehavior interface {
        PaddleFoot(strokeSupply *int)
}

type EatBehavior interface {
        EatBug(strokeSupply *int)
}
```

In this chapter, we will look at manipulating files in the **Google Cloud Platform** (**GCP**). Our interface defines the four behaviors of interest:

```
type GcpHandler interface {
   ListBuckets(flowType domain.FlowType, projectId string) (buckets []domain.Bucket, err error)
   FileExists(fileName string) (fileExists bool, err error)
   DownloadFile(fileName string) (success bool, err error)
   UploadFile(fileName string) (success bool, err error)
}
```

Let's not get confused with the `interface` terminology. We just spoke about a Go interface, whereas when we talk about the interface layer in a layered architecture that is a way of layering our application into separate, cohesive concerns.

This chapter will focus on the mechanics of how we accomplish this task using Go.

What are our best options for decoupling dependencies between high-level and low-level layers?

We'll look at two-candidate solutions, the observer pattern and dependency injection in the upcoming sections.

Hollywood principle

Actors suffer through crushing blows of humiliation in their quest to climb one step higher in the Hollywood hierarchy. Who determines whether an actor winds up as a stage hand or Brad Pitt? The casting director.

Actors audition for a part in a movie and are advised not to ask whether they got the part. The fact is that if the director wants you, he'll find you. That's the Hollywood principle of *"Don't call us. We'll call you"*.

In traditional programming, the actor would audition and then ask the director if they got the part. That's not how the Hollywood Principle works.

What is required for this inversion of control?

We require an API that exposes public functions and a framework where dependent components are bound to a subject during runtime.

What are our framework options?

Observer pattern

The observer pattern is one option. It works by injecting a callback object (observer) into the subject to be observed. The subject simply raises an event in all observers when its state changes.

How the observer reacts to the event is outside the scope or care of the subject.

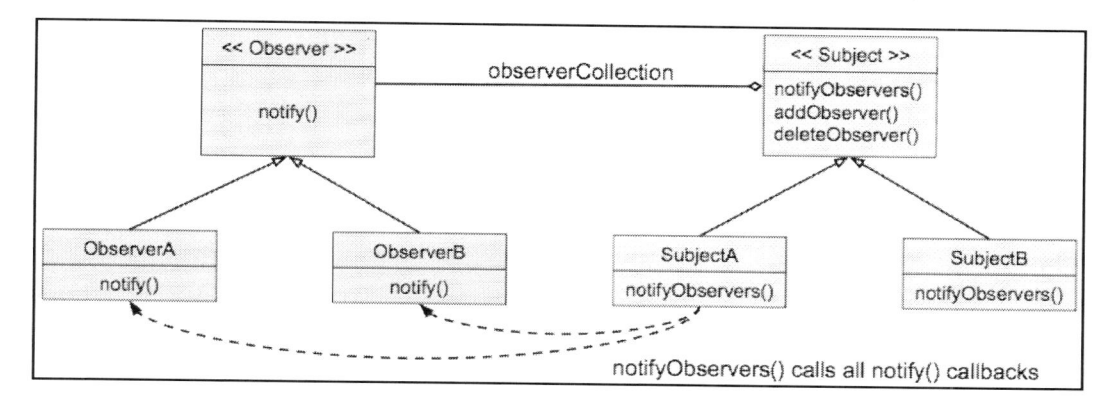

Here's an implementation of that pattern:

```
//main.go

package main

import (
    . "observer"
)

func main() {

    subject := Subject{}
    oa := Observable{Name: "A"}
    ob := Observable{Name: "B"}
    subject.AddObserver(&Observer{})
    subject.NotifyObservers(oa, ob)

    oc := Observable{Name: "C"}
    subject.NotifyObservers(oa, ob, oc)

    subject.DeleteObserver(&Observer{})
    subject.NotifyObservers(oa, ob, oc)

    od := Observable{Name: "D"}
    subject.NotifyObservers(oa, ob, oc, od)
}
```

The observer implements the `Callback` interface. We implement a `Notify` method for the observer receiver. `Notify` is the observer's callback function:

```
// src/observer.go

package observer

type Observable struct {
   Name string
}

type Observer struct {
}

func (ob *Observer) Notify(o *Observable) {
   println(o.Name)
}

type Callback interface {
   Notify(o *Observable)
}
```

The subject implements three methods: `AddObserver`, `DeleteObserver`, and `NotifyObservers`:

```
// src/subject.go

package observer

type Subject struct {
   callbacks []Callback
}

func (o *Subject) AddObserver(c Callback) {
   o.callbacks = append(o.callbacks, c)
}
func (o *Subject) DeleteObserver(c Callback) {
   o.callbacks = append(o.callbacks, c)

   newCallbacks := []Callback{}
   for _, cb := range o.callbacks {
      if cb != c {
         newCallbacks = append(newCallbacks, cb)
      }
   }
   o.callbacks = newCallbacks
}
```

```
func (o *Subject) NotifyObservers(oes ...Observable) {
    for _, oe := range oes {
        for _, c := range o.callbacks {
            c.Notify(&oe)
        }
    }
}
```

The `AddObserver` method is where the subscription, that is, the relationship between the observer and the subject occurs.

The `NotifyObservers` method acts as a simple service locator. It iterates through its list of subscribed observers and executes its callbacks.

The following is the output:

```
A
B
A
B
C
```

When we remove the observer from our service locator by executing `subject.DeleteObserver(&Observer{})`, all subsequent notifications have no effect since there are no observers subscribed to respond to the published events.

Dependency injection

Dependency injection (**DI**) is a form of Inversion of Control and also impacts the flow of control in an application. Although the observer pattern's callback mechanism can modify the flow at many times and in many places in an application, DI typically performs the flow of control configuration during application initialization.

Since this chapter is mainly about a layered architecture and the management of dependencies to prevent circular dependency errors, we will not explore pub/sub architectures and the observer pattern. Instead, we will choose DI to reconcile our dependencies in our main function.

Applying FP at the Architectural Level

A cloud bucket application

Pictures are worth a thousand words, right? Let's use some diagrams to help describe our basic application architecture.

Next, we will see the high-level architecture of our application that we'll call `onion`. (An onion has layers, so we'll use that metaphor to remind us of the layers.) It moves files from the **SOURCE Cloud Bucket** to the local filesystem and then to the **SINK Cloud Bucket**.

The purple API box in the following diagram represents the web services API that our `onion.go` application exposes for the administrative user. The red API represents the Google Cloud Platform storage API:

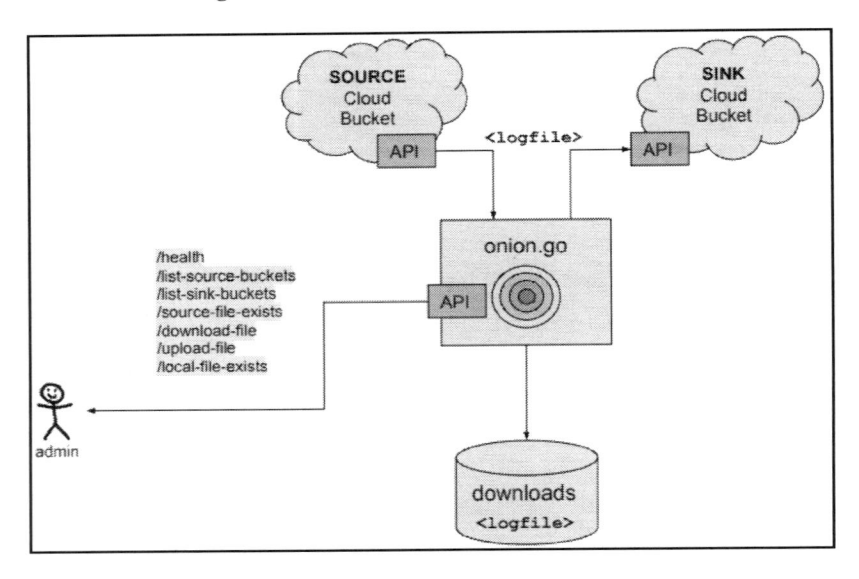

The admin will direct the `onion.go` application to download a log file from the **SOURCE Cloud Bucket** to the local filesystem. The admin can subsequently tell `onion.go` to upload the file to the **SINK Cloud Bucket**.

The purple paths, for example, `/health`, `/list-source-buckets`, and `/list-sink-buckets` are the web service APIs that our onion application exposes to the administrative user.

Directory structure

The directory structure of our application looks like this:

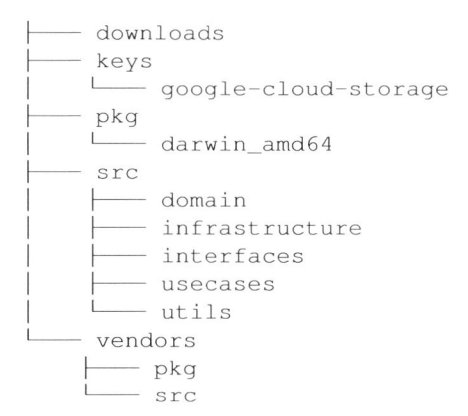

```
├── downloads
├── keys
│   └── google-cloud-storage
├── pkg
│   └── darwin_amd64
├── src
│   ├── domain
│   ├── infrastructure
│   ├── interfaces
│   ├── usecases
│   └── utils
└── vendors
    ├── pkg
    └── src
```

The source code for our project is `main.go`, which lives in the project root. The rest of our application is separated into directories corresponding to our application's architectural layers (domain, use cases, interfaces, and infrastructure).

Before looking into the details of the other layers, let's see how we tie them together. That work is done in our `main.go` file. We start by initializing our configuration options with `GetOptions()`.

main.go

Let's have a look at the contents of `main.go`:

```go
func init() {
    GetOptions()
    if Config.LogDebugInfo {
        InitLog("trace-debug-log.txt", os.Stdout, os.Stdout, os.Stderr)
    } else {
        InitLog("trace-log.txt", ioutil.Discard, os.Stdout, os.Stderr)
    }
    // use a filename in a downloads subdirectory
    fileName = os.Getenv("TEST_FILENAME")
    if len(fileName) == 0 {
        fileName = defaultFileName  // CloudflareLogFilename(time.Now())
    }
    // . . .
    HandlePanic(os.Chdir(Config.ProjectRoot))
}
```

We direct `Debug` statements to standard out if our `log_debug_info` setting is true; otherwise, we discard them. We hardcode the name of the log file for simplicity, but we could have used a config value or a function call to dynamically generate the filename.

The last thing we do in our `init` function is to change our application's working directory to our project root directory. If there is an error doing so, the `HandlePanic()` function from our `utils` package will display a stack trace for debugging purposes.

We find the `HandlePanic()` function in our utils package. Unlike most functions, we do not return an error from `HandlePanic()`. We handle it by adding the filename and line number of the source code file where the error originated and alert.

func HandlePanic

Here is our `HandlePanic()` function:

```
func HandlePanic(err error) {
    if err != nil {
        _, filePath, lineNo, _ := runtime.Caller(1)
        _, fileName := path.Split(filePath)
        msg := fmt.Sprintf("[file:%s line:%d]: %s", fileName, lineNo, err.Error())
        panic(msg)
    }
}
```

It is worth noting that we import our utils package by prefacing it with a period like this:

```
import . "utils"
```

This allows us to reference public functions (starting with capital letters) without including the `utils` package name.

Dependency injection

In the decorator chapter, we looked at inversion of control. We saw how a decorator, for example, the **FaultTolerance**, can be injected into the flow (of main) by our decorator framework using dependency injection.

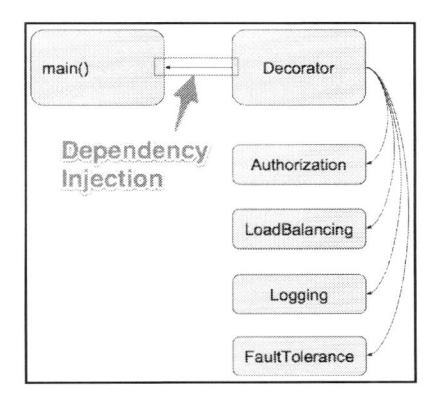

We will use the same concept of dependency injection to wire up our application and to provide control over function calls and the data that flows between our interfaces.

Remember our electrician analogy? This is a great time to revisit the concept. Our work is much like the electrician who first turns off the power to the house: who lays the wires and subsequently turns the power on. After the power is turned on, our electrician can test the switches to verify that the home's electrical system has been wired properly.

We create the interfaces that connect the layers of our application. In the main function we instantiate our interactors. Our interactors use the interfaces through which we call functions and thereby control the flow of data between the parts of our loosely coupled system.

We have two interactors--one for interacting with the Google Cloud Platform, the `GcpInteractor`, and the other, `LocalInteractor`, for reading and writing files to the local filesystem.

func main()

Now, let's go through the `main()` function:

```
func main() {
   gcpi, err := infrastructure.GetGcpInteractor()
   HandlePanic(errors.Wrap(err, "unable to get gcp interactor"))
   li, err := infrastructure.GetLocalInteractor()
   HandlePanic(errors.Wrap(err, "unable to get local interactor"))

   wsh = WebserviceHandler{}
   wsh.GcpInteractor = gcpi
   wsh.LocalInteractor = li
```

We inject both our interactors into our web service handler, which allows our admin user to manipulate our repositories via our public web service APIs, for example, `/list-source-buckets`.

Note that DI occurs at object creation time. Contrast DI with parameterized functions or the use of a context--that contains all pertinent information for a single function invocation—that can be passed through a chain of function calls.

DI typically occurs once during the lifetime of an application. Parameterized functions and the passing of context, occurs many times.

Layers in the architecture

We are building an application framework based on a layered achitecture that will allow us to grow our application with less difficulty.

After building a solid application framework based on a layered architecture, we'll return to pure functional programming topics and techniques in subsequent chapters.

We will separate our Onion application into four layers:

- Domain
- Use cases
- Interfaces
- Infrastructure

We will discuss them in detail in the upcoming sections.

Domain layer

The following diagram illustrates the layers in our layered architecture. The arrow indicates that we only import packages in one direction. Domain will never import from use cases, interfaces, or infrastructure. The red background in the **domain** layer indicates that we're looking into that layer in this section:

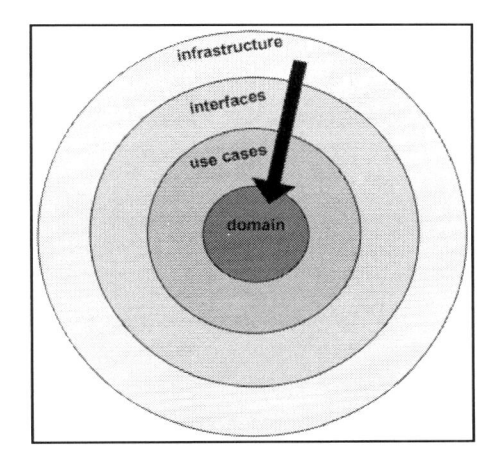

The **domain** layer is where we define our business entities. These are the core business objects that we would initially think of when defining the essence of what our application does.

From our following type definitions, we quickly glean that our application moves files to and from buckets of a cloud storage provider:

```
type (
    HostProvider int
    FlowType    int
)

type CloudStorage struct {
    HostProvider HostProvider //Host location for log files, e.g., google cloud bucket
    ProjectId    string       //Project Id for this GCP storage account
    FlowType     FlowType     //source or sink
}

type LocalRepository interface {
    FileExists(fileName string) (fileExists bool, err error)
}
```

Applying FP at the Architectural Level

```
type BucketRepository interface {
   List(projectId string) (buckets []Bucket, err error)
   FileExists(fileName string) (fileExists bool, err error)
   DownloadFile(fileName string) (success bool, err error)
   UploadFile(fileName string) (success bool, err error)
}

type FileRepository interface {
   Store(file File)
   FindById(id int) File
}

type Bucket struct {
   Name     string `json:"name"`
}
type Buckets struct {
   Buckets []Bucket `json:"buckets"`
}
```

The `LocalRepository` and `BucketRepository` do not refer to specific implementations. The **domain** layer does not care whether the bucket is Google bucket or an AWS bucket. The term repository is used. To the **domain** layer a repository is just a place in which files are persisted and retrieved.

Before moving on, let's look at the contents of the log files we're moving around:

```
// downloads/eventset1.jsonl

{"eventId":1000,"timestamp":1500321544026000125,"description":"something bad
happened","userId":997776,"country":"AF","deviceType":"UD10","ip":"19.123.3
.22","srcPort":80}{"eventId":1001,"timestamp":1500321544026000126,"descript
ion":"something pretty bad
happened","userId":429444,"country":"AL","deviceType":"KG90","ip":"44.74.43
.30","srcPort":80}{"eventId":1002,"timestamp":1500321544026000127,"descript
ion":"something super bad
happened","userId":458696,"country":"NZ","deviceType":"VM30","ip":"101.4.66
.210","srcPort":8000}
```

This `.jsonl` file comprises three JSON objects.

The format of each line is defined in our `domain/log_file.go` file:

```go
// domain/log_file.go
type User struct {
    UserId     int    `json:"userId"`
    Country    string `json:"country"`
    DeviceType string `json:"deviceType"`
    IP         string `json:"ip"`
    SrcPort    int    `json:"srcPort"`
}

type LogFile struct {
    EventId     int    `json:"eventId"`
    Timestamp   int64  `json:"timestamp"`
    Description string `json:"description"`
    User
}
```

We define one function to convert our JSON text into a Go struct:

```go
func NewLogFile(logfileJson string) (logFile *LogFile, err error) {
    err = json.Unmarshal([]byte(logfileJson), &logFile)
    if err != nil {
        return nil, errors.Wrap(err, "unable to unmarshal json")
    }
    return
}
```

We define a method to operate on a `LogFile` object, transforming it into a JSON text representation:

```go
func (lf *LogFile) ToJson() (logFileJson string, err error) {
    logFileBytes, err := json.Marshal(lf)
    if err != nil {
        return "", errors.Wrap(err, "unable to marshal json")
    }
    logFileJson = string(logFileBytes)
    return
}
```

It's worth noting that in both cases we wrap the underlying error with our own more specific error message before returning the error to our function's caller.

Applying FP at the Architectural Level

The fewer packages our application references the easier the job will be to maintain our application. Third-party packages can be frequently updated, which is usually a good thing, for example, if they fix a security issue, but can be a bad thing for our application if they change their public interfaces in such a way as to break our application.

The `github.com/pkg/errors` package is one of the few packages that is worth the trouble. It allows us to add context to the error message without changing or hiding the original error message.

> Package errors (https://github.com/pkg/errors) provide simple error handling primitives. You can also refer to: https://dave.cheney.net/2016/04/27/dont-just-check-errors-handle-them-gracefully.

The `Write` method allows us to write the content of a `LogFile` object to disk:

```go
func (lf *LogFile) Write(logFilename, contents string) (err error) {
    overwrite := true
    flag := os.O_WRONLY | os.O_CREATE
    if overwrite {
        flag |= os.O_TRUNC
    } else {
        flag |= os.O_EXCL
    }
    osFile, err := os.OpenFile(logFilename, flag, 0666)
    if err != nil {
        return errors.Wrapf(err, "unable to open %s", logFilename)
    }
    bytes := []byte(contents)
    n, err := osFile.Write(bytes)
    if err == nil && n < len(bytes) {
        err = io.ErrShortWrite
        return errors.Wrapf(io.ErrShortWrite, "not all bytes written for %s", logFilename)
    }
    if err1 := osFile.Close(); err1 != nil {
        return errors.Wrapf(err, "unable to close %s", logFilename)
    }
    return
}
```

In `file.go`, we define our `File` struct, which comprises file attributes. For example, filename and bytes. It also has the `LogFile` defined as an embedded field.

```
// domain/file.go

type File struct {
    Id          int
    Name        string  `json:"name"`
    ErrorMsg    string  `json:"error"`
    Contents    LogFile `json:"logFile"`
    Bytes       []byte  `json:"bytes"`
}
```

We also define structs for manipulating the `.jsonl` files that we receive from (and send to) GCP buckets:

```
type CloudFile struct {
    Name        string `json:"name"`
}
type CloudFiles struct {
    Names       []CloudFile
}

type CloudPath struct {
    Path        string `json:"path"`
}
type CloudPaths struct {
    Paths []CloudPath
}
```

The `file.go` file also contains the following functions for manipulating a file:

- `NewFile`
- `NameOnly`
- `Exists`
- `Path`
- `Read`
- `Write`
- `Parse`

Our `api.go` file defines the structs we use to communicate whether a file exists or whether operations performed on our files were successful:

```
// domain/api.go

type Existence struct {
   Exists    bool `json:"exists"`
}

type Outcome struct {
   Success   bool `json:"success"`
}

type OutcomeAndMsg struct {
   Success   bool   `json:"success"`
   Message   string `json:"message"`
}

type MultiStatus struct {
   OutcomeAndMsgs []OutcomeAndMsg
}
```

Use cases layer

Let's look at the use cases layer now:

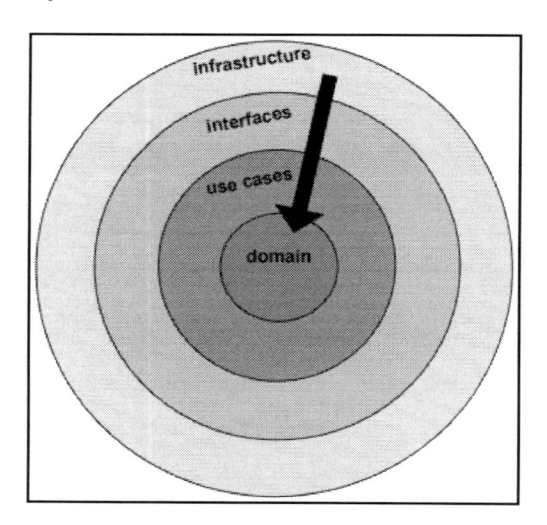

The use cases layer has to do with what the user wants to do, that is, their use cases for using this application.

It references the repositories, local filesystem, and the source and sink buckets in the cloud.

We can directly reference domain entities and we can reference interface entities via the local and GCP interactors.

If we can reference an infrastructure entity in any way, then our design is broken. For example, we should be able to swap out the Google Cloud Platform storage APIs with AWS S3 bucket APIs and without our use case layer changing in any way.

In our application, a user may want to check whether a local file exists or get the file, in order to upload it to a bucket in GCP.

The `LocalInteractor` struct controls the flow to and from the local filesystem:

```
// usecases/usecases.go
type LocalInteractor struct {
    LocalRepository domain.LocalRepository
}

func (interactor *LocalInteractor) LocalFileExists(fileName string)
(fileExists bool, err error) {
    return interactor.LocalRepository.FileExists(fileName)
}
```

The `GcpInteractor` struct controls the flow of files and information regarding files in a cloud bucket. *Doing things* with buckets includes things such as listing the files in a bucket, checking whether a file exists, uploading, and downloading a file:

```
type GcpInteractor struct {
    SourceBucketRepository domain.BucketRepository
    SinkBucketRepository domain.BucketRepository
}
```

There are two types of buckets. One acts as a source of files and the other acts as the sink (or destination) for files.

Note that we can reference the `BucketRepository` struct from the `usecases` package, but there will be no reference to `usecases` in any file in the `domain` package:

```
func (interactor *GcpInteractor) ListSinkBuckets(projectId string) (buckets
[]domain.Bucket, err error) {
    return interactor.SinkBucketRepository.List(projectId)
}
```

The `GcpInteractor` methods in `usecases.go` define the use cases for manipulating files in our Google Cloud account:

```
func (interactor *GcpInteractor) SourceFileExists(fileName string) 
(fileExists bool, err error) {
    return interactor.SourceBucketRepository.FileExists(fileName)
}
```

The `DownloadFile` and `UploadFile` methods are arguably our most important ones:

```
func (interactor *GcpInteractor) DownloadFile(fileName string) (success 
bool, err error) {
    return interactor.SourceBucketRepository.DownloadFile(fileName)
}

func (interactor *GcpInteractor) UploadFile(fileName string) (success bool, 
err error) {
    return interactor.SinkBucketRepository.UploadFile(fileName)
}
```

The logic in this layer is very lean. When we develop more complex applications that have business rules to enforce, these use cases would likely be the best place to put them.

For example, if we had implemented security in our application, we could define the following rules as:

- Only users in the sink group or above can list the files in a sink bucket
- Only users in the `source-downloads` group can download files
- Only users in the `super-admins` group can upload files

Then we'd likely put our authorization logic here in the use cases layer.

Compatible interfaces

In order for the dependency injection to work, our application must have compatible interfaces, for example, `FileExists(fileName string) (fileExists bool, err error)` in `domain.go` and `gcphandler.go`.

The line `return interactor.SourceBucketRepository.FileExists(fileName)` is delegating the `FileExists` behavior to the interface, which is implemented by `gcphandler.go` and then injected into the interactor. Below, we define our interface for our BucketRepository:

```
// domain/domain.go

type BucketRepository interface {
    List(projectId string) (buckets []Bucket, err error)
    FileExists(fileName string) (fileExists bool, err error)
    DownloadFile(fileName string) (success bool, err error)
    UploadFile(fileName string) (success bool, err error)
}
```

The `BucketRepository` interface is compatible with the `GcpHandler` interface:

```
// interfaces/gcpstorage.go

type GcpHandler interface {
    ListBuckets(flowType domain.FlowType, projectId string) (buckets []domain.Bucket, err error)
    FileExists(fileName string) (fileExists bool, err error)
    DownloadFile(fileName string) (success bool, err error)
    UploadFile(fileName string) (success bool, err error)
}
// infrastructure/gcphandler.go
func (handler *GcpHandler) FileExists(fileName string) (fileExists bool, err error) {
    ...
    br, err := handler.Client.Bucket(bucketName).Object(fullPath).NewReader(ctx)
    ...
    return true, err
}
```

Let's not forget the wiring up that occurred in main, that associated the `/source-file-extsts` URL end point with the `GcpInteractor`:

main.go

```
func main() {
    gcpi, err := infrastructure.GetGcpInteractor()
    ...
    wsh = WebserviceHandler{}
    wsh.GcpInteractor = gcpi
    ...
      {Api{wsh.SourceFileExists, "/source-file-exists"},
```

```
"fileName="+fileName}
```

This is the crux of the framework that performs the dependency injection and allows us to write code that spans the layers of our application without violating the dependency rule.

Interfaces layer

In this section, we will be looking at the interfaces layer:

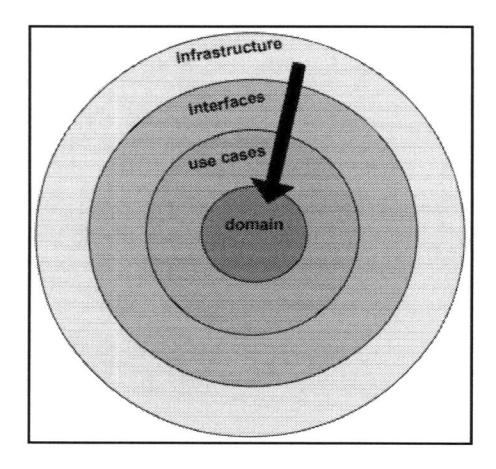

The interfaces layer provides a means to communicate with external repositories, for example, cloud bucket or local files storage. If our external repositories need to communicate events back to our application, for example, out of disk space, these events would flow through this interfaces layer.

We begin by defining our interface, that is, the functions that our interfaces layer supports.

This file contains handlers for interfacing with the **Google Cloud Platform's (GCP)** storage API:

```
// interfaces/gcpstorage.go

type GcpHandler interface {
    ListBuckets(flowType domain.FlowType, projectId string) (buckets []domain.Bucket, err error)
    FileExists(fileName string) (fileExists bool, err error)
    DownloadFile(fileName string) (success bool, err error)
    UploadFile(fileName string) (success bool, err error)
}
```

To simplify our implementation, we'll only define one `GcpHandler` interface for both source and sink buckets. The consequence is that `DownloadFile` will be available, but not useful for the sink bucket and `UploadFile` will not be useful for the source bucket.

Next, we define a structure in which we can register our interface handlers:

```
type GcpRepo struct {
    gcpHandlers map[string]GcpHandler
    gcpHandler  GcpHandler
}

type SourceBucketRepo GcpRepo
type SinkBucketRepo GcpRepo
```

We have two types of GCP repositories. A source bucket and a sink bucket.

Earlier, we provided the interface that satisfies the needs of the use cases. In the following code, we implement the code that injects that actual implementation (at run time):

```
func NewSourceBucketRepo(gcpHandlers map[string]GcpHandler) *SourceBucketRepo {
    bucketRepo := new(SourceBucketRepo)
    bucketRepo.gcpHandlers = gcpHandlers
    bucketRepo.gcpHandler = gcpHandlers["SourceBucketRepo"]
    return bucketRepo
}

func (repo *SourceBucketRepo) List(projectId string) (buckets []domain.Bucket, err error) {
    return repo.gcpHandler.ListBuckets(domain.SourceFlow, projectId)
}

func (repo *SourceBucketRepo) FileExists(fileName string) (fileExists bool, err error) {
    return repo.gcpHandler.FileExists(fileName)
}

func (repo *SourceBucketRepo) DownloadFile(fileName string) (success bool, err error) {
    return repo.gcpHandler.DownloadFile(fileName)
}
// UploadFile is not operational for a source bucket
func (repo *SourceBucketRepo) UploadFile(fileName string) (success bool, err error) {
    return false, nil
}
```

Applying FP at the Architectural Level

How can the code above be improved?

Our NewSinkBucketRepo function could be rewritten as follows:

```
func NewSourceBucketRepo(gcpHandlers map[string]GcpHandler)
*SourceBucketRepo {
    return &SourceBucketRepo{
        gcpHandlers: gcpHandlers,
        gcpHandler: gcpHandlers["SourceBucketRepo"],
    }
}
```

See the difference? Note that, unlike in C, it's perfectly OK to return the address of our local variable `SourceBucketRepo`. When we return our `SourceBucketRepo` composite literal, the expression is evaluated and Go will allocate a fresh instance of `SourceBucketRepo`. So, the storage associated with our `SourceBucketRepo` variable will survive after our `NewSourceBucketRepo` function returns.

The code for wiring up the injection to handle the sink bucket dependencies is very similar to the source bucket code:

```
func NewSinkBucketRepo(gcpHandlers map[string]GcpHandler) *SinkBucketRepo {
    return &SinkBucketRepo{
        gcpHandlers: gcpHandlers,
        gcpHandler: gcpHandlers["SinkBucketRepo"],
    }
}

func (repo *SinkBucketRepo) List(projectId string) (buckets
[]domain.Bucket, err error) {
    return repo.gcpHandler.ListBuckets(domain.SinkFlow, projectId)
}

func (repo *SinkBucketRepo) FileExists(fileName string) (fileExists bool,
err error) {
    return repo.gcpHandler.FileExists(fileName)
}

func (repo *SinkBucketRepo) DownloadFile(fileName string) (success bool,
err error) {
    return false, nil
}

func (repo *SinkBucketRepo) UploadFile(fileName string) (success bool, err
error) {
    return repo.gcpHandler.UploadFile(fileName)
```

```
}

func (repo *SinkBucketRepo) ListFileNamesToFetch(fileName string)
(cloudFiles domain.CloudFiles, err error) {
    return cloudFiles, err
}
```

The local storage interface is similar to the GCP bucket interface. Both have a means to check whether a file exists and to retrieve a file. We have added some logic that shows that this would be a good place to implement a caching mechanism in order to increase performance (at the expense of additional RAM requirements):

```
// interfaces/localstorage.go

type LocalHandler interface {
    FileExists(fileName string) (fileExists bool, err error)
}

var FileCache map[string][]string   //slice of json values, one for each LogFile

type LocalRepo struct {
    localHandlers map[string]LocalHandler
    localHandler  LocalHandler
    fileCache     map[string]domain.File
}

type LocalFileSystemRepo LocalRepo
```

We see the same dependency injection logic in the `NewLocalRepo()` function:

```
func NewLocalRepo(localHandlers map[string]LocalHandler)
*LocalFileSystemRepo {
    localRepo := new(LocalFileSystemRepo)
    localRepo.localHandlers = localHandlers
    localRepo.localHandler = localHandlers["LocalFileSystemRepo"]
    return localRepo
}
```

Next, we implement the `FileExists()` function:

```
func (repo *LocalFileSystemRepo) FileExists(fileName string) (fileExists
bool, err error) {
    return repo.localHandler.FileExists(fileName)
}
```

Applying FP at the Architectural Level

If we want to implement file caching, we could create a `FileCache` global variable in the interfaces layer like this:

```
var FileCache map[string][]string   //slice of json values, one for each LogFile
```

We could initialize it in the `init()` function:

```
func init() {
  FileCache = make(map[string][]string)
}
```

But if we did, what else should we do?

What if two requests occur at the same time to upload a file? What could happen?

What if we implemented a `DeleteFile` function?

Some form of resource locking and race condition mitigation would be needed.

The big win for us is that now we have a place to put this caching logic. The layering helps when the time comes to extend our application's functionality.

Now we'll have a look at the `interfaces/webservice.go` file.

First, let's define an `Api` struct:

```
type Api struct {
    Handler func(res http.ResponseWriter, req *http.Request)
    Url     string
}
```

We've seen how we used the `Api` struct to associate our application endpoints with their corresponding web service implementations.

The `main.go` file defines an `enpoint` struct that embeds this `Api` struct:

```
type endpoint struct {
   Api
   uriExample   string
}
```

In main, we initialize the `endpoints` slice with our web service endpoint (handler and URL):

```
var endpoints = []endpoint{
   {Api{wsh.Health, "/health"}, ""},
   {Api{wsh.ListSourceBuckets, "/list-source-buckets"},
"projectId="+Config.GcpSourceProjectId},
   {Api{wsh.ListSinkBuckets, "/list-sink-buckets"},
"projectId="+Config.GcpSinkProjectId},
   {Api{wsh.SourceFileExists, "/source-file-exists"},
"fileName="+fileName},
   {Api{wsh.DownloadFile, "/download-file"}, "fileName="+fileName},
   {Api{wsh.UploadFile, "/upload-file"}, "fileName="+fileName},
   {Api{wsh.LocalFileExists, "/local-file-exists"}, "fileName="+fileName},
}
```

Later in main, we iterate through our endpoints and associate our URLs with their respective handlers:

```
Info.Println("Example API endpoints:")
{
   for _, ep := range endpoints {
      http.HandleFunc(ep.Api.Url, ep.Api.Handler)
      printApiExample(ep.Api.Url, ep.uriExample)
   }
}
```

We created a `printApiExample()` helper function to print the following in our console:

```
Example API endpoints:
http://localhost:8080/health
http://localhost:8080/list-source-buckets?projectId=rdbx-168418
http://localhost:8080/list-sink-buckets?projectId=rdbx-168418
http://localhost:8080/source-file-exists?fileName=eventset1.jsonl
http://localhost:8080/download-file?fileName=eventset1.jsonl
http://localhost:8080/upload-file?fileName=eventset1.jsonl
http://localhost:8080/local-file-exists?fileName=eventset1.jsonl
http://localhost:8080/get-local-file?fileName=eventset1.jsonl
```

Next, we define our interactor interfaces. There is only one for our local filesystem:

```
type LocalInteractor interface {
   LocalFileExists(fileName string) (fileExists bool, err error)
}
```

Applying FP at the Architectural Level

We define five interfaces for our GCP buckets:

```
type GcpInteractor interface {
    ListSourceBuckets(projectId string) (buckets []domain.Bucket, err error)
    ListSinkBuckets(projectId string) (buckets []domain.Bucket, err error)
    SourceFileExists(fileName string) (fileExists bool, err error)
    DownloadFile(fileName string) (success bool, err error)
    UploadFile(fileName string) (success bool, err error)
}
```

We create a `WebserviceHandler` struct to provide access to both local files and cloud bucket files:

```
type WebserviceHandler struct {
    LocalInteractor LocalInteractor
    GcpInteractor   GcpInteractor
}
```

Health API

Health is a useful, simple utility web service, which is defined as follows:

```
func (handler WebserviceHandler) Health(res http.ResponseWriter, req *http.Request) {
    res.WriteHeader(http.StatusOK)
    res.Header().Set("Content-Type", "application/json")
    io.WriteString(res, `{"alive": true}`)
}
```

If we want the JSON results, it is defined as follows:

```
$ curl http://localhost:8080/health
{"alive": true}
```

If we only need the HTTP header status code, it is defined as follows:

```
$ curl -s -I http://localhost:8080/health
HTTP/1.1 200 OK
Date: Sun, 23 Jul 2017 22:19:03 GMT
Content-Length: 15
Content-Type: text/plain; charset=utf-8
```

File exists APIs

Here's a web service method for checking whether a local file exists:

```
func (handler WebserviceHandler) LocalFileExists(res http.ResponseWriter,
req *http.Request) {
   fileName := req.FormValue("fileName")
   exists, err := handler.LocalInteractor.LocalFileExists(fileName)
   handleExists(sf("Running LocalFileExists for fileName: %s...",
fileName), "find file", req, res, err, exists)
}
```

Here's one for checking whether a file exists in our source cloud bucket:

```
func (handler WebserviceHandler) SourceFileExists(res http.ResponseWriter,
req *http.Request) {
   fileName := req.FormValue("fileName")
   exists, err := handler.GcpInteractor.SourceFileExists(fileName)
   handleExists(sf("Running SourceFileExists for fileName: %s...",
fileName), "file exists", req, res, err, exists)
}
```

Extending functionality

We could easily extend our application by adding `WebserviceHandler` methods that could access both source and sink buckets as well as the local filesystem, all in the same function invocation.

Our design using interfaces is flexible in other ways, too. For example, using a testing configuration setting when starting our application we could instruct our application's main function to use a test mock implementation when wiring up the interactors. This could enable our tests to interact with a speedy test stub bucket interface that provides canned responses to test the control flow within our application rather than taking time to initialize connections and deal with the latency of the network.

Now we'll look at the `interfaces/webservice_helpers.go` file.

First, we define the `sf` variable to be the `fmt.Sprintf` function. This allows us to abbreviate our code, replacing `sf` with `fmt.Sprintf`:

```
var sf = fmt.Sprintf
```

Next, we define one of the few global variables in our application. This is the standard response we return to the web clients when an error is encountered. This value never changes. So, it is for all intents and purposes a constant:

```
var ErrorResponse = []byte("Error")
```

In the following code, we implement a function to determine the format of the data to return to the user:

```
func getFormat(r *http.Request) (format string) {
   //format = r.URL.Query()["format"][0]
   // Hard code json for now
   format = "json"
   return
}
```

Granted, we've hardcoded the value to `json`, but we could have just as easily pulled the value from a query parameter. The idea to remember is that we use a function to return this value. The value returned from the function can change from one request to the next. We do not need to write code to synchronize results to ensure that each format returned corresponds properly with each request. Neither do we need data modification locking logic nor do we need to write code to prevent race conditions.

What if we had defined format to be a global string? What errors might that cause? Could we use it to scale this application horizontally?

The general rule is, only if a value is constant, use a global reference. Otherwise, we should return all results via a function call. Why? Because using global variables that change makes our application state unpredictable.

Why global variables are bad

In `Chapter 1`, *Pure Functional Programming in Go*, we briefly discussed immutable variables, but did not dive much into why they are so bad. Let's do that now that we have a concrete example in mind.

Functional impurity

Also covered in `Chapter 1`, *Pure Functional Programming in Go,* pure functions always return the same result, given the same inputs and never have side effects. Global variables cause any function that references it to be impure.

Code complexity and bugs

Global variables by definition are available to a number of functions. It quickly becomes difficult to understand the cause and effect aspects of program flow when a function behaves differently based on its value and other functions are changing that global value.

Performance and race conditions

Mutable global variables require a locking mechanism to allow only one function at a time to update its value. This is often difficult to program and frequently results in race conditions, where a number of functions, that want to update the global variable, must wait in line.

Testing difficulties

Testing must take into account the value of global variables. This typically means that each tester must be aware of the global variable's existence, it's permissible values, and do the work of initializing the global variable's value prior to running each test.

Format the response

In each web service request handler, we use the `setFormat` function in conjunction with the `getFormat` function to format the response data. We are simply using JSON in our example code, it is easy to see how we could extend our implementation to include formats such as XML and CSV.

(We're still in `interfaces/webservice_helpers.go`.):

```
func setFormat(format string, data interface{}) ([]byte, error) {
   var apiOutput []byte
   if format == "json" {
      output, err := json.Marshal(data)
      if err != nil {
         return nil, errors.Wrap(err, "unable to marshal data to json")
      }
      apiOutput = output
   } else {
      Error.Printf("invalid data format encountered")
      apiOutput = ErrorResponse
   }
   return apiOutput, nil
}
```

The handler helpers are similar in format. Let's first look at how we handle a success or failure.

Our function signature contains seven arguments. That's a lot, which makes it a likely candidate for a refactoring. In the next chapter, we'll study how we can simplify complex APIs by passing functions instead of simple values.

Since `debugMsg` and `msg` are both strings, they share a single `string` declaration. Similarly, `err`, `error`, and `success` are all of the type `bool`; `bool` only needs to be typed once after the list of bool arguments. This is idiomatic Go. It is a style of programming, unique to Go, that helps us write simpler, more easily understood code.

Let's examine the `handleSuccess()` function:

```
func handleSuccess(debugMsg, msg string, req *http.Request, res
http.ResponseWriter, err error, success bool) {
   Debug.Printf(debugMsg)
   response := domain.Outcome{}
   response.Success = success
   if err != nil {
      Error.Printf("Failed to %s. %v", msg, err)
   }
   output, err := setFormat(getFormat(req), response)
   if err != nil {
      output = ErrorResponse
      Error.Printf("Failed to setFormat. %v", err)
   }
   Debug.Printf("string(output): %s", string(output))
   fmt.Fprintln(res, string(output))
}
```

The `handleSuccess()` function is called by the `SourceFileExists()` function in `webservices.go`:

```
func (handler WebserviceHandler) SourceFileExists(res http.ResponseWriter,
req *http.Request) {
   fileName := req.FormValue("fileName")
   exists, err := handler.GcpInteractor.SourceFileExists(fileName)
   handleExists(sf("Running SourceFileExists for fileName: %s...",
fileName), "file exists", req, res, err, exists)
}
```

We start with a `Debug.Printf` statement. It takes the first parameter from a web service handler method such as `SourceFileExists`:

```
sf("Running SourceFileExists for fileName: %s...", fileName)
```

It's worth noting that the `sf` function is defined as a function variable at the top of our `webservice_helpers.go` file:

```
var sf = fmt.Sprintf
```

Prior to calling our `handleExists` helper function, we pull the `fileName` value from a query parameter.

What happens when we call `exists, err := handler.GcpInteractor.SourceFileExists(fileName)` ?

Let's look at the series of function calls that will eventually return our results.

First, we visit `usecases.go` in the `usecases` layer. The `SourceFileExists` is a `GcpInteractor` method linked to `SourceBucketRepository`:

```
func (interactor *GcpInteractor) SourceFileExists(fileName string) (fileExists bool, err error) {
    return interactor.SourceBucketRepository.FileExists(fileName)
}
```

That call to `FileExists` brings us back the interfaces layer and calls the `FileExists` method in the infrastructure layer:

```
func (repo *SourceBucketRepo) FileExists(fileName string) (fileExists bool, err error) {
    return repo.gcpHandler.FileExists(fileName)
}
```

The /source-file-exists API flow of control

The following chart and the upcoming diagram show the call stack starting from main where the `SourceExists` API is called:

The flow of control goes from main.go to		Layer
`webservices.go (SourceFileExists)`	to	interfaces (to user)
`usecases.go (SourceFileExists)`	to 1	use cases
`gcpstorage.go (FileExists)`	to 2	interfaces (to GCP)
`gcphandler.go (FileExists)`	to 3	infrastructure
`file.go (NewFile)`	to 4	domain

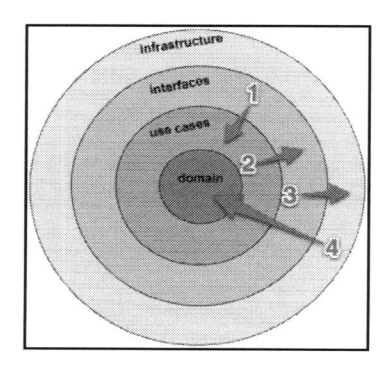

Notice that the interfaces layer is traversed twice during this API call. The function call to `SourceFileExists` in `webservices.go` provides the programmatic interface between the user that requested the `/source-file-exists` end point and the use cases layer's analogous `SourceFileExists` function, which defines what the user wants to do. The next interface in this call stack interacts with the Google Cloud Platform.

The /source-file-exists API call stack

The following screenshot shows a single API call to the `/source-file-exists` web service. The call originates in main, where the web service endpoint is associated with the `SourceFileExists` function in `webservices.go`.

See how the flow of control moves from a user requesting a web service endpoint (in main) and flows upwards, from layer to layer?--`interfaces` | `use cases` | `interfaces` | `interfaces` | `infrastructure` | `domain`.

This is a powerful form of flow control that allows us to build complex applications, with many multidirectional logic flows and still adheres to the dependency rule, that is, we only import packages in one direction:

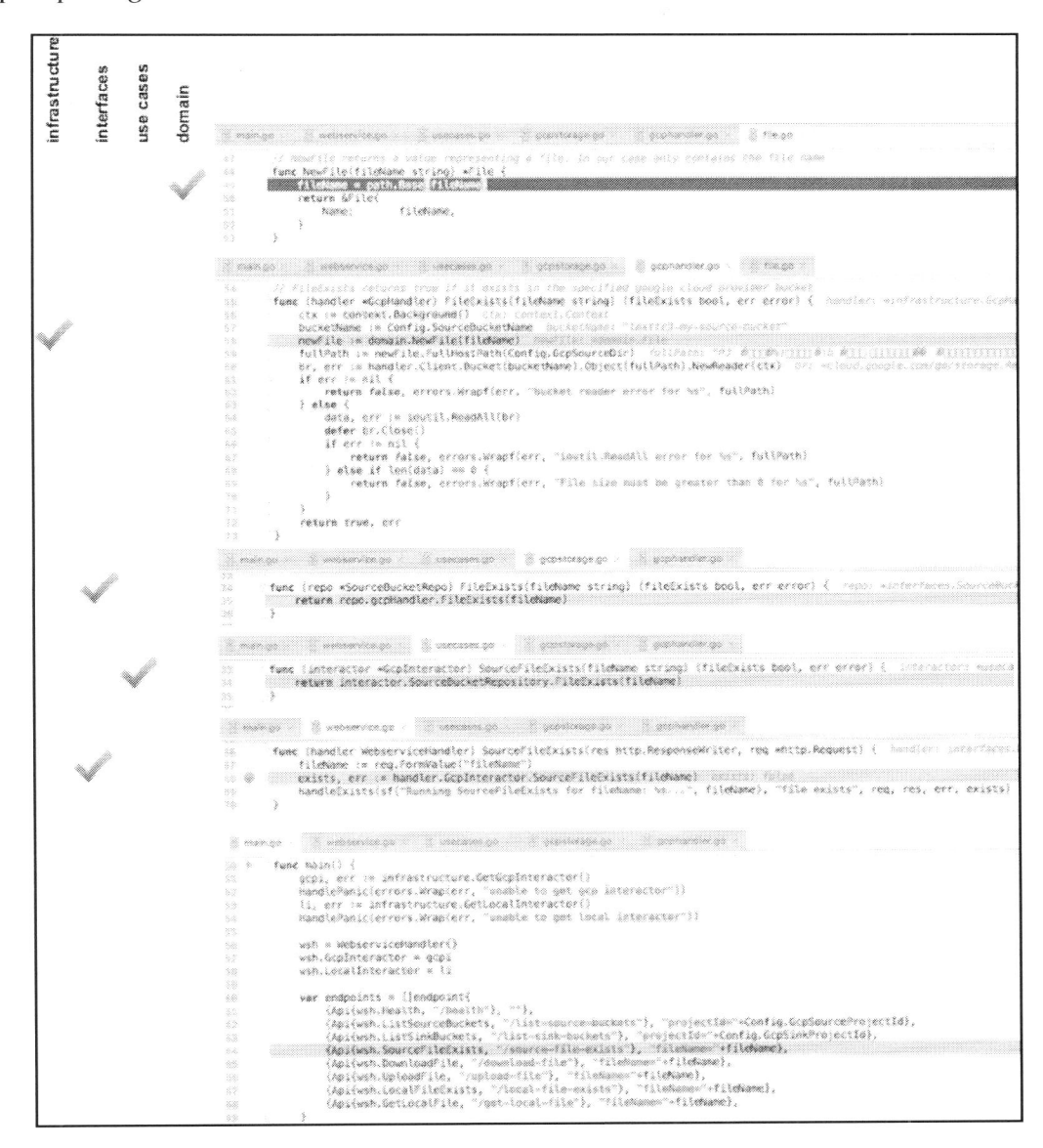

Testing our interfaces

In order to test our application, we'll create an `interfaces_test` directory inside our `interfaces` directory.

Since `interfaces_test` is a different package than `interfaces`, we are unable to access the private functions and other symbols within the `interfaces` package. We are able to change our web service internals without breaking any tests. This also helps us focus on the API. We see just what any other client of our API will see when it's deployed and it simplifies our task of creating tests.

We use the `testing` package from the Go standard library:

```
package interfaces_test

import (
   . "interfaces"
   . "utils"
   "infrastructure"
   "github.com/pkg/errors"
   "io/ioutil"
   "net/http"
   "net/http/httptest"
   "os"
   "strings"
   "testing"
)

const failure = "\u2717"
const defaultFileName = "eventset1.jsonl"

var     fileName                string
var     wsh                     WebserviceHandler
```

We declare `fileName` and `WebserviceHandler` that we populate in our following `init()` function:

```
func init() {
   GetOptions()
   if Config.LogDebugInfoForTests {
      InitLog("trace-debug-log.txt", os.Stdout, os.Stdout, os.Stderr)
   } else {
      InitLog("trace-debug-log.txt", ioutil.Discard, os.Stdout, os.Stderr)
   }
   HandlePanic(os.Chdir(Config.ProjectRoot))
   Debug.Printf("Config: %+v\n", Config)
   // use a filename in a downloads subdirectory
```

```
        fileName = os.Getenv("TEST_FILENAME")
        if len(fileName) == 0 {
            fileName = defaultFileName
        }
        // instantiate interactors
        gcpi, err := infrastructure.GetGcpInteractor()
        HandlePanic(errors.Wrap(err, "unable to get gcp interactor"))
        li, err := infrastructure.GetLocalInteractor()
        HandlePanic(errors.Wrap(err, "unable to get local interactor"))
        // wire up interactors to webservice handler
        wsh = WebserviceHandler{}
        wsh.GcpInteractor = gcpi
        wsh.LocalInteractor = li
    }
```

We reuse the `Api` struct that we used in our main. Instead of associating our APIs with a sample URL, we associate our `Api` with `expectedBody`:

```
    type endpoint struct {
        Api
        expectedBody    string
    }
```

We only need one function to test our end points. We use an anonymous struct and a set of composite literals to create a group to test our data together in a simple, readable format:

```
    func TestEndpoints(t *testing.T) {
        Debug.Printf("fileName: %s", fileName)

        var endpoints = []endpoint{
            {Api{wsh.Health,
                "/health"},
                `{"alive": true}`},
            {Api{wsh.ListSourceBuckets,
                "/list-source-buckets?projectId="+Config.GcpSourceProjectId},
                `{"buckets":[{"name":"my-backup-bucket"},{"name":"my-source-bucket"}]}`},
            {Api{wsh.ListSinkBuckets,
                "/list-sink-buckets?projectId="+Config.GcpSinkProjectId},
                `{"buckets":[{"name":"my-backup-bucket"},{"name":"my-source-bucket"}]}`},
            {Api{wsh.SourceFileExists,
                "/source-file-exists?fileName="+fileName},
                `{"exists":true}`},
            {Api{wsh.UploadFile,
                "/upload-file?fileName="+fileName},
                `{"success":true}`},
            {Api{wsh.DownloadFile,
```

Applying FP at the Architectural Level

```
            "/download-file?fileName="+fileName},
        `{"success":true}`},
    {Api{wsh.LocalFileExists,
            "/local-file-exists?fileName="+fileName},
        `{"exists":true}`},
}
```

As we iterate over our slice of endpoints, we call each `Api.Url`:

```
t.Log("Testing API endpoints...")
{
    for _, ep := range endpoints {
        {
            req, err := http.NewRequest("GET", ep.Api.Url, nil)
            if err != nil {
                t.Fatal(err)
            }
```

We create a `ResponseRecorder` type that satisfies the `http.ResponseWriter` interface to record the response:

```
            rr := httptest.NewRecorder()
            handler := http.HandlerFunc(ep.Api.Handler)
```

Since our handlers implement `http.Handler`, we can call their `ServeHTTP` method directly and fail the test if the status code is not okay:

```
            handler.ServeHTTP(rr, req)
            t.Logf("\tChecking \"%s\" for status code \"%d\"",
                ep.Api.Url, http.StatusOK)
            if status := rr.Code; status != http.StatusOK {
                t.Errorf("\t\t%v handler returned wrong status code: got
                %v want %v", failure, status, http.StatusOK)
            }
```

Lastly, we compare the returned response with the value we stored in the `expectedBody` field of endpoint (`ep`):

```
            t.Logf("\tChecking \"%s\" for expected body", ep.Api.Url)
            Debug.Println("rr.Body.String(): ", rr.Body.String())
            if strings.TrimSpace(rr.Body.String()) != ep.expectedBody {
                t.Errorf("\t\t%v handler returned unexpected body: got
                %v want %v", failure, rr.Body.String(), ep.expectedBody)
            }
        }
    }
}
}
```

The output should look like this:

```
$ go test interfaces/interfaces_test -config ../../../config.toml
webservice_test.go:79: Testing API endpoints...
webservice_test.go:93:      Checking "/health" for status code "200"
webservice_test.go:98:      Checking "/health" for expected body
webservice_test.go:93:      Checking "/list-source-buckets?projectId=rdbx-168418" for status code "200"
webservice_test.go:98:      Checking "/list-source-buckets?projectId=rdbx-168418" for expected body
webservice_test.go:93:      Checking "/list-sink-buckets?projectId=rdbx-168418" for status code "200"
webservice_test.go:98:      Checking "/list-sink-buckets?projectId=rdbx-168418" for expected body
webservice_test.go:93:      Checking "/upload-file?fileName=eventset1.jsonl" for status code "200"
webservice_test.go:98:      Checking "/upload-file?fileName=eventset1.jsonl" for expected body
webservice_test.go:93:      Checking "/download-file?fileName=eventset1.jsonl" for status code "200"
webservice_test.go:98:      Checking "/download-file?fileName=eventset1.jsonl" for expected body
webservice_test.go:93:      Checking "/source-file-exists?fileName=eventset1.jsonl" for status code "200"
webservice_test.go:98:      Checking "/source-file-exists?fileName=eventset1.jsonl" for expected body
webservice_test.go:93:      Checking "/local-file-exists?fileName=eventset1.jsonl" for status code "200"
webservice_test.go:98:      Checking "/local-file-exists?fileName=eventset1.jsonl" for expected body
```

If you have any errors, the output will look something like this:

```
$ go test interfaces/interfaces_test -config ../../../config.toml
Failed to file exists. bucket reader error for source-events/eventset1.jsonl: storage: object doesn't exist
Failed to upload file. unable to get file (eventset1.jsonl) from bucket(lexttc3-my-source-bucket): storage: object doesn't exist
--- FAIL: TestEndpoints (1.45s)
webservice_test.go:79: Testing API endpoints...
webservice_test.go:93:      Checking "/health" for status code "200"
webservice_test.go:98:      Checking "/health" for expected body
webservice_test.go:93:      Checking "/list-source-buckets?projectId=rdbx-168418" for status code "200"
webservice_test.go:98:      Checking "/list-source-buckets?projectId=rdbx-168418" for expected body
webservice_test.go:93:      Checking "/list-sink-buckets?projectId=rdbx-168418" for status code "200"
```

```
webservice_test.go:98:      Checking "/list-sink-
buckets?projectId=rdbx-168418" for expected body
webservice_test.go:93:      Checking "/source-file-
exists?fileName=eventset1.jsonl" for status code "200"
webservice_test.go:98:      Checking "/source-file-
exists?fileName=eventset1.jsonl" for expected body
webservice_test.go:102:         X handler returned unexpected body: got
{"exists":false}
want {"exists":true}
webservice_test.go:93:      Checking "/upload-file?fileName=eventset1.jsonl"
for status code "200"
webservice_test.go:98:      Checking "/upload-file?fileName=eventset1.jsonl"
for expected body
webservice_test.go:93:      Checking "/download-
file?fileName=eventset1.jsonl" for status code "200"
webservice_test.go:98:      Checking "/download-
file?fileName=eventset1.jsonl" for expected body
webservice_test.go:102:         X handler returned unexpected body: got
{"success":false}
want {"success":true}
webservice_test.go:93:      Checking "/local-file-
exists?fileName=eventset1.jsonl" for status code "200"
webservice_test.go:98:      Checking "/local-file-
exists?fileName=eventset1.jsonl" for expected body
FAIL
FAIL    interfaces/interfaces_test 1.475s
```

Infrastructure layer

This section will now talk about the infrastructure layer:

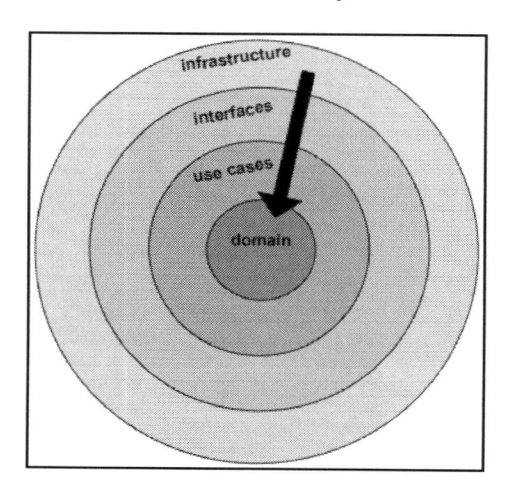

The infrastructure layer is where the code that communicates with the external services exists, such as databases, cloud storage, or even a local filesystem.

Since our code is separated into layers, we should be able to take all the functions from a layer and use them in a different application. The functions in our infrastructure layer have the least to do with our current problem domain, making them more applicable to other applications that need to interact with the Google Cloud Platform.

While our `source` and `sink` functions in our interfaces layer may only make sense to our business and what we want to accomplish, the functions in the infrastructure layer such as `FileExists` and `ListBuckets` are less specific and hence more reusable.

Much of what we find in Go's standard library, as shown in the following list, would belong in the infrastructure layer:

- `database/sql`
- `log/syslog`
- `net/http`
- `net/rpc`
- `net/snmp`
- `net/textproto`

If a package potentially handles interactions with external systems, then it likely belongs in the infrastructure layer.

This function signature is also Go idiomatic. It takes a single parameter and returns two values. The first is the results, while the second is an error:

```
func (handler *GcpHandler) FileExists(fileName string) (fileExists bool, err error) {
    ctx := context.Background()
    bucketName := Config.SourceBucketName
    newFile := domain.NewFile(fileName)
    fullPath := newFile.FullHostPath(Config.GcpSourceDir)
```

The `FileExists()` function returns `true` if the files exist in the specified Google Cloud provider bucket. We build a function call chain to retrieve the bucket reader. In Go idiomatic fashion, it returns two values--one for the bucket reader and the other for a potential error.

Context object

We must pass a context object that is passed to a `withContext` function that creates a new request object, based on the context. However, since the context is empty, this is what we might refer to as **code ceremony**. Note that in the next chapter on functional APIs we'll cover passing request contexts in more depth. In this case, `ctx` is something we must pass so that our code compiles:

```
ctx := context.Background()
. . .
br, err :=
handler.Client.Bucket(bucketName).Object(fullPath).NewReader(ctx)
```

Our `errors` package allows us to wrap our error with a specific error message and not lose the error message from GCP:

```
if err != nil {
   return false, errors.Wrapf(err, "bucket reader error for %s", fullPath)
} else {
```

Again, we see the idiomatic return of two values—the result and the error.

We use another idomatic Go construct using a `defer` call to close our bucket reader. This is yet another example of how Go helps us write better code by making it easy to do the right thing. In languages that do not have a `defer` statement, we must remember to close our connection after performing our work. With Go, we can grab a handle to a data reader and immediately tell the application to close the connection when the function exits:

```
    data, err := ioutil.ReadAll(br)
   defer br.Close()
   if err != nil {
      return false, errors.Wrapf(err, "ioutil.ReadAll error for %s",
         fullPath)
   } else if len(data) == 0 {
      return false, errors.Wrapf(err, "File size must be greater
         than 0 for %s", fullPath)
   }
 }
 return true, err
}
```

Typically, when we encounter an error, it is best practice to wrap the error with a message that makes sense in context and to immediately return the error and whatever makes sense for the result value. In this case, since this is a call to `FileExists`, we return `false` if any error is encountered.

If we make it to the last return statement, then the file in question exists and is of nonzero length. If the GCP API had a public `FileExists` function, we could call it, but this method will suffice for our purposes.

We design each layer to be as simple and concise as possible. The interfaces layer's job is to move and possibly transform data as it flows between use cases and the underlying infrastructure.

Now, we'll look at the `infrastructure/localhandler.go` file. Since there is only one local filesystem in our example, we do not need to provide a key to register `NewLocalHandler`:

```
type LocalHandler struct {}

var LocalInteractor *usecases.LocalInteractor

func NewLocalHandler() *LocalHandler {
    gcpHandler := new(LocalHandler)
    return gcpHandler
}
```

The `FileExists()` function calls the standard library `os.Stat` function. All files in our example application will be stored in the `download` directory. Since the names of two return values have been defined in the `FileExists()` function signature, we only need to set their values where appropriate and execute a bare return statement.

```
func (handler *LocalHandler) FileExists(fileName string) (fileExists bool, err error) {
    _, err = os.Stat(fmt.Sprintf("%s/%s", Config.DownloadDir, fileName))
    if !os.IsNotExist(err) {
        fileExists = true
    }
    return
}
```

The `GetLocalInteractor` function ties its repository (the local filesystem) to its interfaces. Our small example has only one method, `FileExists`:

```
func GetLocalInteractor() (localInteractor *usecases.LocalInteractor, err error) {
    if LocalInteractor == nil {
        localHandler := NewLocalHandler()
        localHandlers := make(map[string] interfaces.LocalHandler)
        localHandlers["LocalFileSystemRepo"] = localHandler
        localInteractor = new(usecases.LocalInteractor)
        localInteractor.LocalRepository =
```

```
    interfaces.NewLocalRepo(localHandlers)
        LocalInteractor = localInteractor
    }
    return LocalInteractor, nil
}
```

Granted, this is a lot of code for wiring up just one method, but a typical enterprise application has external persistence dependencies each with a potentially large number of methods. Our layered architecture provides the structure required to extend a large application with minimal effort.

In a nutshell, a layered architecture:

- Provides the structure required to extend a large application with minimal effort
- Enforces high cohesion, based on a layered approach
- Keeps components loosely coupled by managing function references
- Adheres to the dependency rule
- Uses the Hollywood Principle by injecting dependencies during application initialization

If your application is growing large and you are having issues with cyclic dependencies, the layered architecture is worth your consideration.

Benefits of DDD

The following are the benefits of DDD technique:

Adaptability

DDD makes adding a new ways to interact with our application easy. We simply add a new interactor, that is, our port/adapter, to our `WebServiceHandler`. In our onion.go application, we have two different ways to communicate with our application: the local file system and the Google Cloud Platform.

Sustainability

By decoupling our application business logic from the tools we are using, for example, Google Cloud Platform, we make it less vulnerable vendor lock-in and issues and dependency on services that become defunct or out dated.

Testability

The use of interactors eases the usage of mocks in order to test our applicative services and domain code. Tests can be written for our application service layer before we decide which technology (REST, Messaging, etc.) to be plugged with its corresponding port/adapter.

Comprehensibility

The applicative use case layer clearly indicates our application's functional intentions.

A solid architectural foundation

This layered architecture can form the basis for supporting additional architectural patterns including REST, CQRS, event driven architectures and event sourcing. That's why we focused on DDD.

FP and Micyoservices

Let's look hints of FP philosophies in microservices and related architecturesof event driven architectures, CQRS, Lambda Architecture and functional reactive programming.

The architectures we will consider leverage FP philosophies in different ways to achieve their goals of being:

- Event driven
- Scalable
- Responsive
- Resilient

Applying FP at the Architectural Level

Message passing

These architectures frequently employ fanout strategies to improve performance. For example, an application might have a series of requests that block while performing each request as follows:

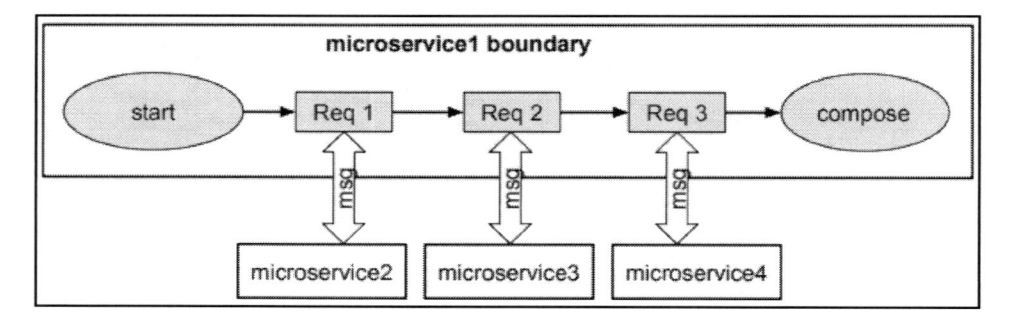

If each request takes 1 second the total time required to send, receive and compose all responses will be 3 seconds.

When possible, we should opt to perform each request asynchronously by fanning out our requests as follows:

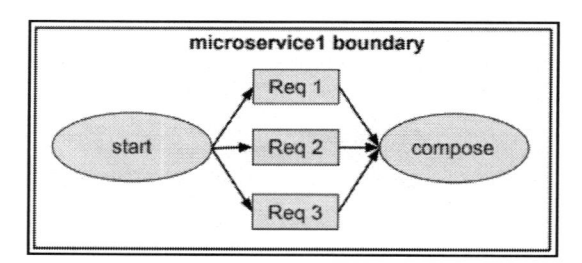

This would reduce the time required to process all requests from 3 seconds to 1 second.

Asynchronous processing takes less time which frees up our resources faster. This minimizes latency and reduces contention for our shared resources. We have just solved one of the biggest hurdles to scalability and improved overall throughput and performance.

All parties must participate

In order to reap the full benefits of non-blocking execution all parts in a request/response chain needs to participate in the non-blocking asynchronous call. If any resource, whether inside or outside the service boundary blocks, then we've got a problem.

What's the problem with blocking?

Usually resources provide access via a processing thread. Threads are limited. If all the threads are busy, subsequent requests must wait until one becomes available.

Asynchronous message passing helps us focus on workflows and interaction patterns between our services.

Communication across boundaries

When communicating between our independent, isolated services we can only request its state. Each service responds to requests with immutable data that reflects its current state.

Polyglot Persistence

Each service may use different storage repository technologies such as:

- Eventlog
- Graph DB
- NoSQL
- RDBMS
- Timeseries DB

The storage technology does not matter. What's important is that each service is responsible for its state, providing access to immutable data only via its API.

Lambda architecture

The Lambda architecture is a generic, scalable and fault-tolerant data processing architecture that handles data at-rest as well as data in-motion. It's comprised of three layers:

Speed

This layer for real time processing. The Realtime views may not be as accurate or complete as the ones eventually produced by the batch layer, but they are available as soon as data is received and can be replaced when the batch layer's views for the same data becomes available.

Batch

This layer can store a large amount of data. Output is typically stored in a read-only database. Any errors can be fixed by recomputing based on a complete data set at which time views can be updated. Apache Hadoop is the de facto standard batch-processing system used in most high-throughput architectures. Response times can be measured in minutes or even hours.

Servicing

Output from the batch and speed layers are stored in the serving layer, which responds to ad-hoc queries by returning precomputed views or building views from processed data.

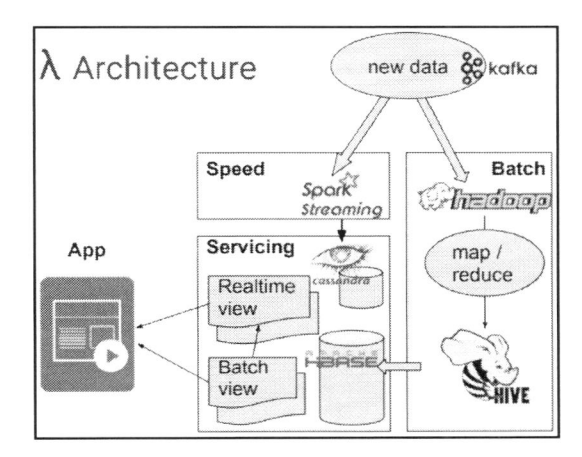

Some Lambda implementations have various storage and technology decisions, but they all have a batch and a real time components that both consume the same data and a real time view that can be updated by corrected data from batch processing.

The problem with this architecture is that the same data is ingested by both the Speed and by the Batch layer and typically stored in two separate databases, Cassandra and HBASE in the example above. Plus, extra processing occurs when the batch jobs return fixed up batch view data that needs to be merged into the related real time views.

Next generation big data architecture

The next generation big data architecture has dropped the batch layer completely. The purely real time system brings stream processing directly into the services architecture where the data is stored via event logging. The most current data is stored in the database and the history of events is stored in the event logs.

CQRS

Command and Query Responsibility Segregation (CQRS) is an architecture style that separates read operations from write operations.

Applying FP at the Architectural Level

Traditionally, the same data model is used to query and update a database. However, more complex applications, problems with this shared data model appear. For example, To satisfy the write requirements our data model need to contain complex validation and business logic. Our read requirements will have no need for that extra logic. Instead, it may need to perform many different queries, using data structures that are needed by our write component. Complexity is increased on both sides.

CQRS addresses these problems by separating reads and writes into separate models, using commands to update data, and queries to read data.

Commands are based on tasks, rather than specific create or update commands. For example, *Upgrade Car*, rather than *append LX* to `model_name` field. Commands are placed on a queue for asynchronous processing.

Queries return plain data objects that have no behavior or domain knowledge.

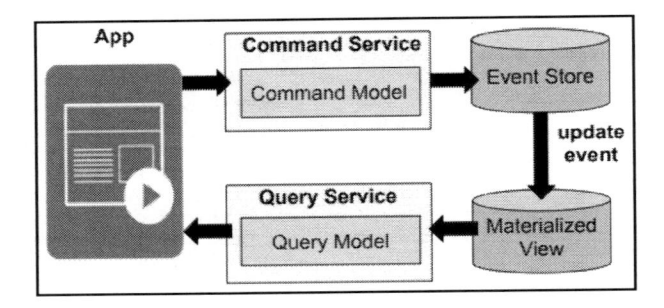

Benefits of CQRS

CQRS **optimizes performance**. The command service/event store side can be optimized for updates while the query service/materialized view side can be optimized for queries.

CQRS **simplifies queries** by storing a materialized view in the read database. Complex joins can be avoided and performance improved.

CQRS **separates** of writing and reading which greatly simplifies the business logic in the query model and puts the complex validation and business logic in the command model where it belongs.

CQRS allows the reads and writes to **scaleindependently**.

CQRS relies on messaging which is a good fit for message-based microservices.

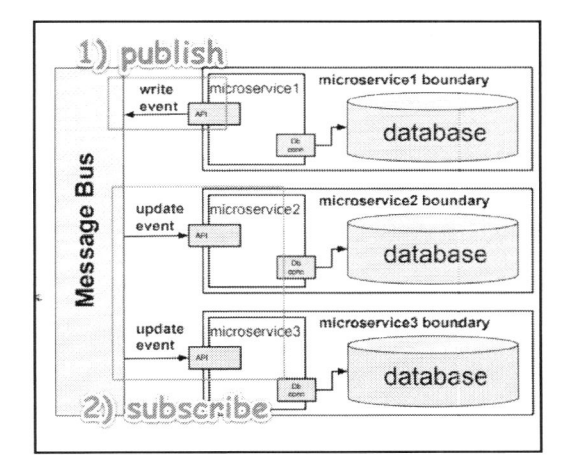

Above, microservice1 writes to its database which publishes a write event. Microservice2 and microservice3 subscribe to microservice1's write event and get updated every time that event occurs.

Infrastructure architecture

Developing an isolated microservice is very easy in comparison to designing, developing and configuring its infrastructure. Infrastructure includes things like:

- Accessing and ingesting logs
- Balancing loads
- Checking application health
- Database replication
- Debugging applications
- Distributing secrets
- Integrating other services
- Monitoring resources
- Mounting storage systems
- Naming and discovering
- Orchestrating/Coordination
- Providing authentication and authorization

- Replicating application instances
- Rolling updates
- Using Horizontal Autoscaling

Share nothing architecture

A share nothing architecture (SN) is a distributed computing architecture where each node is independent and self-sufficient. Nodes do not share data storage and there is no single point of contention across the system. Sounds a lot like a microservice, right?

The problem with SN architectures is that join operation between the nodes can be time consuming.

SN eliminates shared mutable state, minimizes resource contention and increases scalability.

Integrating services

Microservices have no control over other microservices externally or internally. It is important that our digital fabric of microservices agree on acceptable communication protocols.

Agreed upon protocol

The protocol should enforce policies regarding security, the direction and velocity of the flow of data as well as flow control.

Circuit breakers

In order to prevent cascading failures there should be mechanisms in place such as fail fast circuit breakers. Management of retries for failed requests should consider things like:

- How long should we wait to retry?
- Should we monitor the endpoint and wait for it to get back online and then try again?
- When do we notify devops about the failure?

Functional reactive architecture

Functional reactive architecture (FRP) is similar to other architectures in that it embraces many of the FP concepts such as immutable data structures, event streaming and data transformation, but different in that it is a front-end architecture.

Reactive Functional Programming (RFP) incorporates aspects from both Reactive Programming (RP) and Functional Programming (FP).

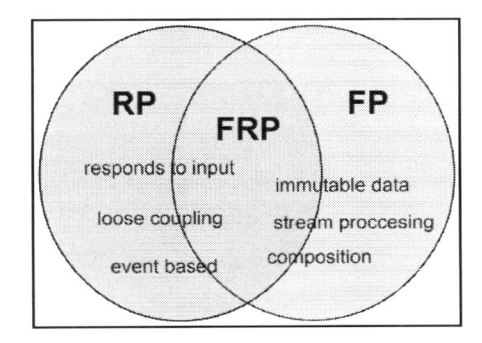

Let's look at an example to get a better appreciation for the connection between FRP and FP.

Suppose we have a User Interface (UI) application that sums two numbers:

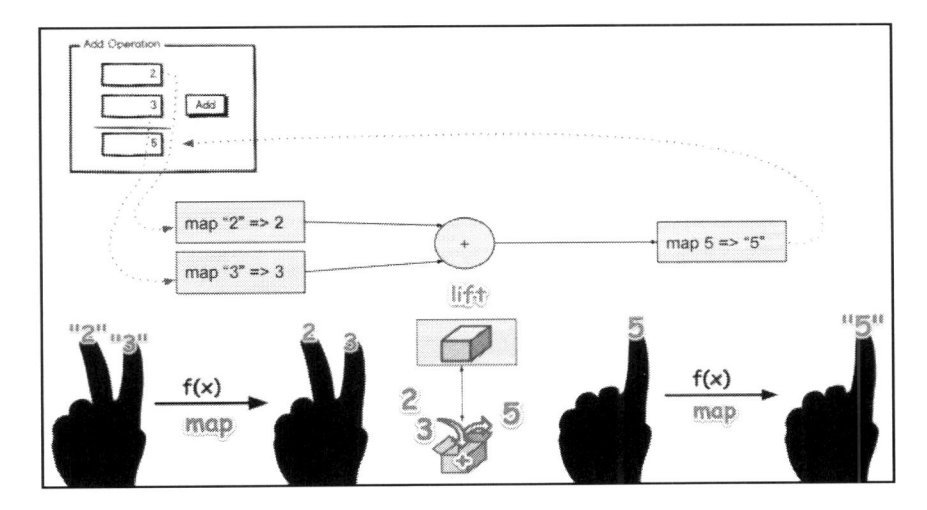

> There is a lot more to RFP (immutable data structures, memoization, state and event management, and so on). Since this is a front end technology the logic will not be Go, but rather JavaScript (which is one of my specialties).
>
> So, if you like my style of writing and would like me to write a book combining Go, ReactJS and some distributed data store technology let me hear from you. Please post your feedback here: `https://www.amazon.com/Learning-Functional-Programming-Lex-Sheehan-ebook/dp/B0725B8MYW`

Go is ideal for building microservices

Distributed computing involves the horizontal scaling our our microservices. We have seen that when we can dramatically improve performance by running our tasks in parallel. In order to manage, order and orchestrate our workloads we need a simple mechanism. What simpler solution exists for creating and running applications concurrently? (Answer: None.)

Here're some of Go's features that make it ideal for microservice environments:

- Simplicity
- Concurrency
- Speed at compile time
- Speed at runtime
- Security
- Networking/gRPC/Protocol buffers
- Systems programming
- Small footprint

Go is built upon the philosophy of simplicity. To write go code is to write practical code.

Concurrency is baked into the Go language in the form of goroutines and channels.

> **TIP**: For a coding example using goroutines and channels see `Chapter 5`, *Adding Functionality with Decoration*.

Go's compile times are extremely fast. Once compiled, Go binaries are native executables.

There are no virtual environments to install, configure, import dependencies from, deploy and manage. The only footprint is a small native executable. That's less surface area for attackers to exploit.

Size matters

Let's face it. Size matters. If you are paying for the resources (CPU, storage, networking, and so on) which would you prefer to pay for:

1,000 of these?

Or 1,000 of these?

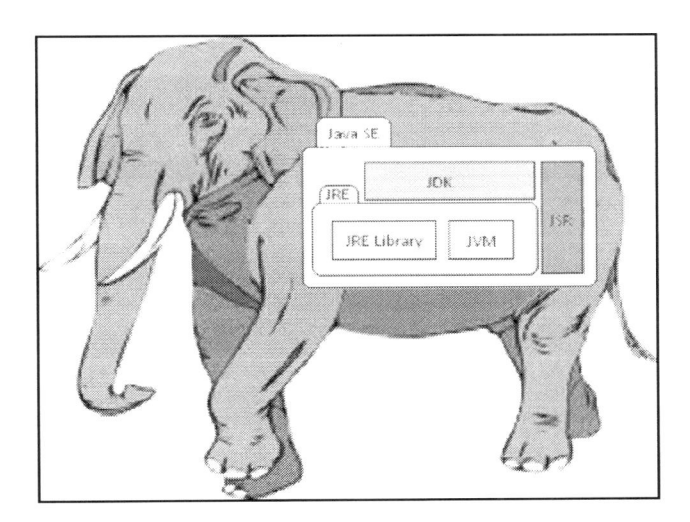

Benefits of gRPC

If you need to employ a request/response architecture, using gRPC with protocol buffers is the way to go. gRPC allow us to easily release SDKs. Now integration is a matter of and asking the other developers to copy-paste example code written in their language. This represents a big win for companies what want to integrate with our products, while not requiring us to implement entire SDKs in all the various languages that our vendors and partners use.

gRPC is built on HTTP/2 HTTP/2's client-side and/or server-side streaming allow for faster response times and support for bulk ingestion and bi-directional streaming. We can asynchronously stream requests/responses; The server would stream back status messages, allowing for easy checkpoint operations. This allows us to process uploads as fast as possible without blocking for confirmations.

By using protocol buffers with gRPC, we'll improve serialization and deserialization performance. Clients receive typed objects rather than free form JSON. This allows our clients can reap the benefits of type-safety, auto-completion in their IDEs, and improved version management.

gRPC enables us to write one interface definition, in the proto format, for both the client and server side of our APIs. Interface driven development enables both development teams to work in parallel. That makes us leaner, providing more value faster.

Who is using Go?

A short list of systems and infrastructure tools being built in Go includes:

- Docker
- Kubernetes
- Packer
- CoreOS
- InfluxDB
- Etcd
- NSQ

Summary

In this chapter, we learned the importance of the dependency rule. We learned that we can only import packages in one direction. We learned how to separate a complex application into layers.

We learned how to use dependency injection to interact between our application layers and implemented an application using a layered architecture.

The key to selecting the right architecture is a deep understanding our system's requirements, existing components and the capabilities of available technologies choices. At the end of the day it's the system engineer's job to ensure the entire system works properly.

In the next chapter, we'll learn about functors, monoids, type classes, and other functional programming concerns.

7
Functional Parameters

While writing this chapter, my mind wandered back a few years to when I used to program in FoxPro. As I recall, I wrote a lot of functions in FoxPro. The functions I wrote were typically singular in purpose and rarely required more than four parameters. After Microsoft purchased Fox Software, newer versions of FoxPro began to be less functional. The UI builder was becoming more like Visual Basic. Functions began to be replaced by classes. Logic that was once readily accessible became hidden behind buttons and GUI objects. The lines of code increased, testing took more time and development cycles took longer. I felt a lack of productivity and could not adequately explain my feelings.

> *"He who does not understand the supreme certainty of mathematics is wallowing in confusion."*
>
> *- Leonardo Da Vinci*

When I discovered Go, it was like paradise regained; A return to simplicity with added benefits of concurrency, networking, great development tools, first class functions as well as the best parts of OOP.

Our goal in this chapter is to do the following:

- Learn a better way to refactor long parameter lists
- Recognize the difference between a dead data object and a functional parameter
- Learn the difference between currying and partial application
- Learn how to apply a partial application to create another function with a smaller arity
- Use a context to gracefully shut down our server
- Use a context to cancel and rollback a long-running database transaction
- Implement functional options to improve our APIs

Functional Parameters

> **TIP**
> If you think it's okay to simplify a long parameter list by either passing pointers to mutable data objects or by calling other functions hidden within your function, please read this chapter with an open mind.

Refactoring long parameter lists

Long parameter lists are typically considered code smell.

How long is too long?

When we look at a parameter list and are unable to keep track of it all, then it's likely too long.

> **Mind's limit found - 4 things at once**
>
> Working memory relates to the information we can pay attention to and grasp. Keeping our parameter lists short helps others easily understand our function's purpose.
> `https://www.livescience.com/2493-mind-limit-4.html`

Four parameters or fewer is the sweet spot, but seven is the maximum.

Consider our telephone numbers. How many digits? Seven. For example: 867-5309

Why do you think the seven digits are separated into two sets of numbers with the largest set having four digits?

What's wrong with a function signature with more than seven parameters?

A function signature should not be so long and complicated that we are unable to comprehend it. Keep it simple. Use thoughtful, reasonable, and meaningful parameter names.

Ever noticed that functions with a long parameter list are typically some type of constructor? And that those functions are prone to get even more parameters over time?

It is natural for software engineers to want to reduce their functions' parameter lists. That's part of what we do when we refactor our application. As long as we keep the goal of comprehensibility in mind, we'll be fine. Sometimes, we might have a function signature that has ten parameters. If other alternatives would make our function signature ambiguous, then go for it. Clarity trumps ambiguity. How many parameters should we use? It depends.

> Refactoring code is the process of changing the structure of our code without changing its behavior. We are not adding features. Instead, we are making our code more readable and more easily maintained. Often, we take large functions (over 200 lines of code) and break them into smaller, more comprehensible units of code.

Some ways of accomplishing this feat are better than others.

Refactoring - the book

Ever read the book *Refactoring*? It covers the topic of refactoring long parameter lists.

The following points are made:

- Methods can query other objects' methods internally for data required to make decisions
- Methods should depend on their host class for needed data
- We should pass one or more objects to simplify our call signature

- We should use a technique called *replace parameter with method* to reduce the number of required parameters
- Pass a whole object with required attributes to reduce the number of required parameters
- Use a parameter object when we have unrelated data elements to pass
- We can send separate parameters when we do not want to create a dependency on a larger parameter object; this is an exception and we should probably not do it
- Long parameter lists will change over time and are inherently difficult to understand

This advice is consistent with the pure object-oriented language design methodology. However, we as good Go programmers should only be in agreement with the last point. Why?

How can it be that the advice that many have followed for almost 20 years could be so horribly wrong?

Edsger W. Dijkstra says OOP is a bad idea

The Dutch computer scientist, Dijkstra, provides the following insight on OOP:

> "Object-oriented programming is an exceptionally bad idea which could only have originated in California."
>
> - *Edsger W. Dijkstra*

What? OOP is an *exceptionally bad idea*? Why?

First, let's understand a little bit more about Edsger W. Dijkstra.

Chapter 7

What else did Edsger W. Dijkstra say?

Dijkstra said things such as:

"The competent programmer is fully aware of the strictly limited size of his own skull; therefore he approaches the programming task in full humility, and among other things he avoids clever tricks like the plague."

- *Edsger W. Dijkstra*

He also said the following:

"Simplicity is prerequisite for reliability."

- *Edsger W. Dijkstra*

Mozart composition

"Neither a lofty degree of intelligence nor imagination nor both together go to the making of genius. Love, love, love, that is the soul of genius."

- *Wolfgang Amadeus Mozart*

Functional Parameters

Dijkstra shared his thoughts about the differing programming styles found in software development. Dijkstra compared the difference between the way Mozart and Beethoven composed music. Dijkstra explained that Mozart began composing with the entire composition in mind. Beethoven, on the other hand, would write parts of the music before the composition was completed and would literally glue the corrections to create the final composition.

Beethoven composition

Edsger seems to prefer Mozart's style of programming. His own approach to programming illustrates that programs should be designed and correctly composed, not just hacked and debugged into correctness.

The reason Mozart was able to perform detailed design before implementation was due to the fact that he was a master of the art of music composition and had a lot of experience. Sometimes, when developing software, we won't have that luxury. When we are unable to identify a framework suited for our project, there will be much more trial-and-error programming.

Personally, when I am not under a tight deadline, I prefer the Beethoven style of development. I think of it as recreational programming. It's self-exploratory in nature. For me, Mozart development requires more discipline. Typically, the end result is the same. Mozart development takes less time to complete, but Beethoven development is more enjoyable. I suppose that's why the developers enjoy R&D projects so much.

The underlying OOP problem

As noted in `Chapter 4`, *SOLID Design in Go*, you learned how Java (and OOP languages) places emphasis on a type hierarchy. The designers of OOP focused on nouns rather than verbs. Everything is an object. An object has attributes (data) and can perform actions (methods).

An inactive noun

One of the underlying problems with OOP is that it promotes storing and hiding data in the object's properties/attributes. It is assumed that our application will eventually want to access this object's data while executing one or more of the object's methods.

OOP inconsistency

An OOP application can recall its hidden information and mutate it. An object's method can be called multiple times during the lifetime of the application. Each call to the same method with the same call signature can produce different results every time. This characteristic of its behavior makes OOP unreliable and difficult to test effectively.

OOP is inconsistent with basic mathematics. In OOP, due to an object's mutable state, we cannot always call a method with the same parameters each time and always get the same results. There is no mathematical model for OOP. For example, if we call `myMethod(1,2)` and get 3 the first time and get 4 the next time, due to the mutable state and internal calls to other objects, then the correctness of an OOP program cannot be defined.

Functional programming and cloud computing

The essence of functional programs is very different from OOP. Functional programs, given the same set of input parameters, will always yield the same results. We can easily run them in parallel. We can chain/compose them in ways that are faster and not possible with OOP.

Our deployment model has changed from in-house servers, where admins would spend so much time configuring and optimizing them that they gave the server pet names. We used to see names follow a pattern such as Greek gods. There's *Zeus*, our database server, and *Apollo* our HR server.

Now that our servers are deployed in the cloud, our admins can add new servers with the click of a button or set up auto scaling: if the average CPU goes above 80%, then add a new server. It looks something like this:

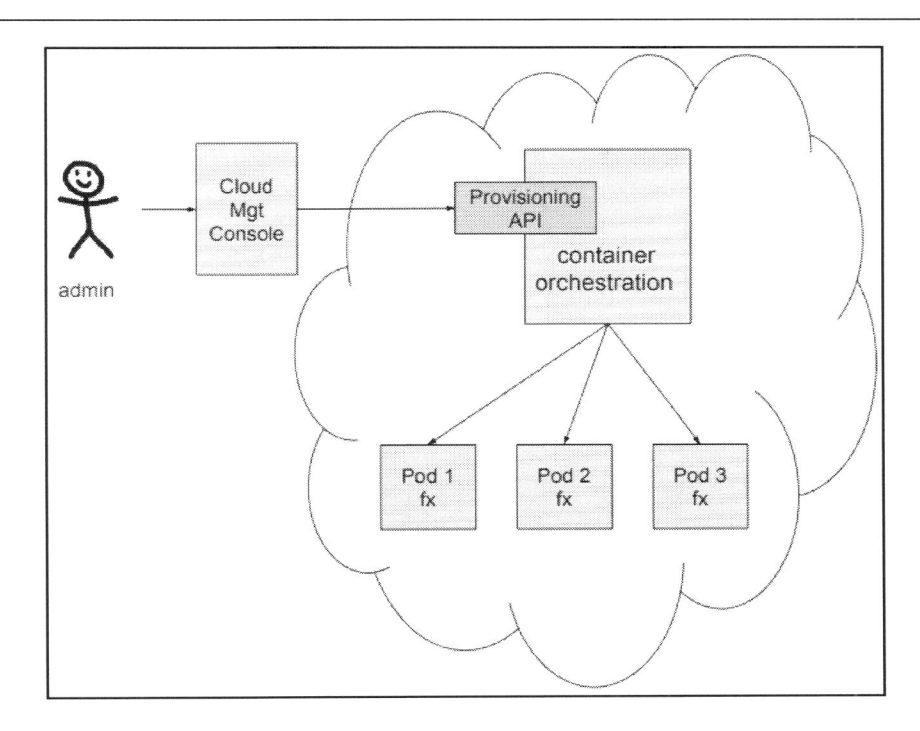

The Pods in the preceding diagram represent a server, which might have a few related containers. One container in the pod would be running our `f(x)` function. If a server crashes, our auto scaling logic that's running in our container orchestrator would be notified and it will automatically start another server to replace it. Pods can quickly be provisioned and can be taken out of service based on our cloud deployment profile settings and our sites' traffic patterns. Since servers come and go so easily and quickly these days, we refer to them as cattle rather than pets. We are more concerned with the health of our herd of servers than we are about any one particular pet server.

> The term *Pod* is taken from Kubernetes. Refer to https://kubernetes.io/docs/concepts/workloads/pods/pod-overview/ to know more.
>
> Pods are the rough equivalent of OpenShift v2 gears and logically represent a *logical host*, where all service containers can communicate with each other via localhost.
>
> Other container orchestrators include Docker Swarm, Mesos, Marathon, and Nomad. Refer to https://github.com/KaivoAnastetiks/container-orchestration-comparison.

Functional Parameters

Applications with FP characteristics behave reliably in our cloud environments; however, applications with OOP characteristics of mutable state do not do so.

A closer look at f(x)

Let's examine a basic function definition, where **f** is the function name and **x** is the input value. Another name for **x** is the input parameter.

The entire expression **f(x)** represents the output value:

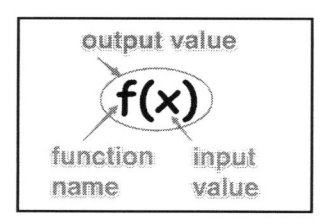

```
        output value
            ↘
          ( f(x) )
           ↙    ↘
      function  input
       name     value
```

If $f(x) = x + 1$, then we know that every time we input the value 2, the output value will always be 3.

This pure and simple characteristic is what makes functional programming so powerful.

If, on the other hand, we had an object with an `AddOne` method that would sometimes return 3 when given the value of 2, then how could we reliably scale our `object.AddOne` method? We can't, and that is the main reason why, in the context of cloud computing, the following equation is true: *FP > OOP*.

A closer look at refactoring

Let's examine each point made in the Refactoring book in the light of functional programming.

Passing every parameter a function requires to do its job is not a good idea

Why wouldn't we want our function signature to indicate the values (parameters) that it needs to make decisions?

How can we reduce the parameters that a function requires?

Methods can query other objects' methods internally for data required to make decisions

So, instead of calling the `GetTravelTime(startLocation, endLocation)` method, it would be better to call `GetTravelTime()`?

Where would we get the `startLocation` and `endLocation` values from?

How can we be sure that there aren't other values, such as `modeOfTransportation`, that would impact our travel time result?

Doesn't that create internal, undocumented dependencies (assuming we document our external APIs)?

Methods should depend on their host class for needed data

Does this mean that we are relying on mutable data that could be updated before and during our function call?

If we want to prevent updates on data during the time our function is running, what extra code must we write to ensure data consistency? What locking mechanisms will we need to implement?

Will this prevent us from writing code that runs in parallel?

Is concurrent programming possible?

Pass a whole object with required attributes to reduce the number of required parameters

So, instead of `GetTravelTime(startLocation, endLocation, speed)`, our call should look like this: `GetTravelTime(info)`.

There are times when a function call like this `Initialize(Config)` makes sense, and it depends on our use case.

However, maybe we should strive to simplify what our function does so that it naturally requires fewer parameters rather than finding ways to jam more parameter values into a single input parameter object.

Replace parameter with method technique to reduce the number of required parameters

This technique instructs us to remove the parameter and let the receiver invoke the method.

Before applying Replace Parameter with Method technique

We start with a `getDiscountedPrice` function that takes two parameter: `lineItemPrice` and discount:

```
lineItemPrice := quantity * itemPrice;
discount := getDiscount();
totalPrice := getDiscountedPrice(lineItemPrice, discount);
```

Replace Parameter with Method aggressively strives to reduce the number of parameters.

In this case we have two parameters. That is clearly fewer than the four parameters. Why reduce this low number of parameters?

After applying Replace Parameter with Method technique

After refactoring our code per our instructions, we have removed a parameter. Now we only have one parameter:

```
lineItemPrice := quantity * itemPrice;
totalPrice := getDiscountedPrice(lineItemPrice);
```

How will code maintainers know that the `totalPrice` can be reduced by a discount?

Does hiding the discount parameter improve understandability or does it actually increase code complexity?

Use a parameter object when we have unrelated data elements to pass

A parameter object contains only fields and crude methods for accessing them (getters and setters). It is a dead data structure used only to transfer data.

If we are passing a lot of unrelated data items into a function, then what are the odds that our function would fail the Single Responsibility Principle?

What if we wanted to add logic that could modify a data value based on our runtime context?

However, if we have a set of parameters that describe a new customer, we could consider grouping them into a data objects. Something like the following could be considered a reasonable thing to do:

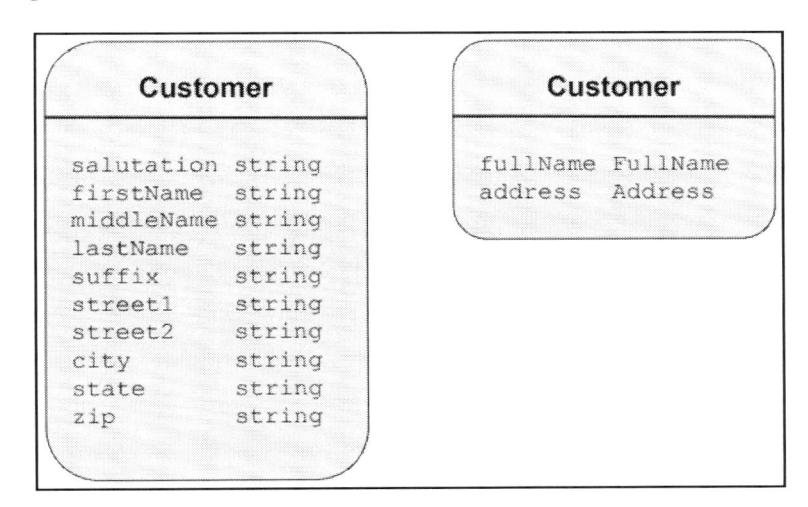

```
Customer
----------------
salutation  string
firstName   string
middleName  string
lastName    string
suffix      string
street1     string
street2     string
city        string
state       string
zip         string


Customer
----------------
fullName  FullName
address   Address
```

We grouped the `FullName` attributes (salutation, firstName, middleName, lastName, suffix) together to form a `FullName` data object. We also grouped address attributes to create an `Address` data object. Now, we can call `CreateCustomer` passing only two attributes:

```
CreateCustomer(fullName, address)
```

The call with two parameters is an improvement over the following one with eight:

```
CreateCustomer(salutation, firstName, middleName, lastName, suffix,
    street1, street2, city, state, zip)
```

So, as with most things in the world, the right thing to do depends on our situation.

Can you think of a problem with this approach?

Doesn't this create a dependency upon the `fullName` and address objects?

What if either the `fullName` or address data objects changed after we began executing our `CreateCustomer` function but before it was complete? What data inconsistencies would we have then?

Long parameter lists will change over time and are inherently difficult to understand

This statement makes a lot of sense. The rest of this chapter will expound on this statement. We'll explore how we can manage an API that could change over time and that might need more than a few parameters to get the information it needs to complete its task(s).

If we compose our application like Beethoven, starting with a general idea of what we want to accomplish and beating our program into shape, then we might not know exactly what parameters an API will need at first.

An action verb

How do we design an API that requires more than a few parameters, yet has the following qualities?

- Provides sensible defaults
- Indicates which parameters are required/optional
- Provides the entire power of language to init complex values rather than relaying via dead structures
- Can grow over time
- Is safe
- Is discoverable
- Is self-documenting
- Is highly configurable

What about passing a configuration struct?

Like the `fullName` and address data objects we saw earlier, passing a configuration data object creates a dependency. The configuration object is retained by both the `caller` and the function `called`.

If we pass pointers to our configuration object that would complicate issues if any mutations occurred, either by the caller or the callee.

The solution

The solution we're looking for would allow a new constructor to accept a variable number of parameters with the following characteristics:

- Predefining default values (where no parameter is passed for that particular setting)
- Only passing values that have meaning
- Harnessing the power of the Go programming language to customize the value of the parameter passed

Much of this design comes from one of Rob Pike's blog posts.

> Refer to self-referential functions and the design of options, by Rob Pike in his blog post at `https://commandcenter.blogspot.com/2014/01/self-referential-functions-and-design.html`.

Kudos for sharing the closure technique of returning a function literal in which we set the value of our server setting. We'll see exactly how this works later in this chapter.

Three ways to pass multiple parameters

Let's keep in mind that there are three ways to pass multiple parameters to a function. We will discuss them in the next sections.

Simply passing multiple parameters

Here, we pass four parameters to the `InitLog` function:

```
func InitLog (
   traceFileName string,
   debugHandler io.Writer,
   infoHandler io.Writer,
   errorHandler io.Writer,
) {
// . . .
}
```

Passing a configuration object/struct that contains multiple attributes

Here, we pass the `ClientConfig` configuration data object and print its values out:

```
func printClientConfig(config *ClientConfig) {
    Info.Printf(" - security params: %v", config.SecurityParams)
    Info.Printf(" - core limit: %v", config.CoreLimit)
    Info.Printf(" - payload config: %v", config.PayloadConfig)
    Info.Printf(" - channel number: %v", config.ClientChannels)
    Info.Printf(" - load params: %v", config.LoadParams)
    // . . .
```

A disadvantage of this approach is that we create a dependency between the caller and the callee. What if the caller or some other part of the caller's system modifies the configuration object while our function is processing?

Sometimes, as in the example provided earlier, it is fairly safe to assume that the configuration object will not change. In that case, passing a configuration object is the right thing to do. It's easy and effective with little chance of a mutation causing an inconsistent state.

But what if the parameter might need to be modified due to the additional complexity that lies inside the called function? Static values from a dead structure can't help.

Partial application

Our third option is called **partial application**. We can accomplish this with currying.

The idea behind currying is to create new, more specific functions from other more general functions by partially applying them.

Consider that we have have an `add` function that takes two numbers:

```
func add(x, y int) int {
    return x + y
}
```

We can create another function that returns the `add` function with one of the parameters pre-inserted. We'll take a simple example of adding one to any other number:

```
func addOnePartialFn() func(int) int {
    return func(y int) int {
        return add(1, y)
    }
}
```

The results of calling `add(1,2)` will be the same as calling `addOne(2)`:

```
func main() {
    fmt.Printf("add(1, 2): %d\n", add(1, 2))
    addOne := addOnePartialFn()
    fmt.Printf("addOne(2): %d\n", addOne(2))
}
```

The following is the output of the preceding code:

```
add(1, 2): 3
addOne(2): 3
```

> **Currying** is the ability of a function to return a new single argument function until the original function receives all of its arguments.
>
> Calling a curried function with only a few of its arguments is called **partial application**.

Function currying is a technique we can use to chop up complex functionality into smaller parts that are easier to reason about. Smaller units of logic are also easier to test. Our application becomes a clean composition of the smaller parts.

However, the solution that we will be pursuing in this chapter will be of the first variety, that is, we will pass all the required parameters. However, we will only need to pass the required parameters and we will use sensible default values for unprovided parameters.

How can we accomplish this? By using functional parameters!

Functional parameters

We'll use the `GetOptions()` utils function as we have in previous chapters and we'll call `GetOptions` and `InitLog` in our init function so that our configuration values and logger will be set up prior to running any commands in the `main` package:

```go
package main

import (
    "server"
    . "utils"
    "context"
    "io/ioutil"
    "net/http"
    "os"
    "os/signal"
    "time"
    "fmt"
)

func init() {
    GetOptions()
    InitLog("trace-log.txt", ioutil.Discard, os.Stdout, os.Stderr)
}
```

Let's subscribe to the `SIGINT` signal using signal `Notify`. Now, we can catch a *Ctrl + C* event before our program abruptly stops. We'll create a quit channel to hold our signal. It only needs to have a buffer size of 1.

When our `quit` channel receives a `SIGINT` signal, we can begin our graceful, orderly shutdown procedure:

```go
func main() {
    quit := make(chan os.Signal, 1)
    signal.Notify(quit, os.Interrupt)
```

Pay close attention to the following code. This is where we pass our functional parameters!

```
newServer, err := server.New(
    server.MaxConcurrentConnections(4),
    server.MaxNumber(256), // Config.MaxNumber
    server.UseNumberHandler(true),
    server.FormatNumber(func(x int) (string, error) { return fmt.Sprintf("%x", x), nil }),
    //server.FormatNumber(func(x int) (string, error) { return "", errors.New("FormatNumber error") }),  // anonymous fcn
)
```

In our example, we chose to provide four parameters (`MaxConcurrentConnections`, `MaxNumber`, `FormatNumber`, and `UseNumberHandler`) to our server's `New` constructor.

Note that the parameter names are self-explanatory. We passed the actual scalar values (4, 256, true) for the first three parameters. We could have chosen to use config values (`Config.MaxConcurrentConnections`, `Config.MaxNumber`, and `Config.UseNumberHandler`) or use environment variables. We could also use environment variables. We'd likely not use an environment variable for `UseNumberHandler`. Mostly, environment variables are used for settings that are likely to vary from development, test, QA and production environments, for example, `IPADDRESS` and `PORT`.

> Here's a handy library for dealing with environment variables in Go:
>
> `https://github.com/caarlos0/env`

The last parameter `FormatNumber` accepts an anonymous function to change the display format of the number:

```
server.FormatNumber(func(x int) (string, error) { return fmt.Sprintf("%x", x), nil })
```

The `%x` argument in the `fmt.Sprintf` statement instructs our handler to display the entered number in binary format.

Functional Parameters

When the user enters the number 2 in their request, this is what's displayed:

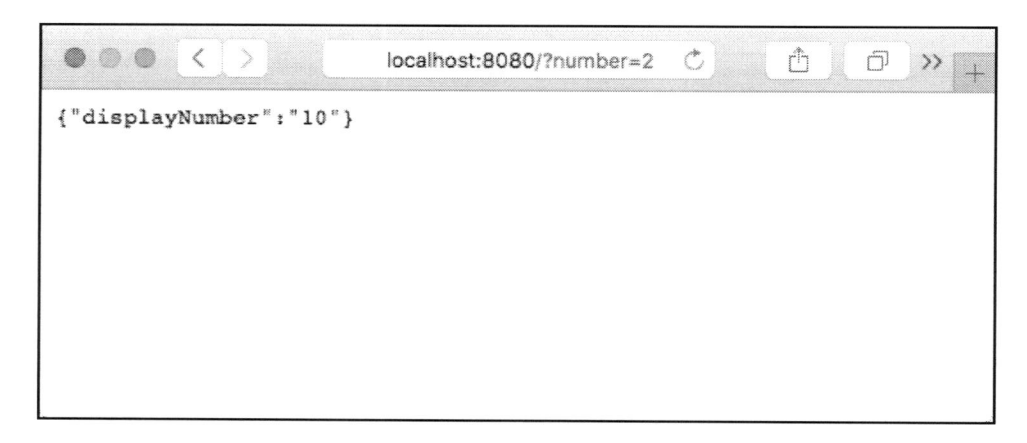

```
localhost:8080/?number=2
{"displayNumber":"10"}
```

If the call to `Server.New` fails, then log the error and exit the program:

```
if err != nil {
    Error.Printf("unable to initialize server: %v", err)
    os.Exit(1)
}
```

Next, we provide the parameters required for a running HTTP server. The `Addr` parameter is the address the server listens on.

Rather than letting the `http.Server` default to using `http.DefaultServeMux` to handle requests, we we pass our `newServer` function type variable to accept our custom `ServerOption` functional parameters to customize its behavior:

```
srv := &http.Server{
    Addr:    ":"+Config.Port,
    Handler: newServer,
}
```

Next, we'll create a Goroutine for an anonymous function call.

Our Goroutine will wait until the user triggers a `SIGINT` interrupt (by pressing *Ctrl* + *C* in the terminal session where the server was started). At that time, the quit channel will receive the signal.

Though `Context` can be used to pass request-scoped variables, we're only going to use it to pass a cancellation signal. We'll go into more detail about `Context` in the next section.

The `quit` channel is closed when the 2 second deadline expires or when the returned `cancel` function is called. As long as the server shutdown logic takes less than two seconds, the defer `cancel()` will be called; otherwise, the deadline will close the `quit` channel:

```
go func() {
   <-quit
   ctx, cancel := context.WithDeadline(context.Background(),
time.Now().Add(2 * time.Second))
   defer cancel()
   Info.Println("shutting down server...")
   if err := srv.Shutdown( ctx ); err != nil {
       Error.Printf("unable to shutdown server: %v", err)
   }
}()
```

The call to `Shutdown` will stop the server without interrupting any active connections. First, `Shutdown` closes open listeners, then it closes idle connections. Without a deadline, it could wait indefinitely for connections to return to idle before shutting them down.

The `ListenAndServe` function listens on the localhost port `Config.Port` and calls serve to handle requests on incoming connections:

```
Error.Println("server started at localhost:"+Config.Port)
err = srv.ListenAndServe()
```

At this point, our server will be listening for requests and our terminal will look like this:

```
2. func-param
~/clients/packt/dev/fp-go/3-functional-concerns/ch08-func-param/func-param $ go-run
Config {Port:8080 LogDebugInfo:true MaxConcurrentConnections:4 MaxNumber:10 UseNumberHandler:true}
server started at localhost:8080
```

Functional Parameters

Note that we can get that config information printed to our terminal by inserting the following as our first line in our `main` function:

```
Info.Printf("Config %+v", Config)
```

The "+" in `%+v` tells the `Printf` function to print the field names as well as the values.

When we press *Ctrl + C*, the code in the following line signals our Goroutine on the `quit` channel:

```
signal.Notify(quit, os.Interrupt)
```

```
● ● ●                                    2. bash
 ~/clients/packt/dev/fp-go/3-functional-concerns/ch08-func-param/func-param $ go-run
Config {Port:8080 LogDebugInfo:true MaxConcurrentConnections:4 MaxNumber:10 UseNumberHandler:true}
server started at localhost:8080
^Cshutting down server...
server shutdown gracefully
 ~/clients/packt/dev/fp-go/3-functional-concerns/ch08-func-param/func-param $
```

The `srv.Shutdown` method runs and then the last line in `main` executes to print `server shutdown gracefully`.

Before diving into more of our `func-param` project code, let's look more closely at to Go's `Context` package functionality.

Contexts

Contexts are primarily used for requests spanning multiple processes and API boundaries. Contexts help maintain background information on the state of the object during different phases of a process life cycle as it traverses various API boundary processes.

Here's an example (from https://blog.golang.org/context) of passing a Context parameter:

```go
func httpDo(ctx context.Context, req *http.Request, f func(*http.Response, error) error) error {
    // Run the HTTP request in a goroutine and pass the response to f.
    tr := &http.Transport{}
    client := &http.Client{Transport: tr}
    c := make(chan error, 1)
    go func() { c <- f(client.Do(req)) }()
    select {
    case <-ctx.Done():
        tr.CancelRequest(req)
        <-c // Wait for f to return.
        return ctx.Err()
    case err := <-c:
        return err
    }
}
```

Passing the Context parameter to every function in every request provides control over timeouts and cancellation for requests that span APIs and process boundaries. Furthermore, it helps to ensure that critical values such as security credentials do not stay in transit longer than necessary.

Third-party libraries and frameworks, for example, Gorilla's (http://github.com/gorilla/context) package, provide a bridge between their packages and others that take a Context request-scoped parameter. This improves interoperability between heterogeneous packages when building scalable services.

We will use an application context to provide control over stopping our server. The deadline ensures that our shutdown process does not exceed a reasonable amount of time (2 seconds in our example). Also, by sending the cancel signal, we provide our server with the opportunity to run its cleanup processes prior to shutting down.

Functional Parameters

Here's an illustration of what's going on with our `Context` parameter:

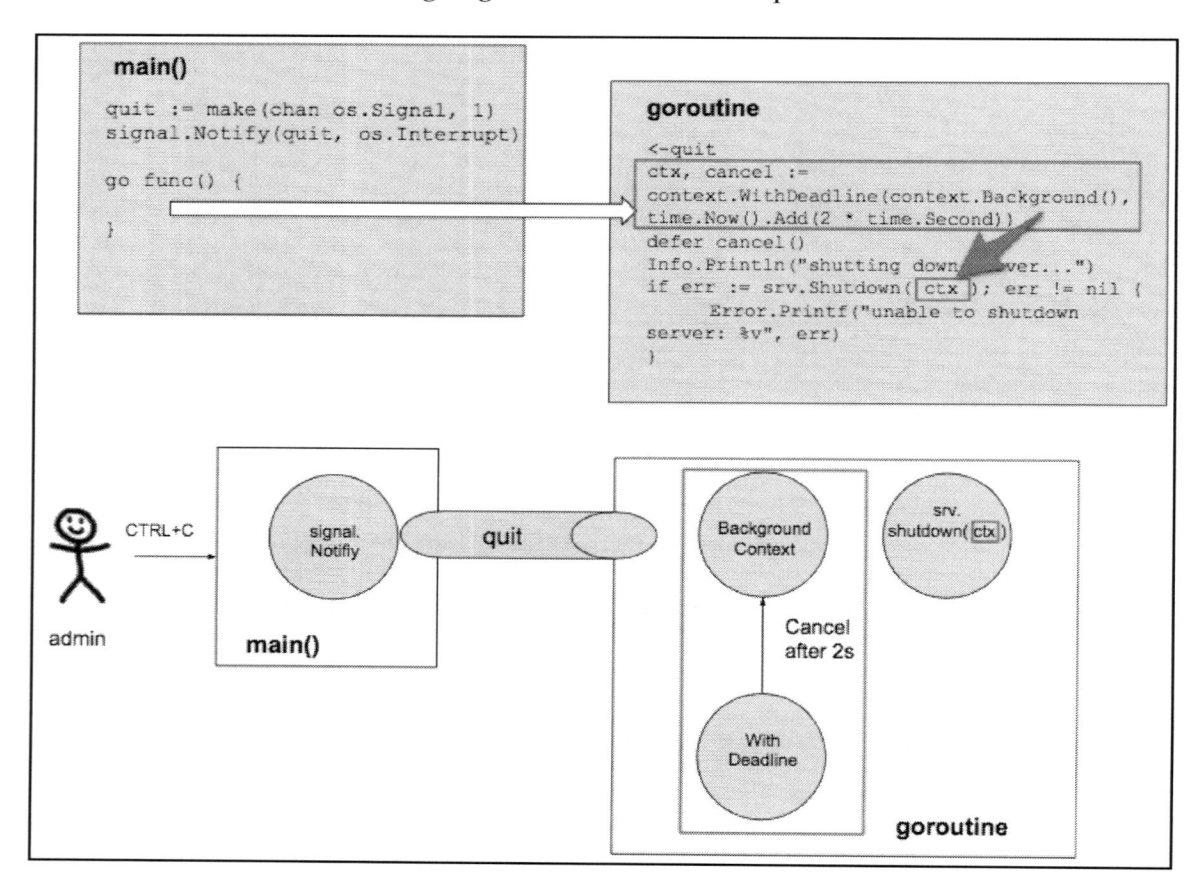

```
main()
quit := make(chan os.Signal, 1)
signal.Notify(quit, os.Interrupt)

go func() {

}
```

```
goroutine
<-quit
ctx, cancel :=
    context.WithDeadline(context.Background(),
    time.Now().Add(2 * time.Second))
defer cancel()
Info.Println("shutting down server...")
if err := srv.Shutdown(ctx); err != nil {
    Error.Printf("unable to shutdown server: %v", err)
}
```

- admin → CTRL+C → signal.Notify → quit → Background Context → srv.shutdown(ctx)
- main()
- Background Context → Cancel after 2s → With Deadline
- goroutine

When the admin user presses *Ctrl + C*, the `os.interrupt` signals the `quit` (buffered) channel. A `Context` (`ctx`) is created with a deadline of 2 seconds. That Context parameter is sent to the `srv.Shutdown` function, where the server's cleanup code is executed. If it takes longer than 2 seconds, then our Goroutine will be canceled. The result is that our server is gracefully shut down and we can be assured that it won't take longer than 2 seconds.

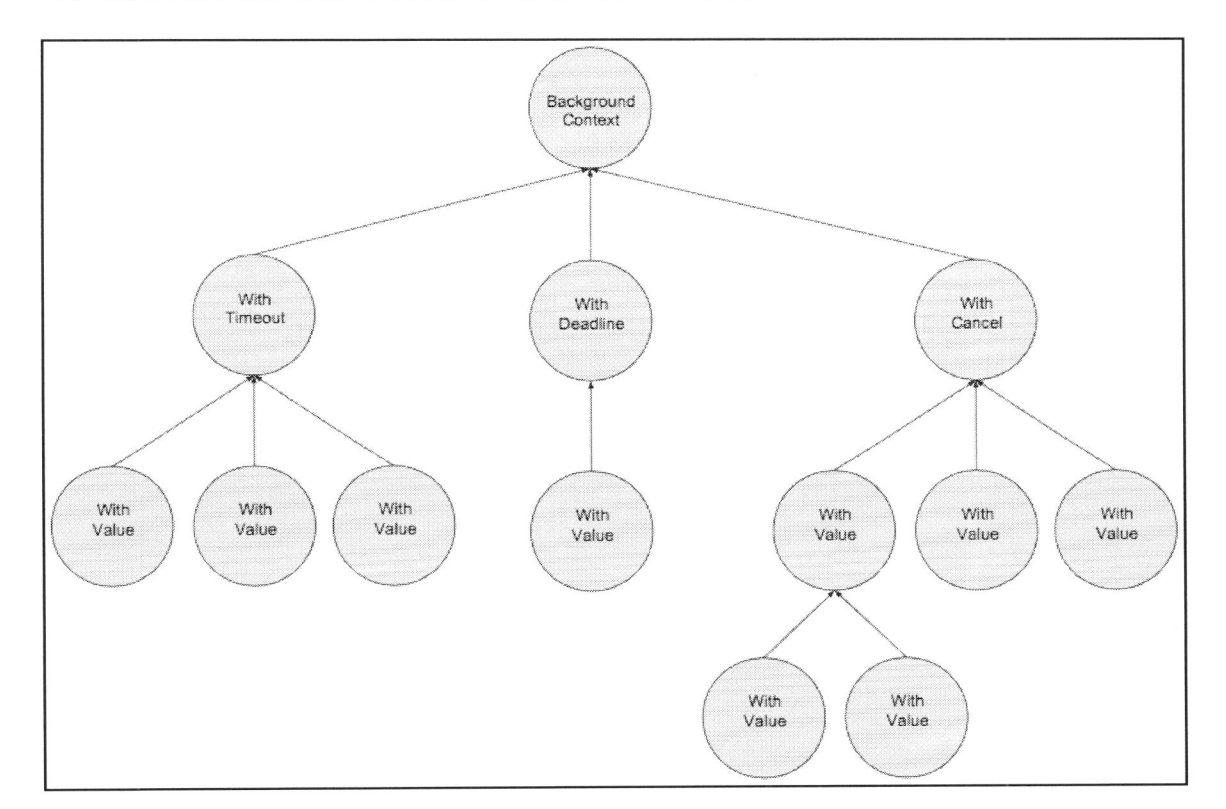

We could build elaborate `Context` trees like the one here:

However, before doing so, we should be aware of our `Context` limitations, which we will discuss next.

Context limitations

Trees can be traversed upward, that is, from children nodes to parent nodes (not the other way).

We should only use values that advise, for example, this user's localname is `en_US`. The `en_US` can be used to enhance the user experience, but not to change the flow of the application. We should not store values that can affect the flow of control in the `Context` package.

Functional Parameters

Report example

As an example of the effects caused by storing the flow of control values in the `Context`, let's consider the following:

```
func Report(ctx context.Context)   {
    reportName, _ := ctx.Value("reportName").(string)
    filter, _ := ctx.Value("filter").(string)
    RunReport(reportName, filter)
}
```

In the preceding example, we passed only the context as a parameter. Inside our `Report` function, we extract the flow of control modifying values, `reportName` and filter. Now, we have the format in which the `Report` function needs to do its job.

Why do some people think that it's a good idea to query other objects' methods internally for data required to make decisions or to make a habit of passing a big amorphous object, filled with data that we must then extract inside our function in order to know what to do next?

It is typically best practice to pass all of the parameters that a function requires. This coding style creates self-documenting APIs. If we find that our parameter list is growing large, that is, over six parameters, then we should consider whether our function should be refactored. Is there any reusable code in our large function? Maybe we can create a helper function and reduce our parameter footprint?

Let's not forget what we discussed in the `Chapter 4`, *SOLID Design in Go*. The *(S)ingle Responsibility principle* states that a class should have only a single responsibility.

If we are passing a ton of parameters, could it be possible that our function is performing more than one task?

Writing good code is not unlike a good game of soccer

Play it simple. Make your passes crisp and short. Be intentional. Maintain control of the ball. Always keep your eye on the ball.

Watch a recreational player and then watch an **elite player** (EP) play the game. What is the the main difference? How well does EP receive the ball? How well does EP pass the ball? Does EP play the ball into space in the path of their teammate or does EP kick long balls in the general direction of the opponent's goal?

Chapter 7

Move (to open space), receive (the ball), then pass (the ball). Teams that do that well consistently win. What are we talking about here? Interfaces. Teams that pass the ball effectively from player to player win more games.

We can learn from this. If we strive to write self-documenting APIs (move to open space) then our API becomes more accessible to our clients. When the APIs that we call are similarly designed (as simple as possible, requiring only mandatory parameters, with sensible defaults) our system will be highly interoperable and efficient.

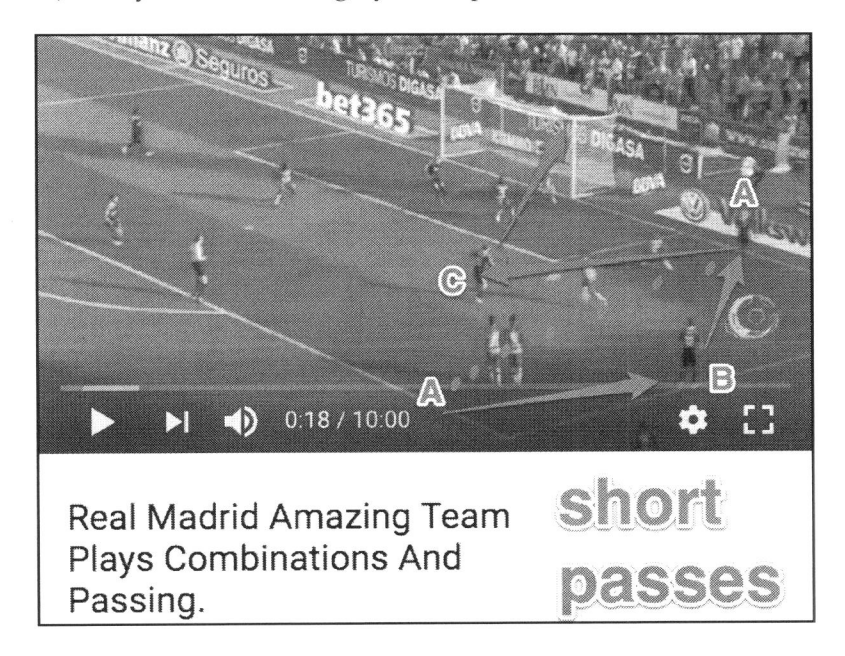

> Real Madrid, an amazing team, plays combinations and passing. Our APIs should interoperate like the Real Madrid team in the video at `https://www.youtube.com/watch?v=b6_IUVBAJJ0`.

Was that a typical use case? Assuming the soccer ball is our data/message, when would we want to pass a message along, avoiding opponents, to move API endpoints and deposit it in the goal unchanged?

Functional parameters - Rowe

Watch the throw-in to Rowe. What Kelyn Rowe does with the ball is like what a functional parameter can do in its callee. Compare that magic with the passing we see in recreational soccer or with passing a dead value in a `Context`.

> Dom Dwyer scored Team USA 1-0 over Panama; refer to this video at https://www.youtube.com/watch?v=CVXPeGhPXkE.

Report example

The values in the `Context` are affecting the control flow of the application. Let's refactor it:

```
RunReport(reportName, filter)
```

In this case, using `Context` to pass values only obfuscates our intention and makes our code less readable. We'd be hard pressed to find a good use case for `Context` values in real-world applications.

A more practical Context use case

A more practical `Context` use case would be to send a `Cancel` message to a long-running function.

Several use cases come to mind when dealing with database transactions.

In some cases a request could generate a number of child requests, each running for varying amounts of time and consuming various resources. If during our database transaction, one of our child requests panics, we could use the `Context` to signal all routines to cancel and to free up all transaction-related resources:

```
import (
    "database/sql"
    "github.com/pkg/errors"
)
```

Provide access to the `sql.DB` commit and rollback:

```
type Transaction interface {
    Commit() error
    Rollback() error
}
```

The `TxFunc` param is a functional parameter provided to the `db.WithTransaction` function. It will execute the given function within the context of the database transaction. If an error occurs, the transaction will be rolled back:

```
type TxFunc func(tx Transaction) error
```

Db uses the `sql.DB` implementation to access the `Begin` and `Commit` transaction:

```
type Dbms struct {
    db *sql.DB
}
```

The `WithTransaction` function is a function that provides a `Transaction` interface that can be used to perform SQL operations in a transaction. If the function returns an error, then the transaction will be rolled back:

```
func (s Dbms) WithTransaction(fn TxFunc) error {
    var    tx           Transaction
    var isCommitted bool
    var    err          error
```

Begin the transaction:

```
tx, err = s.db.Begin()
if err != nil {
    return errors.Wrap(err, "error starting transaction")
}
```

[309]

Functional Parameters

Rollback if an error occurred during the transaction:

```
defer func() {
   if isCommitted != true {
      tx.Rollback()
   }
}()
```

Execute the function that performs the SQL operations in the transaction.

See the `fn(tx)` function?

That's where our functional parameter is executed. That's where the real work is performed. It's where the logic that performs SQL queries runs. It executes in the context of the transaction. So, if any of the queries or subqueries fail, the entire transaction will be rolled back:

```
if err = fn(tx); err != nil {
   return errors.Wrap(err, "error in TxFunc")
}
```

Commit the transaction and set `isCommitted` to true to indicate success:

```
   if err = tx.Commit(); err != nil {
      return errors.Wrap(err, "error committing transaction")
   }

   isCommitted = true
   return nil
}
```

We're done with our look at Context. Now, back to the functional parameters solution...

src/server/server.go

We can skim the imports to get an idea of what we'll be doing in this file. We'll process some HTTP requests, marshal some JSON-converting strings to integers, handle errors, and implement a logger for our server:

```
package server

import (
   "encoding/json"
   "fmt"
   "github.com/pkg/errors"
   "log"
   "net/http"
```

```
    "os"
    "strconv"
)
```

We'll define three constants and use them when defining our default values:

```
const (
    defaultServerMaxMessageSize = 1024 * 1024 * 4
    defaultMaxNumber = 30
    defaultMaxConcurrentConnections = 2
)

var defaultServerOptions = options {
    maxMessageSize:           defaultServerMaxMessageSize,
    maxNumber:                defaultMaxNumber,
    maxConcurrentConnections: defaultMaxConcurrentConnections,
}
```

Our `Server` struct has three fields:

```
type Server struct {
    logger  Logger
    opts options
    handler http.Handler
}
```

Here's the `Logger` type:

```
type Logger interface {
    Printf(format string, v ...interface{})
}
```

We use the handler to provide the `ServeHTTP`, which is a `Handler` that responds to HTTP requests:

```
func (s *Server) ServeHTTP(w http.ResponseWriter, r *http.Request) {
    s.handler.ServeHTTP(w, r)
}
```

New is our server constructor. New is a variadic function that receives an arbitrary number of functional parameters of type `ServerOption`.

Note that the `opt` param is a variadic parameter of type `ServerOption`.

We return a pointer to our newly created `Server` object and the idiomatic `error` value:

```
func New(opt ...ServerOption) (*Server, error) {
```

Functional Parameters

First, we prepopulate our options with default values:

```
opts := defaultServerOptions
```

Then, we iterate through each `ServerOption`. The following is the signature for a `ServerOption`. We see that we use it to define the function type variables that accept a pointer to the options:

```
type ServerOption func(*options) error
```

If an error is found, we wrap our error to be returned and exit this function:

```
for _, f := range opt {
    err := f(&opts)
    if err != nil {
        return nil, errors.Wrap(err, "error setting option")
    }
}
```

Here, we create our `Server` variable and populate it with the functional parameters (`opts`) as well as a `logger`:

```
s := &Server{
    opts:   opts,
    logger: log.New(os.Stdout, "", 0),
}
s.register()
return s, nil
}
```

Before returning a call, our server's `register` method with our HTTP multiplexer (mux). A mux matches the URL incoming requests against registered patterns and calls the handler for the pattern that most closely matches the requested URL.

Here's the the `register` method:

```
func (s *Server) register() {
    mux := http.NewServeMux()
    if s.opts.useNumberHandler {
        mux.Handle("/", http.HandlerFunc(s.displayNumber))
    } else {
        mux.Handle("/", http.FileServer(http.Dir("./")))
    }
    s.handler = mux
}
```

Note that we use the `useNumberHandler` option to determine which handler to associate with our root path "/".

> **TIP**: This is a contrived mux example used to illustrate a use for server options. In production, you're likely better off using packages such as https://github.com/gorilla/mux and https://github.com/justinas/alice on top of https://golang.org/pkg/net/http/.

If `s.opts.useNumberHandler` is `true`, then the mux will call the `http.HandlerFunc` function and pass the `displayNumber` function as its only functional parameter.

The `displayNumber` function in an HTTP that uses a few server options to determine how to handle the `request:handler`:

```
func (s *Server) displayNumber(w http.ResponseWriter, r *http.Request) {
    s.logger.Printf("displayNumber called with number=%s\n",
r.URL.Query().Get("number"))
    if numberParam := r.URL.Query().Get("number"); numberParam != "" {
        number, err := strconv.Atoi(numberParam)
        if err != nil {
            writeJSON(w, map[string]interface{}{
                "error": fmt.Sprintf("invalid number (%v)", numberParam),
            }, http.StatusBadRequest)
        }
```

In the following block of code we compare the number entered by the user to the `maxNumber` server option value. If the entered value is greater than the max value, we display an error message; otherwise, we continue processing:

```
        if number > s.opts.maxNumber {
            writeJSON(w, map[string]interface{}{
                "error": fmt.Sprintf("number (%d) too big. Max number: %d",
number, s.opts.maxNumber),
            }, http.StatusBadRequest)
        } else {
```

If there is no convert function (`convertFn`), then we set the number to be displayed (`displayNumber`) to the value entered by the user.

Functional Parameters

However, if `convertFn` is defined, we pass the number to it, execute it, and assign the return value to `displayNumber`:

```
var displayNumber string
if s.opts.convertFn == nil {
    displayNumber = numberParam
} else {
    displayNumber, err = s.opts.convertFn(number)
}
```

See how we use a function literal in `main()` with the `fmt.Sprintf` command to affect the displayed number?

```
server.FormatNumber(func(x int) (string, error) { return fmt.Sprintf("%x", x), nil }),
```

To see our number in a hexadecimal format, we'll open a web browser and enter this in the address bar: `http://localhost:8080/?number=255`:

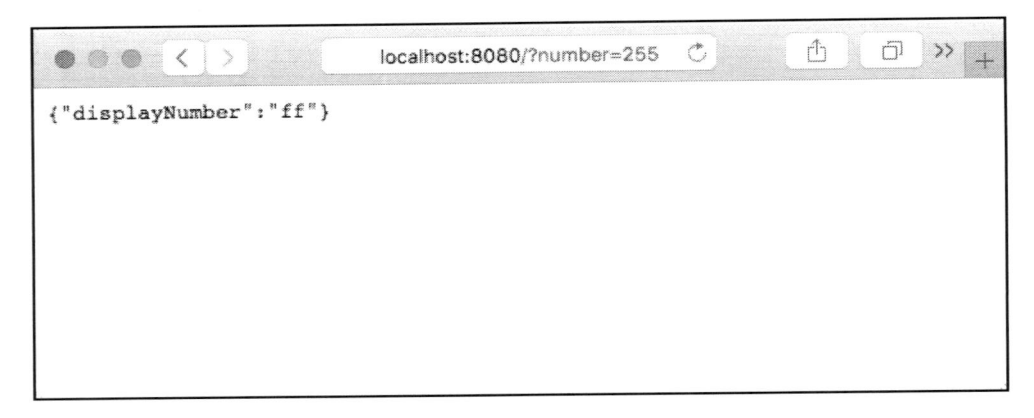

```
{"displayNumber":"ff"}
```

Want to see the `displayNumber` in different format? If so: stop the app by entering *Ctrl + C* in the terminal console. In `main.go`, change `fmt.Sprintf("%x", x)` to `fmt.Sprintf("%b", x)` and restart the app by entering the `go-run` command.

```
server.FormatNumber(func(x int) (string, error) { return fmt.Sprintf("%b", x), nil }),
```

When we go back to our web browser and refresh we see our number 255 in a binary format:

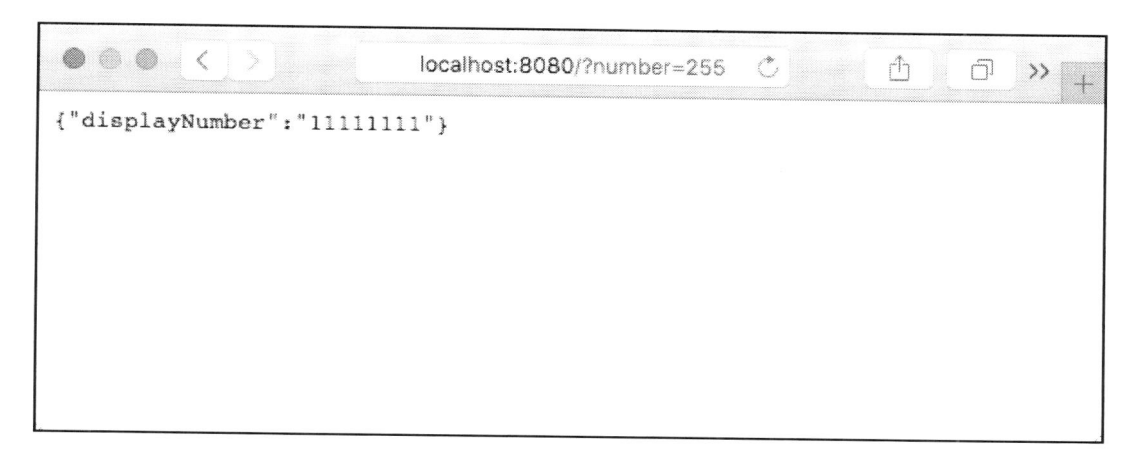

```
localhost:8080/?number=255
{"displayNumber":"11111111"}
```

If we were to comment out the `server.FormatNumber` parameter, we'd get the number entered by the user without formatting:

```
//server.FormatNumber . . .    <= comment out FormatNumber parameter
```

```
localhost:8080/?number=255
{"displayNumber":"255"}
```

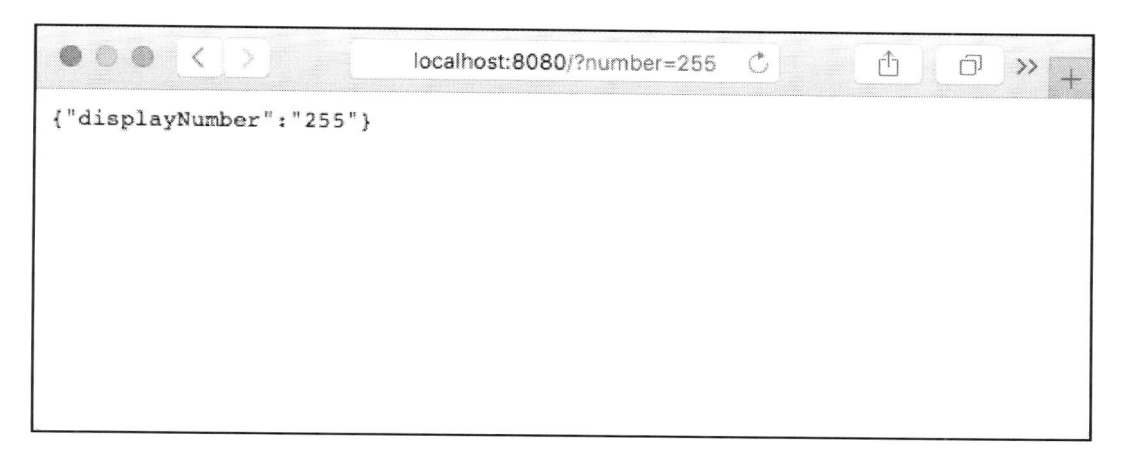

> **TIP**
>
> Refer to the following resource for more `Sprintf` options http://lexsheehan.blogspot.com/search?q=octal+hex+printf.

Functional Parameters

If there is an error, we display it. If there are no errors, we display our (possibly formatted) number:

```
            if err != nil {
                writeJSON(w, map[string]interface{}{
                    "error": "error running convertFn number",
                }, http.StatusBadRequest)
            } else {
                writeJSON(w, map[string]interface{}{
                    "displayNumber": displayNumber,
                })
            }
        }
    } else {
        writeJSON(w, map[string]interface{}{
            "error": "missing number",
        }, http.StatusBadRequest)
    }
}
```

Our last project file that we'll examine contains our `ServerOption` functions.

The src/server/server_options.go file

We'll use the Go standard library errors package because we simply want to create an error object:

```
package server

import (
    . "utils"
    "errors"
)
```

We define a `ServerOption` type to simplify our function signatures:

```
type ServerOption func(*options) error
```

Currying allows functions to yield new functions as their return value. Is that what `MaxNumber` is doing? `MaxNumber` is a function and returns a `ServerOption`. A `SeverOption` is a function. So, yes. We have some currying going on here.

Our first `ServerOption` function is `MaxNumber`. It has a simple responsibility: assigning the value of its argument (n) to our option's `maxNumber` field:

```
func MaxNumber(n int) ServerOption {
    return func(o *options) error {
        o.maxNumber = n
        return nil
    }
}
```

Note that `MaxNumber` is a function that returns a function that returns an error. Since there is no possibility of an error occurring in this function, we simply return nil.

Other `ServerOption` functions can be more complicated and we might run into an error condition in one of those non-trivial functions and have the need to return an error.

The `MaxConcurrenConnections` function has a conditional statement, as shown here:

```
func MaxConcurrentConnections(n int) ServerOption {
    return func(o *options) error {
        if n > Config.MaxConcurrentConnections {
            return errors.New("error setting MaxConcurrentConnections")
        }
        o.maxConcurrentConnections = n
        return nil
    }
}
```

The next two functions provide the ability to format our input number.

The `convert` type is a function type that accepts an int and returns a string and possibly an error:

```
type convert func(int) (string, error)
```

The `FormatNumber` function is another `ServerOption`. Unlike the other ones, which accept scalar input values, `FormatNumber` accepts a function parameter of type `convert`:

```
func FormatNumber(fn convert) ServerOption {
    return func(o *options) (err error) {
        o.convertFn = fn
        return
    }
}
```

Functional Parameters

Let's take another look at `main()`, where `FormatNumber` is called:

```
server.FormatNumber(func(x int) (string, error) { return fmt.Sprintf("%x",
x), nil }),
```

The `FormatNumber` function's argument is passed in as a functional parameter. It is an anonymous function that satisfies the signature of a convert function type:

```
type convert func(int) (string, error)
```

The function accepts an `int` and returns a string and and error.

`FormatNumber` has one statement--the return statement. It returns a `ServerOption` function after it executes the convert function (fn).

Don't be confused by the fact that we know that the convert function receives an int but we do not see it in the anonymous return function: `o.convertFn = fn`.

The line of code, `o.convertFn = fn`, is executed by `main()`; when it runs it creates the `newServer` value:

```
newServer, err := server.New( . . .
```

What it's doing is assigning the `fn` function to the `convertFn` function's `SeverOption` value:

```
func New(opt ...ServerOption) (*Server, error) {
   opts := defaultServerOptions
   for _, f := range opt {
      err := f(&opts)
```

It's not until the user submits a request and that request is handled by the `displayNumber` function that the following line is executed:

```
displayNumber, err = s.opts.convertFn(number)
```

That's where the `int` number is actually passed to the `convertFn` function.

The last `ServerOption` function is `UseNumberHandler`. It is simple, quite like `MaxNumber`:

```
func UseNumberHandler(b bool) ServerOption {
   return func(o *options) error {
      o.useNumberHandler = b
      return nil
   }
}
```

Summary

Go is designed using good ideas from both FP and OOP world. For example, go borrowed interfaces, duck typing, and composition over inheritance from OOP world and functions as first class citizens from the FP world.

Go is a perfect example of being pragmatic. Go took the better principles from both OOP and FP paradigms, while clearly ignoring many ideas from each. Perhaps, this perfectly balanced design is what makes Go so special? In that way, Go is the perfect ratio of software languages.

> See `Chapter 11`, *Category Theory That Applies*, for a discussion about the golden ration.

In the next chapter, we'll delve more deeply into pure functional programming. We'll see how to leverage category theory and class types to abstract away details in order to glean new insights. We'll look at functors along with slightly stronger and more useful versions of functors called applicative functors. You'll also learn how to bring the world of side-effects under control using Monads and Monoids.

8
Increasing Performance Using Pipelining

Often, we feel the need to work on some data and pass it along a series of steps, transforming it along the way before it arrives at its destination. We come across these sort of processes occurring in real-life scenarios, especially in factory assembly line environments.

In this chapter, we will see how the pipeline patterns can be used to build component-based applications. We'll see how we can use function composition data flow programming techniques to create flexible solutions that are not only robust, but also performant in today's distributed processing environments.

Our goal in this chapter is to do the following:

- Be able to identify when to use the pipeline pattern
- Learn how to build a pipeline
- Understand how we can leverage buffering to increase throughput
- Use Goroutines and channels to process data faster
- Improve API readability using interfaces
- Implement useful filters
- Build a flexible pipeline
- See what happens when you change the order of filters and submit invalid data

Increasing Performance Using Pipelining

Introducing the pipeline pattern

The pipeline software design pattern is used in cases where data flows through a sequence of stages where the output of the previous stage is the input of the next. Each step can be thought of as a filter operation that transforms the data in some way. Buffering is frequently implemented between filters to prevent deadlock or data loss when one filter runs faster than another filter connected to it. Connecting the filters into a pipeline is analogous to function composition.

The following diagram depicts the flow of data from a data source, for example, a file. The data is transformed as it passes from one filter to the next, until the result is finally displayed on standard out in the console:

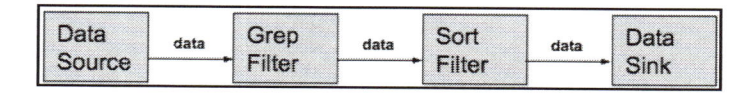

```
Data Source --data--> Grep Filter --data--> Sort Filter --data--> Data Sink
```

Grep sort example

The `/etc/group` file is the data source. Grep is the first filter whose input is all the lines from the `/etc/group` file. The `grep` command removes all lines that do not begin with `"com"`, and then sends its output to the Unix pipe, which sends that data to the `sort` command:

```
$ grep "^com" /etc/group | sort
com.apple.access_disabled:*:396:
com.apple.access_ftp:*:395:
com.apple.access_screensharing:*:398:
com.apple.access_sessionkey:*:397:
com.apple.access_ssh:*:399:
```

Let's be clear. What we're covering in this chapter behaves like Unix pipes, but what we'll study are pipelines that are implemented in Go, mainly using Go channels and Goroutines. Similarly, we will not discuss Go Pipes (https://golang.org/pkg/os/#Pipe) other than to say that they are unbuffered, unstructured streams of bytes.

Pipeline characteristics

The pipeline pattern affords a number of valuable benefits that are desirable in properly engineered applications; these benefits are as follows:

- Provides the structure for a system that processes data
- Divides tasks into sequential steps
- Encapsulates each step in a filter
- Independent filters (run in isolation) with a set of inputs and outputs
- Data passes through a pipeline in one direction
- Configurable modularity (read, write, split, and merge operations)
- High cohesion, where filter logic is self-contained
- Low coupling, where filters communicate through connecting pipes
- Distinction between batch and online processing disappears

The pipeline pattern has many characteristics that make it appealing for a variety of use cases. We see it in use in technologies ranging from constant integration and deployment pipelines, to batch and stream data processing. If there is a need to handle the flow of data in an assembly line fashion, then we should consider using this pipeline pattern.

Let's take a look at the advantages:

- **Extensibility**: Add another filter to the pipeline
- **Flexibility**: Function composition by connecting filters
- **Performance**: Utilizes multi-processor systems
- **Testability**: Easy to analyze, evaluate, and test pipe filter systems

As with any pattern, we must consider its potential issues.

Here are some of the disadvantages:

- Potential data transformation overhead
- Potential deadlock and buffer overflow
- Potential reliability issues if infrastructure loses the data flowing between filters
- Potential reprocessing of data if a filter fails after sending results downstream, but before indicating that processing was successfully completed (design filters in a pipeline to be idempotent)
- Potentially large context, since each filter must be provided with sufficient context to perform its work

Increasing Performance Using Pipelining

Here are some high-level use cases, which if applicable, make this pipeline pattern an attractive design solution candidate:

- Processing requirements can be decomposed into a set of independent steps
- Filter operations can take advantage of multi-core processors or distributed computing
- Each filter has different scalability requirements
- A system that must accommodate reordering of processing steps

Examples

Now, let's look at some examples to help appreciate the value and applicability of this pipeline pattern.

Website order processing

The following diagram depicts the flow of an order from the website that displays the order form to the user. The filters along the way perform various tasks, such as decrypting the request payload, authenticating the user credentials, charging the customer's credit card, sending the customer a confirmation email, and finally, displaying the thank you page:

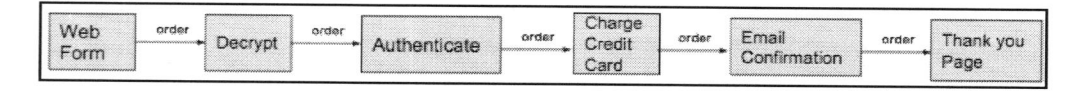

Web Form → order → Decrypt → order → Authenticate → order → Charge Credit Card → order → Email Confirmation → order → Thank you Page

Boss worker pattern

In the boss worker pattern, the **Boss** filter pushes data down to the workers that process the data and merge the results into the **Product**:

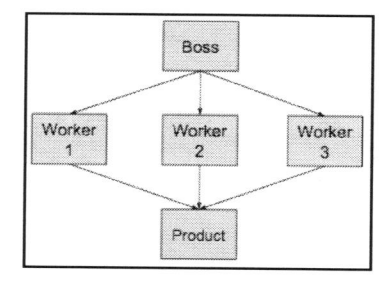

Boss → Worker 1, Worker 2, Worker 3 → Product

Load balancer

The following example shows a **Load Balancer** that takes requests from clients and sends them to the server that has the smallest backlog and is most available to handle the request information packet:

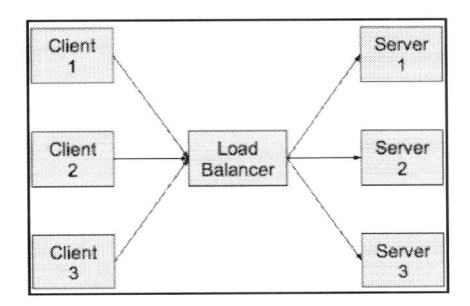

Data flow types

The data flow types can be viewed as **Read**, **Split**, **Merge**, and **Write** operations:

Filter type	Image	Receive	Send	Description
Read			✓	A **Read** filter reads data from the data source and sends the information packet downstream.
Split		✓	✓✓	Multiple functions read from the same channel until that channel is closed. It improves the performance by distributing work among a group of workers to parallelize CPU usage.
Transform		✓	✓	This filter receives data from upstream, transforms it, and sends it downstream.

Increasing Performance Using Pipelining

Merge	![Merge diagram]	✓	✓	This function reads from multiple input channels onto a single channel that's closed when all the inputs are closed. Work can be distributed to multiple Goroutines that all read from the same input channel.
Write	![Write diagram]		✓	This filter receives data from upstream and writes it to the sink.

Building blocks

These are the basic building blocks of a flow-based programming system. With these basic operations, we can build any component-based system:

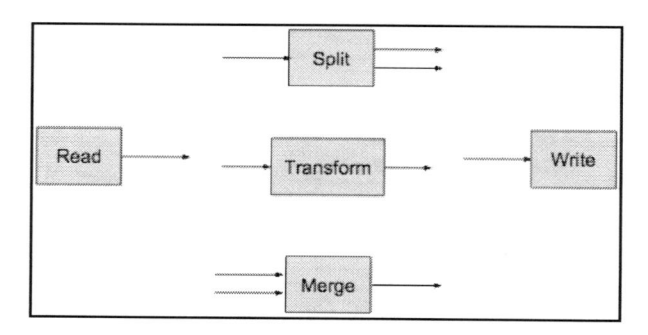

> Flow-based programming is a component-based programming model that defines applications as a network of asynchronous processing operations (aka filters) that exchange streams (https://en.wikipedia.org/wiki/Stream_(computing)) of structured information packets with defined lifetimes, named ports, and separate definitions of connections.

Generalized business application design

The following diagram depicts the component composition diagram for a generalized business application that processes input requests and routes the requests to backend servers. Responses from the servers are subsequently handled, processed, and returned. A few alternate data flows exist for responses that need to be re-routed or re-processed:

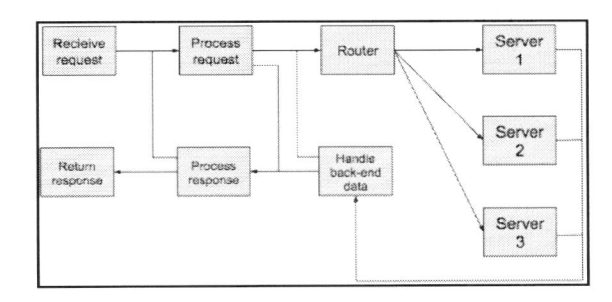

Note that each operation can be swapped, as long as its input and output sets are identical, without impacting the flow of data or overall operation of the application.

Example implementations

Now that we see the value in the pipeline pattern, let's start planning a Go implementation of one.

In Go, pipelines are implemented using a series of stages connected by Go channels. A Go pipeline begins with a data source (aka producer), has stages that are connected via channels, and ends with a data sink (aka consumer).

The data source can be a generator function that sends data to the first stage and then closes the initial outbound channel.

Each filter (step or stage) in the pipeline:

- Consists of one or more Goroutines that run the same function (aka filter)
- Receives upstream data via one or more inbound channels
- Transforms the data in some way
- Sends data downstream via one or more outbound channels
- Closes its outbound channels when all the send operations are completed
- Keeps receiving values from inbound channels until those channels are closed

Example transformer functions include the following:

- Accumulator
- Aggregator
- Delta (to calculate the change between two sample data points of a resource)
- Arithmetic

Example data sinks include the following:

- File storage (for example, NFS and CIFS/SMB protocol access to NAS or DAS)
- Message broker (for example, Kafka, NATS, and RabbitMQ)
- Database (for example, PostgreSQL, MongoDB, and DynamoDB)
- Cloud storage (for example, S3, OpenStack Swift and Ceph)

Imperative implementation

Let's start our coding examples with the simplest form of a pipeline, which of course is implemented using the imperative style of programming.

Decrypt, authenticate, charge flow diagram

We'll base our coding examples on the following flow diagram:

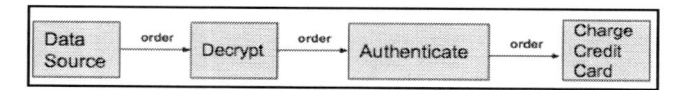

We'll be passing order data from stage to stage until the entire process has been completed. The order data can be transformed along the way, for example, when the **Decrypt** step converts the credit card number into plain text. We'll refer to each stage or step as a filter. In our example, each filter will receive one order from the upstream and send one order downstream. The flow is unidirectional. It starts at the data source and moves to the **Decrypt** filter, then to the **Authenticate** filter, and ends in the **Charge Credit Card** filter:

```
package main

import (
        "fmt"
        gc "github.com/go-goodies/go_currency"
)
```

We'll import the `go_currency` package, which will help us handle the prices in the order line items:

```
type Order struct {
        OrderNumber int
        IsAuthenticated bool
        IsDecrypted bool
        Credentials string
```

```
                CCardNumber string
                CCardExpDate string
                LineItems    []LineItem
        }
        type LineItem struct {
                Description string
                Count       int
                PriceUSD    gc.USD
        }
```

The `GetOrders()` function will be our order generating data source. Note that the credit card numbers are stored in an encrypted format. We'll need to decrypt them later in order to charge the credit card:

```
        func GetOrders() []*Order {
                order1 := &Order{
                        10001,
                        false,
                        false,
                        "alice,secret",
                        "7b/HWvtIB9a16AYk+Yv6WWwer3GFbxpjoR+GO9iHIYY=",
                        "0922",
                        []LineItem{
                        LineItem{"Apples", 1, gc.USD{4, 50}},
                        LineItem{"Oranges", 4, gc.USD{12, 00}},
                        },
                }
```

Note that our credit card number is encrypted and the last field is a slice of `LineItem` structs:

```
                order2 := &Order{
                        10002,
                        false,
                        false,
                        "bob,secret",
                        "EOc3kF/OmxY+dRCaYRrey8h24QoGzVU0/T2QKVCHb1Q=",
                        "0123",
                        []LineItem{
                                LineItem{"Milk", 2, gc.USD{8, 00}},
                                LineItem{"Sugar", 1, gc.USD{2, 25}},
                                LineItem{"Salt", 3, gc.USD{3, 75}},
                        },
                }
                orders := []*Order{order1, order2}
                return orders
        }
```

Increasing Performance Using Pipelining

In our example, we'll only process two orders. We return them from the `GetOrders()` function as a slice of the `Order` structs.

We call the `GetOrder()` function to generate our orders. Next, we range over our orders, running each one in turn through our order processing pipeline:

```
func main() {
     orders := GetOrders()
     for _, order := range orders {
          fmt.Printf("Processed order: %v\n", Pipeline(*order))
     }
}
```

Our pipeline has three steps. Each step is a function that we'll refer to as a filter. There are three sequential filters that our order runs through as it is processed:

```
func Pipeline(o Order) Order {
     o = Authenticate(o)
     o = Decrypt(o)
     o = Charge(o)
     return o
}
```

The following is the output:

```
Order 10001 is Authenticated
Order 10001 is Decrypted
Order 10001 is Charged
Processed order: {10001 true alice,secret
7b/HWvtIB9a16AYk+Yv6WWwer3GFbxpjoR+GO9iHIYY= 0922 [{Apples 1 4.50} {Oranges
4 12.00}]}
Order 10002 is Authenticated
Order 10002 is Decrypted
Order 10002 is Charged
Processed order: {10002 true bob,secret
EOc3kF/OmxY+dRCaYRrey8h24QoGzVU0/T2QKVCHb1Q= 0123 [{Milk 2 8.00} {Sugar 1
2.25} {Salt 3 3.75}]}
```

Since we're starting with the simplest example possible, in each filter is output which filter action is occurring and we pass the order along, in this simple example without transforming it in any way:

```
func Authenticate(o Order) Order  {
     fmt.Printf("Order %d is Authenticated\n", o.OrderNumber)
     return o
}

func Decrypt(o Order) Order {
```

```
            fmt.Printf("Order %d is Decrypted\n", o.OrderNumber)
            return o
    }

    func Charge(o Order) Order {
            fmt.Printf("Order %d is Charged\n", o.OrderNumber)
            return o
    }
```

This is the basic idea of a pipeline. We take a data packet, for example, an order, and pass it from step to step, where each step is a filter function with a specific speciality. The data can be transformed along the way and travels in one direction from the data source to the sink, which ends the process.

Concurrent implementation

In order to increase performance, we should consider running things concurrently. Go has a few concurrency constructs that we can use: Goroutines and channels. Let's give that a try:

```
func main() {
        input := make(chan Order)
        output := make(chan Order)

        go func() {
                for order := range input {
                        output <- Pipeline(order)
                }
        }()

        orders := GetOrders()
        for _, order := range orders {
                fmt.Printf("Processed order: %v\n", Pipeline(*order))
        }
        close(input)
}
```

We created an input channel and an output channel for our pipeline.

Next, we created an immediately executable Goroutine function. Note the open/close parenthesis at the end of the Goroutine block: `}()`. This Goroutine won't exit until we close the input channel in the last line of our main function.

We generate an order, just as in our imperative example. Then, we process each order by passing the next order to the pipeline.

Increasing Performance Using Pipelining

The output is identical to the imperative example and it runs slower. So, we have reduced performance and increased code complexity. We can do better.

Buffered implementation

Let's try using input/output buffers.

In the following diagram, each stage of the pipeline reads from its input buffer and writes to its output buffer. For example, the **Decrypt** filter reads from its instream buffer, coming from the data source and writes its output buffer:

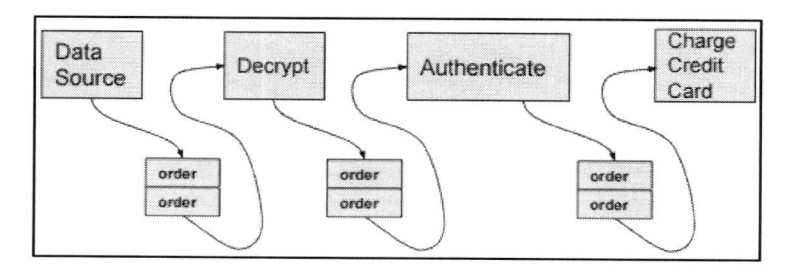

Since there are two orders, the buffer size is two. Since concurrent queues' buffer shared inputs and outputs, if we had four orders, then all filters in the pipeline could execute at the same time. If we had four CPU cores available, then all filters could run concurrently.

As long as there is room in its output buffer, a stage of the pipeline can add the value it produces to its output queue. If the output buffer is full, the producer of the new value waits until space becomes available.

Filters can block, waiting for orders to arrive in its instream buffer or until its input channel has been closed.

Buffers can be effectively used that hold more than one order at a time and this can compensate for variability in the time it takes each filter to process each order.

In the best case scenario, each filter along the pipeline would process its input order in about the same time as the other filters. However, if the **Decrypt** filter takes substantially longer to process an order than the **Authenticate** filter, the **Authenticate** filter will block, waiting on **Decrypt** to send the decrypted order into its input buffer.

Here's how we would modify our program to include buffered channels:

```
func main() {
    orders := GetOrders()
    numberOfOrders := len(orders)
    input := make(chan Order, numberOfOrders)
    output := make(chan Order, numberOfOrders)
    for i := 0; i < numberOfOrders; i++ {
        go func() {
            for order := range input {
                output <- Pipeline(order)
            }
        }()
    }
    for _, order := range orders {
        input <- *order
    }
    close(input)
    for i := 0; i < numberOfOrders; i++ {
        fmt.Println("The result is:", <-output)
    }
}
```

The following is the output:

```
Order 10001 is Authenticated
Order 10001 is Decrypted
Order 10001 is Charged
Order 10002 is Authenticated
Order 10002 is Decrypted
Order 10002 is Charged
The result is: {10001 true alice,secret
7b/HWvtIB9a16AYk+Yv6WWwer3GFbxpjoR+GO9iHIYY= 0922 [{Apples 1 4.50} {Oranges
4 12.00}]}
The result is: {10002 true bob,secret
EOc3kF/OmxY+dRCaYRrey8h24QoGzVU0/T2QKVCHb1Q= 0123 [{Milk 2 8.00} {Sugar 1
2.25} {Salt 3 3.75}]}
```

This is great, right? We increased performance by adding buffered channels. Our solution runs filters concurrently on multiple cores at the same time.

That's great, but what if we process a large number of orders?

Leverage all CPU cores

We could increase the number of buffers by the number of CPU cores available:

```
func main() {
       orders := GetOrders()
       numberOfOrders := len(orders)
       cpus := runtime.NumCPU()
       runtime.GOMAXPROCS(cpus)
       input := make(chan Order, cpus)
       output := make(chan Order, cpus)
       for i := 0; i < numberOfOrders; i++ {
              go func() {
                     for order := range input {
                            output <- Pipeline(order)
                     }
              }()
       }
       for _, order := range orders {
              input <- *order
       }
       close(input)
       for i := 0; i < numberOfOrders; i++ {
              fmt.Println("The result is:", <-output)
       }
}
```

The use of I/O buffers is an improvement on our design, but there is actually a better solution.

Improved implementation

Let's take another look at our order processing pipeline:

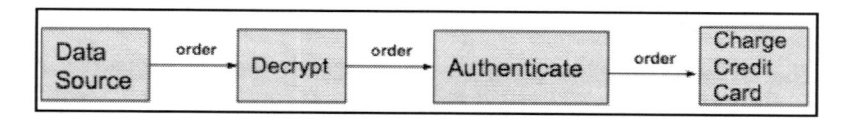

Now, let's implement the **Decrypt, Authenticate**, and **Charge Credit Card** filters with a closer to real life example.

The `Order` and `LineItem` structs will remain the same and so will the `GetOrders()` generator.

Imports

We have more imports. We'll use `go_utils` for its `Dashes` function to anonymize the credit card number. Also, we'll import a number of `crypto` packages for decrypting the credit card number:

```
package main

import (
        "log"
        "fmt"
        gc "github.com/go-goodies/go_currency"
        gu "github.com/go-goodies/go_utils"
        "strings"
        "crypto/aes"
        "crypto/cipher"
        "crypto/rand"
        "encoding/base64"
        "errors"
        "io"
        "bytes"
)
```

BuildPipeline

We have a new function, `BuildPipeline()`, which takes a list of filters and connects them using each filter's input and output channels. The `BuildPipeline()` function lays the pipe, starting with the data source and ending with the sink, that is, the `Charge` filter:

```
func main() {
        pipeline := BuildPipeline(Authenticate{}, Decrypt{}, Charge{})
```

Increasing Performance Using Pipelining

Immediately executable Goroutine

Next, is the immediately executable Goroutine that iterates over the orders that it generates and sends each order to the input of that filter:

```
go func(){
      orders := GetOrders()
      for _, order := range orders {
            fmt.Printf("order: %v\n", order)
            pipeline.Send(*order)
      }
      log.Println("Close Pipeline")
      pipeline.Close()
}()
```

When all of the orders have been sent into the pipeline, it's time to close the pipeline's input channel.

Receive order

Next, we execute the pipeline's `Receive()` function to wait for the orders to arrive on the output channel, and then we print out the order:

```
      pipeline.Receive(func(o Order){
            log.Printf("Received: %v", o)
      })
}
```

The following is the output:

```
order: &{10001 true alice,secret 7b/HWvtIB9a16AYk+Yv6WWwer3GFbxpjoR+GO9iHIYY= 0922 [{Apples 1 4.50} {Oranges 4 12.00}]}
order: &{10002 true bob,secret EOc3kF/OmxY+dRCaYRrey8h24QoGzVU0/T2QKVCHb1Q= 0123 [{Milk 2 8.00} {Sugar 1 2.25} {Salt 3 3.75}]}
Credit card XXXXXXXXXXXX1111 charged 16.50
Credit card XXXXXXXXXXXX5100 charged 14.00
2017/03/08 03:05:36 Close Pipeline
2017/03/08 03:05:36 Received: {10001 true alice,secret 4111111111111111 0922 [{Apples 1 4.50} {Oranges 4 12.00}]}
2017/03/08 03:05:36 Received: {10002 true bob,secret 5105105105105100 0123 [{Milk 2 8.00} {Sugar 1 2.25} {Salt 3 3.75}]}
```

Filterer interface

Our pipeline API is constructed around the `Filterer` interface:

```
type Filterer interface {
        Filter(input chan Order) chan Order
}
```

A Filterer object

A Filterer object has one method, `Filter`, which has an input channel of type `Order` and returns an output channel of type `Order`:

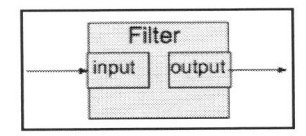

We define types to act as receivers of `Filter` executions. The first filter encountered in the pipeline is the Authenticate filter. The following Authenticate filter has a single input parameter of type `Order` channel and it returns a single value of type `Order` channel.

Authenticate filter

Our authentication logic is hardcoded and simple, that is, not what I'd call production ready. The password `secret` will work for any username. If `Authenticate` encounters `secret` in the `Credentials` field, the order will flow unchanged to the next step in the pipeline. However, if the password is not `secret`, then the order's `isValid` field will be set to `false`. The behavior or subsequent filters in the pipeline can be affected by this value:

```
type Authenticate struct {}
func (a Authenticate) Filter(input chan Order) chan Order {
        output := make(chan Order)
        go func(){
                for order := range input {
                        usernamePwd := strings.Split(order.Credentials, ",")
                        if usernamePwd[1] == "secret" {
                                order.IsAuthenticated = true
                                output <- order
                        } else {
                                order.IsAuthenticated = false
                                errMsg := fmt.Sprintf("Error: Invalid password for order Id: %d", order.OrderNumber)
```

```
                        log.Println("Error:", errors.New(errMsg))
                        output <- order
                }
        }
        close(output)
    }()
    return output
}
```

Decrypt filter

The following `Decrypt` filter has a single input parameter of type `Order` channel and it returns a single value of type `Order` channel:

```
type Decrypt struct {}
func (d Decrypt) Filter(input chan Order) chan Order {
    output := make(chan Order)
    go func(){
        for order := range input {
            creditCardNo, err := decrypt(order.CCardNumber)
            if err != nil {
                order.IsDecrypted = false
                log.Println("Error:", err.Error())
            } else {
                order.IsDecrypted = true
                order.CCardNumber = creditCardNo
                output <- order
            }
        }
    }
```

Note that we handle errors by logging the error. Even though we are told that the `IsDecrypted` field value is always false when it arrives from the source, we play it safe and set `order.IsDecrypted = false` if we encounter an error.

We only process this order if the order is valid. The order can be invalid if the decrypt function fails, refer to the the preceding code. The order can also be invalidated in a previous step in the flow, for example, if the order's `Authenticate` filter failed.

Complete processing

When this filter's processing is complete, we close its output channel:

```
        close(output)
    }()
    return output
```

}

The ChargeCard helper function

The `ChargeCard` function is a helper function used by the `Charge` filter to charge the credit card number found in the order. This implementation simply prints that the credit card was charged. It's a good placeholder for a real charge credit card logic:

```
func ChargeCard(ccardNo string, amount gc.USD) {
        fmt.Printf("Credit card %v%v charged %v\n",
gu.Dashes(len(ccardNo)-4, "X"), ccardNo[len(ccardNo)-4:], amount)
}
```

Charge filter

Like all the other filters in the API, `Charge` accepts an input channel of type `Order` and returns an output channel of type `Order`.

If the order is valid, then we initialize the total to $0.00 using the `total := gc.USD{0, 0}` statement and iterate over the order's line items, executing the `Add` function to arrive at the order's total amount. We then pass that amount to the `ChargeCard` helper function to collect our money:

```
type Charge struct {}
func (c Charge) Filter(input chan Order) chan Order {
        output := make(chan Order)
        go func(){
                for order := range input {
                        if order.IsAuthenticated && order.IsDecrypted {
                                total := gc.USD{0, 0}
                                for _, li := range order.LineItems {
                                        total, _ = total.Add(li.PriceUSD)
                                }
                                ChargeCard(order.CCardNumber, total)
                                output <- order
                        } else {
                                errMsg := fmt.Sprintf("Error: Unable to charge order Id: %d", order.OrderNumber)
                                log.Println("Error:", errors.New(errMsg))
                        }
                }
                close(output)
        }()
        return output
}
```

The encrypt and decrypt helper functions

The `decrypt` helper function in the following code is used by the `Decrypt` filter. We also have the `encrypt` helper function, though not in our pipeline, can be nice to have, to encrypt plain text and for testing purposes.

The `decrypt` function accepts the encrypted string value. The `aes.NewCipher` accepts our 32-byte long AES encryption key and returns an AES-256 cipher block, which is passed to `NewCBCDecrypter`. The `NewCBCDecrypter` function also accepts an initialization vector (`iv`), which it uses to decrypt the block in cipher block chaining mode. Its `CryptBlocks` function is used to decrypt the value, and `RightTrim` is used to slice off the trailing `\x00`. Voila! we've got our decrypted string value:

```go
var AESEncryptionKey = "a very very very very secret key"

func encrypt(rawString string) (string, error) {
        rawBytes := []byte(rawString)
        block, err := aes.NewCipher([]byte(AESEncryptionKey))
        if err != nil {
                return "", err
        }
        if len(rawBytes)%aes.BlockSize != 0 {
                padding := aes.BlockSize - len(rawBytes)%aes.BlockSize
                padText := bytes.Repeat([]byte{byte(0)}, padding)
                rawBytes = append(rawBytes, padText...)
        }
        ciphertext := make([]byte, aes.BlockSize+len(rawBytes))
        iv := ciphertext[:aes.BlockSize]
        if _, err := io.ReadFull(rand.Reader, iv); err != nil {
                return "", err
        }
        mode := cipher.NewCBCEncrypter(block, iv)
        mode.CryptBlocks(ciphertext[aes.BlockSize:], rawBytes)
        return base64.StdEncoding.EncodeToString(ciphertext), nil
}

func decrypt(encodedValue string) (string, error) {
        block, err := aes.NewCipher([]byte(AESEncryptionKey))
        if err != nil {
                return "", err
        }
        b, err := base64.StdEncoding.DecodeString(encodedValue)
        if err != nil {
                return "", err
        }
        if len(b) < aes.BlockSize {
                return "", errors.New("ciphertext too short")
```

```
        }
        iv := b[:aes.BlockSize]
        b = b[aes.BlockSize:]
        if len(b)%aes.BlockSize != 0 {
                return "", errors.New("ciphertext is not a multiple of the
block size")
        }
        mode := cipher.NewCBCDecrypter(block, iv)
        mode.CryptBlocks(b, b)
        b = bytes.TrimRight(b, "\x00")
        return string(b), nil
}
```

Testing how the application handles invalid data

Let's see how our application handles bad data.

Invalid credit card cipher text

Note the XXX that has been appended to the encrypted credit card number value:

```
func GetOrders() []*Order {

        order1 := &Order{
                10001,
                true,
                "alice,secret",
                "7b/HWvtIB9a16AYk+Yv6WWwer3GFbxpjoR+GO9iHIYY=XXX",
                "0922",
                []LineItem{
                        LineItem{"Apples", 1, gc.USD{4, 50}},
                        LineItem{"Oranges", 4, gc.USD{12, 00}},
                },
        }
```

The following is the output:

```
2017/03/08 04:23:03 Error: illegal base64 data at input byte 44
2017/03/08 04:23:03 Close Pipeline
2017/03/08 04:23:03 Received: {10002 true bob,secret 5105105105105100 0123
[{Milk 2 8.00} {Sugar 1 2.25} {Salt 3 3.75}]}
order: &{10001 true alice,secret
7b/HWvtIB9a16AYk+Yv6WWwer3GFbxpjoR+GO9iHIYY=XXX 0922 [{Apples 1 4.50}
{Oranges 4 12.00}]}
order: &{10002 true bob,secret EOc3kF/OmxY+dRCaYRrey8h24QoGzVU0/T2QKVCHb1Q=
```

Increasing Performance Using Pipelining

```
0123 [{Milk 2 8.00} {Sugar 1 2.25} {Salt 3 3.75}]}
Credit card XXXXXXXXXXXX5100 charged 14.00
```

The order that had the invalid credit card number was not fully processed. Note the error message in the log.

Invalid password

Note the XXX that has been appended to the credentials field value:

```
func GetOrders() []*Order {
    order1 := &Order{
        10001,
        false,
        "alice,secretXXX",
        "7b/HWvtIB9a16AYk+Yv6WWwer3GFbxpjoR+GO9iHIYY=",
        "0922",
        []LineItem{
            LineItem{"Apples", 1, gc.USD{4, 50}},
            LineItem{"Oranges", 4, gc.USD{12, 00}},
        },
    }
}
```

The following is the output:

```
order: &{10001 false alice,secretXXX
7b/HWvtIB9a16AYk+Yv6WWwer3GFbxpjoR+GO9iHIYY= 0922 [{Apples 1 4.50} {Oranges
4 12.00}]}
2017/03/08 04:49:30 Close Pipeline
order: &{10002 false bob,secret
EOc3kF/OmxY+dRCaYRrey8h24QoGzVU0/T2QKVCHb1Q= 0123 [{Milk 2 8.00} {Sugar 1
2.25} {Salt 3 3.75}]}
2017/03/08 04:49:30 Error: Error: Invalid password for order Id: 10001
Credit card XXXXXXXXXXXX5100 charged 14.00
2017/03/08 04:49:30 Received: {10002 true bob,secret 5105105105105100 0123
[{Milk 2 8.00} {Sugar 1 2.25} {Salt 3 3.75}]}
```

The order that had the invalid password was not fully processed. Note the error message in the log.

Changing the order of authenticate and decrypt filters

Previously, the order was `Decrypt{},Authenticate{}, Charge{}`:

```
func main() {
        pipeline := BuildPipeline(Authenticate{}, Decrypt{}, Charge{})
```

The following is the output:

```
order: &{10001 false alice,secret
7b/HWvtIB9a16AYk+Yv6WWwer3GFbxpjoR+GO9iHIYY= 0922 [{Apples 1 4.50} {Oranges
4 12.00}]}
2017/03/08 04:52:46 Close Pipeline
order: &{10002 false bob,secret
EOc3kF/OmxY+dRCaYRrey8h24QoGzVU0/T2QKVCHb1Q= 0123 [{Milk 2 8.00} {Sugar 1
2.25} {Salt 3 3.75}]}
2017/03/08 04:52:46 Received: {10001 true alice,secret 4111111111111111
0922 [{Apples 1 4.50} {Oranges 4 12.00}]}
Credit card XXXXXXXXXXXX1111 charged 16.50
2017/03/08 04:52:46 Received: {10002 true bob,secret 5105105105105100 0123
[{Milk 2 8.00} {Sugar 1 2.25} {Salt 3 3.75}]}
Credit card XXXXXXXXXXXX5100 charged 14.00
```

There was difference. In both cases, both invoices were fully processed.

Attempting to charge before decrypting credit card number and authentication

We start by building our pipeline of functions: Charge,Decrypt and Authenticate.

```
func main() {
        pipeline := BuildPipeline(Charge{}, Decrypt{}, Authenticate{})
```

The following is the output:

```
order: &{10001 false alice,secret
7b/HWvtIB9a16AYk+Yv6WWwer3GFbxpjoR+GO9iHIYY= 0922 [{Apples 1 4.50} {Oranges
4 12.00}]}
order: &{10002 false bob,secret
EOc3kF/OmxY+dRCaYRrey8h24QoGzVU0/T2QKVCHb1Q= 0123 [{Milk 2 8.00} {Sugar 1
2.25} {Salt 3 3.75}]}
2017/03/08 04:58:27 Error: Error: Unable to charge order Id: 10001
2017/03/08 04:58:27 Error: Error: Unable to charge order Id: 10002
2017/03/08 04:58:27 Close Pipeline
```

Increasing Performance Using Pipelining

Attempting to charge before authentication

No surprise here either. If we attempt to charge the credit card before we authenticate the request, the charge will not be processed:

```
func main() {
        pipeline := BuildPipeline(Decrypt{}, Charge{}, Authenticate{})
```

The following is the output:

```
2017/03/08 05:10:32 Close Pipeline
2017/03/08 05:10:32 Error: Error: Unable to charge order Id: 10001
2017/03/08 05:10:32 Error: Error: Unable to charge order Id: 10002
order: &{10001 false false alice,secret
7b/HWvtIB9a16AYk+Yv6WWwer3GFbxpjoR+GO9iHIYY= 0922 [{Apples 1 4.50} {Oranges
4 12.00}]}
order: &{10002 false false bob,secret
EOc3kF/OmxY+dRCaYRrey8h24QoGzVU0/T2QKVCHb1Q= 0123 [{Milk 2 8.00} {Sugar 1
2.25} {Salt 3 3.75}]}
```

Further reading

An entire book could be written on the topic of the pipeline pattern.

Some of the topics not covered in this chapter, but you should research on your own, include the following:

- Designing and implementing the `Split` and `Merge` filters
- Understanding how the `sync.WaitGroup` type helps you manage synchronization of channel communication
- Add branching and conditional workflow patterns to the pipeline

> **Good reads:** *Go Concurrency Patterns: Pipelines and cancellation* (https://blog.golang.org/pipelines) and *Go by Example: Channels* (https://gobyexample.com/channels)

Summary

Building applications that have high cohesion and low coupling is a major goal in software engineering. In this chapter, we explored the pipeline pattern and you learned how to build component-based systems using **flow-based programming** (**FPB**) techniques. We studied FPB patterns and use cases that would benefit from applying the pipeline pattern.

We studied an example order processing flow. We progressed from an imperative implementation to a concurrent one using Goroutines and channels. We learned how I/O buffers can effectively be used to hold more than one order at a time and how this can compensate for variability in the time it takes each filter to process each order.

Our last implementation was an improvement upon the prior attempts. We created an elegant API based on the `Filterer` interface. We were able to define and control our entire order processing flow with this one command:

```
pipeline := BuildPipeline(Decrypt{}, Charge{}, Authenticate{})
```

Lastly, we implemented various FPB error handling techniques and tested their effectiveness.

In the next chapter, we'll look at another technique used to improve performance: being lazy.

9
Functors, Monoids, and Generics

"Here's my attempt at functional programming in Go. I think it's a good idea, but I'm really not sure."

I have seen comments like this on over a dozen blog articles. I hope that after reading this chapter and working through the examples, you'll have a new-found love for functional programming (FP). Not because it's so pure that you worry that side-effect programming will send you to hell, but rather, because you feel comfortable with concepts that form the basis of pure FP and you see that its benefits outweigh the costs of learning how to use it.

Our goals in this chapter are as follows:

- Appreciate how the lack of generics support in Go can be a good thing
- Learn how to use a generics code generation tool to solve the boilerplate problem
- Deeply understand how function composition works
- Build a few functors and understand how to map between worlds
- Build a few monoids and learn how to write your own reduce functions

Understanding functors

A functor is a structure-preserving transformation between categories. In other words, a functor is a mappable type. Let's see what that means with an example.

An imperative versus pure FP example

Suppose we start with a slice of ints, `ints := []int{1,2,3}`.

In imperative programming, we write all the scaffold code to implement exactly how to process this slice of ints. In pure FP, however, we tell our functor what we want the loop to do:

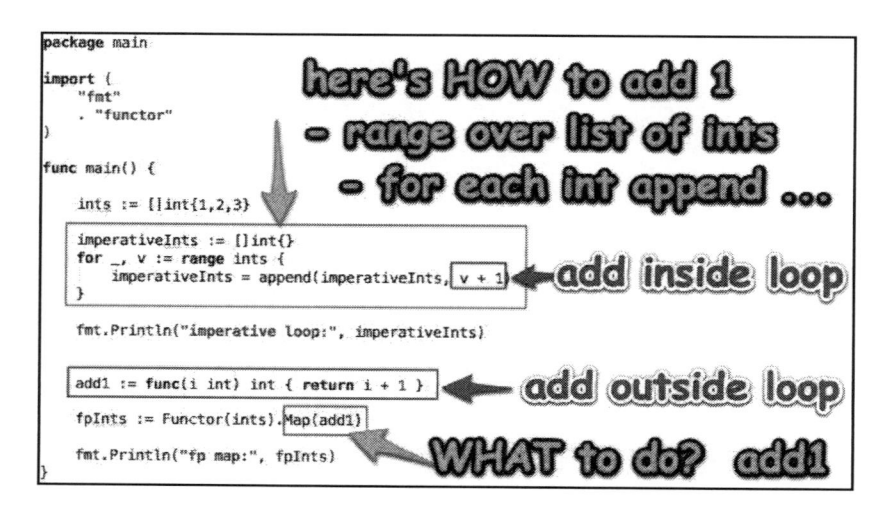

```
package main

import (
    "fmt"
    . "functor"
)

func main() {
    ints := []int{1,2,3}

    imperativeInts := []int{}
    for _, v := range ints {
        imperativeInts = append(imperativeInts, v + 1)
    }
    fmt.Println("imperative loop:", imperativeInts)

    add1 := func(i int) int { return i + 1 }
    fpInts := Functor(ints).Map(add1)
    fmt.Println("fp map:", fpInts)
}
```

here's HOW to add 1
- *range over list of ints*
- *for each int append ...*
← *add inside loop*
← *add outside loop*
WHAT to do? add1

Here's the output:

```
imperative loop: [2 3 4]
fp map: [2 3 4]
```

Let's see how this works.

What did that Map function do for us?

The `Map` function abstracted the loop. We don't have to bother writing the same old range/for looping code. We simply pass in our original `ints` list and tell our functor to map that slice into a slice where each element is one greater than it was before. This is a lot like SQL, where we declare what data we want and let the database engine worry about how to get the data.

What possible benefits can this afford us?

Do we have to change our SQL query code to benefit from a database engine update that increases the query performance? The answer is no, and the same goes for our pure FP code.

What if all we had to do was write `Functor(list).Map(add1)` and define our custom `add1` function? What if `Functor` was part of the Go Standard Library (or another very stable third-party package), and what if the next version of Go came out and it knew how to optimize performance based on the size of the list we passed it? Would that not be an automatic, significant benefit gained from simply compiling with the latest version of Go (or that other, very stable third-party package)?

> **TIP**
> This may not seem like a big win in terms of the lines of code written, or even clarity. In this case, and in smaller utility or administrative programs, it might not be of great benefit. The IMHO place where using FP style offers the greatest benefit is in business use case logic. We look for places where we need to be careful to not clutter business intent with noisy code like for loop scaffolding and error checking code blocks. Those are great places for FP-style programming. Other good places are where we would like to horizontally scale our application without worrying about race conditions or side effects.

A magical structure

A functor can be thought of as a magical structure that can be mapped over, where the magical structure can be thought of as a shape with a constant set of elements accompanied by the ability to apply a transformation operation to each element.

Let's look at some examples.

Functors, Monoids, and Generics

Color blocks functor

A functor consists of a structure, usually a slice in Go, and a transformation operation, that is, the mapping function:

Structure	Eight blocks, each filled with a different color
Transformation operation	`f(x) = x - 30`, where x is the hue

Below, is a functor that maps eight colored blocks to eight corresponding blocks whose color has been altered by applying the transformation operations above to adjust the hue of the color displayed in the boxes.

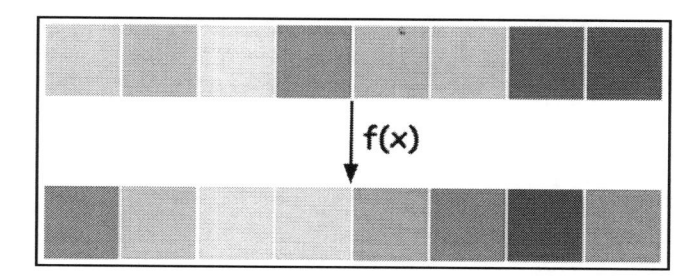

The preceding diagram shows a single **f(x)** arrow to keep the clutter to a minimum, but a more accurate representation would show arrows from each original element to its corresponding, new, transformed element. That's what actually occurs--each element is processed inside the structure and transformed into a new value that is returned inside the structure:

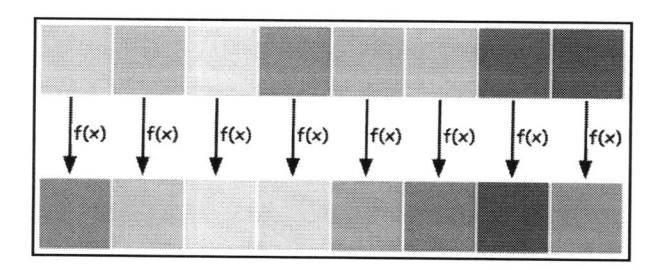

Fingers times 10 functor

As mentioned before, a functor consists of a structure and a transformation operation:

Structure	Five fingers, each representing an integer
Transformation operation	`f(x) = x * 10`

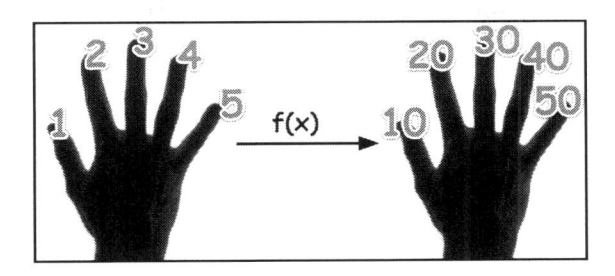

From the last chapter, we know that a category consists of the following:

- Grouping of objects
- **Objects**: Dots/points/a primitive with no properties and no structure
- **Morphism (arrow)**: Something that goes between two objects/elements

Can you see the objects (the numbers on each finger)?

Can you see the mappings (**1** to **10**, **2** to **20**, **3** to **30**, and so on)?

The fact that our category is closed under multiplication, has an identity element, and has a mapping function (times 10), means that we've got a functor. See it?

This is a shape-preserving map that maps from one category to another; hence, the functor is called a category homomorphism. The **f(x)** illustrates that the functor is a function between two categories.

> Counting on our fingers (functors) is more proof that all we really need to know, we are taught in kindergarten!

Definition of a functor in Haskell

We've seen a **functor** in the previous chapter in the type class hierarchy diagram. A functor has only one type class method, `fmap`, which has a type of `fmap :: (a -> b) -> f a -> f b`. It says--give me a function that takes an `a` and returns a `b`, a structure with an `a` inside it, and I'll give you a structure with a `b` inside it. The function is applied to each element inside the structure. The `fmap` function transforms values inside the structure.

We could use the following terms interchangeably:

- Structure
- Container
- Box

The important thing to remember is that a functor operates on the element inside the thing (structure/container/box) and returns the structure with the transformed value (not the raw value).

Kinds of types

Functors in Haskell must have the kind * -> *. Kinds are another layer of types, above the concrete types in Haskell. Kinds allow us to define what behavior types are capable of and then connect them with the appropriate type classes. For example, an **Int** can act like a showable, readable, ordered, or enumerable thing. Values in Haskell can be classified by their type. Let's use Haskell's concise syntax to look at some examples:

Type(Class)	__Kind__	Description
Int	*	* represents concrete types (such as Bool, Char, or Int).
Char	*	* represents concrete types (such as Bool, Char, or Int).
[]	* -> *	[] takes a single type of kind * and returns a new type of kind *.
Maybe	* -> *	A higher-kinded type that takes a single type of kind * and returns a new type of kind *.
Either	* -> * -> *	A higher-kinded type that takes a single type of kind * and either returns a new type of kind * or returns a new type of kind *.
Functor	(* -> *) -> Constraint	A functor is a type class, not a type. We define the behavior of the higher-kinded type that is a functor to be something that takes a kind * and maps it into another kind, *. The constraint refers to the fact that the functor must obey the rules defined in its algebra. A constraint enforces some sort of limitation. For example, a Numeric constraint might constrain all values of the Numeric type to be numeric. 123 passes, but "ABC" fails for the Numeric constraint.

Maybe

Maybe is a functor that maps every type to the same type with an additional Nothing value. Maybe is like an optional value (note that types are the objects in our category):

```
data Maybe a = Just a | Nothing
```

The value of Maybe Int can be either just a number, such as Just 2, or Nothing.

The Maybe type maps types to types. For example, it maps **Char** to **Maybe Char**. fmap, defined in the following snippet, shows how every a -> b function has a corresponding version, Maybe a -> Maybe b, which just returns Nothing when given Nothing and behaves normally otherwise:

```
instance Functor Maybe where
    fmap f Nothing = Nothing
    fmap f (Just x) = Just (f x)
```

Polymorphism at a higher level

Haskell's rich type features (type classes, parameterized algebraic data types, recursive data types, and so on) allow us to implement polymorphism on a much higher level than is currently possible in Go.

It is possible to implement polymorphic behavior in Go. However, due to language limitations (the lack of generics), it requires additional code to specify each type that implements the desired behaviors.

> For a Golang code example that demonstrates how to leverage structs and methods to derive polymorphic behavior, see http://l3x.github.io/golang-code-examples/2014/07/15/polymorphic-shapes.html.

No Generics results in a lot of boilerplate code

Without support for generics, when we implement a list function, we must implement it for each type our application requires. It's a lot of repetitive, boilerplate code. For example, if we must implement a Sum function for int8, int32, float64, and complex128, this is what it might look like:

```go
package main

import (
    "fmt"
)

func int8Sum(list []int8) (int8) {
    var result int8 = 0
    for x := 0; x < len(list); x++ {
        result += list[x]
    }
    return result
}

func int32Sum(list []int32) (int32) {
    var result int32 = 0
    for x := 0; x < len(list); x++ {
        result += list[x]
    }
    return result
}

func float64Sum(list []float64) (float64) {
    var result float64 = 0
    for x := 0; x < len(list); x++ {
        result += list[x]
    }
    return result
}

func complex128Sum(list []complex128) (complex128) {
    var result complex128 = 0
    for x := 0; x < len(list); x++ {
        result += list[x]
    }
    return result
}

func main() {
    fmt.Println("int8Sum:", int8Sum([]int8 {1, 2, 3}))
```

```
        fmt.Println("int32Sum:", int32Sum([]int32{1, 2, 3}))
        fmt.Println("float64Sum:", float64Sum([]float64{1, 2, 3}))
        fmt.Println("complex128Sum:", complex128Sum([]complex128{1, 2, 3}))
}
```

Here's the output:

```
int8Sum: 6
int32Sum: 6
float64Sum: 6
complex128Sum: (6+0i)
```

With generics, we would only need to implement a Sum function similar to the following one. <T> is a placeholder for any type we pass into Sum that supports the + operator:

```
func Sum(list []<T>) (<T>) {
    var ret <T> = 0
    for item := range list {
        ret += item
    }
    return ret
}
```

It would be nice to not have to write all that repetitive boilerplate code. Are there any other options?

Yes. We could use the empty interface{} everywhere and perform reflection and type casting to pull the data out of the list structure and put it back into the generic interface{}, but that is not performant, and it's a lot of extra code.

Solve lack of generics with metaprogramming

Metaprogramming (MP) is about writing code that writes code. In MP, we write programs that treat programs, even themselves, as input data. Our MP will read, analyze, transform, and generate code.

Maybe we can use MP to fix what's missing in Go due to its lack of support for generics?

Maybe. First, let's get a better understanding of what MP is about.

Here are some examples:

- Lexers, parsers, interpreters, and compilers
- **Domain-Specific Languages (DSLs)**
- **Aspect-Oriented Programming (AOP)**
- Attributes (.NET)
- Annotations (Java)
- Generics (.NET, Java)
- Templates (C++)
- Macros (C)
- method_missing (Ruby)
- Reflection (Go, C#, Ruby)

There are several types of MP.

Programs that support the `eval` function can generate new code by concatenating strings that represent executable commands. Note: this can pose security risks and is generally not a best practice.

Some languages, such as LISP, can change their own application code based on state information, which provides the flexibility to make new decisions at runtime.

Other statically typed languages, such as C++, have the ability to evaluate expressions and make compile-time decisions to generate code that can be compiled statically into the final executable. This is the type of MP that we'll look at in the next section.

Reflection is a form of MP where a program can observe and modify its own structure and behavior, such as by determining what type of data a pointer is referring to or returning a list of all the properties of an object.

Go does not come with support for macros or generics, so it looks like we must use reflection. Reflection allows our program to manipulate objects whose types are not known at compile time.

For example, we can create a linked list of items using the empty `interface{}`. That will allow us to put any type of data in our list. When we pull an item out of our list, we must use type assertion to assign a data type to it in order to use it. The problem is that this is not a type-safe operation, it's cumbersome to use, and it is a slow operation. Using reflection is generally not a best practice. Some possible use cases include the following (none of which help us with generics):

- Calling functions

- Recognizing interfaces
- Validating fields

> For more information on reflection in Go, have a look at the following information:
> golang.org/pkg/reflect/
> blog.golang.org/laws-of-reflection
> blog.ralch.com/tutorial/golang-reflection/
> blog.gopheracademy.com/birthday-bash-2014/advanced-reflection-with-go-at-hashicorp/

If we shouldn't use reflection, then how can we solve this problem of repetitive, boilerplate code?

Generics code generation tool

How can we not write all that repetitive code and not take a performance hit, nor lose any type safety of our strongly-typed language?

Let's look at using Go tooling to generate the boilerplate code for us. We'll use it to replace `interface{}` in our code with `<T>`. Here, `<T>` represents any type that works in the context in which it is found.

Since we'll be using real types, we'll get compile-time type safety.

The clipperhouse/gen tool

Though there are several generics code generation tools available, let's look at my personal favorite, clipperhouse/gen.

We get the following functions for free with the clipperhouse/gen tool:

Aggregation	Filter	Map	Misc
Aggregate[T]	All	Select[T]	List
Average	Any	Where	Ring
Average[T]	Distinct		Set
Count	DistinctBy		stringer
Max	First		

Functors, Monoids, and Generics

Max[T]	GroupBy[T]		
MaxBy	Shuffle		
Min	Sort		
Min[T]	SortBy		
MinBy			

> gen is a code-generation tool for Go. It's intended to offer generics-like functionality for your types. Out of the box, it offers LINQ/underscore-inspired methods.
>
> - https://github.com/clipperhouse/gen
> - https://en.wikipedia.org/wiki/Language_Integrated_Query
> - https://en.wikipedia.org/wiki/Underscore.js

Using the gen tool, we'll gain most of the benefits of generics without the performance hits of either reflection or type assertion.

What generics do for us is a lot like code generation. At runtime, when we pass an a of type A to a function, it seems magical that our function can accept the a and do the right thing. What happens most of the time at runtime (by JIT or a regular Go compiler, depending on the situation) is that Go does a code generation replacement operation. What happens at runtime is that our a gets swapped in/out of A-shaped holes in our code. This is the same pattern that our generics code generation tool will use to generate generic code for us:

```
"List <A>".Replace("<A>", a)
```

We'll use our generics generation tool to swap out any type that fits in the T-shaped hole:

```
"List <T>".Replace("<T>", "Foo")
"List <T>".Replace("<T>", "Bar")
```

We can use our gen tool to generate code at development time. It spits out code for us, much like an IDE might do.

We mark up our types using **annotations** in a comment line above the **type** of our code for which we want code generation.

Let's work through an example. First, let's go to the correct directory and initialize our Go environment by sourcing the init script, running glide-update, and pulling gen into our vendors directory.

[358]

Here's the list of the commands we use:

```
cd <DEVDIR>/fp-go/4-purely-functional/ch11-functor-monoid/03_generics_cars
. init
glide-update
go get github.com/clipperhouse/gen
```

This is what our directory structure looks like before running gen:

Functors, Monoids, and Generics

Here's our directory structure after running `gen`:

```
~/dev/02_generics_cars $ find src -type f
src/car/types.go
~/dev/02_generics_cars $ go get github.com/clipperhouse/gen
~/dev/02_generics_cars $ tdml 4
├── bin
├── src
│   └── car
├── vendors
│   ├── pkg
│   │   └── darwin_amd64
│   │       ├── github.com
│   │       └── golang.org
│   └── src
│       ├── github.com
│       │   └── clipperhouse
│       └── golang.org
│           └── x

13 directories
~/dev/02_generics_cars $ cd src/car;gen;cd -
/Users/lex/dev/02_generics_cars
~/dev/02_generics_cars $ find src -type f
src/car/car_slice.go       ← new file
src/car/types.go
~/dev/02_generics_cars $ go-run
cars: [{Honda Accord 3000} {Lexus IS250 40000} {Toyota Highlander 3500} {Honda Accord ES 3500}]
filter cars by 'Honda': [{Honda Accord 3000} {Honda Accord ES 3500}]
Hondas prices: [3000 3500]
Hondas sum(prices): 6500
```

(must cd to src directory with file that has type definitions and run gen)

Now, let's look at our project's code in `src/car/types.go`:

```go
package car

// +gen slice:"Where,Sum[Dollars],GroupBy[string],Select[Dollars]"
type Car struct {
    Make  string
    Model string
    Price Dollars
}

type Dollars int
```

Do you see the `// +gen slice:"Where,Sum[Dollars],GroupBy[string],Select[Dollars]` annotation? It tells our gen tool to generate a slice of `Car` and give us the following methods:

- `CarSlice.Where`
- `CarSlice.SelectDollars`
- `CarSlice.SumDollars`

Chapter 9

When we run gen in the directory with types.go, gen will generate a **src/cars/car_slice.go** file with the following content:

```
// Generated by: gen
// TypeWriter: slice
// Directive: +gen on Car

package car

// CarSlice is a slice of type Car. Use it where you would use []Car.
type CarSlice []Car

// Where returns a new CarSlice whose elements return true for func. See:
http://clipperhouse.github.io/gen/#Where
func (rcv CarSlice) Where(fn func(Car) bool) (result CarSlice) {
    for _, v := range rcv {
        if fn(v) {
            result = append(result, v)
        }
    }
    return result
}

// SumDollars sums Car over elements in CarSlice. See:
http://clipperhouse.github.io/gen/#Sum
func (rcv CarSlice) SumDollars(fn func(Car) Dollars) (result Dollars) {
    for _, v := range rcv {
        result += fn(v)
    }
    return
}

// GroupByString groups elements into a map keyed by string. See:
http://clipperhouse.github.io/gen/#GroupBy
func (rcv CarSlice) GroupByString(fn func(Car) string) map[string]CarSlice {
    result := make(map[string]CarSlice)
    for _, v := range rcv {
        key := fn(v)
        result[key] = append(result[key], v)
    }
    return result
}

// SelectDollars projects a slice of Dollars from CarSlice, typically
called a map in other frameworks. See:
http://clipperhouse.github.io/gen/#Select
func (rcv CarSlice) SelectDollars(fn func(Car) Dollars) (result []Dollars)
```

[361]

Functors, Monoids, and Generics

```
{
    for _, v := range rcv {
        result = append(result, fn(v))
    }
    return
}
```

So, gen is generating all that boilerplate code for us. That keeps our source files clean and tidy. If Go supported generics, our code would be similar to the code we write that works with gen. How similar? Let's see.

Here's our `main.go` file:

```
package main

import (
    "fmt"
    . "car"
)

func main() {
    var cars = CarSlice{
        Car{"Honda", "Accord", 3000},
        Car{"Lexus", "IS250", 40000},
        Car{"Toyota", "Highlander", 3500},
        Car{"Honda", "Accord ES", 3500},
    }
    fmt.Println("cars:", cars)
```

Here's the output:

```
Output:cars: [{honda accord 3000} {lexus is250 40000} {toyota highlander 3500} {honda accord es 3500}]
```

See that `CarSlice` type? That's what gen created for us. We must type in the actual struct types, such as `Car`, and gen will create the `CarSlice` type and all the methods that we tell it to generate for us in our annotation (just above the type definition).

If Go supported generics

This is what the same block of code might look like if Go supported generics:

```
var cars = Slice<Car>{
    Car{"Honda", "Accord", 3000},
    Car{"Lexus", "IS250", 40000},
    Car{"Toyota", "Highlander", 3500},
```

```
        Car{"Honda", "Accord ES", 3500},
    }
    fmt.Println("cars:", cars)
```

Looking at this code block from a lazy programmer's perspective, if Go supported generics, we'd have to type two extra characters, < and >.

It looks like the biggest feature of generic code support has just been neutralized. When we consider this information along with the functions we get for free with gen and the fact that the performance hit is guaranteed to occur at compile time (rather than runtime), it makes Go's direct support of generics seem like a benefit or, at the very least, much less of a problem.

Adding new methods

If we want to add methods that gen does not provide to our `CarSlice`, we can put those in a separate file. The thing we need to remember is to not type any of our source code into the files generated by gen. That's because our code would be overwritten the next time we told gen to run.

Defining a filter function

A few lines down in our `main.go` file, let's define a `filter` function that will return cars whose `Make` is `Honda`. We use our new `Where` method and pass it our `honda` literal function:

```
honda := func (c Car) bool {
    return c.Make == "Honda"
}
fmt.Println("filter cars by 'Honda':", cars.Where(honda))
```

Here's the output:

```
filter cars by 'honda': [{honda accord 3000} {honda accord es 3500}]
```

Cool. Next, let's create a mapping function to return the price field:

```
price := func (c Car) Dollars {
    return c.Price
}
fmt.Println("Hondas prices:", cars.Where(honda).SelectDollars(price))
```

Here's the output:

```
hondas prices: [3000 3500]
```

[363]

Since we have already filtered by Honda, the result only contains the prices of Honda cars.

Aggregation? Sure, we can do aggregation. Let's call the `SumDollars` function that we got for free when we ran our annotation:

```
fmt.Println("Hondas sum(prices):", cars.Where(honda).SumDollars(price))
```

Here's the output:

```
hondas sum(prices): 6500
```

Nums revisited

Remember those four numerics types that we implemented a `Sum` method for without generics? Let's revisit that code and see if we can improve our code base now that we know about gen:

```
cd <DEVDIR>/fp-go/4-purely-functional/ch11-functor-monoid/04_generics_nums
. init
glide-update
```

Note that we need to run glide-update so that the vendors directory will be created for us. It will first be placed in our GOPATH so that when we run the next command, the gen package and its dependencies will go in our vendors directory rather than our project's src directory:

```
go get github.com/clipperhouse/gen
```

Now, let's cd to **~/dev/04_generics_nums/src/num** and run gen:

```
cd src/num;gen;cd -
```

We can see that gen created four files, one for each slice type:

```
~/dev/03_generics_nums $ cd src/num;gen;cd -
/Users/lex/dev/03_generics_nums
~/dev/03_generics_nums $ find src -type f
src/num/complex128_slice.go
src/num/float64_slice.go
src/num/int32_slice.go
src/num/int8_slice.go
src/num/types.go
src/num/vars.go
```

Chapter 9

We have to define each type and annotate that we want gen to create a Sum method for each slice. Note that we never need to create a type for a slice, only the types. Gen creates the slices for each type for us, along with the methods that we request in the gen slice annotations.

Here is the code from `src/num/types.go`:

```
package num

// +gen slice:"Sum[Int8]"
type Int8 int8

// +gen slice:"Sum[Int32]"
type Int32 int32

// +gen slice:"Sum[Float64]"
type Float64 float64

// +gen slice:"Sum[Complex128]"
type Complex128 complex128
```

This is what one of the generated files (`src/num/int8_slice.go`) looks like:

```
// Generated by: gen
// TypeWriter: slice
// Directive: +gen on Int8

package num

// Int8Slice is a slice of type Int8. Use it where you would use []Int8.
type Int8Slice []Int8

// SumInt8 sums Int8 over elements in Int8Slice. See:
// http://clipperhouse.github.io/gen/#Sum
func (rcv Int8Slice) SumInt8(fn func(Int8) Int8) (result Int8) {
    for _, v := range rcv {
        result += fn(v)
    }
    return
}
```

Functors, Monoids, and Generics

Remember the price function that we passed to the `Select<T>` function in our previous cars example? Let's have a look at it:

```
price := func (c Car) Dollars {
    return c.Price
}
fmt.Println("Hondas prices:", cars.Where(honda).SelectDollars(price))
```

That's the kind of function we'll create in our `src/num/vars.go` file:

```
package num

var (
    Int8fn = func (n Int8) Int8 { return n }
    Int32fn = func (n Int32) Int32 { return n }
    Float64fn = func (n Float64) Float64 { return n }
    Complex128fn = func (n Complex128) Complex128 { return n }
)
```

We'll simply return the value that's passed into our literal function definitions in our `fmt.Println` statements:

```
package main

import (
    "fmt"
    . "num"
)

func main() {
    fmt.Println("int8Sum:", Int8Slice{1, 2, 3}.SumInt8(Int8fn))
    fmt.Println("int32Sum:", Int32Slice{1, 2, 3}.SumInt32(Int32fn))
    fmt.Println("float64Sum:", Float64Slice{1, 2, 3}.SumFloat64(Float64fn))
    fmt.Println("complex128Sum:", Complex128Slice{1, 2, 3}.SumComplex128(Complex128fn))
}
```

Here's the output:

```
int8Sum: 6
int32Sum: 6
float64Sum: 6
complex128Sum: (6+0i)
```

Even with this simple sum numbers example, we see that our gen tool saves us from typing the boilerplate loop structures for summing numbers.

We have only used the `Sum` method, but there are about two dozen more to choose from.

> A snippet of documentation describing the `Aggregate` method can be found at https://clipperhouse.github.io/gen/slice/#.

The slice typewriter

The slice typewriter is built into gen by default. It generates functional convenience methods that will look familiar to users of C#'s LINQ or JavaScript's array methods. It is intended to save you some loops, using a pass a function pattern. It offers easier ad hoc sorting.

The annotation looks like this:

```
// +gen slice:"Where,GroupBy[int],Any"
type Example struct {}
```

Here, `Example` is used as a placeholder for your type.

A new type, `ExampleSlice`, is generated, and becomes the receiver for the following methods:

Aggregate[T]

`AggregateT` iterates over a slice, aggregating each element into a single result. `AggregateT` is comparable to LINQ's Aggregate and underscores reduce function.

Here is the signature:

```
func (ExampleSlice) AggregateT(func(T, Example) T) T
```

In the following example, we specify in our comment annotation that we want gen to create an `Aggregate` function that operates over a slice of strings. We define a `join` function that we pass to `AggregateString`, which performs the join operation:

```
// +gen slice:"Aggregate[string]"
type Employee struct{
Name     string
Department string
}

employees := EmployeeSlice {
{"Alice", "Accounting"},
{"Bob", "Back Office"},
```

Functors, Monoids, and Generics

```
        {"Carly", "Containers"},
    }

    join := func(state string, e Employee) string {
        if state != "" {
            state += ", "
        }
        return state + e.Name
    }

    employees.AggregateString(join) // => "Alice, Bob, Carly"
```

Generics implementation options

Below is a decision matrix that can be used to evaluate which generics implementation is best.

Criteria	Weight	Template	Runtime	Copy/paste	Interfaces
Low souce complexity	6	1	1	0	0
Retains static type checking	5	1	0	1	0
Min. runtime performance hit	4	1	0	1	0
Min. increase in compile times	3	0	1	0	1
Min. souce code increase	1	1	1	0	1
Min. executable size increase	1	0	0	0	1
Score		16	10	9	5

There are many aspects to consider when we think about how to implement generics. For example, let's consider the difference between Haskell's parametric polymorphism and C++'s ad hoc polymorphism.

In Haskell, polymorphic functions are defined uniformly for all types. We could call this compile time polymorphism.

In C++, dynamic polymorphism, via substitution, virtual functions and interfaces enable polymorphic behavior, but whether our implementation works for any particular type is decided at runtime when the concrete type is substituted for its parameter.

C++ templates offer a similar functionality without the runtime overhead of dynamic polymorphism. The tradeoff is the fact that the flexibility is fixed at compile time.

Type classes in Haskell allow us to define different behaviors for the same function for different types. In C++, we do this using template specialization and function overloading.

Note that we are only scratching the surface of the issues, and only with a discussion of two languages (C++ and Haskell). There are plenty of edge cases to consider. For example, should the Go compiler perform aggressive optimizations? If so, that would mean specializing polymorphic functions for all types in which they are used, which opens up another level of complexity to manage.

If generics support were added to Go, there would be a cost and risk involved. The cost would come up front, either at compile time or runtime. In all cases, the pros and cons of each approach should be carefully evaluated and we should be careful what we ask for. We'll talk more about generics in the next chapter.

> **TIP**
>
> For more information on generics and Go, including more tools like gen, you can refer to `docs.google.com/document/d/1vrAy9gMpMoS3uaVphB32uVXX4pi-HnNjkMEgyAHX4N4`. Another resource is `golang.org/doc/faq#generics`.

We used the gen tool

We used the gen tool, which is more aligned with the C++/Template approach. While using gen caused us to write a little more code, we were in control, and we got some LINQ-like functionality out of the box, which keeps us from having to write a lot of boilerplate code for handling slices. Nice!

So, does Go support generics? No. But we can use a tool such as gen to solve the big problem of having repetitive boilerplate code. We still have our type safety and do not pay the performance penalty for using reflection.

The shape of a functor

A functor is an algebraic type that accepts a value (or usually, a list of values) and has a map function that applies to each element in the list to produce a new functor of the same shape. What is a shape?

Let's look at an imperative example:

```
ints := []int{1,2,3}
impInts := []int{}
for _, v := range ints {
    impInts = append(impInts, v + 2)
}
fmt.Println("imperative loop:", impInts)
```

Here's the output:

```
imperative loop: [3 4 5]
```

The shape in this example means a slice with three ints. We started with a slice with three ints, ran our imperative code, and ended up with a slice with three ints.

A functor gets the same results (three elements in and three elements out) but a functor does it in a different way.

We give our functor the same slice of three ints. The functor executes `add2` for each int and returns a slice with three ints (each of which is two greater than before):

```
add2 := func(i int) int { return i + 2 }
fpInts := Functor(ints).Map(add2)
fmt.Println("fp map:", fpInts)
```

Here's the output:

```
fp map: [3 4 5]
```

There must be more to a functor than that, right?

Yes. The devil is in the details. So, let's shine some light on it.

Functor implementation

Let's look at our ints functor implementation.

ints functor

Like the good programmers that we are, we declare our interface at the top of our file. Our interface, that is, our contract, has only one function, `Map`. Our `IntFunctor` type accepts a `func(int) int` function and returns another `IntFunctor`.

What? It returns an `IntFunctor`? What is that, and how did it print correctly?

Let's have a look at `src/functor/ints.go`:

```
package functor

import (
    "fmt"
)

type IntFunctor interface {
    Map(f func(int) int) IntFunctor
}
```

One feature of a functor is that it applies that `f` function inside its container. Now, what is a container?

```
type intBox struct {
    ints []int
}
```

That's our functor's container. We'll call it a `box`, because a box is a container, and since we are good, lazy programmers, we prefer names that are short.

Okay. I see the box. What happens in our magical `box`?

```
func (box intBox) Map(f func(int) int) IntFunctor {
    for i, el := range box.ints {
        box.ints[i] = f(el)
    }
    return box
}
```

Firstly, we notice that `Map` is a method and box is the receiver. `Map` takes a function and returns another `IntFunctor`. Ah, so we map from one `IntFunctor` to another? Yes, indeed.

Since a functor needs to map one structure to another one, and since there may be more than one element to map (and when we say map, we mean transform element for element/three in, three out). It's safe to assume we're going to be mapping lists of elements.

How are list shapes in Go usually implemented? With a slice, right? It should be no surprise that the receiver of our `Map` method is a slice. Every slice can be iterated over using `range`, and that's what we use to iterate through our list of elements and apply our function (`f`) to each element and return the `box` we were passed. The difference is that the `box` now contains transformed elements.

Wait a second, what's a `range` with iterator variables `i` and `el`, that are mutating, doing in our pure FP world? And even more disturbing is the fact that we are mutating the contents of our box. That's right, mutations did occur, but only in the box. It's magical, remember? Inside this box is where things can change and not affect our otherwise pure world of FP.

How can we draw a line between pure and impure? This is where we do it:

```
func Functor(ints []int) IntFunctor {
    return intBox{ints: ints}
}
```

That's it. That's the place where we allow our execution to be lowered into the gutter of mutation:

```
fpInts := Functor(ints).Map(add2)
```

See the `Functor(ints)` part in the preceding line? That's where we wrap our `ints` inside the magical box, and that is where we allow the naughty `add2` mutation function to apply itself to each int in our slice.

> **TIP**
> This action of lowering elements into the gutter of mutation is typically referred to as lifting. I would argue that, according to the upcoming analogy, lifting is a misnomer. Lowering would be a more appropriate name for it. For more information, see `https://en.wikipedia.org/wiki/Lambda_lifting`.

What happens in the functor box is not unlike what happens when a person entertains impure thoughts. The structure would be the list of three lovely cows dressed in polka-dot dresses in one's mind. The impure person would allow their thoughts to be lowered to a place where they would apply the `Undress<T>` literal function, where the `T` type in this case would be a Cow:

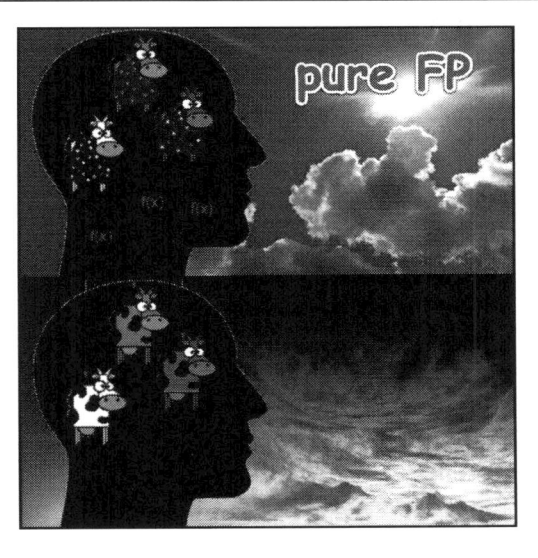

Pure FP goes to Hell

The person may feel safe knowing that their mind is the magical box where all sorts of impure mutations are permitted. When this occurs, a person exercises an `Undress` functor and maps lovely, dressed cows from one world down into another.

> When your Momma says, *"Get your mind out of the gutter!"*, this is exactly what she's talking about.

The last thing we do in `src/functor.ints.go` is create a `String()` method:

```
func (box intBox) String() string {
    return fmt.Sprintf("%+v", box.ints)
}
```

Since we have implemented this one `String()` method, per the duck typing rules of Go, our `IntFunctor` is a `Stringer`:

```
type Stringer interface {
    String() string
}
```

This is a beautiful, one-method interface. `fmt` looks for this interface to print values.

Functors, Monoids, and Generics

The Go Standard Library is very accessible and a great place to go to see how things really work. In our example, we see that we passed v as the verb (when we returned `fmt.Sprintf("%+v", box.ints)`) around *line 577* in the `print.go` file. Here is the snippet from `print.go` that starts on *line 577*:

```
// /usr/local/Cellar/go/1.9/libexec/src/fmt/print.go

// If a string is acceptable according to the format, see if
// the value satisfies one of the string-valued interfaces.
// Println etc. set verb to %v, which is "stringable".
switch verb {
case 'v', 's', 'x', 'X', 'q':
    // Is it an error or Stringer?
    // The duplication in the bodies is necessary:
    // setting handled and deferring catchPanic
    // must happen before calling the method.
    switch v := p.arg.(type) {
    case error:
        handled = true
        defer p.catchPanic(p.arg, verb)
        p.fmtString(v.Error(), verb)
        return

    case Stringer:
        handled = true
        defer p.catchPanic(p.arg, verb)
        p.fmtString(v.String(), verb)
        return
    }
}
```

Functor definition

The `Functor` class is used for types that can be mapped over.

> **TIP**: We'll use Haskell syntax because it so clearly defines FP algebraic data types, including their structures, rules, and logic. `fmap` is the map function. The period `.` notation is the `compose` operator.

Instances of `Functor` should satisfy the following identity and associativity laws:

```
fmap id      ==  id
fmap (f . g) ==  fmap f . fmap g
```

We should recognize these two rules from the previous chapter on category theory.

Identity operation

The identity law of our category says that the identity morphism of **A** is **A**:

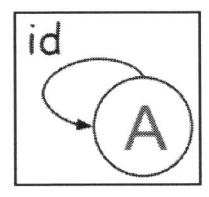

If our operation is a map and the elements in our list are numbers, then the identity morphism is +0. If we add 0 to every element of our input list, our transformed list will consist of the same elements.

> HEADS UP! We are going to hammer home the concept of composition. Your understanding of what composition is and how it works is essential to your ability to be productive in pure functional programming. If you read only a few pages in this book, let your reading begin now.

Composition operation

The composition operation, **g.f** or **g** after **f**, applies function **f** to x (which takes us from **A** to **B**) and passes the result of that to **g** (which takes us from **B** to **C**), and that nested set of operations is equivalent to the composition operation of **g.f**.

In Haskell, we define our composition operation on the first line and request to see the type definition of our composition operation on the second line. The third line is what the composition means:

```
> (.) g f = \x -> g (f x)
> :t (.)
(.) :: (b -> c) -> (a -> b) -> a -> c
```

The a, b, and c above correspond to the **A**, **B**, and **C** in the following diagram.

It says, when we pass the **A** to **B** function (**f**) to the **B** to **C** function (**g**), we get the **A** to **C** function (**g.f**).

[375]

Functors, Monoids, and Generics

This is basic composition. Assuming we start at **A**, this diagram says we can get to **C** either by way of **B** (**A** to **B** to **C**) or by going directly from **A** to **C**. When we choose the short route (**A** to **C**), or **g.f**, we compose **g** and **f** in a nested manner, like g(f(x)), where x is the value that we get from **A**:

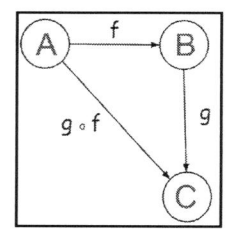

Not quite there? Hang in there. After a few examples you will be.

Composition example in Go

We're going to create two functions, `Humanize` and `Emphasize` (representing f and g), and a composition function of `Emphasize(Humanize(true))` to illustrate the path **A** to **B** to **C**:

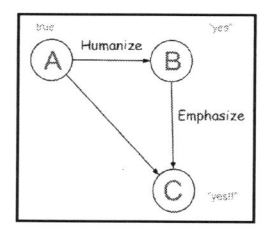

The `src/compose/compose.go` file contains the following code:

```
package compose

func Humanize(b bool) string {
    if b { return "yes" } else { return "no" }
}

func Emphasize(s string) string {
    return s + "!!"
}

func EmphasizeHumanize(b bool) string {
    return Emphasize(Humanize(b))
}
```

`main.go` looks like this:

```
package main

import (
    "fmt"
    . "compose"
)

func main() {
    fmt.Println("A to B - Humanize(true):", Humanize(true))
    fmt.Println("B to C - Emphasize(\"yes\"):", Emphasize("yes"))
    fmt.Println("A to C - EmphasizeHumanizeFG(true)",
EmphasizeHumanizeFG(true))
}
```

If you're using the init script, then your terminal should look like this:

```
~/clients/packt/dev/fp-go/4-purely-functional/ch09-functor-monoid/07_compose_gof $ . init
++ ln -s /Users/lex/clients/packt/dev/fp-go/4-purely-functional/ch09-functor-monoid/07_compose_gof /Users/lex/dev/07_compose_gof
Installed Go version: go version go1.9.2 darwin/amd64
Switching Go to version 1.9.2 ...
GOVERSION: go version go1.9.2 darwin/amd64
CURRENT_GOVERSION: go1.9.2
You should only need to run this init script once.
Add Go source code files under the src directory.
After updating dependencies, i.e., adding a new import statement, run: glide-update
To build and run your app, run: go-run
~/dev/07_compose_gof $ go-run
A to B - Humanize(true): yes
B to C - Emphasize("yes"): yes!!
A to C - EmphasizeHumanize(true): yes!!
A to C - Emphasize_Humanize(true): yes!!
~/dev/07_compose_gof $
```

> If this was a more complicated example that included external packages, then you would have run the following (in this order):
> . `init`, `glide-update`, and `go-run`

Haskell version of compose

We'll cover the Haskell version of composing Humanize and Emphasize:

```
humanize b = if b then "yes" else "no"
emphasize str = str ++ "!"
compose g f = \x -> g (f x)
emphasizeHumanize = compose emphasize humanize
emphasizeHumanize True
```

That's it! Those five lines are equivalent to the 25 lines of Go code!

> I am not at all advocating for any Gophers to switch to Haskell--there are far too many reasons to keep coding and deploying Go solutions to address here. I include the Haskell code for informational purposes. As mentioned earlier in the book, category theory trickles down from the brains of the mathematicians directly into Haskell. So, if we want to be good, pure functional programming Gophers, then we should learn Haskell.

Here's the REPL terminal log of our session:

```
Prelude> humanize b = if b then "yes" else "no"
Prelude> :t humanize
humanize :: Bool -> [Char]
Prelude> emphasize str = str ++ "!"
Prelude> :t emphasize
emphasize :: [Char] -> [Char]
Prelude> compose g f = \x -> g (f x)
Prelude> :t compose
compose :: (t2 -> t1) -> (t -> t2) -> t -> t1
Prelude> :t (.)
(.) :: (b -> c) -> (a -> b) -> a -> c
Prelude> emphasizeHumanize = compose emphasize humanize
Prelude> :t emphasizeHumanize
emphasizeHumanize :: Bool -> [Char]
Prelude> emphasizeHumanize True
"yes!"
Prelude> (.) g f = \x -> g (f x)
Prelude> :t (.)
(.) :: (t2 -> t1) -> (t -> t2) -> t -> t1
Prelude> emphasizeHumanize = (.) emphasize humanize
Prelude> emphasizeHumanize True
"yes!"
Prelude> emphasizeHumanize = emphasize . humanize
Prelude> emphasizeHumanize True
"yes!"
Prelude> emphasizeHumanize False
"no!"
Prelude>
```

Let's look a bit closer at some of the lines.

We can ask our Haskell REPL to tell us the type of what we define using :t <symbol>.

For example, :t humanize tells us that it is a function (->) that takes a Bool and returns a list of characters:

```
:t humanize
humanize :: Bool -> [Char]
```

The \x tells Haskell that compose is a lambda expression. We name our lambda compose and pass the g and f functions as parameters.

The g (f x) says, apply f to x, take that result, and pass it to g:

```
compose g f = \x -> g (f x)
```

Now, let's see what type compose is:

```
:t compose
compose :: (t2 -> t1) -> (t -> t2) -> t -> t1
```

That's a little hard to follow. So, let's see how Haskell says the type is of its default implementation of the compose operator:

```
:t (.)
(.) :: (b -> c) -> (a -> b) -> a -> c
```

We've seen that before:

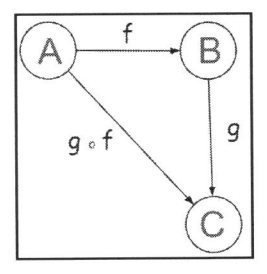

Great! Now we're making progress. Time to define our emphasizeHumanize composition lambda:

```
emphasizeHumanize = compose emphasize humanize
```

Functors, Monoids, and Generics

`compose` is our function, and we pass it two parameters--`emphasize` and `humanize`. Being good, careful programmers, we'll check our function literal's type:

```
:t emphasizeHumanize
  emphasizeHumanize :: Bool -> [Char]
```

Rock solid! It takes a Bool and returns a string.

So far, so good. Now it's time to run this Haskell `compose` function and see if we get the same results as we did in Go:

```
emphasizeHumanize True
  "yes!"
```

Woot!

Given that a lot of Haskellers are mathematicians, we know that they like to use symbols instead of words. Furthermore, we know they like their code to look like math equations. So, let's think like good, math-minded programmers and spice up the syntax.

Let's redefine the composition function name with the `.` symbol (notice that we have to put the `.` in parentheses; otherwise, Haskell complains):

```
(.) g f = \x -> g (f x)
```

And now let's check its type:

```
:t (.)
(.) :: (t2 -> t1) -> (t -> t2) -> t -> t1
```

Okay, we can grok that now...it's basic composition. We can use our period in place of compose:

```
emphasizeHumanize = (.) emphasize humanize
emphasizeHumanize True
  "yes!"
```

But that's not good enough. We can do better. Let's use the infix notation by moving the (.) in between our two parameters, like so:

```
emphasizeHumanize = emphasize . humanize
```

And let's verify that it works:

```
emphasizeHumanize True
  "yes!"
emphasizeHumanize False
  "no!"
```

(g.f)(x) = g(f(x)) composition in Go

This is a graphical representation of our final example of composition in Go:

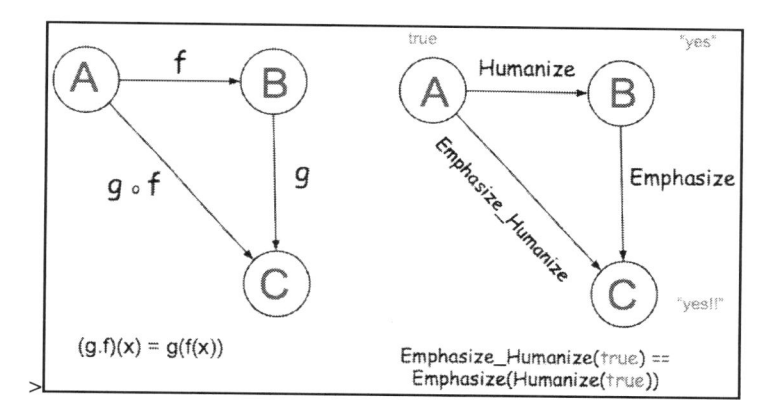

Don't gloss over that diagram. Study it. Let it sink in.

This is composition, the fundamental principle of functional programming.

That **(g.f)(x) = g(f(x))** equation is quite literal. It says that we can execute the **f** function, **Humanize(true)**, and then pass that value **"yes"** to **g** ... **Emphasize("yes")** to get **"yes!!"**.

That **(g.f)(x) = g(f(x))** equation says one more thing. It says that we can nest our functions, **g(f(x))**, which is like going from **A** to **B** and then **B** to **C**, or we can simply go directly from **A** to **C** by executing **EmphasizeHumanize(true)**.

Functors, Monoids, and Generics

So, according to the left-hand diagram, **(g.f)(x) = g(f(x))**, and similarly, according to the right-hand diagram, **EmphasizeHumanize(true) = Emphasize(Humanize(true))**.

Bam!

The (g.f)(x) = g(f(x)) implementation

Now let's take a peek at the code.

Here are the **f** and **g** functions from the preceding diagram:

```
package compose

func Humanize(b bool) string {
    if b { return "yes" } else { return "no" }
}

func Emphasize(s string) string {
    return s + "!!"
}

func EmphasizeHumanize(b bool) string {
    return Emphasize(Humanize(b))
}
```

Now for the new stuff.

We'll create two types. Fbs represents **f** (or **A** to **B**), which takes a bool (true), and returns a string, "yes". Fss represents **g** (or **B** to **C**). Fss takes a string, "yes", and returns a string, "yes!!":

```
type Fbs func(bool) string
type Fss func(string) string
```

Here's our Compose function:

```
func Compose(g Fss, f Fbs) Fbs {
    return func(x bool) string {
        return g(f(x))
    }
}
```

Nested inside our Compose function is an anonymous function. It's our Lambda. In Haskell, it looked like \x -> g (f x).

Lambdas are expressions, and we could pass them around anywhere. We need a function that takes a Boolean and returns a "yes!!" or a "no!!".

Lastly, we define our g.f function literal:

```
var Emphasize_Humanize = Compose(Emphasize, Humanize)
```

A note about composition naming conventions in Go

In Go, we don't have the luxury of renaming a function name with the . symbol or a way to easily convert a function call that looks like **compose(f, g)** to one that looks like **g compose f**, much less one that looks like **g . f**. But no worries! We'll just use the following naming convention to represent a compose function: Emphasize_Humanize (which reads, g . f, where g is Emphasize and f is Humanize). Typically, a camelcased symbol would look like EmphasizeHumanize, but with the _ separating the camel humps, it's obvious that this a special symbol.

Functors, Monoids, and Generics

Here's main.go:

```
package main

import (
    "fmt"
    . "compose"
)

func main() {
    fmt.Println("A to B - Humanize(true):", Humanize(true))
    fmt.Println("B to C - Emphasize(\"yes\"):", Emphasize("yes"))
    fmt.Println("A to C - EmphasizeHumanize(true):",
EmphasizeHumanize(true))
    fmt.Println("A to C - Emphasize_Humanize(true):",
Emphasize_Humanize(true))
}
```

And here's what it looks like when we run it:

```
~/clients/packt/dev/fp-go/4-purely-functional/ch09-functor-monoid/07_compose_gof $ . init
++ ln -s /Users/lex/clients/packt/dev/fp-go/4-purely-functional/ch09-functor-monoid/07_compose_gof
/Users/lex/dev/07_compose_gof
Installed Go version: go version go1.9.2 darwin/amd64
Switching Go to version 1.9.2 ...
GOVERSION: go version go1.9.2 darwin/amd64
CURRENT_GOVERSION: go1.9.2
You should only need to run this init script once.
Add Go source code files under the src directory.
After updating dependencies, i.e., adding a new import statement, run: glide-update
To build and run your app, run: go-run
~/dev/07_compose_gof $ go-run
A to B - Humanize(true): yes
B to C - Emphasize("yes"): yes!!
A to C - EmphasizeHumanize(true): yes!!
A to C - Emphasize_Humanize(true): yes!!
~/dev/07_compose_gof $
```

The directions of the arrows are significant

In the last chapter, we used the following chart to solve $f(x) = x + 2$:

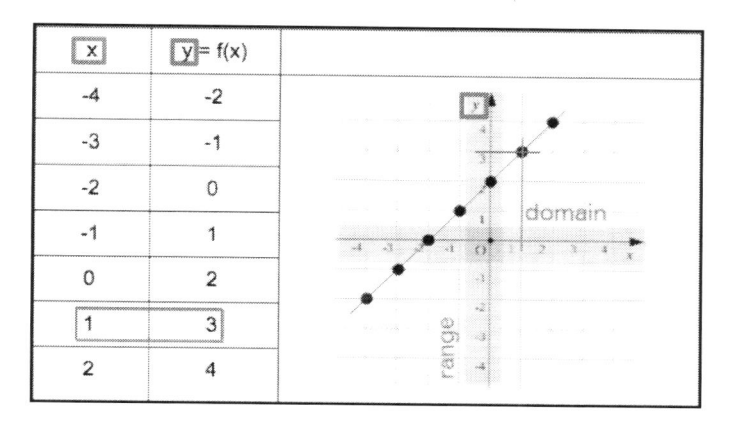

x	y = f(x)
-4	-2
-3	-1
-2	0
-1	1
0	2
1	3
2	4

Remember when we composed $f(x) = x + 2$ with $g(x) = x2 + 1$? We solved **g(f(1)) = 10**:

$$1 \to \boxed{f} \xrightarrow{3} \boxed{g} \xrightarrow{10}$$

We also proved that **f(g(1)) = 4**, which is obviously not **10**. So, we know that function composition is not commutative. The arrows go one way only.

EmphasizeHumanize ordered incorrectly

When we try to reverse the order of operations, this is what we're trying to do:

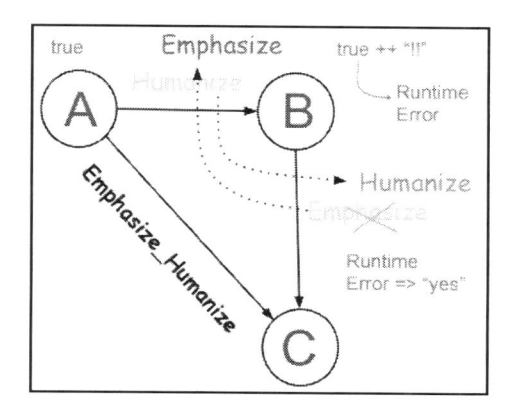

This does not compute.

We start by passing a Boolean **true** to **Emphasize**, but what does that mean? What are we trying to do? We are not changing the direction of the arrows, but we are attempting to change the order in which we call them. Given our context of beginning with a Boolean and trying to get a "yes!!" or a "no!!" out, it only makes sense to apply our Humanize and Emphasize functions in one direction. We are, in effect, trying to compose backwards:

```
func Compose(f Fss, g Fbs) Fbs {
    return func(n bool) string {
        return g(f(n))
    }
}
```

Note that the rest of the code is identical to before. We only swapped the nesting order of **f** and **g** in our return statement.

Our function literal that calls our Compose function looks like this:

```
var EmphasizeHumanizeFoG = Compose(Emphasize, Humanize)
```

That says, *"Emphasize the true and then Humanize the result of that"*, which is clearly not going to work (see the preceding diagram).

This code won't even compile:

```
~/clients/packt/dev/fp-go/4-purely-functional/ch09-functor-monoid/08_compose_fog $ . init
++ ln -s /Users/lex/clients/packt/dev/fp-go/4-purely-functional/ch09-functor-monoid/08_compose_fog /Users/lex/dev/08_compose_fog
Installed Go version: go version go1.9.2 darwin/amd64
Switching Go to version 1.9.2 ...
GOVERSION: go version go1.9.2 darwin/amd64
CURRENT_GOVERSION: go1.9.2
# compose
../../clients/packt/dev/fp-go/4-purely-functional/ch09-functor-monoid/08_compose_fog/src/compose/compose.go:25:35: cannot use Emphasize
 (type func(string) string) as type Fbs in argument to Compose
../../clients/packt/dev/fp-go/4-purely-functional/ch09-functor-monoid/08_compose_fog/src/compose/compose.go:25:35: cannot use Humanize
 (type func(bool) string) as type Fss in argument to Compose
You should only need to run this init script once.
Add Go source code files under the src directory.
After updating dependencies, i.e., adding a new import statement, run: glide-update
To build and run your app, run: go-run
~/dev/08_compose_fog $ go-run
# compose
../../clients/packt/dev/fp-go/4-purely-functional/ch09-functor-monoid/08_compose_fog/src/compose/compose.go:25:35: cannot use Emphasize
 (type func(string) string) as type Fbs in argument to Compose
../../clients/packt/dev/fp-go/4-purely-functional/ch09-functor-monoid/08_compose_fog/src/compose/compose.go:25:35: cannot use Humanize
 (type func(bool) string) as type Fss in argument to Compose
~/dev/08_compose_fog $
```

Function composition is associative

So, function composition does not commute, but it is associative:

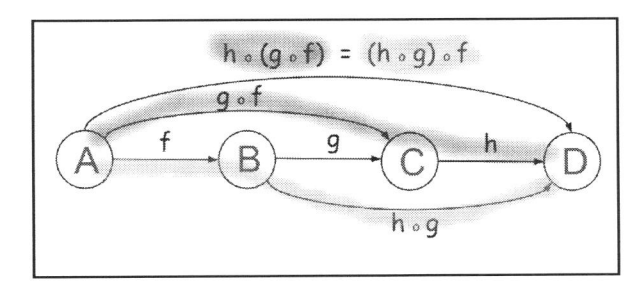

$$h \circ (g \circ f) = (h \circ g) \circ f$$

with the diagram showing $A \xrightarrow{f} B \xrightarrow{g} C \xrightarrow{h} D$, plus arcs labeled $g \circ f$ (from A to C), $h \circ g$ (from B to D), and $h \circ (g \circ f) = (h \circ g) \circ f$ (from A to D).

That diagram says that we can compose our functions to get from **A** to **D** by either choosing the upper (**A→C→D**) path or the lower (**A→B→D**) path.

The idea of a functor is that it translates the diagrams we can draw in one category into diagrams in another category. This often lets us convert ideas and theorems from one category into another.

Let's look at an example of a particular functor, the forgetful functor, to get a better feel for what it means to convert things from one category into another.

Functional composition in the context of a legal obligation

Assume that Larry agreed to pay Lucy $5,000 by 1st October and that date has passed. Lucy wants to get paid $5,000 and Larry wants to pay her, but he does not have the money.

Should Lucy sue Larry to get him to pay?

The following category diagram describes their situation:

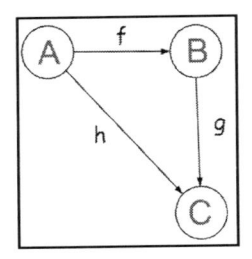

```
    f
A ─────> B
 \       │
  \ h    │ g
   \     │
    ↘    ↓
        C
```

The category states are as follows:

- **A** = Where we are today (12th October)
- **B** = Lucy demands a lawsuit
- **C** = Lucy gets paid

The category morphisms are as follows:

- **f** = Legal expense (for both, $2,000+)
- **g** = Larry pays Lucy $5,000
- **h** = Larry pays Lucy $5,000

Decisions determine state transitions

If Larry, in good faith, communicates the following to Lucy, which path will Lucy take?

> *To be clear, I'm simply asking for more time to pay or for you to allow me to make scheduled payments directly to you without going through the court system.*
>
> *Your thoughts?*
>
> *Larry*

It's obvious that these two will eventually get from **A** to **C**, but which path is the shortest? Which path is more costly, both in terms of time and financial expenses?

Category theory review

We connect two arrows from **A** to **B** and **B** to **C**, and another equivalent arrow from **A** to **C**. **A**, **B**, and **C** are called objects. They can represent anything. In this example, they represent states--beginning (**A**), intermediate (**B**), and final (**C**) states. In the next example, the domain and range represent different court cases, different worlds. The facts of each case make up the structure of each, and the arrows between the two worlds are the mappings the attorneys perform to make their case.

Categorical rules

There are only two rules that must be followed:

- Identity
- Associativity

Results oriented

Category theory is results oriented. It's all about getting from **A** to **C**. The arrows are one-directional. When we compose the two paths (**A** → **B** and **B** → **C**), we get an equivalent path (**A** → **C**). That is what we are doing when we compose functions. We can call one `Compose` function (shown in the following snippet) rather than two functions (`f` and `g`):

```
func Compose(g Fss, f Fbs) Fbs {
    return func(x bool) string {
        return g(f(x))
    }
}
```

The forgetful functor and the law

Suppose Lucy chooses the longer path; how will Lucy's attorneys make the case for their client?

Let's assume there is more to this story. Let's assume that Lucy has injured Larry in some way in the past, and now that Lucy is forcing Larry into a lawsuit, he will in turn choose to convey this new information to his attorney in order to file a counterclaim.

The rule of law

How will the law work when they go to court? The attorneys research the law to find a case from prior court cases that might yield favorable results for their client. They then use that case's ruling as a precedent to win the current case for their client.

It is impossible to refer to the entirety of case history to prove their point. So, attorneys for both sides will use a rhetorical device, known to category theorists as the forgetful functor. The forgetful functor necessarily leaves behind some structure. It is very difficult to find a case from the past that is identical in every way to the case at hand.

Each attorney attempts to convince others that the structure that they present--that is, the one court case that, if chosen, would yield the best results for their client--is the one that should be applied.

The reality is that there is a very large number of court rulings in the past that could apply, but each attorney will try to convince the judge and/or jury that the case that they choose is the way the the law actually is.

The winning side will have effectively mapped a prior court ruling from a world that included different parties (plaintiff, defendants, and case facts) onto the current case. Some of the details will be different, but the winning attorney is the one that best communicates that they have identified the most relevant and applicable case to apply in court today.

Each attorney identifies the bilateral symmetry between an old case that will best help their client and the present court case, and does their part to convince others to apply that case. We might hear the argument begin this way, *"Ladies and gentlemen, the essential structure you need to apply is this one"*.

Lucy's forgetful functor

Given that G is their current case, with its current set of facts, Lucy's attorney maps the facts from the case (E) that helps Lucy the most:

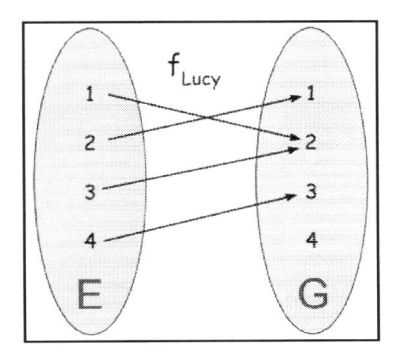

f_{Lucy} is the mapping function from the facts of case **E**, with precedence in favor of Lucy.

Larry's forgetful functor

Larry's attorney maps the facts from the case (**F**) that helps Larry the most:

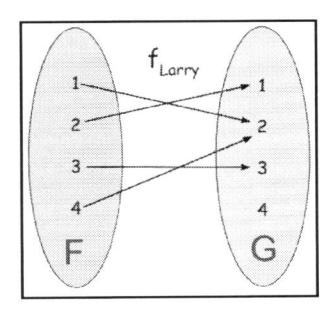

It's up to the judge and/or jury to decide which mapping fits best with the current case under review. The side with the best mapping wins.

It's time to code another functor (pun intended).

Functors, Monoids, and Generics

Build a 12-hour clock functor

We'll build a 12-hour clock functor like this one:

Structure	A clock with 12 places for the hours
Transformation operation	$f(x) = x + 12$, where x is the hour

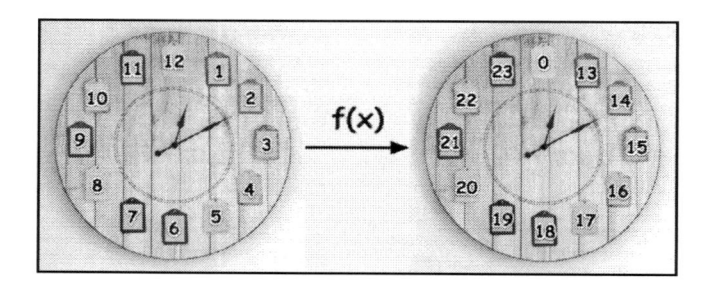

First, let's examine the functor implementation:

```
// src/functor/clock.go

package functor

import (
    "fmt"
)
```

Define our `ClockFunctor` interface to include a single function (`Map`):

```
type ClockFunctor interface {
    Map(f func(int) int) ClockFunctor
}
```

Create a container to hold our list of 12 hours:

```
type hourContainer struct {
    hours []int
}
```

When called, Map will be executed/applied to each element in the container:

```
func (box hourContainer) Map(f func(int) int) ClockFunctor {
   for i, el := range box.hours {
      box.hours[i] = f(el)
   }
   return box
}
```

It's okay for the implementation of Map to be impure, as long as the side effects are limited to variables, such as the loop variables, scoped to the Map function. Notice that return the container, that we call box, whose elements have been transformed in some way by the mapper function, **f**.

Next, we create a function named Functor that wraps our list of 12 hours into the magical box for transformation. This is where we lower our values into the gutter. Some call this process lifting, where the mapping transformation from one world to another occurs (for details, see *Pure FP goes to Hell* earlier in this chapter):

```
func Functor(hours []int) ClockFunctor {
   return hourContainer{hours: hours}
}
```

Clock functor helpers

Towards the end of our clock.go file, we'll add some helpers, as discussed in the following sections.

The Unit function

Our Unit function is our identity function. When applied to elements in the slice, it will have no effect. It's trivial, but it's a requirement to satisfy the functor algebraic laws:

```
var Unit = func(i int) int {
   return (i)
}
```

The AmPmMapper function

This is the mapper we apply when we want to change from AM to PM hours. It will be passed to the `Map` method and applied to each hour contained in the box. It converts an AM hour (1, 2...12) to its corresponding PM hour (13, 14..0).

```
var AmPmMapper = func(i int) int {
    return (i + 12) % 24
}
```

The AmHoursFn helper

We can call this handy function any time we want the list of AM hours. Note that if we create an `AmHours` variable to pass to our clock's functor, its value can be changed. So, this is like a slice constant of AM hours:

```
func AmHoursFn() []int {
    return []int{1, 2, 3, 4, 5, 6, 7, 8, 9, 10, 11, 12}
}
```

> In real-world scenarios, we'll use functors as intended, that is, we will pass an initial slice of values in and allow each functor to transform the slice of values each time a new functor's `Map` function is called. In our `main.go` file, we want to reset the set of hours for learning purposes.

The String helper function

Create a String helper function to use when printing the functor's contents:

```
func (box hourContainer) String() string {
    return fmt.Sprintf("%+v", box.hours)
}
```

main.go

We start with our typical `package main` and `import` statements and the `main()` function:

```
package main

import (
    . "functor"
    "fmt"
)

func main() {
```

Note that we preface our internal `functor` package (found in the `src` directory) with a dot. That allows us to refer to symbols that it exports, such as `Functor` and `Map`.

First, we call our `Functor` method and pass in our slice of `AmHours`. `Functor` wraps our hours structure in a function of type `ClockFunctor`:

```
    fmt.Println("initial state     :", Functor(AmHoursFn()))
```

Here's the output:

```
initial state     : [1 2 3 4 5 6 7 8 9 10 11 12]
```

The `Functor` function is what connects our two worlds: the world of AM hours and the world of PM hours (or vice versa). We can say that `Functor` lowers our hours into a magical box where the transformation mapping function, `amPmMapper`, is applied to each element, transforming it into its corresponding PM (or AM) hour.

Note that the mapper function must be free of any side effects:

```
    fmt.Println("unit application  :", Functor(AmHoursFn()).Map(Unit))
```

Here's the output:

```
unit application  : [1 2 3 4 5 6 7 8 9 10 11 12]
```

We can see that when we pass our functor's identity function, unit, to its `Map` method, it returns what we passed it, that is, the AM hours.

Now for the fun part. Let's pass our mapping function to our functor:

```
    fmt.Println("1st application   :", Functor(AmHoursFn()).Map(AmPmMapper))
```

Here's the output:

```
1st application   : [13 14 15 16 17 18 19 20 21 22 23 0]
```

Awesome! Our list of AM hours has been transformed into a list of PM hours.

Now, let's show off and chain two `Map` calls:

```
fmt.Println("chain applications:",
Functor(AmHoursFn()).Map(AmPmMapper).Map(AmPmMapper))
```

Here's the output:

```
chain applications: [1 2 3 4 5 6 7 8 9 10 11 12]
```

Why was that showing off? It does not look like anything changed. Lame. Right?

Wrong. We're chaining our functors.

The reason why the output doesn't look like it's changed is because it went from AM hours to PM hours and back to AM hours.

Terminal output log

Here's what it looks like in our terminal:

```
~/clients/packt/dev/fp-go/4-purely-functional/ch09-functor-monoid/09_clock_functor $ . init
++ ln -s /Users/lex/clients/packt/dev/fp-go/4-purely-functional/ch09-functor-monoid/09_clock_functor /Users/lex/dev/09_clock_functor
Installed Go version: go version go1.9.2 darwin/amd64
Switching Go to version 1.9.2 ...
GOVERSION: go version go1.9.2 darwin/amd64
CURRENT_GOVERSION: go1.9.2
You should only need to run this init script once.
Add Go source code files under the src directory.
After updating dependencies, i.e., adding a new import statement, run: glide-update
To build and run your app, run: go-run
~/dev/09_clock_functor $ go-run
Initial state     : [1 2 3 4 5 6 7 8 9 10 11 12]
Zero application  : [1 2 3 4 5 6 7 8 9 10 11 12]
1st application   : [13 14 15 16 17 18 19 20 21 22 23 0]
Chain applications: [1 2 3 4 5 6 7 8 9 10 11 12]
Chain applications: [13 14 15 16 17 18 19 20 21 22 23 0]
~/dev/09_clock_functor $
```

Functor summary

Our clock functor comprises a structure (an int slice) that holds 12 hours and a `Map` method that accepts a mapper function that is used to transform each of the 12 hours into the subsequent set of 12 hours (AM/PM). Each time the `Map` method is executed, it returns a new functor; because of this feature, we can chain our `Map` method calls.

In other words, have a look at the following example:

```
Functor([]int{1, 2, 3}).Map(mapperFn).Map(mapperFn))
```

We see that with functors, we wrap and `Map` (and can chain our maps).

The car functor

Let's use a functor to upgrade (and downgrade) some cars! We'll start by opening our `car.go` file in our `functor` package.

The functor package

Let's have a look at `src/functor/car.go`:

```
package functor

import (
    "fmt"
    "strings"
)

type (
    Car struct {
        Make string `json:"make"`
        Model string `json:"model"`
    }
)
```

It's good practice to define our types at the top. Putting them in a type block helps to keep our code clean and tidy. Another good practice is to add JSON annotations to each field of a struct to enable easy (un)marshalling of JSON into our `Car` struct.

> **TIP**
> If you want to omit empty fields from a struct, you can add the `omitempty` clause to the end of your field annotation. For example, if the `Make` was optional or sometimes not included and we didn't want the `json` created from a `Car` struct to include empty `Make` fields, our struct definition would look like this:
>
> ```
> Car struct {
>     Make string `json:"make"`
>     Model string `json:"model,omitempty"`
> }
> ```

Next comes our interface definition that includes the single `Map` method:

```
type CarFunctor interface {
    Map(f func(Car) Car) CarFunctor
}
```

And here's our magical box that consists of the slice we'll be transforming:

```
type carContainer struct {
    cars []Car
}
```

Here's our `Map` method implementation, where we iterate through the elements of the slice of cars in our magical box, applying the mapping function `f` to each element:

```
func (box carContainer) Map(f func(Car) Car) CarFunctor {
    for i, el := range box.cars {
        box.cars[i] = f(el)
    }
    return box
}
```

Here's our `Wrap` method that is used to lower our slice of cars into the magical box for transformation:

```
func Wrap(cars []Car) CarFunctor {
    return carContainer{cars: cars}
}
```

Here we define our helper functions. `Unit` we've seen before--it's our identity morphism. The other two are `Upgrade` and `Downgrade`. We'll keep it simple and simply append an " LX" to the end of the model name when we upgrade or remove it to downgrade a car:

```
var (
    Unit = func(i Car) Car {
        return (i)
    }

    Upgrade = func(car Car) Car {
        if !strings.Contains(car.Model, " LX") {
            car.Model += " LX"
        } else if !strings.Contains(car.Model, " Limited") {
            car.Model += " Limited"
        }
        return car
    }

    Downgrade = func(car Car) Car {
        if strings.Contains(car.Model, " Limited") {
            car.Model = strings.Replace(car.Model, " Limited", "", -1)
        } else if strings.Contains(car.Model, " LX") {
            car.Model = strings.Replace(car.Model, " LX", "", -1)
        }
        return car
    }
)
```

Lastly, we include a `String` method so that our `fmt` package knows how to print our cars:

```
func (box carContainer) String() string {
   return fmt.Sprintf("%+v", box.cars)
}
```

main.go

We'll manipulate strings and some JSON, as well as a `car` functor:

```
package main

import (
   "encoding/json"
   "fmt"
   "functor"
   "strings"
)
```

Create a `cars` variable to hold a `Car` type and initialize it with two cars. Since we annotated our `Make` and `Model` fields with `'json'`, we can easily unmarshal a `Toyota Highlander` into a car:

```
func main() {

   cars := []functor.Car{
      {"Honda", "Accord"},
      {"Lexus", "IS250"}}

   str := `{"make": "Toyota", "model": "Highlander"}`
   highlander := functor.Car{}
   json.Unmarshal([]byte(str), &highlander)
   cars = append(cars, highlander)
```

Now, let's exercise our `car` functor and verify that it works properly:

```
fmt.Println("initial state    :", functor.Wrap(cars))
fmt.Println("unit application:", functor.Wrap(cars).Map(functor.Unit))
fmt.Println("one   upgrade    :", functor.Wrap(cars).Map(functor.Upgrade))
fmt.Println("chain upgrades   :",
functor.Wrap(cars).Map(functor.Upgrade).Map(functor.Upgrade))
fmt.Println("one   downgrade  :", functor.Wrap([]functor.Car{{"Honda",
"Accord"}, {"Lexus", "IS250 LX"}, {"Toyota", "Highlander LX
Limited"}}).Map(functor.Downgrade))
```

Compare one line of FP to a bunch of imperative lines

It takes one line of FP-style code to apply an upgrade and downgrade to a car. Granted, the `Upgrade` and `Downgrade` mapper functions were defined in the `functor` package, but that's a great benefit. We can keep the boilerplate implementation of looping through the slice of cars separate from our business use case logic.

With the imperative implementation style, we first implement the `for...range` iteration block into which we insert our Upgrade/Downgrade logic:

```
// FUNCTIONAL STYLE
fmt.Println("up and downgrade:",
functor.Wrap(cars).Map(functor.Upgrade).Map(functor.Downgrade))

// IMPERATIVE STYLE
cars2 := []functor.Car{}
for _, car := range cars {
   // upgrade
   if !strings.Contains(car.Model, " LX") {
      car.Model += " LX"
   } else if !strings.Contains(car.Model, " Limited") {
      car.Model += " Limited"
   }
   cars2 = append(cars2, car)
}
cars3 := []functor.Car{}
for _, car := range cars2 {
   // downgrade
   if strings.Contains(car.Model, " Limited") {
      car.Model = strings.Replace(car.Model, " Limited", "", -1)
   } else if strings.Contains(car.Model, " LX") {
      car.Model = strings.Replace(car.Model, " LX", "", -1)
   }
   cars3 = append(cars3, car)
}
fmt.Println("up and downgrade:", cars3)
```

See the difference?

Which style of coding will be easier to maintain?

Car functor terminal session

Let's run our car functor example:

```
~/clients/packt/dev/fp-go/4-purely-functional/ch09-functor-monoid/10_car_functor $ . init
++ ln -s /Users/lex/clients/packt/dev/fp-go/4-purely-functional/ch09-functor-monoid/10_car_functor /Users/lex/dev/10_car_functor
Installed Go version: go version go1.9.2 darwin/amd64
Switching Go to version 1.9.2 ...
GOVERSION: go version go1.9.2 darwin/amd64
CURRENT_GOVERSION: go1.9.2
You should only need to run this init script once.
Add Go source code files under the src directory.
After updating dependencies, i.e., adding a new import statement, run: glide-update
To build and run your app, run: go-run
~/dev/10_car_functor $ go-run
initial state    : [{Make:Honda Model:Accord} {Make:Lexus Model:IS250} {Make:Toyota Model:Highlander}]
unit application : [{Make:Honda Model:Accord} {Make:Lexus Model:IS250} {Make:Toyota Model:Highlander}]
one  upgrade     : [{Make:Honda Model:Accord LX} {Make:Lexus Model:IS250 LX} {Make:Toyota Model:Highlander LX}]
chain upgrades   : [{Make:Honda Model:Accord LX Limited} {Make:Lexus Model:IS250 LX Limited} {Make:Toyota Model:Highlander LX Limited}]
one downgrade    : [{Make:Honda Model:Accord} {Make:Lexus Model:IS250} {Make:Toyota Model:Highlander LX}]
up and downgrade: [{Make:Honda Model:Accord LX} {Make:Lexus Model:IS250 LX} {Make:Toyota Model:Highlander LX}]
up and downgrade: [{Honda Accord LX} {Lexus IS250 LX} {Toyota Highlander LX}]
~/dev/10_car_functor $
```

Monoids

Monoids are the most basic way to combine any values. A monoid is algebra that is closed under an associative binary operation and has an identity element.

We can think of a monoid as a design pattern that allows us to quickly reduce (or fold) on a collection of a single type in a parallel way.

Monoid rules

A monoid is anything that satisfies the following rules:

- Closure rule
- Associativity rule
- Identity rule

Let's discuss these rules in brief.

Closure rule

"If you combine two values of same type, you get another value of the same type."

Given two inputs of the same type, a monoid returns one value of the same type as the input.

Closure rule examples

1 + 2 = 3, and 3 is an integer.

1 + 2 + 3 also equals an integer.

1 + 2 + 3 + 4 also equals an integer.

Our binary operation has been extended into an operation that works on lists!

Closure axiom

If a, b ∈ S, then a + b ∈ S.

That says, if a and b are any two values in the set S of integers and if we apply the binary operation + to any two values, then the result of that addition operation will be a value that is also in the set of integers.

Associativity rule

"If you combine several more values, the order in which you combine does not matter"

```
( 1 + 2 ) + 3 == 1 + ( 2 + 3 )    // left and right associativity
```

So, if we have 1 + 2 + 3 + 4, we can transform that into (1 + 2) + (3 + 4).

Note that associativity works for addition and multiplication and string concatenation, but not for subtraction and division.

Identity rule

"There is an identity element that doesn't do anything."

- Identity rule

Functors, Monoids, and Generics

A monoid will take two values of the same type and return one value of the same type.

Identity rule examples

Under the + operator, the set of integers has an identity of 0.

Rule	Example
Left identity	0 + 1 == 1
Right identity	1 + 0 == 1

Notice that the operator is binary, that is, it takes two inputs, and those inputs must be of the same type.

The result of combining the identity element (sometimes called empty or zero) with x is always x.

An identity of 0

Under the * operator the set of integers has an identity of 1.

```
1 * 0 == 0
1 * 2 == 2
```

Writing a reduction function

Given the previous three rules, we can write a reduction function. When we run a reduction on an array of integers using addition, we seed our operation with a 0 (the identity element).

When we run a reduction on an array of integers using multiplication, we seed our operation with a 1 (the identity element).

That's the idea. The following table summarizes a number of possible reductions:

Type	Operation	Unit/zero/neutral value
ints	+	0
ints	*	1
string	+ (concat strings)	""
bool	&&	true
bool	||	false
list	<< (concat list)	[]

A semigroup is a missing neutral value

If we are missing the unit/zero/neutral value, then we don't have a monoid, we have a semigroup. Note that a semigroup can be converted into a monoid.

That was a very interesting discussion of the algebra of monoids, but what the heck are they good for, and why should we care?

Here are a couple of good uses for monoids.

Converting binary operations into operations that work on lists

Consider the following operation:

```
1 + 2 + 3    ⇒    [1,2,3] |> List.reduce(+)
```

Instead of having to write all that code where we type a number, type a +, type another number, and we can feed a list of numbers into our reduce function that applies the + operation to each item and accumulates the sum.

Here's an example of appending strings:

```
"a" + "b" + "c"   ⇒   ["a", "b", "c"] |> List.reduce(+)
```

What was the neutral/identity element used in each of the preceding examples?

> **TIP**: The preceding code is F# code. The `|>` symbol is just a pipe symbol, like we use in a Unix terminal. It allows us to pipe the list of integers `[1,2,3]` or a list strings `["a", "b", "c"]` into `List.reduce(+)`. The greater than symbol is just an indication of the direction of the flow of data, that is, from left to right.

Using monoids with divide and conquer algorithms

Monoids are frequently used to solve large computations. Monoids help us to break our computations into pieces. We can run smaller computations in separate cores or on separate servers and recombine/reduce/fold the results into a single result. We often employ parallel or concurrency techniques along with incremental accumulation of our result.

As a very simple example, if we need to add these numbers: 1 + 2 + 3 + 4.

We can add (1 + 2) on one CPU/core and (3 + 4) on another:

3 + 7 = 10

> **TIP**: Where associativity holds, we can parallelize our computations.

Referential transparency

Identifying when using monoid can help us make design decisions that affect performance.

On day one, we're asked to add 1 + 2 + 3. Then, on day two, we're asked to add 1 more. We don't have to add 1 + 2 + 3 again. We can simply store that and add our new 1 to it: 6 + 1 = 7.

Given that nothing is free, what did it cost us to gain the performance boost of not having to add 1 + 2 + 3? Storage. The question becomes, which is more costly? The answer to that will tell us whether to leverage referential transparency or not. Just because we can do something does not mean we always should.

Handling no data

What if we have no data but we're asked to reduce it? Similarly, what if we have no data but we're asked to incrementally add to it?

This is when the identity element comes in handy! It can be the initial value for missing data.

More examples of monoids

Lists are monoids. The operation to combine them is simply concatenation. Many types of containers are also monoids, including monads.

What are not monoids?

Integers are not monoids, but integers under addition (a way to combine them) are monoids.

Whole numbers (integers starting at 1), and even whole numbers under addition, are not monoids. What is the neutral element for addition? The answer is zero.

Functors, Monoids, and Generics

Invoices are not monoids:

	Garage Name			AUTO REPAIR WORK ORDER				
	Address			NAME				
	city, state, zip, phone			ADDRESS				
W.O. #	1000			CITY, STATE				
	CUSTOMER'S INFORMATION							
Date	YEAR, MAKE, MODEL		HOME PHONE #		MECHANICS RECOMMENDATIONS			
6/10/2012	1978, chevrolet, C10				Turn Flywheel $35.00			
ODOMETER	SERIAL NO.		CELL PHONE #					
10077								
LICENSE NO	MOTOR NO.		BUDGET					

QTY	PART NO.	Description	List Price	Price Each	Total	ACCESSORIES		
1	MU55051	clutch set new 5 pc prfct	$ 223.30	$ 129.78	$ 129.78			
1	MS903142	gasket intake manifold fl	$ 25.82	$ 12.97	$ 12.97			
1	MS9275b	gasket exhaust manifold fl	$ 13.78	$ 9.31	$ 9.31			
2	DEe1608	pnt generl mtrs blu 12 oz	$ 10.31	$ 6.95	$ 13.90			
1	40987	fuel pump airtx	$ 33.23	$ 22.41	$ 22.41			
1	42315	power stering belt	$ 9.78	$ 6.60	$ 6.60			
1	WT857p	switch temp light	$ 26.74	$ 10.96	$ 10.96			
1	VS12869AC	gasket valve cover set fl	$ 25.38	$ 12.38	$ 12.38			
2		Gear oil 80W90 1qt CSTL	$ 7.86	$ 5.30	$ 10.60			
1	MGL9100	oil filter	$ 7.61	$ 4.12	$ 4.12			
5		1 qt motor oil 10w40	$ 5.07	$ 2.70	$ 13.50			
					$ -			
					$ -			
					$ -			
					$ -			
					$ -			
					$ -			
					$ -			
					$ -			
					$ -			
					$ -	TOTAL ACCESSORIES	$	-
					$ -	LABOR ONLY		
				TOTAL PARTS	$ 246.53	PARTS	$	246.53
LUBE, OIL CHANGE, FLUSH TRANS, FLUSH DIFF.						ACCESSORIES	$	-
						MISC.	$	5.88
						SUBLET REPAIRS	$	35.00
						TOTAL	$	287.41
TOTAL				$	-	TAX	7.75% $	22.27
ESTIMATE AMOUNT-PARTS & LABOR				AUTHORIZED BY		TOTAL	$	309.68

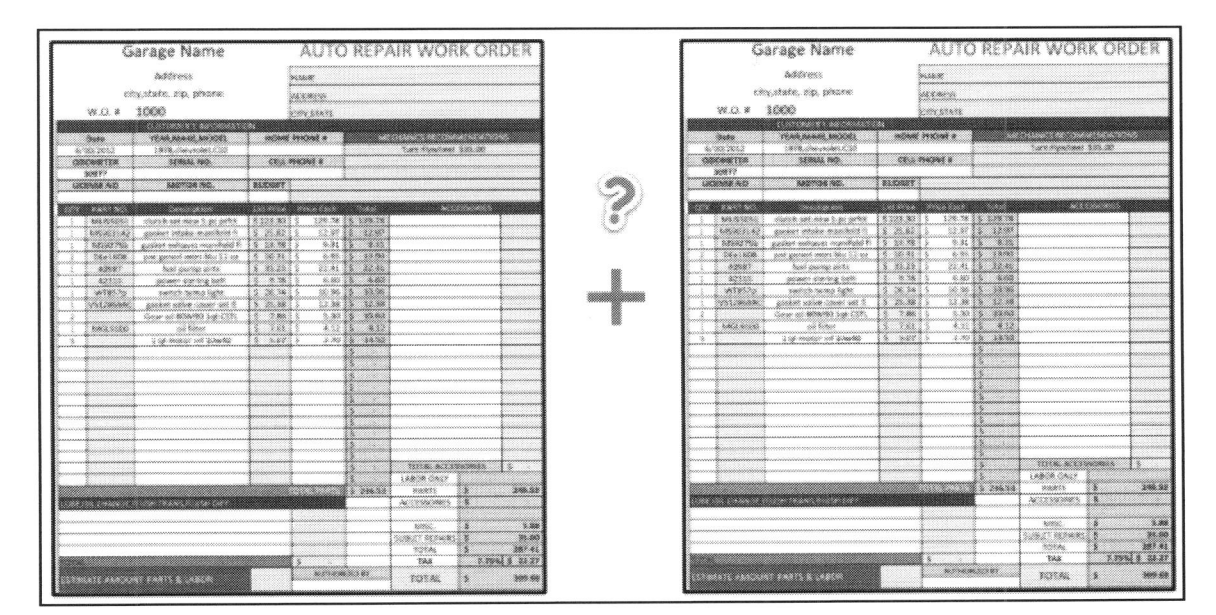

How can we combine two invoices?

What does it mean to add invoices? Are we going to merge the colors or somehow smash them together? If we stack them, how can we do anything with them, other than take the top one off the list? How do we combine the customer addresses? Sure, we can add the work order numbers, 1,000 + 1,000 = 2,000, but what value is that to us?

How could we possibly add invoices? Maybe if we choose some fields that are statistical in nature?

Monoid examples

We'll cover three types of monoid here:

- Name monoid
- Int slice monoid
- Line item monoid

That's right. We're going to turn that invoice into a monoid!

Name monoid

Let's see what we can do with a name. First, we define an interface that has two methods, `Append` and `Zero`. We wrap our name in `nameContainer`.

Our `nameContainer` is a struct with a single string field, `name`. Our `Append` method appends the given name to the long name string it's building up that lives in the magical `nameContainer`. Our zero morphism for our name string is an empty string.

The content of `src/monoid/name_monoid.go` would look as follows:

```go
package monoid

type NameMonoid interface {
    Append(s string) NameMonoid
    Zero() string
}

func WrapName(s string) NameMonoid {
    return nameContainer{name: s}
}

type nameContainer struct {
    name string
}

func (s nameContainer) Append(name string) NameMonoid {
    s.name = s.name + name
    return s
}

func (nameContainer) Zero() string {
    return ""
}

func (s nameContainer) String() string {
    return s.name
}
```

Here's what `main.go` looks like:

```
package main

import (
    "monoid"
    "fmt"
)

func main() {

    const name = "Alice"
    stringMonoid := monoid.WrapName(name)
    fmt.Println("NameMonoid")
    fmt.Println("Initial state:", stringMonoid)
    fmt.Println("Zero:", stringMonoid.Zero())
    fmt.Println("1st application:", stringMonoid.Append(name))
    fmt.Println("Chain applications:",
stringMonoid.Append(name).Append(name))
```

Name monoid terminal session

Let's run our monoid:

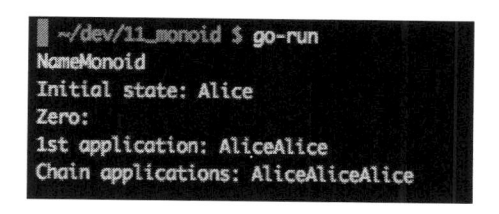

```
~/dev/11_monoid $ go-run
NameMonoid
Initial state: Alice
Zero:
1st application: AliceAlice
Chain applications: AliceAliceAlice
```

Here, we ran our app and got good results. The initial state is Alice, and the **Zero** value is the empty string; after the first append we get **AliceAlice,** and when we chain another we get **AliceAliceAlice.**

Int slice monoid

Let's see what we can do with a slice of ints.

First, we define an interface that has two methods, `Append` and `Zero`. We wrap our int in `intContainer`. `intContainer` is a struct with a single int field, `ints`. Our `Append` method appends the given int slice to the slice of `ints` it's building up that lives in the magical `intContainer`. The `Zero` morphism for a slice is `nil`.

Functors, Monoids, and Generics

Here is the content of `src/monoid/int_monoid.go`:

```
package monoid

type IntMonoid interface {
    Zero() []int
    Append(i ...int) IntMonoid
    Reduce() int
}

func WrapInt(ints []int) IntMonoid {
return intContainer{ints: ints}
}

type intContainer struct {
    ints []int
}

func (intContainer) Zero() []int {
return nil
}

func (i intContainer) Append(ints ...int) IntMonoid {
    i.ints = append(i.ints, ints...)
return i
}

func (i intContainer) Reduce() int {
    total := 0
    for _, item := range i.ints {
        total += item
    }
return total
}
```

That is just about the same logic as the Name monoid, except for that `Reduce` method. The `Reduce` method will allow us to combine all of our ints with our binary operator, addition, and arrive at a sum of all ints in the `intMonoid` container.

The contents of `main.go` are as follows:

```
ints := []int{1, 2, 3}
intMonoid := monoid.WrapInt(ints)
fmt.Println("\nIntMonoid")
fmt.Println("Initial state:", intMonoid)
fmt.Println("Zero:", intMonoid.Zero())
fmt.Println("1st application:", intMonoid.Append(ints...))
fmt.Println("Chain applications:",
intMonoid.Append(ints...).Append(ints...))
fmt.Println("Reduce chain:",
intMonoid.Append(ints...).Append(ints...).Reduce())
```

We call the same list of methods we did for our `nameMonoid` and get correct results. The interesting line is the last one, where we chain our Appends and then call Reduce to sum up our ints:

```
IntMonoid
Initial state: {[1 2 3]}
Zero: □
1st application: {[1 2 3 1 2 3]}
Chain applications: {[1 2 3 1 2 3 1 2 3]}
Reduce chain: 18
```

Int slice monoid terminal session

Lineitem slice monoid

Let's see what we can do with a slice of line items.

First, we define an interface that has three methods, `Append`, `Zero`, and `Reduce`. We wrap our line items in the `lineitemContainer`. Our `lineitemContainer` is a struct with three fields that correspond to our invoice's line items:

```
type Lineitem struct {
    Quantity   int
    Price      int
    ListPrice  int
}
```

Our `Append` method appends the given line item to the slice of line items it's building up that lives in the magical `lineitemContainer`.

The `Zero` morphism for a slice is `nil`.

Functors, Monoids, and Generics

The `src/monoid/lineitem_monoid.go` file will have the following code:

```
package monoid

type LineitemMonoid interface {
    Zero() []int
    Append(i ...int) LineitemMonoid
    Reduce() int
}

func WrapLineitem(lineitems []Lineitem) lineitemContainer {
return lineitemContainer{lineitems: lineitems}
}

type Lineitem struct {
    Quantity   int
    Price      int
    ListPrice  int
}


type lineitemContainer struct {
    lineitems []Lineitem
}

func (lineitemContainer) Zero() []Lineitem {
return nil
}

func (i lineitemContainer) Append(lineitems ...Lineitem) lineitemContainer {
    i.lineitems = append(i.lineitems, lineitems...)
return i
}

func (i lineitemContainer) Reduce() Lineitem {
    totalQuantity := 0
    totalPrice := 0
    totalListPrice := 0
    for _, item := range i.lineitems {
        totalQuantity += item.Quantity
        totalPrice += item.Price
        totalListPrice += item.ListPrice
    }
return Lineitem{totalQuantity, totalPrice, totalListPrice}
}
```

That is just about the same logic as the Int slice monoid, except for that Reduce method. The Reduce method will allow us to combine all of our line item fields with our binary operator, addition, and arrive at a sum total of all line item entries in the lineitemMonoid container.

The main.go file will have the following code:

```
lineitems := []monoid.Lineitem{
    {1, 12978, 22330},
    {2, 530, 786},
    {5, 270, 507},
}
lineitemMonoid := monoid.WrapLineitem(lineitems)
fmt.Println("\nLineItemMonoid")
fmt.Println("Initial state:", lineitemMonoid)
fmt.Println("Zero:", lineitemMonoid.Zero())
fmt.Println("1st application:", lineitemMonoid.Append(lineitems...))
fmt.Println("Chain applications:",
lineitemMonoid.Append(lineitems...).Append(lineitems...))
fmt.Println("Reduce chain:",
lineitemMonoid.Append(lineitems...).Append(lineitems...).Reduce())
```

That's the same stuff we verified with the other monoids. Our feeder value, line items, is a slice of three line item tuples. Verify that the math of the Reduce works.

Int slice monoid terminal session

Looking at the last line of output, we can see that we have called our Reduce function to sum our totals (totalQuantity, totalPrice, and totalListPrice):

```
LineItemMonoid
Initial state: {[{1 12978 22330} {2 530 786} {5 270 507}]}
Zero: {}
1st application: {[{1 12978 22330} {2 530 786} {5 270 507} {1 12978 22330} {2 530 786} {5 270 507}]}
Chain applications: {[{1 12978 22330} {2 530 786} {5 270 507} {1 12978 22330} {2 530 786} {5 270 507} {1 12978 22330} {2 530 786} {5 270 507}]}
Reduce chain: {24 41334 70869}
```

For a quick manual verification, let's look at totalQuantity--*1+2+5+1+2+5+1+2+5 = 24*. Looks good!

Summary

In this chapter, we learned how to use tooling to solve issues that arise in Go because of its lack of support for generics. We were able to use this tooling to generate underscore like features in our Go code by starting with properly defined base types. With no more worries about potential generics support slowing down our runtime executables (as is the case with Java), we jumped for joy with an unexpected productivity boost.

We continued forward into the land of pure FP, where we tackled the concept of function composition. With `g.f(x) == g(f(x))` in our tool belt, we studied functors and learned how to transform lists of items. We chained our maps and even learned how attorneys can use the forgetful functor to win cases in court for their clients.

We wrapped up the chapter with monoids. We not only learned the algebraic laws of monoids, but we implemented them. We chained `Append` methods and even wrote a couple of reductions.

In the next chapter, we'll continue our on our path towards pure enlightenment, and maintain our quest for simpler code and improved error handling.

10
Monads, Type Classes, and Generics

Functional programming in Go:

> *"Not sure if it's a good idea, but let's try it anyway."*
>
> *"Fun to think about; Not sure how to use it."*
>
> *"The Y-Combinator is a theoretical concept with no practical value."*
>
> *"Who can understand the code in this Monad package. Lambda what? Generics?"*

Please put your prejudices aside, work through this chapter, and then ask yourself, How relevant is functional programming in Go?

Our goals in this chapter are as follows:

- Understand how a Monad works
- Learn how to compose functions using the `bind` operation
- Understand how the `Success` and `Failure` paths work
- Understand how a Monad deals with impure operations
- Work through a Monadic workflow implementation in Go
- Learn what Lambda Calculus is and what it has to do with Monads
- See how Lambda Calculus implements recursion
- Learn how the Y-Combinator works
- Use the Y-Combinator to control workflow
- Learn to write concise workflow code and handle all errors at the end

- Understand how Type classes work and implement a few in Go
- Review the pros and cons of generics

Mother Teresa Monad

Who are you? Are you a good person or a bad person? What would other people say? How did you become the person you are now?

Ponder those questions for a few minutes.

What is a Monad?

The explanation is like answering the question: How were you raised as a child and what have you become?

In the following diagram, we explore a Monad:

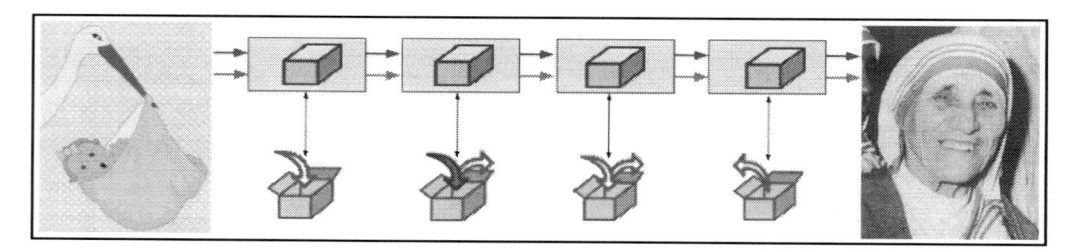

The chain of blue boxes represents moments in the flow of Mother Teresa's life.

The closed blue boxes represent her private time from birth to death. The open boxes represent events in which she opened herself up to interactions with the world around her.

Let's suppose she was nurtured as a baby and received positive input (the blue incoming arrow). Also suppose that along the way, she was exposed to some negative input (the dark incoming arrows) as well as positive input. Her life (the data) was transformed in some way during every interaction. As she grew, her actions were her side effects (the outgoing arrows from the open box).

Success might be defined as entering the gates of Heaven after death (or Hell, for failure).

So, what is a Monad? It's a mechanism into which data flows, interacts with an impure environment, is transformed, and eventually comes out the other end; it's a way to structure and control the workflow in a real application that interfaces with external endpoints, such as log files, external APIs, notifications, and so on.

The previous diagram should prompt a few questions.

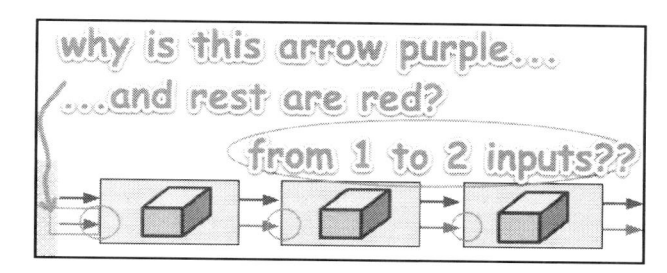

In Chapter 4, *SOLID Design in Go*, we saw how a function **f** receives **a** and returns **b**, but we also recognized that in the real world, where connections fail and RAM and disk space might fill up, errors may occur:

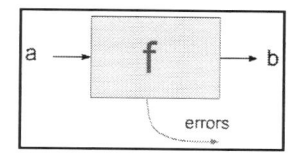

To keep our diagram clean-looking, we'll just move the errors arrow up and shoot it out the right side, rather than underneath. We'll also color the input and output arrows blue. That's our pure, happy path. See? No side effects:

But real programs can have side-effects, right? Real programs interface with external APIs, accept input from users, print invoices, and send emails, right? Where's the real stuff?

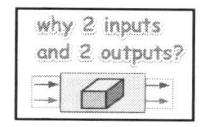

We have two inputs matching our two outputs so that we can easily link our blue boxes into a chain. Remember when we discussed the decomposition of finite state machines? We pulled apart the pieces (**C1**, **C2**, and **C5**) of our application. These are our *reusable components*.

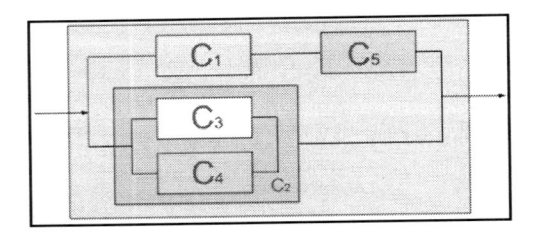

That was done in order to fill our toolbox with individual components, which we can subsequently use to re-compose our application:

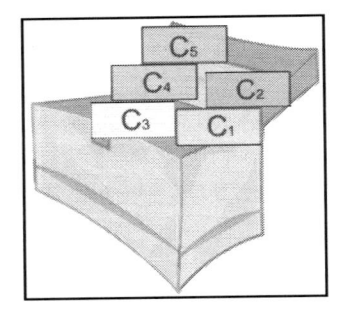

Ever wonder how our pieces will fit back together?

It's not going to work if all our pieces look like this:

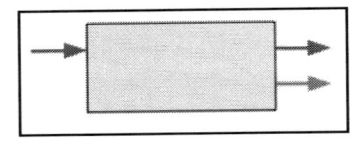

However, consider if the pieces looked like this:

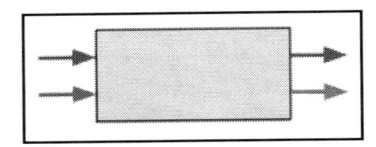

Then they will all fit together like legos! See how they fit together?

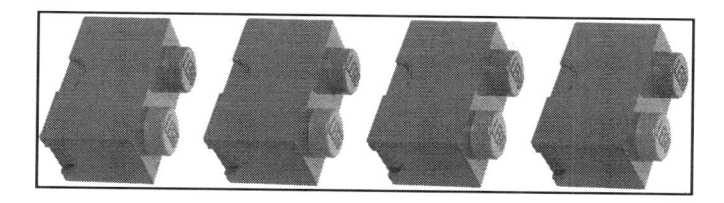

How can we go from a one-input to a two-input thing?

The bind operation

We accomplish this feat using the Monad's bind operation:

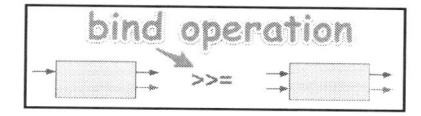

> In Haskell, it's called the `bind` operation. Other names for bind include `flatMap`, `flatten`, `andThen`, `collect`, and `SelectMany`. (That's part of what makes functional programming confusing--different languages use different names for the same thing.) The Lexical Workflow calls it `Next`.

More descriptive names might be adapt, link, or even hard shove. (In our code example, we'll use the name `Next`, because it makes the most sense in the context of moving to the `Next` step.) Bind is a pattern that adapts the one-input, two-output block to a two-input, two-output block.

Now, let's talk about the two paths--the top blue path is the `Success` path. That's our *Happy Path*, through which our data flows, as long as all goes well. The bottom red path is where errors go.

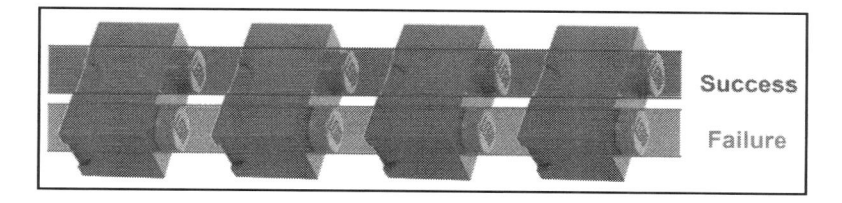

The lift operation

Let's examine what happens when an error occurs in the lift operation of our second component in the chain:

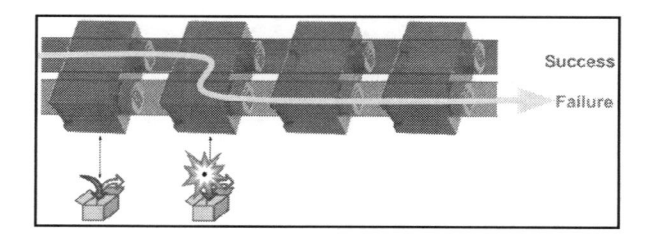

Lifting lifts a function into a *wrapped* type. Lift connects our functions from one world and another.

> A functor lifts single parameter functions. An applicative functor lifts second multi parameter functions.

This is the type definition of the the lift operation in Haskell:

```
liftA2 :: Applicative f => (a -> b -> c) -> f a -> f b -> f c
```

See the following terminal console for an example of using the lift operation (`liftA2`) to transform the the `replicate` function into a wrapped type. We're using the *applicative style* since we are lifting with an arbitrary number of arguments.

```
~/clients/packt/dev/haskell/ghci $ ghci
GHCi, version 8.2.1: http://www.haskell.org/ghc/  :? for help
Prelude> replicate 2 "A"
["A","A"]
Prelude> :t replicate
replicate :: Int -> a -> [a]
Prelude> import Control.Applicative
Prelude Control.Applicative> :t liftA2
liftA2 :: Applicative f => (a -> b -> c) -> f a -> f b -> f c
Prelude Control.Applicative> (liftA2 replicate) [1,2] ["A", "B", "C"]
[["A"],["B"],["C"],["A","A"],["B","B"],["C","C"]]
Prelude Control.Applicative> :t liftA2
liftA2 :: Applicative f => (a -> b -> c) -> f a -> f b -> f c
Prelude Control.Applicative>
```

Notice that we do not throw an exception (or panic); instead, we move our application flow from the `Success` path to the `Failure` path. Practically, what this means is that we no longer need to check for errors after executing each command that could possibly fail in our code. Using the monad pattern, we are able to redirect program flow to the `Failure` path and handle all of our errors for this execution chain at the tail end.

Now that we understand why and how we got two inputs and two outputs, let's look at what's going on under our chain of blue boxes:

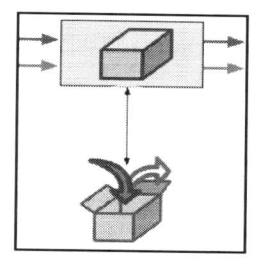

See the open box with the arrows coming in and going out? Those are impure arrows.

Remember our discussion about the action of lowering elements into the gutter of mutation in `Chapter 9`, *Functors, Monoids, and Generics*, in the section about functors?

This is where our monad allows us to open our box outside the pure world of FP. Our monad is a functor, and here, we're using the functor operation of lifting.

> For details about lifting, see the previous chapter.

The in arrow represents interactions with the external world. Things like:

- Managing state
- Reading log files
- Accepting input from external APIs
- Concurrent processing

The out arrow represents interactions with the external world. Things like:

- Managing state
- Writing log files
- Sending output to external APIs
- Concurrent processing

Remember, in pure functional programming, if a program receives a certain input value, then it will always return the same output. However, when a program writes to a log file, how could it possibly have the same timestamp each time? Monads allow pure FP programs to remain pure and still interact with an impure world.

what happens in the box?

This is where the mapping/data transformation function is applied to the data.

In our Mother Teresa life monad example, this (in the box) is where the positive interactions, perhaps with her loving mother, occurred, which helped to point her in a positive direction. What other interactions might have occurred to transform her life?

How can any useful application not manage state? How can an FP application manage state and remain pure? Monads. (See the state monad in the upcoming table.)

Why use Monads to manage state? Monads allow the manipulation of state in an elegant, type-safe, constrained, deferred, and controlled manner.

Elegant? What's elegant about a Monad? Elegance is in the eye of the beholder. Elegance gets out of the way. It is simple, obvious, straightforward, and allows us to very little intellectual effort to immediately understand our code's purpose:

```
step := Get(lineBase64)
step = Next(step, Base64ToBytes)
step = Next(step, BytesToData)
step = Next(step, TimestampData)
step = Next(step, DataToJson)
```

That's a Monad. It's clutter-free and it's easy to see what the workflow does.

Deferred? What are we talking about? Why not just bake in all the control flow logic up front? We know what should happen in all our use cases. Why not write all our if/then/else logic and for loops and bake them all into a single executable?

With Monads, we attempt to write our applications using as many pure, side effect free functions as possible. This style of programming mostly defers the decisions about how and when to mutate states until the moment they are required. That's what happens when we open the box.

Constrained? What's constrained? Well, that's an overloaded term. From a framework perspective, we are constraining/quarantining our side effect causing and real-world interfacing code to this little, purposeful box. Its job is to perform the specific data mapping transformation functions that have been provided to it. If any errors occur, the framework will capture them and package the errors for us, and will ensure that they quickly travel down the `Failure` path until they get spit out the end of the execution pipe, where all errors for this execution chain are handled. From a data perspective, we use our type system to constrain the input to only valid data types. (If we have a division operation, we can constrain our input type to be `PositiveNumbers` to ensure that a divide by zero exception will never occur.) From a type class perspective, our operations are constrained by the laws of Monads.

What operations? What laws? The operations are the sequences of tasks that we chain together to perform various operations on our data. If we start with a list of cars, we might want to transform our list by applying the following transformations:

```
Filter(ByDomestic()).Map(Upgrade()).Reduce(JsonReducer())
```

And finally, what do we mean by controlled? This is where the Monad shines. The Monad provides the structure for chaining the transformation operations. It provides the `Success` and `Failure` paths. Now, rather than littering our code with `if err != nil` error checking blocks, we can put all of our error handling logic at the end of all of the steps we need to perform for our particular use case.

One more time: What is a Monad? A Monad is a design pattern that provides a way of chaining operations together. The `bind` function is what links the operations together in a chain; it takes the output from one step and feeds it into the next one.

We can write the calls that directly use the `bind` operator, or we can use a sugar syntax, in a language like Haskell, which makes the compiler insert those function calls for use. But either way, each step is separated by a call to the `bind` function.

> Since Haskell is a fully baked pure functional programming language, we'll often refer to its FP in order to think about how we can best incorporate that method of thinking/design into our Go solutions.

In Haskell, there are many kinds of monads. What makes each monad unique and especially useful is what it does in addition to the `bind` operation. We can use the following table of monads found in Haskell as a starting point for building a package of monads in Go:

Monad	Description
Either	The `Either` type is similar to the `Maybe` type, with one key difference--it can carry attached data of both `Success` and `Failure`. The `Left` return value to indicates failure, and `Right` indicates success. Here's a useful pun: use *Either* to get the *Right* answer.
Error	Allows us to define exactly how exception handling works for our application. For example, we can choose to ignore a specific exception if a similar one has been handled in the past 60 seconds.
Eval	Used for modularizing parallel code by separating the algorithm from the parallelism, allowing us to change the way we parallelize our code by replacing the `Strategy` function. `Eval` and the swappable `Strategies` leverage lazy evaluation to express parallelism.
Failure	Aborts the chain of execution steps automatically without requiring an `if err != nil` conditional error check after every function call.
Free	Allows us to construct a monad from an arbitrary type. The free monad allows us to abstractly specify control flow between pure functions and separately define an implementation. We use monads to glue together pure functions with special purpose control-flow, such as fail fast error handling (`Maybe`/`Either`) or asynchronous computation.

Identity	The `Identity` monad is a monad that does not embody any computational strategy. It simply applies the bound function to its input without any modification. Computationally, there is no reason to use the `Identity` monad instead of the much simpler act of applying functions to their arguments. The purpose of the `Identity` monad is its fundamental role in the theory of monad transformers. Any Monad transformer applied to the `Identity` monad yields a non-transformer version of that Monad. The `Identity` monad is like the number zero in addition. You cannot increase another number with zero, but zero comes in handy when you need to write a `Reduce` function.
If	Provides simple control flow to evaluate the results of a clause if the logic condition is true, or else it will evaluate the false block (if one is provided).

IO	Separates I/O from the rest of the (pure) language. In Haskell, it's the return statement that takes the impure I/O and puts it into the `IO` Monad. It allows access to impure I/O sources, such as memory, global variables, network, native operating system calls, standard input, and so on. The following example Haskell code illustrates the IO monad:
	`loveGo :: IO Bool`
	`loveGo =`
	`do putStrLn "Do you love Go? (yes/no)"`
	`inpStr <- getLine`
	`return ((inpStr) == "yes")`

Lazy	It's the same as the `StateThread` (ST) monad, except that this monad delays the evaluation of state operations until a value depending on them is required.
List	We can make each step return a list of results. Our bind function can iterate over the list, feeding each one into the next step. This eliminates the need to write looping constructs to iterate over lists of elements. Write it once and reuse it.
Maybe	Used to deal with nil values, as it deals with computations that might not return results. Instead of returning nil (or throwing an exception/panic), monadic operations return a `Just` value or `Nothing`. Errors are propagated down the monad structure until they reach the exit point at which all errors are handled. Here's how it's defined in Haskell: `data Maybe a = Nothing	Just a`

Option	Used as the return type for data that might otherwise return a nil/null value. If the data is invalid, `None` is returned inside the `Option` monad, or else `Some` is returned with the valid data inside of it. The monadic functions will then chain fail states, so if a function requires the data is valid but receives an `Option` with `None` in it, it will simply return `Option None` to the `Next` function. This pattern is similar to returning `Null` in an imperative language and it solves the `Billion Dollar Mistake`.
Par	Used for modularizing parallel code by requiring the programmer to provide more details about the data dependencies. Par provides more control and does not rely on lazy evaluation to manage parallel tasks.
Parser	Used to create a parser. For example, our grammar might look like this: `addop = "+"	"-".` `digit = "0"	"1"	...	"8"	"9".` `expr = term { addop term }.` `factor = "(" expr ")"	number.` `mulop = "*".` `number = ["-"] digit { digit }.` `term = factor { mulop factor }.` We could use our Parser monad to perform math operations such as: `ghci> 1+2` `3`
Pause	Used when computations need to be interrupted and resumed. Could provide a step function, which runs the computation until it calls the yield function where the computation is paused, returning to the caller enough information to resume the computation later. For an example of about a dozen possible implementations, see `stackoverflow.com/questions/10236953/the-pause-monad`.
Reader	Provides access to the global state. During initialization, an application can read configuration into a single context that can be passed along to subsequent steps. Also known as **Environment**.
State	Provides access to state values. A run function that performs some computation will update the state and return the final state. For example, in an online first person shooter video game, the player needs to know the state of the player during every phase of the game: their health, amount of ammo, types of weapons on hand, location, or an overlay a map of the surrounding area. State is not global, but rather, a new state created in each step of the game. Since the state is not actually performing destructive updates, reverting to an older version or performing undo operations is easier.

ST	Allows us to safely work with a mutable states. For example, we can thaw an immutable/frozen array and modify it in place and freeze a new immutable array. ST also allows us to create data structures that we can then modify, as we can do in imperative languages. Also known as a **State Thread monad**.
STM	The **Software Transactional Memory (STM)** monad helps us with the problem of synchronizing multiple tasks by preventing us from accidentally performing non-transactional I/O operations that may cause deadlocks. In order to perform concurrent programming in imperative programming, we use threads that must share data. We must be careful that the different threads don't improperly update the shared data. We often lock data blocks using a a technique called a **semaphore lock**. With STM, we don't need to worry about semaphores since our code contains no locks. Note that in Go, the language constructs we use to perform concurrent programming include Goroutines, channels, and `sync.WaitGroup`.
Writer	Used to signal some side effect. Often used for logging or debug printing.

In addition to learning from Haskell's implementation of Monads, other features we can learn from include:

- Lazy evaluation
- Type classes
- Syntax based on layout
- Pattern matching on data structures
- Bounded and Parametric polymorphism

Check out more about Haskell at the following resources:

- `https://en.wikipedia.org/wiki/Haskell_(programming_language)`
- `https://www.haskell.org/`
- `http://learnyouahaskell.com/`
- `https://www.huffingtonpost.com/aaroncontorer/haskell-the-language-most_b_4242119.html`

Monadic functions

Monads are implemented as a type class with two methods, `return` and bind (`>>=`):

```
class Monad m where
  return :: a -> m a
  (>>=)  :: m a -> (a -> m b) -> m b
```

Note that `m` refers to a type constructor, such as `Either` or `Maybe`, that implements the `Monad` type class.

We'll include a few more monadic functions from the Standard Library in the following table:

Function	Description
fail	The fail function supports a monad's implementation of failure. We get the `fail` function from the `Monad` type class, and it enables a failed pattern matching to result in a failure in the context of the current monad instead of a program crash. For example, the `fail` function is called when pattern matching fails in a do expression. `fail :: Monad m => String -> m a`
fmap	`fmap` comes from the Functor type class. `fmap` applies a function over ordinary values `a -> b`, and lifts them to become a function over containers `f a -> f b`, where `f` is the container type: `fmap :: Functor f => (a -> b) -> f a -> f b`

mplus mzero	`MonadPlus` is a type class which extends a `Monad` class and provides `mzero` and `mplus`:
	`class Monad m => MonadPlus m where`
	`mzero :: m a`
	`mplus :: m a -> m a -> m a`
	`mplus` combines two results into one.
	`mzero` represents an empty result.

return	Return is our lift function. Don't confuse `return` with what return means in Go. Think of it like this: **Return** a pure value **a** (of type **A**) into a monad **m a** (of type **Monad A**). The Lexical Workflow Solution calls this function `Get`.

| (>>=) | (>>=) runs an action and then passes its result to a function that also returns an action. Both actions are run and the final result is the result of the second action. We can think of (>>=) as our chaining function:<br>main.hs:<br><br>```
module Main (main) where
 import Lib
 main :: IO ()
 main = do
 putStrLn "Enter your first name:" >>
 getLine >>=
 (\yourName -> putStrLn $ "Hello, " ++ yourName)
```<br>Add the following to your Haskell ghci console:<br>```
*Main Lib> main
 Enter your first name:
 CocoPuff
 Hello,
CocoPuff
```<br>(>>=) is also known as **bind**. The Lexical Workflow Solution calls this function Get.<br>Here's its type definition:<br>`(>>=) :: Monad m => m a -> (a -> m b) -> m b` |
| (>>) | (>>) performs two actions in sequence. The result of the first action is discard. What we keep is the result of the second operation:<br>```
*Main Lib> putStr "Hello, " >> putStrLn "CocoPuff"
 Hello, CocoPuff
```<br>(>>) is defined in terms of the `bind` operation that discarded its argument. The following says that (>>) has a left and right argument that are monadic with types m a and m b:<br>`(>>) :: Monad m => m a -> m b -> m` |
```

Basic monadic functions

The following table consists of some of the more frequently used Monads (for composition, looping, and mapping):

Function	Description

forM	`forM` acts like an iterator that maps an action over a list and returns the transformed list. `forM` serves the same purpose as `mapM` and exists for readability. The rule of thumb is that if there are multiple lines of code in the for loop, then use `forM`. For example:
	`results <- forM items $ \item -> do`
	`    -- A big do-block using `item`.`
	`forM :: (Monad m, Traversable t) => t a -> (a -> m b) -> m (t b)`

forever	`forever` is a combinator used to repeat an action `forever`, as follows: `forever :: Applicative f => f a -> f b`
mapM	The `map` operation performs mutations when it transforms elements in a list, right? But how can that be? Pure functions cannot mutate variables. We're able to execute actions indirectly by using `mapM`. `mapM` can change the element's values in the list because it runs in the IO monad, as follows: `mapM :: (Monad m, Traversable t) => (a -> m b) -> t a -> m (t b)`
sequence	Used to evaluate each action in the sequence from left to right and collect the results, as follows: `sequence :: (Monad m, Traversable t) => t (m a) -> m (t a)`
void	Used to discard the return value of an IO action, as follows: `void :: Functor f => f a -> f ()`
(=<<)	This is the same as `>>=` but with the arguments interchanged, as follows: `(=<<) :: Monad m => (a -> m b) -> m a -> m b`
(>=>)	Used to compose monads via left-to-right Kleisli composition, as follows: `(>=>) :: Monad m => (a -> m b) -> (b -> m c) -> a -> m c`
(<=<)	This is the same as `>=>` but with the arguments interchanged (using right-to-left Kleisli composition), as follows: `(<=<) :: Monad m => (b -> m c) -> (a -> m b) -> a -> m c`

Note that `functionName_` functions not listed here are used for side-effects. For example, when we want to evaluate such a list for effects, we use `sequence_` and `mapM_`, which discard the results.

Monadic list functions

The thing to remember with lists is that they model non-determinism. A list of values a represents a number of different possibilities for the value of a.

Function	Description
filterM	Used in place of `filter` inside a monad, as follows: `filterM :: Applicative m => (a -> m Bool) -> [a] -> m [a]`
foldM	Used in place of foldl where monadic computations built from a list are bound left-to-right, as follows: `foldM :: (Monad m, Foldable t) => (b -> a -> m b) -> b -> t a -> m b`

join	Used to flatten the nesting of groups, as follows:
	`> join [[[1]]]`
	`[[1]]`
	`> join [[1]]`
	`[1]`
	`join :: Monad m => m (m a) -> m a`

msum	A list based concat function that is best described by the following example:
	`> msum [Nothing, Nothing, Just "A", Just "B"]`
	`Just "A"`
	
	`> msum [[],[1,2],[],[3]]`
	`[1,2,3]`
	`msum :: (MonadPlus m, Foldable t) => t (m a) -> m a`

replicateM	Used to perform an action n times and gather the results, as follows: `replicateM :: Applicative m => Int -> m a -> m [a]`
zipWithM	Used to merge two lists together, applying a special rule in the process. `zipWithM` is a monadic version of the `zipWith` function on lists. It is useful when only the side-effects of the monadic computation matter, as follows: `zipWithM :: Applicative m => (a -> b -> m c) -> [a] -> [b] -> m [c]`

Monadic workflow implementation

Let's start by reading our car data in from a file with base64 encoded text strings that represent cars, found in `cars.base64`:

```
4-purely-functional/ch10-monads/01_car_steps/data/cars.base64
eyJjYXIiOnsidmluIjoiREc1NDVIRzQ5NDU5WiIsIm1ha2UiOiJUb3lvdGEiLCJtb2RlbCI6Ikh
pZ2hsYW5kZXIiLCJvcHRpb25zIjp7Im9wdGlvbl8xIjoiSGVhdGVkIFNlYXRzIiwib3B0aW9uXz
IiOiJQb3dlciBTdGVlcmluZyIsIm9wdGlvbl8zIjoiR1BTIn19fQ0K
eyJjYXIiOnsidmluIjoiMzQ4NTQzOTg1QVpERCIsIm1ha2UiOiJMZXh1cyIsIm1vZGVsIjoiSVM
gMjUwIiwib3B0aW9ucyI6eyJvcHRpb25fMSI6Ik5vaWNrIFNoaWZ0Iiwib3B0aW9uXzIiOiJNb2
9uIFJvb2YiLCJvcHRpb25fMyI6IkxlYXRoZXIifX19DQo=
eyJjYXIiOnsidmluIjoiTUZORkg2NkZCWlE5OSIsIm1ha2UiOiJIb25kYSIsIm1vZGVsIjoiQWN
jb3JkIiwib3B0aW9ucyI6eyJvcHRpb25fMSI6IkdQUyIsIm9wdGlvbl8yIjoiQWxsb3kgV2hlZW
xzIn19fQ==
```

Our car processing monad will take that base64 text, timestamp it, and output JSON, as shown in the following code:

```
{
  "car": {
    "vin": "MFNFH66FBZQ99",
    "make": "Honda",
    "model": "Accord",
    "options": {
      "option_1": "GPS",
      "option_2": "Alloy Wheels"
    }
  },
  "timestamp": "20171030003135"
}
```

Let's start by looking at `main.go`. We import two project packages, `workflow` and `utils`. We also import `bufio` and `os` from the Go Standard Library for processing our `base64` text file.

We put our project packages at the top of our list of imported packages. We import *workflow* and *utils*. In this book, we use the logging and configuration features from the utils package a lot. In order to be lazy, we'll just remember that we can use the `Config` object anywhere we want and refer to a value from our `config.toml` file. Similarly, to use our info logger, we can simply type `Info.Println`.

In Go, it is considered best practice to write tests first. That's called **test driven development**. We discussed that in the first chapter. You should code your applications that way. However, after Chapter 2, *Manipulating Collections*, example code is more frequently found in the `main.go` file (with no test files). I did that because I am a lazy programmer and don't like to type more than is absolutely necessary, and I think it conveys the lesson quicker/better. I used similar reasoning when I chose to eliminate the package reference requirement when calling Config and the Info, Debug, and Error loggers. Should you use a global logger and config object at your job? Probably not. Why? Because they are dependencies that should be explicitly passed into each function that uses them. Chapter 7, *Functional Parameters*, illustrates how this can can accomplished. For more information, see `http://peter.bourgon.org/go-best-practices-2016/`.

In the following `main.go` we import packages and run our initializer.

```
package main

import (
    "workflow"
    . "utils"
    "bufio"
    "os"
)

func init() {
    GetOptions()
    InitLog("trace.log", os.Stdout, os.Stdout, os.Stderr)
    Info.Println("AppEnv:", Config.AppEnv)
}
```

The `init` function will be executed before our `main` function. We call `GetOptions` to read the values in our `config.toml` file into a global `Config` variable.

Yes. It's a global variable. And there're more. For example, Debug, Info, and Error are our global loggers.

Are you wondering why I would dare put global variables in an example application using a pure FP concept like Monads?

This book is about improving the way you approach application development. Go is a multi paradigm language and allows us to mix pure FP with our existing code. The `01_car_steps` application consists of an imperative framework with a global logger object, as well as some pure FP code to handle workflow.

> This is a small application, so having one global logger is convenient. If this were a larger project, it would be better to have one logger for each instance of your service.

While this book does cover theory as well as some of the history of pure FP, this book's main goal is to be practical. I hope you will be able to use some of the code in this book in your own projects (or at least some of the concepts) to build better applications yourself.

Debug, Info, and Error are each assigned a `log.New` object (https://golang.org/pkg/log/#New) that returns a `*Logger`. If you want to use it concurrently from various goroutines, you should pass those logger objects around as pointers.

We can adjust our application settings in the `config.toml` file as follows:

```
# Full path to the file containing the base64 car strings
data_filepath = "./data/cars.base64"

# Runtime environment
app_env = "development"

# Level options: panic, error, info, debug
log_level = "debug"

# The character(s) used to preface debug lines
log_debug_chars = ">>"

# Whether to include timestamps and log level on all log entries
log_verbose = true

# Enable or disable logging of utils/TimeTrack() (For benchmarking/debugging)
log_timetrack = true

# i18n translation file name, see github.com/nicksnyder/go-i18n
```

```
i18n_filename = "en-us.all.json"
```

The last setting can tell our application which translation file to use. Later in this chapter, we'll see how we can use `go-i18n` to use message IDs to reference the appropriate message, and how to change the translation text based on the appropriate language/locale. We won't add the internationalization (I18N) of error messages in this first example to keep things simple, and so that we can focus on understanding how monads work.

The `log_ settings` can affect what gets logged as our application runs. We'll see a few examples of how to use them later in this chapter.

Our `main` function initializes a `carCntr` to count how many cars we've processed. Next, we open our data file using the `Config.DataFilepath` value set in our config file.

> An idiom is a manner of speaking that is natural to the native speakers of a language. In English, idioms often have figurative meanings, utilizing pictures to help us visualize that meaning. For example, *Hit the nail on the head*, *A hot potato*, *It takes two to tango*, and so on.

The following `if` statement that opens a file in idomatic style Go.

The `Config.DataFilepath` value, `./data/cars.base64`, comes from our `config.toml` file:

```
# Full path to the file containing the base64 car strings
data_filepath = "./data/cars.base64"
```

Let's look closely at that line of code to see what we can learn:

```
                    execute os.Open statement
        if file, err := os.Open(Config.DataFilepath); err == nil {
                                                      assign err value
```

We start with the if statement, like in a typical `if...then` else statement, but rather than immediately checking for a Boolean (true/false), after the `if`, we execute a statement that opens our data file. That statement assigns err a value. If `err == nil`, then we know the file opened successfully. This particular idiom is used about 100 times in the Go standard library. The coding styles we find in the Go Standard Library should be emulated, especially ones that appear that many times.

Monads, Type Classes, and Generics

> The goal of this book is not to remove idiomatic Go from your toolbox, but rather to add simple yet powerful FP tools to it. *If your only hammer is imperative in programming, then every iterative nail looks like a for loop.* That's just not the case. Some iterative tasks are better solved with maps, filters, reductions, functors, monoids, and/or monads.

In the following `main` function we initialize our car counter and open our configuration file.

```
func main() {
    carCntr := 0
    if file, err := os.Open(Config.DataFilepath); err == nil {
```

After opening a file, it's best practice to immediately defer the closing of the file. (The Go standard library uses defer over 100 times.) This way, we won't forget to close our file, which is a frequent mistake that causes memory leaks and can be difficult to troubleshoot. defer is another delightful tool Go gives us to help us write better code.

We execute bufio's `NewScanner` command to open the file and load its contents into the scanner variable in order to read the file line by line.

For simplicity, we chose to read cars from a file, but we could read our data from a stream of input coming from another I/O source such as:

- ActiveMQ
- NATS
- Kafka
- Kestrel
- NSQ
- RabbitMQ
- Redis
- Ruby-NATS
- ZeroMQ

What's important is that the interface to the source you read from needs to implement the `Reader` interface. If we look at the `NewScanner` implementation in the Go standard library, we can see it takes an `io.Reader`:

```
// NewScanner returns a new Scanner to read from r.
// The split function defaults to ScanLines.
func NewScanner(r io.Reader) *Scanner {
    return &Scanner{
        r:              r,
```

```
        split:          ScanLines,
        maxTokenSize: MaxScanTokenSize,
    }
}
```

The `io.Reader` is an interface with one method, `Read`. So, in other words, the API that we get our data from needs to have a `Read` method:

```
type Reader interface {
    Read(p []byte) (n int, err error)
}
```

This is another pattern that we should learn to emulate from the Go Standard Library: *Program to the interface*. Here, the interface of interest is an object with a `Read` method.

We can use the scanner's `Scan` method in a for loop. We will continue to iterate until there are no more lines to be read:

```
    defer file.Close()
Info.Println("----")
    scanner := bufio.NewScanner(file)
    for scanner.Scan() {
        carCntr += 1
    Info.Println("Processing car #", carCntr)
        line :=  scanner.Text()
        Info.Println("IN :", line)
```

Now, we're in the loop and have printed out the first line read (the first car):

```
Processing car # 1
IN :
eyJjYXIiOnsidmluIjoiREc1NDVIRzQ5NDU5WiIsIm1ha2UiOiJUb3lvdGEiLCJtb2RlbCI6Ikh
pZ2hsYW5kZXIiLCJvcHRpb25zIjp7Im9wdGlvbl8xIjoiSGVhdGVkIFNlYXRzIiwib3B0aW9uXz
IiOiJQb3dlciBTdGVlcmluZyIsIm9wdGlvbl8zIjoiR1BTIn19fQ0K
```

Next, we call our monad to execute the workflow required to process our input line (our first car):

```
    err, carJson := workflow.ProcessCar(line)

    if err == nil {
    Info.Println("OUT:", carJson)
    }
```

Monads, Type Classes, and Generics

After we process our input, we check for errors and output the result:

```
OUT:
{"car":{"vin":"DG545HG49459Z","make":"Toyota","model":"Highlander","options
":{"option_1":"Heated Seats","option_2":"Power
Steering","option_3":"GPS"}},"timestamp":"20171030145251"}
```

The remainder of `main` prints a few dashes, checks for scanner errors and closes another if else block.

```
      Info.Println("----")
    }
    if err = scanner.Err(); err != nil {
      Error.Error(err)
    }
  } else {
    Error.Error(err)
  }
}
```

The output for the preceding code is as follows:

```
AppEnv: development
----
Processing car # 1
IN :
eyJjYXIiOnsidmluIjoiREc1NDVIRzQ5NDU5WiIsIm1ha2UiOiJUb3lvdGEiLCJtb2RlbCI6Ikh
pZ2hsYW5kZXIiLCJvcHRpb25zIjp7Im9wdGlvbl8xIjoiSGVhdGVkIFNlYXRzIiwib3B0aW9uXz
IiOiJQb3dlciBTdGVlcmluZyIsIm9wdGlvbl8zIjoiR1BTIn19fQ0K
OUT:
{"car":{"vin":"DG545HG49459Z","make":"Toyota","model":"Highlander","options
":{"option_1":"Heated Seats","option_2":"Power
Steering","option_3":"GPS"}},"timestamp":"20171030145251"}
----
Processing car # 2
IN :
eyJjYXIiOnsidmluIjoiMzQ4NTQzOTg1QVpERCIsIm1ha2UiOiJMZXh1cyIsIm1vZGVsIjoiSVM
gMjUwIiwib3B0aW9ucyI6eyJvcHRpb25fMSI6IlN0aWNrIFNoaWZ0Iiwib3B0aW9uXzIiOiJNb2
9uIFJvb2YiLCJvcHRpb25fMyI6IkxlYXRoZXIifX19DQo=
OUT: {"car":{"vin":"348543985AZDD","make":"Lexus","model":"IS
250","options":{"option_1":"Stick Shift","option_2":"Moon
Roof","option_3":"Leather"}},"timestamp":"20171030145251"}
----
Processing car # 3
IN :
eyJjYXIiOnsidmluIjoiTUZORkg2NkZCWlE5OSIsIm1ha2UiOiJIb25kYSIsIm1vZGVsIjoiQWN
jb3JkIiwib3B0aW9ucyI6eyJvcHRpb25fMSI6IkFsbG95IFdoZWVscyIsIm9wdGlvbl8yIjoiUG
93ZXIgU3RlZXJpbmcifX19
```

[440]

```
OUT:
{"car":{"vin":"MFNFH66FBZQ99","make":"Honda","model":"Accord","options":{"o
ption_1":"Alloy Wheels","option_2":"Power
Steering"}},"timestamp":"20171030145251"}
----
```

Let's see what happens when we run this line:

```
err, carJson := workflow.ProcessCar(line)
```

We import `utils` so that we can log errors:

```
//src/workflow/process_car_steps.go

package workflow

import (
    . "utils"
)
```

Our `ProcessCar` function clearly expresses our business intent. It accepts a base64 encoded string and, in idiomatic Go style, returns an error and result (`carJson`). If all goes well, our error will be nil and `carJson` will be populated.

The workflow embodies our business logic. The rest of our code is framework.

Notice that `ProcessCar` is not cluttered with error checking code, but rather, each step in the workflow is self-explanatory.

This diagram illustrates each step in our workflow:

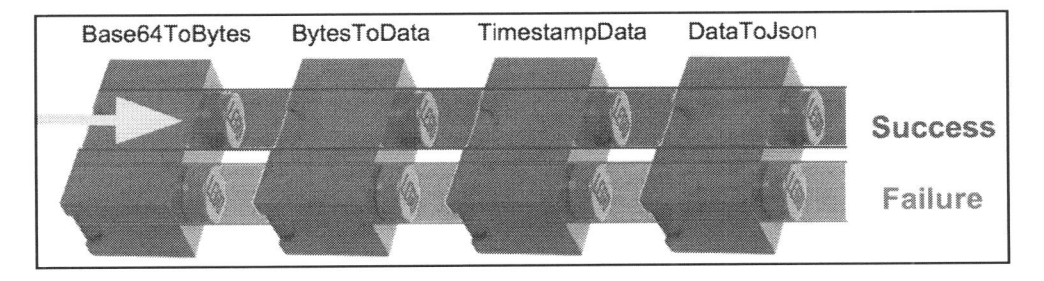

We initialize our step variable by calling the `Get` function with our input `lineBase64`. This starts our workflow:

```
func ProcessCar(lineBase64 string) (err error, carJson string) {
   step := Get(lineBase64)
   step = Next(step, Base64ToBytes)
   step = Next(step, BytesToData)
   step = Next(step, TimestampData)
   step = Next(step, DataToJson)
   json, err := step(nil)
   if err != nil {
      Error.Error(err)
   } else {
      carJson = json.(string)
   }
   return
}
```

Let's look in `monad.go` for the `Get` function's implementation:

src/workflow/monad.go

```
package workflow

type Data interface{}
```

That's the empty interface! Look out for pirates!

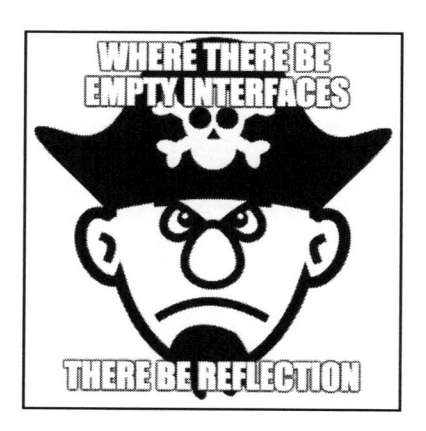

This pirate is right. In our example, we do use reflection in our toolbox of functions. For example, in order to get the filename to pass to the `ioutil.Readfile` function, we must downcast our filename argument from the empty `interace{}` data to a string.

Here is a snippet from `src/workflow/toolbox.go`:

```
func Base64ToBytes(d Data) Monad {
    dString := d.(string)
    return func(e error) (Data, error) {
        return base64.StdEncoding.DecodeString(dString)
    }
}
```

If Go supported generics, we would not need to do this. We'd just need to modify our code slightly to accept generic data types. So, the above `ReadFile` function would look something like this:

```
func Base64ToBytes(<T>) Monad {
    return func(e error) (Data, error) {
        return base64.StdEncoding.DecodeString(T)
    }
}
```

That's about 30% less code, and it will run faster because typecasting is a relatively expensive operation. In this case, if Go supported generics, the compiler would create a string shaped hole in the compiled `ReadFile` function, into which we could pass our string.

In this case, if Go supported generics, we'd have about 30% less code to write and our code would be type-safe and very fast.

It's easy to see why so many programmers are making such a big deal about this topic.

If the runtime cost of reflection is too much to bear, then we can leverage meta-programming tools like `clipperhouse/gen` to generate the repetitive, boilerplate code necessary to handle all the data types that reflection would otherwise handle for us. (If we went down this type-safe route, and we compared the code necessary to support type-safe, reflection free code to what we'd need to write if Go supported generics, we'd likely find that we'd have around 80% less code to maintain than if we had generics.)

> **TIP**
> Before you start thinking about jumping onto the Haskell or Java bandwagon for generics, consider what is good about Go: simplicity, performance, concurrency support, and so on. It's easy enough to use tools to generate type-safe code, and when Go does one day (fingers crossed) support generics, we should be able to fairly easily remove our generated boilerplate code and simply use generics.

Monads, Type Classes, and Generics

Here is our `Monad` type. It is a function that accepts an `error` and returns transformed `Data` and an `error`:

```
type Monad func(error) (Data, error)
```

What can we guess about the way a `Monad` works? Maybe if it gets an error, it will fail fast and pass the error along, or otherwise, it will continue processing and pass the data along with nil for the error?

Sounds a bit like `Continuation Passing Style` (`CPS`) programming, but how does it work? Remember in `Chapter 4`, *SOLID Design in Go*, when we learned that Monads are purple?

We saw a composition of functions like this:

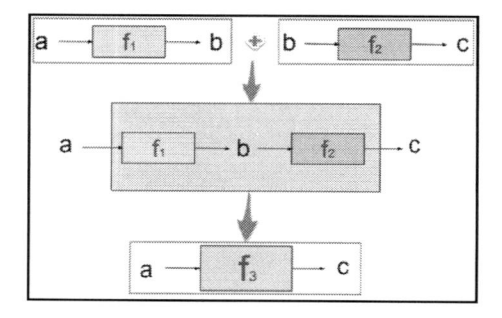

We learned that in order to be a Monad, we need our functions to accept **a** and return a like this:

That would give us associativity:

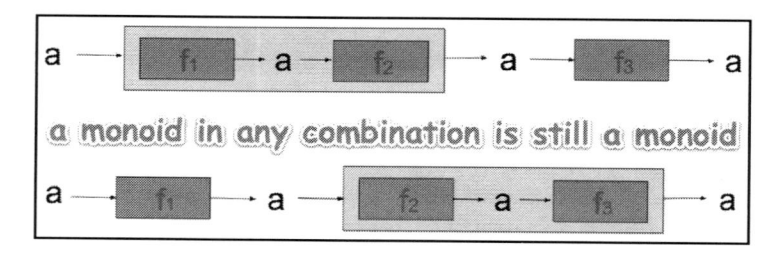

a monoid in any combination is still a monoid

We'll call the Get method that lifts our data into the world of pure FP. It accepts data and returns a Monad. Note that our Data, d, is curried:

```
func Get(d Data) Monad {
    return func(e error) (Data, error) {
        return d, e
    }
}
```

This is where we put our data in the first blue box in our monad chain:

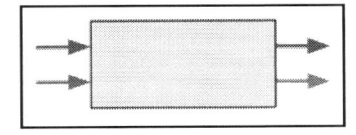

After initializing our step, we call our first data transformation function, Base64ToBytes (in workflow/process_car_steps.go):

```
step := Get(lineBase64)
```

Let's jump back to monad.go and look at Next function's implementation:

```
func Next(m Monad, f func(Data) Monad) Monad {
    return func(e error) (Data, error) {
        newData, newError := m(e)
        if newError != nil {
            return nil, newError
        }
        return f(newData)(newError)
    }
}
```

The Next function accepts a monad and a function that returns a monad and itself returns a monad.

That's it. This is how we get purple Monads that take a and return a.

The first line in our `Next` function looks familiar:

```
return func(e error) (Data, error) {
```

That's because that line is exactly the same as the first line in our Get method. In the line that follows, we call our monad, passing our error as its parameter, and get transformed data, `newData`, as well as the `newError` value in return:

```
newData, newError := m(e)
```

It is here that our stack fills up with `workflow.Next` monad functions. Our call stack will look like this:

```
workflow.Next (Base64ToBytes)
workflow.Next (BytesToData)
workflow.Next (TimestampData)
workflow.Next (DataToJson)
workflow.ProcessCar
main.main
```

This is where we wire up our steps and jump back to `Get` to grab our data (in the return statement):

```
func Get(d Data) Monad {
    return func(e error) (Data, error) {
        return d, e
    }
}
```

If we were electricians, we'd turn off the power, wire up the lights in the house, and turn the power back on to see if our wiring was correct.

As soon as execution returns from the `return d, e` statement, we hit the `if newError != nil` error check block:

```
func Next(m Monad, f func(Data) Monad) Monad {
    return func(e error) (Data, error) {
        newData, newError := m(e)
        if newError != nil {
            return nil, newError
        }
        return f(newData)(newError)
    }
}
```

If an error occurs, then we return nil for the data and the `newError`; all subsequent error checks will pass the same `newError` along until our execution spits out the error at the end of the monad chain.

If an error does not occur, the last return is executed: `return f(newData)(newError)`. What is this? Ever seen a function call like this before?

```
someFunction(val1)(val2)
```

This language construct is known as the Y-Combinator. Before diving into the details of the Y-Combinator implementation in Go, let's think about what it is and its origin, the Lambda Calculus.

Lambda calculus

The Lambda calculus defines what a function is from a computational perspective. It's comprised of three things:

- Variables (x, y, z, and so on)
- A way of creating functions (with the "\" notation)
- A way to apply functions (substitution)

Everything else is defined in terms of encoding those three things.

Monads, Type Classes, and Generics

In `Chapter 7`, *Fu*nctional Parameters, we defined a function where **f** is the function name, **x** is the input value, and the result is the whole expression **f(x)**:

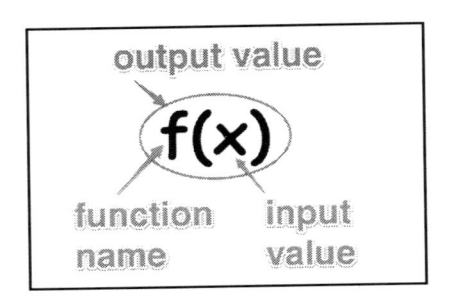

[diagram: f(x) with labels "output value", "function name", "input value"]

If *f(x) = x + 2*, then we know that every time we input the value three, five will always be the output value. So, functions are like black boxes where we put values in and get different values out. There's neither internal hidden data nor side-effects.

However, in lambda calculus, we use anonymous, unnamed functions. How would we express *f(x) = x + 2* in lambda calculus?

The way we build functions in lambda calculus is with expressions, as shown in the following diagram:

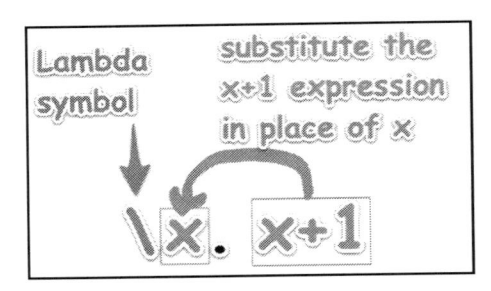

[diagram: \x. x+1 with labels "Lambda symbol" and "substitute the x+1 expression in place of x"]

The period after \x is just a notation that separates our function signature (its arguments, x) from its body (x+2 in our example).

In the following example, 3 is the input parameter:

    (\x. x+2) 3

The result is 5.

In math class, we're used to writing function applications like this: f(3). In lambda calculus, we say (f 3).

The function application associates to the left, so `(f a b c) = (((f a) b) c)`.

When a function is applied, we are simply substituting our parameter for x in our body, where the computation, such as x+2, is performed. Let's try another one that takes two parameters:

```
(\x.\y. (x+y)/2) 3 5
```

This returns one parameter function that also returns one parameter function, which then returns the result:

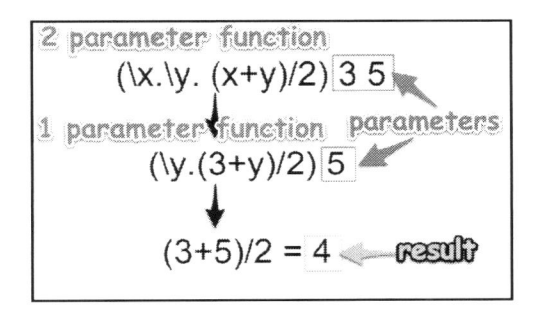

```
2 parameter function
(\x.\y. (x+y)/2) 3 5
          ↓
1 parameter function   parameters
(\y.(3+y)/2) 5
          ↓
(3+5)/2 = 4  ← result
```

What we just did was called **currying**, where functions of multiple arguments are really just higher order functions that take one argument and return function(s).

The numbers we used earlier (2, 3, 5) and the operators (+, /) are not part of lambda calculus. We just used them to encode computations.

Lambda calculus does not have data types, but we can represent data types by using functions. Let's create the Boolean data type:

Boolean functions	Description
`true := \x.\y.x`	The `true` function is a function of two parameters (x and y) and returns the first parameter (x).
`false := \x.\y.y`	The `false` function is a function of two parameters (x and y) and returns the second parameter (y).

Monads, Type Classes, and Generics

Let's define the logical negation function, not:

Boolean expressions	Description
(\b. b false true) true	lambda b b applied to false and true returns true
(\b. b true false) false	lambda b b applied to true and false returns false

We've seen that the Fibonacci function is recursive:

```
func fib(x int) int {
    if x == 0 {
        return 0
    } else if x <= 2 {
        return 1
    } else {
        return fib(x-2) + fib(x-1)
    }
}
```

We defined the `fib` function in terms of itself. That makes the fib function recursive.

Let's start by defining a for loop using Lambda Calculus.

Maybe we could form an expression a that would call itself, as in, apply the function to itself. That would that look like?

```
forLoop := (\x.x x) (\x.x x)
```

Let's see how that works:

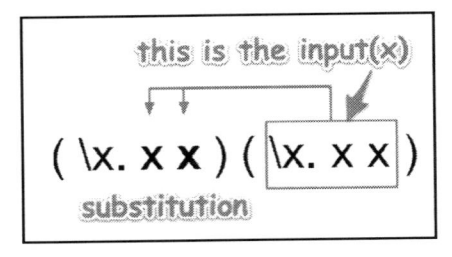

(\x. x x) (\x. x x)
substitution — this is the input(x)

\x.x x takes input x and applies x to itself. Our function takes x as its input and makes two copies of x. That's called self application.

Recursion is about defining something in terms of itself.

Let's see what it looks like when we perform recursion twice:

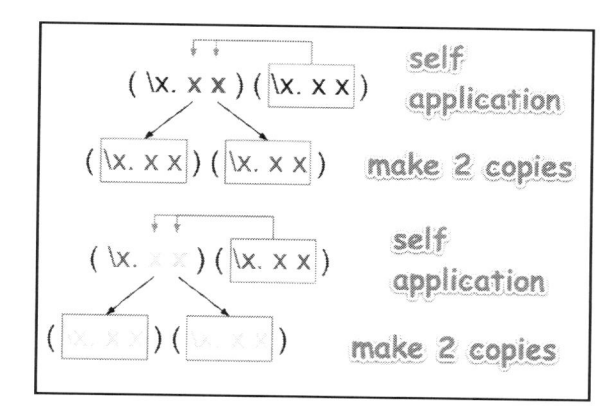

[Diagram showing lambda calculus self-application and making 2 copies, repeated twice]

We can see how this process can continue indefinitely. This is how we encode for loop behavior using Lambda calculus.

Now that we know how to encode a for loop, how can we encode recursion?

Let's define a general recursive function as follows:

```
recursive f = f(recursive f)
```

That reads, recursive `f` equals `f` applied to recursive `f`.

When we run this function, it will repeatedly apply `f` and we'll get: `f(f(f(...)))`. The following is the Y-Combinator:

```
Y = \f.(\x.f(x x)) (\x.f(x x))
```

It's not recursive, but it encodes recursion. This is how we can implement recursion in a language that does not support recursion.

Ready to see how to implement the Y-Combinator in Go?

But wait, there's more.

Let's stop to think about where the Y-Combinator could be used in bioengineering. The recursive genome function could be modeled using the Y-Combinator. What proof is there that the Lambda Calculus is practical? Look in the mirror:

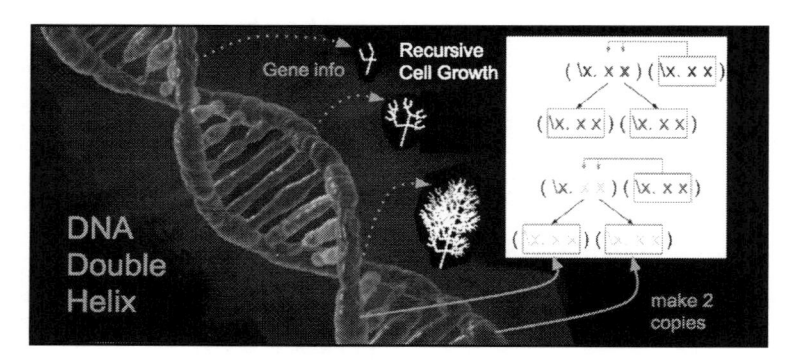

For more information on the *Recursive Genome Function - the Pellionisz Principle*, see `http://www.junkdna.com/recursivegenomefunction/`.

Did you know that your genes can be sequenced and anomalies detected to indicate your predisposition to certain diseases, like Parkinson's Disease? The sooner you know, the sooner preventative measures can be taken.
See `https://en.wikipedia.org/wiki/Disease_gene_identification`.

The Lambda Calculus (which provides recursion) and Monads (which control the composition of operations) are deeply woven into the fabric of life. What happens when we sleep? Have you ever worked long hours to solve a problem without success, only to wake the next morning with the solution in mind? Did you know that we are about 25% more susceptible to illness when we are sleep deprived? What do you think causes DNA mutations that lead to cancerous cell growth? What is it about restorative time (sleep) that allows our body to compose properly?

When we follow basic rules, we thrive.

> *"Early to bed, early to wise makes a man healthy wealthy and wise."*

> *- Benjamin Franklin*

Chapter 10

Y-Combinator

The Y-combinator is one of most beautiful ideas in all of programming. This code demonstrates how amazingly powerful the simple ideas of functional programming are. The Y-Combinator is a higher order function. It accepts a single argument, which is a function that isn't recursive. It returns a copy of the function which is recursive. It requires that our language supports first class functions and that functions be named or anonymous. Go supports all of that.

The Y in Y-Combinator

Ever wonder the Y in the Y-Combinator comes from?

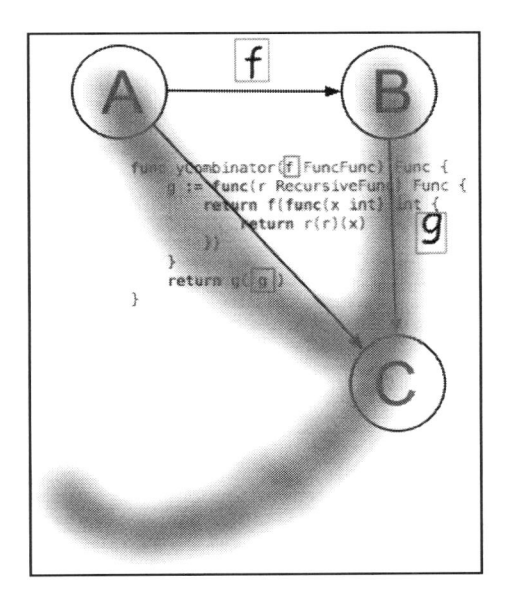

See how **A** and **B** and **C** connect the dots to form the top part of the "y"?

[453]

How the Y-Combinator works

The diagram below illustrates how the Y-Combinator works:

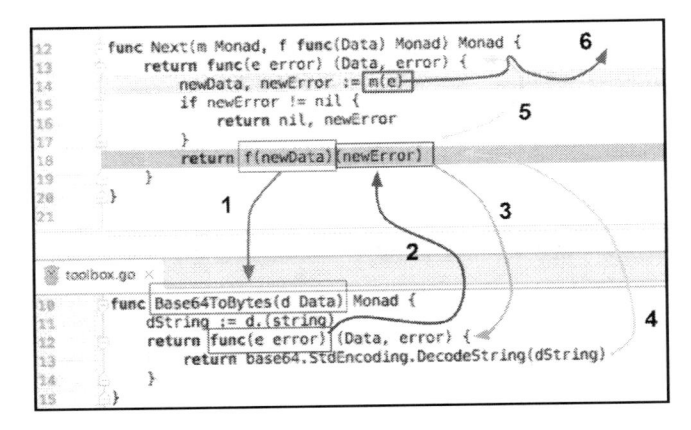

The following are the steps to wire up the Y-Combinator:

1. `f(newData)` calls `Base64ToByes` with the `base64` encoded text. `dString` is downcast into a string.

2. The `return func(e error) (Data, error) {` statement is executed and returns execution back to the return statement in the `Next` function.

3. At that time, `f(newData)`, which itself is a function, has its `newError` parameter populated and can now be executed.

4. Runtime execution returns to the `return func(e error) (Data, error)` line in `Base64ToBytes` and enters its code block, which is the return statement that decodes the `base64` string into a regular string.

5. Execution again returns to `Next`, in the last return line. This is where recursion happens. It calls itself, passing the error value.

6. On *line 14* we call our next monad. This is where continuation passing happens.

We wrote a recursive function of one bound variable using only functions of one variable and no assignments. The Y-combinator performs the magic of associating the anonymous inner function (`func(e error) (Data, error) {`) with the parameter name (`newError`) of the function (`f`) that was originally passed to `Next`.

Now that we know how one of our reusable functions in `toolbox.go` works, we don't need to go through the rest of them. They all work the same way. We can simply move on to the `Next` step through each line of our workflow until we come out the other end. If an error is encountered in any of our reusable functions, we simply kick the can down the road.

This makes it easy and simple to handle errors. Errors only need to be handled at the very end of the process, in one place. Simple.

The Lexical Workflow solution

Here's our entire `ProcessCar` workflow:

```
func ProcessCar(lineBase64 string) (err error, carJson string) {
    step := Get(lineBase64)
    step = Next(step, Base64ToBytes)
    step = Next(step, BytesToData)
    step = Next(step, TimestampData)
    step = Next(step, DataToJson)
    json, err := step(nil)
    if err != nil {
        Error.Error(err)
    } else {
        carJson = json.(string)
    }
    return
}
```

How's that for clarity? Each step one after the next and error handling at the very end.

> This Go idiomatic Monadic workflow solution needs a label, and because I thought of it first, its name is The Lexical Workflow. It's how we can do Monadic composition of impure components in Go. Lex means **law**, and since it controls and rules over our workflow, the name fits. (The fact that it has my name in it must be purely coincidental!)

Is our ProcessCar method idomatic Go code?

Let's start with what's not idiomatic.

The non idiomatic parts

There are no if `err != nil` error checks until the end of our processing pipeline. That's by design.

The benefits of using a monadic pipeline are as follows:

- Enables us to clearly express business logic without the clutter
- Eliminates if `err != nil` error checks after every operative line of code
- Provides structure for pipeline processing
- Orders all of our `Next` steps in our workflow
- Provides a framework for plugging in reusable components

The idiomatic parts

We have a typical if `err != nil` error check at the end of our pipeline:

```
if err != nil {
    Error.Error(err)
} else {
    carJson = json.(string)
}
```

This is where we should perform error checking, so having an error check is natural.

We could choose to implement an `Either` monad to wrap our response in a struct that might look like this:

```
type Either struct {
    Value interface{}
    Error error
}
```

We could include a sum or union type which would return only either `Success()` or `Failure()`:

```
type SuccessOrFailure interface {
    Success() bool
    Failure() bool
}
```

Then we would have to create another interface to convert our `Either` to a `Success` or a `Failure`. It might look something like this:

```
type Either interface {
    SuccessOrFailure
    Succeeded() StringOption
    Failed() ErrorOption
}
```

But we'll no longer pursue these monadic error handling techniques. The Go idiomatic error check works great for our purposes (to handle errors for this workflow) and it does so without the added complexities of additional layers of interfaces or other external dependencies (that we'll discuss at the end of this chapter).

An alternative workflow option

Suppose we have a text file that looks like this:

```
4-purely-functional/ch10-monads/02_error_checker/alphabet.txt
ABCDEFGHIJKLMNOP
```

This code will read three sets of two characters:

```
func main() {
    file, err := os.Open("alphabet.txt")
    if err != nil {
        log.Fatal(err)
    }

    byteSlice := make([]byte, 2)
    numBytesRead, err := io.ReadFull(file, byteSlice)
    if err != nil {
        log.Fatal(err)
    }
    logInfo(numBytesRead, byteSlice)

    byteSlice = make([]byte, 2)
```

```
            numBytesRead, err = io.ReadFull(file, byteSlice)
            if err != nil {
                log.Fatal(err)
            }
            logInfo(numBytesRead, byteSlice)

            byteSlice = make([]byte, 2)
            numBytesRead, err = io.ReadFull(file, byteSlice)
            if err != nil {
                log.Fatal(err)
            }
            logInfo(numBytesRead, byteSlice)
```

We can improve our code by defining a struct with an error field and an `io.Reader` field:

```
     type twoByteReader struct {
         err      error
         reader  io.Reader
     }
```

You might remember from Chapter 3, *Using High-Order Functions*, that the `io.Reader` interface only requires one method, read. So, we implement that and add the `logInfo` call:

```
     func (tbr *twoByteReader) read() (numBytesRead int, byteSlice []byte) {
         if tbr.err != nil {
             return
         }
         byteSlice = make([]byte, 2)
         numBytesRead, tbr.err = io.ReadFull(tbr.reader, byteSlice)
         logInfo(numBytesRead, byteSlice)
         return
     }
```

Now, our code to print three sets of two bytes looks like this:

```
         tbr := &twoByteReader{reader: file}
         byteSlice = make([]byte, 2)
         tbr.read()
         tbr.read()
         tbr.read()
     }
```

Much better! But that is more like a utility function than a workflow solution. It simplifies our code and reduces the number of `if err != nil` blocks.

However, for every step in our workflow, if possible, we'd need to create a separate utility function, and each would have its own `if err != nil` blocks.

Compare that to our monad workflow pipeline that only requires one `if err != nil` block.

Business use case scenarios

The monad workflow provides a solution for business use case scenarios. If we work with a team that implements application features or manages tasks using use case scenarios, the steps in the monad workflow pipeline would likely correspond directly to our task's requirements. Using this workflow could simplify testing, as well as development.

Here's an example that requires five steps:

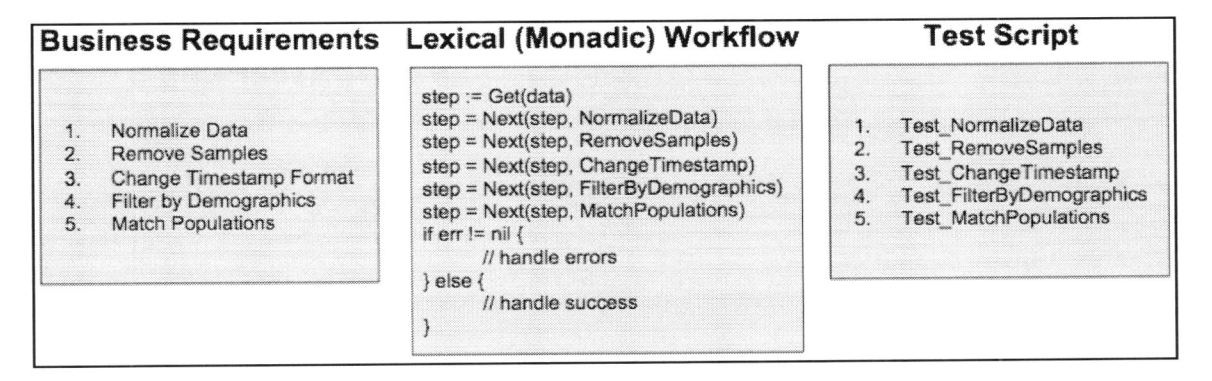

Business Requirements	Lexical (Monadic) Workflow	Test Script

1. Normalize Data
2. Remove Samples
3. Change Timestamp Format
4. Filter by Demographics
5. Match Populations
	step := Get(data)
	step = Next(step, NormalizeData)
	step = Next(step, RemoveSamples)
	step = Next(step, ChangeTimestamp)
	step = Next(step, FilterByDemographics)
	step = Next(step, MatchPopulations)
	if err != nil {
	    // handle errors
	} else {
	    // handle success
	}
		1. Test_NormalizeData
		2. Test_RemoveSamples
		3. Test_ChangeTimestamp
		4. Test_FilterByDemographics
		5. Test_MatchPopulations

Each requirement maps directly to a workflow step (as well as a test).

If we make it through the last step with no errors, then we downcast our data into a string. It will contain JSON and look something like this:

```
{
  "car": {
    "vin": "348543985AZDD",
    "make": "Lexus",
    "model": "IS 250",
    "options": {
      "option_1": "Stick Shift",
      "option_2": "Moon Roof",
      "option_3": "Leather"
    }
  },
  "timestamp": "20171030205535"
}
```

Y-Combinator re-examined

Let's look at another Y-Combinator example in Go to improve our grasp of the topic. Remember the `Fibonacci` function in Chapter 1, *Pure Functional Programming in Go*? It looked like this:

```
func fib(x int) int {
    if x == 0 {
        return 0
    } else if x <= 2 {
        return 1
    } else {
        return fib(x-2) + fib(x-1)
    }
}
```

If it passes a 0, 1, or 2, it simply returns a value (0 or 1). Otherwise, it will call itself (recursion) with two functions that look like this--`fib(x-2) + fib(x-1)`. Since values are continually being decremented by two or one, processing will eventually complete, at which time the accumulated values will be summed up.

The following diagram illustrates this recursive processing. The orange and red boxes highlight functions that only need to be executed once. Referential integrity allows us to store the value of those functions. Subsequent execution only needs to look up the stored value, rather than re-execute the function:

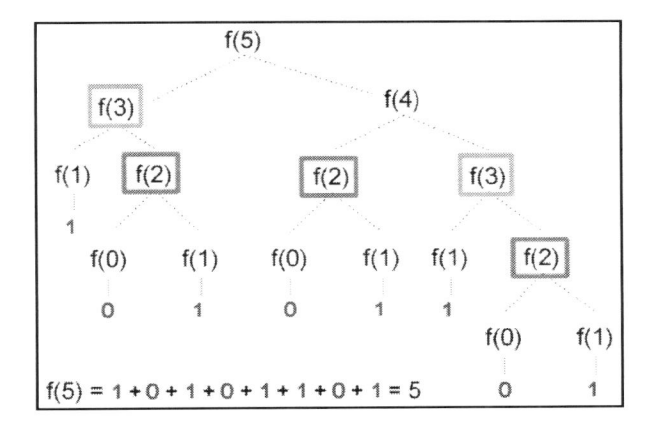

```
                            f(5)
                   ┌─────────┴─────────┐
                 f(3)                 f(4)
              ┌───┴───┐           ┌────┴────┐
            f(1)    f(2)        f(2)      f(3)
             │    ┌──┴──┐      ┌──┴──┐   ┌──┴──┐
             1   f(0)  f(1)   f(0) f(1) f(1)  f(2)
                  │     │      │    │    │   ┌─┴─┐
                  0     1      0    1    1  f(0) f(1)
                                              │    │
                                              0    1
f(5) = 1 + 0 + 1 + 0 + 1 + 1 + 0 + 1 = 5
```

We define three function types in `main.go`, as follows:

- `Func`: A simple function that takes an int and returns an `int`
- `FuncFunc`: A function that takes a function of type `Func` and returns a function of type `Func`
- `RecursiveFunc`: A function that takes a `RecursiveFunc` function and returns a function of type `Func`

```
//4-purely-functional/ch10-monads/03_y_combinator/main.go

package main

import "fmt"

type Func func(int) int
type FuncFunc func(Func) Func
type RecursiveFunc func (RecursiveFunc) Func
```

Let's look at what happens when we initialize the `yCombo` variable:

```
yCombo := yCombinator(fibFuncFunc)
```

The `yCombinator` function is called and we initialize our `g` variable with a recursive lambda expression.

Monads, Type Classes, and Generics

Let's take a closer look at the wiring that occurs when we initialize the `yCombo` variable:

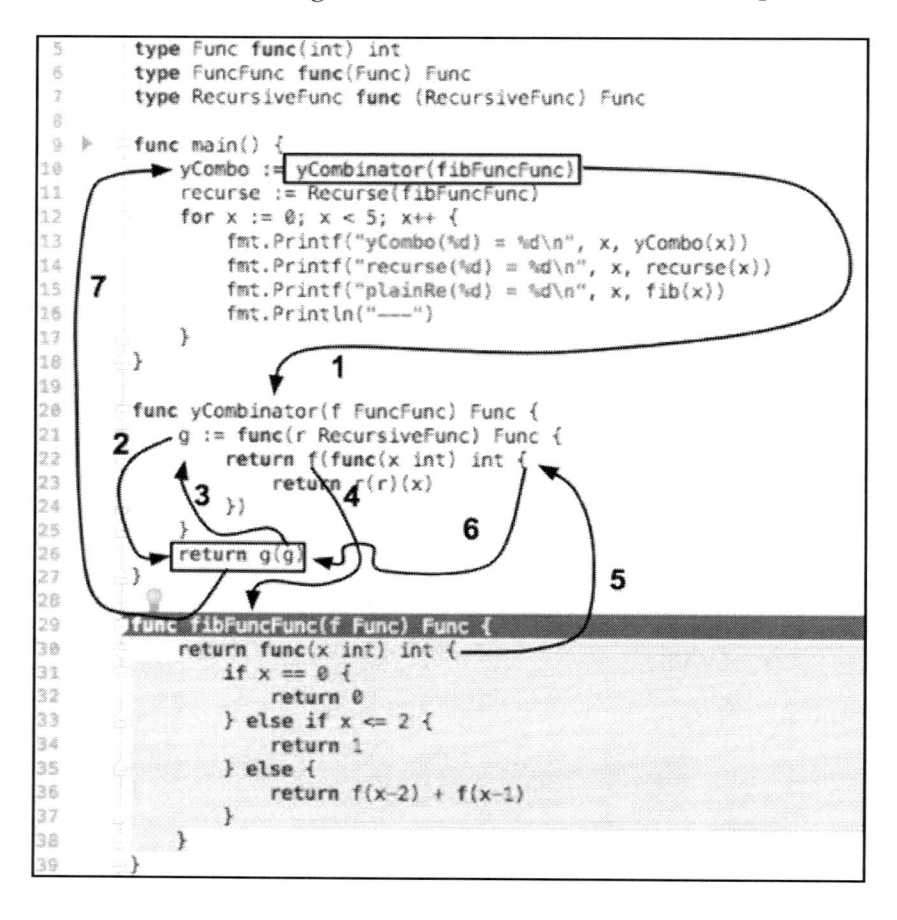

```
 5    type Func func(int) int
 6    type FuncFunc func(Func) Func
 7    type RecursiveFunc func (RecursiveFunc) Func
 8
 9    func main() {
10        yCombo := yCombinator(fibFuncFunc)
11        recurse := Recurse(fibFuncFunc)
12        for x := 0; x < 5; x++ {
13            fmt.Printf("yCombo(%d) = %d\n", x, yCombo(x))
14            fmt.Printf("recurse(%d) = %d\n", x, recurse(x))
15            fmt.Printf("plainRe(%d) = %d\n", x, fib(x))
16            fmt.Println("----")
17        }
18    }
19
20    func yCombinator(f FuncFunc) Func {
21        g := func(r RecursiveFunc) Func {
22            return f(func(x int) int {
23                return r(r)(x)
24            })
25        }
26        return g(g)
27    }
28
29    func fibFuncFunc(f Func) Func {
30        return func(x int) int {
31            if x == 0 {
32                return 0
33            } else if x <= 2 {
34                return 1
35            } else {
36                return f(x-2) + f(x-1)
37            }
38        }
39    }
```

Compare that to the minimal wiring required for the basic recursive variable initialization:

```go
func main() {
    yCombo := yCombinator(fibFuncFunc)
    recurse := Recurse(fibFuncFunc)
    for x := 0; x < 5; x++ {
        fmt.Printf("yCombo(%d) = %d\n", x, yCombo(x))
        fmt.Printf("recurse(%d) = %d\n", x, recurse(x))
        fmt.Printf("plainRe(%d) = %d\n", x, fib(x))
        fmt.Println("----")
    }
}

func yCombinator(f FuncFunc) Func {
    g := func(r RecursiveFunc) Func {
        return f(func(x int) int {
            return r(r)(x)
        })
    }
    return g(g)
}

func fibFuncFunc(f Func) Func {
    return func(x int) int {
        if x == 0 {
            return 0
        } else if x <= 2 {
            return 1
        } else {
            return f(x-2) + f(x-1)
        }
    }
}

func Recurse(f FuncFunc) Func {
    return func(x int) int {
        return f(Recurse(f))(x)
    }
}
```

Monads, Type Classes, and Generics

The execution path looks to be nearly the opposite when we evaluate our Lambda expressions on *line 13* and *line 14*. The slightly wider red lines are the two steps the yCombo function requires to evaluate the expression. The thinner black lines are the eight (plus one) steps that it takes to evaluate the regular recursive function:

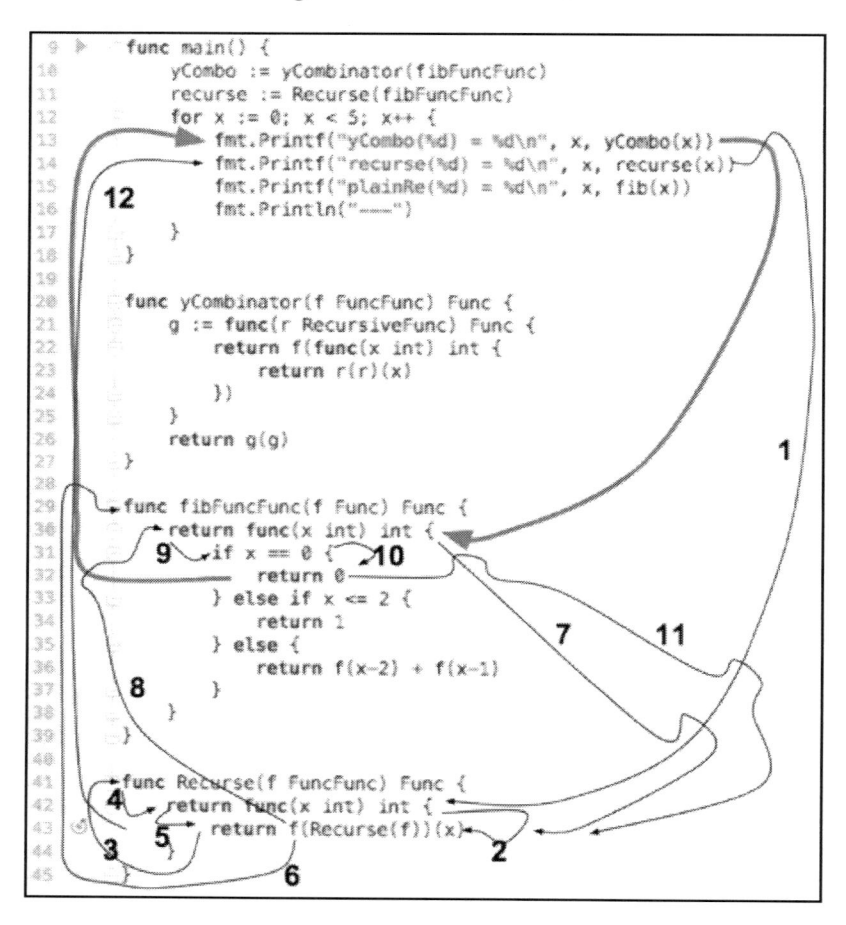

```go
func main() {
    yCombo := yCombinator(fibFuncFunc)
    recurse := Recurse(fibFuncFunc)
    for x := 0; x < 5; x++ {
        fmt.Printf("yCombo(%d) = %d\n", x, yCombo(x))
        fmt.Printf("recurse(%d) = %d\n", x, recurse(x))
        fmt.Printf("plainRe(%d) = %d\n", x, fib(x))
        fmt.Println("-----")
    }
}

func yCombinator(f FuncFunc) Func {
    g := func(r RecursiveFunc) Func {
        return f(func(x int) int {
            return r(r)(x)
        })
    }
    return g(g)
}

func fibFuncFunc(f Func) Func {
    return func(x int) int {
        if x == 0 {
            return 0
        } else if x <= 2 {
            return 1
        } else {
            return f(x-2) + f(x-1)
        }
    }
}

func Recurse(f FuncFunc) Func {
    return func(x int) int {
        return f(Recurse(f))(x)
    }
}
```

These patterns of execution indicate major differences. The yCombinator (lambda expression) does hold on to state and only references the argument (x). In contrast, the regular recursive function holds on to the state of x after arriving at the Recurse function (*step 2*). When Recurse gets to *step 6* (*line 43*), the value for x is supplied from *line 42* (left there from *step 2*).

Since the `yCombinator` (lambda expression) has been prewired, when it's time to evaluate the lambda expression (*line 13*), only two steps are required. Compare that to the twelve steps required to evaluate the regular recursive function (`Recurse`).

Since recursion is necessary in our lambda expression implementation, now would be a good time to re-emphasize the need for the Go compiler to support **Tail Call Optimization (TCO)**. *Chapter 3*, *Using High-Order Functions*, mentioned that TCO avoids creating a new stack by making the last call in a recursion the function itself.

What is tail recursion?

Recursion is where a function calls itself. Tail recursion is where a recursive call is the last line of our function. For example, the last line of our `fib` function calls itself twice:

```
func fib(x int) int {
    if x == 0 {
        return 0
    } else if x <= 2 {
        return 1
    } else {
        return fib(x-2) + fib(x-1)
    }
}
```

In this case, there is no reason to preserve the state. There are no other lines of code left to execute in the function and we don't care about any values of any variables that may have been assigned prior to reaching our return statement.

If our return statement occurred in the middle of our function, the Go runtime would need to remember our function's address in order to return to it, and it would need to store function-local variable values for when our recursive call completes and returns to resume execution.

The problem we currently have is that Go treats all recursive calls the same. Even though tail recursion has no need for a return address or to access any other function-local variable values, Go does it anyway.

If Go were tail call optimized, then it would not allocate additional space on the stack but would instead execute a `GOTO` statement from the tail call directly to itself. That would improve performance and save stack space.

Why not optimize tail calls? One reason is that inserting `GOTO` statements could make debugging stack frame information more difficult.

When was the last time you debugged a stack frame? I'm sure system programmers debug stack frames all day, but most of us don't. It's probably safe to assume that we all care about performance. Perhaps a trade-off would be to allow functional programmers to add an annotation above a tail call to indicate to the compiler to perform TCO for us?

Without TCO, we need to be aware of recursion depth, because in Go each level of recursion means another layer of information that Go runtime needs to store on the stack.

If we are traversing a binary tree, our recursive algorithm will likely be **O(log n)**, which means that we will likely not run into runtime performance issues.

However, if our recursion depth is **O(n)**, this could lead to some troubles with stack. Anything over that should be avoided.

Big-Oh notation

Big-Oh notation is frequently used to indicate the relative complexity of algorithms.

It's used to indicate the order of an algorithm. For example, if we have three algorithms, one O(n), one O(n log n), and one O(n2), the times for various n are:

n	O(n)	O(n log n)	O(n2)
10	10	33	100
100	100	664	10000
500	500	4483	250000
1000	1000	9966	1000000
5000	5000	61438	25000000

Let's assume our unit of measurement is one second per operation. The first line in the table tells us that executing 10 operations takes from 10 seconds for an **O(n)** algorithm to about 1.5 minutes for a **O(n2)** algorithm. The last line tells us that executing 5,000 operations would take from 1.4 hours for the **O(n)** to around three quarters of a year for the **O(n2)** algorithm. Order of magnitude matters.

What does this have to do with tail recursion? Recursive function calls make our stack grow linearly **O(n)**. So, the lack of TCO probably won't make our applications crash, but it will definitely slow them down. Performing computations with an order of magnitude greater than **O(n)** would be difficult at best.

In other words, when we use recursive function calls, we can quickly run out of stack space. TCO can reorganize/optimize our code so that our program uses constant stack space, which will prevent our stack from growing too large and will reduce stack errors.

The benefits of TCO are:

- Improved execution speed, since no stack pushes and pops are required
- Function recursion depth is no longer a constraint
- Stack overflow runtime errors will not be an issue

The languages that support TCO are:

- Common Lisp
- JavaScript (ECMAScript 6.0)
- Lua
- Python
- Scheme
- Racket
- Tcl
- Kotlin
- Elixir
- Perl
- Scala

Where's Haskell? Haskell performs more optimized optimizations than just the tail call elimination. Haskell uses *guarded* recursion. It's a lazy runtime system that does not evaluate a thunk unless it has to.

There are a few reasons to not include it. With TCO enabled, calls would no longer be clearly delineated, making debugging stack frames more difficult. How would TCO affect defer statements?

What if Go supported an annotation (such as `//@tco`) that would allow us to turn on TCO for a particular function call?

> **TIP**
> See the *How to Propose Changes To Go* section of the appendix for more information about Go and TCO.

InternationalizatioN (I18N) package

Remember earlier in the chapter when we looked at the monad workflow and saw how we could push all errors that occurred in any step into the error pipe and wait until the very end to process them?

One thing we might need to do when we process errors is to localize the error messages for the language of the individuals tasked with reading them.

This sample application explores how we might do that using the `go-i18n` library.

> The Go package **go-i18n** (`https://github.com/nicksnyder/go-i18n`) a command (`https://github.com/nicksnyder/go-i18n#goi18n-command`) that helps you translate Go programs into multiple languages. It supports pluralized strings (`http://cldr.unicode.org/index/cldr-spec/plural-rules`) for all 200+ languages in the **Unicode Common Locale Data Repository (CLDR)** `http://www.unicode.org/cldr/charts/28/supplemental/language_plural_rules.html`.

In `main.go`, we import the `github.com/nicksnyder/go-i18n/i18n` library as well at the text/template library from Go's Standard Library:

```
package main

import (
"os"
    "text/template"
    "github.com/nicksnyder/go-i18n/i18n"
    "fmt"
)
```

Here, we initialize the `funcMap` function with the `"T"` key, and give it the value `i18n.TranslateFunc`:

```
var funcMap = map[string]interface{}{
"T": i18n.IdentityTfunc,
}
```

Next, we define our templates:

```
var tmplIllegalBase64Data =
template.Must(template.New("").Funcs(funcMap).Parse(`
{{T "illegal_base64_data" .}}
`))
var tmplUnexpectedEndOfJson=
template.Must(template.New("").Funcs(funcMap).Parse(`
{{T "unexpected_end_of_json_input"}}
`))
var tmplJsonUnsupportedValue =
template.Must(template.New("").Funcs(funcMap).Parse(`
{{T "json_unsupported_value" .}}
`))
```

We define their corresponding functions:

```
func illegalBase64(T i18n.TranslateFunc, bytePos string) {
    tmplIllegalBase64Data.Execute(os.Stdout, map[string]interface{}{
        "BytePos":    bytePos,
    })
}
func unexpectedEndOfJson(T i18n.TranslateFunc) {
    tmplUnexpectedEndOfJson.Execute(os.Stdout, map[string]interface{}{
    })
}
func jsonUnsupportedValue(T i18n.TranslateFunc, bytePos string) {
    tmplJsonUnsupportedValue.Execute(os.Stdout, map[string]interface{}{
        "Val":    bytePos,
    })
}
```

Notice that if our error message accepts parameters, then we define them in the body of the Execute function. For example, `illegalBase64` defines `BytePos`. Here's how it might be output:

```
illegal base64 data at input byte 136
```

Monads, Type Classes, and Generics

In our main function, we load our translation files. In this sample application, we'll show the support for English and German:

```
func main() {
    i18n.MustLoadTranslationFile("en-us.all.json")
    i18n.MustLoadTranslationFile("de-de.all.json")
```

Next, we range over a list of our two languages, en-US, and de-DE, printing out three messages for each language:

```
    for _, locale := range []string{"en-US", "de-DE"} {
        fmt.Println("\nERROR MESSAGES FOR", locale)
        T, _ := i18n.Tfunc(locale)
        tmplIllegalBase64Data.Funcs(map[string]interface{}{
            "T": T,
        })
        tmplUnexpectedEndOfJson.Funcs(map[string]interface{}{
            "T": T,
        })
        tmplJsonUnsupportedValue.Funcs(map[string]interface{}{
            "T": T,
        })

        illegalBase64(T, "136")
        unexpectedEndOfJson(T)
        jsonUnsupportedValue(T, "+Inf")
    }
}
```

This is where we tell `i18n` which translation to use:

```
T, _ := i18n.Tfunc(locale)
```

Three lines follow, in which we assign our en-US translation function to the "T" key of our `tmplIllegalBase64Data` variable:

```
tmplIllegalBase64Data.Funcs(map[string]interface{}{
    "T": T,
})
```

When it is evaluated, the `Funcs` method in `text/template/template.go` is executed and is passed to our `funcMap` variable.

This is what Funcs looks like (mine is in /usr/local/Cellar/go/1.9/libexec/src/text/template/template.go):

```go
func (t *Template) Funcs(funcMap FuncMap) *Template {
    t.init()
    t.muFuncs.Lock()
    defer t.muFuncs.Unlock()
    addValueFuncs(t.execFuncs, funcMap)
    addFuncs(t.parseFuncs, funcMap)
    return t
}
```

Notice that since Func is a method of *Template and returns a *Template, Func can be chained.

At the end of the range loop, we call our error message printing functions:

```
illegalBase64(T, "136")
unexpectedEndOfJson(T)
jsonUnsupportedValue(T, "+Inf")
```

The output is as follows:

```
ERROR MESSAGES FOR en-US
illegal base64 data at input byte 136
unexpected end of JSON input
json: unsupported value: +Inf

ERROR MESSAGES FOR de-DE
ungültige base64-Daten am Eingangsbyte 136
unerwartetes Ende der JSON-Eingabe
json: nicht unterstützter Wert: +Inf
```

The English translation file 4-purely-functional/ch10-monads/04_i18n/en-us.all.json has the following content:

```json
{
  "illegal_base64_data": {
    "other": "illegal base64 data at input byte {{.BytePos}}"
  },
  "json_unsupported_value": {
    "other": "json: unsupported value: {{.Val}}"
  },
  "unexpected_end_of_json_input": {
    "other": "unexpected end of JSON input"
  }
}
```

Monads, Type Classes, and Generics

The German translation file `4-purely-functional/ch10-monads/04_i18n/de-de.all.json` has the following content:

```
{
  "illegal_base64_data": {
    "other": "ungültige base64-Daten am Eingangsbyte {{.BytePos}}"
  },
  "json_unsupported_value": {
    "other": "json: nicht unterstützter Wert: {{.Val}}"
  },
  "unexpected_end_of_json_input": {
    "other": "unerwartetes Ende der JSON-Eingabe"
  }
}
```

> **TIP:** I used Google Translate. Just type sentences in your native language in the left pane (English) and select the language you want it translated to (German) in the right pane's drop-down.

We can use Google Translate to translate sentences into other languages:

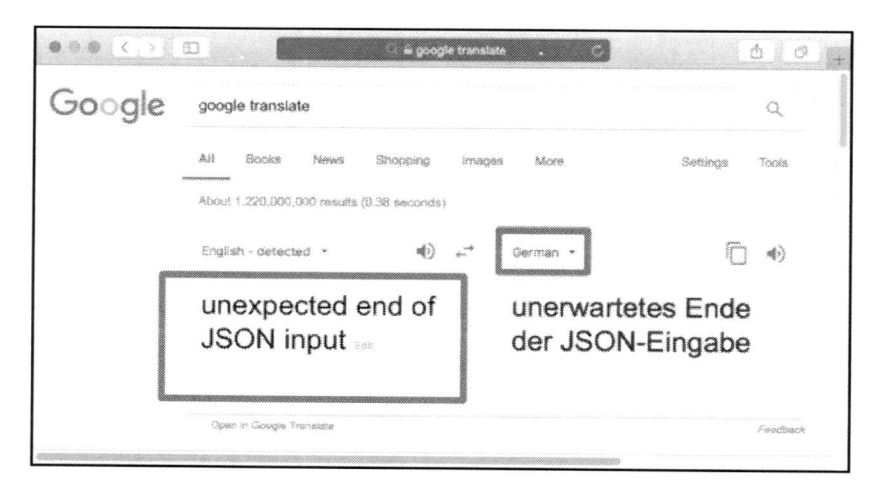

Assuming you are using the init script that is included in every Go project for this book, you should have the `get-go-binary` Bash function loaded in your shell and ready to use.

Here's the workflow to initialize our project and install i18n:

```
~/clients/packt/dev/fp-go/4-purely-functional/ch10-monads/04_i18n $ . init
++ ln -s /Users/lex/clients/packt/dev/fp-go/4-purely-functional/ch10-monads/04_i18n /Users/lex/dev/04
_i18n
Installed Go version: go version go1.9.2 darwin/amd64
Switching Go to version 1.9.2 ...
GOVERSION: go version go1.9.2 darwin/amd64
CURRENT_GOVERSION: go1.9.2
You should only need to run this init script once.
Add Go source code files under the src directory.
After updating dependencies, i.e., adding a new import statement, run: glide-update
To build and run your app, run: go-run
~/dev/04_i18n $ glide-update
~/clients/packt/dev/fp-go/4-purely-functional/ch10-monads/04_i18n ~/dev/04_i18n
[INFO]  Generating a YAML configuration file and guessing the dependencies
[INFO]  Attempting to import from other package managers (use --skip-import to skip)
[INFO]  Scanning code to look for dependencies
[INFO]  --> Found reference to github.com/nicksnyder/go-i18n/i18n
[INFO]  Writing configuration file (glide.yaml)
[INFO]  You can now edit the glide.yaml file. Consider:
[INFO]  --> Using versions and ranges. See https://glide.sh/docs/versions/
[INFO]  --> Adding additional metadata. See https://glide.sh/docs/glide.yaml/
[INFO]  --> Running the config-wizard command to improve the versions in your configuration
[INFO]  Downloading dependencies. Please wait...
[INFO]  --> Fetching updates for github.com/nicksnyder/go-i18n.
[INFO]  Resolving imports
[INFO]  --> Fetching updates for github.com/pelletier/go-toml.
[INFO]  --> Fetching updates for gopkg.in/yaml.v2.
[INFO]  Downloading dependencies. Please wait...
[INFO]  Setting references for remaining imports
[INFO]  Exporting resolved dependencies...
[INFO]  --> Exporting github.com/nicksnyder/go-i18n
[INFO]  --> Exporting github.com/pelletier/go-toml
[INFO]  --> Exporting gopkg.in/yaml.v2
[INFO]  Replacing existing vendor dependencies
[INFO]  Project relies on 3 dependencies.
vendor packages have been moved to /Users/lex/clients/packt/dev/fp-go/4-purely-functional/ch10-monads
/04_i18n/vendors and your GOPATH: /Users/lex/clients/packt/dev/fp-go/4-purely-functional/ch10-monads/
04_i18n/vendors:/Users/lex/clients/packt/dev/fp-go/4-purely-functional/ch10-monads/04_i18n
~/dev/04_i18n
~/dev/04_i18n $ get-go-binary github.com/nicksnyder/go-i18n/goi18n
~/dev/04_i18n/tmp_dir_4581 ~/dev/04_i18n
~/dev/04_i18n
~/dev/04_i18n $ goi18n -help
Merge translation files.

Usage:

    goi18n merge [options] [files...]
```

The i18n site describes a workflow we can use if we are sending our files out to a translation service.

Type classes

Type classes allow us to define behavior on types.

As discussed in `Chapter 3`, *Using High-Order Functions*, type classes add an additional layer to our type system.

We accomplish this by:

1. Defining behavior using Go interfaces (parent type class)
2. Declaring a new type (base type class) to wrap base types
3. Implementing behavior on our new type classes

Let's look at our `Equals` type class implementation.

Parent class definition:

```
//4-purely-functional/ch11-monads/05_typeclasss/src/typeclass/equals.go
package typeclass

import (
    "strconv"
)
type Equals interface {
    Equals(Equals) bool
}
```

Equals is our parent type class. All base classes must implement the `Equals` method.

Base class definitions

We'll define two base types, `Int` and `String`.

Int base class

The `Equals` method of Int will check whether other types are equal, using whatever logic we deem appropriate:

```
type Int int

func (i Int) Equals(e Equals) bool {
    intVal := int(i)
    switch x := e.(type) {
    case Int:
        return intVal == int(x)
    case String:
        convertedInt, err := strconv.Atoi(string(x))
        if err != nil {
            return false
        }
        return intVal == convertedInt
    default:
        return false
    }
}
```

String base class

It's just like the `Int` class, but for strings:

```
type String string

func (s String) Equals(e Equals) bool {
    stringVal := string(s)
    switch x := e.(type) {
    case String:
        return stringVal == string(x)
    case Int:
        return stringVal == strconv.Itoa(int(x))
    default:
        return false
    }
}
```

Our main.go file

We start by importing our typeclass code (located in the `src` directory, where we store all project-local packages):

```
package main

import (
    "typeclass"
    "fmt"
)

func main() {
    int42 := typeclass.Int(42)
    str42 := typeclass.String("42")
    fmt.Println("str42.Equals(int42):", str42.Equals(int42))
```

The output is as follows:

```
str42.Equals(int42): true
```

Sum parent type class

Let's create another type class to sum values:

```
4-purely-functional/ch10-monads/05_typeclasss/src/typeclass/sum.go
package typeclass

type Sum interface {
    Sum(Sum) int64
}
```

Sum is our parent type class. All base type classes must implement the `Sum` method.

Sum base classes

Here are our base classes:

```
type Int32 int32
type Int64 int64
type Float32 float32
type IntSlice []int
```

We can see from our type definitions that we will be able to sum any two of these base types.

Here's the `Int32` implementation of `Sum`:

```
func (i Int32) Sum(s Sum) int64 {
    it := int64(i)
    switch x := s.(type) {
    case Int64:
        return it + int64(x)
    case Int32:
        return it + int64(x)
    case Float32:
        return it + int64(x)
    case IntSlice:
        sum := int64(0)
        for _, num := range x {
            sum += int64(num)
        }
        return it + sum
    default:
        return 0
    }
}
```

Notice that we return zero if the value we are trying to add our `Int32` to is not in the accepted list of types.

> Another option would be to implement a result type, like Haskell's Either type. This is a recent Golang specification addition which was rejected. For details, see https://github.com/golang/go/issues/19991.

The Sum implementations for `Int64` and `Float64` are similar:

```
func (i Int64) Sum(s Sum) int64 {
    it := int64(i)
    switch x := s.(type) {
    case Int64:
        return it + int64(x)
    case Int32:
        return it + int64(x)
    case Float32:
        return it + int64(x)
    case IntSlice:
        sum := int64(0)
        for _, num := range x {
            sum += int64(num)
        }
        return it + sum
```

[477]

Monads, Type Classes, and Generics

```
        default:
            return 0
        }
    }

    func (i Float32) Sum(s Sum) int64 {
        it := int64(i)
        switch x := s.(type) {
        case Int64:
            return it + int64(x)
        case Int32:
            return it + int64(x)
        case Float32:
            return it + int64(x)
        case IntSlice:
            sum := int64(0)
            for _, num := range x {
                sum += int64(num)
            }
            return it + sum
        default:
            return 0
        }
    }
```

In our implementation for int slices, we implement a range iteration for each type we wish to add to our slice of ints:

```
    func (i IntSlice) Sum(s Sum) int64 {
        it := i
        switch x := s.(type) {
        case Int64:
            sum := int64(0)
            for _, num := range it {
                sum += int64(num)
            }
            return int64(x) + sum
        case Int32:
            sum := int64(0)
            for _, num := range it {
                sum += int64(num)
            }
            return int64(x) + sum
        case Float32:
            sum := int64(0)
            for _, num := range it {
                sum += int64(num)
            }
```

```
            return int64(x) + sum
    case IntSlice:
        sum := int64(0)
        for _, num := range it {
            sum += int64(num)
        }
        for _, num := range x {
            sum += int64(num)
        }
        return sum
    default:
        return 0
    }
}
```

Here, we exercise our Sum type classes:

```
    int64One := typeclass.Int64(1)
    int64Two := typeclass.Int64(2)
    fmt.Println("int64Two.Sum(int64One):", int64Two.Sum(int64One))

    int32One := typeclass.Int32(1)
    fmt.Println("int32One.Sum(int64One):", int32One.Sum(int64One))

    float32Five := typeclass.Float32(5)
    fmt.Println("int32One.Sum(int64One):", float32Five.Sum(int64One))

    int64Slice123 := typeclass.IntSlice([]int{1, 2, 3})
    int64Slice234 := typeclass.IntSlice([]int{2, 3, 4})
    fmt.Println("int64Slice123.Sum(int64Slice234):",
int64Slice123.Sum(int64Slice234))
}
```

The output is as follows:

```
int64Two.Sum(int64One): 3
int32One.Sum(int64One): 2
int32One.Sum(int64One): 6
int64Slice123.Sum(int64Slice234): 15
```

Generics revisited

In the last chapter, we discussed some of the benefits of generics:

- Type safety
- Eliminates the need to write repetitive, boilerplate code

Monads, Type Classes, and Generics

- Reuses and shares code for different types
- Enforces consistent APIs across different types
- Time spent optimizing generic code has more impact
- Don't need to re-implement algorithms that are hard to get right
- Able to specify domain constraints

Given the following type definitions:

```
type Car struct {
    Make, Model string
    Price Dollars
}
type Truck struct {
    Make, Model string
    BedSize int
    Price Dollars
}
price := func (c T) Dollars {
    return c.Price
}
```

Instead of writing both of these:

```
type CarSlice []Car
func (rcv CarSlice) SumDollars(fn func(Car) Dollars) (result Dollars) {
    for _, v := range rcv {
        result += fn(v)
    }
    return
}

type TruckSlice []Truck
func (rcv TruckSlice) SumDollars(fn func(Truck) Dollars) (result Dollars) {
    for _, v := range rcv {
        result += fn(v)
    }
    return
}
```

We can print the price sums as follows:

```
fmt.Println("Car Prices:", cars.SumDollars(price))
fmt.Println("Truck Prices:", trucks.SumDollars(price))
```

If Go supported generics, we could write it once. It would look something like this:

```
func (rcv []T) SumDollars(fn func(T) Dollars) (result Dollars) {
    for _, v := range rcv {
        result += fn(v)
    }
    return
}
```

We can print the price sums as follows:

```
fmt.Println("Car Prices:", cars.SumDollars(<Car>))
fmt.Println("Truck Prices:", trucks.SumDollars(<Truck>))
```

> **Covariance and contravariance** (https://www.ibm.com/developerworks/library/j-jtp01255/index.html) refers to the ability to use a less specific or more more specific type than originally specified. Covariant and contravariant generic type parameters provide greater flexibility when assigning and using generic types.

Considering that example code, what's not to love about generics?

> Go's fast compilation speed is partly due to incremental compilation. Incremental compilation is not possible with generics because the concrete type only knows where the generic function is used at runtime, not where it is defined.

Not counting the fact that the implementation of generics into the Go compiler would be incredibly complex, in terms of both semantics and implementation, here are some of the disadvantages of adding generics to Go from a developer's perspective:

- Generic algorithms tend to accumulate features (affecting code quality).
- It's difficult to optimize generic algorithms.
- It's difficult to debug generic code.
- Error handling complexities.
- Usage complexities: covariance, contravariance, erasure.
- Slows down compile time (or runtime).
- Generic/existing non-generic code incompatibilities.

The fourth and the seventh disadvantage and 7 are the most concerning.

Monads, Type Classes, and Generics

First, let's better understand what is meant by error handling complexities. What about `Maybe`, `Either`, and `Option` solving the nil pointer errors?

In order for pure FP monadic error handling to work, all the packages referenced in our applications would need to return a monadic error type, like Either. (Either it succeeded or not, but nil would never be returned.)

Granted, that would eliminate the need for the the following ubiquitous error check:

```
if err != nil {
    return nil, err
}
```

However, we would now need to change the way we handle errors, using new language extensions like `Maybe` monads, `Either`, `Option`, `Nothing`, `Just`, and so on. (For some code examples, see `2-design-patterns/ch04-solid/02_maybe`.) That's another layer of complexity.

Furthermore, how would we integrate this new error handling paradigm into existing applications? If we were creating a new application, but wanted to use any standard library packages or any package that had not been converted to use generics-compatible error handling, would we write an adapt layer? That's another layer of complexity.

The impact of going generic would be signification. What percentage of the Go Standard Library would need to change?

Do we replace the ubiquitous slice with a collection type? How much existing code would be affected by that?

How would support for generics affect concurrency?

How would performance be impacted if go were to lose type erasure and implement reification in order to add explicit type annotations to generic arguments?

Impact of Golang

A minimal set of language constructs that would need modification includes:

- Type assertions
- Type switches
- Range statements
- Function calls

They are all deeply impactful, and the last one is deep and broad.

The entire type system will likely need an overhaul.

Personal opinion

Before writing this book, I was of the opinion that the benefits of generics far outweighed its disadvantages. Writing this book forced me to really think about it.

I thought about the pros and cons as well as alternatives, such as using metaprogramming and code generation tools (see the clipperhouse/gen tool in the last chapter).

I thought about how monadic error handling works and its similarities to Go's `return successValue, err error` handling idiom (as well as its similarities to the Unix `stdout` / `stderr`). I found a way to get the most significant feature from pure FP (Monads) to work in Go while maintaining Go's error handling idiom.

The benefits of using The Lexical (Monadic) Workflow Solution in Go are:

- Type-safe
- No empty interfaces/unboxing/downcasting/reflection required
- Expressive, easy-to-understand workflow code
- `Get(data)` then `Next(step), Next(step)` until done
- Mostly idiomatic error handling in one place (at the end)
- Directly mirrors business requirements
- Allows us to compose new workflows easily using reusable components (see `toolbox.go`)
- Designed to be optimized for horizontal scaling
- Does not impose any requirements on external packages
- Does not require additional Monadic error handling logic

Since this solution uses a lambda expression, there is recursion, and since Go currently does not provide TCO, there is a performance hit, but the recursion is limited to controlling the workflow.

The burden is that I must manually create repetitive code or generate the generic code (using a tool like clipperhouse/gen) to avoid the performance penalty of using the empty `interface{}` and reflection.

I concluded that generics are a trade-off between compilation time, runtime, and my time. Given the risk and the list of disadvantages of adding generics to Go, I'm okay with doing a little more work.

> *"Simplicity and elegance are unpopular because they require hard work and discipline to achieve and education to be appreciated."*
>
> - Edsger Dijkstra

Summary

Function programming in Go is a paradigm shift, a fundamentally different approach to the way we write software. Just like we can get the results we want with an imperative Turing Machine or with Lambda Calculus, we can choose to code imperatively with idiomatic Go or declaratively using the FP style of programming.

We began our journey with a light introduction to FP. We learned how to write intermediate functions like `Map`, `Filter`, and `Sort`, as well as terminal functions like `Reduce` and `Join`, to transform collections. We saw how to use tools like Gleam and Itertool and implemented lazy evaluation using Go routines and a Go channel.

We thought about the characteristics of FP and worked through examples of function composition, closures, and high order functions.

We studied both the imperative-functional and pure-functional styles of software design (and later mixed both styles). We learned how the Reader/Writer interface in Go implements the single responsibility principle. Just one whiff of OOP gave us an appreciation for the simplicity (and honesty) of pure FP. (FP contracts don't lie.) The secret to function composition was revealed to us: Monads chain continuations.

We learned how `Map` and `Reduce` work. As the constant flow of diagrams began to heighten our awareness of the value of FP, we were tossed back to the world of imperative programming using functions.

Duck typing, embedding, the decorator, strategy, and pipeline patterns, inversion of control, dependency injection, the use of channels to control the flow of events in a concurrent program... we even learned how to avoid circular dependencies using a layered application architecture. We learned the difference between currying and partial application and how to implement functional parameters to improve our APIs.

Category theory was presented in a way never seen before: using over 100 images, 17 tables of information, and code samples, along with simple and concise wording. We led you through the history of functional programming and learned the deep connection between category theory, logic, and type theory. We learned that the math we learned in grade school, middle school, and high school is applicable to functional programming. (Maybe that even inspired someone to send their old math teacher a note of appreciation?)

With a solid understanding of category theory, we embarked on a pure FP journey where we learned how to map between worlds using functors. We built a few monoids and learned how to write a reduce function. We also learned how to use a generics code generation tool to solve the boilerplate problem.

Armed with the knowledge of pure and imperative functional programming, we dove into the world of Monads. We learned about Lambda Calculus and how the Y-Combinator works, and how to use it to control workflow.

We implemented the Lexical Workflow Solution that leveraged the Y-Combinator to control a sequence of impure operations. We witnessed our data as it was transformed from one step to the next. We saw how the `Success` and `Failure` pipes work and how we could handle all errors at the end of the pipeline using the idiomatic Go techniques. We gained a much better understanding of the pros and cons of adding generics to Go.

Where to go from here

Here are some ideas:

- Look for places to use the Lexical Workflow Solution to control data transformation workflows
- Build a reusable set of components, to put in your toolbox, that you can use in our workflows
- Build your own type classes, monads and pure FP components in Go
- Support the request to add TCO to Go (see the `Appendix`, *Miscellaneous Information and How-To's*)

I hope the information you found in this book is useful for what you're building both today and tomorrow and that it inspires you to continue to improve upon these ideas so that we can all build even better applications going forward.

"Talk is cheap. Show me the code."

- Linus Torvalds

11
Category Theory That Applies

In kindergarten, we learned how to read time. In advanced math, we learned how to abstract a 12-hour clock and called it a monad.

In elementary school, we learned geometry, logical reasoning, and functions.

Category Theory That Applies

In high school, we learned algebra, linear, and quadratic equations. We were so busy going through the motions deep in the minutiae of our problems that we could see no use for any of it.

> **TIP:** Check out the learning material used in K-12 education here: https://www.ixl.com/math/kindergarten/match-analog-clocks-and-times.

Fast forward to our day job. To appear smart, we often ask, *Will it scale?* No matter what *it* is.

Wondering how reading time and horizontal scaling are related? They are, deeply. We'll find out how in this chapter.

Our goal in this chapter is to do the following:

- Gain a working understanding of the category theory
- Appreciate the deep connection between category theory, logic, and type theory
- Understand what binding, currying and application means in the context of a lambda expression
- Understand the different categories of homomorphisms and how to use them
- Learn to use composition techniques from category theory
- Understand what interface-driven development is about
- See the value of knowledge driven systems
- Apply our understanding of category theory to build better apps

Our goal

By the end of this chapter, we will see value in those math classes we took back in school. We'll understand how the things we learned in our high school math classes can be applied when horizontally scaling our software solutions.

The following diagram implies that **Category Theory**, functional programming, and logic are equivalent:

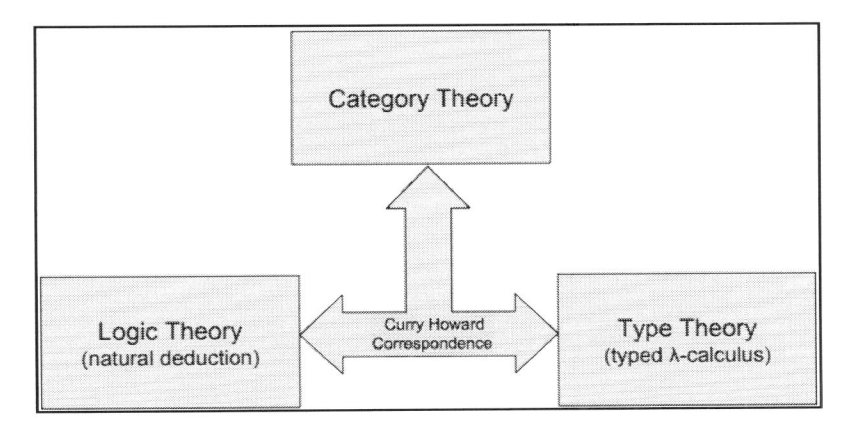

[Diagram: Category Theory at top, connected by arrow to a two-way arrow between Logic Theory (natural deduction) and Type Theory (typed λ-calculus), labeled "Curry Howard Correspondence"]

Huh?

I thought Category Theory was about a sets of objects and the arrows that connect them and that *Proof Theory* was about using logic to prove something. And we all know that function programming is about software. How can all three things be related?

This seems about as useful as all those math classes we had to take in school, right?

Your pessimism is understandable. Please proceed with an open mind and remain seated. Mathematics, logic, and computation. They are just three different ways to approach solving the same problems.

How can Category Theory, Proof Theory, and functional programming be the same thing? (and why care?)

> "Scientists derive satisfaction from figuring out the puzzle. It's about the quest, not the grail."
>
> -Isaac Asimov

Break it down

Let's break each part down to get a firm grasp of the breadth of our problem:

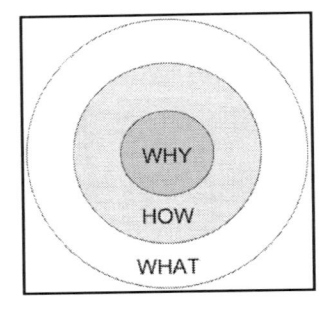

[Diagram: concentric circles labeled WHY (innermost), HOW, WHAT (outermost)]

If the **WHY** is the motivation for building your application, then the **HOW** describes how our application is better, and the **WHAT** is our end product/application.

The **HOW** relates to how we, as humans, reason. This is the realm of the Category Theory.

The **WHAT** pertains to the specifics of what it is. This is the realm of mathematics and computation. We will use algebra to help define the **WHAT**. Later, we'll see that our work in algebra is directly transferable to functional programming.

Algebra and the unknown

Algebra is a branch of mathematics that is very similar to arithmetic. It uses the four main operations that math uses: addition, subtraction, multiplication, and division (+, -, /, *). Algebra also introduces a new element: the unknown. In math, the unknown is on the right-hand side of the equation. Remember math problems like *2 + 3*. The answer is unknown until we perform the math operation on the operands (2 and 3). In algebra, we use symbols in place of the unknown placeholder. An algebraic equation would be *2 + 3 = x*. That is an algebraic equation that states both sides of the equals sign are equivalent. The operands 2 and 3 operands are known and the *x* is the unknown.

```
2 + 3 = __   ← arithmatic
2 + 3 = x    ← algebra
```

The goal in algebra is to solve the equation by determining the value(s) of the unknown symbol(s):

$$\text{add} \begin{array}{l} 2 + 3 = x \\ 5 = x \end{array}$$
$$\text{solution} \rightarrow x = 5$$

Remember what our math teachers would do next?

$$2 + x = 3$$

They would swap the symbol and a number to make the problem more difficult for us to figure out! Then, they would give us more and more complicated equations like this:

$$3x + 2 = 17$$

They forced us to perform multiple steps to simplify our problem. Since both sides must remain equal, we can visualize the problem using a weight balance:

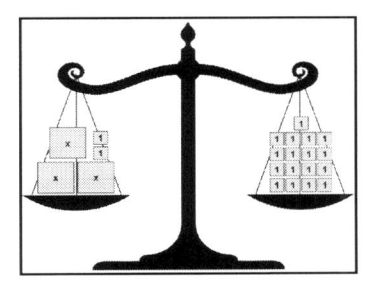

How did we solve the more complicated problem? Answer: By chopping it up into smaller pieces that are easier to work with, as shown in the following figure:

$$\begin{array}{r} 3x + 2 = 17 \\ -2 = -2 \\ \hline (\div)\ 3x = 15\ (\div) \end{array}$$
$$\text{solution}\ \boxed{x = 5}$$

Category Theory That Applies

Algebra, not unlike in the real world, relies on rules for things to work properly. Here are the few rules:

- **Rule 1:** The variable x in an algebraic equation cannot represent two different values in the same equation at the same time

    For example, if we have the equation, $x + x = 6$, the following is true: $1 + 5 = 6$; However, since x cannot represent the two different values in the same equation, the only value that would work for x is 3 (using 1 and 5 for x would violate *Rule 1*).

- **Rule 2:** If we want two variables to represent two different values, we must use two different symbols. For example, $x + y = 6$.
- **Rule 3:** When the same variable symbol is used multiple times in the same equation, it represents the same value.
- **Rule 4:** The default operation is multiplication. 2 * x is the same as 2x. So, if there is no operator, we can assume we are dealing with the default operation, multiplication.
- **Rule 5:** Parenthesis can be used to group terms. If we see 3(2), that is the same as 3 * (2) which is the same as 3*2. All three groupings of terms are equal to 6 (not 32).

$$3(2x - 3) - 7x = -14$$

    Our job now is to break this problem down into smaller steps and figure out what the value of x is. (Hint: you've seen it before.)

- **Rule 6:** Different symbols can represent the same value in the same equation, but they don't have to.

As we saw, x and y have the same value, but only in the second if statement. As the value of x varies (from 0 to 1 to 2), the value of y varies (from **2** to **1** to **0**). That's the main reason why the symbols x and y are called **variables**. They can vary.

The way variables are handled in a Turing-based language as opposed to a Lambda calculus (pure functional programming) language is very different.

In a Turing-based language like C, the value of a variable x is stored in a specific location in the memory in the computer running the C program. It can be a global variable, which means other running procedures can access and change (aka *mutate*) its value:

```
        x + y = 2   value varies
if x == 0 then y == 2
if x == 1 then y == 1  ← same
if x == 2 then y == 0
```

In a pure functional language like Haskell, values are never stored. New ones can be created and passed along the execution chain.

Real-world application of algebra

Ever wondered what good are these equations?

They can be useful when trying to model things in the real world. Let's take some algebraic equations and graph their solutions. Graphing an equation is like using the results of equations (output of functions) to draw lines and curves that can be used to illustrate and/or predict things in real life.

Linear equation and the law of demand

Linear equations can be used to describe things with straight line slopes:

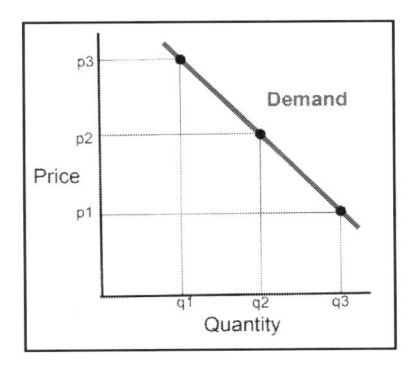

Category Theory That Applies

The law of demand states that as the price of a product increases, the demand for that product will decrease. That's because people naturally avoid buying a product that will force them to forfeit the purchase of something else that they value more. The graph indicates that the demand curve is a downward slope. The lower the price, the more products will be sold.

Building architects use linear equations to determine slopes of roof lines and Google Maps uses linear equations to tell you how long your trip will take.

What do we know about linear equation functions like $f(x) = 3x + 2$?

For every input x, we get one and only one result. That's why if we were to input every possible number (as the value x), we get a line! And that's why vertical lines are difficult to achieve in geometry.

Quadratic equations all around us

Equations like the following are said to be linear:

$y = x + 2$

This is because all the variables are to the power of one.

Given the **x** values of **-4** to **2**, we can easily calculate the **y** values, as follows:

x	y = f(x)
-4	-2
-3	-1
-2	0
-1	1
0	2
1	3
2	4

If we were to input every possible *x* value (including those with decimals like 0.1, 0.11, 0.12, and so on), we'd get a straight line. We can say that the *domain* is the set of all possible *x* values and the *range* is the set of all possible *y* values. Note that any non-vertical or non-horizontal line is a function with its domain and range consisting of all real numbers.

It's easy to see that our preceding *f(x)* function is just a mapping from one set of numbers to another.

When we use exponents of 2 or greater, then the equation is said to be quadratic. Here's an example:

$y = x^2 + 1$

Function composition with linear and quadratic functions

Let's compose our $f(x) = x^2 + 1$ quadratic equation with our $g(x) = x + 2$ linear equation table. Here's one way we could compose our two functions: $y = f(g(x))$. We'd say *y* equals *f-compose-g of x* or $y = f \circ g$ where o is our composition operator. The way it works is that we assign a value for *x*, then we plug that value into *g*, compute g(x), and then plug the result into *f*.

We input **1** to **g** and to express that as **g(1)**. We input **g(1)** to **f** to get **f(g(1))**.

$$1 \rightarrow \boxed{g} \rightarrow g(1) \rightarrow \boxed{f} \rightarrow f(g(1))$$

Let's make it work by replacing **g(1)** with the value that maps from **1** to **g(1)**, which is **3**:

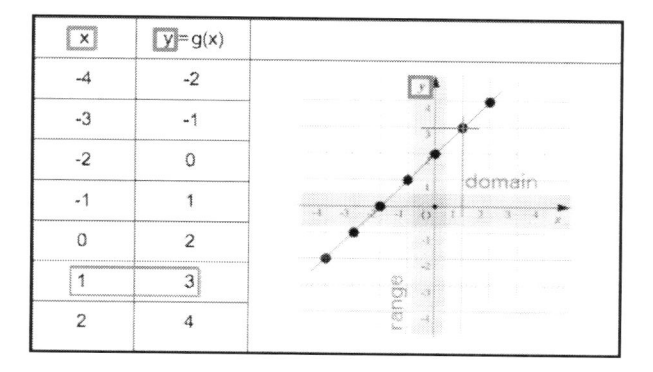

x	y = g(x)
-4	-2
-3	-1
-2	0
-1	1
0	2
1	3
2	4

Category Theory That Applies

Replacing **g(1)** with **3**, we get the following:

$$1 \rightarrow \boxed{g} \rightarrow g(\cancel{1})^3 \rightarrow \boxed{f} \rightarrow f(g(1))$$

When we input **3** to **g**, we evaluate the $x^2 + 1$ or $3^2 + 1$ expression, which equals **10**:

$$1 \rightarrow \boxed{g} \rightarrow g(\cancel{1})^3 \rightarrow \boxed{f} \rightarrow f(\cancel{3})^{10}$$

So, **f(g(1))** equals **10**.

What if we reverse our nesting of functions like **g(f(1))**? Will we get the same answer?

$f(1) = x2 + 1 = 1 + 1 = 2$
$g(2) = 4$

> ℹ️ We got *f(2)=4* from the preceding linear equation table.

Since $g(f(1)) = 10$ and $f(g(1)) = 4$, we know that composing the same functions in a different order will likely give different results.

We also see that when we compose, we are either replacing a function/value with the corresponding/mapped value from a table or we are evaluating a function expression and replacing with that value. We've already seen how the referential integrity characteristic of our functions allow us to cache its value. So, after a function is evaluated the first time, all we're doing is a bunch of value replacements when we compose functions.

> "If A equals success, then the formula is A equals X plus Y and Z, with X being work, Y play, and Z keeping your mouth shut."
>
>   - Albert Einstein

Chapter 11

More examples of quadratic equations

Are all of the following quadratic?

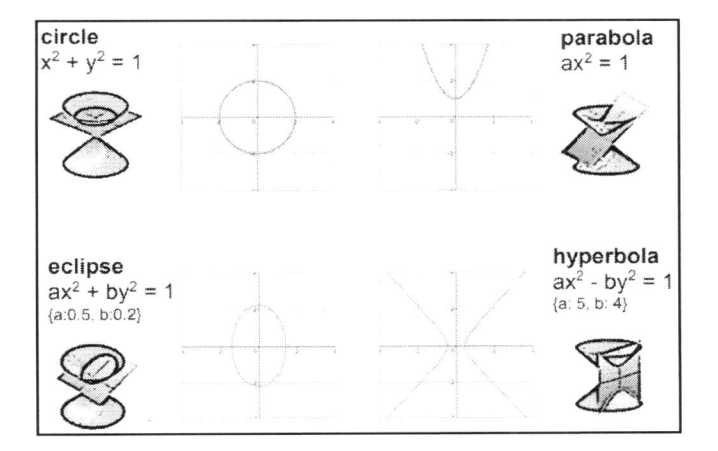

circle $x^2 + y^2 = 1$	**parabola** $ax^2 = 1$
eclipse $ax^2 + by^2 = 1$ {a:0.5, b:0.2}	**hyperbola** $ax^2 - by^2 = 1$ {a: 5, b: 4}

TIP: Plot your own equations online at: `https://www.desmos.com/calculator`

The golden ratio

Let's look at one more fascinating quadratic equation. The Greeks believed that the rectangular shape, which had the most aesthetic proportions, was one where the large and the small rectangles have the same proportions.

This became known as the *golden rectangle*. The solution to $x^2 + x = 1$ is $x = 1.61803398875$, which we'll shorten to $x = 1.61$.

[497]

Category Theory That Applies

The Greeks weren't the only ones that thought the golden ratio was perfect.

When we look closely, we'll see the Golden Ratio in business:

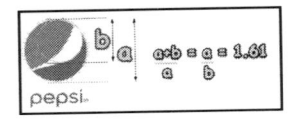

Remember the Fibonacci sequence and its relationship to recursion from Chapter 1, *Pure Functional Programming in Go*? 0, 1, 1, 2, 3, 5, 8, 13, 21, 34, 55, 89. In this sequence, each term is the sum of the previous two terms. If we look closely, we'll see this sequence in nature. For example, lilies have 3 petals, buttercups 5, marigolds 13, asters 21. Most daisies have 34, 55 or 89 petals.

The seeds of a sunflower head radiate from its center in two families of interlaced spirals, one winding clockwise and the other counterclockwise. There are usually 34 spirals twisting clockwise and 55 in the opposite direction.

The more we learn about the relationship between mathematics, programming, the arts and sciences and nature, the more evidence we find of the hand of a master architect at work around us.

The more we understand how systems around us work, the more patterns we see. Later, when we look closer at the category theory, we'll study the important patterns of decomposition (chopping problems up into small, comprehensible pieces) and composition (putting those pieces back together again). FP allows us to break a monolithic application down into a set of Lego building blocks that can be assembled in different configurations for different systems if desired, and we do can do so in an easy-to-understand, declarative manner.

Given the guarantees of immutability and referential transparency, the time at which an operation occurs is much less of a concern. This simplifies the combinatorial complexity of coding concurrent solutions. This also allows performance to be improved harmlessly by the use of parallelism, and it pays off in distributed systems, where time is not even perfectly defined.

Basic laws of algebra

Study these basic laws of algebra. We'll see them again soon!

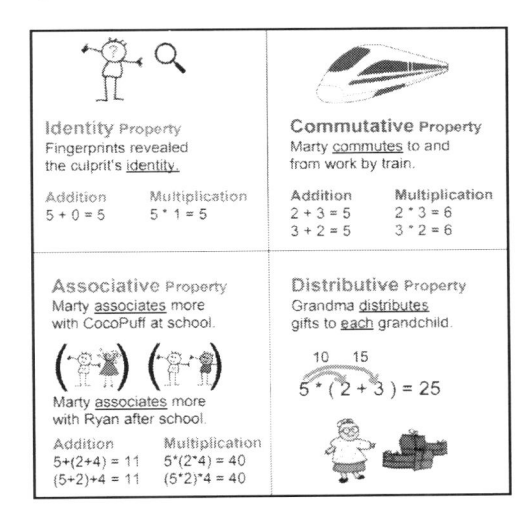

Identity Property Fingerprints revealed the culprit's identity.	Commutative Property Marty commutes to and from work by train.
Addition 5 + 0 = 5	Multiplication 5 * 1 = 5	Addition 2 + 3 = 5 3 + 2 = 5	Multiplication 2 * 3 = 6 3 * 2 = 6

Associative Property Marty associates more with CocoPuff at school. Marty associates more with Ryan after school.	Distributive Property Grandma distributes gifts to each grandchild. $5 * (2 + 3) = 25$
Addition 5+(2+4) = 11 (5+2)+4 = 11	Multiplication 5*(2*4) = 40 (5*2)*4 = 40	

Later, you'll learn that function composition has the following features:

- It is associative
- It is typically not commutative
- It is distributive via $(g+h) \circ f = g \circ f + h \circ f (g + h) \circ f = g \circ f + h \circ f$
- It is typically not distributive via $f \circ (g + h) = f \circ g + f \circ h$

Correspondence in mathematics

The category theory presents mathematics as abstractly as possible and removes all nonessential properties, providing a framework for all mathematics.

Remember your math classes? Here are a few of the classes:

Branch of mathematics	Description
Algebra	Algebra describes relationships between its elements using laws, for example, associative, commutative properties. There are different types of algebra, such as, linear, lie, commutative, and abstract. In algebra, we often replace numbers with letters in an equation. For example, The $1 + 2 = 3$ form becomes $x + y = z$. Boolean algebra is another type of algebra in which the variables are truth values (true and false) instead of numbers.
Geometry	Geometry studies the properties of shapes and position in space. It provides formulas for determining things such as the circumference of a circle ($c = 2\pi r$) and determining the area of various shapes.
Logic	Logic provides rules of mathematical reasoning. Boolean algebra is a form of mathematical logic.
Numerical analysis	Numerical analysis provides algorithms to approximate solutions to mathematical problems. It typically uses computing power to quickly get close to the true solution that might not be solvable manually.
Calculus	Calculus is the application of the results proven in analysis.

Mathematics is the study of data structures: shapes, numbers, groups, sets, and so on. We study their structure, their behaviors, and how they interact with each other.

Curry, Howard, and Lambek discovered that all branches of mathematics are the exact same thing! They realized that at a certain level of abstraction, the structure of all mathematical theories are the same. We can morph the structure of our logic into category classes and we can change that structure into type theory. All morphisms, and hence all activities, in the universe can be described by the category theory.

For example, when we consider a photon particle in an electromagnetic field, a soccer ball in flight, and a bouncy C (musical note), they don't seem to have much in common until we provide context. From the point of view of wave theory, they are all the same problem. Now, change or context to centripetal force; again, they are all the same problem, only in a different context. When we abstract away all the non-essential details, what remains is the mathematical structure.

The advantage of using abstraction in this way is that we begin to see connections between things that were previously hidden from view. When can create and use tools that allow us to contextualize problem sets in different ways. We have the full power of category theory to enlighten our way. Software engineers who understand these concepts are better equipped to perform data analytics. Software engineers who learn to apply functional programming concepts build more reliable solutions that scale horizontally across multiple cores and across multiple compute instances in their cloud native clusters. It's not difficult to see what all the fuss regarding functional programming is about, right?

Proof theory

Proof theory is a branch of mathematics where we make assumptions and apply logic to prove something. For example, if a and b can be proven to be true, then a is true and so is b.

Logical connectives

The following table depicts logical connectives, in order of precedence:

Symbol	Math name	English name	Go operator	Example	Meaning
$\neg$	Negation	NOT	!	$\neg a$	not a
$\wedge$	Conjunction	AND	&&	$a \wedge b$	a and b
$\oplus$	Exclusive disjunction	exclusive or (XOR)	NA	$a \oplus b$	either a or b (but not both)

Category Theory That Applies

∨	Disjunction	OR	||	a ∨ b	a or b
∀	Universal quantification	∀ x: A(x) means A(x) is true for all x	NA	∀a:A	all values a of type A
∃	Existential quantification	∃ x: A(x) means there is at least one x such that A(x) is true	NA	∃a:A	there exists some value a of type A
⇒	Material implication	Implies	NA	a ⇒ b	if a then b
⇔	Material equivalence	a ⇔ b is true only if both a and b are false, or both a and b are true	NA	a ⇔ b	a if and only if b
≡	Is defined as	a ≡ b means a is defined to be another name for b	NA	a ≡ b	a is logically equivalent to b
⊢	Turnstile	a ⊢ b means a is provable from b	NA	a ⊢ b	a is provable from b

NA = Not Applicable, that is, there is no symbol for this in Go.

> There are other logic symbols, but these are some of the more important ones.

In software, we use logic by combining these symbols and other terms like variables to prove whether something is true.

The following is an example using quantification symbols:

`f: A ⇒ B` means ∀a:A∃b:B such that `b = f(b)`

In other words, there is a function from *A* to *B*, where for all values a of type *A*, there exists some value b of type *B* such that *b* = *f(a)*.

[502]

Logical inconsistency

The following function signature represents a function with logical inconsistency:

```
def factorial(i int) int
```

The problem is that factorial is not defined for negative integers.

Partial function

If our function is not defined/consistent for all values in our domain, it's said to be a partial function (as opposed to a total function). If our function is inconsistent, then we run the risk of running into unexpected errors during runtime.

There are two main ways to solve this problem:

- We can solve this inconsistency by reducing the size of our domain to only positive integers
- We can use failure monads like either validation or disjunction to capture things that go wrong

Truth table

The truth tables contains interpretations of a proposition. An interpretation is the calculation of the value of a proposition:

a	b	¬a	¬b	a ∧ b	a ∨ b	a ⊕ b	a → b	a ↔ b
T	T	F	F	T	T	F	T	T
T	F	F	T	F	T	T	F	F
F	T	T	F	F	T	T	T	F
F	F	T	T	F	F	F	T	T

> "The opposite of a correct statement is a false statement. The opposite of a profound truth may well be another profound truth."
>
> - Niels Bohr

Conditional propositions

The following propositions say the same thing:

- *If a, then b*
- *a implies b*
- $a \rightarrow b$
- $a \Rightarrow b$

The variable a is the hypothesis and b is the conclusion. The conclusion is always true, except when a is true and b is false. One way of thinking about this is: "If pigs could fly, then..." anything you conclude is true after such an obviously false statement. If a and b are both true, then obviously going from a to b will be true. However, if a is true and b is false, then when going from a to b we'll end up with a false value.

Logical equivalence

Now, we can use our truth table to determine the outcome of compound propositions. Since $\neg a \vee b$ and $a \rightarrow b$ have the same truth values, they are said to be logically equivalent and we express that with the $\neg a \vee b \equiv a \rightarrow b$ equation.

a	b	¬a	¬a ∨ b	a → b
T	T	F	T	T
T	F	F	F	F
F	T	T	T	T
F	F	T	T	T

A logically equivalent statement could be, "*If Jenny were sitting at her desk then she'd be at home.*" That is a logical statement. A logical equivalent statement might be, "*If Jenny were not at home, then she would not be sitting at her desk.*"

We create logical equivalences by creating a hypothesis and its conclusion. The preceding hypothesis is: "*If Jenny were sitting at her desk,* and the conclusion is "*she'd be at home.*" We determine the truth of each and compare their truth (true or false).

Converse of a conditional proposition

Let's use a truth table to prove the $(a \to b) \land (b \to a) \equiv a \leftrightarrow b$ equation:

a	b	a → b	b → a	(a → b)∧(b → a)	a ↔ b
T	T	T	T	T	T
T	F	F	T	F	F
F	T	T	F	F	F
F	F	T	T	T	T

In other words, a biconditional proposition $(a \leftrightarrow b)$ is equivalent to the conjunction of a conditional proposition $(a \to b)$ and its converse $(b \to a)$.

Order matters

Remember the statement: *"If Jenny were sitting at her desk, then she'd be at home?"*

Its converse would be, *"If Jenny were at home then she'd be sitting at her desk."* The converse is created by swapping the hypothesis and conclusion. How does the converse change the logic of the sentence? (*Could "Jenny be at home, but not at her desk?"*) The same words in a different order can change the resulting truth value.

Similarly, the inverse of a conditional can also change the logic. For example, consider the negative form of *"If Jenny were sitting at her desk, then she'd be at home,"* which is *"If Jenny were not sitting at her desk, then she would not be at home."* (Could Jenny be at home, but not at her desk?)

See how we can use truth tables to combine statements and determine its resulting truth value?

The Curry Howard isomorphism

The Curry Howard Isomorphism said that types are propositions and programs are their proofs. A proposition is an assertion (declarative statement), which is either true or false (but not both).

Examples of propositions

Consider the following examples of propositions:

- The equation 2 * 3 = 5
- If it is storming outside, then I take an Uber to class; otherwise, I walk, and if it is sunny, then I ride my bicycle:

Variable	Clause
a	It is storming outside
b	I take an Uber to class
c	I walk
d	It is sunny
e	I ride my bicycle

The following is the **written logic version**:

a implies b and ((not a) implies (c and (d implies e)))

The following is the **logical symbols version**:

$(a \Rightarrow b) \wedge (\neg a \Rightarrow (c \wedge (d \Rightarrow e)))$

Not propositions

The following are the examples of not propositions:

- $x = 5$ (this is not an assertion of truth, it's an assignment)
- $x + y = 5$ (not enough information to be an assertion, answer depends on missing data)

Propositions can combine terms using connectives (and, or not).

Lambda calculus

Alonzo Church brought formal logic, called **untyped Lambda calculus**, to computer science that includes substitution, abstraction, and application. Let's remember these terms and use them when implementing a lambda expression in Go later in this chapter.

Why so formal?

Why do we care about adhering to the formalism and rules of logical (and algebraic) equations?

"The irony is that the constraints of formalism is what liberates us to be our best."

The importance of protocol

Respecting your elders, saying "Yes, Ma'am" and "Yes Sir" is not just social formalism. That's called *following protocol*. It helps us communicate in a consistent way. Following formalisms helps us to act appropriately. Examples of practicing the civil virtues include things like these:

- Being honest
- Maintaining self-control
- Showing kindness toward fellow human beings

When we lead through an example of serving one another with transparency and kindness and to guard against greed and other forms of evil, we can freely engage with others in ways that are less likely to offend.

How does offensive language and inappropriate behavior from our leaders affect the strength of our society? What good comes from showing blatant disrespect toward officers of the law?

When everyone understands the importance of being polite and showing guarded generosity, we live in a strong social system in which we all have the opportunity to thrive. When we transfer this concept to our software development efforts, we end up with better solutions. The way we implement this system is through logic. If our systems are logically sound, then they will reliably help us achieve our goals.

Historical Events in Functional Programming

The history of functional programming is nothing short of fascinating. Functional programming languages are based on an elegant yet simple mathematical foundation, Lambda calculus.

"To understand a science, it is necessary to know its history."
- Auguste Comte

Let's look at the discoveries that led up to Lambda calculus.

George Boole (1815 - 1864)

Logic came from ancient Greeks such as Aristotle and Euclid. Prior to Boole, logic was literally in Greek; it was expressed in the form of language. Boole was the first to translate logic into algebraic symbols:

- *true = 1*
- *false = 0*
- *and = product (AxB)*
- *or = sum(A+B)*

Augustus De Morgan (1806 - 1871)

De Morgan's Law stated that all logical operations can be expressed in terms of *and*, *or*, and *not*. Furthermore, all logical operations can also be expressed in terms of just *and* and *not*, or just *or* and *not*:

$a \wedge b = \neg ((\neg a) \vee (\neg b))$
$a \vee b = \neg ((\neg a) \wedge (\neg b))$

The first equation says that *a* and *b* are both true if and only if at least one of *a* or *b* is false. The second equation says that at least one of *a* or *b* is true if and only if both a and b are false.

Friedrich Ludwig Gottlob Frege (1848 – 1925)

Frege was a German mathematician who is considered by many as the father of analytic philosophy. He studied the use of functions in logic and was the first to use currying. Frege invented axiomatic predicate logic. Axioms are statements/propositions that we accept as true; they are so self-evident that no other reasoning could make it plainer. They are simple truths.

Modus Ponens

The following rule of propositional logic is called **Modus Ponens**:

$\{ a \rightarrow b, b \} \vdash b$

1. If the tree is still on the power line, then we have no power
2. The tree is still on the power line
3. We have no power

Charles Lutwidge Dodgson (1832 –1898)

Charles Dodson (pen name: Lewis Carroll) authored several books in which he stripped away intuition and any preconception by manipulating logic, even if it seems like nonsense. Let's look at the literary nonsense in his fiction book, *Alice in Wonderland*. Dodson often defied common sense by creating an entirely new world through the manipulation of language. The story maintained a balance between sense and nonsense, remaining logical, even though it appeared at times to be completely illogical. For example, as Alice moves within the back-to-front world of *Looking-Glass Land*, she discovers a book written in a seemingly unintelligible language:

Twas brillig, and the slithy toves

Did gyre and gimble in the wabe:All mimsy were the borogoves,

And the mome raths outgrabe.

"Beware the Jabberwock, my son!

The jaws that bite, the claws that catch!Beware the Jubjub bird, and shun

The frumious Bandersnatch!"

In *Through The Looking Glass*, Alice tries to keep up with the Red Queen; though constantly running, she remains in the same spot. Alice remarked:

Well, in our country, said Alice, still panting a little, *you'd generally get to somewhere else—if you run very fast for a long time, as we've been doing.*

The Red Queen's race is often used to illustrate deep concepts such as these:

- Time travel
- The relativistic effect on light from galaxies near the edge of the expanding observable universe
- Our efforts in the IT industry to adopt new technologies in an effort to keep up with our competitors (though years later, when looking back, we realize we did not actually improve our systems, we merely changed technologies sometimes to our detriment)

We'll later look at an FP library named **Fantasy Land**, which likely gets its name from the nonsense logic found in works such as Alice in Wonderland.

Alfred Whitehead and Bertrand Russell (1903)

In a letter Russell wrote to Frege, the proposed the *Barbers Paradox* found a problem with Frege's logic:

Given that a town's only barber shaves everybody, except those who shave themselves. We can deduce two things:

- If a person does not shave her/himself, the barber will
- If person shaves her/himself, the barber won't

The paradox is: *The barber cannot be shaven.*

The first statement says that if the barber does not shave himself, then barber will shave himself. However, the second statement directly contradicts that first statement.

Russell and Whitehead collaborated to prove/solve the Barber's Paradox and to prove that mathematics is a formal, logical framework. In 1912, they arrogantly produced a work entitled Principia Mathematica (that's the same name that Isaac Newton used to name his works that included the laws of motion, forming the foundation of classical mechanics, the law of universal gravitation, and a derivation of Kepler's laws of planetary motion).

Russell and Whitehead's work proved to be impractical (it includes a 450-page proof to show that *1 + 1 = 2*). The irony is that logical substitution was not formalized in their Principa Mathematica. (We'll look at what logical substitution means when we look at Lambda calculus.)

Moses Schonfinkel (1889–1942)

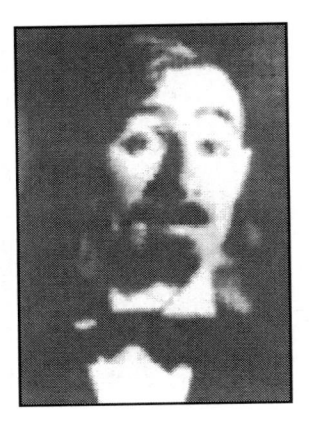

Schonfinkel was a Russian mathematician who invented combinatory logic around 1924. A combinator is a higher order function that uses only function application and earlier defined combinators to define a result from its arguments. This replacement technique reduced multiple function arguments to a single argument, and was later known as currying, after Haskell Curry.

The following table explains Schonfinkel combinators:

Definition	Acroymn - German	Function Type
λx. x	I - Identitatsfunktion	Identity
λx,y. x	K - Konstanzfunktion	Constant
λx,y,z. xz(yz)	S - Verschmelzungsfunktion	Amalgamation
λx,y,z. xzy	T - Vertauschungsfunktion	Exchange
λx,y,z. x(yz)	Z - Zusammensetzungsfunktion	Composition

Haskell Curry - 1927

Haskell Curry introduced Combinatory Logic in 1927 that eliminated the use of variables that change. It is based on combinators. A combinator is a higher order function that uses function application and previously defined combinators to produce a result from its arguments. Alonzo Church later devised a similar formalism called **The Lambda Calculus**, where lambda expressions represent functional abstractions are replaced by a limited set of combinators. For details, see *The Lambda Calculus* section later in this chapter.

Gerhard Gentzen (1936)

In 1936, a German mathematician named Gerhard Gentzen provided proof that first-order arithmetic (addition and multiplication) is consistent using primitive recursive arithmetic. Gentzen used sequent calculus, which is a conditional tautology (a series of true statements) to build arguments according to rules and procedures of inference (https://en.wikipedia.org/wiki/Inference) with zero or more assertions. Note that sequent calculus is very similar to natural deduction, which is composed of one or more assertions.

Alonzo Church (1930, 1940)

Church read the Principa Mathematica and decided to improve upon it. Church applied formal mathematical logic to computer science using function abstraction and application using variable binding and substitution. In 1930, Church's released the first version of Lambda calculus, which formed the basis of what he called *effectively computable functions*.

In 1935, Kleene and Rosser proved that it was logically inconsistent. Church quickly responded with an improved version named *simply typed Lambda calculus* that fixed the issue of non-terminating programs with a typed system that defined the syntax of high order logic, but did not include recursive functions. Later, in 1940, Church invented The Lambda Calculus, which is composed only of functions, which does not concern itself with concrete values like strings and numbers. It works with only functions.

Functions can take functions and return functions. Haskell Curry intended Lambda calculus to be a foundation for mathematics. You need some form of recursive type to write any interesting kind of program in it. Haskell Curry's work with combinatory logic is a foundation of the functional programming language.

Alan Turing (1950)

At about the same time as Alonzo Church published his Lambda calculus, Alan Turing introduced the Turing machine, which could perform any computational task, that is, anything Lambda calculus could calculate. Turing completeness is an abstract statement of ability, rather than a prescription of specific language features used to implement that ability. The features used to achieve Turing completeness can be quite different; Fortran systems would use loop constructs or possibly even `goto` statements to achieve repetition. Pure functional languages like Haskell and Prolog use recursion.

MacLane and Eilenberg (1945)

Saunders Mac Lane (left) and Samuel Eilenberg (right) introduced the concepts of categories, functors, and natural transformations in 1945 with their paper titled, *A general theory of natural equivalences*. In their study of algebraic topology, they gave explicit definitions for objects, maps, and composition of maps, with the goal of understanding the processes that preserve mathematical structure.

John McCarthy (1950)

Next came John McCarthy who published the paper *Recursive functions of symbolic expressions and their computation by machine, Part I* (http://dl.acm.org/citation.cfm?id=367199). In 1958, one of his students wrote an interpreter based on McCarthy's teachings, which became a programming language based on pure mathematics called Lisp. Lisp was the first functional language. The first popular computer languages based on type systems were Fortran and Cobol, which emerged in the 1950s.

Curry-Howard-Lambek Correspondence (1969)

Curry, Howard, and Lambek (CHL) discovered the one-to-one correspondence between objects in category theory, propositions in logic, and types in programming languages.

CHL looked at the types of rules for natural deduction rules and typed Lambda calculus and discovered that they are identical.

	Gentzen's Natural Deduction	Church's Typed Lambda Calculus
Structural Rules	$\dfrac{}{A \vdash A}\text{Id}$	$\dfrac{}{x : A \vdash x : A}\text{Id}$
Introduction Rules	$\dfrac{\Gamma, B \vdash A}{\Gamma \vdash B \to A}{\to}\text{-I}$	$\dfrac{\Gamma, x : B \vdash t : A}{\Gamma \vdash \lambda x.t : B \to A}{\to}\text{-I}$
	$\dfrac{\Gamma \vdash A \quad \Delta \vdash B}{\Gamma, \Delta \vdash A \wedge B}\wedge\text{-I}$	$\dfrac{\Gamma \vdash t : A \quad \Delta \vdash u : B}{\Gamma, \Delta \vdash (t, u) : A \wedge B}\wedge\text{-I}$
Elimination Rules	$\dfrac{\Gamma \vdash B \to A \quad \Delta \vdash B}{\Gamma, \Delta \vdash A}{\to}\text{-E}$	$\dfrac{\Gamma \vdash t : B \to A \quad \Delta \vdash u : B}{\Gamma, \Delta \vdash t(u) : A}{\to}\text{-E}$
	$\dfrac{\Gamma \vdash A \wedge B}{\Gamma \vdash A}\wedge\text{-E}_1$	$\dfrac{\Gamma \vdash t : A \wedge B}{\Gamma \vdash t.fst : A}\wedge\text{-E}_1$
	$\dfrac{\Gamma \vdash A \wedge B}{\Gamma \vdash B}\wedge\text{-E}_2$	$\dfrac{\Gamma \vdash t : A \wedge B}{\Gamma \vdash t.snd : B}\wedge\text{-E}_2$

Category Theory That Applies

If we remove the red terms in the preceding table, they are identical. Hence, Church's lambda types correspond one-to-one with Gentzen's logical formulas. Type checking is the same as proof checking.

- Logic includes **and, or** and **implication** constructs
- Programming has data records and function constructs
- Category theory has arrows which are functions (that can also be data)

As an example of how they relate, consider that a proposition in logic can be true or false. Similarly, a type can be either inhabited or not. True propositions are inhabited. The void type is false. If we can produce an element of a type, then we have proven our proposition.

CHL realized that Cartesian closed categories, intuitionistic propositional logic, and the simply typed Lambda calculus are all essentially the same thing.

Let's have a look at the correspondence table:

Category theory	Logic theory	Type theory/Lambda calculus
Objects	Propositions	Types
Morphisms	Proofs	Functions
Equivalences between morphisms	Equivalences between proofs	Beta-eta equivalences between Lambda calculus term

All three areas of study arrived at the same discoveries independently, from different perspectives, but the mathematical structures they describe in each case are essentially identical.

Roger Godement (1958)

In 1958, Roger Godement wrote a book on the sheaf theory that first introduced the concept of monads. Sheaves are objects that capture local data about a manifold, yet in doing so, allows one to see global properties of space as a whole. What's a manifold? It's a geometric object, for example, the Earth. From where you stand or walk, it looks like it goes on for ever. However, if you walk around the Earth enough times, you'll realize that it's a sphere. What Godement called a **standard construction** was subsequently called a **monad** by Saunders Mac Lane, and that name stuck.

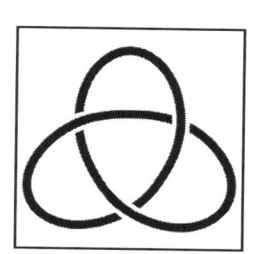

Moggi, Wadler, Jones (1991)

In 1991, Eugenio Moggi wrote *Notions of computation and monads*, which introduced the concept of categorical semantics of computation in order to understand features in new programming languages. Languages often add new features to solve particular problems, but the features are rarely specified carefully in a formal way. In order to understand programs written in these languages, we need a framework to help us understand how information flows through our applications.

Moggi described a category C and an endomorphic functor f with an object A.

- A is a type in C, where members are values of type A
- f applies to A and returns another A

It is amazing how far we have gone with so little. Less really is more!

Philip Wadler and Simon Peyton Jones and others began to use monads and it trickled down into the Haskell language. Now, monads are part of its standard library. Uses for monads include the following:

- Chain/link/connect/compose functions
- Handling input
- Handling side effects

- Asynchronous/concurrent processing
- Logging
- Error handling

Gibbons, Oliveira (2006)

Gibbons and Oliveira explored an FP solution to the OOP iterator pattern. They used imperative iterations patterns and observed that data is mapped element-by-element with accumulation and can return an object of the same shape, that is, a transformed list of elements.

They took Kernighan and Ritchie's imperative wordcount program (in the following C# code) and created an alternative implementation using traversal operators and applicative functor techniques:

```
public static int[] wc<char> (IEnumerable<char> coll) {
    int nl = 0, nw = 0, nc = 0;
    bool state = false;
    foreach(char c in coll) {
        ++nc;
        if(c == '\n') ++nl;
        if (c == ' ' || c == '\n' || c == '\t') {
            state = false;
        } else if (state == false) {
            state = true;
            ++nw;
        }
    }
    int[] res = {nc, nw, nl};
```

Category Theory That Applies

```
        return res;
}
```

Here's an iteration example in Go:

```
is250 := &Car{"Lexus", "IS250"}
accord := &Car{"Honda", "Accord"}
cars := []*Car{is250, accord}
upgradedCars := []*Car{}
count := 0
for _, car := range cars {
    upgradedCars = append(upgradedCars, car.Upgrade())
    count ++
}
```

same shape — map
accumulate

Given that different traversals perform different functions:

Function	Map element	Create state	Mapped dependent on state	State dependent on element
`collect`	X	X		X
`disperse`	X	X	X	
`measure`	X	X		
`traverse`	X	X	X	X
`reduce`		X		X
`reduceConst`		X		
`map`	X			

The computation is in this form (K is the type of computation and T is data type): `K[T]`

The nature of the following FP computations:

Computation	Description	New computations	Use computations	Functor map
Option[T]	0 || 1 element	Some(t)	Some(3)	change value
List[T]	>= 0 elements	List(t)	List(1, 2, 3)	change values
Future[T]	perform later	future(t)	future(sum)	change later
State[S, T]	dependency on state	state(s => (s,t))	state(s => (s, s+2))	change t_x
IO[T]	external effects	IO(t)	IO(putStr("hi"))	modify action

Starting with this applicative: `f(a, b) ==> f(K[a], K[b])` with this pointed `f(a:A, b:B):C ==> fk: K[A => B => C]` and with currying:

```
K[A => B => C]  <*>
K[A]            <*> K[B]
K[B => C]       <*> K[B] == K[C]
```

Then, apply **f** to **a** and **b inside K**: K(**f**) <*> K(**a**) <*> K(**b**)

We can use applicative composition to compose functions with Traversables and show that transformations on iterators are applicative.

That's the big picture. For the details, read their paper: https://www.cs.ox.ac.uk/jeremy.gibbons/publications/iterator.pdf.

The history of FP in a nutshell

In the 1930s, two very different approaches to solve computing problems emerged . The first school of thought rallied behind Alonzo Church. (Church developed Lambda calculus around 1929.) Church said that design should be top-down rather than bottom-up. He said we should start by treating all computation as the evaluation of mathematical functions and then remove abstractions to move toward the machine-level operations. The ability to control complexity via composition was arguably the main concern (definitely not performance). Languages that sprang from this line of thinking include ML, Lisp, SmallTalk, Erlang, Clojure and Haskell.

The other computing solution came from Alan Turing (a former student of Church, developed the Turing machine around 1937). Turing said that software design should first consider the hardware upon which the software would run. Later, abstraction could be as needed to achieve the desired result. Performance was their paramount concern. Languages that sprang from this line of thought include Fortran, C, C++, C#, Pascal, and Java.

Lambda calculus and Turing Machines are both Turing Complete. A Turing Complete machine is basically a general purpose computer (has if, then, else, branching logic and looping constructs like for or while loops and a way to read and write data) that can help us solve problems. Church proved that a Turing Machine can be implemented using Lambda calculus.

The Lambdas warned against the fragility of locking down the software design based on hardware that may be obsoleted. Until recently, the bottom up approach has won out. With the recent advent of multi-core computers and distributed processing environments, Lambda calculus is gaining ground.

Recently, Turing-based languages have begun to embrace the top down approach. For example, we began to see FP characteristics in Java 7. More and more FP features are added to each subsequent version. We're also seeing FP constructs being added to Python, C++, C#, PHP, and more.

What is the most important concern today? Raw performance, or the ability to control complexity? As usual, It Depends, but given the industry shift to cloud computing environments, the ever increasing need to integrate with third-party libraries and even with other in-house departments, it looks like functional programming is not only catching on, it's taking over.

Where to go from here

As the need to run applications concurrently in distributed cloud environments rises, so will the demand to build and maintain those solutions. We know that pure FP scales, but how can we use FP to improve overall performance and control its complexity?

Knowledge is power. Keep learning. And apply what you know to build a better future.

Functional Programming Resources:

https://www.cambridge.org/core/journals/journal-of-functional-programming/

Check out today's FP giants here:

- https://scholar.google.com/citations?view_op=search_authorshl=enmauthors=label:functional_programming
- http://learnyouahaskell.com/
- http://learnyousomeerlang.com/

Programming language categories

Here, we can see four categories of programming languages. The two big categories are imperative and declarative. When programming in a declarative language, we tell the computer what we want. For example, in the following declarative code, we tell the computer that we want to find a `Highlander` car.

A declarative example

The following is an example of declarative programming language:

```
car, err := myCars.Find("Highlander")
```

Contrast that with an imperative language with all code ceremony where we must construct a `for` loop.

An imperative example

The following is an example of an imperative programming language:

```
func (cars *Cars) Find(model string) (*Car, error) {
    for _, car := range *cars {
        if car.Model == model {
            return &car, nil
        }
    }
    return nil, errors.New("car not found")
```

}

An OOP example

Object-oriented programs (OOP) consists of stateful objects that support object-related operations, called **methods**, whose implementation and internal structure is hidden. This means you can evolve or replace the internals of an object without the clients of that object also having to change. It also means that changes can occur to the hidden data without your knowledge, which, as we've seen, can be a bad thing. OOP also includes the idea of inheritance, where a new object could base its state and implementation on another object higher up in its hierarchy, which can cause your program to become rigid and more difficult to change. Here is a `Car` object and its `Add` method:

```
type Car struct {
  Model string
}

func (cars *Cars) Add(car Car) {
  myCars = append(myCars, car)
}
```

Venn diagram of four programming paradigms

Note that Go supports all three of those styles of programming. Originally, *idiomatic* Go programming style directed us to code using for loops. That is beginning to change. Similarly, Java was originally a mix of object-oriented and imperative coding styles. Java supported Generics in 2004 to provide type safety for collections and to eliminate the need of typecasting. 8 years later, Java added support for lambda expressions. The JDK's `java.util.stream` package leverages FP language features to provide aggregate operations on data structures like collections and arrays in a declarative and parallel-processing-friendly manner.

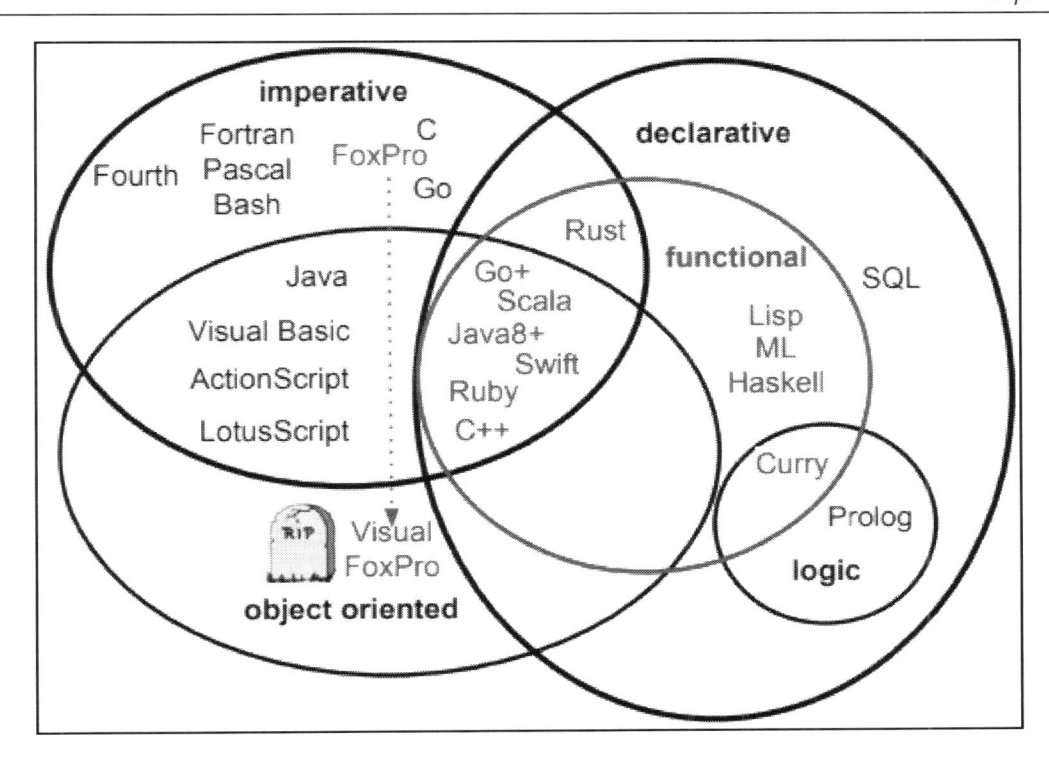

Five generations of languages

Another way to group programming languages is by their *generation*.

The first generation (1GL) language consists only of 1's and 0's which represent the on and off positions of electrical switches. The 1GL machine language is difficult for humans to understand.

Assembly language (2GL) allows the programming to user words to represent operations and operands, for example, CMP means compare the data in the AX register with the number 99. The result is stored in the the EFLAGS register and used by the jump (JL) command. 2GL's are specific to a particular processor family, that is, they are machine dependent.

Category Theory That Applies

A 3GL is a higher level language and most are not machine dependent. For example, Go is a 3GL. Go abstracts more details than a 2GL and allows us to program in more familiar notations. Go provides curly braces { } to indicate blocks of code, control structures like if, switch and range and other abstractions such as functions and interfaces.

A 4GL language are declarative. They allow us to declare what we want to compute, rather than telling the computer how to do it. This is yet another higher level of abstraction. For example in SQL we may write `SELECT * FROM USERS` which says, give me all the columns and all the rows of data in the `USERS` table. We did not have to include and looping, order, parsing or any other details, we just said what we wanted.

A 5GL languages allow use to program using human languages like English. They are typically built on Lisp and emulate human-like qualities such as learning, reasoning, seeing and communicating.

1GL	2GL	3GL	4GL	5GL

101010101
010101001
110100101
 	
Machine Language
	CMP AX,99
	JL DONE
	SUB AX,11
	
	Assembly Language
		C, C++, Go, Java, Lisp, Fortran, Pascal, Ruby, ...	SQL
			LINQ
			PowerBuilder
			Visual FoxPro
			Appcelerator...
				Prolog
				Mercury
				Op
				Based on Lisp

The Forth language

Let's look at the Forth language. It is imperative, but incorporates key FP aspects, such as abstraction, replacement and chaining functions. We can open a forth console and start typing commands and get results. Rather than hide the fact that the runtime will use a stack to push and pop operators and operands on and off the stack, it's built into the language. There are no anonymous functions. Forth uses *words* which act like named functions. Words can reference other words which provides a very elegant form of abstraction. Common stack operations in Forth work with the top two or three values on the stack and can change the order of things or duplicate things.

Let's look at an example:

```
~/clients/packt/dev/fp-go $ gforth
Gforth 0.7.3, Copyright (C) 1995-2008 Free Software Foundation, Inc.
Gforth comes with ABSOLUTELY NO WARRANTY; for details type `license'
Type `bye' to exit
: squared ( x -- x-squared ) dup * ;  ok
: sumOfSquares ( x y -- z ) squared swap squared + ;  ok
3 squared . 9  ok
2 3 sumOfSquares negate . -13  ok
```

We define our a function name/word starting with a colon. Comments are enclosed in parentheses. (x -- x-squared) says our function/word will take one input off the stack (x) and return that value squared. We define a second word that takes the top two values from the stack and returns a result. To test, we type 3 squared ., the "." means evaluate this expression. The result is 9 (3 duplicated and multiplied). Next, we type 2 3 sumOfSquares negate . this pushes 2 and 3 on the stack, executes squared (which returns 9 since 3 is on the top), swaps 3 with 9 and runs square which takes the next value (2) and then evaluates "+" which takes the top two values on the stack (9 and 4). We chain the builtin word to get our result: -13.

> If you're using a mac then you can install forth using `brew install forth`. For details and more Forth references, visit: https://github.com/lawrencewoodman/awesome-forth

Unlike the FP languages, Forth is untyped. Also, Forth directly uses values on the stack rather than passing parameters. Forth is a compiled language with a small footprint and is often used for embedded programming application, for example, NASA space crafts. We'd probably not consider Forth for enterprise system development since it lacks type safety.

The LINQ language

Most languages are multi-paradigm, meaning that depending on our coding style, we can use declarative, object-oriented and imperative features in the same program. Knowing when to use which style is more of an art than science. The more we learn, the better equipped we will be to make the right design choice, and the sooner in our development process we do it, the better. One final not, see the dotted line from imperative/declarative FoxPro to object-oriented Visual FoxPro? That's Microsoft killing its competition; FoxPro was once a well designed multi-paradigm language. FoxPro's procedural language was extended using **Language Integrated Query** (**LINQ**). LINQ added query expressions similar to SQL to the FoxPro language. For example, the scatter and gather commands were used with the prebaked context of manipulating a database table:

```
select User
scatter memvar
select Customer
gather memvar
```

These **4th generation language** (**4GL**) features increased developer productivity and code consistency.

Type systems

What comes to mind when we see the word *type*? Data type? Like integer, string, date, or a composite type (struct in Go) that can contain multiple fields of various data types..

What are they good for? When we compile our program, strongly typed language compilers can catch errors that might cause runtime errors or possibly worse, incorrect results that don't crash the program. For example, JavaScript uses type coercion to dynamically change data types of variables during runtime. The statement *MyBalance + 100.00* will equal *MyBalance100.00*, which might not be what we really want and may cause problems that are caught by online bank customers that complain that their balances don't add up. Weakly typed languages such as JavaScript and Ruby require much more rigorous testing than strongly typed language alternatives. Type systems not only detect errors in programs prior to running them, thereby increasing code quality, but they also help IDEs provide useful code navigation features.

The Lambda Calculus

Lambda calculus is a logical system of rules for expressing computation using variable binding, abstraction, and function application. We can define anonymous functions and apply those functions. Lambda calculus would be limited if it weren't for recursion. Pure functional programming languages derived from lambda calculus include LISP, Haskell, and ML.

Lambda Expressions

A lambda expression is an instance of a functional interface consisting of a set of terms. These terms can be variables like x, y, and z. These are not mutating variables, but rather placeholders for values or other lambda terms. The variable inside of x is applied to whatever it is bound to. The variable x is inside the term t. The lambda abstraction is defined as $\lambda\ x.t$.

For example, if we have the equation `f(x) = x2` and replace x with 5, we have $f(5) = 5^2$.

When the function f is applied to x, we get x^2. In our example, the function f is applied to the argument 5 and we get 52.

We can eliminate the parentheses for brevity and we have the term f applied to another term 5: `f 5 = 52`.

When we abstract, we remove information that we don't need: *Lambda of x where x^2 is applied to 5*: `(λx.x2)  5 = 52`.

We could use a term that is not a constant or a variable in place of 5. *Lambda of x where x2 is applied to lambda of y + 1*: `(λx.x2) (λy.y + 1) = λy.(y + 1)2`.

Now, we have a new function. We passed a function to a function and got a function.

Since the lambda expression is an instance of a functional interface, when we write our code as though it were data we are effectively generating code with code.

When we only need to use a function once, it is usually more convenient to not give the function a name. In that case, it would be an anonymous function. Another name for the anonymous function is a *lambda expression*. Why create a new local function and then refer to the named function, when we can simply use a lambda expression?

Anonymous function example and type inference

First, let's look at what we mean by the term *anonymous function*.

```
package main

func addTwo(x int) int {         named function
    return x + 2
}

func main() {
    println(addTwo(5))                     // named function

    println(func(x int) int {return x + 2}(5))  // anonymous function

    val := func(x int) int {return x + 2}(5)    // function expression
    println(val)
}
```

Function literals in Go require us to declare its type (`int` in our preceding example). In pure functional languages like Haskell and even Java 8 and above, the compilers of those languages are able to infer the type of the lambda expression without requiring use to declare it inline. Those compilers need minimal information to infer the types of expressions at runtime. If the compiler sees an expression with an argument of 5 and the "+" operator, a language with type inference will not require us to specifically indicate that we are dealing with integers.

> **TIP**
> Check out an example of lambda expression type inference in Java 8 here: `https://www.youtube.com/watch?v=a8jvxBbswp4`.

Lambda expression ingredients

A lambda expression is an unnamed block of code with parameters.

A lambda expression consists of three things:

- A block of code *x + 2*
- Parameters *x*
- Values for the free variables (not defined inside the code block) *5*

Lambda calculus uses the following three concepts to describe how to perform a unit of computation:

- Abstraction (defining a *function*)
- Binding (defining a *variable*)
- Application (executing a *function*)

Variables that are unbound are referred to as *free variables*. Computation is achieved by performing single steps of reduction:

1. Alpha reduction
2. Beta reduction
3. Eta reduction

Consider the following untyped Lambda calculus statement:

$(\lambda x.xx) (\lambda x.xx)$

The lambda symbol (from whence the name is derived) "λ" binds the name. In the example, the first parenthetical captures a statement that binds the name x. The second parenthetical serves as an argument. During beta-reduction, when we are applying the function, the parameter is bound to the name x. This is just substitution.

Confused? That's understandable, since we are using a mixture of Greek and English to describe what the code does. Let's look at some Go code that performs these steps for clarity:

> **TIP**
> Refer to the *Lambda calculus Reduction steps* post for a more detailed description of the 3 steps: https://stackoverflow.com/questions/34140819/lambda-calculus-reduction-steps

Now that we've got some formalism out of the way, let's look at what it means in practice.

Visualizing a lambda expression

This is what happens when we evaluate a lambda expression:

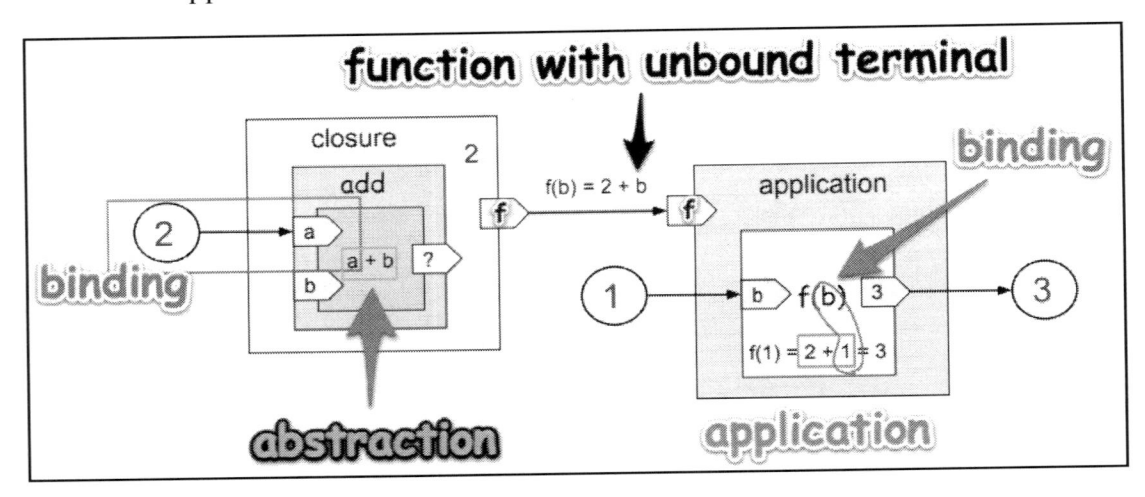

![Diagram showing closure with add function, binding of 2 to a, abstraction producing f(b) = 2 + b, and application where b is bound to 1, yielding f(1) = 2 + 1 = 3]

Let's describe our visualization.

First, we define our function as the *abstract* operation of $a + b$. This operation requires two values, a and b. Second, when we execute *add2 := add(2)*, we are binding the value 2 to the variable a. (*a* is technically a variable, but we treat it like a constant. Remember? Functional programming does not permit mutation.) Since our inner, anonymous function closes over a, the a variable's value is stored in the context of our closure structure and remains available for use later when we apply b and finally evaluate our $a + b$ expression.

We define our add function to be of type *lambda*, that is, a function that accepts an int and returns an int. (Note that unlike our abstract add operation that requires two values, all of our functions accept only one argument and return only one value.) The output of our closure structure returns an expression representing the function definition $f(b) = 2 + b$.

We call our closure when we execute *three := add2(1)*, where *three* is a lambda, that is, it is a function that accepts an input function. That input function accepts an int, that is, 1 in our example. 1 is bound to the unbound terminal b. Now that we know that all of our variables are bound, that is, they all have values, we can evaluate our expression $2 + 1$ and return the result *3*:

```go
package main

type lambda func(int) int

func add(a int) lambda {
    return func(free int) int {
        return func(b int) int {
            return a + b
        }(free)
    }
}

func main() {
    add2 := add(2)
    three := add2(1)
    println("Pass 1 to to add2 expression to get:", three)
    four := add2(2)
    println("Pass 2 to to add2 expression to get:", four)
}
```

1) define function
2) bind to variable
3) execute function

The following is the output:

```
Pass 1 to to add2 expression to get: 3
Pass 2 to to add2 expression to get: 4
```

In *step 1*, we define our add function. The add function accepts the argument a of type int and returns an anonymous function of type lambda.

In *step 2*, we call our lambda function and pass the integer 2. 2 is accepted as argument a. We can say that add is partially invoked in this step and that the value 2 stored in a is curried. What we return is a *closure*, that is, a function that *closes over* the a variable.

In *step 3*, we pass our free variable 1 to our add2 lambda function. This is where the magic happens. add2 is a variable that contains a function with the curried value 2. When we pass 1 to that lambda, it assigns 1 to the free argument, which next gets assigned to the *b* argument of the inner, anonymous, application function where our *a + b* expression is evaluated and returned.

Pretty cool, huh? Go allows us to directly implement lambda expressions. Maybe this lambda closure application functionality will become part of Go's standard library one day. There's not much code here, but understanding it and then implementing it was challenging. However, now that we have it, we can reuse our add2 function and pass it around like a variable. A variable that contains contextual data and logic. Sweet!

Granted our example was rudimentary, but consider all the naturally scalable reuse and compositional capabilities that we now have in our arsenal!

A Lambda calculus is like chocolate milk

The closure is like the shot glass, chocolate syrup is like our curried variable *a*. Every shot glass partially filled with chocolate syrup is like our partially invoked lambda expression that we set aside, just waiting for the milk.

When we add good ole' milk and stir, that's like passing the 1 and executing 2 + 1. The result (that is, 3) is a tasty treat called chocolate milk. For our lactose intolerant friends, we can take a glass of chocolate syrup (partially invoked function with curried chocolate syrup) and add almond milk. For our crazy lactose intolerant uncle, we can take another curried glass of chocolate syrup and add hemp milk. See, Lambda calculus isn't confusing after all; it's delicious!

Lambda examples in other languages

Let's look at the same `add2` lambda function in a few other languages:

JavaScript

Since JavaScript is a weakly typed language, we don't need to specify that the type of our *a* and *b* variables are integers:

```
var add = function (a) {
  return function (b) {
      return a + b;
  };
};
add2 = add(2);
```

JavaScript (ES6)

ES6 provide arrow functions (also known as *fat arrow* functions) that provide a more concise syntax for writing function expressions. Fat arrows indicate an anonymous function and allow us to not type the keywords `function` and `return`:

```
const add = a => b => a + b;
add2 = add(2);
```

Ruby

Let's study lambda expressions in Ruby; it's quite insightful.

Ruby lets us define an anonymous lambda function in two ways. One uses the `lambda` keyword:

```
add = lambda {|a, b| a + b}
```

The other uses the stabby symbol:

```
add = -> a, b{a + b}
```

In the IRB console, we can call the lambda expression like this:

```
>> add.call(2, 1)
=> 3
```

There's a lot we can do just with Ruby lambda. A Ruby lambda is a special kind of closure. Like Ruby blocks and procs, a Ruby lambda acts like a code snippet that can be passed around.

Where do we often see lambdas used with Ruby in real world applications? Ever worked with Rails? Ruby on Rails is a web application framework with an **Object Relational Mapping (ORM)** library named `ActiveRecord`. Ruby classes of type `ActiveRecord::Base` map to database tables. We call those Ruby classes models. They have a method named `scope` used for retrieving rows from their associated tables. We can define a scope using a lambda, as follows:

```
class Make < ApplicationRecord
end

class Car < ApplicationRecord
    belongs_to :make
    scope :by_make, -> (id) { where(:make_id => id) }
end
```

Category Theory That Applies

Consider seeding our tables, as follows:

```
Make.create({name: 'Lexus'})
Make.create({name: 'Honda'})
Car.create({make_id: 1, model: 'IS250'})
Car.create({make_id: 2, model: 'Accord'})
Car.create({make_id: 2, model: 'Highlander'})
```

We can use our `by_make` scope to retrieve only records containing Honda cars, as follows:

```
>> ar.by_make(2)
Car Load (1.2ms) SELECT "cars".* FROM "cars" WHERE "cars"."make_id" = $1
+----+---------+------------+
| id | make_id | model      |
+----+---------+------------+
| 2  | 2       | Accord     |
| 3  | 2       | Highlander |
+----+---------+------------+
```

In the preceding, we are able to pass the key `id` value for a Honda (2) which the scope method passes to the lambda function.

In order to leverage the full power of lambda expressions in Ruby, we'll need to curry our function. For example, to call our `add` function from earlier with one parameter like we did in the JavaScript examples, we add the `curry` method to create a lexical scope for our anonymous lambda function. Next, we store it in a variable named `add2`:

```
add2 = add.curry.call(2)
```

The lambda provides a closure, that is, an anonymous, first class literal function that we store as a variable `add`. The curry adds a special ability to access other variables local to the scope in which that lambda was created.

We can call the lambda expression in the `add2` variable by executing its call method:

```
>> add2.call(1)
=> 3
```

Look at the following call to the anonymous function:

```
>> add.call(2, 1)
```

What is immediately obviously different between that and the following call to the curried function?

```
>> add2.call(1)
```

Curried functions take one argument.

Why use currying instead of a regular function with multiple arguments?

A: How many arguments can you pass to the *regular* function?

In this case it's rigidly set to two. However, if we use currying we can easily add more without breaking our interface. This is a powerful tool in our toolbox of composition. We can easily replace the pieces in our chain of function calls with more easily reusable functions.

Thus, we learned that a lambda expression is a curried, anonymous function. We just saw how those two concepts (anonymous and curried function) are defined and accessed in Ruby. In other languages, such as Go, while the syntax varies, the concepts remain the same.

The importance of Type systems to FP

The purpose of a type system is to reduce bugs by defining the interfaces between the different functions in a program and verifying that those functions can be reliably connected. Types can be a simple as strings, ints, and booleans or can be a complex data structure with embedded fields and interfaces. Types can be checked at compile time or runtime.

The Lambda Calculus was originally untyped, but Alonzo Church found that that though it was more expressive, it caused inconsistencies. So, Church introduced a typed version to simplify computation. We use type systems for similar reasons, that is, to improve determinism and to help prevent bugs.

Since in FP a function is a data type, we need to define our functions' type for the type system.

A type system can also increase our programs' runtime performance. Go is a statically compiled language, so the data types are known at compile time. This makes type erasure possible. So, Go does not have to require our programs to carry around explicit type annotations. Contrast this to languages that support Generics. Generics employs a process called reification that allows programmers to pass generic data types, along with explicit type annotations, so that called functions that need to know their type can make the generic data a first class citizen, that is, convert it to an actual data type that the program recognizes.

The added complexity of reification and the performance degradation of using generics contradict Go's core principles of simplicity and performance.

Static versus dynamic typing

In Go and other statically typed languages, such as C, C++, Java, and Scala, the compiler will catch type mismatches at compile time. In contrast, dynamically typed languages such as Ruby, SmallTalk, and Python catch these type errors at runtime and rely more on error handling to keep our programs from crashing.

In statical yet dynamic typed languages, we can easily write a function definition without mentioning the data types, like this:

```
def add(a, b)
    a+b
end
```

This works great when we pass it the correct data:

```
>> add(1,2)
=> 3
```

However, runtime exceptions occur when we pass types that are compatible:

```
>> add(1,Time.now)
TypeError: Time can't be coerced into Integer
```

Type inference

Type inference is the process of determining the appropriate types for expressions based on how they are used.

Go can determine that the type of the variable a in the following examples is `int`:

```
var a = 5
a := 5
```

Go properly infers data types in many scenarios, such as the one here:

```
a := 1.8
b := math.Floor(a + 1)
fmt.Println("b:", reflect.TypeOf(b))
```

The following is the output:

```
b: float64
```

However, since Go does not fully implement the Hindley-Milner type system, Go fails to infer the type of b in this example:

```
a := 1
b := math.Floor(a + 1.8)
println(b)
```

Rather than inferring that the type of b is float64, Go reports the following compile errors:

```
constant 1.8 truncated to integer
cannot use a + 1.8 (type int) as type float64 in argument to math.Floor
```

While it's unfortunate that Go's type system implementation is not perfect, it is understandable why it does not fully implement the HM type system. HM supports polymorphic functions. Go supports neither generics or polymorphic functions, nor parametric polymorphism. However, polymorphic list manipulation can be achieved in Go using the `interface{}` for any unknown types. We can store that in a slice of `interface{}`, that is, `[]interface{}` and use normal slice operations (append, copy, shift, and so on) on the list. When we later retrieve them from the slice, we'll need to cast the items to their appropriate type.

Haskell

Functional programming has been popularized largely as a result of Haskell (named after Haskell Curry), which is a programming language that was designed by a group of academics that are intimately familiar with the category theory. Since Haskell syntax is so clear and closely aligned with the original formal logical notations, we may see a few example in the following texts to help express category theory concepts.

Category Theory That Applies

Things are a bit different in Haskell than they are in Go. For example, Haskell variables are immutable, that is, they are not allowed to change. We use them only as bindings to expressions.

> **TIP**
> I highly recommend learning Haskell. It's a great, pure, functional programming language. Here are some good resources to get you started:
> - http://www.happylearnhaskelltutorial.com/
> - http://learnyouahaskell.com/chapters
> - http://haskellbook.com/
> - https://wiki.haskell.org/Tutorials

In Haskell, we don't implement the steps in our algorithms. Instead, we declare what our functions do. Consider the following example:

- The sum of a list of numbers is zero plus the sum of all the numbers
- The product of a list of numbers is one times the product of all the numbers
- The factorial of a number is the product of all the numbers from 1 to that number
- Our new list is the result of adding two to all the numbers in our original list of numbers

In Haskell, the our functions can only calculate a value and return it. This feature enables referential integrity. If a function is called more than once with the same parameters, it's guaranteed to return the same result every time. This allows the compiler to reason about our program's behavior and to improve its performance. This feature also allows us to compose our functions together to build more complex functions.

Haskell boils away the syntax and code ceremony that is non-essential.

Learning a bit of Haskell will help open our minds up to the new functional programming paradigms that we will cover in `Chapter 10`, *Monoids, and Type Classes, and Generics*.

Type classes in Haskell

Haskell is strongly typed and fully supports the HM type type system. Haskell has an additional layer above what we normally think of as a type. Recall that a type defines the structure of the data stored in a variable of that type (`string`, `int`, user defined struct, and so on). A type class allows us to be more specific and specify not only what the data is, but also how it behaves.

Type classes define the sets of operations. A particular object may be an instance of a class and will have a method corresponding to each operation. Type classes may be arranged hierarchically, forming notions of superclasses and sub classes and permitting inheritance of operations/methods. A default method may also be associated with an operation.

Type classes are not objects; there is no internal mutable state. Type classes are type-safe; any attempt to apply a method to a value whose type is not in the required class will be detected at compile time. In other words, methods are not *looked up* at runtime, but are simply passed as higher order functions.

Like an interface declaration, a type class declaration defines a protocol for using an object, rather than defining an object itself. For example, a type is an instance of the Functor class if it is parameterized by another type where its values can be modified using the fmap function.

Looking at Haskell's type class hierarchy here, we can see that a Monad is a Monoid, as well as an Applicative. So, we know that a Monad inherits operations from both.

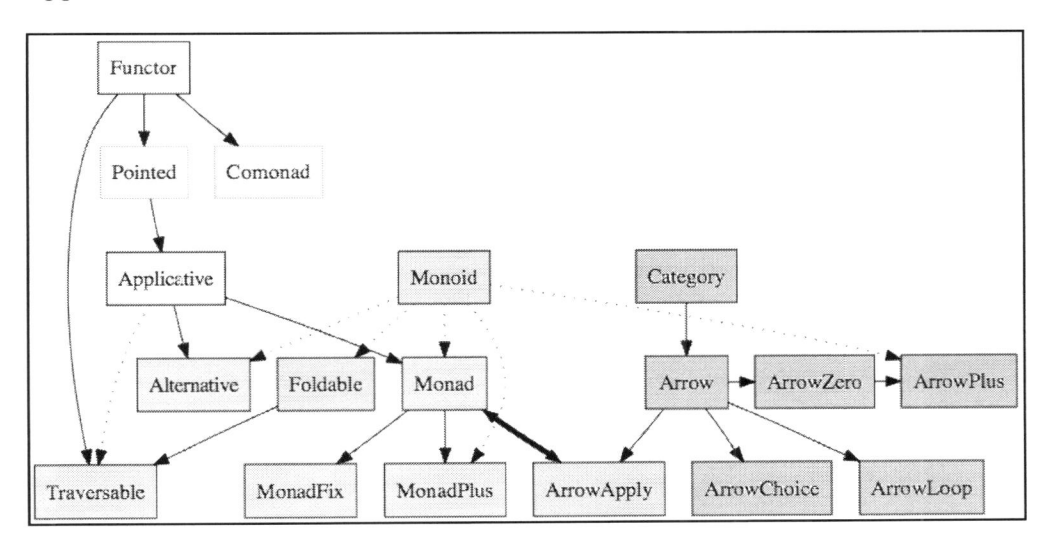

So, we don't need to add the int type to the argument signatures and we still get the type safety features to catch errors at compile time. The following defines a lambda function that adds 2:

```
(\a -> a + 2)
```

Category Theory That Applies

On the following, we're in a Haskell REPL console, where we can enter Haskell commands interactively:

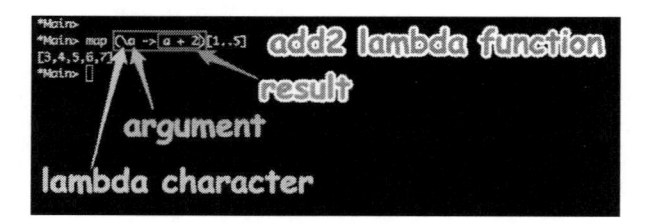

The lambda character allows us to define an anonymous function that performs the curry operation. We pass our lambda function to map, which is a high order function. Map transforms each element in our original list to a new list that results from adding 2 to each item in the list.

Domains, codomains, and morphisms

If we look closely, we can find ordered pairs of data all around us. Let's look at some statistics of Lionel Messi. The following table shows how many goals Messi scored for 10 consecutive years:

Composition Table		Ordered Pairs	Correspondence
Year (Domain A) x	Goals Scored (Range B) f(x)		
2007	10	(2007, 10)	
2008	6	(2008, 6)	
2009	8	(2008, 8)	
2010	5	(2010, 5)	
2011	8	(2011, 8)	
2012	5	(2012, 5)	
2013	5	(2013, 5)	
2014	7	(2014, 7)	
2015	6	(2015, 6)	
2016	10	(2016, 10)	

[544]

We say that the domain is **set A**: {2007, 2007, 2007, 2010, 2011, 2012, 2013, 2014, 2015, 2016} and the range (or codomain) is **set B**: {5, 6, 7, 8, 10} and that the ordered pairs are { (2007,10), (2008, 6), (2008, 8), (2010, 5), (2011, 8), (2012, 5), (2013, 5), (2014, 7), (2015, 6), (2016, 10) }.

Each year maps to a number of goals scored.

If the year where x and y was calculated by calling a function named *f*, we could get y by calling f(x). For example, *f(2010)* = 5 and *f(2016)* = 10.

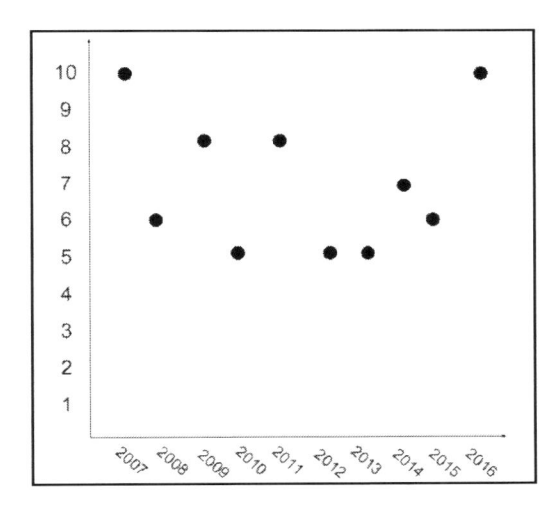

Does the following relation make sense?

How can Messi score exactly 6 goals and exactly 7 goals and exactly 10 goals in the same year? That makes no sense, right? (Right!)

We can say that the relation of *{(2007, 6), (2007, 7), (2007, 10)}* which is defined by our arrows is not a function because it contains ordered pairs with the same *x* value.

Category Theory That Applies

Set theory symbols

Before moving forward with category theory, let's get familiar with the symbols of set theory:

Symbol	Symbol name	Meaning/definition	Example
{ }	Set	A collection of objects (also known as elements)	$A = \{5,6,7,8\}$, $B = \{5,8,10\}$
|	Such that	So that	$A = \{x \mid x \in \mathbb{R}, x<0\}$
A∩B	Intersection	Objects that belong to set A and set B	$A \cap B = \{5,8\}$
A∪B	Union	Objects that belong to set A or set B	$A \cup B = \{5,6,7,8,10\}$
A⊆B	Subset	A is a subset of B. Set A is included in set B	$\{5,8,10\} \subseteq \{5,8,10\}$
A⊂B	Proper subset / Strict subset	A is a subset of B, but A is not equal to B	$\{5,8\} \subset \{5,8,10\}$
A⊄B	Not subset	Set A is not a subset of set B	$\{8,15\} \not\subset \{8,10,25\}$
a∈A	Element of	Set membership	$A = \{5,10,15\}$, $5 \in A$
x∉A	Not element of	No set membership	$A = \{5,10,15\}$, $2 \notin A$
(a,b)	Ordered pair	A collection of 2 elements	
A×B	Cartesian product	A set of all ordered pairs from A and B	
|A|	Cardinality	The number of elements of set A	$A = \{5,10,15\}$, $\|A\|=3$
Ø	Empty set	$\emptyset = \{\}$	$A = \emptyset$
↦	Maps to	f: a ↦ b means the function f maps from the element a to the element b	$f: a \mapsto f(a)$
U	Universal set	set of all possible values	

$\mathbb{N}_0$	Natural numbers / Whole numbers set (with zero)	$\mathbb{N}_0 = \{0, 1, 2, 3, ...\}$	$0 \in \mathbb{N}_0$
$\mathbb{N}_1$	Natural numbers / Whole numbers set (without zero)	$\mathbb{N}_1 = \{1, 2, 3, 4, ...\}$	$5 \in \mathbb{N}_1$
$\mathbb{Z}$	Integer numbers set	$\mathbb{Z} = \{... -2, -1, 0, 1, 2, ..\}$	$-5 \in \mathbb{Z}$
$\mathbb{R}$	Real numbers set	$\mathbb{R} = \{x \mid -\infty < x < \infty\}$	$5.166667 \in \mathbb{R}$

In set theory, we look at elements in a set. For example, set **A** may have 2 elements: {5, 6} and set **B** may have 3 elements: {7, 8, 10}. A Cartesian product has every possible combination of each: { (5, 7), (5, 8), (5, 10), (6, 7), (6, 8), (6, 10) }.

In category theory, we no longer look at elements inside sets, we only look at the relationships between sets. In other words, we only look at the arrows.

Category theory

Category theory is a branch of mathematics that deals with structure, rather than with particulars. It deals with the kinds of structures that make programs composable.

Category theory is a branch of mathematics that is similar to Set theory. A basic example of a category is the category of sets, where the objects are sets and the arrows are functions from one set to another. Objects of a category need are typically sets, and arrows are typically functions. Any way of formalizing a mathematical concept so that it meets the basic conditions on the behavior of objects and arrows is a valid category.

I could not find an easy-to-understand resource for learning category theory. Most of what's out there is geared toward mathematicians. Though I did take a good number of advanced math classes in college, I am not a practicing mathematician. While understanding the logical and mathematical formalism is important (and we'll cover the enough to be conversant), what I really wanted was something that I could wrap my head around. I wanted practical information. I wondered, how can I implement this Lambda calculus in Go? How can I build better scalable software using these lambdas? How can I tease apart the details and compose a better application from smaller, simple pieces? Can I use this new found knowledge to better architect my big data/data analytics project? I hope this chapter does that for you.

Algebra of functions

Category theory is the abstract algebra of functions. In fact, the Lambda calculus is a calculus for specifying, manipulating, and calculating functions. There is a deep connection between Lambda calculus and category theory. We're looking at the same thing from two different perspectives--from the logical, syntactic way on the Lambda calculus side and from a more algebraic, geometric perspective from category theory.

Abstract functions

Abstract functions are any process, expression or assignment that can be read in a functional way. This is an abstract algebra of abstract functions.

We'll look at set theoretical functions on sets in order to arrive at the basic principles of category theory.

We'll look at functions on set. Given sets are **A**, **B**, and **C**. And a function *f* going from *A* to **B**:

f: A -> B

Official definition of a function

A function is a subset of Cartesian product of A and B, which is relation of *AxB* (*A cross B*):

f is equal to or subset of AxB

Here, f is a subset of pairs.

For all of A, there is a unique B (b:B) such that the subset <a,b> is a relation of that relation f:

<a,b> ∈ f

Intuitive definition of a function

In a more intuitive way, we'll think of the function f as: *taking an element of set A and returning an element of set B.*

Function composition with sets

Function composition is where we take the output of one function (f: A → B) and use it as input for another (g: B → C). Through the law of associativity, we know that if A → B → C, then this is true: A → C. (We can go from A to B to C or we can go from A directly to C.)

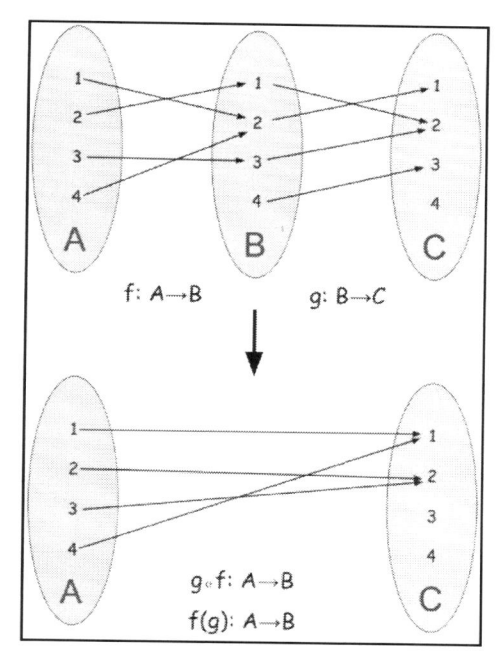

Category Theory That Applies

Composition operation example using travel expenses

In the following composition table, we enter our budget for travelling from the US to Europe:

	Composition Table		
	Dollars (Set A) x	Euros (Set B) f(x)	Peso (Set C) g(x)
Hotel 7 days	1820	1514.96	32429.31
Airplane Ticket	1135	944.77	20223.77
Meals 7 days	560	466.14	9978.25
Transportation	140	116.54	2494.56

If we travel from the US to Europe, we use the **f** arrow (function) to convert dollars to euros. If we travel from Europe to Mexico, we use the g arrow to convert euros to pesos. Here, the output of function f is the input to function **g**; this is called function composition.

If we decided to not travel to and from Europe and travel directly to Mexico from the US, we use the gof arrow. Either way, f($) → g(€) → ₱ or f(g($)) → ₱, we still should get the same amount of pesos for our dollar!

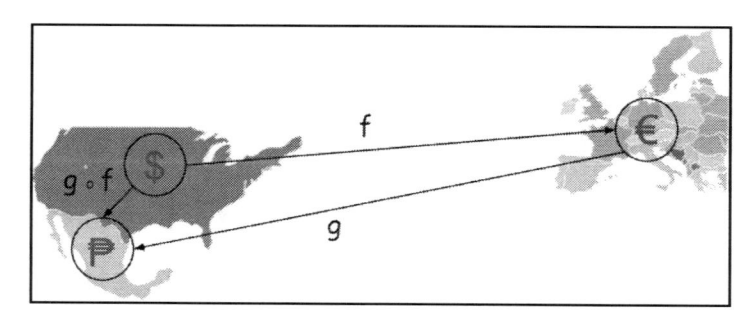

A Category

A category is defined by its objects and the arrows that connect the objects and all compositions.

For every two arrows (f and g), we must define their composition (**g** o **f**).

The elements/data of a category theory include:

- **Categories/sets**: is a grouping of objects
- **Objects**: dots/points/a primitive with no properties no structure
- **Morphisms**: (arrows) something that goes between two objects/elements

We write objects with upper case letters (such as A, B, C, and so on). We write arrows in lower case letters (such as f, g, h, and so on).

Arrows have a beginning and an end. Objects in the beginning of the arrow are in the domain; arrows at the end arrows are in the range (also known as **codomain**).

Category axioms

For each f, we have an arrow that goes from the domain of f to the codomain of **f**:

$f: dom(f) \to cod(f)$

For each A, we have an identity arrow that goes from A to A:

$1A: A \to A$

For each composable pair, $A \to B \to C$ we have a composition operation from $A \to C$.

Category laws

The following are the category laws:

- **Associativity**: $h \circ (g \circ f) = (h \circ g) \circ f$
- **Identity**: $f \circ 1A = f = f \circ 1B$
- **Unit**: Every composite is equal to itself

We'll look more closely at those laws later in this chapter.

More rules
Here are some more rules that apply to categories:

- We can have zero or more arrows between objects.
- There can no more than one arrow from any object in the domain. Remember? x values must not be repeated.
- We can put all compositions in a composition table (how we compose morphisms).
- Different compositions will give you different categories.
- Objects and arrows have no structure and no information; the composition has the information.
- Category theory is based on the more general notion.
- The s value of objects and morphisms. Objects generalize types and morphisms generalize functions.
- A category does not take time into account.
- There is also a spacial relationship between objects.

When it comes to programming and computers, time is important. For example, if we are studying the motion of a soccer ball in flight, the ball moves in an three dimensional (x,y,z) space with respect to time. If we wish to know the exact position of the ball with respect to time, we need to take time into account in our calculations.

More examples
Here're a few examples to help get a better intuition about what a category is, what it means to be a category, what things are required, and what rules must be obeyed.

Invalid categories
Here, we have two valid categories. The first one is of a car. The objects include the car itself, the car's model name, and the car's age. We show two identity morphisms. One arrow goes from a car to itself (upgrade a car and it's another car). The other arrow goes from the integer object to itself (the "++" operator means add one to the current value). We left off the arrow from the model name to itself, but it exists (a name is a name):=

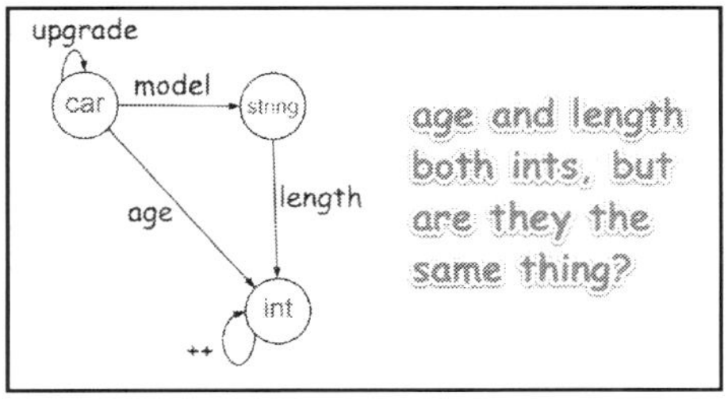
upgrade
car
model
string
age
length
int
++
age and length both ints, but are they the same thing?

Why is this invalid? It looks like it composes, but does it really?

The next example should be a bit more obvious. (Funny, but obviously not a category.)

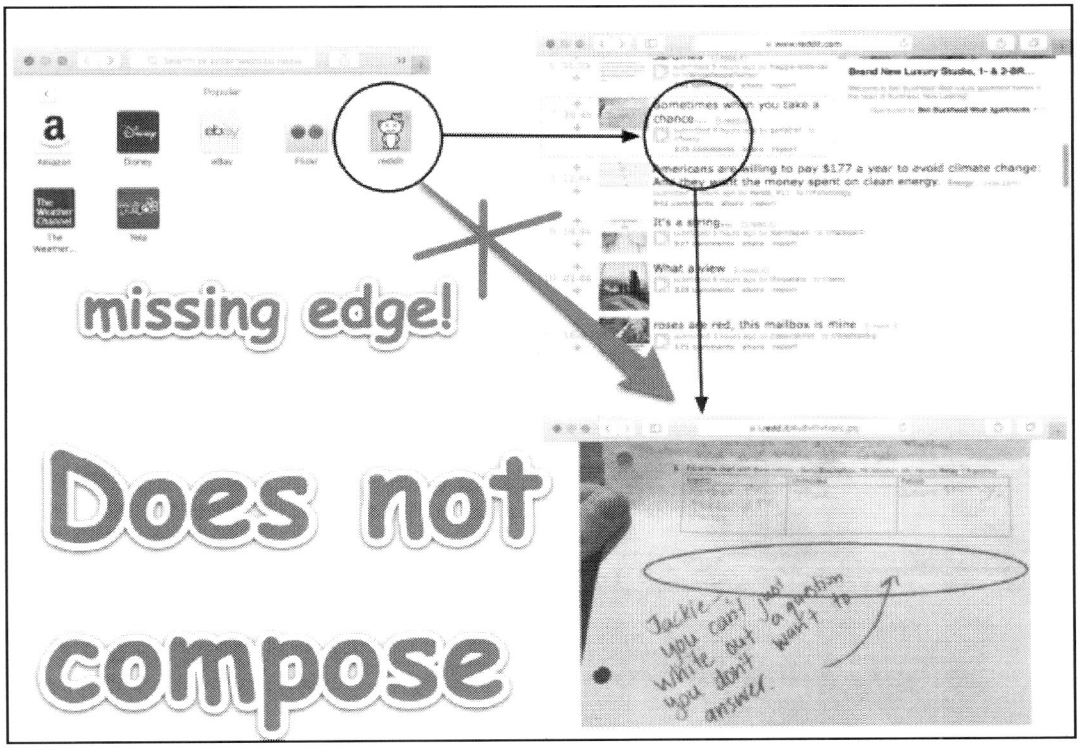
missing edge!
Does not compose

There's a link from the Favorite's page (A) to the link on the Reddit home page (B), and one from there to the image (C), but not one from the Favorite's page (A) to the image (C).

Morphisms

A morphism is an arrow from one object (A, B, C in our example) in a category (our grouping of A, B, C). There can be more than one arrow from A to B (or from B to C, or A to C). Also, arrows can go from any object to itself; this is called the identity morphism.

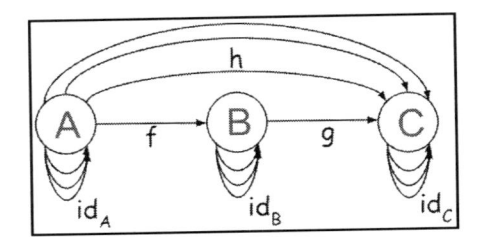

- f:A→B statement is a morphism (f) from A to B
- Hom(A,B) is the collection of all arrows from A to B
- Hom(A,B) is also known as the Hom-Set of A to B
- idA:A→A is a morphism from A to A

The behaviors of morphisms

Let's look at at a couple things we can do with morphisms. W can compose them and run the identity morphism to verify an object's identity.

Composition operation

Below, is our basic composition operation.

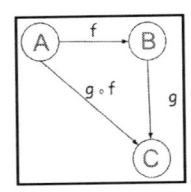

The composition operation is *g o f*, *g after f* applies arg x (from **A**) to give us g applied to f applied to x: $(g \circ f)(x) = g(f(x))$.

If $f(g(x)) = g(f(x))$ for all x, then we can say that **f** and **g** commute under composition.

However, that's not typical. Function composition is generally not commutative.

Let's take an example. Remember when we composed $f(x) = x + 2$ with $g(x) = x2 + 1$ earlier in the chapter? We solved $g(f(1)) = 10$, but what about $f(g(1))$? Does that also equal 10? Let's see now:

$g(1) = 1^2 + 1 = 2$ and $f(2) = 4$

So, no, our functions f and g are not associative: $g(f(1))\; != f(g(1))$.

Identity operation

Identity law of our category says the identity morphism of A is A.

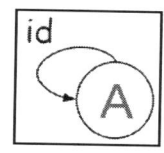

Every object has a morphism pointing back to itself.

When we have more than one object, we denote which ID we're talking about with a subscript, for example, **idA**.

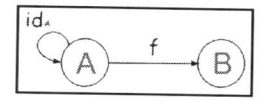

This graph says $f \circ idA = f$.

In other words, the morphism of **f** after **idA** is the same as the morphism of **f**. Here's a concrete example:

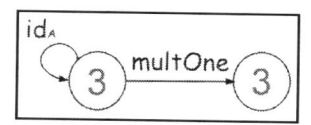

Category Theory That Applies

The identity morphism for the natural number 3 is a function that multiplies any number by

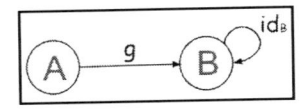

There is a symmetric identity morphism: $idA \circ g = g$

Law of associativity

In the following diagram, we see that we can get from A to C by way of the $g \circ f$ composition.

From **C**, we can get to **D** using the **h** arrow, which we can write as $ho(gof)$.

Note that this is the same as **h(f(g))**. This notation seems more intuitive than using the composition operation, but they mean the same thing.

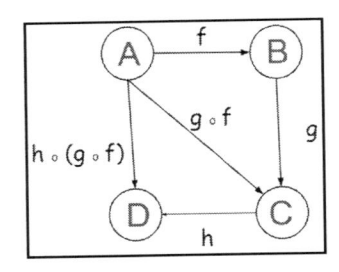

From the following diagram, we see that **ho(gof)** is the same as **(hog)of**.

So, our category obeys the law of associativity. The next diagram is another illustration of the associativity of composition:

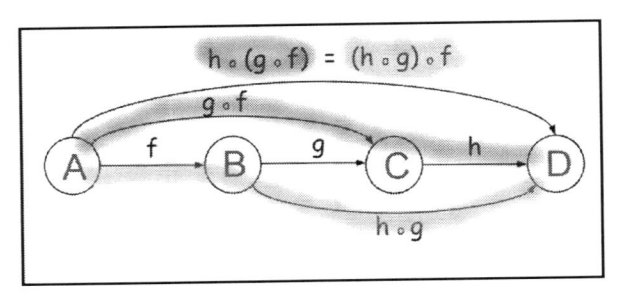

[556]

That diagram says that if the arrows exist from A→B→C→D, then if we start at A, we can use composition of functions to shortcut a set either by choosing the red path **ho(gof)** or the green path **(hog)of**.

Associativity helps us manage complexity. It is the basis for composition.

Only concerned with morphisms

In a category theory, we only have objects and arrows between them.

We can compose functions by applying a function to an argument to get a result. Then, we apply another function to the result and so on, until we end up where we started.

We put all of our compositions in a table and only concern ourselves with the morphisms. It is the morphisms that define the interface for our application. What's important is how objects are connected/mapped.

Interface-driven development

One concept of the category theory that we can use when we develop software is that our design should be concerned only with interfaces, that is, the arrows/morphisms. We have seen the theme of composition repeated throughout this book. From Mozart compositions to function compositions with linear and quadratic functions, and later with finite state machines. We've seen that the way to solve complex problems is to break them apart into understandable pieces. We can then reach into our toolbox of pieces and compose elegant, reliable solutions. We design our **application programming interfaces** (**APIs**) to connect our pieces and can leverage concurrent programming constructs and concurrency-aware frameworks to arrange how the pieces work together to arrive at our desired result.

> Design the architecture, name the components, document the details. Clear is better than clever. Don't communicate by sharing memory; share memory by communicating. Channels orchestrate; mutexes serialize. The bigger the interface, the weaker the abstraction.
>
> For more Go proverbs, visit: https://www.youtube.com/watch?v=PAAkCSZUG1c, and for *Concurrency Is Not Parallelism*, visit: https://www.youtube.com/watch?v=cN_DpYBzKso.

Category Theory That Applies

More morphisms

The example below shows two identity morphisms and a morphism from A to B.

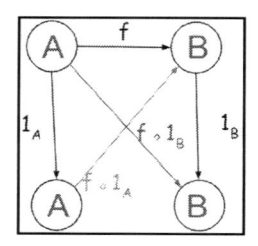

If we take A and any f to B and the Identity on **A (1A)**, then this composite f after the identity on A (**f o 1A**) is equal to f.

Here's another way to look at it:

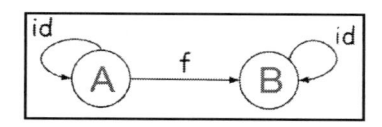

If we take **A** and any **f** and we take the identity on **A**, then this composite **f** after the identity on **A** is equal to **f**.

Here's the morphism f from A to B:

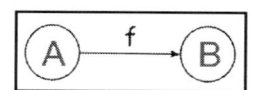

And here's a concrete example:

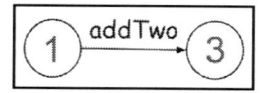

The identity axiom says that if there is an arrow f from the identity of **A** to **B** and there is an arrow f from the identity of **B** to **B**, then the arrow from **A** to **B** is the same arrow f.

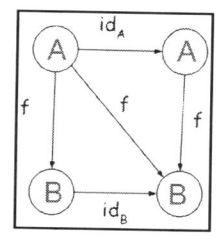

The associativity axiom says that the composition of arrows is associative, which is another way of saying the diagram is commutative.

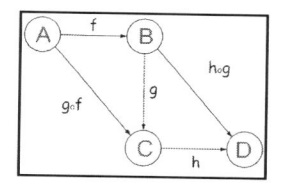

Therefore, for all arrows, $f : a \to b$, $g : b \to c$, and $h : c \to d$, $h \circ g \circ f$ denotes $h \circ (g \circ f)$.

And it follows the this is true: $h \circ (g \circ f) = h \circ g \circ f = (h \circ g) \circ f$.

A review of Category theory

Category theory is about composing functions.

A, B, C = type = algebras/mathematical structure(homomorphisms)

Note that we no longer concern ourselves with the objects/elements inside the sets (only the arrows).

f = function = arrow that goes between objects (and maintains algebraic structure)

The **f** variable is a function that accepts arguments of type A and can, for example, return objects of type B.

Identity arrow (idA) goes from A to A and does nothing. **f;g** (*composition* of 1 arrow after another) is a function that accepts arguments of type A and B, and returns C.

$idA; f = f; idB = f$

Category Theory That Applies

There are three ways to compose two things: $(f;g);h = f;(g;h)$.

C *(category C)* = *set* of all arrows in Category from A to C is in C.

Even more correspondence

Remember the filter types (Read, Split, Transform, Merge, and Write) from our flow-based programming discussion in `Chapter 6`, *Building on an Onion Architecture* (*increase performance with pipelining*)? Let's see how flow-based programming corresponds to category theory, logic, and types.

- Logic has and, or, and implication operations
- Programming has data records and function operations
- Flow-based programming has merge, split, and transform operations

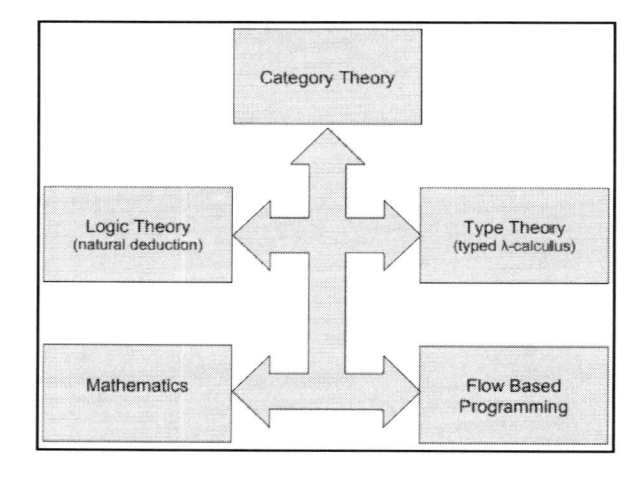

Category theory has arrows that are functions (that can also be data).

Just like a proposition in logic can be true or false, a type can be either inhabited or not. True propositions are inhabited. The void type is false. If we can produce an element of a type, then we have proven our proposition.

Table of morphisms

The following table summarizes our basic operations, as well as our initial and terminal states:

Category Theory		Logical Theory		Type Theory		Flow Based	
				I/O Monad		Read	
Product	(diagram)	Or	∨	Filter	A×B	Split	
Morphism	(diagram)	Imply if...then	⇒	Map	A → B	Transform	
Sum	(diagram)	And	∧	Reduce	A + B	Merge	
				I/O Monad		Write	
initial object	(diagram)	false		Empty Space	Void	Beginning	
terminal object	(diagram)	true		Unit Type one element	()	End	

Morphism examples

The $a \to b$ statement says that if we provide an element a to our function, then our function will produce an element of b. The same goes for logical implication: if a is true then b is true.

If we have a function type $a \Rightarrow b$ and pair it with an element of a, we get an element of b.

Modens ponens

In Latin, modens ponens means, "the mode of affirming".

Category Theory That Applies

Type theory version
$((a \Rightarrow b), a) \to b$ says that if we have function $(a \Rightarrow b)$ and an argument a, it will produce b.

Logic version
If we know b follows from a and that a is true, then you can prove b.

$a \Rightarrow b \wedge a \to b$

This is called Modens ponens also known as an implication.

Correspondence between logic and type theory
Do you see the one-to-one correspondence between logic and type theory?

Add the category theory correspondence and we get the Curry Howard Lambek correspondence.

Cartesian closed category
A cartesian closed category, where a product exists for any two elements and an exponential exists for any two elements, is a model for logic and type theory.

Though many categories have products and sums, only a few have map objects. Such categories are called cartesian closed categories.

There is a deep connection between λ-calculus, logic, and cartesian closed categories.

A **cartesian closed category** (**CCC**) is an abstraction having a small vocabulary with associated laws:

The *category* part means we have a notion of *morphisms* each having a domain and codomain object. There is an identity morphism for and associative composition operator.

The *cartesian* part means that we have products, with projection functions and an operator (`fst` or `snd` in Haskell) to combine two functions into a pair-producing function

The *closed* part means that we have a way to represent morphisms via objects, referred to as *exponentials*.

The corresponding operations are curry and apply. These exponential objects are first class functions.

Lambda expressions can be systematically translated into the CCC vocabulary.

A *CCC* is a category that is closed with respect to both products and exponentials.

This is what it looks like in terms of products and sums of objects:

```
a × (b + c) = a × b + a × c
(b + c) × a = b × a + c × a
```

See the correspondence to the following distributive law?

$(a \vee b) \wedge c = (a \wedge c) \vee (b \wedge c)$

The objects in a CCC represent the types of the language, for example, strings, integers, and floats. The morphisms represent computable functions, for example, length(string). Exponential objects allow us to consider computable functions as the input to other functions.

Joachim Lambek discovered that the models of the simply typed λ-calculus (STLC) are exactly the cartesian closed categories (CCCs).

The generic type mechanism in Java is based on the generic type systems that originated in Lambda calculus. In fact, Java uses the Hindley-Milner Lambda calculus type inference, which is based on CCC.

We will revisit the topic of CCCs when we cover Mondads in a later chapter.

Unit type

A tuple is a list of items that are ordered and immutable. You can select an element based on its position.

A unit type has exactly a one value. It is also known as the identity. The unit for multiplication is 1, for addition is 0, and for string concatenation, it is the empty string.

How many values can a type defined as a tuple of type `int` contain? Infinite (-∞, ..., 0, 1, 2... ∞).

How many values can a type defined as the empty tuple contain? One. The *unit* is also represented as `()` in Haskell.

Category Theory That Applies

The value of a unit type is that you can use it in places where we might otherwise return nil (or null). We return a unit when we don't care what the value is. We don't return nil, we return a value; the unit value. All functions return values; no more null pointer exceptions! Now, we can chain functions and never worry that one on the middle with throw a null pointer exception and crash our program.

Homomorphism

Here's a Venn diagram depicting how the different categories of homomorphisms relate to one another:

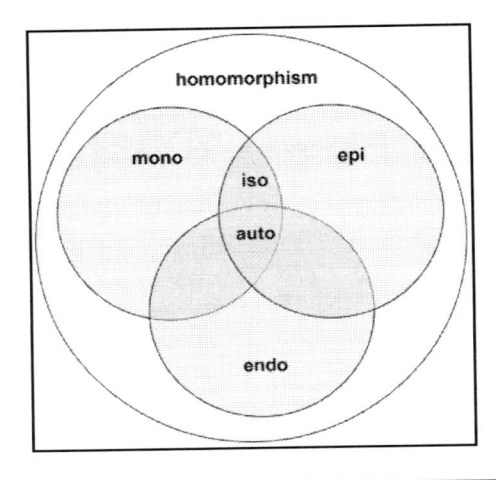

Abbreviation	Description
Mono	Set of monomorphisms (injective)
Epi	Set of epimorphism (surjective)
Iso	Set of isomorphisms (bijective)
Auto	Set of automorphisms (bijective and endomorphic)

A homomorphism is a correspondence between set A (the domain) and set B (the codomain or range), so that each object in A determines a unique object in B and each object in B has an arrow/function/morphism pointing to it from A.

If operations, for example, addition and multiplication, are defined for A and B, it is required that they correspond. That is, $a * b$ must correspond to $f(a) * f(b)$.

Homomorphisms preserve correspondence

Correspondence must be as follows:

- **Single-valued**: The morphism must at least be a partial function
- **Surjective**: Each a in A has at least one f(a) in B

Homomorphism is a way to compare two groups for structural similarities. It's a function between two groups that preserve their structure. Suppose we have two groups, G and H. G and H have different group operations. Let's also suppose that **G** has the group operation ☆ and H has the group operation (heart). Given any two elements in G: $a, b \in G$. And let's suppose a ☆ b = c. We also have a function f that maps **G** to H: $f\colon G \to H$. The elements a, b, and c are mapped to elements in H. The a variable maps to f(a), b maps to f(b), and c maps to f(c):

- $f\colon a \mapsto f(a)$
- $f\colon b \mapsto f(b)$
- $f\colon c \mapsto f(c)$

The purpose of homomorphism is to find the structural similarities between two groups.

So, if in G, a ☆ b = c, then we like f(a) (heart) f(b) = f(c) in the group H.

a ☆ b = c ⇒ f(a) (heart) f(b) = f(c) and since a ☆ b = c, we can substitute to get the definition of a homomorphism:

f(a) (heart) f(b) = f(a ☆ b)

There's a way to compare two groups.

Let's look at an example. G is a group of real numbers ($\mathbb{R}$) with a group operator of addition (+) and identity operator 0, and H is a group of real numbers ($\mathbb{R}$) with a group operator of multiplication (*) and identity operator 1.

We can define the homomorphism that maps elements of G to H that maps element *a* to *ea*.

$f\colon G \mapsto H$

$a \mapsto ea$

Category Theory That Applies

Let's ensure that this is a homomorphism by verifying that f(a + b) = f(a) * f(b).

By the definition of f given above, this says that:

ea + b = ea * ea

This is true. It is a rule of exponents. So, f is a homomorphism.

Homomorphic encryption

Homomorphic encryption allows operations to be performed on ciphertexts without the knowledge of corresponding plaintexts:

```
EncryptFcn(a) (heart) EncryptFcn(b) = EncryptFcn(a ☆ b)
```

An example of homomorphic encryption

Alice downloads a snippet of music she likes from an untrusted source and wants to use it to find the name of the song.

Bob has a song recognition capability and could identify the song for Alice.

The problem is that Alice and Bob do not trust each other.

Alice fears that if she gives Bob her snippet of music, Bob might turn her into the authorities. Bob could give Alice his music catalog but fears that she may sell it to his competitors.

The solution is for Alice to encrypt her music snippet and send that to Bob. Bob could find the encrypted result and send that back to Alice to decrypt.

Lesson learned

We can perform complex collaborative operations without revealing private information through the use of cryptography and category theory.

Isomorphism

Sometimes, groups are more than just similar. If they are identical, they are isomorphic. Isomorphism is comprised of two Greek words that mean equal and form. In mathematics, isomorphism is a perfect one-to-one, bijective mapping between two groups (structures or sets). Every object in group A maps directly to an object in group B.

In an isomorphism, every object in A is mapped to an object in B. The morphisms are also injective because no two objects from A map to the same object in B. So, if the objects in A are x, y, and z, then the following are not possible: `f(x) = f(y)`, `f(x) = f(z)`, `f(y) = f(z)`. The only mappings we find are `x -> f(x)`, `y -> f(y)`, and `z -> f(z)` and none of those three values are the same.

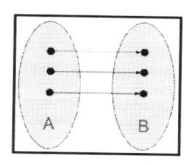

This morphism is also surjective, since every object in codomain B has at least one mapping from domain A. Furthermore, since we have a one-to-one correspondence between every object in A and B. We can see that we've got both surjection and injection; this is also called a bijection.

Injective morphism

An injective morphism is where every object in A maps to different object in B. Mappings to the same object in B are not allowed.

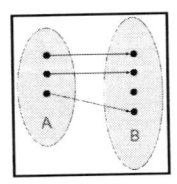

Surjective morphism

Surjective morphism is where every object in the codomain B is connected to a morphism from the domain A. In other words, every object in B has the value of f(x), where x is in A. This mapping is called *many-to-one*, since there are more than one mappings from A to a single object in B.

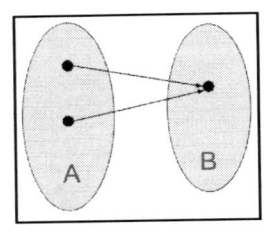

Endomorphism

If the objects are in the same set, the morphism is known as an endomorphism. In other words, the morphism maps back onto itself. An example of this would be a domain A of natural numbers (positive integers), morphisms comprised of addition and multiplication operations, and a range of B, which will consist of natural numbers. Another example would be the set of numbers 1 to 12 on a 12-hour analog clock.

SemiGroup homomorphism

A semigroup is a set with an associative operation. Adding any two positive integers results in another positive integer; hence, addition is an associative property for natural numbers.

Another example is a monoid with a unit morphism that acts as the identity operator. For example, the set of natural numbers and multiplication morphisms, whose unit morphism is the mutliplyByOne function, or the set of natural numbers and addition morphisms, whose unit morphism is the addZero function.

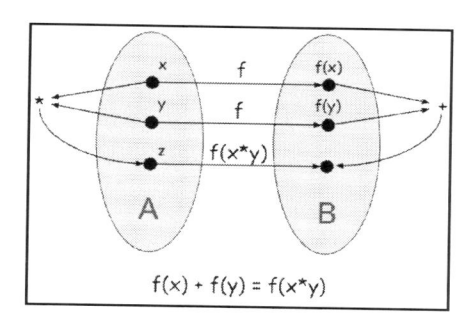

SemiGroup Homomorphism Algebra

Consider that we're given semigroups (A, *) and (B, +) and a function f: A => B. Then f is a semigroup homomorphism if `f(x) + f(y) = f(x*y)`.

Note that "+" is the operation in range B and "*" is the operation in the domain A.

So, a semigroup homomorphism is a mapping between two semigroups that preserve the semigroup operation.

Homomorphism table

The following table contains the categories of homomorphisms that correspond to the Venn diagram of homomorphisms.

A → A

Morphism	Description	Diagram	Example
Epi-	Surjective "onto"	A → B ⇉ C	

Category Theory That Applies

Mono-	Injective "1 to 1"	$C \rightrightarrows A \to B$	
Iso-	Bijective "onto" and "1 to 1" Bijective = Injective + Surjective Each element in the domain will have a corresponding element in the range (aka "codomain").	$A \rightleftarrows B$	An isomorphism between G and H. Ordered pairs: f(a) = 1, f(b) = 6,... f(j) = 7
Endo-	From a structure to itself. An endomorphism is an homomorphism whose domain equals the range.	$A \to A$	Same pixels, rearranged.

Auto-	Bijective endomorphism is an endomorphism that is also an isomorphism; an isomorphism with itself. Automorphism = Bijective + Endomorphism	

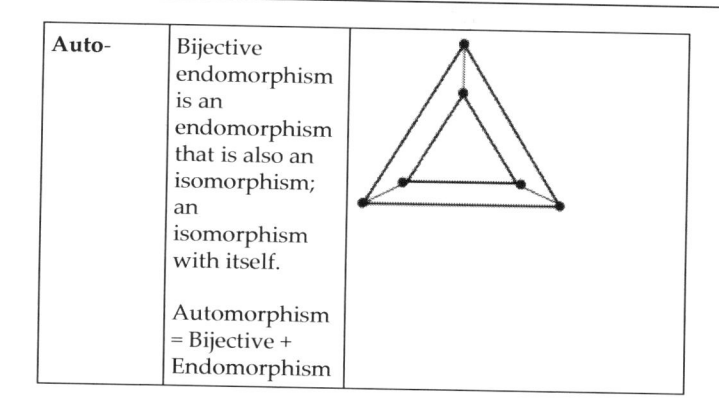

Car crash analogy

We are looking at the same structures/ideas (decomposition, composition, transformation, and so on) from different points of view. Whether it's from a mathematical/algebraic/geometric, logical/syntactic, Lambda calculus or flow-based perspective, it's all the same thing. We just express the same concepts using different notations. It's sort of like asking four different individuals what they saw immediately after a car crash. They all saw the same thing, but the way it's expressed is differently. Considering all points of view can bring more clarity and provide better understanding.

Composable concurrency

Functional programming is not only about composing functions and algebraic data structures--it makes concurrency composable--something that's virtually impossible with other programming paradigms.

How can we take what we've learned about morphisms and apply it to creating highly concurrent processing models? Suppose we start with a monolithic application with a single binary executable.

What if we can focus only on the morphisms, that is, the interface of inputs and outputs, in our system?

Consider that we're given the following:

- Inputs and outputs can be mapped through isomorphisms
- The state exists in the groupings of our objects
- Morphisms are stateless

Finite state machines

Can we assume that the finite state machines (FSMs) of our system exist within our groupings? (Where the FSM would be like the A and B groupings that we looked at previously.)

Let's imagine systematically decomposing our FSMs into the smallest possible components.

Starting with our context component C, by observing behavior/morphisms and applying the Schreier Refinement Theorem and what we know about isomorphism, can we systematically decompose a large FSM into a grouping of the smallest possible FSMs of equivalent behavior?

Here's the first decomposition:

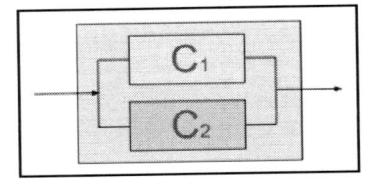

Here's the second decomposition:

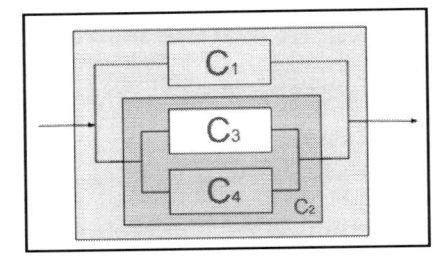

We have been wiring up our components in parallel; we can also (de)compose them in serial:

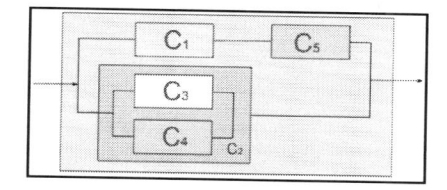

Now that we have a complete set of FSMs that comprise our system, we have filled our toolbox with the building blocks of our system. Now, we can rebuild our system by re-wiring our simple components and fitting them together in a distributed, microservice-based environment. Once we've tested our new configurations, we'll be in a position to deploy our building blocks and scale them horizontally.

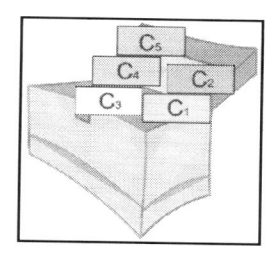

This power and flexibility comes at some cost. In order to put our components to good use, we must build a framework to glue them together and sequence the work. We'll need to think about the following:

- Compatibility of interfaces
- Determining how to partition our work
- Scheduling morphisms
- Managing resources

Category Theory That Applies

Graph Database Example

Suppose we just got hired to build a graph database solution for a local college. First, we should build the information model. It might look something like this:

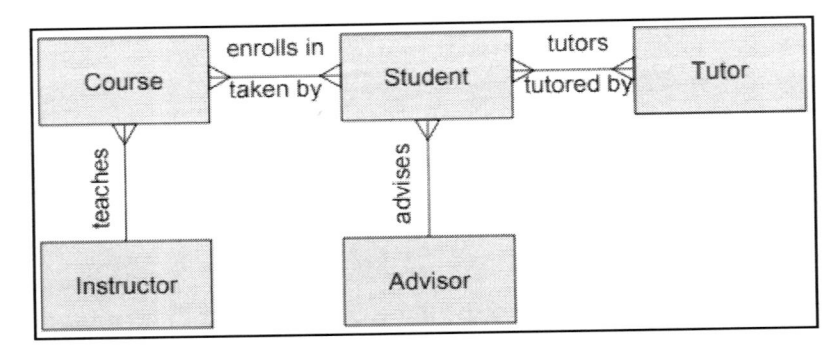

Every course has one instructor and many students.

An instructor can teach more than one class.

An advisor has more than one student, but a student can have only one advisor.

A student may have more than one tutor, and a tutor may help more than one student.

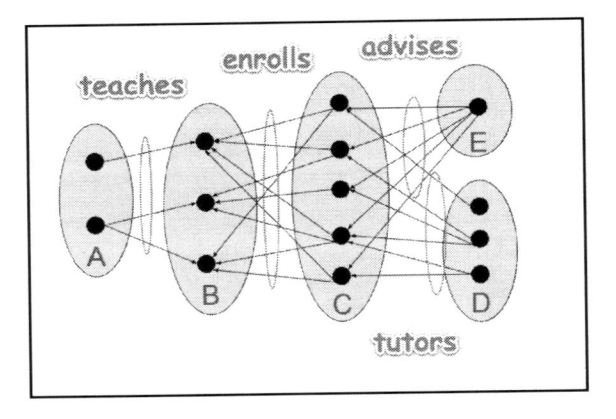

We have five sets of objects:

Set	Description
A	Instructors
B	Courses
C	Students
D	Tutors
E	Advisor

Our actual database schema could look something like this:

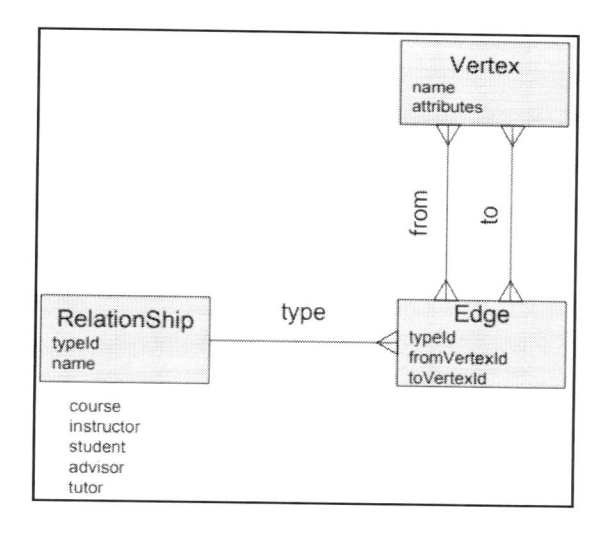

Using mathematics and category theory to gain understanding

Let's work with something we can relate to soccer!

How can we know the position of a ball in the air as it moves from Messi's foot into the goal?

Note that due to spin on the ball and the imbalance of air pressure, when in the air, the ball may curve left to right and up and sharply down.

Category Theory That Applies

> Check out Messi's curving goals here:
> - `https://www.youtube.com/embed/CmSwaK6RsB4?start=11end=15M`
> - `https://www.youtube.com/watch?v=rNlGmhFSkxw`

Suppose we have a small soccer field with the dimensions of 50 yards X 100 yards and a net that is 8 feet tall. The height of the goal is the z dimension:

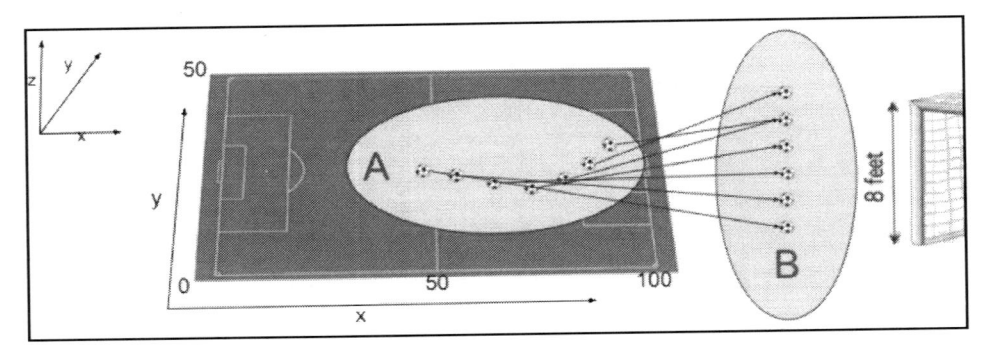

If the sun is directly overhead and makes a shadow on the field, then we can know the x, y coordinates. If we can also measure the height of the ball as it moves, then we know the z coordinate. Combining both of those pieces of information, we can know the ball's position in the three-dimensional space.

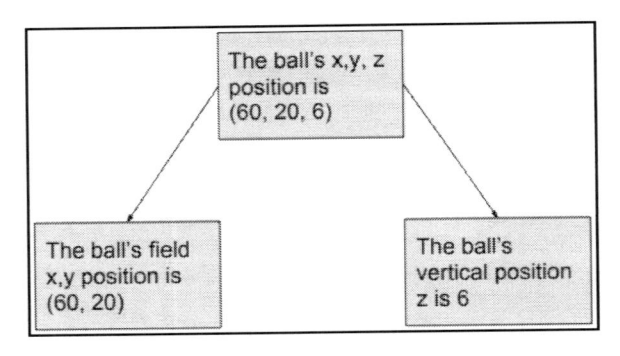

```
            The ball's x,y, z
            position is
            (60, 20, 6)
           /              \
The ball's field      The ball's
x,y position is       vertical position
(60, 20)              z is 6
```

The following diagram says that if we know A and B, then we also know C.

In category theory, this is called a product <f,g> of two sets of arrows, f and g.

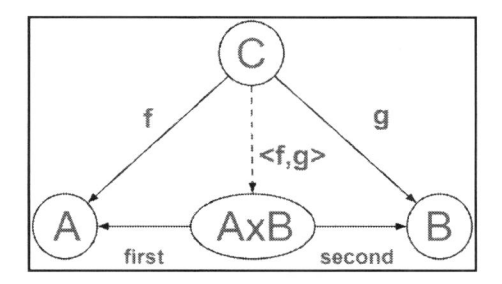

[Diagram: C at top with arrows f to A (left), g to B (right), and <f,g> down to AxB in the middle. AxB has arrows "first" to A and "second" to B.]

Given that first extracts A from AxB and second extracts B from AxB and h = <f,g>, we can say that `<f,g>; first = f` and `<f,g>; second = g`.

So, we have a commuting diagram. In other words, we have two paths <f,g> from C to AxB and first to A is equal to f, which goes from C to A, and vice versa for g.

The Universality Condition says that the only way to get from C to AxB is to apply <f,g> to C.

This diagram says that any arrow <f,g> is in one-to-one correspondence with the f and g arrows.

The cartesian product of the sets (C,A) x (C,B) is equal to the set (C, AxB).

In logic, this means if A is true and B is true then we know that A and B is true. So, the product is logical conjunction.

The identify function is depicted in the table. It says that the identity function of AxB is AxB. While this seems simple, it is important. The identity function is also known as the unit, which we've already discussed as it relates to types and will encounter again in the chapter about monads.

We've seen the following laws for multiplication in elementary school:

Law	Example
Identity	A x 1 = A and 1 x A = A
Associative	A x (B x C) = (AxB) x C
Commutative	A x B = B x A
Distributive	A x (B + C) = (A x B) + (A x C)

Category Theory That Applies

The following diagram depicts the identity law for a product in category theory. It says that the identity of AxB is the arrow pair of <first, second>:

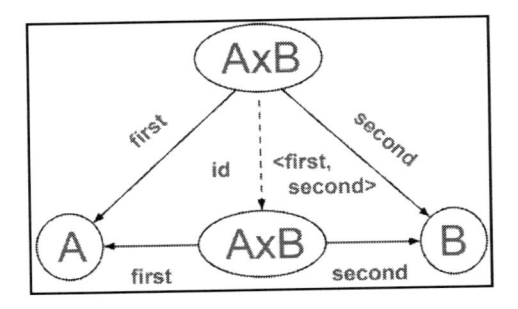

The following diagram depicts the sum operation:

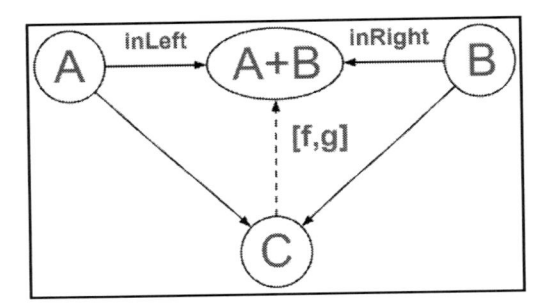

It says that there are two ways to build a sum, with inLeft or inRight.

In code, we'd need a case statement or an if/then statement to get the result.

The bracket in [f,g] indicates that the result is either f or g.

Our morphism must terminate if we are to have either a true sum or a true product.

Our diagram also says that an arrow from A+B is isomorphic with an arrow from A to C paired with an arrow from B to C; or formally, (A,C) x (B,C) = (A+B, C)

So, if we know A or we know B, we have proof of C. (This is also known as disjunction.)

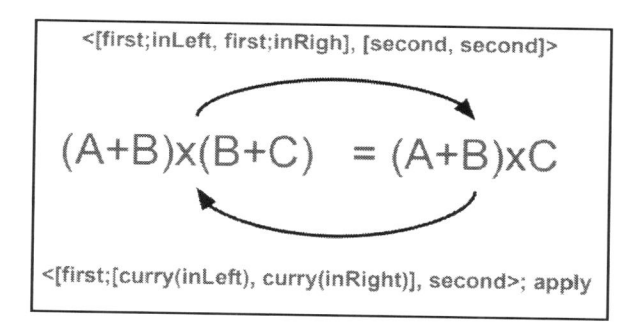

```
        <[first;inLeft, first;inRigh], [second, second]>
                        ─────────►
        (A+B)x(B+C)       =      (A+B)xC
                        ◄─────────
        <[first;[curry(inLeft), curry(inRight)], second>; apply
```

The set theory equation is A ∪ (B∩C) = (A∪B) ∩ (A∪C)

> For more information on distributive law, visit: https://ncatlab.org/nlab/show/distributive+law.

Laws of exponentials for building a lambda expression

Laws of exponentials for building a lambda expression are as follows:

$$\frac{\Gamma, x: A \vdash N: B}{\Gamma \vdash (\lambda x: A.N): [A \Rightarrow B]} \qquad \frac{\Gamma \times A \xrightarrow{f} B}{\Gamma \xrightarrow{curry(f)} [A \Rightarrow B]}$$

$$\frac{\Gamma \vdash L: [A \Rightarrow B] \quad \Gamma \vdash M: A}{\Gamma \vdash LM: B} \qquad \frac{\Gamma \xrightarrow{f} [A \Rightarrow B] \quad \Gamma \xrightarrow{g} A}{\Gamma \xrightarrow{<f,g>} [A \Rightarrow B] \times A \xrightarrow{apply} B}$$

Category Theory That Applies

Table legend

Gamma (Γ) represents the environment, that is, free variables paired with a bunch of types. We give names to free variables (for example, x of type A in the context, y of type B,...) and their type.

Turnstile ($\vdash$) a $\vdash$ b means a is provable from b.

The term (M) represent expressions we write in a programming language.

We show types A and B.

For the top right law...

Consider f represents the semantics (above) and curry(f) and we pair f and g to get A to B with a and apply it, categorically, exponentials give us implication $A \Rightarrow B$.

For the bottom left law:

How do we know A implies B? By assuming A, we can prove B and we know A implies B.

If we know A implies B and we know A, then we can conclude B.

This is also known as modus ponens.

Sums and products

What can we see when we compare the diagrams for sums and products?

If we were to flip the arrows, then they would be identical!

This is called a **Dual**. We say the *co* of a dual is the thing we started with.

Negation in logic is an example of a dual.

> Category theory jokes:
>
> What are the morphisms in the category of cars? AUTO morphisms
>
> A Priest, a Rabbi, and an Automorphism walk into a bar.... "I think we should talk, one-to-one", "We can't... He's onto us."
>
> What does a categorical mathematician call a coconut?

Chapter 11

Isomorphic equations

We have learned the following isomorphic equations:

- $(C,A) \times (C,B) = (C, A \times B)$
- $(A,C) \times (C,B) = (A+B, C)$
- $(C \times A, B) = (C, [A \Rightarrow B])$

In first equation, what does it mean to have an arrow from C to AxB?

A: We have a pair of arrows, an arrow from C to A and an arrow from C to B.

Similarly for 2 and 3.

If C is a finite set with exactly C objects in it, and A is a finite set with exactly A things in it, then how many ways are there to get from C to A?

Answer: There are A X C different ways of getting from C to A

How many functions are there from n variables onto 2?

Answer: 2^n

Do you see the direct correspondence between the categorical isomorphic equations and the laws of exponents we learned in high school?

$$A^C \times B^C = (A \times B)^C$$
$$C^A \times C^B = C^{(A+B)}$$
$$B^{(C \times A)} = (B^A)^C$$

[581]

Category Theory That Applies

Fun with Sums, Products, Exponents and Types

Here's the sum of cows with tigers and elephants:

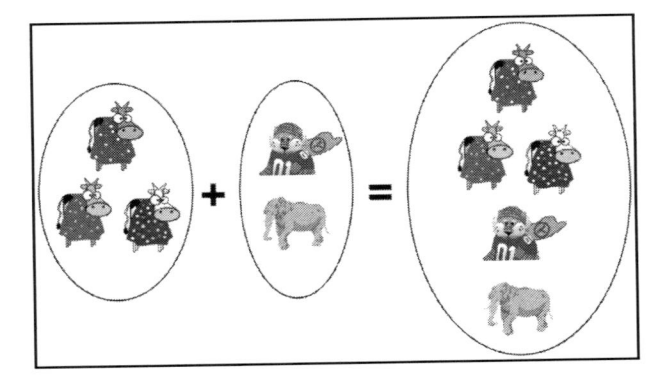

Here's a product of cows with tigers and elephants:

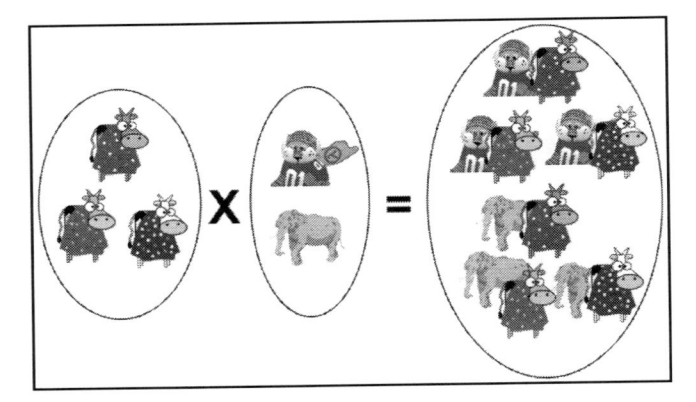

Here's the exponents of cows with tigers and elephants:

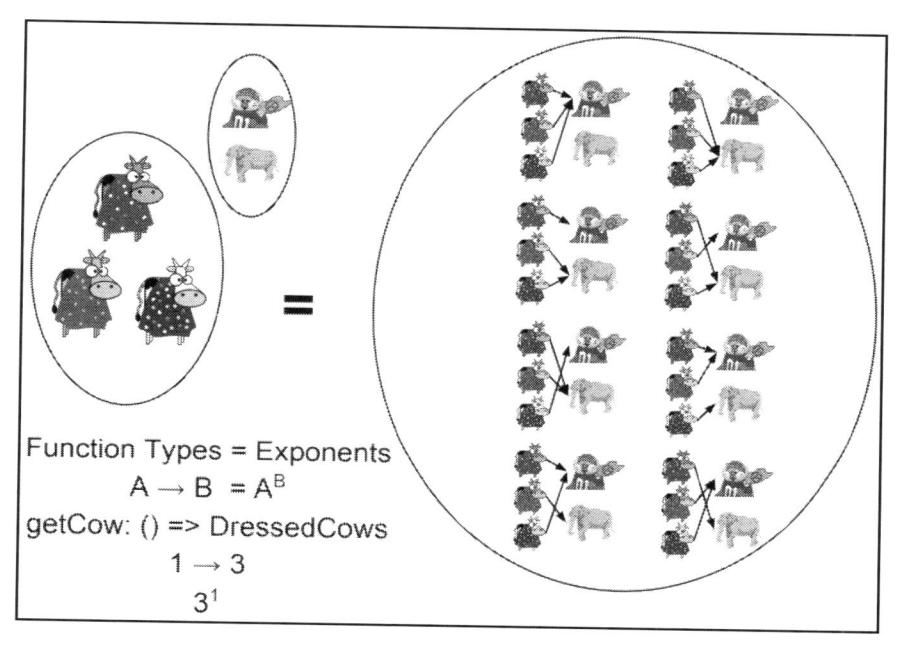

Function Types = Exponents
$A \rightarrow B = A^B$
getCow: () => DressedCows
$1 \rightarrow 3$
3^1

If we have a getCow method that will return DressedCows and if we have 3 types of DressedCows then if we call getCow then there are 3^1 possible DressedCows that it can return.

Note that functions with no arguments are Units. A Unit is a singleton type that carries no information. In `Chapter 9`, *Functors, Monoids, and Generics*, we'll see how Units are useful when we build a 12-hour clock functor and when writing a reduce function. A Unit is our identity morphism.

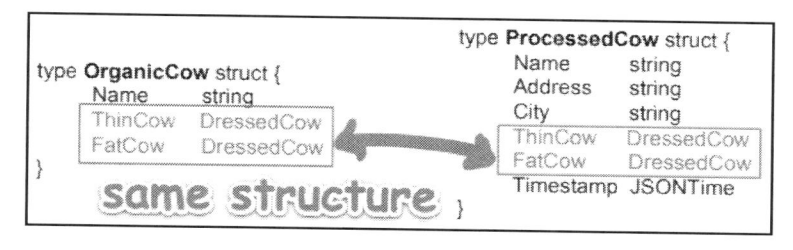

```
type OrganicCow struct {              type ProcessedCow struct {
    Name     string                       Name      string
    ThinCow  DressedCow                   Address   string
    FatCow   DressedCow                   City      string
}                                         ThinCow   DressedCow
         same structure                   FatCow    DressedCow
                                          Timestamp JSONTime
                                      }
```

Looking at structures algebraically lets us find matching structure.

Category Theory That Applies

Once we've identified an isomorphism we have proven ways to optimize for memory usage, performance or data augmentation.

Proving what our code allows us to us it.

Proving what our code isn't prevents errors.

In this way, types are a fundamental part of functional programming.

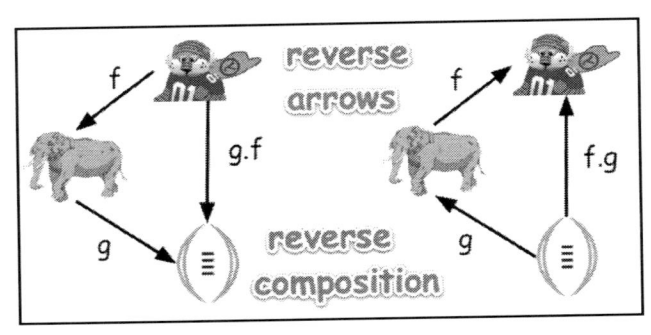

Our sums are isomorphic to products. The tiger on the left and the tiger on the right are *dual* to each other. Same for the elephant and the football. A tiger's dual is called a cotiger. Similarly sums are called coproducts.

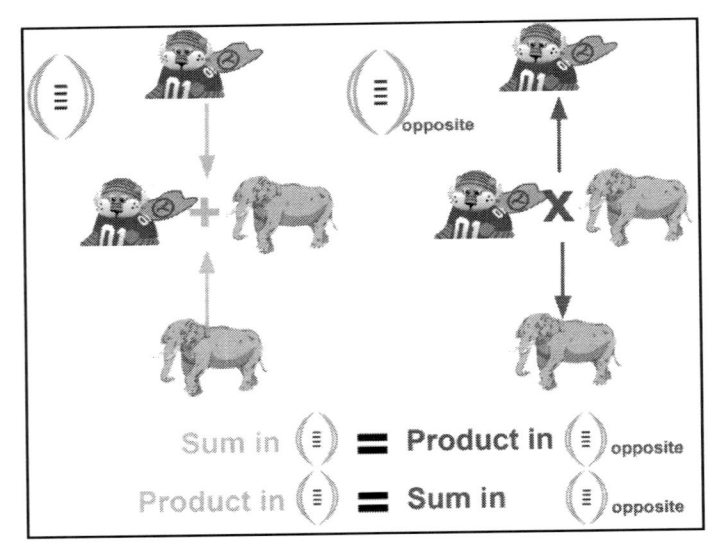

A monomorphism is shown below. **f** is *monic*:

if f.g = f.h then g = h

An epimorphism is shown below. **f** is *epic*:

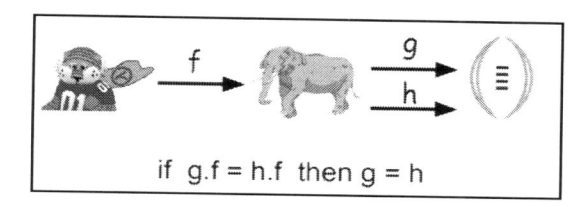

if g.f = h.f then g = h

The following diagrams shows that monomorphisms are dual to epimorphisms.

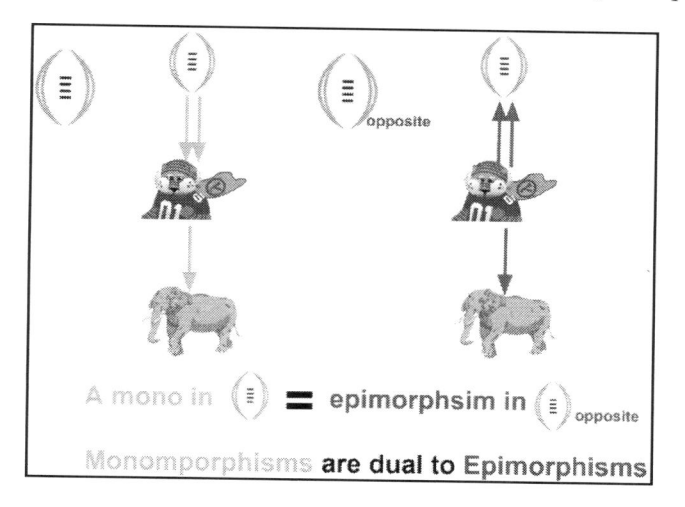

A mono in (≡) = epimorphsim in (≡) opposite

Monomporphisms are dual to Epimorphisms

Category Theory That Applies

If we don't lose data going from tigers to elephants to tigers:

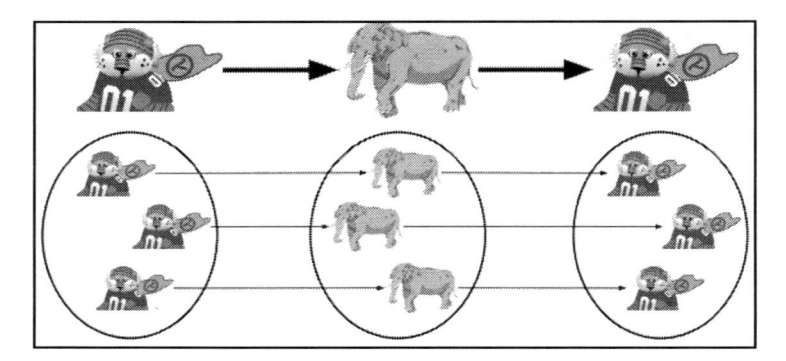

Also, we don't lose data going from elephants to tigers to elephants:

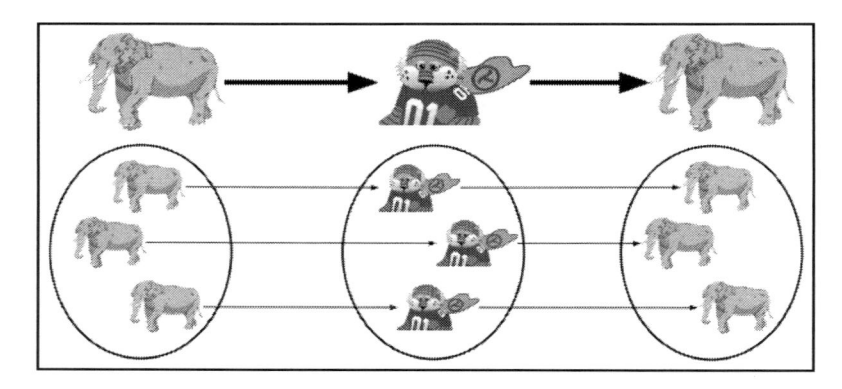

Then, our morphism are isomorphic.

Algebraic data structures give us certainty when move, map and transform data that we won't lose data.

It is essential to understand how our data structures are preserved during our workflows.

Functional programming brings us the certainty we need for data integrity as well as the composition we need to help manage complexity.

Chapter 11

When Aubie goes to buy his tickets to the Iron Bowl he enters is order data...

```
┌─Order Ticket─────────────┐
│   Your name    [Aubie Tiger]│
│   Your phone   [ 867-5309 ]│
│                           │
│   Game         Iron Bowl 2017│
│   No. Tickets       [    4]│
│   Price              $500  │
│                    ─────── │
│   Total           $ 2,000  │
│                           │
│   Credit card  [4012888888]│
│   Exp date     [11/25]    │
│                           │
│                 [Submit]  │
└───────────────────────────┘
```

When he clicks the **Submit** button the data flows from one endpoint to another. As the data flows, it may be transformed in some way but the structure of the data is kept intact:

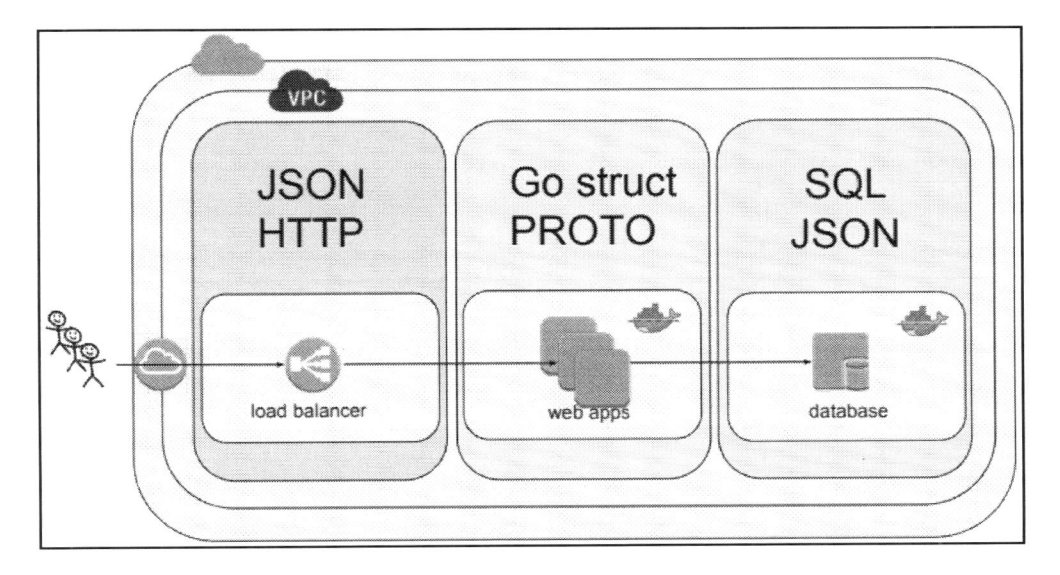

VPC

| JSON | Go struct | SQL |
| HTTP | PROTO | JSON |

load balancer → web apps → database

[587]

Isomorphisms guarantee data integrity (no data loss). Computation uses data types to map morphisms. Interface definitions (using data types) allow us to connect functions. Immutable data structures can leverage memoization, improve concurrency, and reduce memory usage. Using FP in Go helps us to simplify our development process. We no longer need to worry about a whole classification of data/interface incompatibility issues.

Benefits of using FP an Go include better:

- performance
- data reliability
- component reuse
- management of complexity
- resource utilization

Big data, knowledge-driven development, and data visualization

Big data implies there's a lot of data. When there is a lot of data, it becomes difficult to find meaning. The category theory helps us to remove the unimportant details and see the meaningful information that is there waiting to be discovered.

Data visualization

How can we apply what we've learned in the real world?

Composition sounds great but how can we go from this:

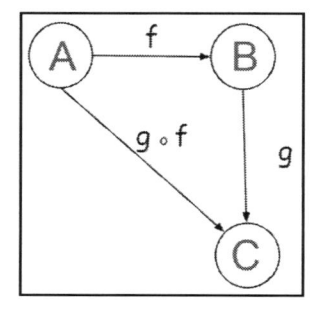

And an I/O Monad:

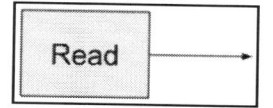

To something useful.

We can read data from server logs and integrate a graphical user interface (GUI) that renders a presentation that our users can view and derive an understanding from the data that is presented in a meaningful way.

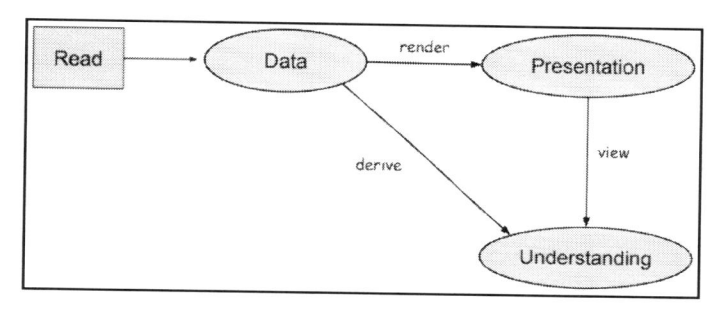

What if our data had a corresponding schema?

Can we generalize the presentation of the data to different layouts? For example, spreadsheet programs allow their users to display different types of graphs based on the same set of rows and columns (pie charts, bar charts, and so on). If we can do that, then the following is feasible:

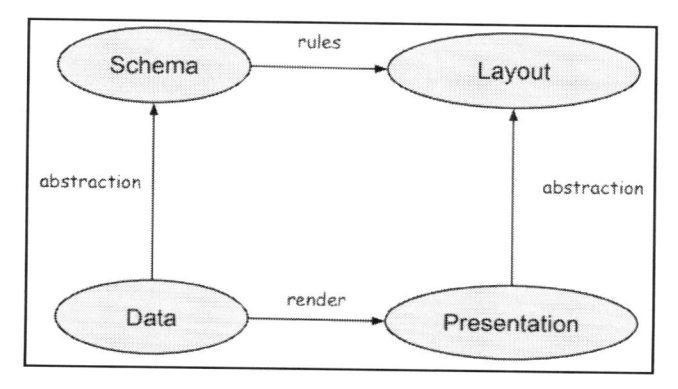

Category Theory That Applies

From the practical side of things, the data from our log files might feed into tables with rows and columns, much like a spreadsheet. From the category side, we could say that our schema is a Cartesian product of object instances and their attributes: Schema = Instances x Attributes.

We can then combine our diagrams to get this:

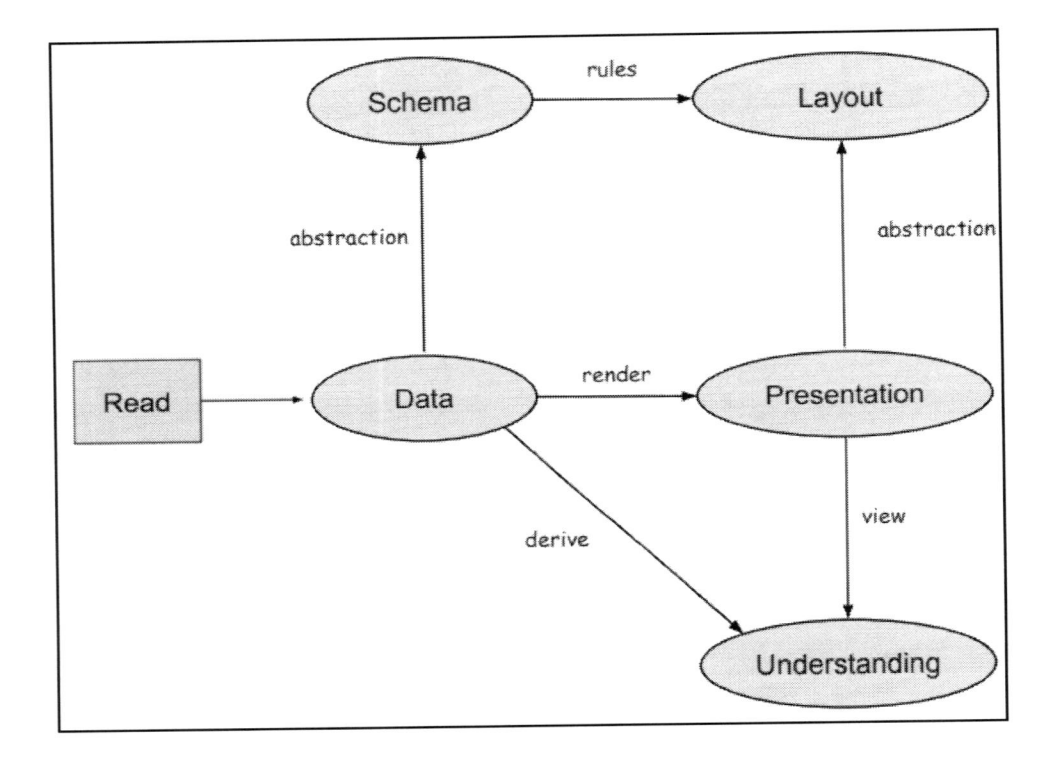

Now, if we want to allow our users to input queries to gain a working knowledge of their domain, we could arrive at the following diagram:

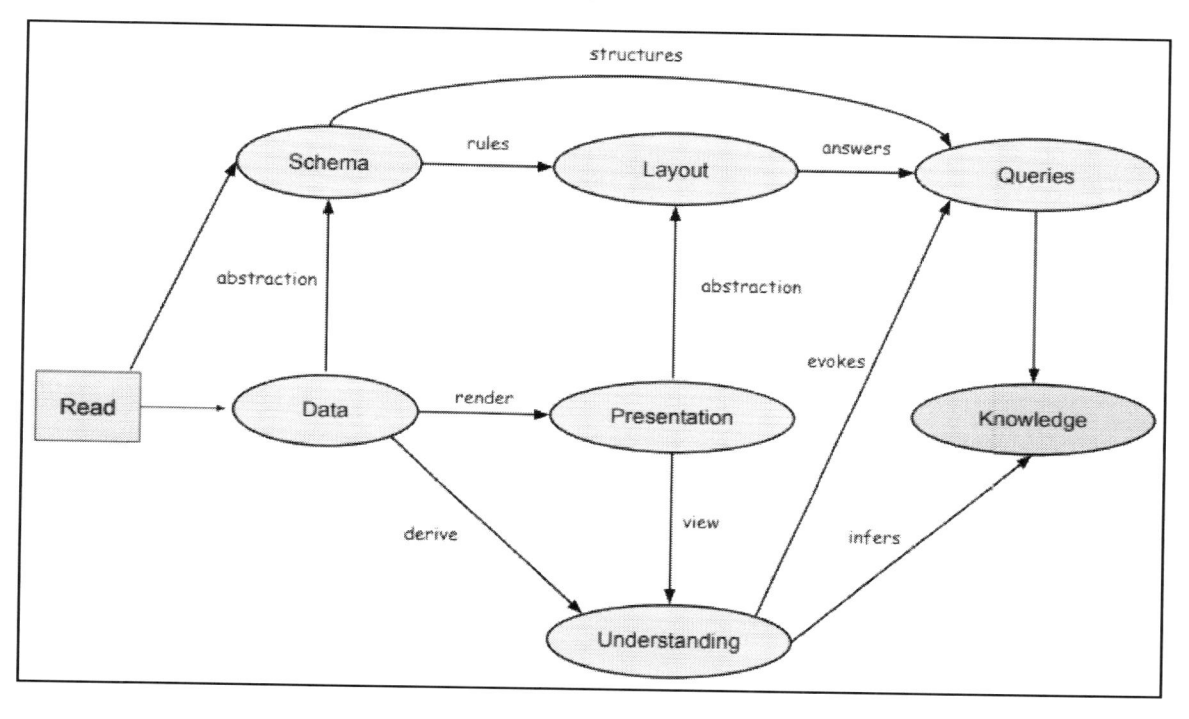

Category Theory That Applies

The category shown here defines a well-formed vizualisation process; if the arrows, objects, and data are accurate, then the diagram will commute. We can be confident that the knowledge we gain is reliable.

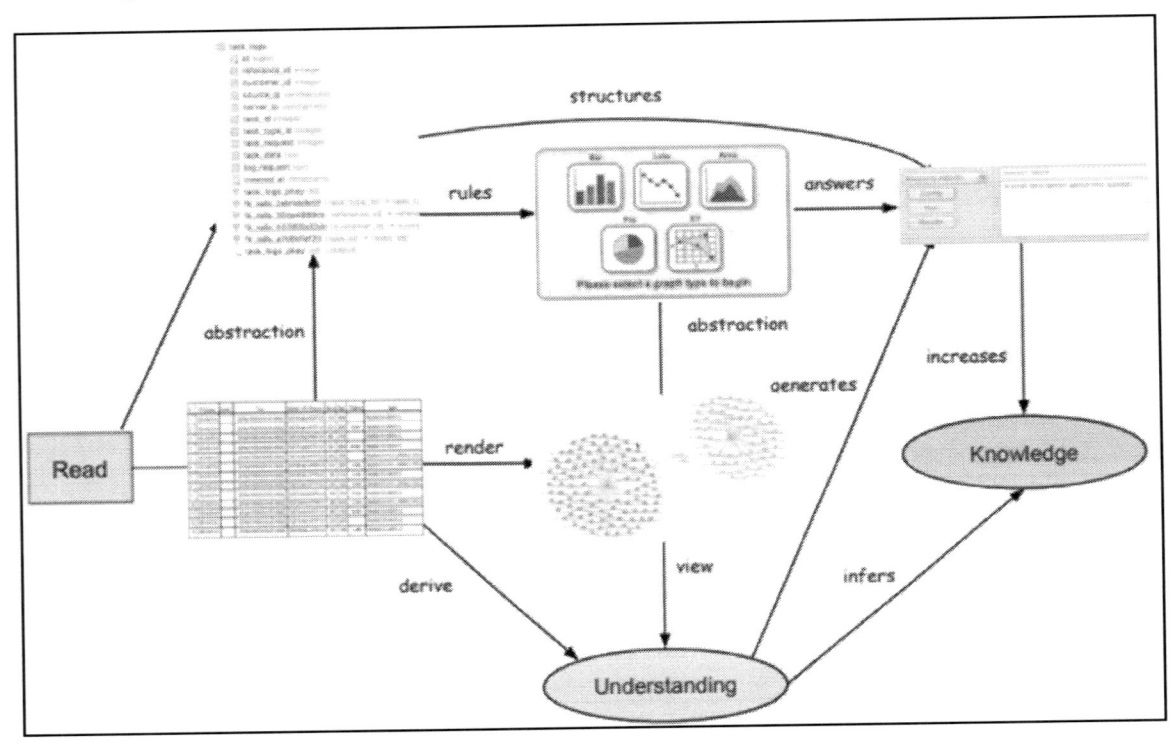

Knowledge-driven systems can make the difference between success and failure. Our proverbial hay stack could be every interaction, every gesture of body language/facial expression, words spoken, commitments kept/broken, and so on. If our key performance indicator is the health of our relationship, a knowledge-based system could sift through the minutia and highlight the one remark that mattered, "*I wish you would stop work and greet me when I arrive.*"

Sometimes, we need to start with the correct data set. If our goal is to find the next great location to build a shopping mall, we could gather two data sets, one for all cell phone records and another of population demographics. Though both sets of data have copious amounts of data that don't provide guidance, if we build our system with rules designed to find the actionable needles of truth, the given geolocation information of both cell phone records and demographics combined with income statistics, our system could bring to light the most ideal locations for our investors.

You might be thinking, "*I can do that with my imperative language.*" Perhaps, but will it scale?

Summary

In this chapter, you learned what we need to know about category theory to be dangerous. We walked through history together, learning how functional programming came to be what it is today. We looked at logical propositions and proofs, sets, objects, and arrows as well as Lambda calculus. We shared in the amazement of the correspondence between category theory, logic, and Lambda calculus. And you saw how to apply what you learned in real-world scenarios (such as the flight of a soccer ball and doing business with untrusted partners). Lastly, we gained insight into how to design knowledge-based systems to derive value from big data.

In the next chapter, we'll dig deeper into pure functional programming. We'll see how to leverage category theory and class types to abstract away details in order to glean new insights. We'll look at functors, along with slightly stronger and more useful versions of functors called applicative functors. We'll also learn how to bring the world of side-effects under control using monads and monoids.

Miscellaneous Information and How-Tos

This appendix has four sections:

- How to build and run Go projects
- How to propose changes to Go
- FP Resources
- Minggatu-Catalan Number

How to build and run Go projects

There are various ways to build and run Go applications. In this section, I'll show you what I used to build the example Go projects for this book.

TL;DR

Use the `cd` command to direct to your project root directory. Run `. init` once.

Ready to run your app? Did you change a (non-standard library) import statement? If so, run `glide-update`.

To run your app, execute `go-run`.

Development workflow

This is what our development workflow looks like:

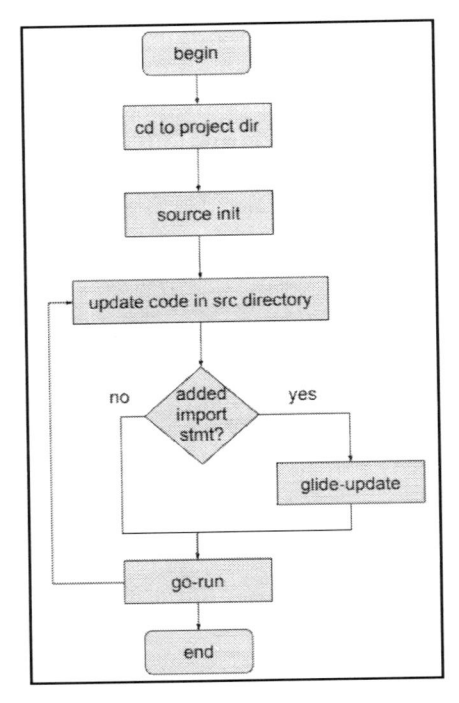

We put `cd` into our project source code root directory and run `init`. Then, we updated code, run the `glide-update` and `go-run` commands, and repeat until done. Note that if we only added imports for packages from Go's standard library, we won't need to run the `glide-update` command, though running the `glide-update` command won't hurt.

Dot init features and benefits

The *dot init* solution will do the following:

1. Create a link to this project root directory in your `MY_DEV_DIR` directory.
2. Verify that you are running the correct version of Go.
3. Verify that you have a `src` directory (it will create one if you don't have one).
4. Simplify references to project-local packages.

5. Verify that you have a `toml` config file (if you set `USES_TOML_CONFIG_YN` to yes).
6. Create aliases for your convenience.
7. Verify that you have glide installed.

In *step 1*, it's nice to have one place to go `MY_DEV_DIR`, for example, `~/myprojects` to see all the projects I've worked on. I can sort by date and easily delete the links to inactive projects.

Use *step 2* to avoid messing with GOPATH, GOROOT, or GOBIN.

As explained in *step 3*, the `src` directory is where we put our project-local package source files. We also have a file (typically named `main.go`) in our project root directory with the `main()` function in the main package.

Perform *step 4* so that we no longer need to include the full GitHub repository path for project-local packages!

Instead of `".github.comlearn-fp-go/2-design-patterns/ch05-decoration/02_decorator/decorator"`, we simply use `". decorator"`. Note that if you just really do not want to use *dot init*, you'll need to go through the source code and replace all of the simple project-local package references with the full repository path references and move the code. You may also need to move the code out of the project-local package's `src` directory up a level; it won't conflict with your global GOPATH's `src` directory.

In *step 5*, the `toml` config file (https://github.com/BurntSushi/toml) is the default config file solution. The `.init` file includes the `toml` config file runtime flag automatically (as long as you set this in the `init` script: `USES_TOML_CONFIG_YN=yes`).

Aliases available

Here're the available alias commands:

```
alias go-test='go test  ./... 2>&1 | grep -v "$(basename $(pwd))\t\[no test files"'
</span>alias go-test-bench='go test -bench=. ./... 2>&1 | grep -v "$(basename $(pwd))\t\[no test files"'
alias glide-ignore-project-dirs="printf \"ignore:\n$(find ./src -maxdepth 1 -type d | tail -n +2 | sed 's|./src\/||' | sed -e 's/^/- \.\//')\n\""
alias mvglide='mkdir -p vendors && mv vendor/ vendors/src/ && export GOPATH=$(pwd)/vendors:$(pwd);echo "vendor packages have been moved to $(pwd)/vendors and your GOPATH: $GOPATH"'
```

Miscellaneous Information and How-Tos

```
alias glide-update='if [ ! -z $(readlink `pwd`) ]; then export LINKED=true
&& pushd "$(readlink `pwd`)"; fi;rm -rf {vendor,vendors};rm glide.*;export
GOPATH=$(pwd):$(pwd)/vendors && export GOBIN=$(pwd)/bin && glide init --
non-interactive && glide-ignore-project-dirs >> glide.yaml && glide up &&
mvglide && if [ $LINKED==true ]; then popd;fi'
alias prune-project="(rm -rf bin pkg vendors;rm glide.lock;rm -rf
./src/mypackage;sed -i -e '/mypackage/ s/^#*/\/\///' main.go) 2>/dev/null"
alias show-path='echo $PATH | tr ":" "\n"'
alias prune-path='export PATH="$(echo $PATH | tr ":" "\n" | uniq | grep -v
"$(dirname $ORIG_DIR)" | tr "\n" ":")"; if [[ "$PATH" =~ ':'$ ]]; then
export PATH="${PATH::-1}";fi'
alias find-imports='find . -type f -name "*.go" -exec grep -A3 "import" {}
\; -exec echo {} \; -exec echo --- \;'
alias go-fmt='set -x;goimports -w main.go src/*;{ set +x; } 2>/dev/null'
```

In summary, dot init will allow you to update your dependencies with one command (`glide-update`) and compile and run your application with one other command (`go-run`). All you have to do to start using it is make sure that the init script exists in your project root directory and run `. init` one time. The `.init` initialization reduces the code you have to write and maintain, and it keeps building and running your Go app as simply as possible.

Functions available

Here're the functions available:

```
tdml() {
    if [ -z $1 ]; then LEVEL=2; else LEVEL=$1;fi
    tree -C -d -L $LEVEL
}
get-go-binary() {
    GO_BINARY_URL="$1"
    if [ -z $GO_BINARY_URL ]; then
        echo "Missing GO_BINARY_URL.  Usage: get-go-binary <GO_BINARY_URL>
Example: get-go-binary github.com/nicksnyder/go-i18n/goi18n"
        return
    fi
    TMP_DIR="tmp_dir_$RANDOM"; mkdir "$TMP_DIR"; pushd "$TMP_DIR"; export
GOPATH="$(pwd)"; go get -u $GO_BINARY_URL; popd; rm -rf "$TMP_DIR"
}
```

Appendix

Motivation for using goenv

> **TIP**: If you always use the latest version of Go or if do your development work on a non-Macintosh computer, you can skip this section.

If we need to support multiple go runtimes, we put our Go project code in different directories. To help us manage our go runtime environments, let's look at a little utility script named `goenv` and the init script found in our project root directories.

> This section assumes that you are using a Mac computer. Manage your Go runtime environment with `goenv`; visit: https://github.com/l3x/goenv. For more information on the `go` command, visit: https://golang.org/cmd/go

Motivation for using the init script

The `init` script and the alias commands that it provides has one purpose:

To make building and running our Go apps easy.

Managing dependencies (third-party packages) can be a pain. Import statements can be too long for our local source files. Always keeping our `GOPATH`, `GOBIN`, `PATH`, and so on up to date can also be a pain.

I created the init script to simplify the process of building and running the example apps in this book. I found it so useful that I use it for other projects too. I hope it works well for you, too.

Ways to manage Go dependencies

There are over a dozen ways to manage Go dependencies. We can do so with the tools that we will discuss in this section.

The go get tool

When I started developing in Go, I used the `go get` tool. Here's a snippet from its help message:

```
go get --help
...When checking out or updating a package, get looks for a branch or tag
that matches the locally installed version of Go. The most important rule
is that if the local installation is running version "go1", get
searches for a branch or tag named "go1". If no such version exists it
retrieves the default branch of the package...
```

I soon learned that it would get the most recent version of all packages. Not what I wanted.

I was looking for something more like Ruby's **Gemfile** or the **npm** package manager where I could specify the specific version of each package and create a `.lock` file to keep it from changing every time I run my build tool.

The Godep tool

I used Godep for a while. And it worked fine, but it was a hassle to use.

Godep created a `Godeps.json` file in a Godeps directory in the root of my project. Godep then created copies of all of my third-party packages into the Godeps directory at the root of my project. I typically checked those third-party packages into version control with the rest of my code.

Godep requires a number of steps that I find quirky. For example, to update a project's dependency, you will have to update it in your `GOPATH` via the `go get -u github.com/another-thirdparty/package` command, and then copy it from my `$GOPATH` to my project's Godeps directory via the `godep save github.com/another-thirdparty/package` command.

In my humble opinion, having to modify a dependency using `$GOPATH` is quirky. Modifying dependencies of multiple projects using different versions of dependencies concurrently is even more quirky (quirky = more user errors).

I like simple, not quirky.

Appendix

Vendoring in Go

Vendoring in Go was introduced in Go 1.5. It allows Go apps to fetch dependencies not only from `$GOPATH/src`, but also from a child folder named vendor, located at the root your project. Previously, you had to save your third-party packages in the globally shared `$GOPATH` path. Now, you can place your dependencies into your project's vendor folder.

I was still looking for a way to pin down the version of each package or to specify a `MAJOR.MINOR` version and have my package manager grab the latest `MAJOR.MINOR.PATCH` version.

> For more information, visit `https://docs.google.com/document/d/1Bz5-UB7g2uPBdOx-rw5t9MxJwkfpx90cqG9AFL0JAYo/edit`

Glide - the modern package manager

I found Glide and appreciated its features and the fact that it's under active development/improvement. It reminded me of Ruby's Gem package management. It's great, but still a lot to remember.

> Glide references
> - `https://github.com/Masterminds/glide`
> - `https://glide.sh/`
> - `https://glide.readthedocs.io/en/latest/getting-started/`
> - `https://glide.readthedocs.io/en/latest/commands/`

I just wanted to run one command to build my code and one command to run my code. I wanted something simple, so I created the init script and its aliased commands to wrap the functionality of Glide.

I find the `init`, `glide-update`, and `go-run` set of commands super easy to use. Hopefully, you will too. Granted, when you use it to build very large projects, you will initially need to deal with import/dependency errors, as with any dependency management tool, but I find Glide to be the best one out there. So, what you see in this appendix is a simple set of build and run commands that's built on top of the full featured build tool, Glide.

Miscellaneous Information and How-Tos

Each dot init step in detail

First, use the `cd` command to direct to the project directory with our source code. Let's look at the `01_dependency-rule-good` source code. This happens to be the first code project from Chapter 7, *Functional Parameters*. Next, let's run `goenv info`, which will inform us about our Go environment.

The cd command to project root directory

Before using **dot init**, you might see invalid settings for `GOROOT`, `GOPATH`, and `GOBIN`:

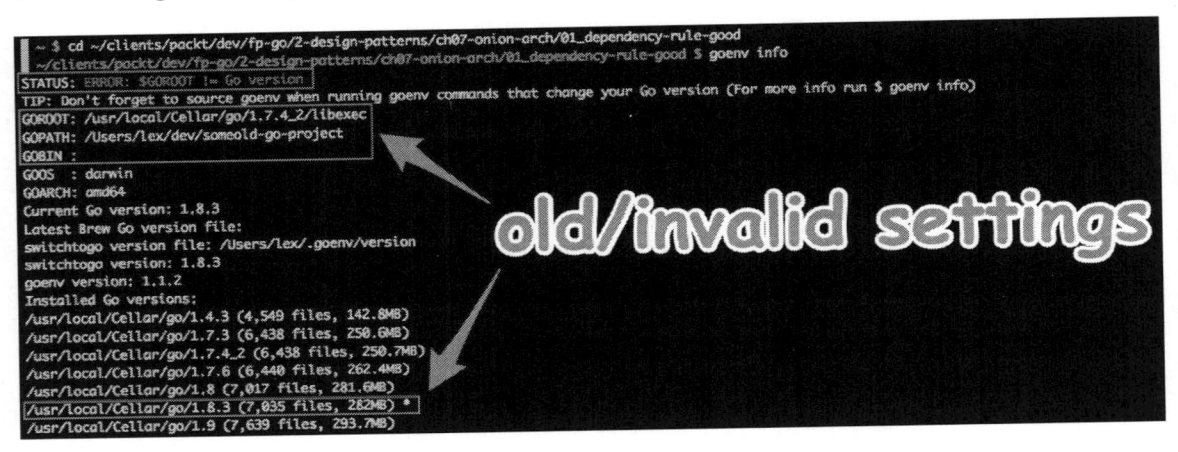

The * on the last line of output in the preceding screenshot indicates that our Go version is set to version 1.8.3. Note that running `go version` returns `go1.9 darwin/amd64`, which was the most recent version of Go when our book was published.

We see that our `GOPATH` is not properly set and that we have three versions of Go installed.

Using homebrew to install Go

On a Mac, we can use homebrew to install and manage our Go installations:

```
brew search go
```

> Running the preceding command might return result like this:
>
> go
> go@1.4
> go@1.5

[602]

```
go@1.6
go@1.7
go@1.8
```

The checks indicate which versions of Go are already installed. To install go version 1.5, we can run `brew install go@1.5`. To install the latest version of go (currently 1.9), run `brew install go`.

Examining the initial directory structure and files

Let's examine our initial directory structure and files:

```
~/clients/packt/dev/fp-go/2-design-patterns/ch07-onion-
arch/01_dependency-rule-good $ tree -C -d -L 2; find . -type f
.
└── src
    ├── packagea
    └── packageb

3 directories
./.bash_exports
./config.toml
./glide.yaml
./init
./main.go
./src/packagea/featurea.go
./src/packageb/featureb.go
```

The init script contents

Before we run our `init` script, let's look at the contents of our init script:

```
#!/bin/bash
# Author : Lex Sheehan
# Purpose: This script initializes a go project with glide dependency
management
# For details see:
https://www.amazon.com/Learning-Functional-Programming-Lex-Sheehan-ebook/dp
/B0725B8MYW
# License: MIT, 2017 Lex Sheehan LLC
MY_DEV_DIR=~/dev
CURRENT_GO_VERSION=1.9.2
USES_TOML_CONFIG_YN=no
```

Miscellaneous Information and How-Tos

```
LOCAL_BIN_DIR=/usr/local/bin/
# ------------------------------------------------------------
# Verify variables above are correct.  Do not modify lines below.
if [ -L "$(pwd)" ]; then
    echo "You must be in the real project directory to run this init
script.  You are currently in a linked directory"
    echo "Running:   ln -l \"$(pwd)\""
    ls -l "$(pwd)"
    return
fi
CURRENT_GOVERSION="go$CURRENT_GO_VERSION"
ORIG_DIR="$( cd "$( dirname "${BASH_SOURCE[0]}" )" && pwd )"
DEV_DIR="$MY_DEV_DIR/$(basename $ORIG_DIR)"
PROJECT_DIR_LINK="$MY_DEV_DIR/$(basename $ORIG_DIR)"
if [ -L "$PROJECT_DIR_LINK" ]; then
    rm "$PROJECT_DIR_LINK"
fi
if [ ! -d "$MY_DEV_DIR" ]; then
    mkdir "$MY_DEV_DIR"
fi
# Create link to project directory in MY_DEV_DIR
set -x
ln -s "$ORIG_DIR" "$PROJECT_DIR_LINK"
{ set +x; } 2>/dev/null
cd "$PROJECT_DIR_LINK"
export GOPATH=$ORIG_DIR
export GOBIN=$ORIG_DIR/bin
if [ -e "$GOBIN" ]; then
    rm "$GOBIN/*" 2>/dev/null
else
    mkdir "$GOBIN"
fi
#[ $(which "$(basename $(pwd))") ] && { echo "An executable named
$(basename $(pwd)) found on path here: $(which $(basename $(pwd))).
Continue anyway? (yes/no)"; read CONTINUE_YN; if [[ "$CONTINUE_YN" =~
^(yes|y)$ ]]; then echo 'Okay, but when you run go-run it may run the pre-
existing binary.'; else echo "You might want to rename this project
directory ($(basename $(pwd))) to a name that does not match a pre-existing
binary name."; return; fi; } 2>/dev/null
APP_NAME=$(basename $(pwd))
GOVERSION=$(go version)
echo "Installed Go version: $GOVERSION"
if [[ $(type goenv) ]]; then
    # Attempt to automatically set desired/current go version.  This
requires goenv.
    . goenv "$CURRENT_GO_VERSION"
    echo "GOVERSION: $GOVERSION"
    echo "CURRENT_GOVERSION: $CURRENT_GOVERSION"
```

Appendix

```
        if [ -z "$GOVERSION" ] || [[ "$(echo $GOVERSION | awk '{print $3}')" !=
"$CURRENT_GOVERSION" ]]; then
            echo "Expected Go version $CURRENT_GOVERSION to be installed"
            return
        fi
    else
        if [ -z "$GOVERSION" ] || [[ "$(echo $GOVERSION | awk '{print $3}')" !=
"$CURRENT_GOVERSION" ]]; then
            echo "Expected Go version $CURRENT_GOVERSION to be installed.
Consider using github.com/l3x/goenv to manage your go runtimes."
            return
        fi
fi
command -v goimports >/dev/null 2>&1 || { echo >&2 "Missing goimports.  For
details, see: https://github.com/bradfitz/goimports"; return; }
command -v glide >/dev/null 2>&1 || { echo >&2 "Missing glide.  For
details, see: https://github.com/Masterminds/glide"; return; }
if [ ! -e ./src ]; then
    mkdir src
fi

if [ ! -e ./src/mypackage/ ]; then
    mkdir ./src/mypackage
fi

if [ ! -e ./src/mypackage/myname.go ]; then
    cat > ./src/mypackage/myname.go <<TEXT
package mypackage

func MyName() string { return "Alice" }
TEXT
fi

if [ ! -e ./main.go ]; then
    cat > ./main.go <<TEXT
package main

import (
    "mypackage"
)

func main() {
    println("hello from main.go")
    println(mypackage.MyName() + " says hi from mypackage")
}
TEXT
fi
```

```
if [ ! -e ./.gitignore ]; then
    cat > ./.gitignore <<TEXT
# Binaries for programs and plugins
*.exe
*.dll
*.so
*.dylib

# Test binary, build with `go test -c`
*.test

# Output of the go coverage tool, specifically when used with LiteIDE
*.out

# Project-local glide cache, RE:
https://github.com/Masterminds/glide/issues/736
.glide/

# Temporary backup file created by sed in prune-project alias
main.go-e
TEXT
fi

if [ "${PATH/$GOBIN}" == "$PATH" ] ; then
  export PATH=$PATH:$GOBIN
fi

if [[ "$USES_TOML_CONFIG_YN" =~ ^(yes|y)$ ]]; then
    if [ ! -e ./config.toml ]; then
        echo You were missing the config.toml configuration file...
Creating bare config.toml file ...
        echo -e "# Runtime environment\napp_env = \"development\"" >
config.toml
    fi
    ls -l config.toml
    alias go-run="go install && $APP_NAME -config ./config.toml"
else
    alias go-run="go install && $APP_NAME"
fi
alias go-test='go test  ./... 2>&1 | grep -v "$(basename $(pwd))\t\[no test
files"'
alias go-test-bench='go test -bench=. ./... 2>&1 | grep -v "$(basename
$(pwd))\t\[no test files"'
alias glide-ignore-project-dirs="printf \"ignore:\n$(find ./src -maxdepth 1
-type d | tail -n +2 | sed 's|./src\/||' | sed -e 's/^/- \.\//')\n\""
alias mvglide='mkdir -p vendors && mv vendor/ vendors/src/ && export
GOPATH=$(pwd)/vendors:$(pwd);echo "vendor packages have been moved to
$(pwd)/vendors and your GOPATH: $GOPATH"'
```

```
alias glide-update='if [ ! -z $(readlink `pwd`) ]; then export LINKED=true
&& pushd "$(readlink `pwd`)"; fi;rm -rf {vendor,vendors};rm glide.*;export
GOPATH=$(pwd):$(pwd)/vendors && export GOBIN=$(pwd)/bin && glide init --
non-interactive && glide-ignore-project-dirs >> glide.yaml && glide up &&
mvglide && if [ $LINKED==true ]; then popd;fi'
alias prune-project="(rm -rf bin pkg vendors;rm glide.lock;rm -rf
./src/mypackage;sed -i -e '/mypackage/ s/^#*/\/\//' main.go) 2>/dev/null"
alias show-path='echo $PATH | tr ":" "\n"'
alias prune-path='export PATH="$(echo $PATH | tr ":" "\n" | uniq | grep -v
"$(dirname $ORIG_DIR)" | tr "\n" ":")"; if [[ "$PATH" =~ ':'$ ]]; then
export PATH="${PATH::-1}";fi'
alias find-imports='find . -type f -name "*.go" -exec grep -A3 "import" {}
\; -exec echo {} \; -exec echo --- \;'
alias go-fmt='set -x;goimports -w main.go src/*;{ set +x; } 2>/dev/null'
tdml() {
    if [ -z $1 ]; then LEVEL=2; else LEVEL=$1;fi
    tree -C -d -L $LEVEL
}
get-go-binary() {
    GO_BINARY_URL="$1"
    if [ -z $GO_BINARY_URL ]; then
        echo "Missing GO_BINARY_URL.  Usage: get-go-binary <GO_BINARY_URL>
Example: get-go-binary github.com/nicksnyder/go-i18n/goi18n"
        return
    fi
    TMP_DIR="tmp_dir_$RANDOM"; mkdir "$TMP_DIR"; pushd "$TMP_DIR"; export
GOPATH="$(pwd)"; go get -u $GO_BINARY_URL; popd; rm -rf "$TMP_DIR"
}
echo You should only need to run this init script once.
echo Add Go source code files under the src directory.
echo After updating dependencies, i.e., adding a new import statement, run:
glide-update
echo To build and run your app, run:   go-run
```

All we need to do is verify that the preceding variables the dotted line are correct:

```
MY_DEV_DIR=~/dev
CURRENT_GO_VERSION=1.9.2
USES_TOML_CONFIG_YN=no
LOCAL_BIN_DIR=/usr/local/bin/
```

If we don't change anything, the script will work using go version 1.9 and it will create a ~/dev directory if it does not already exist.

Running the init script

To get our project ready for development, in our terminal, just run `.` `init`.

```
▌ ~/clients/packt/dev/fp-go/2-design-patterns/ch07-onion-arch/01_dependency-rule-good $ . init
+++ basename /Users/lex/clients/packt/dev/fp-go/2-design-patterns/ch07-onion-arch/01_dependency-rule-good
++ PROJECT_DIR_LINK=/Users/lex/dev/01_dependency-rule-good
++ ln -s /Users/lex/clients/packt/dev/fp-go/2-design-patterns/ch07-onion-arch/01_dependency-rule-good /Users/lex/dev/01_dependency-rule-good
Installed Go version: go version go1.9 darwin/amd64
Switching Go to version 1.9 ...
Exported GOBIN=/Users/lex/clients/packt/dev/fp-go/2-design-patterns/ch07-onion-arch/01_dependency-rule-good/bin
You should only need to run this init script once.
Add Go source code files under the src directory.
After updating dependencies, i.e., adding a new import statement, run: glide-update
To build and run your app, run: go-run
▌ ~/dev/01_dependency-rule-good $ tree -C -d -L 2; find . -type f
.
└── src
    ├── packagea
    └── packageb

3 directories
./config.toml
./glide.yaml
./init
./main.go
./src/packagea/featurea.go
./src/packageb/featureb.go
```

Note that `source` and "." do the same thing; they run the following command in the context of the current shell environment.

Note that our current directory path is shorter. We're in a newly linked directory. It's a link file in `MY_DEV_DIR`. A benefit or side-effect of running this script is that we can go to our `MY_DEV_DIR` to see what projects we've worked on lately. It's also nice not to have such a long path name in our terminal (assuming we display our full, current directory path in our shell prompt).

Re-examining the initial directory structure and files

We also ran the tree command to see our project directories and ran the file command to see our files.

The only new file the init script created is `PROJECT_DIR_LINK` (in this example, `/home/lex/dev/01_dependency-rule-good`).

The goenv shows what's been updated

That init script must have done something else for us, right? Let's run our goenv info command again to see what else it did:

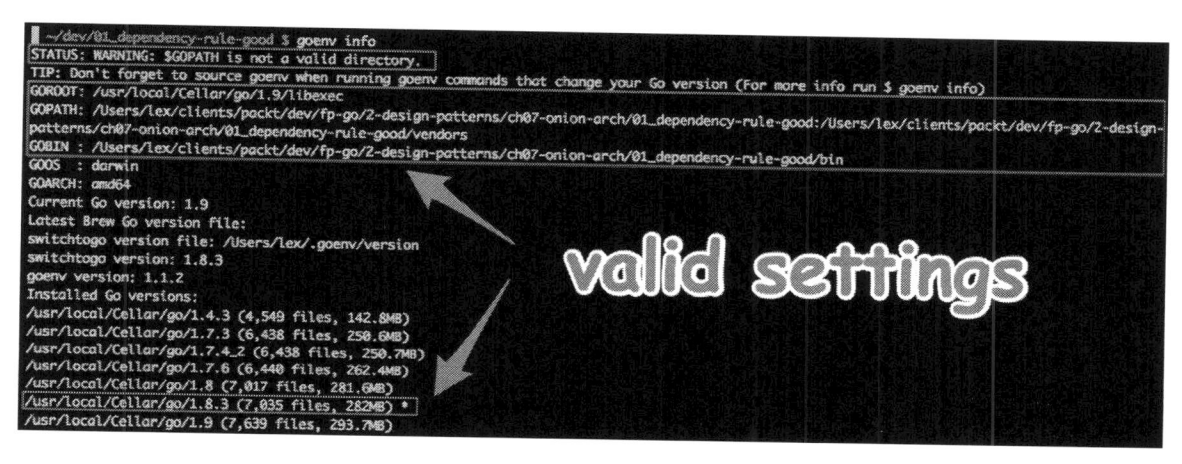

```
 ~/dev/01_dependency-rule-good $ goenv info
STATUS: WARNING: $GOPATH is not a valid directory.
TIP: Don't forget to source goenv when running goenv commands that change your Go version (For more info run $ goenv info)
GOROOT: /usr/local/Cellar/go/1.9/libexec
GOPATH: /Users/lex/clients/packt/dev/fp-go/2-design-patterns/ch07-onion-arch/01_dependency-rule-good:/Users/lex/clients/packt/dev/fp-go/2-design-patterns/ch07-onion-arch/01_dependency-rule-good/vendors
GOBIN : /Users/lex/clients/packt/dev/fp-go/2-design-patterns/ch07-onion-arch/01_dependency-rule-good/bin
GOOS  : darwin
GOARCH: amd64
Current Go version: 1.9
Latest Brew Go version file:
switchtogo version file: /Users/lex/.goenv/version
switchtogo version: 1.8.3
goenv version: 1.1.2
Installed Go versions:
/usr/local/Cellar/go/1.4.3 (4,549 files, 142.8MB)
/usr/local/Cellar/go/1.7.3 (6,438 files, 250.6MB)
/usr/local/Cellar/go/1.7.4_2 (6,438 files, 250.7MB)
/usr/local/Cellar/go/1.7.6 (6,440 files, 262.4MB)
/usr/local/Cellar/go/1.8 (7,017 files, 281.6MB)
/usr/local/Cellar/go/1.8.3 (7,035 files, 282MB) *
/usr/local/Cellar/go/1.9 (7,639 files, 293.7MB)
```

valid settings

We get a warning because the GOPATH is actually a path. (Most other vendor solutions will not work properly if GOPATH is anything other than a single directory.) Our GOPATH is constructed just like our PATH environment variable. It's composed of paths appended together, separated by a colon character.

Our GOPATH is comprised of two values: the src path (with our project source files) and the vendors path (with our third-party dependency source files).

Running glide-update to get third-party dependency files

After we add files to our src directory and have some import statements and before we run our Go app, let's ensure that Go has all the source files for our dependencies that it requires to build our application.

Miscellaneous Information and How-Tos

Anytime we update any import statement (and before we run our application), we run `glide-update`.

```
 ~/dev/01_dependency-rule-good $ glide-update
~/clients/packt/dev/fp-go/2-design-patterns/ch07-onion-arch/01_dependency-rule-good ~/dev/01_dependency-rule-good
[INFO]	Generating a YAML configuration file and guessing the dependencies
[INFO]	Attempting to import from other package managers (use --skip-import to skip)
[INFO]	Scanning code to look for dependencies
[INFO]	Writing configuration file (glide.yaml)
[INFO]	You can now edit the glide.yaml file. Consider:
[INFO]	--> Using versions and ranges. See https://glide.sh/docs/versions/
[INFO]	--> Adding additional metadata. See https://glide.sh/docs/glide.yaml/
[INFO]	--> Running the config-wizard command to improve the versions in your configuration
[INFO]	Downloading dependencies. Please wait...
[INFO]	No references set.
[INFO]	Resolving imports
[INFO]	Downloading dependencies. Please wait...
[INFO]	Setting references for remaining imports
[INFO]	No references set.
[INFO]	Exporting resolved dependencies...
[INFO]	Replacing existing vendor dependencies
[INFO]	Project relies on 0 dependencies.
vendor packages have been moved to /Users/lex/clients/packt/dev/fp-go/2-design-patterns/ch07-onion-arch/01_dependency-rule-good/vendors and your
GOPATH: /Users/lex/clients/packt/dev/fp-go/2-design-patterns/ch07-onion-arch/01_dependency-rule-good:/Users/lex/clients/packt/dev/fp-go/2-design-
patterns/ch07-onion-arch/01_dependency-rule-good/vendors
~/dev/01_dependency-rule-good
 ~/dev/01_dependency-rule-good $ go-run
A
B
```

We can run our Go application by typing `go-run`. This will compile our application (putting the binary in our `GOBIN` directory) and run it. Our application outputs two lines with the characters **A** and **B**.

Running `glide-update` will create the typical `vendor` directory and quickly rename it to vendors (which is a further indication that this is not a standard glide installation). We don't have to be a glide expert to get our dependencies managed by glide. Anytime we update dependencies (and change an import statement), we just run the glide-update alias and all the dependencies' code will go into the vendors directory and our `GOPATH` will know to look there when it compiles. Also note that if you use a fancy IDE that requires you to enter your `GOROOT`, `GOBIN`, and `GOPATH`, you just need to run `goenv-info` to see what our project correct settings are.

If `glide-update` reports any errors, it will be up to us resolve them.

Adding standard library imports

We'll add the `fmt` package to the import statement in `packagea`:

```
package packagea

import (
    b "packageb"
    "fmt"
)

func Atask() {
    fmt.Println("A")
    b.Btask()
}
```

We'll add the log package to the import statement in `packageb`:

```
package packageb

import (
    "log"
)

func Btask() {
    log.Println("B")
}
```

After adding our imports, we source init:

```
~ $ cd /Users/lex/clients/packt/dev/fp-go/4-appendix/02_dependency-with-import
~/clients/packt/dev/fp-go/4-appendix/02_dependency-with-import $ . init
+++ basename /Users/lex/clients/packt/dev/fp-go/4-appendix/02_dependency-with-import
++ PROJECT_DIR_LINK=~/Users/lex/dev/02_dependency-with-import
++ ln -s /Users/lex/clients/packt/dev/fp-go/4-appendix/02_dependency-with-import /Users/lex/dev/02_dependency-with-import
Installed Go version: go version go1.9 darwin/amd64
Switching Go to version 1.9 ...
Exported GOBIN=/Users/lex/clients/packt/dev/fp-go/4-appendix/02_dependency-with-import/bin
You should only need to run this init script once.
Add Go source code files under the src directory.
After updating dependencies, i.e., adding a new import statement, run: glide-update
To build and run your app, run: go-run
```

Next, we update our dependencies:

```
~/dev/02_dependency-with-import $ glide-update
~/clients/packt/dev/fp-go/4-appendix/02_dependency-with-import ~/dev/02_dependency-with-import
[INFO] Generating a YAML configuration file and guessing the dependencies
[INFO] Attempting to import from other package managers (use --skip-import to skip)
[INFO] Scanning code to look for dependencies
[INFO] Writing configuration file (glide.yaml)
[INFO] You can now edit the glide.yaml file. Consider:
[INFO] --> Using versions and ranges. See https://glide.sh/docs/versions/
[INFO] --> Adding additional metadata. See https://glide.sh/docs/glide.yaml/
[INFO] --> Running the config-wizard command to improve the versions in your configuration
[INFO] Downloading dependencies. Please wait...
[INFO] No references set.
[INFO] Resolving imports
[INFO] Downloading dependencies. Please wait...
[INFO] Setting references for remaining imports
[INFO] No references set.
[INFO] Exporting resolved dependencies...
[INFO] Replacing existing vendor dependencies
[INFO] Project relies on 0 dependencies.
vendor packages have been moved to /Users/lex/clients/packt/dev/fp-go/4-appendix/02_dependency-with-import/vendors and your GOPATH: /Users/lex/cl
ients/packt/dev/fp-go/4-appendix/02_dependency-with-import:/Users/lex/clients/packt/dev/fp-go/4-appendix/02_dependency-with-import/vendors
~/dev/02_dependency-with-import
```

Now, we can run our app:

```
~/dev/02_dependency-with-import $ go-run
A
2017/10/03 18:06:06 B
```

The only difference is that the `log.Println` command adds a time stamp. We see that it works, but what about the dependencies? Does the vendor's directory now have some files?

```
~/dev/02_dependency-with-import $ tree -C -d -L 2; find . -type f
├── bin
├── pkg
│   └── darwin_amd64
├── src
│   ├── packagea
│   └── packageb
└── vendors
    └── src

8 directories
./bin/02_dependency-with-import
./config.toml
./glide.lock
./glide.yaml
./init
./main.go
./pkg/darwin_amd64/packagea.a
./pkg/darwin_amd64/packageb.a
./src/packagea/featurea.go
./src/packageb/featureb.go
```

Nope. Still no files. Why?

That's because `fmt` and `log` are both from Go's standard library.

The Go standard library

The Go standard library is a set of core packages that enhance and extend the language. By *core*, we mean that every time we compile our Go app, we'll get that pkg directory and it will be filled with the Go standard library packages.

Go standard library packages have the following features:

- They add no extra overhead
- They are guaranteed to always exist
- They are guaranteed to always be backwards compatible (won't break between release cycles)

Using packages from Go's standard library will make our code easier to manage and more reliable.

Example packages include the following:

- log
- fmt
- encoding/json
- database/sql/driver
- net/http

> For details regarding Go's Standard Library, refer to: https://golang.org/pkg/

Adding third-party imports

For this example, we'll import a simple third-party utility package, go-goodies/go_utils. I created go-goodies/go_utils back in 2015 (when I was still very much learning the language). I have not modified much of the code in a while, so that I can look back to see how much I've learned. It all should still work properly, but in many cases, there are better ways to accomplish things. You've been warned, so please don't judge.

Importing statement referencing go_utils

Let's add a third import, u "github.com/go-goodies/go_utils".

Note that we use the preceding u in the Atask function to reference the PadLeft function:

```
package packagea

import (
    b "packageb"
    "fmt"
    u "github.com/go-goodies/go_utils"
)

func Atask() {
    fmt.Println(u.PadLeft("A", 3))
    b.Btask()
}
```

We can use the grep command on our source files for import statements:

```
~/dev/03_with-third-party-import $ find . -type f -name "*.go" -exec grep -A3 "import" {} \; -exec echo {} \; -exec echo --- \;
import (
        a "packagea"
)
./main.go
---
import (
        b "packageb"
        "fmt"
        u "go-goodies/go_utils"
./src/packagea/featurea.go
---
import (
        "log"
)
./src/packageb/featureb.go
---
```

Since we updated an import statement, we need to run `glide-update` before we run our app:

```
~/dev/03_with-third-party-import $ glide-update
~/clients/packt/dev/fp-go/4-appendix/03_with-third-party-import ~/dev/03_with-third-party-import
[INFO] Generating a YAML configuration file and guessing the dependencies
[INFO] Attempting to import from other package managers (use --skip-import to skip)
[INFO] Scanning code to look for dependencies
[INFO]  --> Found reference to github.com/go-goodies/go_utils
[INFO] Writing configuration file (glide.yaml)
[INFO] You can now edit the glide.yaml file. Consider:
[INFO]  --> Using versions and ranges. See https://glide.sh/docs/versions/
[INFO]  --> Adding additional metadata. See https://glide.sh/docs/glide.yaml/
[INFO]  --> Running the config-wizard command to improve the versions in your configuration
[INFO] Downloading dependencies. Please wait...
[INFO]  --> Fetching github.com/go-goodies/go_utils.
[INFO] Resolving imports
[INFO]  --> Fetching github.com/margnus1/go-deepcopy.
[INFO]  --> Fetching github.com/nu7hatch/gouuid.
[INFO] Downloading dependencies. Please wait...
[INFO] Setting references for remaining imports
[INFO] Exporting resolved dependencies...
[INFO]  --> Exporting github.com/go-goodies/go_utils
[INFO]  --> Exporting github.com/margnus1/go-deepcopy
[INFO]  --> Exporting github.com/nu7hatch/gouuid
[INFO] Replacing existing vendor dependencies
[INFO] Project relies on 3 dependencies.
vendor packages have been moved to /Users/lex/clients/packt/dev/fp-go/4-appendix/03_with-third-party-import/vendors and your GOPATH: /Users/lex/c
lients/packt/dev/fp-go/4-appendix/03_with-third-party-import:/Users/lex/clients/packt/dev/fp-go/4-appendix/03_with-third-party-import/vendors
~/dev/03_with-third-party-import
```

Miscellaneous Information and How-Tos

This time, we can see that `glide-update` pulled in the third-party (`go_utils`) files under the vendor's directory:

```
~/dev/03_with-third-party-import $ tree -C -d -L 2; find . -type f
├── src
│   ├── packagea
│   └── packageb
└── vendors
    └── src

5 directories
./config.toml
./glide.lock
./glide.yaml
./init
./main.go
./src/packagea/featurea.go
./src/packageb/featureb.go
./vendors/src/github.com/go-goodies/go_utils/contains.go
./vendors/src/github.com/go-goodies/go_utils/file.go
./vendors/src/github.com/go-goodies/go_utils/golang-gopher-utils.png
./vendors/src/github.com/go-goodies/go_utils/LICENSE
./vendors/src/github.com/go-goodies/go_utils/num_conversions.go
./vendors/src/github.com/go-goodies/go_utils/README.md
./vendors/src/github.com/go-goodies/go_utils/singleton.go
./vendors/src/github.com/go-goodies/go_utils/types.go
./vendors/src/github.com/go-goodies/go_utils/utils.go
./vendors/src/github.com/go-goodies/go_utils/utils_test.go
./vendors/src/github.com/margnus1/go-deepcopy/.gitignore
./vendors/src/github.com/margnus1/go-deepcopy/deepcopy.go
./vendors/src/github.com/margnus1/go-deepcopy/deepcopy_test.go
./vendors/src/github.com/margnus1/go-deepcopy/LICENSE
./vendors/src/github.com/margnus1/go-deepcopy/Makefile
./vendors/src/github.com/margnus1/go-deepcopy/README.md
./vendors/src/github.com/nu7hatch/gouuid/.gitignore
./vendors/src/github.com/nu7hatch/gouuid/COPYING
./vendors/src/github.com/nu7hatch/gouuid/example_test.go
./vendors/src/github.com/nu7hatch/gouuid/README.md
./vendors/src/github.com/nu7hatch/gouuid/uuid.go
./vendors/src/github.com/nu7hatch/gouuid/uuid_test.go
```

We can see that the `go-goodies/go_utils` references the following third-party packages:

- http://github.com/margnus1/go-deepcopy
- http://github.com/nu7hatch/gouuid

When we run our app, we see the effect of using the `PadLeft` function:

```
~/dev/03_with-third-party-import $ go-run
  A
B
~/dev/03_with-third-party-import $
```
u.PadLeft("A", 3)

> You can use the init script and the aliases it provides with confidence that they will not touch your source files (well, except prune-project will comment out lines in `./main.go` that reference `mypackage`). The files they modify include the soft linked directory file in your `~/dev` directory and the `bin`, `pkg` and vendors directories.

Development workflow summary

How you manage your dependencies, build, run, and deploy your applications is a matter of preference. It's often a good idea to get all of the developers in your team to build applications the same way. The techniques shared in this section demonstrate the way I built the demo applications for this book. I kept it simple. However, the rest of the story is that I rarely build applications in isolation like I did for this book. Nearly every time, I use Docker in my `development/test/deployment` workflow. Note that the use of Docker is out of scope of this book.

Troubleshooting dot init

This is how I resolved the build errors that occurred when converting Chapter 4, *SOLID Design in Go*, to the dot init technique.

First, I used the `cd` command to direct to the project's root directory (where the `project` is Chapter 4, *SOLID Design in Go*, source code):

```
 ~/clients/packt/dev/fp-go/1-functional-fundamentals/ch03-hof/01_hof $ . init
+++ basename /Users/lex/clients/packt/dev/fp-go/1-functional-fundamentals/ch03-hof/01_hof
++ PROJECT_DIR_LINK=/Users/lex/dev/01_hof
++ ln -s /Users/lex/clients/packt/dev/fp-go/1-functional-fundamentals/ch03-hof/01_hof /Users/lex/dev/01_hof
Installed Go version: go version go1.9 darwin/amd64
Switching Go to version 1.9 ...
You should only need to run this init script once.
Add Go source code files under the src directory.
After updating dependencies, i.e., adding a new import statement, run: glide-update
To build and run your app, run: go-run
```

Miscellaneous Information and How-Tos

Next, I ran `glide-update` to tell Glide to put the dependencies in the vendors directory:

[Terminal screenshot showing main.go with annotation "Dot init: change import to 'hof'" and glide-update output with errors about unable to checkout github.com/l3x/fp-in-go]

But, that failed because the `import` statement was incorrect:

```
~/dev/01_hof $ find src -type f
src/hof/cars.csv
src/hof/cars.go
src/hof/generator.go
src/hof/more_cars.csv
src/hof/restful.go
src/hof/types.go
src/hof/utils.go
```

(annotation: "created hof dir and moved files")

Appendix

Here's what the imports look like now:

```
~/dev/01_hof $ find-imports
import (
    . "hof"
    "log"
    "os"
)
./main.go
---
import (
    "fmt"
    s "strings"
    "regexp"
)
./src/hof/cars.go
---
import (
    "sync"
    "log"
)
./src/hof/generator.go
---
import (
    "fmt"
    "github.com/julienschmidt/httprouter"
    "net/http"
)
./src/hof/restful.go
---
import (
    "path/filepath"
    "encoding/csv"
    "os"
)
./src/hof/utils.go
---
```

import ". hof" in main.go

3rd party package

Tell Glide to put third-party packages in the vendor's directory.

```
~/dev/01_hof $ glide-update
~/clients/packt/dev/fp-go/1-functional-fundamentals/ch03-hof/01_hof ~/dev/01_hof
[INFO]    Generating a YAML configuration file and guessing the dependencies
[INFO]    Attempting to import from other package managers (use --skip-import to skip)
[INFO]    Scanning code to look for dependencies
[INFO]    --> Found reference to github.com/julienschmidt/httprouter
[INFO]    Writing configuration file (glide.yaml)
[INFO]    You can now edit the glide.yaml file. Consider:
[INFO]    --> Using versions and ranges. See https://glide.sh/docs/versions/
[INFO]    --> Adding additional metadata. See https://glide.sh/docs/glide.yaml/
[INFO]    --> Running the config-wizard command to improve the versions in your configuration
[INFO]    Downloading dependencies. Please wait...
[INFO]    --> Fetching updates for github.com/julienschmidt/httprouter.
[INFO]    Resolving imports
[INFO]    Downloading dependencies. Please wait...
[INFO]    Setting references for remaining imports
[INFO]    Exporting resolved dependencies...
[INFO]    --> Exporting github.com/julienschmidt/httprouter
[INFO]    Replacing existing vendor dependencies
[INFO]    Project relies on 1 dependencies.
vendor packages have been moved to /Users/lex/clients/packt/dev/fp-go/1-functional-fundamentals/ch03-hof/01_hof/vendors an
d your GOPATH: /Users/lex/clients/packt/dev/fp-go/1-functional-fundamentals/ch03-hof/01_hof:/Users/lex/clients/packt/dev/f
p-go/1-functional-fundamentals/ch03-hof/01_hof/vendors
~/dev/01_hof
```

Miscellaneous Information and How-Tos

Compile and run:

```
~/dev/01_hof $ go-run
-bash: 01_hof: command not found
```

Bummer! `.init` can't find the binary.

No worries, just cd back to the original project root directory and re-source init:

```
~/dev/01_hof $ cd -
/Users/lex/clients/packt/dev/fp-go/1-functional-fundamentals/ch03-hof/01_hof
~/clients/packt/dev/fp-go/1-functional-fundamentals/ch03-hof/01_hof $ . init
+++ basename /Users/lex/clients/packt/dev/fp-go/1-functional-fundamentals/ch03-hof/01_hof
++ PROJECT_DIR_LINK=/Users/lex/dev/01_hof
++ ln -s /Users/lex/clients/packt/dev/fp-go/1-functional-fundamentals/ch03-hof/01_hof /Users/lex/dev/01_hof
Installed Go version: go version go1.9 darwin/amd64
Switching Go to version 1.9 ...
You should only need to run this init script once.
Add Go source code files under the src directory.
After updating dependencies, i.e., adding a new import statement, run: glide-update
To build and run your app, run: go-run
~/dev/01_hof $ go-run
main.go:7:2: cannot find package "github.com/julienschmidt/httprouter" in any of:
        /usr/local/Cellar/go/1.9/libexec/src/github.com/julienschmidt/httprouter (from $GOROOT)
        /Users/lex/clients/packt/dev/fp-go/1-functional-fundamentals/ch03-hof/01_hof/src/github.com/julienschmidt/httprouter (from $GOPATH)
```

> **TIP**: If you run `go-run` and you see *command not found*, just rerun `init`, `glide-update`, and `go-run`.

Still more problems!

Appendix

Oh, right. I forgot to read the init's message and failed to run `glide-update`. Let's do that next:

```
 ~/dev/01_hof $ glide-update
~/clients/packt/dev/fp-go/1-functional-fundamentals/ch03-hof/01_hof ~/dev/01_hof
[INFO]    Generating a YAML configuration file and guessing the dependencies
[INFO]    Attempting to import from other package managers (use --skip-import to skip)
[INFO]    Scanning code to look for dependencies
[INFO]    --> Found reference to github.com/julienschmidt/httprouter
[INFO]    Writing configuration file (glide.yaml)
[INFO]    You can now edit the glide.yaml file. Consider:
[INFO]    --> Using versions and ranges. See https://glide.sh/docs/versions/
[INFO]    --> Adding additional metadata. See https://glide.sh/docs/glide.yaml/
[INFO]    --> Running the config-wizard command to improve the versions in your configuration
[INFO]    Downloading dependencies. Please wait...
[INFO]    --> Fetching updates for github.com/julienschmidt/httprouter.
[INFO]    Resolving imports
[INFO]    Downloading dependencies. Please wait...
[INFO]    Setting references for remaining imports
[INFO]    Exporting resolved dependencies...
[INFO]    --> Exporting github.com/julienschmidt/httprouter
[INFO]    Replacing existing vendor dependencies
[INFO]    Project relies on 1 dependencies.
vendor packages have been moved to /Users/lex/clients/packt/dev/fp-go/1-functional-fundamentals/ch03-hof/01_hof/vendors an
d your GOPATH: /Users/lex/clients/packt/dev/fp-go/1-functional-fundamentals/ch03-hof/01_hof:/Users/lex/clients/packt/dev/f
p-go/1-functional-fundamentals/ch03-hof/01_hof/vendors
~/dev/01_hof
 ~/dev/01_hof $ go-run
2017/10/04 generator.go:78:
Generated Cars (1 to 4)
-------------------------
2017/10/04 generator.go:83: car: Honda Accord ES2
2017/10/04 generator.go:83: car: Lexus IS250
2017/10/04 generator.go:83: car: Honda CR-V
2017/10/04 utils.go:15:
GenerateCars(1, 3)
-------------------------
2017/10/04 utils.go:17: car: Honda Accord ES2
2017/10/04 utils.go:17: car: Honda CR-V
2017/10/04 utils.go:17: car: Lexus IS250
2017/10/04 generator.go:78:
Generated Cars (1 to 15)
-------------------------
2017/10/04 generator.go:83: car: Ford F-150
2017/10/04 generator.go:83: car: Lexus IS250
2017/10/04 generator.go:83: car: Lexus SC 430
2017/10/04 generator.go:83: car: Honda Accord ES2
2017/10/04 generator.go:83: car: Toyota Highlander
2017/10/04 generator.go:83: car: Honda CR-V
2017/10/04 generator.go:83: car: Chrysler Pacifica
2017/10/04 generator.go:83: car: Toyota 86
2017/10/04 generator.go:83: car: Dodge Charger
2017/10/04 generator.go:83: car: Dodge 330
2017/10/04 generator.go:83: car: GM Oldsmobile Cutlass Supreme
2017/10/04 generator.go:83: car: GM Hummer H3
2017/10/04 generator.go:83: car: Toyota RAV4
2017/10/04 generator.go:83: car: GM Hummer H2
2017/10/04 utils.go:15:
GenerateCars(1, 14), Domestic, Numeric, JSON
-------------------------
2017/10/04 utils.go:17: car: {"car": {"make": "Ford", "model": " F-150 XL"}}
2017/10/04 utils.go:17: car: {"car": {"make": "GM", "model": " Hummer H3 X"}}
2017/10/04 utils.go:17: car: {"car": {"make": "GM", "model": " Hummer H2 X"}}
```

Miscellaneous Information and How-Tos

Success!

What might happen when we try to run our tests?

When we `cd` into our `02_fib` example application and type `go test -bench=. ./...`, we might run into a few errors:

```
~/myprojects/fp-go/1-functional-fundamentals/ch01-pure-fp/02_fib $ go test -bench=. ./...
# _/Users/lex/myprojects/fp-go/1-functional-fundamentals/ch01-pure-fp/02_fib
package testmain
        imports testing/internal/testdeps: cannot find package "testing/internal/testdeps" in any of:
        /usr/local/Cellar/go/1.7.3/libexec/src/testing/internal/testdeps (from $GOROOT)
        /Users/lex/clients/kryptos/dev-lean/go/src/testing/internal/testdeps (from $GOPATH)    ← invalid
FAIL    _/Users/lex/myprojects/fp-go/1-functional-fundamentals/ch01-pure-fp/02_fib [setup failed]
```

This could happen if our `GOROOT` and/or `GOPATH` gets set to an invalid value.

There are two obvious errors here. The environment variables, `GOROOT` and `GOPATH`, are both invalid.

We find the path for `GOROOT` on a Mac computer by typing `brew info go|grep Cellar|grep -v export`:

```
~/myprojects/fp-go/1-functional-fundamentals/ch01-pure-fp/02_fib $ brew info go|grep Cellar|grep -v export
/usr/local/Cellar/go/1.4.3 (4,549 files, 142.8MB)
/usr/local/Cellar/go/1.7.3 (6,438 files, 250.6MB)
/usr/local/Cellar/go/1.7.4_2 (6,438 files, 250.7MB)
/usr/local/Cellar/go/1.7.6 (6,440 files, 262.4MB)
/usr/local/Cellar/go/1.8 (7,017 files, 281.6MB)
/usr/local/Cellar/go/1.8.3 (7,035 files, 282MB)
/usr/local/Cellar/go/1.9 (7,639 files, 293.7MB) *     ← most current
 ~/myprojects/fp-go/1-functional-fundamentals/ch01-pure-fp/02_fib $ export GOROOT=/usr/local/Cellar/go/1.9/libexec
 ~/myprojects/fp-go/1-functional-fundamentals/ch01-pure-fp/02_fib $ export GOPATH=$(pwd)              ← reset env vars
 ~/myprojects/fp-go/1-functional-fundamentals/ch01-pure-fp/02_fib $ export GOBIN=$GOPATH/bin
```

We just happen to know that we need to add the `libexec` directory to the path that returned the result as shown in previous screenshot, to set our `GOPATH`. We'll set our `GOPATH` to the root directory of our current application, that is, our current directory. We also set the `GOBIN` path to tell Go where to store the executable file that gets created when we compile our source code.

> Since we won't need to handle any third-party packages in this chapter, we don't need to deal with dependency management. There are more than a dozen Go dependency management tools available. For subsequent chapters, we'll use Glide (https://github.com/Masterminds/glide) for package management and a very lightweight wrapper dot init that further simplifies our build and run processes. For details, see the Appendix.

Note that dot init eliminates the possibility of these sort of errors.

That was a lot of information for a tool that is supposed to simplify things. True, but nearly every time, all you need to know is in the *TL;DR* section.

How to propose changes to Go

I am certain that Generics are not supported in Go (not even in Go 2.0), and as mentioned in the summary, I'm okay with that.

However, the feature that we'd benefit most greatly from, if Go had it, is **Tail Call Optimization (TCO)**.

The first step - search specs

Is it possible that Go already supports TCO? Time to find out.

First, I looked at the Go language specification for any mention of a TCO feature (https://golang.org/ref/spec).

I found nothing about TCO.

Miscellaneous Information and How-Tos

Second step - Google search

Next, I did the requisite Google search, and found this:

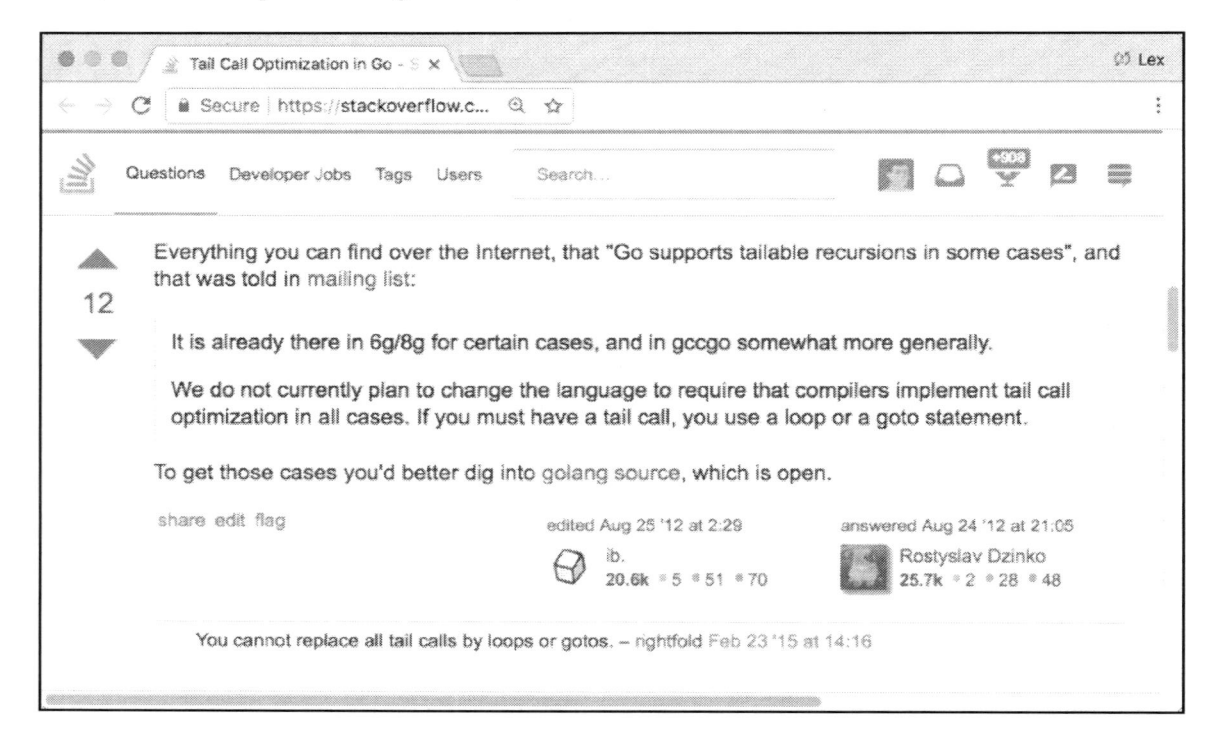

The official Golang change proposal process

Then, I learned about the process of proposing changes to Go (`https://github.com/golang/proposal/`).

Appendix

Search for existing issues

Here's the process.

First, visit `https://github.com/golang/go/issues` and search the language feature you'd like to be added to go, for example, type `tail call optimization`, as shown in the following screenshot:

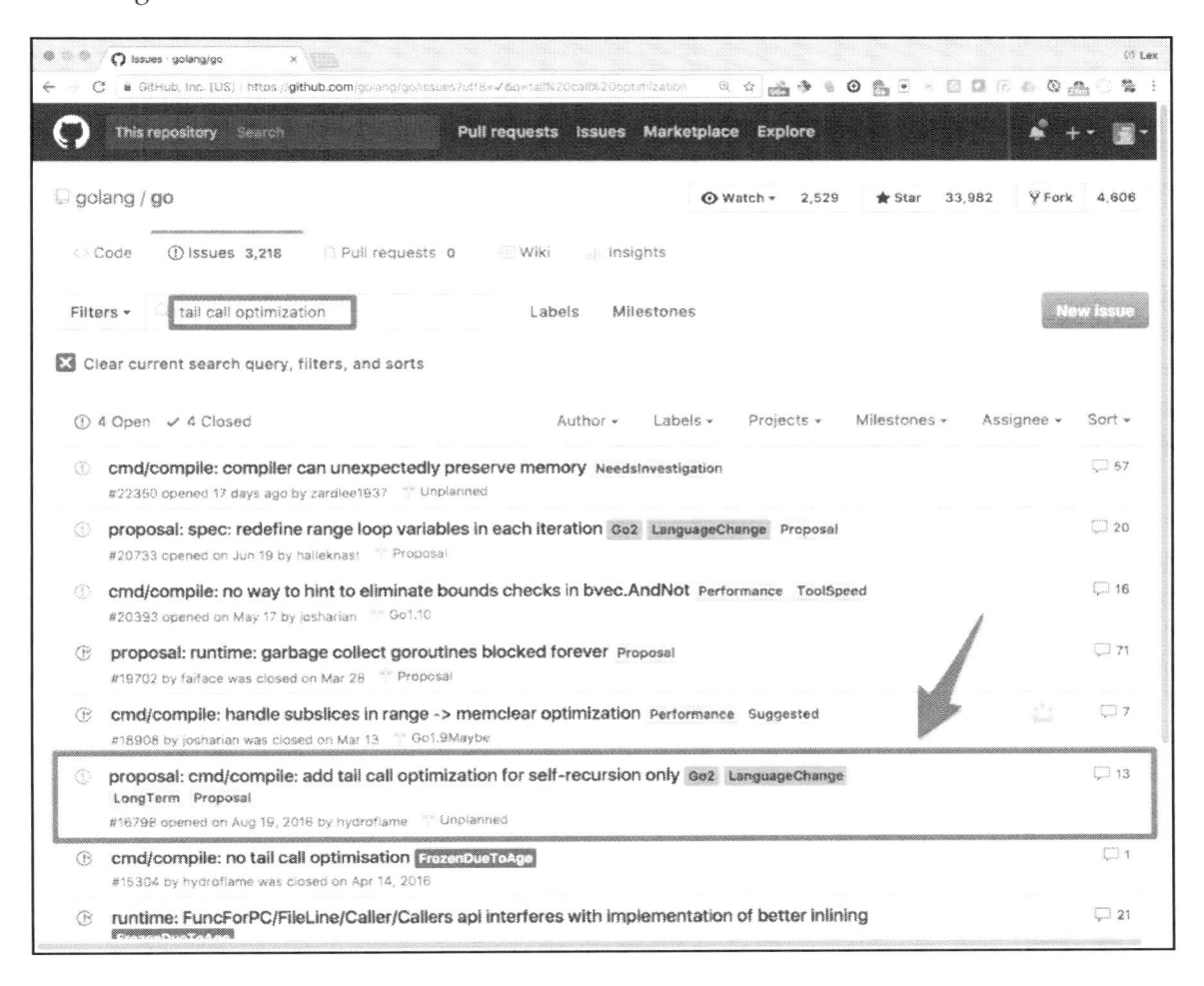

Miscellaneous Information and How-Tos

Reading existing proposals

I clicked on the line (with 13 comments) to see details:

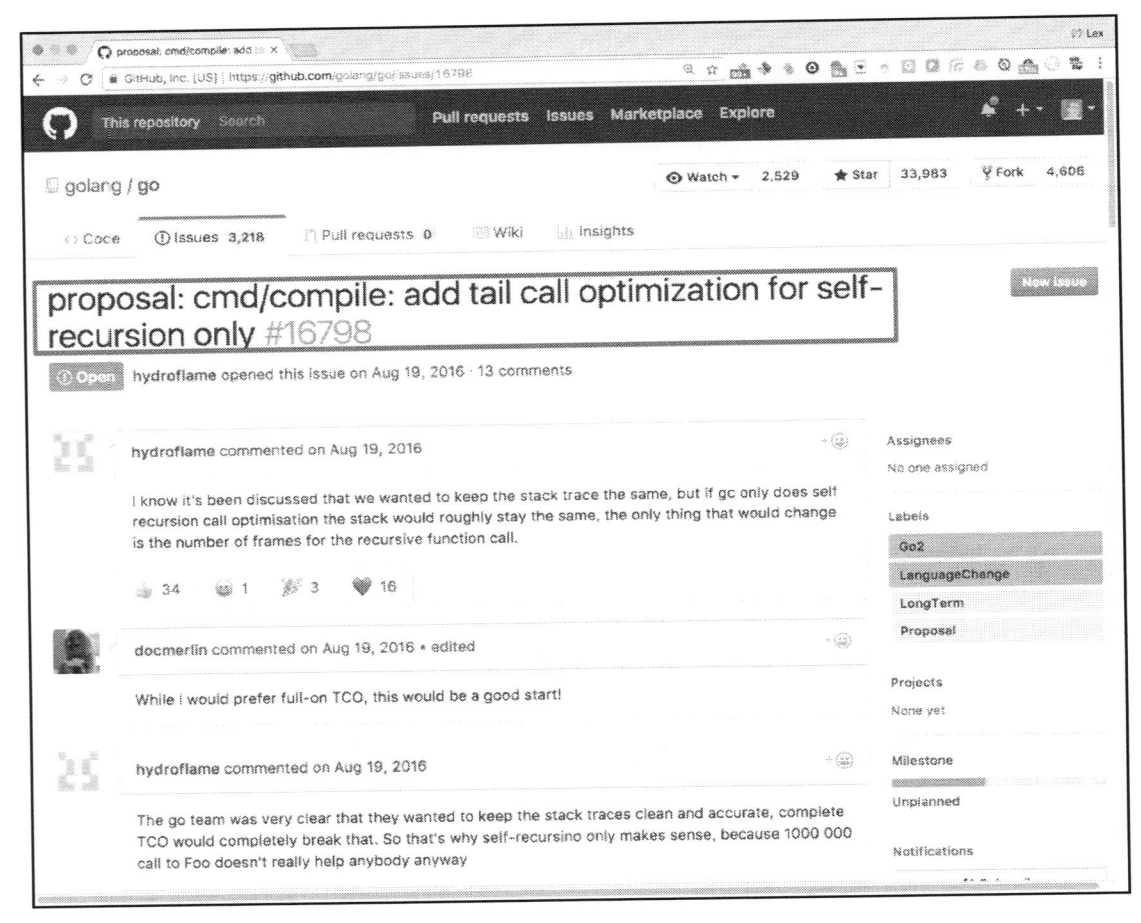

This is the feature that would dramatically improve our recursive function calls, for example, the Y-Combinator.

Remember our benchmark test results from running the `SumRecursive` function in `Chapter 1`, *Pure Functional Programming in Go*? It was about three times slower that the imperative version. The lack of TCO is the single most important reason why using FP on Go today is generally not recommended. Adding TCO to the list of Go's compiler features would solve this problem. That is why this low impact, high reward feature is so important.

There are other proposals that included more information in the initial post, which is a better way to present our idea. However, when we read the subsequent comments, details become more apparent. When I read the following comments, I was convinced that this proposal gets my vote:

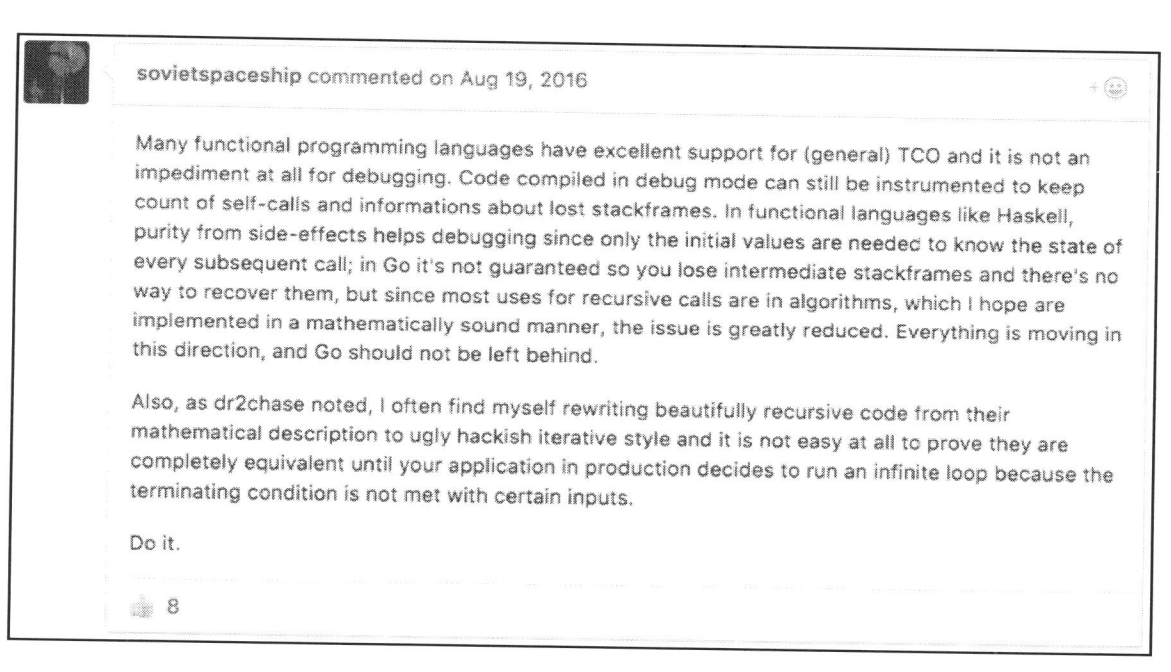

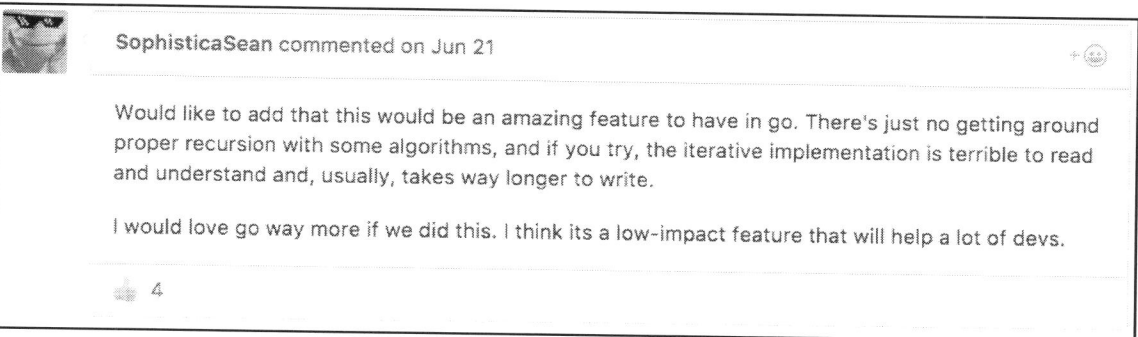

> **sovietspaceship** commented on Aug 19, 2016
>
> Many functional programming languages have excellent support for (general) TCO and it is not an impediment at all for debugging. Code compiled in debug mode can still be instrumented to keep count of self-calls and informations about lost stackframes. In functional languages like Haskell, purity from side-effects helps debugging since only the initial values are needed to know the state of every subsequent call; in Go it's not guaranteed so you lose intermediate stackframes and there's no way to recover them, but since most uses for recursive calls are in algorithms, which I hope are implemented in a mathematically sound manner, the issue is greatly reduced. Everything is moving in this direction, and Go should not be left behind.
>
> Also, as dr2chase noted, I often find myself rewriting beautifully recursive code from their mathematical description to ugly hackish iterative style and it is not easy at all to prove they are completely equivalent until your application in production decides to run an infinite loop because the terminating condition is not met with certain inputs.
>
> Do it.
>
> 👍 8

> **SophisticaSean** commented on Jun 21
>
> Would like to add that this would be an amazing feature to have in go. There's just no getting around proper recursion with some algorithms, and if you try, the iterative implementation is terrible to read and understand and, usually, takes way longer to write.
>
> I would love go way more if we did this. I think its a low-impact feature that will help a lot of devs.
>
> 👍 4

I think sharing an example of the `@tco` annotation I have in mind could bring more attention to this proposal. But it is about a month before my book is published. Do I enter the following comment in now and say, "*wait for my book to get all, the glory details.*" or wait? What the heck, I'm going for it.

Miscellaneous Information and How-Tos

Adding a comment to the existing TCO proposal

You can read the comment at `https://github.com/golang/go/issues/16798`.

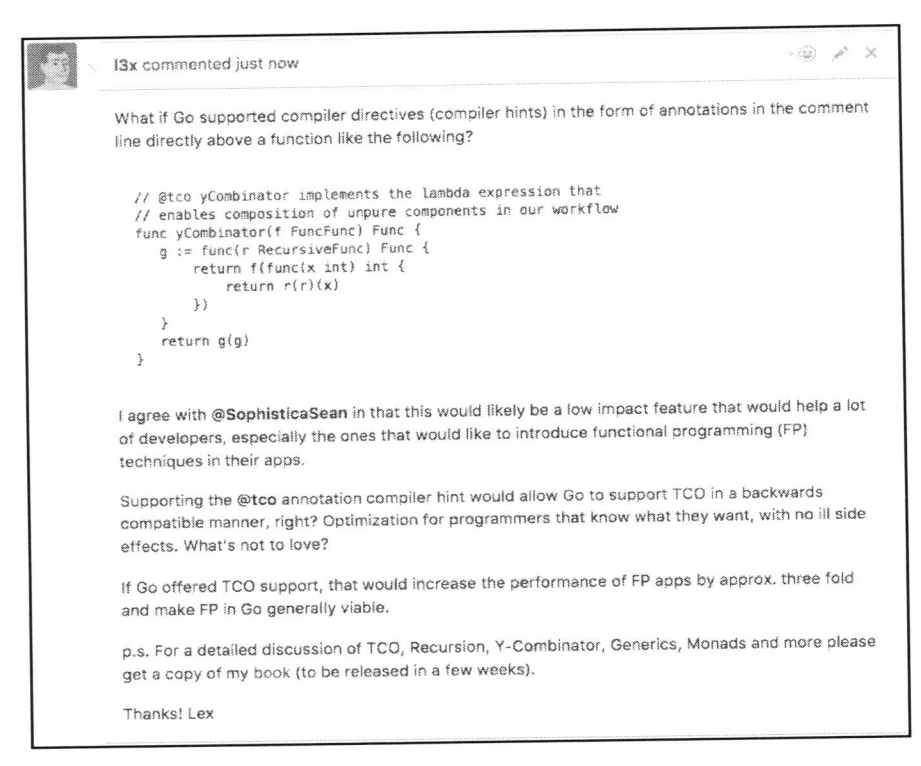

> **l3x** commented just now
>
> What if Go supported compiler directives (compiler hints) in the form of annotations in the comment line directly above a function like the following?
>
> ```
> // @tco yCombinator implements the lambda expression that
> // enables composition of unpure components in our workflow
> func yCombinator(f FuncFunc) Func {
>     g := func(r RecursiveFunc) Func {
>         return f(func(x int) int {
>             return r(r)(x)
>         })
>     }
>     return g(g)
> }
> ```
>
> I agree with **@SophisticaSean** in that this would likely be a low impact feature that would help a lot of developers, especially the ones that would like to introduce functional programming (FP) techniques in their apps.
>
> Supporting the **@tco** annotation compiler hint would allow Go to support TCO in a backwards compatible manner, right? Optimization for programmers that know what they want, with no ill side effects. What's not to love?
>
> If Go offered TCO support, that would increase the performance of FP apps by approx. three fold and make FP in Go generally viable.
>
> p.s. For a detailed discussion of TCO, Recursion, Y-Combinator, Generics, Monads and more please get a copy of my book (to be released in a few weeks).
>
> Thanks! Lex

Now, I wonder if my request warrants a separate proposal for the compiler directive? For example, *Proposal: Add compiler hints in the form of comment annotations.*

We'll just leave that comment as is and see what happens.

The comment turned into a new proposal (`https://github.com/golang/go/issues/22624`).

The conversation is ongoing as this book goes to the press.

Appendix

Creating a new proposal

If I had not found this existing proposal, this is what I would have done. Go to `https://github.com/golang/go/issues/new` to create an issue:

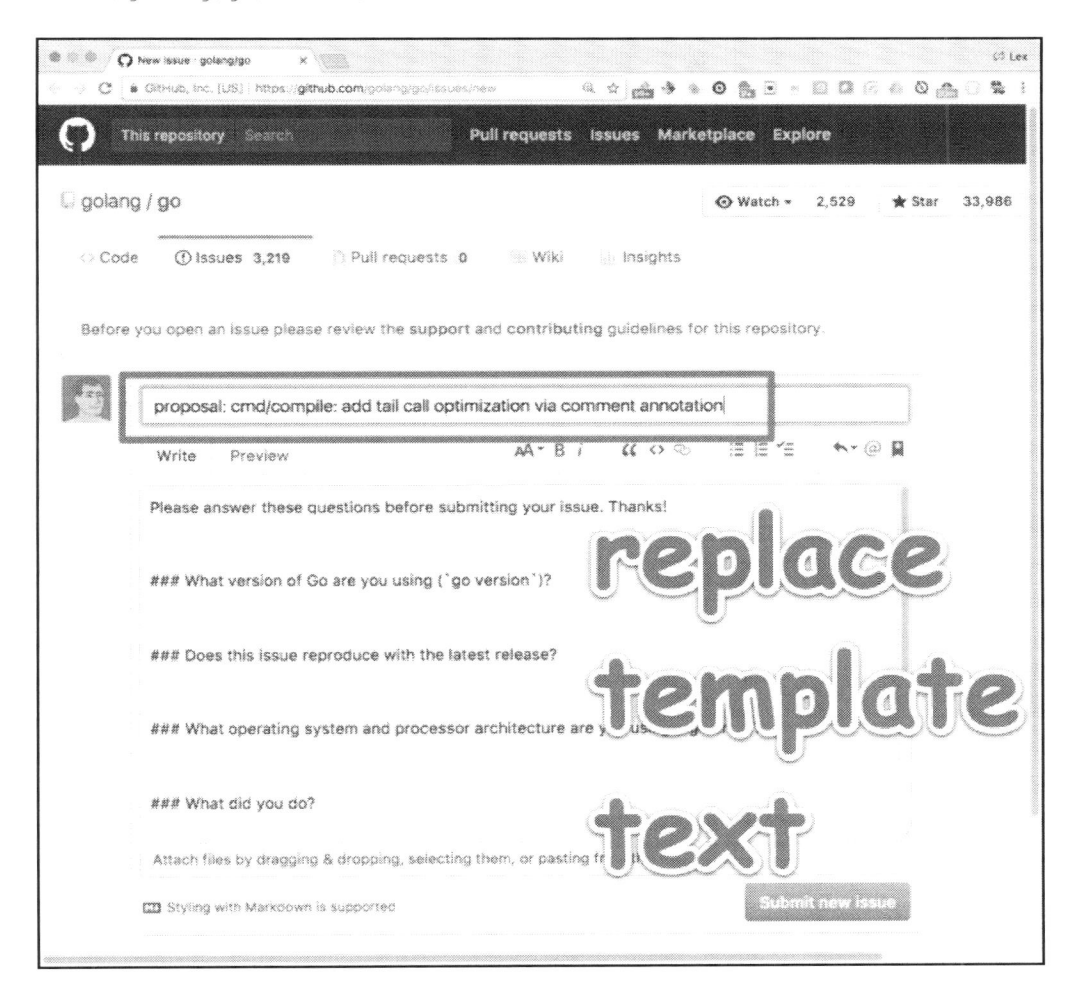

Assuming after writing the proposal, if it becomes obvious from the questions that I failed to clearly define the proposal in the proposal message, I could then create a design document to help clarify the request.

Creating a design document

I would go here, `https://github.com/golang/proposal/` click on the **Create new file** button, and save it as `design/NNNN-tco-annotation.md`, where NNNN is the GitHub issue number and `tco-annotation` is its short name. For example, `15292-generics.md` (`https://github.com/golang/proposal/blob/master/design/15292-generics.md`).

The design doc should follow the design template format at: `https://github.com/golang/proposal/blob/master/design/TEMPLATE.md`.

Sending an email to notify the golang-dev group

After saving the design document, I would post a NEW TOPIC to the `golang-dev` mail group, as follows:

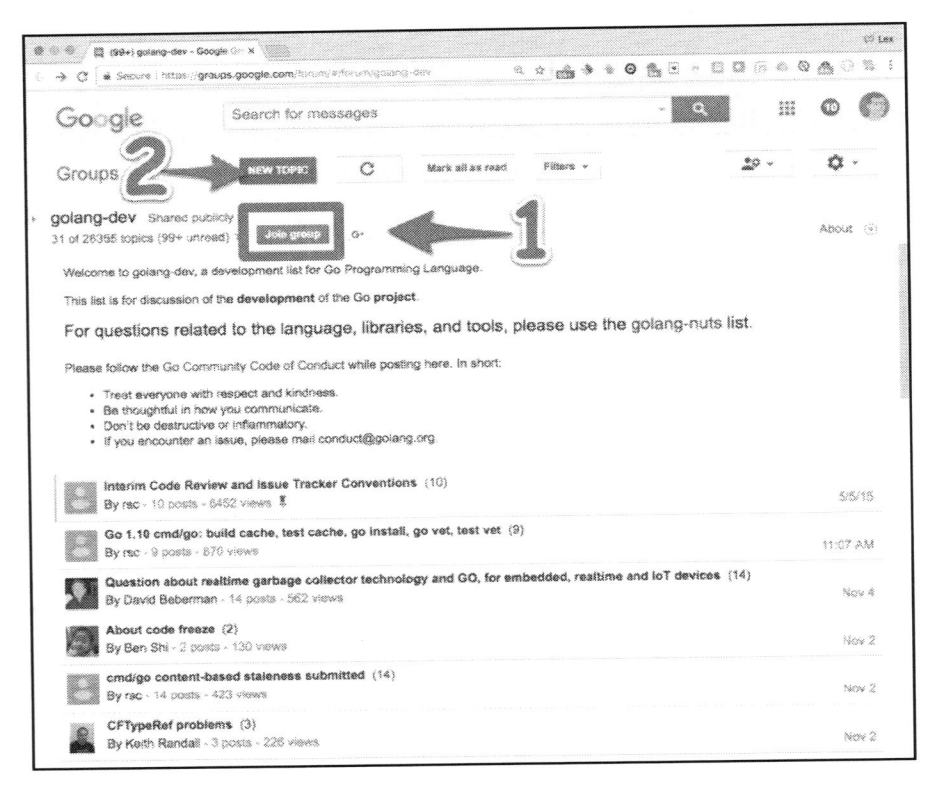

An example proposal

Here's an example of the notification email for a well-written proposal:

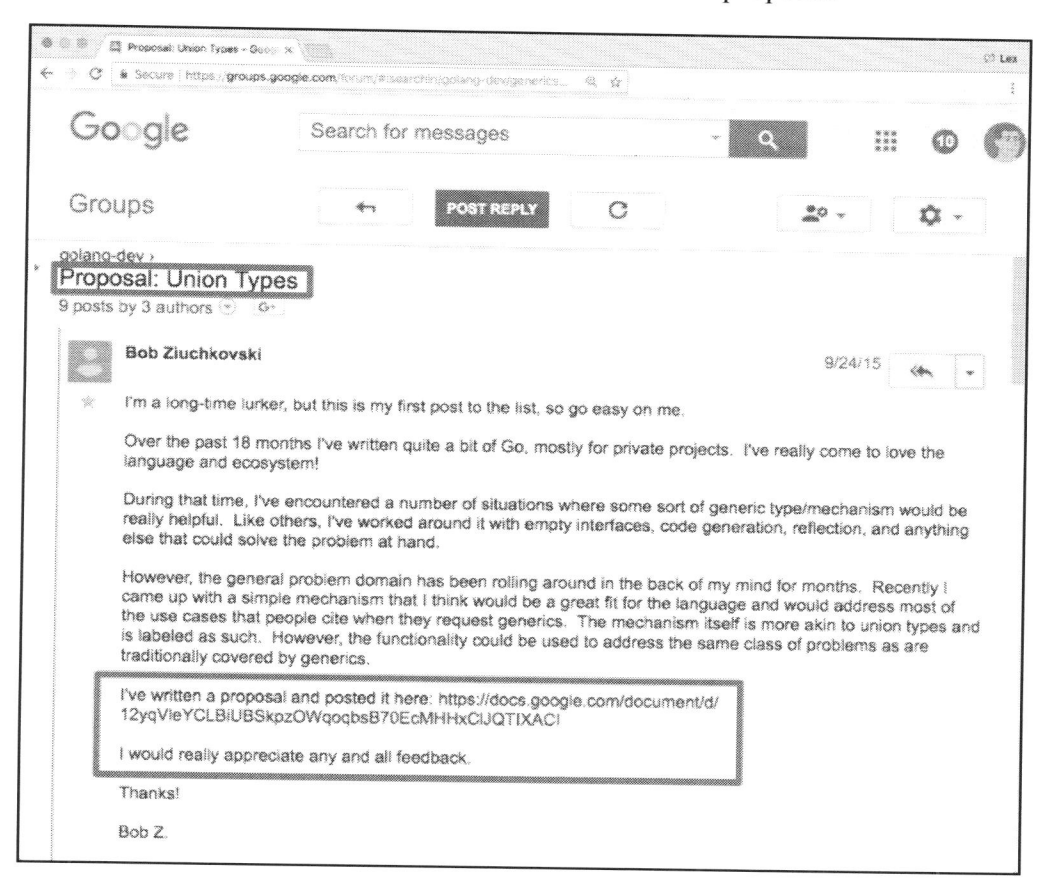

![Screenshot of a Google Groups email from Bob Ziuchkovski titled "Proposal: Union Types" posted to golang-dev on 9/24/15. The message reads: "I'm a long-time lurker, but this is my first post to the list, so go easy on me. Over the past 18 months I've written quite a bit of Go, mostly for private projects. I've really come to love the language and ecosystem! During that time, I've encountered a number of situations where some sort of generic type/mechanism would be really helpful. Like others, I've worked around it with empty interfaces, code generation, reflection, and anything else that could solve the problem at hand. However, the general problem domain has been rolling around in the back of my mind for months. Recently I came up with a simple mechanism that I think would be a great fit for the language and would address most of the use cases that people cite when they request generics. The mechanism itself is more akin to union types and is labeled as such. However, the functionality could be used to address the same class of problems as are traditionally covered by generics. I've written a proposal and posted it here: https://docs.google.com/document/d/12yqVIeYCLBiUBSkpzOWqoqbsB70EcMHHxCIJQTIXACl I would really appreciate any and all feedback. Thanks! Bob Z."]

Monitoring a proposal until the resolution is reached

I would monitor my inbox for new messages regarding the proposal to check whether I needed to add clarification. Once comments and revisions on the design doc wind down, there will be a final discussion about the proposal and it will either be accepted or declined.

FP resources

Rather than compiling a list of functional programming resources that would interest Go developers here, I'll make a github repo that can be updated over time:

```
https://github.com/l3x/fp-resources
```

If you are aware of any missing links, feel free to submit a pull request so that I can update the information for everyone to see.

Minggatu - Catalan number

The discovery of the Catalan number is generally credited to Eugene Catalan in 1844, even though it was actually originally discovered more than 100 years earlier by the Chinese mathematician Minggatu (1730).

The nth Catalan number can be represented by the following equation:

$$Cn = (2n)!/(n+1)!n!$$

The first few Catalan numbers for n = 0, 1, 2, 3, 4, 5, 6 are 1, 1, 2, 5, 14, 42, 132.

The Catalan numbers are a sequence of numbers that appear in many counting and computer science solutions.

Appendix

The easiest way for me to explain the concept is by answering, How many *mountain tops* can you form with n upstroke and n downstroke that all stay above the original line?

The variable C_n number of mountain tops containing n pairs of matching /\ characters:

```
                              /\
             /\      /\ /\    /\      /  \
 /\/\/\,   /\/  \,  /  \/\,  /  \,   /    \
```

Let's use use textual delimiters (of open and close parenthesis) to represent containers.

Catalan numbers are a fundamental concept of containment often used to assist the conceptualization and design of new software and hardware architectures based in combinatory logic.

The variable C_n is the number of expressions containing n pairs with matching parentheses:

```
    () () () ,  () (()) ,  (()) () ,  (() ()) ,  ((()))
```

The connection to lambda calculus is that that combinatory logic of matching parenthesis is sufficiently expressive to formalize recursive functions, and we know from our study of the Y-Combinator that recursive functions are fundamental.

For a better intuition, consider that in most programming languages, code is represented internally by the interpreter or compiler using an **abstract syntax tree (AST)**. An AST decomposes blocks of code into its smallest parts, making it easy to transform, analyze, or execute the code:

```
if b !=0 {
    result := a/b
} else {
    result := NaN
}
return result
```

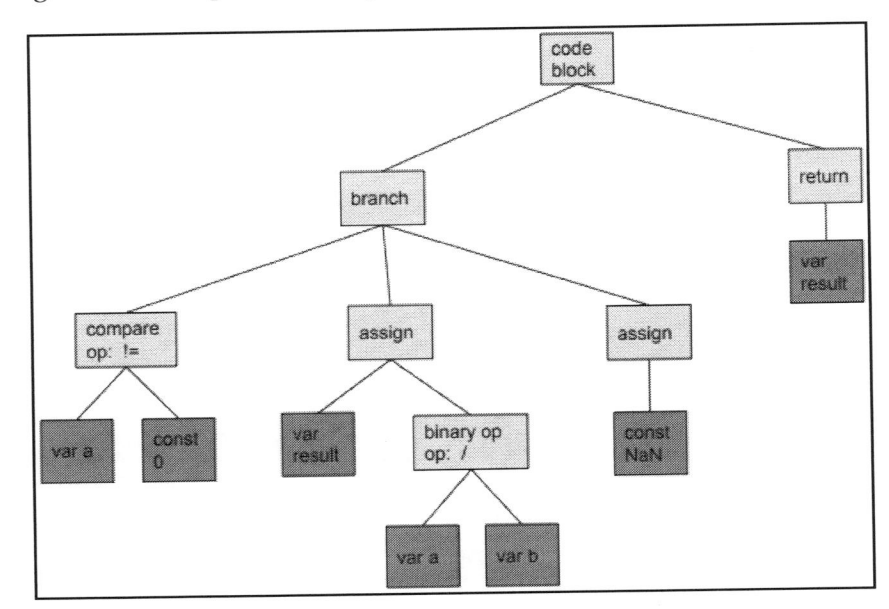

The following AST chart represents the preceding code block:

Here's about what that code block looks like in LISP:

```
(if (b != 0) ( / a b) (NaN) )
```

We use parentheses to represent the AST. An open parenthesis, "(", means step down a level of the tree, and a close parenthesis, ")", means step back up a level of the tree.

There are other ways we could represent a tree structure in code.

An explanation and call to action

Though this information is directly applicable and meaningful to functional programming, it was not placed in the *History of Functional Programming* because the discovery dates were not in line with the sequence of events that lead directly to the invention/discovery of The Lambda calculus by Alonzo Church.

This serves to show that people often think along the same lines, but for lack of communication/collaboration, nobody knows and nobody benefits from each other's work.

Today, we are neither bound by distance nor by planes, trains, or automobiles, but by human nature.

I believe that if it were up to software engineers and mathematicians, we would all share equally and rapidly. We are eager to share what we have learned and created (and love), but it's the corporation owners and governments (motivated by greed and power) that shut our mouths.

I would like to acknowledge the great thinkers around the world like Minggatu and urge my fellow engineers, of all nations, to join in an effort to replace the lust for power with our love and passion for science.

f(x) is pure. Humanity can be impure.

The Lambda Calculus (refer to the Y-Combinator and DNA Double Helix section in the last chapter) is empirical proof that we (Chinese, Russian, Korean, Indian, African, Arab, American, and so on) are all more alike than we are different.

We are all created equal. Let's substitute the love for power with the power of love. Let's put our differences aside and collaborate, whenever possible, to make a better world.

Peace,

Lex

Index

1
12-hour clock functor
  building 392
  helpers 393

4
4th generation language (4GL) 530

A
abstract syntax tree (AST) 633
Aggregate method
  reference 366
Alan Turing 515
Alfred Whitehead 511
algebra
  about 490
  laws 499
  real-world application 493
  rules 492
Alonzo Church 514
alternative workflow option 457
annotations 358
application architectures
  about 208
  functionality 208
  importance 211
  performance 208
  reference 208
  scalability 208
application programming interfaces (APIs) 557
Aspect-Oriented Programming (AOP) 356
Augustus De Morgan 509
authenticate and decrypt filters
  charging, before credit card number decryption 343

B
base class
  Int base class 475
  main.go file 476
  string base class 475
  sum base class 476, 479
  sum parent type class 476
Bash commands
  piping 44, 45
Bertrand Russell 511
big data 588
Big-Oh notation 466
boilerplate code
  for lack of generics 354
buffered implementation, pipeline pattern
  CPU cores, leveraging 334
business use case
  scenarios 459

C
car functor
  about 397
  example, executing 402
  main.go file 400
  one line of FP, comparing to bunch of imperative lines 401
  package 398
category theory
  about 489, 547, 559
  abstract functions 548
  as algebra of functions 548
  composition operation example, using travel expenses 550
  elements 551
  function composition, with sets 549
  function, defining 548

function, intuitive definition 549
  using 575
category
  about 550
  axioms 551
  examples 552
  invalid categories 552
  laws 551
  rules 552
cd command
  for projecting root directory 602
chapter4 application code
  about 102, 104
  build and runtime instructions 103
  Filter function 105, 107
  FilterFunc 107
Charles Lutwidge Dodgson 510
clipperhouse/gen tool
  about 358, 362
  filter function, defining 363
  generics, supported by GO 362
  new methods, adding 363
closure rule, monoid
  axiom 403
  examples 403
codomain 544, 551
collection of cars
  Contains() method 69
  empty interface 68
  iterating over 68
collection
  iterating through 42, 43, 44
composable concurrency
  about 571
  finite state machines 572
composition operation
  (g.f)(x) = g(f(x)) composition, implementing 382
  (g.f)(x) = g(f(x)) composition, in Go 381
  about 375
  arrow directions 385
  example, in Go 376
  function composition, as associative 387
  Haskell version 378
  incorrect order of EmphasizeHumanize 385
  naming conventions 383

concurrency
  managing, WaitGroup variable used 121
container orchestrator
  reference 290
contains 67
contexts
  about 302
  functional parameters 308
  good code, writing 306
  limitations 305
  reference 302
  report example 306, 308
  src/server/server.go 310, 313
  src/server/server_options.go file 316, 318
  use case 309
converse of a conditional proposition
  about 505
  orders 505
credit card number
  charging, before authentication 344
Curry Howard Isomorphism
  about 505
  examples, of not propositions 506
  examples, of propositions 506
  Lambda calculus 506
Curry-Howard-Lambek (CHL) Correspondence 517
currying
  about 118
  example 120, 297
customer relationship management (CRM) 211
cyclic dependency
  about 221
  error code 222
  Golang difference 223
  solution 224
  working code 221

D

data visualization 588, 593
decorator pattern
  about 176
  decorator.go file 190
  implementation 180
  main.go file 180

requestor.go file 200
simple_log.go file 182
type hierarchy UML 177
decorator.go file
  authorization decorator 192
  client request, wrapping up with decorators 191
  framework, for injecting dependencies 191
  graph 198
  LoadBalancing decorator 193
  Logging decorator 192
  trace log, examining 200
Decrypt filter
  ChargeCard helper function 339
  complete processing 338
Dependency Injection (DI) 195
dependency injection, Onion Architecture
  about 233
  func() main 234
dependency rule
  cyclic dependency 221
design document
  creating 630
development workflow
  about 617
  dot Init, troubleshooting 617, 623
directed acyclic graph (DAG) 78
directory structure, Onion Architecture
  func HandlePanic 232
  main.go 231
domain entities 225
Domain-Specific Languages (DSLs) 355
domains 544
duck typing
  about 150
  design 171

E

Eilenberg 516
elite player (EP) 306
empty interface-based Map function
  testing 71, 72
endomorphism 568
environment
  about 428
  variables, reference 299

error handling 128
example proposal 631
examples, quadratic equations
  about 497
  golden ratio 497, 499

F

f(x) 290
FantasyLand JavaScript specification
  about 142
  Ord algebra 143
  Setoid algebra 142
FaultTolerance 233
Feature Oriented Software Development (FOSD) 141
filter function 61, 63, 67
first in, first out (FIFO) 42
forgetful functor
  about 391
  and law 390
  rule of law 390
Forth language 528
function signature, with more than seven parameters
  issues 283
functional composition
  about 388
  category theory, result oriented 389
  category theory, review 389
  category theory, rules 389
  forgetful functor 390
  state transitions, determining 388
functional Inversion of Control (IoC)
  example 179
  procedural design 178
functional packages 76
functional parameters 298, 302
functional programming (FP)
  about 11, 81
  characteristics 81
  closure 96
  expressions, using 101
  first-class functions 95
  functional programming 288
  generics 94

history, in nutshell 523
immutable state 98
motivation 12
reference 524
resources 632
functors
  about 45, 54, 347, 349
  benefits, of using map function 349
  color blocks functor 350
  defining, in Haskell 351
  definition 374
  fingers times 10 functor 350
  identity operations 375
  imperative, versus pure FP example 348
  implementation 370
  implementing, with ints functors 370
  intermediate functions 54
  map function 348
  Reduce example 54
  shape 369
  terminal functions 56
  types 352

G

Gang of Four (GOF) 176
gen
  reference 358
GenerateCars function
  finishing up 121
generics code generation tool
  about 357
  clipperhouse/gen tool 357
  nums 364
generics
  about 479
  reference 369
Gibbons 521
Gleam
  about 78
  collections, processing 79
  LuaJIT, FFI library 78
  reality check 106
  Unix pipe tools 78
glide-update
  executing, for obtaining third-party dependency
    files 609
Glide
  reference 601
Go dependencies
  Glide 601
  managing, with go get tool 600
  managing, with godep tool 600
  vendoring 601
Go interfaces
  used, for type embedding 163
Go projects
  building 595
  dependencies, managing 599
  development workflow 596
  dot init features 596
  dot init step 602
  executing 595
  goenv, using 599
  init script, using 599
  standard library imports, adding 611
  third-party imports, adding 613
Go proverbs
  reference 557
Go
  advantages 76
  changes, proposing 623
  disadvantages 76
  distributed computing solution, implementing 77
  error handling idiom 164
  functional programming style 76
  generics 70
  Google search 624
  map function 71
  Reader and Writer interfaces 170
  Reader and Writer interfaces, examples 171
  reference 61
  specs, searching 623
goenv
  reference 599
  updated scenarios, displaying 609
Golang 482
Golang change proposal process
  comment, adding to existing TCO proposal 628
  existing Issues, searching for 625
  existing proposals, reading 626

reference 624
golang-dev group
  notifying, by sending email 630
Gorilla's package
  reference 303
Goroutine
  currying 118
graph database
  example 574

H

Haskell Curry 513
Haskell
  reference 429, 541
  type classes 542
helpers, 12-hour clock functor
  AmHoursFn helper 394
  AmPmMapper function 394
  main.go 395
  String helper function 394
  summary 397
  terminal output log 397
  Unit function 393
high-order functions (HOF) 82
historical events, functional programming 507,
    509, 510, 511, 512, 513, 514, 515, 516, 517,
    519, 520, 522
HOF application
  about 101
  chapter4 application code 103
  example 123
  RESTful resources 108
homebrew
  used, for installing Go 602
homomorphism encryption
  about 566
  example 566
homomorphism
  about 564
  car crash analogy 571
  categories 569
  encryption 566
  preserve correspondence 565

I

identity rule, monoid
  examples 404
  identity of 0 404
imperative implementation, pipeline pattern
  charge flow diagram 328
improved implementation
  Authenticate filter 337
  BuildPipeline 335
  Charge filter 339
  Decrypt filter 338
  decrypt helper function 340
  encrypt helper functions 340
  executable Goroutine 336
  Filterer interface 337
  Filterer object 337
  imports 335
  order, receiving 336
inference
  reference 514
infrastructure layers, Onion Architecture
  about 262
  context object 264
init script
  contents 603
  executing 608
init, features
  aliases 597
  functions 598
initial directory structure and files
  examining 603
  reexamining 608
interface composition 170
interface layers, Onion Architecture
  about 244
  global variables, limitations 252
  interface, testing 258
  response, formatting 253
interfaces
  used, for creating design 172
intermediate functions
  about 54
  filter 55
  map 55

[641]

      mapping example 55
      sort 55
  InternationalizatioN (I18N) package 468, 472
  invalid data, handling
      about 341
      attempt to charge, before credit card number
          decryption 343
      authenticate and decrypt filters, order change
          343
      credit card charging attempt, before
          authentication 344
      invalid credit card cipher text 341
      invalid password 342
  invariant 144
  Inversion of Control (IoC) 195
  isomorphism 567
  Itertools
      about 72, 73
      Go channels, used by new function 74
      iterators, testing for element equality 75
      map function, testing 74

J

  Java
      loathing 125
      loathing, reasons 127
  John McCarthy 516
  Jones 520

K

  Keep It Simple Stupid-Glide (KISS-Glide) 181, 188
  knowledge-driven development 588

L

  Lambda calculus
      about 506, 513, 531
      formalism 507
      importance of protocol 507
      reference 533
  lambda expressions
      about 531
      anonymous function example 532
      building, with laws of exponentials 579
      contents 532
      describing 536

      in JavaScript 536
      in JavaScript (ES6) 537
      in other languages 536
      in Ruby 537
      reference 532
      type inference 532
      visualizing 534
  lambda lifting 372
  Language Integrated Query (LINQ) 530
  laws of exponentials
      for building lambda expression 579
      isomorphic equations 580, 581
      table legend 580
  layers, Onion Architecture
      infrastructure layer 262
      interfaces layer 244, 248
      use cases layer 240
  lazy evaluation 54
  Liskov substitution principle
      about 144
      code example 146
      dependency inversion principle (DIP) 152
      duck typing 150
      FP function 145
      inheritance 150
      interface segregation principle 152
      OOP method 144
  LoadBalancing decorator
      about 193
      dependency injection 195
      easy-metrics graph 196
      first failure 196
      Inversion of Control (IoC) 195
      strategy pattern 193
      trace log file, groking 197
  logical connectives
      about 501
      function 503
      partial function 503
  long parameter lists
      refactoring 282, 283

M

  MacLane 516
  Map function

about 61, 63, 67, 111
  performance 112
MapReduce
  about 154
  example 155
mathematics
  correspondence 500
  using 575
maybe functor 353
memoization 55
metaprogramming (MP)
  used, for solving lack of generics 355
methods 526
Minggatu-Catalan Number 632
Modus Ponens
  about 509
  logic version 562
  type theory version 562
Moggi 520
monad
  about 153, 519
  activities 157
monadic functions
  fail 430
  fmap 430
  forever 432
  forM 432
  mapM 432
  mplus 430
  mzero 430
  return 431
  sequence 432
  void 432
monadic list functions
  filterM 433
  foldM 433
  join 433
  msum 433
  replicateM 433
  zipWithM 433
monadic workflow implementation
  about 434, 439, 444
  Lambda Calculus 447, 452
Monads, Haskell
  Error 426

Eval 426
Failure 426
Free 426, 427
Identity 427
If 427
IO 427
Lazy 427
List 427
Maybe 427
Option 428
Par 428
Parser 428
Pause 428
Reader 428
Software Transactional Memory (STM) 429
ST 429
State 428
Writer 429
monoid
  about 402
  examples 407, 409
  name monoid 410
  no data, handling 407
  not monoids 407
  reduction function, writing 404
  referential transparency 406
  rules 402
  semigroup 405
morphism
  about 544, 554, 558
  cartesian closed category (CCC) 562
  composition operation 555
  correspondence 560
  correspondence, between logic and type theory 562
  examples 561
  focusing on 557
  identity operation 555
  injective morphism 568
  interface-driven development 557
  law of associativity 556
  operations 561
  subjective morphism 568
  unit type 563
Moses Schonfinkel 512

Mother Teresa Monad 425
  about 418
  bind operation 421
  lift operation 422, 423
multiple parameters
  configuration object/struct, passing 296
  partial application 297
  passing, ways 296
  simply pass 296

N

name monoid
  about 410
  Int slice monoid terminal session 415
  Lineitem slice monoid 413, 415
  terminal session 411, 412
new proposal
  creating 629
non-functional requirements (NFRs) 12

O

Object Relational Mapping (ORM) 537
Object-Oriented Programming (OOP)
  about 135, 526
  cloud computing 288
  inconsistency 288
  issue 287
  limitation 284
Oliveira 521
Onion Architecture
  about 230
  client-server architecture 209
  cloud architecture 210
  dependency injection 233
  dependency injection (DI) 229
  dependency rule 220
  directory structure 231
  domain statement 224
  hollywood principle 226
  implementing 207
  infrastructure 224
  interface-driven development 225
  layers 234
  observer pattern 226
  use cases 224
  using 224
open/closed principle
  about 138
  expression problem 143
  FantasyLand JavaScript specification 142
  in functional programming 141
options, for implementing generics
  about 368
  gen tool 369

P

package errors
  reference 238
partial application 297
pipeline pattern
  about 322
  advantages 323
  buffered implementation 332
  characteristics 323
  concurrent implementation 331
  data flow types 325
  disadvantages 323
  example implementations 327
  examples 324
  generalized business application design 326
  grep sort example 322
  imperative implementation 328
  improved implementation 334
  invalid data handling, by application 341
  load balancer 325
  reference 344
  website order processing 324
Pod
  reference 289
polymorphism
  at higher level 353
post conditions 145
precondition 145
predicates
  about 57, 58, 59, 60
  combinator pattern 61
  reflection 60
problem
  splitting up 490
procedure design

comparing, to functional Inversion of Control (IoC) 178
  example 179
programming language
  2GL 527
  3GL 528
  4GL 528
  5GL 528
  categories 525
  declarative category 525
  first generation (1GL) language 527
  imperative category 525
  imperative example 525
  type systems 530
programming paradigms
  Venn diagram 526
proof theory
  about 501
  logical connectives 501
  truth table 503
proposal
  monitoring 631

R

Reader and Writer interfaces
  using 174
real-world application, algebra
  about 493
  law of demand 493
  linear and quadratic functions 495
  linear equation 493
  quadratic equations 494, 497
Recursive Genome Function
  reference 452
refactoring
  considerations 290, 292, 294
  solution 295
reflection, Go
  reference 356
Replace Parameter with Method
  applying 292
requestor.go file
  about 200, 201
  channels, used for managing lifecycle 202
  DI framework 205

  job, declared in main() function 201
  makeRequest goroutine, launching 204
  request, completing 204
RESTful resources
  about 108
  cars, adding 110
  chaining functions 109
  concurrency, handling 122
  GenerateCars function 116
  generators 115
  high-order functions 114
  Map function 111
  Reduce functions 113
  RESTful server 116
Roger Godement 519
rules, monoid
  associativity rule 403
  closure rule 403
  identity rule 404

S

self-referential functions
  reference 295
semaphore lock 429
semiGroup homomorphism
  about 568
  algebra 569
set theory symbols 546
simple_log.go file
  about 183
  easy-metrics GUI, used for explaining statistics 187
  InitLog calls example 183
  main package 184
single responsibility principle
  about 136
  function composition 138
SINK Cloud Bucket 230
slice typewriter
  about 367
  Aggregate[T] 367
software architecture 209
software design
  bad design 134
  good design 133

good, versus bad design over time 134
methodology 132
software product line
  reference 141
Software Transactional Memory (STM) 429
SOLID design principles
  about 135
  Liskov substitution principle 144
  open/closed principle 138
  single responsibility principle 136
SOURCE Cloud Bucket 230
Sprintf options
  reference 316
standard construction 519
standard library imports
  adding 611
  Go standard library 613
State Thread (ST) monad 429

T

tail recursion 465
tail-call optimization (TCO) 77, 82, 465
terminal functions
  about 56
  Collect, Join, GroupB 56
  ForEach 56
  GroupBy example 57
  Join example 56
  Reduce 56
  Reduce example 57
third-party imports
  statement referencing go_utils, importing 614
toml config file
  reference 597
truth table
  about 503
  conditional propositions 504
  converse of conditional proposition 505

logical equivalence 504
type classes
  about 474
  base class definitions 474
type system implications
  Haskell 541
  static, versus dynamic typing 540
  type inference 540

U

Unicode Common Locale Data Repository (CLDR)
  reference 468
Unified Markup Language (UML) 133
untyped Lambda calculus 506
use cases layers, Onion Architecture
  about 240
  compatible interfaces 242

V

Viva La Duck application
  about 158
  executing 165, 167
  pass by reference 162
  pass by value 162

W

Wadler 520

Y

Y-Combinator
  about 453, 460, 465
  big-Oh notation 466
  idiomatic 456
  Lexical Workflow solution 455
  not idiomatic 456
  tail recursion 465
  working 454